THE BARONIAL OPPOSITION TO EDWARD II

ITS CHARACTER AND POLICY

THE BARONIAL OPPOSITION TO EDWARD II

ITS CHARACTER AND POLICY

A Study in Administrative History

JAMES CONWAY DAVIES

LONDON AND NEW YORK

First published by
FRANK CASS AND COMPANY LIMITED
by arrangement with Cambridge University Press.

First edition	1918
New impression	1967

Published 2006 by Routledge
2 Park Square, Milton Park, Abingdon, Oxfordshire OX14 4RN
711 Third Avenue, New York, NY 10017

First issued in paperback 2014

Routledge is an imprint of the Taylor and Francis Group, an informa business

ISBN 13: 978-0-714-61466-3 (hbk)
ISBN 13: 978-0-415-76046-1 (pbk)

PREFACE

THE baronial opposition to Edward II was more than an opportunist outburst of oligarchical tendencies, though the circumstances of the time were suitable for an opposition of such a nature. It was more than a reaction from the policy of Edward I. Its basis was not personal. It was a conflict of principles, contradictory and irreconcilable. On one side stood the royal, on the other the baronial. The principles which moved the royal policy found their expression in the administration.

It was against the royal system of administration that the barons stood in the reign of Edward II. A consideration of the features of that system of administration is therefore of the utmost importance in determining the character and policy of the baronial opposition. A study of the administration as controlled by the household is important for two chief reasons. It gives the objective of the baronial attack. It explains the strength of the king's position and therefore supplies the reason for the failure of the barons.

The second part of the thesis is concerned with the various attacks of the barons upon the royal position. The methods employed were not new. There were precedents upon which the barons proceeded. But the methods were directed by the nature and capabilities of the administrative system which they sought to destroy or capture.

In the circumstances, therefore, it was inevitable that the bulk of the material upon which the thesis is based should be administrative records of the chancery and exchequer. The K. R. and L. T. R. Memoranda Rolls of the Exchequer have been little used since the time of Madox. The extent to which the present thesis is built upon material supplied by these is apparent from the frequency of the references. The value of the material obtained, especially of the writs of privy seal addressed to the treasurer and barons, and entered on the memoranda rolls, is great and has provided new light upon points of administrative interest as well as upon problems connected with the present subject. King's Remembrancer Accounts, Miscellanea, Writs and Bills have also supplied useful material. The Issue Rolls for the reign have been searched and have supplied information concerning both the "curialists" and the administrative officers.

Of the chancery records, the files of Chancery Warrants have been of considerable value, especially in the consideration of the various manifestations and activities of the council, while the Chancery Miscellanea have added points of interest on a variety of topics.

The volumes of Ancient Correspondence have been invaluable and have added to the knowledge of the administrative, constitutional and political history of the reign. The knowledge of the part which Pembroke took in the administration after 1312 is derived to a considerable extent from writs of privy and secret seal addressed to him and preserved in the Ancient Correspondence. The activity of the younger Despenser in respect to Gascony in the closing years of the reign is also portrayed in this collection. Of other classes in the Special Collections those of the Parliamentary and Council Proceedings have been drawn on to some extent.

A number of wardrobe books among the British Museum manuscripts have been used, especially Stowe MS. 553. The manuscript collections in Cambridge University Library and the Library of Canterbury Cathedral and of Corpus Christi College, Cambridge, have supplied additional information of value.

Among printed sources the publications of the Record Commission and the Calendar Series have been used to a great extent. The chronicles in the Rolls Series have also been employed. The chronicles have been used principally to illustrate and portray character and no important point is based solely upon the authority of a chronicle. An exception must however be made of the important documents incorporated in some chronicles. The publications of various learned societies, especially of the Selden Society, have been used. The volumes in the publications of the Selden Society edited by Professor Maitland and others have supplied information and suggestions of the utmost value to the development of the thesis.

Amongst private sources the most helpful has been Professor T. F. Tout's book on *The Place of Edward II in English History.* My general plan was well advanced and my materials collected before the publication of the book, but its appearance encouraged me in the plan I was pursuing and the suggestions it made proved of the utmost importance. A preface can contain no suitable expression of thanks for the counsel and advice which Professor Tout gave me ungrudgingly and the extent to which I have availed myself of his weighty judgment will be made apparent in the numerous references to his work. The appendices to his book, especially those of the lists of officials for the reign, though not complete, have been of great service as a source of reference. With a number of the conclusions Professor

Tout reached I have been unable to agree. One naturally hesitates in expressing difference of opinion from such an authority, and it is hoped that sufficient reasons have been given for the difference.

The general scheme of the thesis is new, and the arrangement also is original. In the preparation of the scheme and in its development the advice and aid of Mr G. T. Lapsley, Fellow of Trinity College, have placed me under a deep obligation to him and I desire to express my gratitude. The extent of the original treatment in the detailed working out of the thesis is shown in the footnotes. The extent to which it is based upon manuscript authorities relieves me of the burden of labouring this point. A number of the more important documents are included in an appendix.

Among the more important of the points which have received new light from the investigation of new material and re-reading of the old are those surrounding the activity of the earl of Pembroke during the reign. The dual nature of the baronial policy as expressed by Lancaster and Pembroke is emphasised and some additional information upon the action of the middle party during the reign is sketched. Frequent reference is made to the pre-eminent interest and importance of the earl of Pembroke, and the decisive part which he took in the administration between 1312–1315 given a prominence which it has not hitherto had. Indeed the great attraction of the character of Pembroke, who alone of the men of the reign seems to be worthy a biography, is convincing.

There is little new light to be thrown upon the character of Edward II, though it would appear that he was not as foolish or useless as he has been painted. Edward II stood for a system and that he did not fit into the scheme that system demanded was not altogether his fault. Additional evidence has yielded some light upon the place of the younger Despenser in the administration.

The space that has been devoted to the "administrative" council seems justified by the importance of that body in the household system and the lack of treatment it has hitherto received. The problem of the council *at* and *with* the exchequer also has a direct bearing upon the main thesis and had to be treated at some length.

The "additional" ordinances have, it is believed, been treated at length for the first time. The additional evidence upon the conduct and part of Lancaster after the battle of Bannockburn seems to justify the separate treatment of that point. The committee set up at the parliament of Lincoln has been treated at some length and the suggestion that the letter of Lancaster of June, 1317, giving the names of a committee appointed to guide the king, referred to the committee set up at Lincoln in February, 1316, is new.

In the final chapter points of importance have been discussed; and the material which the K. R. and L. T. R. Memoranda Rolls of the Exchequer furnished seemed to warrant the conclusions which have been reached upon the appointment of sheriffs. It was necessary that the treatment of the exchequer reforms of the concluding years of the reign should be brief, but some new facts relating to them have been introduced. The writ of privy seal ordering the division of the exchequer in 1324, and other writs such as that concerning the appointment of an escheator of cities and boroughs are new.

The few points referred to give examples of the nature and value of the material supplied by the documents at the Record Office. For most of the new light, I am indebted to them, though printed sources have been little less useful. It is to be regretted that the removal from London of many valuable records has prevented a final revision of a few of the documents. The thesis, here printed after revision, was awarded the Thirlwall Prize, in the University of Cambridge, in 1917.

The Master and Governing Body of Emmanuel College and other members of the College have throughout taken the greatest practical interest in the preparation and publication of the work and my obligations to them are numerous and vast. The financial assistance which the College provided in aid of the costs of publication of an exceptionally long dissertation has enabled me to deal at greater length with the documents examined than might otherwise have been possible.

Finally I desire to express my deep obligations to Mr Hilary Jenkinson of the Public Record Office for the invaluable advice which he was always willing to give and for the many suggestions which he offered. Mr Ratcliffe of the Public Record Office also rendered me valuable assistance. I have to thank the officials of the Public Record Office, and the University Library for their kindness and courtesy; Dr Hazeltine, Reader in English Law, for advice and discussion and Mr P. W. Wood, Librarian of Emmanuel for the facilities he granted me in the use of books from the College Library. Mr J. A. Struthers, St John's College, has given much time ungrudgingly to the proofs and to the compilation of the index, and my sincere gratitude is due to him. I am deeply indebted to the authorities of the University Press for the care and attention they have bestowed upon the work.

J. C. D.

July, 1918

CONTENTS

PART II

THE CONSTITUTIONAL AND ADMINISTRATIVE ACTION OF THE BARONIAL OPPOSITION

INTRODUCTION

The history of England during the fourteenth century was singularly devoid of any of those great movements in the growth of the constitution which had marked the two previous centuries. There was no great period of legal reform and definition like the reigns of Henry II and Edward I. There was no great movement which was to culminate in a Magna Carta or a Model Parliament. This absence of great events and outstanding movements does not prove that regarded strictly from the view-point of constitutional history the century was not of great importance. The constitution is built upon precedent, upon rights slowly acquired and privileges laboriously won, upon the extension of functions and the adoption of new ones, and not solely or chiefly upon great combats between opposing theories and conflicting parties. Constitutional progress can take place without great disturbance, without a great directing mind or a strong controlling hand. The fourteenth century had constitutional problems of its own; not perhaps as imposing or attractive as those before or after, but no less important on that account. It has been said that "the whole constitutional struggle of the fourteenth century raged round the vexed question of the royal prerogative[1]." On the one hand stood the king possessing great power and large prerogatives, on the other hand stood the barons anxious to weaken or control that power and lessen the prerogatives which supported and were supported by it.

The problem of discovering the character and policy of a baronial opposition and the theory on which that policy was established, upon which it proceeded and which it developed involves some consideration of the royal theory and practice of government with which it came into conflict. Of the various theories of government which obtained in the middle ages the royal theory was the most potent. It was more consistent than its rivals and had attained, by its continuity, a higher standard of development. Moreover it was supported by a strong and practical machinery. Too often

[1] J. N. Figgis, *The Divine Right of Kings*, 2nd edit. [1914], p. 28.

large theoretical rights are hampered by lack of suitable machinery or weakness of executive power. So extensive were the prerogatives of the king in England at the beginning of the fourteenth century and so considerable were his administrative powers that any successful issue of a baronial opposition seemed improbable. As long as the king cared to remember that "to the crown belongs not only cruelty and rigour of justice, but still more pity and mercy[1]" opposition to the royal authority was not likely to become overpowering. The instruments of royal policy however, and royalty itself are fallible and from personal failures opposition drew strength.

As illustrative of the extent and immensity of the royal prerogative a number of directions in which it exerted itself will be briefly reviewed. In a discussion on the royal prerogative, two considerations must be borne in mind, the sources whence the king had obtained his prerogative and the dynamic nature of the prerogative. It may be broadly stated that the personal rights the king had obtained as a legacy from the Anglo-Saxon kingship, the tenurial rights from the Norman kings, and the judicial rights developed by the Angevins. There was too, a constant tendency for precedent, custom and law to take the place of the king's pleasure. The matters to be considered deal with the king's rights and privileges, with those things which concerned "lestat et le dreyt de sa coroune[2]" or "lestat le dit nostre seigneur le roy, et sa coroune, et sa dignite[3]" for the king was careful that nothing should be done that would prejudice his right and his crown[4], and his officials were equally careful of his dignity[5] and saw that nothing was permitted which proceeded to the injury of his estate[6]. These powers of the king covered also those who surrounded him. His household had a prerogative court and his officials and clerks possessed various privileges[7]. A king's burgess could claim trial by battle against the burgess of any other lord, but the latter could not claim it against the former[8]. When a plea touched the person of the king an increased number of compurgators was necessary[9]. Once a thing was appurtenant to

[1] *Registrum Johannis Peckham* [Rolls Series], vol. III, Appendix, p. 955.
[2] D. Wilkins, *Concilia* [1737], vol. II, pp. 312–313. [3] Ibid.
[4] Public Record Office, Chancery Warrants, File 113, no. 5528.
[5] *Calendar of Documents relating to Scotland*, ed. J. Bain, vol. III, p. 55.
[6] Publications of the Selden Society, vol. XXVII [1912], *Eyre of Kent*, vol. II, p. 77. *Cal. Inquisitions post mortem*, vol. V, p. 276.
[7] Vide below, pp. 199–206.
[8] Seld. Soc. vol. XVIII [1904], *Borough Customs*, vol. I, p. 35.
[9] Ibid. p. 46.

the crown it could never be removed without a special grant from the king[1]. Words spoken in contempt of the king and to his scandal[2], or deeds done to his contempt such as riding armed to the terror of the people[3] or for a party to a law suit to strike his opponent in the presence of the justices[4] were considered offences of considerable magnitude.

Actions, administrative, judicial and financial were often said to be done of the king's pleasure or special grace. The city of Winchester was held at favour "quamdiu Regi placuerit[5]." Grants of pavage were made of the king's grace[6]. The sentence of execution passed against Roger Damory for participation in the troubles of 1321–2 "le Roy de sa grace et de sa realte met en respit execucion de cel jugement a sa volunte[7]." The pardon and release of those convicted of homicide in self defence was similarly at the king's pleasure[8]. Certain writs were issued only by the king's special grace and by his special warrant[9]. Despite the prohibition of Magna Carta, writs of praecipe were still issued "ex gratia speciali[10]." Releases from prison[11], mainprises[12], compensations[13] were made by the king's special grace; and arrangements to hold parliament were made only if it was pleasing to the king[14]. Amercements for serious offences were said to be "ad voluntatem regis[15]." A great deal of the administration depended upon the king's will, and before the necessary arrangements were made requests were addressed to him in some such form as "sil plest au Roi de recomande ses voluntes a[16],"

[1] *Year Book* 20–21 *Edward I* [Rolls Series], p. 54.

[2] P. R. O. King's Remembrancer Memoranda Roll, no. 88, m. 158 d. Lord Treasurer's Remembrancer Memoranda Roll, no. 85, Recorda Trinitatis, m. 6 d.

[3] Wm Salt Soc., *Collections*, vol. x [1889], pp. 70–71.

[4] Ibid. vol. VI, Pt i, p. 295.

[5] T. Madox, *Firma Burgi*, p. 18.

[6] *Rotuli Parliamentorum*, vol. I, p. 397.

[7] *Abbreviatio Placitorum*, p. 351.

[8] Seld. Soc. vol. XXIV [1909], *Eyre of Kent*, vol. I, pp. lxxi, 88. Wm Salt Soc., *Coll.* vol. VI, Pt i [1885], p. 258; vol. VII [1886], p. 111.

[9] *Cal. Close Rolls*, 1272–79, p. 583.

[10] W. S. McKechnie, *Magna Carta*, 2nd edit. p. 353.

[11] *Cal. Close Rolls*, 1313–18, p. 379.

[12] K. R. Mem. Roll, no. 96, m. 37 d.

[13] H. Cole, *Documents illustrative of English History in the Thirteenth and Fourteenth Centuries*, p. 53.

[14] *Cal. Doc. Scotl.* vol. III, p. 9. T. Madox, *History of the Exchequer*, vol. II [1769], p. 237.

[15] *English Historical Review*, vol. XXII [1907], 'Amerciament of Barons by their Peers,' L. W. V. Harcourt, p. 734.

[16] P. R. O. Chancery Miscellanea, Bundle 24/3 (16).

the reply to petitions and such requests commencing "Le Roi voet[1]."

This slight consideration of instances in which actions were undertaken by the king's grace or pleasure suggests an analysis of the king's prerogatives as they affected his position to justice, the course of justice, his tenurial rights, his financial privileges, and his rights in legislation and administration. Merely illustrative instances of the king's rights in these different directions will be given, the instances not being intended to convey more than a hasty outline of a few of the spheres in which the king's prerogatives extended abundant influence. Before the prerogative rights are considered it would be well to note that so important were considered the king's rights that the law courts and parliament showed an unwillingness to decide matters during the minority of a king. During the minority of Henry III matters before justices had been postponed[2]: and various petitions presented at the first parliament of Edward III were postponed "tanqe a lage le Roi[3]." This was to protect the king's rights and the same object appears in the declaration in 1218 that the king was incapable of disposing of property[4].

The king's prerogatives were extensive and for the purposes of administration he delegated certain of his powers to officials. These officials derived their authority from the powers delegated to them by the king and their administration was subject to the king's supervision and surveillance. Thus the king's powers originally exercised by himself and the *curia regis*, as administration increased in bulk and complexity, were divided among various bodies. The exchequer was set up for the financial business of the crown and various powers were given to the head of that department—the treasurer. Similarly to the chancery and bodies of justices other powers were delegated. The council continued to exercise some degree of supervision over those bodies, but the council itself was subject to the supervision of the king. In the council the various departments and their officials met, for the officials took part in the general administration of the realm as well as in the specialised work of their particular departments. Thus justices of assize were chosen by the chancellor and treasurer[5]. For short periods during his absence the king delegated a considerable number of his rights to

[1] P. R. O. Ancient Petition, no. 2064.
[2] *Bracton's Note Book*, ed. F. W. Maitland, vol. III, cases 1500, 1639.
[3] *Rot. Parl.* vol. II, pp. 11, 12.
[4] *Cal. Patent Rolls*, 1216–25, p. 177.
[5] Ancient Petition, no. 3982.

keepers of the realm, including issuing licences to elect, granting royal assents, making restitution of temporalities, collating and presenting to prebends and other ecclesiastical benefices and dealing with wardships and marriages[1].

In the first stages of the delegation of justice the king continued to take an active control in his courts, and even in the reign of Edward II there are instances of the king actually deciding cases[2]. The reason for the appointment of justices was stated to be "pur ceo qe nous ne suffisoms mie en nostre propre persone a oier et terminer totes les quereles de poeple aundite auoms partie nostre charge en plusours parties[3]." Henry II established itinerant justices in eyre, "dividing the realm into large circuits, for the purpose of the delegated exercise of the prerogative royal jurisdiction[4]." The justices in eyre had a larger measure of delegated power than any other body. They alone could try writs of *quo waranto*. "None else were so sufficiently clothed with the king's persona as to have authority to hear and determine them[5]." They were in fact clothed with the *persona* of the king himself[6]; they were in a very special sense impersonations of the king and in addition to holding pleas they had authority to provide remedy for complaints made to them[7]. It was only the court of king's bench that was not superseded by the eyre[8]. They were in a better position than the justices of the common bench and could do many things for which the latter were not competent[9]. On the opening of the eyre the sheriff surrendered his wand of office to the justices and having been charged to do his duty faithfully it was returned to him[10]. The king's protection was not allowable in answer to the common summons of the eyre[11]. Yet the powers of the justices in eyre were limited. Though their commissions were but temporary and for a specific purpose, the king reserved to himself some of his prerogatives. The justices, for instance, could not take fines for alienations in mortmain without the king's licence[12].

[1] *Cal. Pat. Rolls*, 1307–13, p. 43.

[2] W. S. Holdsworth, *History of English Law*, vol. I, p. 73. Wm Salt Soc., *Coll.* vol. x [1889], p. 9.

[3] Corpus Christi College MS. no. 258, f. 1.

[4] *Select Essays in Anglo-American Legal History*, vol. II, 'Sources of English Law,' Brunner, p. 25.

[5] Seld. Soc. vol. XXIX [1913], *Eyre of Kent*, vol. III, pp. xxxii–xxxiii.

[6] Ibid. p. xxxiv.

[7] Ibid. vol. II, pp. xxviii–xxix.

[8] Ibid. pp. xlvi, 205.

[9] Ibid. pp. 198–9.

[10] Ibid. vol. I, p. 4.

[11] Ibid. pp. 25, 54.

[12] Ibid. p. 91.

The delegated authority exercised by the chancery was both administrative and judicial. A royal official who found that the commission he had was not full enough for the required purpose asked the chancellor "ordiner especial garant accordant au cas[1]," and it was from its function as the maker of writs that the jurisdiction of the chancery grew, and though there was a tendency to give statutory powers to the chancery to issue writs without reference to the king[2], its powers really rested upon the delegation of authority. A high royal official who had to make inquest into the conduct of certain subordinates who were in prison besought the chancellor for a writ for their release[3], no reference being made to the king though the matter was one which touched the prerogative. Moreover the king sometimes sat in his chancery[4]. The Statute of Westminster II gave them authority to make writs *in consimili casu* and writs falling within that statute devised by the common counsel of the clerks in chancery were maintained in the courts[5]. Indeed when the justices abated a writ the clerks of chancery summoned the chief justice before them to explain his conduct and they maintained the writ[6].

In the local administration of England and in the administration of Ireland which had its own great departments and judiciary similar delegations were made. The justice of Ireland, however, could not pardon the king's suit of peace for death or felony, nor seal the pardon with the seal of Ireland without the king's special warrant under one of the seals of England[7]. He could not conduct purveyance there without the advice and assent of the greater part of the king's council in Ireland unless he had a writ from England[8]. On the other hand both in Ireland and Wales the king expressed an unwillingness to remove any of his officials there without his justice to whom he had given power to ordain concerning his officers in those parts according to the king's need[9]. The sheriff was the important delegate in the local administration, though the constant commissions sent by the king for the purpose of inquiry and justice robbed him of the full exercise of his delegated authority.

[1] P. R. O. Ancient Correspondence, vol. XXXV, no. 207.
[2] *Statutes of Realm*, vol. I, p. 253. *Stat. Westm.* I, I Ed. III, § 3.
[3] Ancient Correspondence, vol. XXXVI, no. 35.
[4] Chan. Warr., File 108/5018 d.
[5] Seld. Soc. vol. XIX [1904], *Year Bk* 2–3 *Ed. II*, pp. 157–161.
[6] Seld. Soc. vol. XX [1905], *Year Bk* 3 *Ed. II*, p. 19.
[7] *Stat. of Realm*, vol. I, p. 194.
[8] Ibid. p. 193.
[9] Ancient Petition, no. 11856.

The extent of the delegation to the council in its various phases has a vital connection with the central problem of the reign. The endorsements to petitions presented to the king were generally decided by it. The evidence relating to a petition for release from prison was to come before it[1]. In petitions relating to lands the inquisition was returned to the king and council[2], or the result was certified to the king[3]. The king even ordered the council to advise on petitions in matters of grace[4], though petitions were frequently endorsed "coram Rege quia tangit ipsum[5]" or "coram Rege quia tangit ius regni[6]." A request was made for a confirmation of liberties and other favours. The charters were to be inspected by the council which was to advise if the liberties sought "est grantez bonement a user sans prejudice faire a la corone ou ne mye et lour avisement de ceo reportant au Roi[7]." The obligation to report to the king on occasion before execution provided a safeguard; but even without this there was not necessarily any serious danger in the delegation of considerable authority to various bodies. Such delegation tended to efficiency and therefore made the administration more smooth-working and opposition less likely. The delegated bodies would almost invariably be strong supporters of the royal policy and prerogatives. Even if the contrary happened to be the case, the general nature of the system of government which then obtained was such that all danger was negligible.

In justice the king had all the rights of the chief lord and by virtue of his prerogative he was in a higher position than any chief lord[8]. He was chief lord and king[9]. He was higher than his writ[10] and his command was as binding as statute[11]. The dispensing and suspending power was his[12]. Appeals were made to him to ordain a remedy by his prerogative and right[13]. The king it was claimed could do anything to do justice to the parties[14]. The king was prerogative and therefore no prescription of time ran against him[15],

[1] Ancient Petition, no. 2282. [2] Ibid. nos. 10895, 4605.

[3] Ibid. no. 160. Oxford Historical Society, *Collectanea*, vol. III [1896], p. 116.

[4] K. R. Mem. Roll, no. 81, m. 35 d. L. T. R. Mem. Roll, no. 78, m. 68 d. Vide Appendix of Documents, no. 3.

[5] *Rot. Parl.* vol. I, p. 421. Ancient Petition, no. 361.

[6] Ancient Petition, no. 3841.

[7] H. Cole, *Doc. illustr. Eng. Hist. in 13th and 14th Cent.* p. 46.

[8] Seld. Soc. vol. XXII [1907], *Year Bk* 3–4 *Ed. II*, p. 122. [9] Ibid. p. 120.

[10] Ibid. pp. 120, 123. [11] Seld. Soc., *Eyre of Kent*, vol. I, p. 175.

[12] Holdsworth, *Hist. of Engl. Law*, vol. II, p. 366.

[13] *Rot. Parl.* vol. I, p. 274. [14] *Liber Assisarum* 8 *Ed. III* [1678], p. 27.

[15] *Year Bk* 20–21 *Ed. I* [Rolls Series], p. 68.

a doctrine which was stated by Bracton in the phrase "nullum tempus occurrit regi[1]." If prescriptive right was claimed against the king it could be met with the claim that "no lorde can be more auncienter than the kynge, for all was in hym and came from hym at the begyninge[2]." When the king brought an action against a man he ought to be answered whether he did so with or without a writ[3]. Against the king "qui vos sequitur ex officio" the accused could claim no right to have a counsel[4]. The king could elect whether he would bring a writ in his own name or whether he would make a man answer for a trespass done to him by a writ brought in the name of another person[5]. Parallel with these prerogatives when the king stood as plaintiff was the difficulty of making the king appear as the defendant. Proprietary and possessory writs could not be served against the king: such suit should be brought against him by will[6]. Even in Bracton's time there was no assize against the king unless the disseisin was plain and even then the remedy was of grace[7]. The king bound himself to no one in warranty[8], and he could not be vouched to warranty[9]. When, on account of the trespass of the holder, lands were in the king's hands, the king would not entertain legal process concerning those lands[10]. Complainants could not plead with the king as they could with other people[11]. "If the king's rights are concerned, his pleasure must be taken; he has no superior, he cannot be summoned, none may give him orders; therefore no action will lie against him[12]." There was but one way left and that was by petition. A petition was presented to the king who if he so desired directed the justices to inquire into the matter. This the justices would do but on occasion they could not proceed to a final decision until the king gave leave. A further order from the king was therefore necessary ordering them to proceed to judgment. Judgment was thereupon delivered "saluo semper iure

1 Bracton, *De legibus et consuetudinibus Angliae* [Rolls Series], vol. I, pp. 444–5. Seld. Soc. vol. II [1888], *Select Pleas in Manorial Courts*, ed. F. W. Maitland, p. xxiv.

2 Stanford, *An exposition of the Prerogative* [1567], p. 10.

3 *Year Bk* 20–21 *Ed. I* [Rolls Series], p. 56.

4 *Year Bk* 30–31 *Ed. I* [Rolls Series], p. 530.

5 *Year Bk* 21–22 *Ed. I* [Rolls Series], p. 74.

6 *Year Bk* 33–35 *Ed. I* [Rolls Series], p. 470.

7 *Bracton's Note Book*, cases 76, 401.

8 *Year Bk* 30–31 *Ed. I* [Rolls Series], p. 98

9 *Year Bk* 21–22 *Ed. I* [Rolls Series], p. 286.

10 Ancient Petition, no. 119.

11 *Year Bk* 20–21 *Ed. I* [Rolls Series], p. 112.

12 *Bracton's Note Book*, ed. Maitland, vol. I, p. 129. Cf. case 1108, vol. III, pp. 127–8: "Dominus Rex non potest summoneri nec preceptum sumere ab aliquo cum non habeat superiorem se in regno suo."

domini Regis[1]." The special privileges of the king in matters which directly touched him were a matter of complaint and among the abuses set forth by the *Mirror of Justices* were to make a man answer to the king's suit when he was not indicted or appealed[2] and to suffer judges to be plaintiff for the king[3]; and the writer urged that remedy should be provided in the king's courts even against him[4].

Though where a subject had good cause he might act against the king's request he could not act in opposition to the king's command[5]. The king commanded the justices that no inquisition should be made on a certain behalf[6]. A case of covenant which related to lands held in chief of the king was not prosecuted because there was no commission from the king[7]. Execution against land in the king's hand was stayed until the judges obtained the necessary warrant from the king[8]. The tenants of lands which had been seized into the king's hands were immune from suits because the justices would entertain no plea concerning such land until the king commanded them to do so[9]. Frequently pleas had to wait until the plaintiff had made suit to the king[10], until the justices had communicated with the king[11] or spoken to him on that behalf; and then before judgment was pronounced the finding had to be certified to the king[12]. When execution was respited until the king authorised the justices to issue it "the king notwithstanding his seisin of that kind never in such a case allows any person's right to be delayed by reason of his seisin[13]" for the king would be guided by law[14]. In consideration of the intimate connection between the king and his justices and the extent of his prerogatives it is not surprising that they were often "entirely the king's creatures, their decisions to be

[1] Oxford Hist. Soc. vol. XXXI [1896], *Cartulary of the Monastery of St Friedeswide*, vol. II, pp. 129–134. Cf. Chan. Misc., Bdle 64/1 (28).

[2] Seld. Soc. vol. VII [1893], *Mirror of Justices*, ed. F. W. Maitland, p. 160.

[3] Ibid. p. 161.

[4] Ibid. p. 11.

[5] *Year Bk* 14 *Ed. III* [Rolls Series], p. 310.

[6] Wm Salt Soc., *Coll.* vol. VII [1886], p. 21.

[7] Seld. Soc. vol. XXVI [1911], *Year Bk* 4 *Ed. II*, p. 149.

[8] *Year Bk* 21–22 *Ed. I* [Rolls Series], p. 406.

[9] *Year Bk* 30–31 *Ed. I* [Rolls Series], p. 162.

[10] Seld. Soc., *Year Bk* 4 *Ed. II*, pp. 16–17. Wm Salt Soc., *Coll.* vol. IX [1888], p. 34. *Year Bk* 20–21 *Ed. I* [Rolls Series], p. 388.

[11] *Year Bk* 33–35 *Ed. I* [Rolls Series], pp. 186, 538. Wm Salt Soc., *Coll.* vol. VI, Pt i, pp. 111, 207, 291; vol. VII, pp. 6, 73, 153.

[12] Chan. Misc., Bdle 64/6 (143).

[13] *Year Bk* 30–31 *Ed. I* [Rolls Series], pp. 188–190.

[14] *Year Bk* 32–33 *Ed. I* [Rolls Series], p. 36.

moulded entirely to his will[1]." For the justices might be summoned to appear in person before the king to explain their conduct[2]. Great as was the respect paid to the royal writ or order, much greater was the reverence with which a royal charter was treated. The justices consistently refused to do judgment on a royal charter[3]. A royal charter would serve for seisin[4] and against it "nulla inquisitio patrie est admittenda[5]."

In the customs which governed the place of suing the king had special privileges. It was the king's right to be answered where he pleased, in the court of common pleas or king's bench[6]. He could vary the courts indiscriminately. A writ of contempt for neglect to appear to a writ in king's bench could be brought on his behalf in the common bench[7]. He could transfer a case from the common bench[8] to the king's bench, and by his orders a case was adjourned from before the coroner to the justices of the bench[9]. The king could sue in the bench if he so wished though the subject of the suit was in Wales[10]. An action could be entertained and verdict proceeded to in the king's bench without the warrant for original suit[11] and the common bench had no power to undo what was done there[12].

Closely connected with the judicial privileges of the crown were certain tenurial privileges. Their degree over all other tenurial rights is forcibly illustrated by a petition concerning the advowson of a church in Cornwall which the petitioner urged "soit aportenante a la countee de Cornwaille et ne mie autrement a la corone" which advowson "feurent en les meyns des Rois Dengleterre come en les meyns des contes de Cornewaille" and the church "ne est pas founde en terre qe soit ou onqes feust apartenante en chief et seueralment a la corone eynz est en terre apartenante a la countee de Cornewaille[13]." It was by reason of his prerogative that the king obtained

[1] Seld. Soc., *Eyre of Kent*, vol. I, p. lxxxiii.

[2] *Year Bk* 33–35 *Ed. I* [Rolls Series], p. 138.

[3] *Bracton's Note Book*, cases 857, 1236. Holdsworth, *Hist. Engl. Law*, vol. II, p. 198.

[4] *Year Bk* 32–33 *Ed. I* [Rolls Series], p. 50.

[5] Seld. Soc. vol. V [1891], *Leet Jurisdiction in Norwich*, ed. W. Hudson, p. lxxxviii.

[6] *Year Bk* 14–15 *Ed. III* [Rolls Series], p. 94.

[7] *Year Bk* 15 *Ed. III* [Rolls Series], pp. 346–8.

[8] Wm Salt Soc., *Coll.* vol. VII, p. 14; vol. IX, p. 65.

[9] Seld. Soc. vol. IX [1895], *Select Coroners Rolls*, pp. 20–21.

[10] *Year Bk* 33–35 *Ed. I* [Rolls Series], p. 414.

[11] Seld. Soc., *Year Bk* 3–4 *Ed. II*, p. 115.

[12] Ibid. p. 122.

[13] Ancient Petition, no. 361.

the wardship of the lands held in chief of him[1] and it was stated that order should be taken by the king's council lest wardship and marriage should be delivered out of the king's hands to his disinheritance[2]. All escheats within cities accrued as of right to the king irrespective of what lord the lands were held[3]. It seemed to the king that since his ancestors had been seised since time out of memory with a certain wardship and marriage, that he also ought to be seised of the body of the heir as of his lands "especialment par reson de nostre prerogatiue[4]." When doubt was expressed as to the extent of the grant of franchises, those which were not specifically mentioned were held to remain with the king by his prerogative[5]. When a man's land was forfeited to the king his widow was debarred thereby from obtaining dower[6]. Those who had entered into recognisances with the man whose lands were forfeited could have nothing since the lands were in the king's hands[7]. On the other hand a plea started though not decided before the forfeiture was allowed to continue[8]. As it was the king's right to grant liberties and franchises, so when it pleased him he could reply to a petition seeking rights "Le Roi nest pas uncore auise de grauntir nulles fraunchises[9]."

The same general principles ruled the nature of the king's prerogatives in financial matters. In addition to the income from his demesne, the king had such useful financial rights as purveyance, pre-emption, and prisage[10]. The maltolt which was levied in Scotland[11] as well as in England was of the same character. The king had the right of tallaging his ancient demesne. That right was annexed to the crown of England and could not be separated therefrom except by special deed making express mention of it[12]. The king maintained as a prerogative the right of regulating the currency[13]. Finally it was urged that what belonged to nobody else belonged to the king "propter fisci privilegium[14]."

Legislation and administration were so closely connected in the thirteenth and early fourteenth centuries that they can scarcely be

[1] *Cal. Inq. P. M.* vol. VI, p. 34. [2] Ibid. p. 379.
[3] Seld. Soc., *Eyre of Kent*, vol. I, p. 93.
[4] K. R. Mem. Roll, no. 84, m. 31.
[5] Wm Salt Soc., *Coll.* vol. VI, Pt i, pp. 193–4. [6] Ancient Petition, no. 4719.
[7] Ibid. no. 4660. [8] Ibid. no. 5656. [9] Ibid. no. 5911.
[10] S. Dowell, *History of Taxation and Taxes in England*, 2nd edit. vol. I, p. 17.
[11] *Eng. Hist. Rev.* vol. XXVI [1911], pp. 328–9.
[12] T. Madox, *Firma Burgi*, pp. 248–250.
[13] W. J. Ashley, *Economic History*, vol. I, Pt i, pp. 167–8.
[14] Seld. Soc. vol. VIII [1894], *Bracton and Azo*, ed. F. W. Maitland, p. 105.

considered apart. In Bracton and in a law case in his note book the Statute of Merton is called "noua gracia[1]." What the king had granted of his grace he could interpret and on occasion he did so interpret debated points himself[2]. The matter contained in the Statute of Templars was enacted by the king of his regal authority with the assent of the barons[3]. There were a number of administrative processes which could only be undertaken by the special warrant of the king, such processes touching some such matter as the integrity of the crown[4] or its tenurial rights[5]. Moreover the king possessed the right of intervening at any or every stage in administrative processes. If an official disobeyed the king's mandate and was convicted of it he could be imprisoned until he made fine with the king[6]. What is important to the present purpose is not the king's right to interfere but the fact that he had at his hands the machinery for interference. The administration was the king's; when it pleased him he could interfere, delay, pardon, respite. He had the machinery to exercise and influence in normal times and on normal occasions, in times of stress and on exceptional matters and on matters touching the prerogative.

Before the baronial theory of government and the theories and devices with which they sought to meet the royal theory are discussed the theories and rights of other competing authorities in England will be briefly considered. Though archbishop Stratford could state grandiloquently as late as 1341 that there were "two things by which the world is chiefly governed, the Holy Pontifical Authority and the Royal Power...who doubts but that the Priests of Christ ought to be considered both fathers and masters of Kings and Princes[7]," the king of England had always maintained a strict supervision over the ecclesiastical power. Provincial councils were enjoined to maintain and guard all the things which touched the king's estate, crown, and dignity. They were to do nothing, on pain of forfeiture, to the blemishment of the royal estate or of any of his subjects[8]. The execution of papal letters to the king's prejudice was forbidden[9]. Letters concerning lands and chattels which were

[1] *Bracton's Note Book*, vol. I, pp. 83, 89. [2] Ibid. case 1182.
[3] *Stat. of Realm*, vol. I, p. 196.
[4] Wm Salt Soc., *Coll.* vol. VI, Pt i, pp. 248–9.
[5] *Cal. Inq. P. M.* vol. VI, p. 405.
[6] *Year Bk* 20–21 *Ed. I* [Rolls Series], p. 148.
[7] L. O. Pike, *Constitutional History of the House of Lords*, p. 188.
[8] Wilkins, *Concilia*, vol. II, pp. 312–313.
[9] *Cal. Close Rolls*, 1323–27, p. 523.

not of testament or marriage were prohibited[1] and Stratford was ordered not to convey to the realm or use anything to the prejudice of the king[2]. The keepers of bishoprics vacant by translation, were ordered to deliver the temporalities to the pope's nominee on condition that he renounced such words contained in the papal letters as were prejudicial to the crown[3]. In jurisdiction similarly the king maintained his position. Citations to the Roman curia were held to be contrary to the custom of England and in contempt of the king and those who procured them were imprisoned by the marshal[4]. In a plea which the petitioner stated was to the prejudice of the king and his crown the king ordered the issue of letters to the pope and cardinals[5]. Sometimes however if the pleadings were to be held within the realm and nothing was attempted in derogation of the king's royal dignity they were allowed[6].

The anti-royal writer of the *Mirror of Justices* in his hatred of the royal policy and enactments went so far as to state that a chapter of the Statute of Westminster II was void because it had not received the assent of the pope or the emperor[7]. The general English view however was that the king of England was within his own realm an *emperor vel quasi*[8]. The realm of England had always been free of any imperial subjection[9] and therefore any notary exercising office by imperial authority was not to be admitted[10]. Proclamation of the suspension of such notaries was ordered and duly made[11].

Inasmuch as royal jurisdiction was constantly growing at the expense of feudal franchises by imposing limits to the competency of feudal courts by withdrawing certain pleas[12], it is difficult to fix upon a normal franchise and see what the king's powers with reference to it were, for the king's powers were progressive. The feudal principle that every lord with sufficient tenants to form a court could hold one was not controverted by the royal justices[13]. On the other hand the theoretical limitation of the king's court to pleas touching tenants in chief, defaults of justice, and pleas of the crown was much narrower than practice. Exception was becoming the

[1] *Cal. Close Rolls*, 1313–18, p. 596. [2] Ibid. 1323–27, p. 141.
[3] *Cal. Pat. Rolls*, 1307–13, pp. 4, 6; 1313–17, p. 84.
[4] *Abbrev. Placit.* p. 343. [5] *Rot. Parl.* vol. I, pp. 374–5.
[6] *Cal. Close Rolls*, 1323–27, pp. 91–92.
[7] Seld. Soc., *Mirror of Justices*, pp. 195, xxxiv. [8] Ibid. p. xxxv.
[9] *Foedera*, vol. II, p. 423: "licet regnum nostrum Angliae ab omni subjectione imperiali sit immune et ab origine mundi extiterit alienum." [10] Ibid.
[11] Ibid. *Chronicles of Edward I and Edward II*, vol. I, *Annales Paulini*, p. 288.
[12] Seld. Soc., *Pleas in Manor. Courts*, pp. liii, lix. [13] Ibid. p. xli.

rule and rule the exception[1]. Even in the greatest of English franchises, the palatinate of Durham, royal interference was frequent and decisive. If the bishop failed to do justice there was an appeal to the king[2]. The procedure of producing inhabitants of the palatinate in the royal court allowed the bishop only a slightly increased privilege. A special writ from the king instead of a judicial writ was required to compel the bishop to produce the person required[3]. Restrictions upon the competence of the palatine courts proceeded from the regular process of law and from the royal prerogative[4]. In lesser franchises the royal prerogative exercised a still greater influence. Even if the criminal was pardoned by the person against whom the crime was committed, that is in whose liberty the crime was committed, the king's writ of pardon under the great seal was still necessary[5]. If the bailiff of a lord failed to make the necessary amends a writ of "non omittat propter libertatem" was issued to the sheriff, to whom further execution then belonged[6]. The king treated in a similar manner the franchises of cities and boroughs. He refused to receive the man who had been chosen mayor of Bristol and ordered the townspeople to choose another[7]. The constant attempts of the citizens of London to infringe upon the royal prerogative were resolutely opposed. An inquiry was ordered as to who had taken upon themselves to appoint guardians of the peace there, an action which had usurped the king's prerogative[8]. The commonalty of London brought an action for trespass against a man for being a common forestaller. The action was dismissed because charges of general misconduct could only be made in the king's behalf and in the eyres: "otherwise every man might have this suit whereas it belongs to the king and to his crown which is not to be dismembered[9]." The city however sometimes got round charters of exemption granted by the king by getting the grantees to swear on admission to contribute to all the city charges[10]. The way in which the king was able to keep within limits competing or subordinate authorities suggests that theoretically the barons would have a very difficult task in overcoming the might of the royal prerogatives. The king's practical resources were even more difficult to overcome or evade.

[1] Seld. Soc., *Pleas in Manor. Courts*, p. liii.
[2] G. T. Lapsley, *The County Palatine of Durham*, p. 237.
[3] Ibid. pp. 218–219.
[4] Ibid. pp. 213–215.
[5] Anc. Corresp. vol. XXXV, no. 47.
[6] Wm Salt Soc., *Coll.* vol. IX, pp. 39, 69.
[7] T. Madox, *Hist. of Excheq.* vol. II, p. 94.
[8] *Calendar Letter Books, City of London, D*, p. 282.
[9] Seld. Soc., *Year Bk 2–3 Ed. II*, p. 120.
[10] *Cal. Letter Books, E*, p. 16.

Opposed to the royal position with its large rights and privileges stood the baronial opposition and for it the feudal period had not yet passed. Baronial aims had altered but they were still essentially baronial if no longer feudal and separatist. The barons were assailing a position which was theoretically strong and supported by powerful resources and a well organised administrative system. There were three essentials of success, a political theory of opposition which would successfully combat the royal, force with which to introduce and maintain such a theory and an equally well organised system to take the place of that which existed. It was not sufficient for the barons to maintain that their rank and dignity entitled them to a part in the government of the country and to win that part for themselves by exercising restraint or control over the king. Such a contention had to be worked into the existing political theory, and such a contention could only obtain an opportunity to realise itself if the barons had sufficient practical power to enforce it.

The feudal theory of each baron obtaining sovereign power within his land with no more connection with the central government than an oath of homage to an overlord had ended with the failure to realise baronial aspirations in that direction. The strong monarchy of Henry II had killed the hopes of realising in England the disruptive and separatist tendencies of feudalism. The feudal theory had given place to the oligarchical. The monarchy was a stern reality and the barons sought to wrest from it some share in the government of the land. They endeavoured to make themselves a governing caste. The king was over-strong and there were no limits to his powers. The barons were still the only section in the realm who could stand against him. Parliament was in its infancy. It was necessary that rights should be gained from the king which should eventually become the property of parliament. This the barons did, for their struggles in their own interests as a ruling class finally turned to the profit of parliament.

The important principle which underlay the whole of Magna Carta, that the king was under the law[1] did not obtain when Bracton wrote his *De Legibus et Consuetudinibus Angliae*. Bracton gave a high theory to the kingship. Every person was under the king yet he was under no person. He had no peer in his kingdom. The king ought not to be subject to man but to God and the law, for law made the king. He should therefore give to that law what the law gave

[1] McKechnie, *Magna Carta*, pp. 123–4.

him—dominion and power. Where will and not law had dominion there was no king; yet the king's power should not be restrained[1]. Again the king ought to surpass all his subjects in power. He ought not to have a peer much less a superior. Yet he was not to rule by will but by law for his power was of justice and not of injustice and he was called king from ruling well[2]. When however Bracton discussed the adjudication of an act of the king or a charter the existing text makes him say that the king has a superior, his court, his earls, called counts because they were the king's associates. He who has an associate has a master. If therefore the king was without restraint, that is without law, they ought to put a bridle upon him[3]. The contradiction was glaring and touched the most vital point in politics in Bracton's time. It has therefore been suggested that this latter passage was no part of the original text of Bracton but an interpolation[4]. Its date must have been early as it was incorporated in *Fleta*[5] which was written about 1290[6].

The importance of this point for the present purpose lies in the use of this addition or interpolation by John de Longuevill[7], who was a justice of assize, oyer and terminer and gaol delivery in the reign of Edward II, in a gloss on Bracton attributed to him. To the first passage of Bracton treating of the kingship in which he said that the king had no peer John de Longuevill added as a marginal note:

> Rex ideo sibi associat comites, barones et milites et alios ministros ut sint participes honoris et oneris, quia per se non sufficit sibi ipsi ad regendum populum. Rex enim dicitur a regendo, et qui regere debet praecipere oportet et non praecipi, quia aliter sequeretur quod non esset regens et gubernatus[8] set potius rectus et gubernatus quod quidem non est verum, et satis hoc probatur in littera, quia parem non habet nec superiorem, set hoc videtur instantiam recipere, quia Comites dicuntur socii Regis, et sic arguo: Qui habet socium habet magistrum: Rex habet socium, scilicet, Comitem, ergo Rex habet magistrum, et ultra: Qui habet magistrum habet superiorem: Rex habet magistrum, ergo Rex habet superiorem[9].

Such a use of the view coming in the reign of Edward II is of great interest. The *comites* were those who Bracton said drew their

[1] Bracton, *De Legibus*, vol. I, pp. 38–41. [2] Ibid. vol. II, pp. 172–5.
[3] Ibid. vol. I, pp. 268–9. [4] *Bracton's Note Book*, vol. I, pp. 31–33.
[5] John Selden, *Fleta* [1647], p. 17.
[6] *Britton*, ed. F. M. Nichols [1865], vol. I, Introd. p. xxvi. This date is accepted by Pollock and Maitland, *History of English Law*, 2nd edit. vol. I, p. 210, *Bracton's Note Book*, vol. I, p. 33.
[7] *Britton*, ed. Nichols, vol. I, pp. lxi–lxiii. Vide also *Bracton's Note Book*, vol. I, p. 32. [8] [Corr. gubernans].
[9] Cambridge University MS. Dd. vii. 6, f. 179 b. Seld. Soc., *Bracton and Azo*, p. 125.

name from their companionship or association with the king and who might also be called *consules*, from consulting, for the king had associated with himself such persons for consultation and to govern the people[1]. This Longuevill combined with the other famous passage and proved his point in syllogistic form. The king had earls, associates, masters, superiors.

This would appear to have been the theory held by the barons in the time of Edward II. It involved the view that the king was under the law. The laws could not be altered without the common consent and counsel of all those by whose consent and counsel they were promulgated[2]. A note added to Britton contained the same principle. The king could change the law and establish new ones but not without the assent of the earls and others of his council "quia ubi voluntas unius in toto dominatur ratio plurimum succumbit[3]." Among the rubrics of another Bracton manuscript was *lex parem non habet in Regno*[4]. This position however had not been accepted by the king or his justices. The first and sovereign abuse named by the *Mirror of Justices* was that the king was beyond the law whereas he ought to be subject to it[5]. The king's special command should not override common law[6]; no special ordinance ought to exceed common law[7]; the king should pray for nothing contrary to the law[8], for all these were abuses to the author of the *Mirror*. On the other hand the king's justices who tried the dispute between the earls of Gloucester and Hereford in Edward I's reign when told that there was no legal precedent for making magnates give evidence on oath, replied that the king for the common usefulness by his prerogatives was in many cases above the law and customs used in his kingdom[9]. Gilbert de Roubiry, a justice of the king's bench, said in court towards the close of Edward I's reign that the king was so prerogative in his land that he would have none above him[10], and William de Bereford, chief justice of the common bench under Edward II, made use of the dictum *Le roy est sur la ley*[11]. It was still a debated question whether

[1] Bracton, *De Legibus*, vol. I, pp. 36–37. [2] Ibid. pp. 6–9.

[3] Camb. Univ. MS. Dd. vii. 6, f. 92. *Britton*, ed. Nichols, vol. I, p. 2. Cf. also Selden, *Dissertatio ad Fleta*, p. 468.

[4] Camb. Univ. MS. Ee. iv. 4, f. 2 b.

[5] Seld. Soc., *Mirror of Justices*, p. 155. [6] Ibid. p. 161.

[7] Ibid. p. 184. [8] Ibid. p. 188.

[9] Cf. *Cal. Chancery Rolls (Various)*, 1272–1327, pp. 334–349. *Rot. Parl.* vol. I, pp. 70–77. *Abbrev. Placit.* p. 227.

[10] *Year Bk* 33–35 *Ed. I* [Rolls Series], p. 406.

[11] Seld. Soc. vol. XVII, *Year Bk* 1–2 *Ed. II*, 1307–9, ed. F. W. Maitland, Introd. p. xlv, note 4.

or not the king was under the law; and here was room for dissension and conflict, and even if theoretically the king was under the law, its machinery could not be set in motion against him.

Those whom the addition to the text of Bracton desired to associate with the king in the government of his realm were the earls who Bracton elsewhere had stated were in a special kind of relationship with the king. In contemporary writings and actions there is much to suggest that the earls were recognised as having a greater claim to participate in the government of the country than the barons, and they actually took a preponderating part in the baronial opposition to Edward II. The earls were frequently called *consules* in the writers. A mystical significance was found for the earl's belt[1]. A high position was also assigned to the earls in the *Mirror of Justices* which sought an origin for their power in the coming of the English. According to the number of the king's companions the kingdom was divided into districts, and a district was given to each companion to hold and defend against enemies. It was moreover agreed as law that the king should have his companions to hear and determine in the parliaments all the writs and complaints concerning wrongs done by the king, his family and officials. The companions were now called *comites* and their districts *comitatus*[2]. Very little was said of the barons, and the prelates seemed to have nothing to do with temporal affairs[3]. The writer's political ideal was undoubtedly a narrow oligarchy. The unhistorical nature of his origins does not concern us, it is sufficient to show that the idea of the earls having a part in the administration and being the judges of the wrongs committed by the king was current. The abuses mentioned in the *Mirror* included that ordinances which ought to be made by the common counsel of the king and his earls were then made by the king and his clerks[4]. Without the assent of his earls the king could not change, impair or amend his money nor make money of anything but silver[5].

If there was no mystical interpretation about girding the earl with his sword it had its practical importance, for it was only after the earl had been girded with the sword of the earldom that he was entitled to receive the fee of the third penny of the county in the name of the earldom[6]. In Edward II's day the payment of those sums was

[1] Seld. Soc., *Bracton and Azo*, p. 63.
[2] Seld. Soc., *The Mirror of Justices*, pp. 6–7.
[3] Ibid. pp. xxxviii–xxxix. [4] Ibid. p. 155. [5] Ibid. p. 11.
[6] Cf. *Cal. Close Rolls*, 1272–79, p. 383; 1323–27, p. 390.

in arrear[1]. Earldom was in fact a distinct tenure[2]. The earl of Lincoln held the third penny of his county by service of earldom (*comitatus*)[3] and also manors and liberties as part of the earldom of Salisbury by service of earldom[4]. The earl of Warwick held the castle and office of sheriff of Worcester with other liberties there and other lands in England by service of a whole earldom[5]. The borough and castle of Warwick were also held by him by service of earldom[6]. Such service was to be distinguished from knight's service, as a manor in Warwickshire was said to be held of the king by earldom and by knight service[7]. The earl of Arundel held the castle and borough with other liberties pertaining to the honour of Arundel of the king in chief by service of a fourth part of an earldom[8]. Unfortunately no indication is given of the nature of the service, though originally it must have included some obligations. There was then in the position of earl a difference in status from the baron which, whatever its origin, seemed to imply greater political rights.

During the reign of Edward II the earls take the lead in all political movements. Whether this was due to their tenurial position, their official position as the nominal heads of counties, their personal dignity, or whether it had any connection with the high position which Bracton and others had assigned them is not discoverable. The fact remains that they were the leaders, and it is important to note that it was in 1321 that they first were styled peers[9]. The chronicles speak of the action of the baronial opposition as if it were the action of the earls alone. There were eight earls among the ordainers while the barons numbered but six. In consideration of the difference in total numbers of earls and barons this preponderance was disproportionate. It was the earls that pursued and brought to his death the favourite Gavaston[10]. The song-writer adjured the earls to destroy all traitors[11]. At times too the king acted on the advice of earls alone, though such cases were exceptional, since

[1] *Cal. Close Rolls*, 1307–13, pp. 160, 285. K. R. Mem. Roll, no. 87, m. 3.

[2] Cf. Pollock and Maitland, *Hist. Engl. Law*, vol. I, p. 520: "Often enough has office become property, or rather (for this we believe to be nearer the truth) rights which older and vaguer law had regarded as half official, half proprietary, have become proprietary. Earldoms and serjeanties belong to this category; but we can not distinguish between the lands which the earl has as earl and those which he has as man."

[3] *Cal. Inq. P. M.* vol. V, p. 153. [4] Ibid. pp. 153, 155. [5] Ibid. p. 397

[6] Ibid. pp. 399–400. [7] Ibid. p. 399. [8] Ibid. vol. IV, pp. 56–57.

[9] *Stat. of Realm*, vol. I, pp. 181–4.

[10] Camden Soc. vol. VI [1839], *Political Songs*, ed. T. Wright, p. 261.

[11] Ibid. p. 216.

he was resolutely opposed to the schemes which they tried to enforce upon him. In May, 1315, however, the earls of Pembroke, Warwick, Arundel, Richmond and Hereford were associated with the king about the payment of a debt to the widow of one who had served on the king's side in war[1]. The erection as earl and the fall of Andrew de Harclay illustrate this view of the earl. In the parliament of York in 1322 for his victory over Lancaster at Boroughbridge he was created earl of Carlisle with a grant of 1000 marks a year of lands to maintain his status[2] and he also received a grant of £20 by the style and name of the earl of Carlisle[3]. In a few months he had endeavoured to make a treaty with the Scots, against the will or knowledge of the king, to obtain support for his plans in Lancaster and elsewhere[4]. The attempt was in fact made against the king's direct prohibition[5] and this may have weighed with the king in his subsequent action. He had acted independently as an earl and the first stage of his punishment was to be degradation. He was to be stripped of his dignity by being deprived of the sword he had received from the king[6]. The motive power of the baronial opposition was found in a small number of powerful earls who seemed to desire to form themselves into a ruling class to direct and control the king. Over the barons they had a superiority in dignity and resources and their position was theoretically maintained by high doctrines of the origin and functions of earls. The personal influence of some of the earls had an equally decisive effect upon the barons and throughout the reign the barons appear to have been content to follow the direction of one of the earls.

Of a similar nature was an attempt made by Lancaster to obtain power. Early in the reign of Edward II after search had been made in the rolls in the exchequer for details of the office of steward[7] the stewardship of England was granted to him as appurtenant to the earldom of Leicester[8]. The stewardship had become hereditary in the earldom of Leicester and after the death of Montfort that earldom was held by the earls of Lancaster. Montfort had extended the

[1] Anc. Corresp. vol. XLV, no. 186. Vide App. of Doc. no. 120.

[2] *Cal. Pat. Rolls*, 1321–24, p. 93 (25 March, 1322).

[3] *Cal. Charter Rolls*, 1300–26, pp. 442–3 (30 April, 1322).

[4] *Chron. Ed. I and Ed. II*, vol. II, *Auctore Bridlingtoniensi*, pp. 81–83. *Victoria County History, Lancaster*, vol. II, p. 202.

[5] *Cal. Close Rolls*, 1318–23, p. 692.

[6] *Chronicle of Lanercost* (ed. Maxwell), pp. 244–5.

[7] K. R. Mem. Roll, no. 81, m. 36.

[8] *Cal. Pat. Rolls*, 1307–13, p. 68 (9 May, 1308).

importance of the office and made it almost an administrative one[1]. Thomas of Lancaster was not merely the holder of the Montfort lands; he was the upholder of the Montfort traditions. He saw potentialities of exaggerating his office of steward of England and making it a means of exercising restraint upon the king. He wished to become to England what the steward of Durham was to the palatinate, its chief administrative officer[2]. The theory of the Lancastrian stewardship which was developed to support these claims[3] is of the greatest interest and importance in a consideration of the baronial opposition and its policy. When there was dissension between the king and Lancaster in 1317, the king was at York, the earl at Pontefract. The king ordered his army to meet him at York. It hastened to the king but was not allowed to cross with arms. The earl kept the bridge and prevented any armed men or arms from crossing. He declared that he did this because he was steward of England whose duty it was to protect the interests of the kingdom. If the king wished to take up arms against anyone, he ought to warn the steward immediately[4].

This claim grew still larger. The marshal of England appointed the deputy marshal of the household[5]. On this analogy Lancaster claimed to appoint the steward of the household as his deputy. At the parliament of York in 1318 he had presented a charter on a claim he had made concerning the stewardship of England[6], but it was not until the following year that his claims reached their high water mark. When in the parliament of 1318 the barons had proceeded to nominate the steward of the king's household Lancaster had challenged that appointment[7]. At the parliament of York in 1319 the earl again prayed the king to grant him the stewardship of his household which he claimed belonged to him by reason of the honour of Leicester of which he had been seised by the king[8]. This claim was of the utmost importance. The steward was the great officer of the household and with such an appointment in the hands of the leader of the baronial opposition the king would have been held in the strictest tutelage. The whole case erected in support of the

[1] L. W. V. Harcourt, *His Grace the Steward*, pp. 115–128. Cf. *Eng. Hist. Rev*. vol. I [1886], p. 162.

[2] Lapsley, *Pal. of Durham*, pp. 77–80.

[3] Ibid. pp. 141–169.

[4] *Chron. Ed. I and Ed. II*, vol. II, *Auctore Malmesberiensi*, p. 230.

[5] J. H. Round, *King's Serjeants*, p. 85.

[6] Cole, *Doc. illustr. Eng. Hist. in 13th and 14th Cent.* p. 8.

[7] Ibid. p. 3.

[8] Ibid. p. 48.

theory of the Lancastrian stewardship[1] had as its object control of the king. It was one of the methods by which the barons sought to find a theoretical basis for their schemes against the king to exercise restraint upon his powers.

Another of the theories which the barons sought to use during the reign of Edward II was that of a distinction between the king and the crown. The doctrine of capacities was not new to England. It first manifested itself in the distinction between the spiritual and temporal position of ecclesiastics. Immediately after the Norman conquest Odo, bishop of Bayeux, had asserted his clerical privilege and had said that he was a clerk and that it was not lawful to condemn a bishop without the judgment of the pope. William I replied by saying that he condemned him not as bishop but as earl[2], for Odo was also earl of Kent. Doomsday Book itself had distinguished between the ecclesiastical lands which a bishop held and the lands he had inherited from his father[3]. In Richard I's day Hugh de Nunant, bishop of Coventry, was cited to answer for acting against his fealty. The king's council adjudged that if he should fail to appear within forty days he should be subject to the judgment of the bishops inasmuch as he was a bishop, and to the judgment of laymen inasmuch as he had been a royal sheriff[4]. A clear distinction was drawn between his position as an ecclesiastic and as a royal official. Bracton too had laid it down that the king had power to direct processes against bishops by reason of their baronies[5]. A dispute between the archbishop of York and Anthony de Bek, bishop of Durham, in Edward I's reign was called to the king's court where the king's serjeant stated that the bishop of Durham "habet duos status, videlicet statum episcopi quoad spiritualia et statum comitis palacii quoad tenementa sua temporalia[6]." The archbishop admitted this and said that all bishops had a twofold capacity, a spiritual office and a secular dignity. The reign of Edward II opened with the enforcement of this doctrine against Walter de Langton, bishop of Coventry and Lichfield, Edward I's treasurer. He was arrested and cast into

[1] Harcourt, *His Grace the Steward*, pp. 148–151.

[2] *Ordericus Vitalis* (Patrologia, Migne, vol. CLXXXVIII), Pt III, Bk VII, § vii, pp. 529–530.

[3] Pollock and Maitland, *Hist. Engl. Law*, vol. I, p. 506.

[4] *Chron. R. de Houeden*, vol. III, p. 242. Cf. Pike, *Const. Hist. of House of Lords*, p. 180.

[5] Bracton, *De Legibus*, vol. VI, pp. 370–1, 492–3.

[6] *Rot. Parl.* vol. I, pp. 102–5. *Cal. Close Rolls*, 1288–96, pp. 330–4. Lapsley, *Pal. of Durham*, pp. 53, 191. T. Madox, *Baronia Anglica* [1741], pp. 150–2.

prison for abuses he was charged with during his tenure of office, and kept in prison[1] despite the protests of bishops[2].

Early in the reign of Edward I the doctrine of capacities was applied to the official and private capacities of the chancellor. One of the baronial adherents of Montfort's time applied that he might redeem his lands according to the Dictum of Kenilworth. The other party claimed that a charter had been made offering to redeem the lands at £50,000 and that the charter had been acknowledged before the chancellor and enrolled on the chancery roll. Against this it was claimed that the charter was made under duress in prison. The chancellor had come to him in a room where he was lying in strict custody, laid before him the writing and asked if it had been made by him. He had acknowledged it out of bodily fear. He therefore pleaded that the acknowledgment should not bind him "because it was made when the chancellor was remote from his court and when he had neither clerks with him nor the rolls of Chancery, but had come alone into a chamber where he was lying a prisoner, not as a chancellor but as a private person of the people[3]." A still more important application of the doctrine, this time by the king in his own favour, was made by Edward I. After his accession to the throne he sought to revoke a grant of a franchise he had made as prince to the earl of Warenne. The line he took, though it made no direct distinction between the king and the crown, was one which was dangerous, for it drew a distinction between what was done as prince and as king and by implication this would be made to apply to a distinction between king and crown. The king pleaded that he was then of another state than when he made the grant and was as if another person[4]. The earl urged that he was one and the same person when in the kingly state as when in the state in which he was commonly called lord Edward[5]. This all prepared for the use which was to be made of the doctrine by the barons in the reign of Edward II.

It has been said that at this period "the rights of the king are conceived as differing from the rights of other men rather in degree

[1] Vide below, I, pp. 55–56.

[2] Vide *Regist. Palat. Dunelm.* vol. I, pp. 38–39. Surtees Soc. [1906], vol. CXIII, *The Records of Northern Convocation*, pp. 53–54. Canterbury and York Soc. vol. VII [1911], London, vol. I, *Regist. R. de Baldock*, p. 74.

[3] Wm Salt Soc., *Coll.* vol. VI, Pt i, *Coram Rege Rolls, Trin.* 2 *Ed. I*, pp. 63–64: "non quasi cancellarius sed quasi privata persona de populo."

[4] *Placita de Quo Warranto*, pp. 429–430: "est alterius condicionis quam prius fuit et quasi altera persona."

[5] Ibid.: "Una et eadem persona est tam in statu regis quam in statu quo vocabatur communiter dominus Edwardus."

than in kind[1]." His rights were private rights amplified and intensified[2]. The lands he held as a private person and by strict hereditary right, "and between the lands and the kingship it would be hard to distinguish[3]." No marked line was drawn between those proprietary rights which the king had as king and those which he had as a private person[4]. The growth of the doctrine of capacity was a slow process but some step in this direction had been made, especially when the king relied upon it in a case in his own court. It remained for the barons to make the important application of it to the distinction between king and crown.

Unfortunately much cannot be argued from the use which the barons made of the doctrine, for they did not apply it consistently. In 1308 they applied it in proceedings which they made in parliament against Gavaston as a result of which he was exiled[5]. In 1321 when they were preparing a process of exile against the two Despensers they made the first count of the charge that when the younger Despenser had been angered with the king he had entered into a bill with a number of barons to constrain the king by harsh means to do his will[6]. The tenor of the bill was given and it agrees with the form which had been used in the baronial action against Gavaston. Either the barons detected no inconsistency or thought that the body of barons could do in the public interest what an individual baron could not do in his private interest, for what they had used as a weapon to condemn Gavaston they made as a charge against Despenser. The doctrine ran:

> Homage and oath of allegiance is more by reason of the crown than by reason of the king's person and is more bound to the crown than to the person and this appears in that before the estate of the crown hath descended no allegiance is due to the person, wherefore if the king by chance be not guided by reason, in right of the crown, his lieges are bound by oath made to the crown to guide the king and the estate of the crown back again by reason, and otherwise the oath would not be kept. The question now arises how one ought to guide the king whether by suit of law or by constraint: by suit of law one cannot have redress because he will have no judges but the king's in which case if the king's will be not according to reason he will have nothing but error maintained, wherefore it behoveth in order to save the oath that when the king will not redress the matter or remove that which is evil and damaging for the people at large and for the crown, it is to be adjudged that the matters shall be removed by harsh

[1] Pollock and Maitland, *Hist. of Engl. Law*, vol. I, p. 512.
[2] Ibid. p. 231. [3] Ibid. p. 513. [4] Ibid. p. 518.
[5] *Ann. Paul.* pp. 153–4. *Auct Bridl.* pp. 33–34.
[6] *Stat. of Realm*, vol. I, p. 812. *Auct. Bridl.* p. 65.

measures for he is bound by oath to govern his people and his lieges, and his lieges are bound to govern in his aid and in his default[1].

The doctrine was a complete assault upon the king's position. Everything had previously been considered personal to him. To take but one instance, justice was personal to the king. When he died his peace died with him. A man who had committed a trespass before a king's death could not be impleaded in the reign of his successor[2]. Now a distinction was to be drawn between what was personal and what was official. The whole tendency of the theory accorded rather with the policy and aims of the baronial opposition than with those of a royal favourite. The younger Despenser was never a mere favourite and the use of this political principle shows him as no mere servile supporter of the royal position. For this theory admitted and advocated, equally with the principles and action of the baronial opposition, the doctrine of coercion and restraint; if the king was not guided by reason his lieges were bound by their oaths to lead him. The oaths of allegiance were made to the crown and not to the king and in their fidelity to and protection of the crown and its rights the barons must exercise restraint upon the king who through his action injured the rights of the crown. This doctrine would seem to underlie the Ordinances. The Ordinance which forbad gifts of lands by the king without the consent of the barons in parliament[3] may be taken as an instance. The king had given grants to the damage of the crown. It was therefore the duty of the barons to step in and prevent the crown from being damaged. This they did by repealing all grants that had been made after a certain day and forbidding grants to be made in future without the assent of the barons in parliament. In 1315 Roger de Mortimer of Chirk, to whom the king had granted the lands and castles of Blaenllyfni and Dinas which he had purchased from John the son of Reginald, a grant made after the appointed day and therefore resumed, petitioned for the recovery of the lands and castles. He based his petition upon the fact that the lands did not pertain to the crown but had been purchased by the king from John the son of Reginald and that therefore the Ordinances did not apply[4]. This petition drew a clear distinction between the lands which belonged to the crown and those which belonged by purchase or otherwise to the king.

[1] *Stat. of Realm*, vol. I, p. 182.
[2] Cf. Seld. Soc., *Year Bk* 3 *Ed. II*, p. 104.
[3] Ordinance 7.
[4] *Rot. Parl.* vol. I, p. 305.

In almost every direction in which the baronial opposition desired to exercise restraint upon the king and take a share in his government the theory which drew a distinction between the king and the crown would have benefited them. They could by its means have distinguished between the administrative departments of the chancery, exchequer, and courts of justice, and the household departments of the privy seal, wardrobe and marshalsea court. When the king's administration of the departments of government became bad, or when he failed to get rid of the abuses which had crept in, according to this theory the barons could well intervene and amend the administration. It was in fact their duty to do so. The public and personal departments were not distinctly marked off. They had all descended from the king's court. They shaded off into one another. The barons under Edward II did not confine their attentions to the reform of the administrative departments. Their constant demand was for reform of the household. If however the personal and official functions of the king were to be distinguished the barons should have concentrated their attention upon the administrative departments and allowed the king full and free control over his household. This was clearly impossible as the two were but different manifestations of one system. The barons were attacking a system and wherever theory interfered with the efficacy of the attack it had to be discarded.

The theory was not altogether a source of strength to the barons. Feudalism was based upon the personal relation of lord and vassal and hence the whole of the system erected upon feudalism was personal. Fealty and obedience was however becoming less and less of a personal thing. Peaceful accessions of kings, lack of competitors for the crown, the strength of the royal power and the multitude of its resources all tended to make the division between reigns less in point of time, and of diminishing importance. The necessity of getting charters renewed on the accession of each king was disappearing. What one granted was regarded as binding upon his successors. Here however the fiscal question came in and complicated and delayed the natural course of events. Fines for confirmation of charters formed a fruitful source of revenue. Yet while it aimed a serious blow at the personal power of the king this theory did not impair the prerogative. Abuse of a right by the king did not condemn the right. It simply meant that measures had to be taken to prevent the abuse in the future and to maintain its proper use in the present. All this could be done without detracting from the prerogatives of the crown. The theory was prepared to see the prerogatives of the crown maintained, but at the cost of the practical and personal power of the king.

The unfortunate part of this theory as of all others was that there was no tribunal which could decide what pertained to the crown and what to the king. The king was the one interpreter. This was an impossible position and the only solution of the schemes and theories of baronial opposition lay in the exercise of coercion—a solution which was only justified by its complete and continual success. The doctrine was however to have no future in English history or political theories. The successful end of the baronial process of exile against the Despensers in which the barons had condemned the use of the doctrine by a baron rendered it in Coke's phrase "a damnable and damned" doctrine[1]. In the reign of Edward II it had a certain importance. It was used by the barons in the condemnation of a favourite. It was used by a favourite in an endeavour to impose restraint upon the king. As a justification of restraint and coercion it had considerable force. As a political theory it had much in common with the aims and action of the baronial opposition and in the circumstances it is surprising that its use was not more general.

No charge was made more consistently against Edward II than that he employed evil counsellors and acted on their advice. "Evil counsel" was used by the barons as a convenient phrase to express discontent with and disapproval of the king's policy. Anyone who advised the king contrary to the baronial desire was an evil counsellor. Lancaster's opposition was based upon the fact that the king neglected the advice which he and his associate barons had to offer in favour of other counsel. The pope accordingly besought Edward to remove from court anyone whose presence was displeasing to Lancaster, upon which the pope felt sure that the earl would prove himself a faithful subject[2]. The wrongs which the king did were attributed to those who were around him and who advised him, and from this point of view the baronial cry against evil counsellors may be regarded as an anticipation of the doctrine of the responsibility of ministers. The writer who sang against the king's taxes prayed, in order that the king might prosper, that his false advisers should be cursed[3]. The wickedness which prevailed on every side ought not to

[1] Coke, *Reports* [1608], 7th Part, pp. 11–12, Calvin's Case. John Allen, *Enquiry into the Rise and Growth of the Royal Prerogative* [1830], pp. 84–86.

[2] *Cal. Papal Letters*, 1304–42, p. 434.

[3] Camd. Soc., *Political Songs*, p. 182.

be laid to the charge of the king but to the bad counsellor and his rapacity[1]. It was by evil counsellors that the king had caused the temporalities of various bishops to be seized into his hands[2]. The king alone was excepted from the song writer's curse of those who were responsible for the commissions of trailbaston[3]. Sometimes the king was classed with others, and the shutting of the gates of London in November, 1323, was attributed to the plots of the king and other evil men[4].

The iteration and reiteration of the phrase *evil counsel* during the reign becomes monotonous. At every stage of baronial opposition it was made. The advice of anyone not acceptable to the barons was considered of necessity as derogatory to the king and crown and prejudicial to themselves. Gavaston drew the charge upon himself, and his exile when he went to Ireland was attributed to the evil counsel he had given the king[5]. The elder Despenser, Nicholas de Segrave, William de Bereford and William Inge who had given Gavaston some measure of support[6] therefore drew down the baronial wrath upon themselves, and their removal from the king's counsel and presence was ordered[7]. The barons found the occasion for the Ordinances in the bad and deceitful counsel that had been given the king[8]. One of the Ordinances ordered the removal of the bad counsellors who had evilly guided and counselled the king[9], and the appointment of ministers by the barons was ordained because of the evils which had arisen from bad counsellors and officials[10]. When the earl of Pembroke was in charge of the administration and Anthony Pessaign, who was closely associated with him, had been given the charge of the tin mines of Cornwall the sheriff of that county stated in full county court that the king had bad counsellors and was evilly counselled when he made that gift[11]. When the king in 1313 failed to meet the barons in parliament the blame for his failure was placed upon the evil counsellors whose advice he followed[12]. The king's miseries were due to his court for the courtiers were consumed by avarice[13]. The conduct of his officials was also reprehensible[14]. The Despenser war was caused by the fact that the father and son were

[1] Camd. Soc., *Political Songs*, p. 184.
[2] *Stat. of Realm*, vol. I, p. 255.
[3] Camd. Soc., *Political Songs*, p. 231.
[4] *Ann. Paul.* p. 306.
[5] *Chron. Murimuth*, p. 12.
[6] *Chron. Lanerc.* p. 187.
[7] *Ann. Paul.* p. 264.
[8] *Stat. of Realm*, vol. I, p. 157.
[9] Ordinance 13.
[10] Ordinance 14.
[11] K. R. Mem. Roll, no. 86, m. 76 d. L. T. R. Mem. Roll, no. 83, Rec. St. Hill. m. 1 d. Vide App. of Doc. no. 19.
[12] *Auct. Malm.* p. 194.
[13] Ibid. p. 223.
[14] Ibid. p. 239.

evil counsellors and the seducers of the king[1]. They were exiled and the process against them was one long indictment based upon the evil counsel they had given the king. Yet after their banishment the earl of Lancaster called an assembly, in November, 1321, to treat for the reformation of the evils that he alleged had arisen from the king's evil counsellors[2].

The crushing of the barons in 1322 caused a lull, but the charge was to be revived with increasing frequency as the preparations for the revolution of 1326 were hastened and as that revolution took its path. The revolution sought its justification in the evil counsel the king had followed and the evil counsellors he had allowed to guide him. The younger Despenser was then the special object of attack[3], though Despenser the elder, the earl of Arundel, the bishop of Exeter and Master Robert de Baldock, the chancellor, also came in for their share of odium[4]. The queen stated her object was to remove from the king the evil counsellors who had committed such harm and she proceeded against him because he would not dismiss them[5]. The magnates of the kingdom joined because of the hatred they bore the king's evil counsellors[6]. The Londoners sided with her for the ill will which they harboured against the king for his evil counsel[7]. The whole kingdom rejoiced because the knell of the king's false counsellors was being sounded[8]. The writs which the queen issued stated the purpose for which she had come[9] and in the processes against the Despensers the evil counsel which they had given the king was recounted[10]. The first parliament of Edward III kept up the cry. The knights who had taken part in the quarrel of the two Despensers "et les autres malveis conseilers le Roi et Enemys de la Terre" were pardoned[11]. The commonalty showed certain grievances which the king had made "par maveys consail et abbet" of the two Despensers, Arundel, Baldock and other evil counsellors[12] which included taking lands by fraud and force[13]. This parliament made one of the most shameless applications of the cry of evil counsel when they said that the Despensers came to England after their exile "by evil counsel

[1] *Chron. H. Knighton*, vol. I, p. 421.

[2] *Cal. Close Rolls*, 1318–23, pp. 505–6.

[3] *Flores Hist.* vol. III, p. 216: "nequissimo consiliario suo."

[4] *Ann. Paul.* pp. 317–321. *Auct. Bridl.* pp. 86–87. *Chron. Murimuth*, p. 47. *Chronica Monasterii de Melsa*, vol. II, pp. 350–2. *Memorials of St Edmund's Abbey*, vol. II, pp. 327–9.

[5] *Chron. Lanerc.* pp. 250–1.

[6] *Chron. Knighton*, vol. I, p. 432.

[7] Ibid. p. 434.

[8] Ibid. p. 435.

[9] *Abbreviatio Originalium*, vol. I, p. 303.

[10] *Ann. Paul.* pp. 317–318. *Auct. Bridl.* pp. 87–89.

[11] *Rot. Parl.* vol. II, p. 6.

[12] Ibid. p. 8.

[13] Ibid. pp. 11, 12.

which the king had then near him without the assent of the peers and commons of the realm[1]." In view of the revocations which had been made in due form in the parliament of York in 1322 of the process of exile made by the coercive action of the barons against them and the king this statement was grossly unfair. It resolves itself in fact into the usual meaning of the charge that the barons considered that counsel evil which was opposed to their wishes.

A less biassed view of the counsel which the king followed is found in the letters which the pope wrote to the king on this matter. The pope urged him to remove those friends whose youth and imprudence injured the affairs of the realm[2]. He was enjoined to choose counsellors and officials who loved truth and justice and to beware lest backbiters or malicious flatterers caused the good feeling which then existed between the king and Lancaster to end[3]. The advice which the king followed was frequently unsatisfactory. His advisers were often foolish. It was a political and constitutional grievance that the barons made when they attacked the evil counsellors. Many of them were personally objectionable to the barons and personal motives played no small part in baronial actions. Yet the cry of evil counsel was based upon a constitutional grievance.

The barons claimed that it was their right to have a share in the administration of the country. The evil counsellors prevented them from coming into their own. They were usurping functions of government which the barons claimed belonged to them. The only advice that could be good was that which the barons gave, and government could only be well administered when the barons had a decisive share in and control over the government. The grievance of evil counsellors involved the whole of the household position, for it was owing to the personal or household system of government and its strength that such counsel could be given. The efficiency and execution of such advice was due to the household system which allowed unofficial persons, favourites, and friends to become the supreme influence on the mind of the king and hence in the affairs of government. For the phrase seems to have been applied especially to the small circle of intimate personal advisers that the king had gathered round him. That circle was not composed entirely or principally of favourites and their followers. It contained a number of official persons, important and unimportant, justices, clerks of chancery and household officials. The "administrative" council would appear at times to

[1] *Stat. of Realm*, vol. I, p. 251.
[2] *Cal. Pap. Letters*, 1304–42, p. 430.
[3] Ibid. p. 444.

have been included in the charge. A general cry of this nature had many benefits. It was sufficiently indefinite to be applied under varying circumstances and in a diversity of cases with equal effect. The cry was not new. In previous times it had been directed against favourites, foreigners and the new officials, who usurped rights which the barons claimed, or prevented the barons claiming their demands. In the reign of Edward II the cry was directed especially against the household system and all that it involved.

It had been made the chief charge against the Despensers in the process of exile[1] against them that they had accroached royal power, and the same charge was repeated against them after their deaths though Baldock and Arundel were then added[2]. These four had usurped royal power and the king did nothing and would do nothing except as they counselled him[3]. The king, with more truth, made it a charge in the process against Lancaster in 1322 that he had usurped royal power[4]. It was against the royal prerogative as exercised, controlled or exploited by such ministers as the Despensers that the barons stood in opposition. For the time being the question of the advisability or otherwise of the prerogative was neglected. The barons dealt with practical questions in a direct way. Their immediate object was to supply a remedy for the Despensers' encroachment on royal power and prerogative. The immediate object was ever the first consideration and the process of exile contained no attack upon the prerogative, but merely upon its abuse by irresponsible persons. The primary motive was the expulsion of the Despensers from the royal counsel and from the kingdom, and this was achieved. In doing this as in the Ordinances the barons claimed to be vindicating the royal power. The amount of justification which they had can be illustrated from one count in the charge against the Despensers—that of procuring the death of Llewelyn Bren, the Welsh rebel[5]. He had rebelled in Glamorgan in 1316 and had been forced to surrender to the earl of Hereford and Roger Mortimer of Wigmore, a surrender made under certain conditions. He was led a prisoner to the Tower where he remained for two years. Meanwhile Despenser the younger had obtained possession of the land of Glamorgan in the right of his wife. He secured the person of Llewelyn Bren from the Tower and led him to Cardiff where he was executed. The barons maintained, with justification, that the execution was in great despite of the king. Llewelyn had been received under

[1] *Stat. of Realm*, vol. I, pp. 181–4. [2] Ibid. p. 251. [3] Ibid.
[4] *Rot. Parl.* vol. II, p. 4. [5] *Stat. of Realm*, vol. I, p. 183.

conditions and Hereford and Mortimer had promised him grace, and the king had received him under like conditions. Despenser moreover had seized jurisdiction in a case in which according to reason he could have none. Even if Llewelyn was guilty and had been received without condition, as the rebellion had taken place when Glamorgan was in the king's hands, Despenser had no jurisdiction in the matter. The barons therefore considered that he had accroached royal power and exercised jurisdiction "that pertained to the crown in disinheritance of the crown, dishonour of the king and of the lords of Hereford and Mortimer[1]." The Despensers had usurped royal power by virtue of the position they held near the king. They owed that position to the personal or household system of government. If the barons wished to control the king they had to consider what means they could discover to overcome that system.

The barons claimed a share in the direction of royal policy and in the decision of royal acts. Bracton had said that what had the force of law in England was not "quod principi placuit" but "quicquid de consilio et consensu magnatum et reipublicae communi sponsione, auctoritate regis sive principis praecedente, iuste fuerit definitum et approbatum," though he held that the magnates consented if they did not dissent[2]. The barons might have claimed to have been carrying out this principle and to be insisting that the king no less than his people was subject to the rule of law. To the royal partizans on the other hand the aim of the barons was something very much worse; it was to make the king dependent upon and subservient to the will of the baronage. To them it seemed that the vital question was, which was to hold sovereign power—king or barons? The barons urged that their assent was necessary to various acts of the king, administrative and otherwise. Instances in which the chronicles state that the assent of the barons was given or not given indicate to some extent the baronial policy and demands. Edward II was stated to have succeeded to the throne "non tam jure haereditario quam unanimi assensu procerum et magnatum[3]." The queen crossed to France in 1314 "ex assensu regis et procerum[4]." The truce with Scotland in 1323 was made by the assent of the prelates and barons[5]. On the other hand it was noted that Gavaston was made earl of Cornwall "contra voluntatem omnium nobilium

[1] *Stat. of Realm*, vol. I, p. 183. [2] Seld. Soc., *Bracton and Azo*, pp. 11–13.
[3] T. Walsingham, *Historia Anglicana*, vol. I, p. 119.
[4] *Auct. Bridl.* p. 85.
[5] *Chronica H. de Blaneford*, p. 134.

regni[1]" though the earl of Lincoln seems to have assented[2]. The king adhered to foreigners, the barons of the realm not being consulted[3]; and the exile of the Despensers was annulled without parliament and the assent of the barons[4].

It is true that on occasion when it suited his purpose the king declined to proceed upon some action because he could not have the necessary deliberation with his prelates and barons[5], but this was only a convenient excuse for dismissing an unpleasant topic. It is equally true that the king claimed to undertake various deeds connected with the Scottish war[6], the siege of Berwick in 1319[7] for instance, by the assent of the magnates. Commands to justices of assize even were made "de lassent de touz les grauntz de nostre roiaume qi sount pres de nous[8]" and the earls and barons with the king gave their counsel and assent on other matters[9] and the Ordinances give a list of the matters on which the barons considered their assent should be required and given. The king might accept such claims under stress, but he certainly was not prepared to subscribe to the baronial theory. The king's obedience was conditional upon baronial strength, and therefore it is important to consider the organisation of that force.

A number of the theories and motives which influenced baronial action have been considered; it is now necessary to consider what general means the baronial opposition adopted to achieve its purposes. It will be seen that the methods employed by the barons were all dependent upon force. The theory of the opposition was founded upon force. The first question which confronted them was how the force at their disposal could be best organised. The question of method practically resolved itself into a question of the organisation of force.

By the time of Edward II the feudal contract, as far as military service was concerned, was breaking down, and greater reliance was being placed upon the written contract in the form of a bond or indenture. The protection of the Scottish march was provided for by indentures made between the king and barons by which the barons promised, in return for a certain fee, to retain an agreed

[1] *Ann. Monast.* vol. III, *Ann. Mon. de Bermundeseia*, p. 469.
[2] *Auct. Malm.* p. 155.
[3] *Auct. Bridl.* pp. 32–33.
[4] *Chron. Mon. de Melsa*, vol. II, p. 339.
[5] *Cal. Close Rolls*, 1272–79, pp. 197–8.
[6] *Rotuli Scotiae*, vol. I, pp. 133, 159, 160.
[7] Chan. Warr., File 108/5067. *Cal. Doc. Scotl.* vol. III, p. 124.
[8] Chan. Warr., File 108/5059.
[9] Anc. Corresp. vol. XLIX, no. 6.

number of men in the defence of the Scottish march. The indenture was made before the king's council and on the royal part sealed with the privy seal[1]. This was a dangerous precedent to set as it helped to break down the personal bond between king and vassal and gave the barons an appropriate method upon which to found opposition to the king. The king even employed the plan in local administration. He entered into an indenture with John Darcy the nephew in 1323 by which the latter received the office of sheriff of Lancaster and promised to stay in the safeguard of the county and to grieve the king's enemies with 40 men at arms, 6 knights and 20 hobelers at the king's wages for which he was to receive £78. 8*s*.[2] The disordered state of Lancaster after the baronial rising of 1322 was probably the cause of such a measure but a method of this nature was dangerous when applied to local administration.

The king applied it in even more personal matters. At Boulogne in January, 1308, the barons who had accompanied him to France, including the earls of Lincoln, Warenne, Pembroke and Hereford and Robert de Clifford, entered into a solemn agreement to defend the king's person and the rights of his crown and to redress what was amiss[3]. Hugh D'Audley the younger bound himself in writing to aid the king to the utmost of his power and to do whatever the king should require of him. When he took part against the Despensers in 1321 the king forfeited his lands on the plea that he had adhered to the barons against his oath[4]. In the last crisis with the barons the king made use of the same device. The king granted the earl of Athol a certain manor and castle in consideration of his service to the king and in December, 1321, the earl bound himself in writing to adhere to the king and maintain his quarrel against all men. If he failed to do this the castle, manor and honour were to be resumed[5]. In June, 1322, the earl of Pembroke, on account of suspicions which the king held of him, entered into a bond "of his free will and without coercion sworn upon the gospels to be obedient aiding and counselling to the king as his liege lord in all his matters and all his enterprises whatsoever and to come to him at all times when ordered,

[1] *Cal. Doc. Scotl.* vol. III, pp. 31–32, etc., gives a considerable number of such indentures. The originals are found in P. R. O. Exchequer Accounts, King's Remembrancer, 68/2. Vide App. of Doc. no. 46. For an instance of Ed. III's reign vide Surtees Soc. vol. CXVII [1909], *Percy Cartulary*, p. 272.

[2] K. R. Account, 68/2, no. 17. Vide App. of Doc. no. 47.

[3] Dugdale, *Baronage* [1675], vol. I, p. 183, quoting a Cotton MS.

[4] *Cal. Close Rolls*, 1318–23, p. 365. *Cal. Pat. Rolls*, 1317–21, pp. 572–3, 575. *Auct. Malm.* p. 256.

[5] *Cal. Close Rolls*, 1318–23, pp. 509–510.

without excuse, unless prevented by illness or other sufficient excuse, and to aid and maintain the king in time of peace and war against all men and not to ally himself or make alliance with any one against the king or against any one whom the king will maintain and to suppress with all his power any disobedience against the king," he charged his body, lands and goods and found mainpernors for the observance[1].

This procedure was too good to be neglected by the barons. It gave them an opportunity to consolidate their resources against the king and to bind themselves to work for a common purpose. In the hands of the barons it could be and was used as a powerful instrument against the king. The confederacy of earls and barons that put Gavaston to death in 1312 made use of the device in mutual protection against the anger they knew the deed would arouse in the king. Lancaster and Warwick entered into bonds to defend and save the earl of Hereford with all their power from the damages which could happen to him in the quarrel touching Gavaston as well towards the king as towards all others. Gavaston was to be regarded as the enemy of the king, his kingdom and his people. They promised to live and die in aid and defence of the earl of Hereford and in testimony of this swore upon the gospels[2]. An equally powerful use of the method by Lancaster was the indenture which the earl of Angus and others made with him on 28 June, 1321, to maintain the quarrel which the marcher lords had begun against the Despensers, a confederacy made at the meeting at Sherburn[3].

What could be used against the king could, in the circumstances produced by the household system, be used in his favour. Between the use of this method by the barons and its use by the court party came the application by a number of members of the middle party. The bond by which Pembroke, Badlesmere and Damory bound themselves in 1317 to exercise restraint upon the king[4] did not aim brutally to coerce the king as did the endeavours of the baronial opposition or to provide a force to operate against the baronial opposition and to maintain the royal system. It was a sincere effort to save the king from the extremity of the Lancaster faction though

[1] *Cal. Close Rolls*, 1318–23, pp. 563–4 (22 June, 1322).

[2] The letter of Lancaster is preserved in P. R. O. Duchy of Lancaster, Ancient Correspondence, no. 13. Vide App. of Doc. no. 138. For Warwick's letter vide *Cal. Doc. Scotl.* vol. III, p. 54. The letters are dated 18 June, 1312.

[3] Brady, *Continuation of Complete History* [1700], p. 128. Vide below, pp. 477–8.

[4] *Parliamentary Writs*, vol. II, Pt ii, App. p. 120. Vide below, pp. 433–4.

they were well aware that what they were doing was not in accordance with the king's dignity. Badlesmere obtained pardon for his part in it in August, 1321, when the marcher barons had successfully coerced the king[1].

The use of the method by the court party under Despenser must have been very general. After 1322 the country seems to have been ruled largely by recognisance. Those who had been adherents of the barons in 1322 were forced to enter into recognisance with the king to pay fines, hundreds of such recognisances being made[2]. These recognisances were made to the king but the Despensers also used them on their own behalf[3]. They found recognisances useful instruments in their policy of acquiring lands[4]. After the accession of Edward III, Elizabeth de Burgh, widow of Roger Damory, was released from two recognisances into which her husband had entered with the Despensers. It was found upon investigation that the recognisances were not made by reason of debt but "pur seurte dacort faire entre les parties[5]." An indenture into which the younger Despenser had entered with John Gifford, Richard de Grey and others was made a charge in the process of exile against him[6]. Despenser observed a greater show of constitutional form in his indentures than did the barons. One made in 1316 with Peter de Overdale, knight, for serving with him with ten men at arms for the term of his life in peace and war in England, Scotland and Wales, in case of default £400 having to be paid to Despenser, made a saving clause of the fealty of the king and the father of the knight[7]. The commonalty prayed in the first parliament of Edward III that the bonds into which Edward II by false counsel had forced many to enter, "par escritz de venir au Roi a force et armes en chascun tens qil furent maunde sur peyne de vie et de membre et de quant qil puissent forfere," should be rendered void[8], the burden of which was granted[9]. It was enacted that "the king considering that such writings were made to the king's dishonour, since that every man is bound to do to the king, as to his liege lord, all that pertaineth to him without

[1] *Cal. Pat. Rolls*, 1321–24, pp. 15–21. *Parl. Writs*, vol. II, Pt i, p. 264. *Foedera*, vol. II, p. 454 (20 August, 1321).

[2] *Cal. Fine Rolls*, 1319–27, pp. 152–173, 233–5, 240, 280–1, 293–5. Cf. *Rot. Parl.*, vol. II, p. 5.

[3] *Cal. Close Rolls*, 1323–27, p. 647. Wm Salt Soc., *Coll.* vol. IX, p. 91.

[4] Cf. *Cal. Close Rolls*, 1323–27, p. 174. Vide P. R. O. Exchequer Miscellanea, 3/6.

[5] Ancient Petition, no. 1725.

[6] *Stat. of Realm*, vol. I, p. 182.

[7] *Descriptive Catalogue of Ancient Deeds*, vol. IV, p. 252 (30 August, 1316).

[8] *Rot. Parl.* vol. II, p. 10.

[9] Ibid. p. 12.

any manner of writing, willeth, that from henceforth no such writing be made[1]." In view of the oath which those who attended this parliament were forced to swear at its beginning this high doctrine was incongruous. They had to swear that they would safely guard the person of the queen and her son and maintain with all their power the quarrel begun against Despenser, Baldock and their adherents[2].

The object of the bonds and indentures into which the barons entered was that they might exercise restraint upon the king. The object of the illegal assemblies and confederacies in which these bonds and indentures were made or those assemblies and confederacies which resulted from their making was the same. These assemblies and confederacies may be compared to the "bands" or associations which the Scottish nobles formed so frequently in the fifteenth century[3] for an object which had much in common with the objects of the baronial assemblies and confederacies of Edward II. When the king in 1313 was induced to pardon Lancaster and his confederates for their actions against him the formation of confederacies was specified[4]—a reference to the confederacy which murdered Gavaston. Though such confederacies were an important feature in the history of the baronial opposition they were not avowed. When in 1317 the king complained to Lancaster of the assemblies and confederations he was making, his excuse was that they were made at the king's order in readiness for the approaching muster for the Scottish war[5], and even when Lancaster acted with the king he advocated moderate measures against the confederacies which the magnates made[6]. The baronial success against the Despensers in 1321 was largely due to the frequent assemblies and elaborate confederations which the barons had made in preparation[7]. Yet they had the effrontery to place in the forefront of their charges the use of those means, as in the Ordinances they had charged Gavaston with making alliances of people to live and die with him against all men[8]. At the same time they demanded pardons for their pursuit of the Despensers because, since they had no legal remedy, they had allied themselves together by an oath in writing[9]. Later in 1321 in preparation for the

[1] *Stat. of Realm*, vol. I, pp. 256–7.

[2] *Parl. Writs*, vol. II, Pt ii, p. 354. *Litera Cantuar.* vol. II, pp. 204–7.

[3] Andrew Lang, *History of Scotland*, vol. I, pp. 303, 321–2.

[4] *Cal. Pat. Rolls*, 1313–17, p. 21 (16 Oct. 1313). Cf. *Auct. Malm.* p. 182.

[5] *Chron. Murimuth*, App. pp. 271–4. *Auct. Bridl.* p. 50.

[6] Anc. Corresp. vol. XXXIV, no. 106. Vide App. of Doc. no. 101.

[7] *Cal. Close Rolls*, 1318–23, pp. 355–6. *Le livere de Reis de Brittanie*, p. 338. Vide below, pp. 474–9.

[8] Ordinance 20.

[9] *Parl. Writs*, vol. II, Pt ii, App. p. 164.

approaching storm Lancaster called a meeting at Doncaster but the king prohibited him and others attending any assembly made, without the king's authority, to treat of matters touching the king and his realm[1]. When the battle of Boroughbridge was imminent the king continued to regard the baronial action as that of making assemblies and confederations; though when his success was consummated he called it treason. Sheriffs were ordered to pursue, arrest and imprison all tenants of Lancaster and others who were making leagues or assemblies in aid of the earl or other contrariants, and to cause them to be hindered and aggrieved in every possible way[2]. A few days later it was announced that the rebellious barons were conspiring for the king's shame and were hastening a confederacy made by them with the Scottish rebels contrary to their allegiance[3]. Even after the fall of the baronage in 1322 minor confederacies and conventicles were still made in various counties[4] and as time progressed their number increased and their force swelled until the revolution of 1326[5].

This formation of confederacies was a marked feature of the time and was not only a baronial device. It was widespread throughout the kingdom and general orders prohibiting illegal confederacies were frequently issued[6]. The germs of that system which did so much to produce and continue the Wars of the Roses were already in being and the stimulus of the Hundred Years' War and the policy of Edward III were alone needed to produce the result. The barons made assemblies to restrain the king. They were also affecting the course of justice by their conspiracies to maintain parties and procure false judgments against right and justice, by interference with fines and inquests and by threats; a state of affairs which drew piteous petitions from the commonalty[7]. When the eyre was to be held in London in 1321 confederacies were made amongst the citizens of London by covenants, oaths and other unlawful means to sustain each other in their suits[8]. Certain English merchants at Bruges made a confederacy to restore the staple to that town and to hinder merchants transferring themselves to Saint Omer[9]. The London clergy in 1317 formed a confederacy on account of the simplicity of some rectors and curates and the non-observance of the synodal

[1] *Cal. Close Rolls*, 1318–23, pp. 505–6 (12 Nov. 1321).
[2] Ibid. pp. 516–517 (28 Feb. 1322).
[3] Ibid. pp. 525–6 (1 Mar. 1322).
[4] Cf. ibid. 1323–27, p. 28.
[5] Ibid. pp. 456, 533.
[6] Ibid. 1307–13, pp. 195, 540, 548, 553; 1313–18, p. 469. *Cal. Pat. Rolls*, 1317–21, pp. 95–97. *Cal. Letter Books, D*, p. 295.
[7] *Rot. Parl.* vol. 1, pp. 289, 371.
[8] *Cal. Close Rolls*, 1318–23, p. 286 (14 Jan. 1321).
[9] Ibid. pp. 186–7.

statutes of the city archdeaconry[1]. The prevalence of the idea of confederacy can be illustrated from two of the clauses of the oath of the king's council. If one had entered into alliance with lords or others whereby he could not fulfil the oath without breaking his alliance he was to inform the king thereof, and he was not henceforth to ally himself by oath to anyone without the king's permission[2].

The question of making such oaths, bonds and indentures, which led to the meeting of assemblies and the formation of armed confederacies against the king, involved the question whether the barons had the right to declare war upon the king and whether such a right was recognised. It is important to remember that in many of the baronial actions, barons of the Welsh march had a preponderating influence upon baronial policy. Edward I's struggle with the earls of Gloucester and Hereford about the right of private war in the marches though it had ended in the complete triumph of the king[3] had proved that private war could not be maintained in the marches against the king's direct prohibition rather than that such war could never be maintained[4]. The earls had maintained private war and had entered into a private truce[5]. In the reign of Edward II Despenser the younger gave his men of Cantrev Mawr licence to take a distress from the men of John Gifford of Cantrev Bychan for several grievances that they had suffered from them[6]. Gifford did not complain of this to the king but asked Despenser to order his men to be at peace with the men of Cantrev Bychan[7]. The rights which the barons enjoyed in the marches they would tend to exercise elsewhere. In the reign of Henry III the barons had made their *diffidatio*, and reasonable terms had been granted in the *Dictum de Kenilworth*. It was pleaded in the king's court as justification for trespasses committed that they were done *tempore guerre*[8]. Though the prelates, earls, barons and commonalty of the realm assembled in parliament in 1313 had stated that it was the king's prerogative to forbid the carrying of arms and all other force against his peace[9] it would seem that ideas of the baronial right to rebel in due form still survived, and in the renunciation of homage by William Trussell

1 *Vict. Co. Hist.*, *London*, vol. I, p. 203.

2 *Parl. Writs*, vol. II, Pt i, p. 4; Pt ii, p. 3.

3 *Cal. Chan. Roll*, 1272–1327, pp. 344–9. *Rot. Parl.* vol. I, 70–77.

4 Pollock and Maitland, *Hist. of Engl. Law*, vol. I, p. 302.

5 T. Madox, *Formulare Anglicanum* [1702], p. 84.

6 Anc. Corresp. vol. XXXVII, no. 6. 7 Ibid.

8 *Bracton's Note Book*, case 857. *Eng. Hist. Rev.* vol. XXIV [1909], 'The Commune of Bury St Edmunds,' H. W. C. Davis, p. 313.

9 *Cal. Pat. Rolls*, 1313–17, p. 26. *Stat. of Realm*, vol. I, p. 170.

to Edward II in 1327[1] has been seen a use of the *diffidatio* in his reign[2]. Robert de Cliderou, rector of Wigan, who had been a chancery clerk for thirty years, in 1321–2 preached in his church telling the people that they were the liege men of the earl of Lancaster and bound to assist him against the king, as the earl's cause was just and that of the king unjust[3]. Though he denied the charge he was found guilty by the jury[4]. In Edward III's reign he admitted that he had caused prayers to be said in his church for the earls that they might be given grace as pillars of the land to maintain the crown and peace of the land[5].

The theory that the tenants had to follow their immediate lord even against the king also found expression in the wearing of the lord's robes and its consequences[6]. In accordance with the pardon which had been granted to the barons in August, 1321, at the parliament of Westminster, Roger Damory wrote to the king asking pardon for his followers, "tesmoigne par son sermeit et la feaute qe fait a nostre seigneur le Roi qil furont de sa aerdance et a sa compaignie[7]." The king did not call those who were opposed to him rebels but "contrariants," a word which would be far more in accord with the idea of the *diffidatio*. In the conduct of the campaign of 1321–2 the king's constant order was for the proclamation of his peace. The siege of Leeds Castle was "to punish the disobedience and contempt against the Queen committed by certain members of the household of Bartholomew de Badlesmere[8]." Proclamation was to be made that the king was not going there by reason of any war or disturbance in the realm but to punish disobedience and contempts and to inhibit anyone attempting anything in breach of the peace. Proclamation to maintain the peace was to be made[9]. The king wished to impress most strongly that he was not moving "by reason of war or disturbance of the realm, but in order to provide a remedy for divers trespasses inflicted upon his people in divers counties by malefactors[10]." Proclamation for the maintenance of the king's peace was to be made[11],

[1] *Ann. Paul.* p. 324. *Auct. Bridl.* p. 90. *Auct. Malm.* p. 290. *Chron. Knighton*, vol. II, pp. 441–2.

[2] Allen, *Inquiry into Royal Prerog.* p. 79.

[3] *Parl. Writs*, vol. II, Pt i, pp. 360–1; Pt ii, App. pp. 240–1. [4] Ibid.

[5] *Rot. Parl.* vol. II, p. 406. Vide also *Vict. Co. Hist., Lancaster*, vol. II, p. 201.

[6] Cf. *Cal. Close Rolls*, 1318–23, pp. 571–3, 582, 596, 603–4, 641, 650. *Rot. Parl.* vol. I, 389–390, 411–412.

[7] Anc. Corresp. vol. XXXIII, no. 120.

[8] *Cal. Close Rolls*, 1318–23, pp. 504–5 (16 Oct. 1321).

[9] Ibid. Cf. *Ann. Paul.* p. 299.

[10] *Cal. Close Rolls*, 1318–23, p. 506 (15 Nov. 1321). [11] Ibid. pp. 506, 507.

and anyone doing anything to the contrary was to be arrested[1], and the arrest was ordered of those who, notwithstanding the proclamation, had subsequently attacked the king's subjects[2]. The king seemed most anxious to bring the actions of those who had been opposing him within the scope of the common law. Time after time he insisted that he had made proclamations for the keeping of the peace and his aim was to punish trespasses and oppressions. After Bridgenorth had been captured and burnt, castles had been taken and royal servants killed, and although the sheriffs were ordered to capture Hereford, Mortimer and others, proclamation was still ordered "that the king is journeying through the realm in force for the purpose of punishing such trespass and not by reason of any disturbances among the people or by reason of war to be made in the land[3]." Later the sheriffs were ordered to raise hue and cry after those who notwithstanding the proclamation for the preservation of the peace were committing various trespasses[4]. Though these orders may in part be due to the king's desire to maintain the people in a state of calm there seems to have been more than this behind them. The same idea was contained in other and independent quarters. A petitioner complained that he had been treated as if he had been "encontre nostre seigneur le Roy[5]," and another petitioner in order to prove his innocence recounted his occupation during "tut le temps qe les dites contriauens chevacherent et furent les damages qe il furent encountre la volonte et la pees le Rey[6]." An inquisition stated how numerous horse and foot had levied war against the king and later recounted certain action undertaken *contra pacem regis*[7]. Lancaster was inhibited from receiving the rebels or assisting them and was informed if he disobeyed he would render himself guilty of treason[8]. When the barons had been defeated the king charged them with treason and the processes against the Mortimers recounted that they had "countre vostre homage foi et ligeaunce et encontre nostre seigneur le Roi vostre seigneur lige leuastes de guerre[9]," an anticipation of the statute of 1352 which made the levying of war against the king in his realm an act of treason[10].

[1] *Cal. Close Rolls*, 1318–23, p. 507 (30 Nov. 1321). [2] *Cal. Pat. Rolls*, 1321–24, p. 62.

[3] *Cal. Close Rolls*, 1318–23, pp. 513–514 (15 Jan. 1322).

[4] Ibid. p. 512 (11 Feb. 1322). [5] *Rot. Parl.* vol. I, p. 393. [6] Ibid. p. 404.

[7] *Abbrev. Placit.* p. 345. [8] Ibid. pp. 515–516 (8 Feb. 1322).

[9] P. R. O. Exchequer Miscellanea, 24/12. Vide App. of Doc. no. 44. The charge varied. A minor offender was found "encontre sa ligeance nostre seigneur le Roy" (*Rot. Parl.* vol. I, p. 415), while John Gifford was as a "tretour treterousement et feloneusement" committing various acts (Chan. Misc., Bdle 59/3 (99)).

[10] Pollock and Maitland, *Hist. Engl. Law*, vol. II, p. 505.

The barons endeavoured to maintain the fiction that they were acting on the king's behalf, and doing all things for his honour and profit[1]. When they proceeded against the Despensers in 1321 they marched under the king's banners[2] and on various other occasions they made use of the same device.

The methods and action of the barons eventually rested upon the employment of force. They were all founded upon the principle of coercion. The theory which had drawn a distinction between the king and crown was in effect little more than an attempt to justify coercion. The legalisation of coercion which the executive clause of Magna Carta[3] had allowed, which had approached "more nearly than any other statute of English History to giving legal sanction to the right of resistance and making government and obedience truly a matter of compact[4]," had given the barons the right not merely to resist the king's tyranny but also to compel him to act in the proper manner. Obedience it seemed was to be due only as long as the king fulfilled his portion of the compact; obedience was conditional upon the behaviour of the sovereign. If the king did not abide by his words the barons might obey, resist or coerce. The grant of Magna Carta was however made entirely under duress and what was granted under coercion could only be temporary in its application. For government by coercion must be anarchy. The position which the doctrine of coercion had held during the reign of Henry III was expressed by Matthew Paris when he chronicled how the earl of Chester had carried a certain great sword at the king's coronation and had power to coerce the king if he acted unjustly[5]. In Edward II's reign the barons had in Scotland a first-hand illustration of the rightness of might; Bruce was king of Scotland despite all theories. After the battle of Bannockburn he was called king "because he had acquired Scotland by force of arms[6]." If force could win a crown against the feudal rights which the English crown claimed over Scotland surely force applied by the properly constituted authority could impose its will upon the person who held the crown.

[1] Cf. *Cal. Close Rolls*, 1318–23, p. 525. *Chron. Lanerc.* p. 229. *Chron. Mon. de Melsa*, vol. II, p. 341. This is well brought out in the attempt of Hereford and the Mortimers to obtain possession of Bristol stating they were acting on the king's behalf. The citizens wrote to the king on the matter. Anc. Corresp. vol. XXXIII, nos. 58, 59. Vide App. of Doc. no. 100.

[2] *Parl. Writs*, vol. II, Pt ii, App. p. 164.

[3] Magna Carta, § 61.

[4] Figgis, *Divine Right of Kings*, p. 26.

[5] Matthew Paris, *Chronica Majora*, vol. III, pp. 337–8. Vide Pollock and Maitland, *Hist. of Engl. Law*, vol. I, p. 182, note 5.

[6] *Chron. Lanerc.* p. 210.

The properly constituted authority was the earls with the assistance of the baronage. There was no other means by which the king could be restrained but coercion.

Once the king had been coerced the constitutional scheme of continuous coercion took the form of restraint. Inasmuch however as in the discussion of restraint as a means of government, administrative and constitutional questions are closely interwoven with those of baronial theory this problem will be postponed to be brought into more direct relation with the administrative system and the action which the baronial opposition directed against it. It is but important to remember at present that restraint was the consummation of the baronial policy of coercion. Coercion was spasmodic, restraint sought to be permanent.

The barons saw but imperfectly that a victory won by coercion could only be maintained by additional coercion. The king had a complete remedy for what he did under constraint. Grants made when the king was in durance were void[1]. When the governor and head of the law was in prison the law itself was in prison and there was then no law[2]. The king by his own grant could do nothing in restraint of the royal power[3]; much less could an outside authority exercise such restraint. Whatever was done under coercion was ipso facto null and void. Whatever was done against law, reason and the custom of the realm in prejudice of the crown and royal dignity was worthless and repealed[4]. In these circumstances the action of the royal party in the first parliament of Edward III in deciding that the repeal of the exile of the Despensers had been made by duress and force and should therefore be annulled for evermore[5] was hypocritical in the extreme. In the circumstances of 1322 the only person who was in a position to exercise coercion was the king himself. The action of the advisers of the new king in re-establishing and legalising a process of exile that had been attained by the worst instance of coercion in the late reign was unfortunate as one of the first public acts of the new sovereign. But the revolutionary party of 1326 was restrained by no considerations of policy or scruples. They were out for revenge at all costs. The weak and vacillating Edward II who had ruled by the advice of evil counsellors was a better preserver of the dignity and entirety of the royal power than the government which came to free the king and kingdom of abuses.

[1] *Plac. de Quo Warr.* p. 766. [2] *Year Bk* 20–21 *Ed. I* [Rolls Series], p. 192.
[3] Seld. Soc., *Eyre of Kent*, vol. III, pp. 172–3. [4] *Stat. of Realm*, vol. I, p. 187.
[5] Ibid. p. 252. *Stat. Westm.* I, 1 Ed. III, § 2.

Towards the end of the reign of Edward I the attempts of the smaller freemen, church and baronage in the palatinate of Durham to coerce the bishop were unsuccessful until supported by the king's aid[1]. The attempts of the barons in England to coerce the king proved unsuccessful, but there was no sovereign power to interfere on their behalf. The efficiency of coercion depended essentially upon the force brought to bear upon the king and upon the continual pressure that force exercised. As a system of government or as a basis for stability coercion was impossible. Once the king had gained sufficient confidence and power the whole result achieved by coercion would vanish. It was the obvious answer to something extorted by force to say that what had been conceded under coercion was not binding. This was exactly what the king did. The high royal doctrine was that no one ought to resist in anything any bailiff, or official of the king or hinder him in anything according to the law and custom of the realm[2]. Much less ought the king himself to be resisted. Coercion moreover might prove very dangerous to the barons themselves on the ground that "qui in legem committit frustra invocat legis auxilium[3]." A section of the baronage saw that compulsion by physical force was useless and resorted to coercion by moral persuasion. This was the object at which the middle party aimed. They considered that the king's good will was essential to effective reform.

There is however this much to be said in support of coercion— that it was entirely in accord with the spirit of the time. In private life as in public policy everything was based upon force. Those frequent tournaments which the king found it necessary to prohibit for the well-being of his kingdom provided suitable opportunities for holding illegal assemblies and making confederacies and gave an outlet to the turbulence of the time[4]. Assaults were committed even in parliament and in the king's presence. At a parliament held at Berwick a royal official had been assaulted[5]. At the parliament of Lincoln in 1316 Hugh le Despenser the son attacked and wounded

[1] Lapsley, *Palat. of Durham*, p. 134.

[2] Chan. Misc., Bdle 64/3(78): "nullus debeat alicui balliuo seu ministro domini Regis in aliquo resistare nec in officio suo faciendo secundum legem et consuetudinem regni etcetera contradicere...."

[3] Cf. Seld. Soc., *Eyre of Kent*, vol. I, p. lxxv.

[4] *Cal. Close Rolls*, 1307–13, pp. 52, 126, 155–6, 158–9, 233–4, 257, 269, 314, 344, 354, 442, 457, 478, 555, 561. *Cal. Pat. Rolls*, 1307–13, pp. 97, 110, 302, 520, 521, 525, 557. Wilkins, *Concilia*, vol. II, pp. 437–8.

[5] *Cal. Close Rolls*, 1288–96, pp. 488–9.

another baron[1]. A man drew a knife to attack another even in the great hall of Westminster[2]. John de Somery was charged with obtaining such mastery in the county of Stafford that no one could obtain law or justice there. He had made himself more than king and no one could dwell there unless he bought protection from him either by payment of money or by assisting him to build his castles. Unless people made fine for his protection he attacked them in their own houses with intent to kill[3]. All the leading families in the county were involved in acts of rapine and violence[4], and though the state of Stafford on account of its proximity to the Lancaster influence was worse than most counties, disorder was widespread and general. Lords kept retainers who interfered with the course of justice[5]. Vagrants disturbed the peace of the city of London[6]. The populace of London assembled in force and endeavoured to interfere with the election of the mayor[7]. Because of the disorder strangers entering Chester were to be scrutinised and those of whom evil was suspected were to be refused admission[8]. Even the princes of the church were not safe from attack, though the royal power was sufficient to punish the outrage on the cardinals[9]. In such an atmosphere as this a policy based upon coercion was not incongruous; it was the natural outcome of the state of society.

In the theories upon which the baronial opposition partly based its action and in the methods founded upon those theories there was little consistency. The king stood on one side, the barons on the other, yet it was not entirely a conflict of two radically opposing theories. Both sides possessed reactionary tendencies and both had impulses towards reform. There was no attempt on either side to work out a consistent theory but each seized what was best suited to its immediate purpose. The king and barons were too practical to allow any ideal to sway them for long. They were dealing with living problems and when a point in the enemy's programme seemed useful it was borrowed immediately. The way in which the barons in 1308 exploited the distinction between the king and the crown and in 1321 condemned it, judging it a fit charge for exile, is but characteristic of the trend of royal as well as baronial policy. The king and

[1] *Rot. Parl.* vol. I, pp. 352–3. [2] *Cal. Close Rolls*, 1313–18, pp. 114–115.
[3] *Cal. Pat. Rolls*, 1307–13, p. 369.
[4] Wm Salt Soc., *Coll.* vol. VII, Pt ii, pp. 23–26.
[5] *Cal. Close Rolls*, 1318–23, p. 227. *Lit. Cantuar.* vol. I, pp. 121–3.
[6] *Cal. Letter Books, D*, p. 215. [7] *Cal. Close Rolls*, 1313–18, p. 235.
[8] *Cal. Pat. Rolls*, 1317–21, p. 200.
[9] *Ann. Paul.* pp 280–2. *Auct. Bridl.* p. 52. *Reg. Pal. Dunelm.* vol. IV, pp. 394–5

barons left theory behind and came to grips upon the personal and household system of government. The barons here had something tangible to grapple. There were abuses to attack and reforms to effect. Hence the struggle of the reign is not concerned with the virtues of this or that theory but with the question whether the barons were to obtain a share in the administration or whether the country was still to be administered by the household system.

Inasmuch therefore as the theories were constructed to meet practical needs and those practical needs were a legacy from the feudal system, these theories were but English manifestations of current political ideas. Constitutional development was the result of economic and political necessity, and though it may have been particular in detail it was in broad outlines and in general principles not insular but universal. The causes and environment were practically the same throughout Western Europe. Necessity of a similar nature as had induced Edward I to call his model parliament prompted the summoning of the states general by the king of France in his struggle with the papacy.

In England as elsewhere there was a conflict between feudal theory and political actuality. Inasmuch as political theories in England were "the product far more of practical necessity than of intellectual activity[1]" this conflict should not have been severe. There was still sufficient room for vagueness and impracticability to enter. It was not necessary that a theory should be correctly founded upon facts for it to be effective. Its effect depended upon appropriateness and opportunities. The theories were retained only as long as they promoted some immediate and practical end, as the revolution which overthrew Edward II showed. When personal interests conflicted with political theory or practical policy personal interests were victorious. To the writer of the *Mirror of Justices* it seemed "humbug to make constitutions which were not obeyed[2]." Yet when necessity conflicted with theory necessity won. What was founded upon necessity, when the need altered had to give way to the same force. Deduction of theory from the circumstances of a particular case, or the needs of a certain faction had its advantages. It tended to make the theory practical though it might easily sink to mere expediency. Its effect could only be transitory, and, even for a short time, inadequate. It was narrow, built on a notion of class supremacy. It could not impart a higher standard to political action. In the reign of Edward II though the theory may have met the needs of the time

[1] Figgis, *Divine Right of Kings*, p. 4. [2] Seld. Soc., *Mirror of Justices*, p. 183.

as far as its negative qualities went it was far removed from political actuality because it had no constructive scheme to offer. It had defects too on its negative side for it failed to take into account the practical strength of the household system against which it made its attacks.

One feature which was especially shown in baronial policy was the respect given to legal and political form. Almost consistently throughout their opposition the barons claimed to be acting on the king's behalf. They were the true exponents of law and reason. Whatever coercive action may have preceded the appointment of the ordainers they were anxious that the proper form should be observed and that the appointment should be made at least nominally of the king's free will. Whatever coercive action may have driven the king from his throne and cast him into a prison the deposition had to be effected by the king's consent[1]. The narrow spirit in which the barons acted is illustrated by the obstinate refusal of Lancaster to do homage to the king for the Lincoln earldom outside the realm[2]. Close obedience to legal and political form was maintained on every occasion as long as possible; then eventually they resorted to coercion.

In conflicts between king and barons one great weakness in the political system always manifested itself—the absence of an efficient body before which the differences between king and barons could be decided and adjudicated. "Between king and barons there was no impartial judge and therefore in our sense very little law[3]." The great problem was to find an impartial judge. In 1264 appeal had been made to Louis IX. The result of that experiment the barons could not have considered satisfactory. In 1312 the opinion of French jurists upon the Ordinances was sought but their objections to them did not convince the earls[4]. The pope suggested Charles, count of Valois, as a suitable mediator[5]. The absence of an impartial adjudicator resulted in the resort to coercion. This was most unhappy, for the king had at his command a whole array of resources of which the barons could not deprive him, even by a series of assaults.

[1] The parliament of 1327 was held "per consensum et voluntatem regis" (*Ann. Monast.* vol. III, *Ann. de Bermund.* p. 471) and his resignation of the crown was, as far as form went, voluntarily undertaken (*Chron. de Murimuth*, p. 51; *Auct. Bridl.* pp. 90–91; *Chron. Lanerc.* pp. 254–6). The official view was expressed in the words "quod pater Regis nunc de regimine regni sui se demisit" (Wm Salt Soc., *Coll.* vol. XI [1890], p. 10).

[2] *Chron. Lanerc.* p. 192.

[3] Seld. Soc., *Select Pleas in Manorial Courts*, p. lx.

[4] *Chron. Ed. I and Ed. II*, vol. I, *Annales Londonienses*, pp. 211–215.

[5] *Cal. Pap. Letters*, 1304–42, p. 420.

The system of government centring in the king's household was of such strength that it could easily overcome all baronial attacks. Before the baronial opposition and its action can be appreciated the strength and influence of the household system in its various phases will have to be considered. The reason of the baronial failure can then be explained.

The greatness of the king's prerogative must always be a consideration of the utmost importance in a study of any baronial opposition. It was of special importance in the reign of Edward II because the theoretical prerogatives of the king were put into full practice in the system of administration by which England was governed. The assumption of the king's prerogatives by irresponsible favourites and advisers was a contributory cause to the baronial opposition. The crown had delegated its authority and prerogatives in certain spheres to officials and various phases of the council. It was the obvious course for the barons to pursue to endeavour to capture or control the officials and bodies which exercise the delegated authority. The chief obstacle to the success of this plan was found in the household system. The barons therefore concentrated in the first place upon the capture or reform of that system, though it must be remembered that there was a dual object in baronial policy throughout the reign. They desired to reform the household and to capture the executive. These two objects were intimately connected. The reform of the household was a means by which they might capture the executive, and to capture the executive was the surest means of effecting reform in the household. Just as the household system and the administration displayed the royal policy and prerogatives put into practice so the constitutional and administrative action of the barons was the practical side of the baronial theories.

PART I

THE HOUSEHOLD SYSTEM AND THE ADMINISTRATION

CHAPTER I

THE IMPORTANCE OF THE REIGN OF EDWARD II

Edward I had set a high standard for his successors. In every sphere of his activity he had shown outstanding ability. As a warrior he had subdued Wales and nearly conquered Scotland. As a legislator he had defined matters of procedure and produced settlement in the realm of common law. As an administrator he had made a strenuous endeavour to increase the royal revenue, upon which the efficiency of administration was dependent, but had not met with complete success. He developed and improved the machinery of local and central government. He had provided the Model Parliament. The country had been rescued out of the chaos into which it had fallen under Henry III and the prosperity of the land as well as the strength of the kingship had been increased. He had done more than secure reforms; he had laid down the lines of future development. In many directions the work of his successor would have to be the maintenance of Edward I's reforms. In one direction, partly because Edward I had failed to grapple successfully with the problem, partly because of the reforms he had introduced, important work awaited the new king. The administration was in need of reform. The state of the exchequer in particular required drastic amendment.

The reign of Edward II derives its first importance from the work his predecessor had achieved, with the incomplete character of many of its features and its failure in a number of directions. First of all must be considered the way in which the reign of Edward I influenced certain movements, the results of which are of vital importance to our problem.

The reign of Edward I had accelerated the general transformation of feudalism. Political feudalism had received its transformation by the time of Magna Carta. From that time the barons applied themselves to the problems of central government, and an oligarchic policy gradually took the place of disruptive feudalism. The efficacy of feudalism as a military system was ending[1]. The feudal levy had become unsuited to the needs of warfare and hopelessly small. The king had to seek new methods of finding troops. Indentures[2], commissions of array[3], levies from Wales[4], grants of fencible men from each township[5] were the new forms employed. Already, too, the Edwardian castle was doomed—almost before completion. The social aspect of feudalism had been dependent upon its political and military aspects. When feudalism lost its force as a political and military power its decline as a social system was inevitable. The empty chivalry of the fourteenth century was not unconnected with feudalism but was a feudalism greatly transformed. The general transformation of feudalism had ended by its becoming merely tenurial. Even in its purely tenurial aspect feudalism was to have an influence upon the administration and upon the king. The rights and inheritance of the crown had been assimilated to the position of an ordinary fief. Edward II became king immediately after his father's death because "the pressure of circumstances and the influence of feudal land law brought about the triumph of the notion that the right of inheritance is the only essential element in making a king[6]."

The transformation of feudalism affected the administration, for in part the administrative system seems to have been built upon feudalism. The great officers of the king's household, the marshal, the constable, the chamberlain, the steward, had certain lands attached to them by tenure of grand serjeanty. The offices had become hereditary and had passed with the lands. Minor offices of the administration had also been serjeanties, offices such as carrying royal writs and keeperships of forests. It would seem as if serjeanty had been an immature expression of the household system, possessing the fatal weakness of being hereditary. The grand serjeanties had become

[1] On this point see Sir F. Palgrave's preface to *Parl. Writs*, vol. II, Pt i.

[2] The class of "Indentures of War," K. R. Accounts, 62/1, commences with the reign of Edward I. Vide above, pp. 33–34.

[3] Vide Oman, *Art of War in the Middle Ages*, pp. 513–514.

[4] Vide J. E. Morris, *Welsh Wars of Edward I*, passim.

[5] Vide below, pp. 413–414, for grant made in parliament of Lincoln, 1316; *Cal. Pat. Rolls*, 1321–24, p. 113, for grant made in parliament of York, 1322.

[6] Figgis, *Divine Right of Kings*, p. 27. Note in the proclamation of Edward II's peace: "nostre Seignur Sire Edward son fuiz et son heir soit ia Roi d'Engleterre par descente de heritage" (*Parl. Writs*, vol. II, Pt ii, App. p. 1).

merely ceremonial offices. The effective offices in the household were held either by deputy, as in the case of the marshal, who retained a larger number of official duties than his brother officers, or by entirely new officials such as the steward and chamberlain of the household. Other of the serjeanties had been commuted for a money payment.

In addition to the great offices of the household there were such grand serjeanties as being larderer in the king's household[1], of finding a larderer yearly[2] and of carrying the wand of the marshalsea in the king's household[3]. Other serjeanties consisted in holding positions in the local administration. John de Hastings held a manor by serjeanty of being the steward of the liberty of St Edmund's[4]. Others held land by serjeanty of being the king's bailiff in a wapentake[5], of being the king's forester[6], of finding a bedel to serve a hundred[7], of keeping a gaol[8]. Some held land by service of making attachments at the king's court[9], or of finding a hundreder to serve the king, levy his peace, make distraints for the king's justices and sheriffs[10]. Serjeanty by service of carrying the king's treasure was frequent[11], and one tenant held his land by service of finding a man to carry the king's writs in his war in England for forty days at his own charges[12].

Offices other than local were held in serjeanty. The earl of Warwick held certain lands by being the king's chamberlain[13], and other lands by service of finding a chamberlain at the king's exchequer[14]. The office of usher of the exchequer was similarly held. In 1291 Edward I ordered the treasurer and barons of the exchequer to give seisin of that serjeanty to Simon, the son and heir of Laurence de Scaccario, as he had done homage for it[15]. On Simon's death the serjeanty was divided, John de Dagworth holding one-third, which he granted to his mother[16], and Simon's daughter another third, her kinsman John de Dagworth being her heir[17]. The office was held of the king in chief by homage and service of finding four criers in the common bench, two ushers in the exchequer, and two marshals in each judicial eyre throughout England[18]. The fee attached to the

[1] *Cal. Inq. P. M.* vol. v, p. 285.
[2] Ibid. vol. vi, p. 140.
[3] Ibid. pp. 14–15; vol. vii, p. 337.
[4] Ibid. vol. v, p. 231.
[5] Ibid. vol. vi, p. 288.
[6] Ibid. vol. v, p. 207; vol. vi, pp. 1, 141.
[7] Ibid. vol. v, pp. 211, 277; vol. vi, pp. 1, 141.
[8] Ibid. vol. vi, p. 2.
[9] Ibid. vol. v, pp. 211–212.
[10] Ibid. p. 9.
[11] Ibid. vol. iv, p. 270; vol. vi. pp. 3, 63, 289–290.
[12] Ibid. vol. iv, p. 189.
[13] Ibid. vol. v, p. 398.
[14] Ibid. p. 400; vol. iv, p. 232.
[15] *Cal. Close Rolls*, 1288–96, p. 162.
[16] *Cal. Inq. P. M.* vol. v, p. 4.
[17] Ibid. vol. vi, p. 402.
[18] Ibid. vol. v, p. 4.

office was 5*d.* a day as long as the exchequer was open and the fees due and accustomed from all those pleading and being impleaded in those places[1]. The whole serjeanty eventually fell into Dagworth's hands[2]. This instance of an administrative office held by serjeanty supports the suggestion that it would seem as if serjeanty was an early manifestation of the method of government which afterwards became established in the household system. The weighers, melters and like offices at the exchequer were similarly hereditary serjeanties[3]. It is not suggested that it was complete but that its aim was similar and that there was a similarity in tendency.

The general commutation of serjeanties had taken place before the time of the *Testa de Nevill*[4], the serjeanty according to Madox being changed into another kind of service because the service or duty of a serjeanty had been left unperformed[5]. The grand serjeanty of being one of the king's butlers was commuted in the time of king John[6], but it was under Henry III, when Robert Passelewe was sent to rate the serjeanties, that the general commutation took place[7]. A serjeanty of carrying the king's writs for forty days was rated by Passelewe at 15*s.*[8] In the household system which supplied the administration with its officers the king had a far more efficient system of administration than serjeanties had been able to afford him. The transformation of serjeanty was but one phase of the general transformation of feudalism. It has been laboured because it has some relation with the problem of the household system.

This transformation of feudalism which the reign of Edward I had accelerated, or indeed in commutation of serjeanties completed and formalised, is of considerable importance in an endeavour to estimate the problem of Edward II's reign. It has an influence upon the administration; and it is administrative problems that were to strike the keynote of that reign. Administration had outgrown its machinery. Feudalism could no longer provide it with an adequate system. The king had for some time been turning to his household to supply the need, but the barons were determined to see that such a system should not obtain without a struggle. It was natural that in the decay of the feudal polity the king should turn for guidance to

[1] *Cal. Inq. P. M.* vol. VII, p. 310. [2] Ibid.

[3] Cf. *Eng. Hist. Rev.* vol. XXVI, 'The Weighers of the Exchequer,' J. H. Round, pp. 724–7.

[4] *Testa de Nevill*, pp. 15–16, 32–33, 88–89, etc.

[5] Madox, *Baronia Angl.* p. 33. [6] *Cal. Inq. P. M.* vol. IV, p. 11.

[7] *Testa de Nevill*, pp. 15–16, 32–33, 86–87, etc.

[8] *Cal. Inq. P. M.* vol. V, p. 135.

those lower officials of his own household who had never been drawn into the vortex of the feudal system and should use them as his instruments in the general administration of his kingdom. Edward II entered into an administrative inheritance[1] both theoretically and practically. It was his lot to continue and develop that inherited system to meet the growing needs of administration. It is therefore important to insist that there was no essential break between the reigns.

On account of the marked contrast which the reign of Edward II offered to that of his illustrious predecessor, there has been a tendency to exaggerate the break between the two reigns. It has been stated that all the old and experienced ministers of his father were dismissed by the new king and their places filled by less worthy friends of Edward II[2]. This however is not accurate. The administration went on unaltered. Edward I died on 7 July[3] and up to the 25th of that month the chancellor was still sealing writs in the name of the dead king[4]. The bishop of London was followed as chancellor in August by the bishop of Chichester[5], who had previously been chancellor under Edward I, and the change would not seem to have been the result of caprice.

It was inevitable that the household officials of the prince should on his accession become the household officials of the king, for the prince's household became expanded into the king's. Yet even in the household some of Edward I's officials were retained and others found posts in the administrative departments. John de Benstede, controller of the wardrobe for many years under Edward I, and later chancellor of the exchequer, received well deserved promotion to the keepership, while John de Drokensford, the late king's keeper soon became, for a short period, chancellor of the exchequer, afterwards resuming his place at the wardrobe. Miles de Stapleton, the prince's steward, became steward of the king's household; Walter Reynolds, keeper of the prince's wardrobe, became treasurer; William de Melton, controller of the prince's wardrobe[6], became controller of the king's wardrobe[7]. Other clerks and laymen of the prince's

[1] Edward II's administrative inheritance is considered at length by Professor T. F. Tout in *The Place of Edward II in English History*, § 2, pp. 36–73.

[2] *Chron. Lanerc.* p. 185.

[3] *Ann. Paul.* p. 256. *Auct. Malm.* p. 155.

[4] Lord Campbell, *Lives of Lord Chancellors*, vol. 1, p. 184.

[5] He was acting on 18 August (Chan. Warr., File 58/2).

[6] Ibid.

[7] The changes are treated at length by Prof. Tout, *The Place of Ed. II*, pp. 76–81.

household[1], Ingelard de Warle, Nicholas de Hugate, Robert de Haustede, Oliver de Bordeaux, John de Cherleton found places in the king's household at his accession or soon after.

The changes in the administrative departments too were greatly exaggerated by the chronicler who stated that the barons of the exchequer, the justices and other ministers of the king were removed[2]. The issue rolls of the first year of Edward II prove that there was a continuity of personnel in the lower offices in the administration which was far greater than could have been expected[3]. If the exchequer is taken as an instance, though it received a new treasurer in Reynolds, and, in John de Sandale, chamberlain of Scotland under Edward I[4], a new chancellor of the exchequer[5], it was practically the same administrative officers that held the lower offices. Of the new barons of the exchequer, William de Carlton, Roger de Hengham and Thomas de Cambridge[6], Carlton and Hengham had been barons under Edward I. As chamberlain of the exchequer, Henry de Ludgershall was appointed in the place of William de Buckhill[7]. John de Kirkeby, remembrancer of the exchequer and Hugh de Nottingham[8], keeper of the great roll were maintained in their offices[9]. Of the three chancery clerks who acted most frequently as keepers of the great seal, Adam de Osgodby and Robert de Bardelby had acted as keepers under Edward I[10], while the third, William de Ayremynne had also received favour from that king[11]. The chronicler's statement is probably founded upon the fact that Edward II issued new patents of appointment to all his administrative officers. Thus the chief justice and his six associates of the common bench received patents of appointment[12], yet they had all acted as justices under Edward I. The one direction in which changes were made was in the keepership of castles, for in August, 1307, many barons, including the earl of Lincoln, John

[1] Addit. MS. 22,923 passim. Vide also *Ninth Report Deputy Keeper of Records*, App. II, pp. 248–9.

[2] *Ann. Paul.* p. 257.

[3] P. R. O. Issue Rolls, nos. 141, 143 passim.

[4] *Cal. Doc. Scotl.* vol. II, pp. 442, 488.

[5] *Cal. Pat. Rolls*, 1307–13, p. 6.

[6] Ibid. p. 7. They were appointed on 10 Sept. and attended before the treasurer and William de Bereford to take the oath on 20 Sept. (K. R. Mem. Roll, no. 81, m. 14; L. T. R. Mem. Roll, no. 78, m. 16).

[7] K. R. Mem. Roll, no. 81, m. 14. L. T. R. Mem. Roll, no. 78, m. 16. *Cal. Pat. Rolls*, 1307–13, p. 7.

[8] His appointment as treasurer's remembrancer is noted below, p. 123.

[9] K. R. Mem. Roll, no. 81, m. 14. L. T. R. Mem. Roll, no. 78, m. 16. Vide also *Cal. Close Rolls*, 1307–13, p. 2.

[10] *Cal. Close Rolls*, 1288–96, p. 454; 1302–7, pp. 235, 313.

[11] K. R. Mem. Roll, no. 81, m. 7.

[12] *Cal. Pat. Rolls*, 1307–13, p. 2.

Botetourte, Robert de Clifford and John de Crombwell, received the custody of castles[1].

The greatest change made by Edward II on his accession was the dismissal and imprisonment of Walter de Langton, bishop of Coventry and Lichfield. This the new king did almost immediately, the motive being attributed to revenge for the part he had taken against Gavaston[2]. The chronicler admits there was some reason in the king's action, because as was said, after the death of Edward I more of the king's treasure was found in Langton's possession than was in the treasury[3]. Though this was not the real reason, the king's action appears to have been actuated largely by administrative abuses charged against the late treasurer and would not have been unpopular with a section of the community[4]. Edward II insisted that Langton should appear before a court of justices over which William de Bereford was to preside and should be tried for the "trespas, et mesprisiouns et damages quil fist a nostre piere en son temps et a nous et as altres." The treasurer and barons of the exchequer were to search all memoranda and make a schedule of all the ills and losses which the bishop had committed while in office, the extortions, false enrolments, and obtaining of false judgments and the appropriation of a great amount of treasure which he made the officials of the kingdom pay at his household and elsewhere at his will instead of at the exchequer of receipt[5]. Among the points upon which the exchequer had already given their advice to the king on this matter were the agreements the treasurer had made with sheriffs that they might remain in their offices, the extortions he had made by power of his office, the sales of woods and other land which he had made, the appointment of insufficient persons as sheriffs and other officers on payment of gifts, lands and rents, the grants made by chancery writs when Edward I had been out of the kingdom, and various other matters[6]. Proclamation was made in London that those who had complaints against him were to make them in writing and deliver them to Bereford's

[1] *Cal. Fine Rolls*, 1307–19, pp. 2–3.

[2] *Ann. Paul.* p. 257. *Auct. Bridl.* p. 28. *Chron. Murimuth*, p. 11. *Chron Lanerc.* pp. 184–5. J. de Trokelowe, *Annales*, pp. 63–64. *Chron. W. de Hemingburgh*, vol. II, pp. 271–3. *Flores Hist.* vol. III, p. 140.

[3] *Chron. Lanerc.* pp. 184–5.

[4] *Chron. Ed. I and Ed. II*, vol. I, Intro. pp. cxi–cxii. *Cal. Letter Books, D*, pp. xx–xxi.

[5] K. R. Mem. Roll, no. 81, m. 18. L. T. R. Mem. Roll, no. 78, m. 21 (27 Nov. 1307). Vide App. of Doc. no. 2. Cf. Madox, *Hist. of Exch.* vol. II, p. 47.

[6] P. R. O. Exchequer of Pleas, Plea Roll, no. 31, m. 21. This roll deals entirely with proceedings relating to Langton.

clerk, and speedy justice would be done them[1]. The officials of the late treasurer were also dismissed or imprisoned[2]. His clerk and familiar, William de Eston, was imprisoned in the Tower of London[3]; while Walter de Norwich, who had been treasurer's remembrancer, was dismissed[4].

The commission of justices composed of Roger le Brabazon, William de Bereford, Roger de Hengham and William Inge[5] sat at Windsor, and various cases were decided against the bishop. Some citizens of Chester complained of minerals he had seized and had conveyed to London from a mine rented by them from the earl of Warenne. The decision was given against the bishop, and the citizens had judgment of £48 to be levied on the bishop's property in Stafford[6]. Another from Stafford had petitioned the king in a certain matter and Langton, who was then treasurer, was ordered to afford him a remedy. Because he would give him no gift the bishop refused to do him right[7]. William Tuchet received £500 as damages from the bishop for trespasses he had committed upon him without Temple Bar in London[8]. Sufficient was established against him to maintain the king's action. The view that the king raged against the ministers of his father and replaced them by nominees of his own is exaggerated.

The administrative departments went on their course unaltered by the change of reign. The personnel was substantially the same though the heads of some departments were changed. The bulk of the officials was the same and administrative policy and tradition remained unaltered. The normal course of exchequer and chancery administration was pursued and there was no break between the two reigns. The two benches of justices were without exception precisely the same. The alteration in the household was natural and was of personnel rather than of policy and administration. On every side in administrative history the reign of Edward II started where that of Edward I had ended. There was no gulf, no breach in continuity.

In addition to the administrative inheritance into which Edward II entered he also inherited a legacy of trouble. This legacy of trouble

[1] *Cal. Letter Books, C*, p. 156. Riley, *Memorials of London* [1868], p. 63.
[2] L. T. R. Mem. Roll, no. 78, m. 36 d.
[3] K. R. Mem. Roll, no. 81, m. 45. L. T. R. Mem. Roll, no. 78, m. 42.
[4] Vide below, pp. 123–4. [5] Cf. *Abbrev. Placit.* p. 337.
[6] Chan. Misc., Bdle 51/1 (14).
[7] Wm Salt Soc., *Hist. Coll. Staff.* [1911], ed. J. G. Wedgwood, p. 292.
[8] P. R. O. King's Bench, Class 138, no. 68, m. 1. Wm Salt Soc., *Coll.* vol. x, p. 8. Vide also Chan. Misc., Bdle 68/8 (187).

accentuated and complicated the main problem of his reign. Had Edward I bequeathed the question of administration alone as requiring solution it would have been a sufficiently difficult problem to solve. But in addition to this main consideration other questions of the most serious consequences awaited decision. These problems had proved too much for the great Edward; they would certainly overcome his lesser son. They acted as external complications to the main problem and the king's attempts to grapple with them diverted his energies and dissipated his resources.

In the indictment made against Edward II on his fall it was stated that he had lost Scotland and other lands and seignories in Gascony and elsewhere, which his father had left him in peace[1]. This statement did more than justice to Edward I at his son's expense. Edward I died leaving disputes unsettled and claims undefined. He had died at the very moment when making another effort to enforce his will upon the Scots. The legacy of troubles which he left the new king from Scotland alone was sufficient to overwhelm a weak man. Gascony, despite the political marriage of Edward II, was also a source of trouble which was to hamper his action. Though Edward II immediately reconciled archbishop Winchelsey that churchman's struggle with Edward I had coloured his policy and he became one of the most active and insistent of the ordainers. In his conquest of Wales complete success seemed to have crowned Edward I's efforts. The danger from the Welsh had been removed but that removal had increased the danger from another source. The subjection of Wales had increased the power of the marcher barons, and the barons were to prove the greatest obstacle that Edward II had to encounter.

There is in fact much to be said in favour of regarding the reign of Edward II as a reaction by the barons against the general tendency of Edward I's policy against their rights. His policy in acquiring the great earldoms of Cornwall and Norfolk had been apparent to his own day[2]. His anti-feudal legislation could not have been popular with the baronage. The *quo waranto* proceedings, though they had resulted in a compromise[3], were strongly disliked by the barons. Edward's decision in the parliament of Carlisle in 1306 when he declared that after the grant he had made to the earl of Lincoln for

[1] Twysden, *Decem Scriptores*, vol. II, c. 2765. *Foedera*, vol. II, p. 650. Cf. also the articles of the barons before the Ordinances, below, pp. 358–9.

[2] *Chron. Ed. I and Ed. II*, vol. II, *Commendatio Lamentabilis J. de Londonia*, pp. 8–9. Vide also *Auct. Malm.* pp. 212–213.

[3] Vide Seld. Soc., *Select Pleas in Manorial Courts*, p. lxxvii, note C. Holdsworth, *Hist. of Engl. Law*, vol. I, pp. 489.

life of the return of writs in certain hundreds he "would not grant a similar franchise as long as he lived, to any one excepting his own children[1]," expresses the trend of his policy towards liberties and the feudal position in general. In consequence of the increased power of the marcher lords it was possible that Edward's policy might produce a reaction. The central problem of Edward II's reign did not revolve round this reaction but, in conjunction with other and more vital causes, it may have aided to produce the baronial opposition or to account for its strength.

The great struggle during the reign centred round the administration. The baronial opposition was concerned with matters which touched its interests closely. Yet such external events as the Scottish war had an intimate relation with the central problem. Such matters complicated the general situation. Defence of his kingdom was not a matter which the king could neglect, but the baronial opposition did so on frequent occasions. The Scots afforded them in extremity a potential ally against the king. The financial pressure of the Scottish wars increased the disorder in the exchequer. They made demands upon the financial resources of the kingdom which could not be met. The ravages over the north of England decreased the amount of revenue the exchequer could expect from that portion of the kingdom[2]. The efficiency of administration was impeded by the frequent necessity of transferring the central departments from London to York. Northern magnates and prelates failed to attend parliament because of the invasions[3]. The loss which people endured by the removal of chancery, exchequer and law courts to the north was considerable[4]. After the Scottish raids of 1316 Northumberland remained a desert for fifteen years, lifeless[5]. Again the Scottish wars gave the barons an opportunity and excuse for retaining armed followers[6]. In the same way, though to a less degree, other events entered in to complicate the general situation, among them being the condition of Ireland, the relations with France and Gascony and the famines and murrains of the reign.

[1] *Rot. Parl.* vol. I, p. 211. *Cal. Close Rolls*, 1302–7, p. 531.

[2] Cf. *Rot. Parl.* vol. I, pp. 433, 438. *Cal. Pat. Rolls*, 1317–21, p. 160. *Cal. Close Rolls*, 1318–23, pp. 436, 460. Madox, *Firma Burgi*, p. 243.

[3] *Reg. Pal. Dunelm.* vol. I, pp. 384–5; vol. II, pp. 952–3.

[4] Ancient Petition, no. 4106: "Tute ceste bosoigne qe feust autrefoiz respondu est perdue par la maladie Lauantdit Robert et par la longe demoere la Chauncellerie au North."

[5] *Chron. Mon. de Melsa*, vol. II, p. 333.

[6] *Chron. Murimuth*, App. pp. 271–2. *Auct. Bridl.* p. 50.

However important may have been these difficult obstacles which Edward I left his son to overcome, the great struggle of the reign was between the king and barons over the administration. It is out of this struggle, with its tremendous consequences, that the reign of Edward II derives its real importance in English history. This struggle can only be appreciated when the reign is regarded as a period of definition and differentiation. It was in administration that such definition and differentiation were especially noticeable and important in their consequences, but the same tendencies were visible elsewhere.

In the realm of law Professor Maitland has emphasised the importance of this time as a period of definition and differentiation. "To whatever quarter we look the law seems to be emerging into clearness out of a confused and contentious past. The courts are drawing a line between franchises and feudal rights; but it is no easy task and violence must be done to the facts and theories of former times[1]." There was the same tendency towards definition and differentiation in administration. There was confusion between the administration of the household and the administration of the country[2]. All the administrative departments had sprung from the king's court and there had been no necessity to distinguish between the part of the administration which was immediately personal to the king and the part concerned with the government of the country. No differentiation was made between the king's rights to his lands and his rights to his kingdom. For a long time no distinction was possible. By the reign of Edward II events were leading towards such a distinction. The need for differentiation was becoming apparent. Professor Tout has said that for the first time "the marked differentiation of what may roughly be called 'court administration' and 'national administration' became accentuated[3]." It was impossible for anyone to see any distinction clearly. It was doubtful where the "national administration" could be said to begin and the "court administration" to end. The importance lay in the fact that the beginnings of differentiation were visible. The theoretical distinction between king and crown had its counterpart in a practical differentiation in administration.

[1] Seld. Soc., *Select Pleas in Manorial Courts*, vol. I, p. xxiv.

[2] Stubbs, *Constitutional History*, vol. II [1880], Library Edition, pp. 337–8, has noticed "the antagonism between the court and the administration, between the *curia* and the *camera*, or in modern language the court and the cabinet." In the fourth edition [1896] the text is amended. Cf. vol. II, p. 325.

[3] Tout, *The Place of Ed. II*, Pref. p. vii.

It is difficult to determine the precise causative relation between the differentiation in administration and the baronial opposition. What is quite clear is that the action of the baronial opposition was administrative rather than constitutional, that there was need of administrative reform and that when that reform was undertaken it tended to definition and differentiation. It is equally certain that the barons found the greatest obstacle to the successful issue of their plans in the administrative machinery the king had at his disposal; and the motive power of that machinery was to be found in the king's household. The confusion between the respective spheres of the household and the general administrative system gave rise to a conflict between the "curial" and the "national"—"national" being used as a wider term than that small body of friends and officials who formed the king's court, and not meaning anything more than the general administration of the country as opposed to the particular administration of the household. Before this struggle can be appreciated it will be necessary to consider what the "curial" or household system was. Then all that conflict involved can be seen more clearly.

CHAPTER II

THE HOUSEHOLD SYSTEM

The system of government which prevailed in England during the middle ages may fairly be described as personal. The king with his court was not merely the centre of the government; he was the whole government. The king was not only the head of the law, he was the law. When the king died his peace died with him and trespasses committed before his death could not be punished afterwards unless the accused had been impleaded previously[1]. The force of such favours as licences to alienate died with him and they could not be used after his death[2].

The payment of taxation was personal and if a tenant died taxes could not be levied on his moveables though they were in the hands of his executors[3]. Taxes paid were the personal property of the king. Langton, as executor of Edward I, issued his orders to the collectors of the twentieth and thirtieth in the county of York ordering them to pay the sum which had been assigned to the wardrobe to him, "(nous) auoms fait parler a nostre seigneur son fuz le Roi qui ore est de choses que tuchent le testament son peire et il voet et ad comaunde que tutes les dettes que furent dues a son peire soient assignees a nous et nos coexecutours a fournir le testament et la dareine volunte du mort[4]." A sum of 20,000 marks was ordered to be paid to the executors out of the treasury[5] and on petition of the council the king ordered a writ of liberate, made by Edward I to one who had served him in Gascony, to be paid[6]. As in finance so all phases of administration were considered the personal affair of the king. The curia in its various

[1] Seld. Soc., *Year Bk 3 Ed. II*, p. 104. *Eng. Hist. Rev.* vol. XXVI [1911] p. 253. Likewise after the death of an archbishop a decree of excommunicatior could not be pleaded as valid in the law courts (Seld. Soc., *Eyre of Kent*, vol. II pp. 185–6).

[2] Stanford, *Exposit. of King's Prerog.* p. 306.

[3] L. T. R. Mem. Roll, no. 78, m. 97.

[4] Anc. Corresp. vol. L, no. 5 (23 July, 1307).

[5] P. R. O. Liberate Roll, no. 84, m. 4 (1 Oct. 1307).

[6] Ibid. m. 3 (1 April, 1308).

manifestations treated of every aspect of the affairs of the realm in the broad outlines or general principles and in the minutest details of administration.

The system of personal government succeeded the local system of Anglo-Saxon times and the hardly less local system of early Norman feudal times, and was followed by the parliamentary system which first became a force under the Lancastrians. The essential feature of a system of personal government was the king's household, which expanded with the needs of administration. Its rise in England was not unique, though the particular form which personal government took here had definite features of its own. It was but one manifestation of a universal tendency, and a tendency which was no less apparent in the administration of their lands by the nobles than in the conduct of affairs of the realm by the king.

In England, for example, the household of a noble was conducted in the same manner as the royal chamber and wardrobe. Pembroke ordered his clerk to allow £32. 2*s*. 8*d*. in a farm which had been delivered into his household by Walter, his chaplain[1], just as the king sent his writ of privy seal to the treasurer and barons of his exchequer ordering them to allow to one who held land or an office, sums paid into the wardrobe or chamber for the expenses of the royal household[2]. The household of Lord and Lady Willoughby d'Eresby had its seneschal who was to audit the accounts of the wardrobe keeper, its marshal, and its clerks to write letters and the accounts of the wardrobe[3], resembling the corresponding officials of the royal household. The earl of Lancaster sent the process relating to the holy life and miracles of Winchelsey to the pope by one of his household[4], just as the king employed his household in his embassies to foreign powers.

The growth of a household system of government was almost a necessary concomitant of a strong monarchy, the administration of which was too vast and detailed to be carried on by one person. It was natural that the king should look round him and delegate some of his functions, or use as his instruments in the administration of his land, those personal servants of his whom he found constantly round him, persons who were agreeable to him, devoted to his interests and obedient to his will. It was out of the king's household that the

[1] Exch. Misc. 4/1. Vide App. of Doc. no. 41.
[2] Vide below, pp. 145–6.
[3] Chan. Misc., Bdle 3/33. Vide App. of Doc. no. 51.
[4] *Lit. Cantuar.* vol. 1, pp. 50–53.

great departments of state grew. The exchequer, the chancery, the great council, the two benches of justices had gradually obtained a separate existence, as necessity arose from the complexity of administration. The parent body remained, to exercise a supervisory control over the various offshoots and to provide new departments when necessary. The wardrobe, which had become an active organisation under John and took its definite shape and system in the early part of the reign of Henry III[1], though it never separated itself from the person of the king, was in some danger of becoming more than a department of the household and less than a department of government.

By the time of Edward II most of the great departments of government had obtained officials of their own though some which had grown up latest still retained a more intimate connection with the household, especially for instance the customs department. The chamberlain, who superintended the collection of wine customs answered and accounted through the wardrobe[2]. The chamberlain was also the king's butler[3]. Of the great officers of state the justiciar alone never became connected with the household[4]. The great officers of the administration never became feudalised but they originated as members of the royal household. The chancellor and the treasurer were practically always men in holy orders[5]. Moreover they were too intimately connected with the administrative side of the court and required not high titles or great wealth to uphold their offices, but rather technical skill and administrative ability. The development of the household system can in fact be regarded as an effort on the king's part to rid himself of those feudalised officers like the steward and chamberlain of England, and to make the administration entirely dependent upon the royal will. In this effort the natural place to look for officials to take charge of the administration was in the household.

It must not be thought that the king saw or drew any distinction between his household and the administration. In practice there was none; in theory there was none. In view of the differentiation which was already taking effect and of the ultimate distinction which

[1] *Eng. Hist. Rev.* vol. XXIV [1909], 'The Chief Officers of the King's Wardrobe down to 1399,' T. F. Tout, p. 496.

[2] H. Hall, *Customs Revenues*, vol. II, p. 4.

[3] *Munimenta Gildhallae Londoniensis*, vol. II, Pt i, p. 296, Eyre in the Tower, 14 Ed. II: "Et nota quod Botellarius Domini Regis, et Camerarius domini Regis, et Coronator, idem sunt."

[4] Harcourt, *His Grace the Steward*, p. 25.

[5] Stubbs, *Constit. Hist.* vol. I, pp. 381–2.

was drawn, that portion which concerned the government of the country can be called the administration and that portion which concerned the government of the king's private matters and domestic arrangements the household. A clear and precise distinction is impossible, but this difference will suffice for the present. This relation between administration and household was general; the palatinate of Durham is an unique instance in which the officers of government and the officers of the household were never identical even in name and in which those of the household never had any governmental function[1].

The same phenomenon as accounts for the growth of the administrative departments in England during the twelfth and thirteenth centuries accounts for the origin of the "comes palatii" of the Merovingian period[2], and similar circumstances account for the growth of their position and jurisdiction under the Carolingians. The "comes palatii" were royal officers whose position depended upon the strength of the monarchy; and it was the strength of the monarchy in England which enabled the kings to establish the various departments.

The Norman conquest[3] provided the scope for the development of the household system, though it was not until the reign of Henry I that an outcry was caused by the attention which the king bestowed upon, and the power which he gave to, a new class of official which was obtaining some amount of control, the men whom the chroniclers call the "novi homines." The old hereditary officials were being displaced by another class of officials[4], persons of lower birth and little wealth[5] but of great administrative ability, who acted as a counterpoise to the baronial families[6]. The plan of displacing the feudal baronage by men of low rank was a feature of the history of feudalism. It was after the accession of Henry II that the great impetus to the progress of the household system was given. The kingly power was greater and the baronial power correspondingly less. There was the opportunity for the development of this system;

[1] Lapsley, *Palat. of Durham*, p. 77. [2] Ibid. pp. 3–4.

[3] For the personal element in the Witan and the consideration of the question in Anglo-Saxon times vide Stubbs, *Constit. Hist.* vol. I, pp. 138–9. Vide also H. M. Chadwick, *Origin of the English Nation* [1907] and *Studies in Anglo-Saxon Institutions* [1905].

[4] Stubbs, *Constit. Hist.* vol. I, pp. 338–9.

[5] Ordericus Vitalis, Bk XI, Chap. II, c. 787: "Alios econtra, favorabiliter illi obsequentes, de ignobili stirpe illustravit, de pulvere, ut ita dicam, extulit, dataque multiplici facultate, super consules et illustres oppidanos exaltavit."

[6] Stubbs, *Constit. Hist.* vol. I, p. 339.

there was also the necessity. The reforms undertaken and achieved by Henry II rendered it imperative that there should be an efficient body of administrators capable and willing to work in the spirit of the reformer. Angevin efficiency was dependent upon the strength of the monarchy but its continuance and its crystallisation into a permanent system could only be secured by the skill and training of the royal curia.

The growth of the household system was then the natural outcome of the Angevin system of government. That was a system too complicated for the lay mind to grasp and for the lay hand to execute. Well-trained administrators were essential. There was only one place where such training could be secured—the king's household. Moreover, since the reforms were anti-baronial in their intent, the persons who were to carry them out had to be drawn from another class. A strong monarchy, free from danger of baronial interference, yet ever seeking to increase its strength and the security of its position at the expense of the barons, extending its influence by the expedition of its judicial processes and the improvement of its remedies—that was, in brief, the aim of the Angevin system of government. All this involved a growing complexity of administration. The number of cases attracted to the royal courts by the novelty and speed of its remedies demanded more trained justices. The new writs and assizes presupposed a wider knowledge of the law than the baron or his untrained steward possessed. The financial aspect of the increased jurisdiction, the development of scutage and the new methods of taxation of the early Angevin kings added to the work of the exchequer and complicated it.

Exceptional qualities of administration were required to ensure the smooth working of this already complex machinery; and its complexity was steadily growing. It was important that the administrators should be in complete harmony with the spirit of the reforms; it was of equal importance that their knowledge should be full, and their training complete. The clerks trained in the king's court fulfilled both these conditions. It was a result of the efficient training and skill of the royal court and a tribute to it, that the administrative machinery should be kept going, that the inherent developments should be allowed to take place without impediment, and that the improvements which suggested themselves or were necessitated should all be the result of the care of officials who had been trained there.

There was no other source whence such a body of men could be obtained. The royal court stood in a position of complete advantage. It had a monopoly of administrative talent. There was a demand for efficient officials: it alone could supply that demand. The barons' administration of their lands was not efficient. There was one other field of potential administrative talent—the church. But however able and efficient the administrators of abbeys or dioceses might be, entirely different qualities and a very different training were necessary to qualify for a position in the administration of a kingdom such as England was in the second half of the twelfth century and in the thirteenth century. Moreover the king could not afford to have men of divided allegiance working the newly constructed machinery. The church did not provide the king with officials; the king's court was the shortest avenue to ecclesiastical preferment. With the growing bulk of administration, its efficiency depended more and more upon the officials, especially upon the subordinate officials. However perfect a system may be, its ultimate success depends upon the diligence and skill of its administrators. The king could no longer exercise any considerable amount of supervision over the various departments of his government. Even the head of the department, often a bishop with many calls upon his time, could not exercise sufficient supervision, and it was essential that the clerks who held minor though responsible positions should be well trained.

All this but points to the fact that the personal system of government which was in being at the commencement of the fourteenth century was inevitable. Though doubtless liable to serious faults there was no alternative to the household system and while reform in various directions was probably necessary and would have done nothing more than increase its efficiency, the breakdown of the system would have meant administrative anarchy. There was as yet nothing to replace the king's control of the administration.

As the various departments separated from the parent body the king's direct control over them decreased considerably. As time proceeded, without any other authority intervening, his control became more and more indirect. There was however a body which sought to intervene on every possible occasion and diminish if not end the control of the king over the great departments of government. This was the new phase which baronial opposition, answering to the needs of the time, had taken. The barons' attitude towards the wardrobe was characteristic of their whole policy. The wardrobe was during the thirteenth century "the special mouthpiece of the personal will of the king[1]." Fven over this department the barons during the reign of Edward II[2] sought control. The king's policy in reply to these assaults was but natural. He retreated from one line of defence to another. His plan of fortification was concentric. When the outer ring had been carried or even when it was in danger of being carried, the king retreated to an inner ring. The whole time he was building within. He was rearing new ramparts to replace the old which had been broken.

The core of the system of personal or household government was the king's chamber. It is necessary from the outset to draw a distinction between the king's chamber and the *aula*[3]. The chamber was where the king lived; the *aula* where his household lived. It is true that the same purveyors provided for the king's hall and his chamber[4]. This but suggests a connection between them. The chamber was the centre of government, the hall a subsidiary office of the chamber with little but a household significance[5]. In its widest sense the term "chamber" can be expanded to mean the whole of the king's court including even the departments of government. This use of the word suggests the source of those departments; and in the time of the first two Norman kings, at least, the curia and the chamber were equivalent, and co-equal. The prior and convent of Canterbury objected to send representatives to parliament because they were summoned to a secular court, that is, the parliament of the king, which began and ended in the royal chamber[6]. In its narrowest sense the chamber is but the place in which the king lived, ate, and slept, and this was its meaning in the payments entered on the issue rolls of the exchequer, "in camera regis[7]." The meaning which it is proposed to give the chamber here will be more apparent after some features of its various activities have been considered. At the present stage it can briefly be described as the place of the king's residence, where, surrounded by his personal followers, he made known

[1] *Eng. Hist. Rev.* vol. XXIV [1909], p. 496.

[2] Cf. Ordinance 14. Vide below, pp. 371–2; pp. 383–4.

[3] L. O. Pike, *Constit. Hist. of House of Lords*, p. 27, note 1, points out that *aula regis* and *curia regis* have been employed as synonyms. The *aula* was but a small part of the *curia*.

[4] Cf. Chan. Warr., File 1703 passim, where are given warrants for commissions to purveyors for "Aula et Camera Regis" and "por la sale et chaumbre."

[5] The exception is the court of the *aula* with its pleas before the steward and marshal, which is discussed below, pp. 199–203.

[6] "In eo quod ad Curiam secularem, puta Domini Regis parliamentum, quod in Camera ejusdem Domini fuit inchoatum et per dies aliquot continuatum" (*Parl. Writs*, vol. II, Pt ii, p. 139).

[7] Vide Issue Rolls of Ed. I passim.

his will, and whence, through these same personal followers, the royal influence radiated to every department of government.

Among the activities of the chamber, its relation to the great seal is of considerable interest and importance. The great seal, the most formal and frequently used instrument of administration, the issue of which was carefully guarded, was regularly surrendered to and received from the king in his chamber[1]. After it had been received by the king it was generally delivered into the hands of the keeper of the wardrobe for safe-keeping[2]. The delivery was made in the presence of those persons who happened to be in the king's chamber at the time. The chancellor delivered the seal to the king in January, 1308[3], when the king was about to set out for France for his marriage, in the presence of William Inge, knight[4], William de Melton and Adam de Osgodby, clerks[5]. The delivery of the seal to Robert de Baldock in 1323 was made in an equally personal group, before Despenser, Sir Henry de Clif and Sir William de Herlaston[6]. On occasion, however, the assembly was much bigger, more imposing

[1] *Cal. Close Rolls*, 1296–1302, pp. 58, 150, 253, 594, 601, 610; 1307–13, pp. 18, 258; 1323–27, p. 134.

[2] Ibid. 1296–1302, pp. 150, 295, 594, 601, 610; 1302–7, p. 313; 1307–13, pp. 18, 258.

[3] Ibid. 1307–13, p. 18.

[4] William Inge was at this time a justice of assize and was closely connected with the king as one of his council (Madox, *Hist. of Exch.* vol. II, pp. 30, 57). He had been a king's serjeant as early as 1289 (Camd. Soc., *State Trials* 1289–90, ed. T. F. Tout [1906], Introd. p. xxv). He had been attached to Edward's household when prince of Wales and was referred to by the king as "nostre cher bachiler" (Exch. Misc. 5/2, m. 2). When the council of Edward I had appointed him as a justice in Scotland the prince had made strenuous endeavours to retain him near him (Exch. Misc. 5/2, m. 15). He was a "curialist" who during the early years of the reign took a considerable share in administrative work (cf. *Cal. Doc. Scotl.* vol. III, pp. 33, 39; Foss, *Judges of England*, vol. III, pp. 268–270). He is frequently found assisting the exchequer officials at their work. As early as November, 1307, he was engaged in receiving and examining petitions (L. T. R. Mem. Roll, no. 78, m. 20; Chan. Warr., File 58/33). A little later a petition was to be examined before the treasurer and barons of the exchequer "et Wilhelmi Inge et aliis de consilio eis assidentibus" (K. R. Mem. Roll, no. 81, m. 86). He obtained grants of lands (ibid. no. 82, m. 13), acted as messenger to the chancery (*Cal. Close Rolls*, 1307–13, p. 27) and in the critical period following the Ordinances acted as the mouthpiece of the council to the king (Issue Roll, no. 159, m. 5). In fact he was in much the same position as such friends of the king as Guy Ferre and the count of Savoy who took part in administration (K. R. Mem. Roll, no. 81, mm. 40 d, 43 d) perhaps watching over the king's interests. He was subsequently appointed a justice of common pleas (*Cal. Pat. Rolls*, 1313–17, p. 181).

[5] William de Melton was controller of the wardrobe and Adam de Osgodby a clerk of chancery.

[6] *Cal. Close Rolls*, 1323–27, p. 134

and formal. In 1310 at Woodstock the bishop of Chichester, chancellor, delivered the seal to the king in the presence of the bishop of Worcester, the earls of Gloucester, Lincoln, Warenne, Cornwall and Arundel, Despenser, Clifford, Thomas de Berkley, Henry de Beaumont, Robert fitz Payn, Guy Ferre, knights, Ingelard de Warle, keeper of the king's wardrobe, Sandale, Melton and others[1]. In 1305 the archbishop elect of York, who had to go to Rome about his election, told the king of this in his chamber at Lincoln, before his council; and there a custodian was appointed[2]. It was not essential that the seal should be delivered in the chamber; it was usually done, however, in the king's presence; and in 1324 when Baldock, chancellor, desired to return to his house for rest, the seal was delivered to the king "in the forest of Windsor where the king was for the sake of hunting[3]," while in 1302 the seal was delivered to Edward I in his chapel[4].

There is evidence also of deeds being delivered to the king in his chamber. Gavaston in 1309 restored the castle of Knaresborough and other lands to the king, and the deed of conveyance was delivered by Gavaston to the king in his chamber in the house of the Friars Preachers at Stamford. After enrolment on the chancery roll the deed was given to the keeper of the wardrobe to be kept therein[5]. Side by side with the delivery of important official instruments into the chamber should be taken the delivery of *medicinalia* therein which were received by Sir Thomas de Useflet[6], the king's private clerk[7], and this is useful as acting as a reminder of the other side of the chamber. The chronicler's statement that when Gavaston returned to England, after his banishment in 1311 in accordance with the Ordinances, he went about cautiously and endeavoured to hide himself now in the king's chamber, now at Wallingford and now in the castle of Tintagel[8], also emphasises the other side of the chamber.

Actual business also was transacted in the king's chamber. It was in his chamber at Westminster in his parliament that Edward I in 1305 offered John de Warenne the marriage of Joan his grand-

[1] *Cal. Close Rolls*, 1307–13, p. 258.
[2] Ibid. 1302–7, p. 313.
[3] Ibid. 1323–27, pp. 306–7.
[4] Ibid. 1296–1302, p. 602.
[5] Ibid. 1307–13, p. 225. This deed was witnessed by the earls of Gloucester, Lincoln, Surrey and Richmond, Hugh le Despenser, Henry de Percy, Robert son of Walter, Robert son of Payn, William de Bereford, William Inge. Stamford, 26 July, 1309.
[6] Sir Thomas de Useflet was one of the most important officials of the chamber. Vide below, p. 232.
[7] *Cal. Doc. Scotl.* vol. III, pp. 142–3.
[8] *Auct. Malm.* p. 174.

daughter[1], an offer willingly accepted[2]. It was in the king's parliament at Westminster in the presence of bishops, and ecclesiastical dignitaries, earls and barons and others that Alexander, king of Scotland, came to the king in his chamber and offered to become his liege man and do homage to him, and this was done[3]. The restoration of the castle and honour of Knaresborough, as well as the delivery of the deed, took place in the king's chamber in June, 1308, when Gavaston appeared before the king in his chamber at Langley[4]. The notarial instrument conveying the Templars' lands to the Hospitallers in 1313 was made in the king's chamber at Westminster, though the witnesses, while including household officials and followers, like Edmund de Mauley, king's steward, John de Cherleton and William de Montague, also numbered the archbishop of Canterbury, Sandale, treasurer, Pembroke and Despenser[5].

Matters of importance were occasionally tried and decided in the king's chamber before the king and his council. After the destruction of the walls of the Tower by the citizens of London[6], John de Gisors, mayor, with aldermen and citizens, came before the king in his chamber in the palace of Westminster and before him and his council submitted themselves and on their knees begged grace. The king after a short deliberation with his council restored the mayor and citizens to their former state[7]. Again in 1326 the mayor, sheriffs and aldermen of London appeared in the king's chamber in the Tower of London and were charged by the king in person to maintain peace within the city of London[8].

The importance of the chamber depended not upon the activity displayed therein. Its influence upon the administration was of a subterranean nature. It worked under the great departments of government, asserting its influence in a manner unseen to the outside world. The officers of the chamber, officially nothing more than the body servants of the king, were employed by him in the business of government. The valets of his chamber were sent outside the court on the king's secret business[9], on business not merely personal to

[1] *Cal. Close Rolls*, 1302–7, p. 321.

[2] Ibid. The marriage took place in June, 1306 (*Ann. Lond.* p. 146).

[3] *Cal. Close Rolls*, 1272–79, p. 505.

[4] Ibid. 1307–13, pp. 67–68.

[5] K. R. Mem. Roll, no. 87, m. 89 d: "hec apud Westmonasterium in camera viridi dicti domini Regis."

[6] Cf. *Ann. Lond.* pp. 216–217. *Ann. Paul.* p. 272. Camd. Soc. vol. XXVIII [1844], *Chroniques de London*, ed. G. J. Aungier, p. 37.

[7] *Cal. Close Rolls*, 1313–18, p. 308.

[8] Ibid. 1323–27, p. 563 (20 June, 1326) *Foedera*, vol. II, p. 631.

[9] Cf. Brit. Mus. Stowe MS. 553, Liber Garder, Ed. II, ff. 28, 28 b, 31 b, e.g.

the king but having administrative intent. The higher officers, William de Langley, clerk[1], Giles de Beauchamp, squire of the chamber, were employed on similar missions. The king's confessor took part in definitely administrative processes. He took to the chancellor letters patent which the king ordered to be confirmed under the great seal[2], and in company with the bishop of Worcester, treasurer, he acted as bearer of the king's commands to a provincial council of Canterbury in 1309[3]. An account of the officials of the chamber and the detail of the methods in which the chamber and the household influenced the administration must be postponed; here the problem must be stated in brief outline.

The activity of the chamber was not as important as that of the other household office—the wardrobe. The importance of the chamber lies in the fact that it was the core of the system. It was the source whence in times of stress the king could draw new supplies. There he obtained new safeguards to replace the old which were weakening under the weight of opposition. The chamber, therefore, was of special importance during the reign of Edward II, for then it was developed as a strong defence against the power of the baronial opposition. Important as was the chamber from this point of view, administratively, the influence of the wardrobe was very much greater. The chamber was essentially a personal rather than household department. The wardrobe was a household department which had a large place in administration.

Some slight indication of the influence of the chamber and wardrobe has been given. Without anticipating too much it may be said the officers of the household system exercised a potent and continuous influence upon the administration. There was a perpetual danger that court influence would become predominant and tyrannous. There was a danger of a strong man exercising a great influence over a weak king. The danger was unlikely to arise from the officials of the chamber or household. Their interests ran in lines parallel to those of the king. They might, they doubtless did, exploit their position, but such petty exploitation could not have very serious effects upon the person or position of the king. The real danger lay in an outside influence obtaining the king's confidence and ruling king and kingdom solely or chiefly for personal aggrandizement. This

f. 28, J. le Barber valet of king's chamber: "eunti extra curiam in negociis domini Regis secretis."

[1] Cf. Brit. Mus. Stowe MS. 553, Liber Garder, Ed. II, f. 28 b.

[2] Chan. Warr., File 106/4853 (p.s. 11 Sept. 1318).

[3] Wilkins, *Concilia*, vol. II, p. 328.

danger was realised in the control which the younger Despenser obtained over the king, and the charges which the barons levelled against him, of accroaching royal power, and controlling the king's presence[1], were their interpretation of the problem. How court influence and chamber government worked may be illustrated by a single instance. A meeting of the council was deemed necessary. The king by Despenser ordered a third person to summon a fourth person to be at the Friars Preachers in London at a certain time to discuss certain urgent matters. The nature of this business the king had ordered Despenser to communicate[2].

Everywhere the personal interfered or could interfere with the administrative. A conflict over the control of the personal and governmental departments was bound to come, and there were very special reasons why it came in the reign of Edward II, when the reforms of Henry II had been seconded by the work of Edward I. The growth of the personal system and its various manifestations determined the line of baronial opposition, and therefore administrative history is important here. The conflict of the reign of Edward II may be regarded as that of the "curial" and the "baronial" which gradually from the time of Magna Carta for succeeding centuries may be said to merge into, or at least take upon itself some aspects of, the "national[3]." The great governmental departments were still curial to a considerable extent. The differentiation was only becoming accentuated for the first time. It was to the advantage of the barons that the differentiation should become more marked and finally complete. The king sought to perpetuate and extend the influence of the purely curial upon wider lines. The barons claimed that the curial should not control the governmental; but that they themselves should do so. There was here a definite issue between king and barons, an issue which could be complicated by various causes but which in its main outline would remain constant under all changes of time, place and advantage.

There were definite causes which precipitated the crisis under Edward II. The aim and object of the author of the *Mirror of Justices*, who represents views very closely akin to those of the baronial opposition, have been described by Maitland: "the strain that dominates the whole book is the dislike of the king's officers

[1] *Stat. of Realm*, vol. I, pp. 181–4.

[2] Anc. Corresp. vol. XXXVII, no. 88. Vide App of Doc. no. 113.

[3] Professor Tout distinguishes between "court administration" and 'national administration" (*The Place of Edward II*, p. vii). "Curial" and "baronial" appeared to fit in more accurately with this thesis.

and their ways. Corrupt are they and become abominable in their doings; there is none that doeth good, no not one. From the chancellor and the false judges downwards, they are all guilty of offences, which, to give them their plain names, are perjury, larceny and murder....The system of government is as bad as those who administer it[1]." The state of the administration and the conduct of the administrative officers were dependent upon the household system of government. The causes which precipitated the crisis were largely personal and are to be found in the character of the king and in the personal opposition which the promotion of Gavaston aroused amongst the barons. In part they were a reaction from the legislative and administrative policy of Edward I; in part the result of opportunism, or the fruition of baronial opposition.

The extent to which the problem of Edward II's reign ranged round the household is emphasised by the letters written to the king by the pope. The pope exhorted him to lessen the expenses of his household[2], and urged him not to waste the goods of his realm in sloth, feasting and presents[3]. He was besought to choose counsellors fit to help him in the government of his realm, good judges and a resident steward who would keep account of his expenses[4]. The pope appeared to realise that the problem of the reign centred round the household and rejoiced that the king had reformed himself and his household[5]. Reform of the household formed one of the chief motives of the Ordinances of 1311 as well as of subsequent baronial experiments. In the parliament of York in 1318 the community of the realm petitioned the king on a matter touching the wardrobe[6], and the reforms undertaken after 1322 were largely concerned with the household. These facts will be clearer at the end of the thesis than now, but their statement at this stage is necessary so that it may be realised from the outset how important a consideration of the administration of the household and its relation to the administrative departments is to the main purpose.

There were two methods by which the king could have met the attacks of the baronial opposition. They may be broadly distinguished as the positive and the negative, or the aggressive and the defensive. The positive side appears to have been developed under Edward I, and the son merely assumed the policy and position which

[1] Seld. Soc., *Mirror of Justices*, p. xlvi.

[2] *Cal. Pat. Letters*, 1304–42, p. 430.

[3] Ibid. p. 434.

[4] Ibid. p. 414.

[5] Ibid. p. 433.

[6] Cole, *Doc. illustr. Eng. Hist. in 13th and 14th Cent.* p. 27.

his father had attained. There were, of course, a few additional developments, but the majority of these occurred after the collapse of the baronial opposition in 1322, and took the shape of reform of various departments of administration, especially of the exchequer. The far greater portion of the royal policy was negative[1] and defensive in its intent, though there are a few instances of counter attack on the part of the king. The king generally entrenched himself safely in his household, in his chamber, and all baronial attempts to dislodge him proved futile. When the baronage gained some advantage in the control of one of the great departments of government, the king undermined that control through the household. Under the pressure exercised by the baronial opposition the king placed greater reliance upon his personal system.

There were two reasons why the king could rely upon the negative side. He had a well-established system, complete, self-sufficing, possessing great resources, and he retained throughout complete executive power. As long as the personal system remained the king could retain entire control of the executive. The second reason is to be found in the completeness of the royal prerogative, though this would have been valueless without the practical power of the household system.

[1] Daines Barrington, *Observations upon the Statutes* [1766], p. 169: "Upon the whole, (to consider Edward II as a legislator) though it cannot be said that any law passed during his reign of great importance to the subject, yet he seems to have had the negative merit of never having attempted to introduce any statute, which in any measure tended to derogate from their just rights and liberties."

CHAPTER III

THE PERSONAL ASPECT OF THE REIGN

In determining the policy of a government ruled from the king's household, the character of the king and his principal advisers is of the utmost importance[1]. The policy was largely their wills and interests translated into action. The household system of government permitted the caprices and foibles of the king to influence administrative policy and machinery. The character of the king and its detailed consideration is therefore of profound importance. Edward II lacked the qualities necessary for an efficient working of the personal or household system. The system which Edward I had built up required certain characteristics in the ruler which could not be found in a weak king[2]. Edward II had not these essential characteristics.

Hardly less important than the king's character are the characters of the favourites upon whom he bestowed his affection and to whom did they desire it, the king was prepared to give the direction of the affairs of his realm. The household system was a perfect machinery for a strong-minded and able favourite to work his will in the government of the land. The characters of those with whom Edward II surrounded himself, and especially of the king's prime friends, Gavaston and Despenser, are of far reaching importance and must be treated in detail.

The character of the barons was as important in determining the nature and course of their opposition as was the king's in determining the policy of the government. Those qualities of selfishness, pride and faction which are found as the salient features in baronial opposition were present in the barons of Edward II, and present in an unusual degree. With the transformation of feudalism in its governmental aspect and as a military system had come the loss of

[1] Holdsworth, *Hist. of Engl. Law*, vol. II, p. 238: "Edward and his great minister (Burnell) knew well that the character of the servants of the crown was as important as the character of the measures taken to settle the constitution of the country."

[2] Stubbs, *Constit. Hist.* vol. II, pp. 324–5.

those sterner qualities which feudalism bred. Chivalry was decaying, and the decay influenced the minds and actions of the barons. There was already a narrowness of aim and a pettiness of purpose which was to culminate in the destruction of the baronage and the devastation of the kingdom.

There was a serious depreciation in the conduct and the character of bishops and barons[1] at the beginning of Edward II's reign. Henry de Lacy, earl of Lincoln, appeared to survive as a reminder of a better age in which fidelity and sincerity were more frequent and certainly better appreciated. The low state of personality was not a characteristic of one faction, it was general, though there were a few men of pure motive and disinterested action. Still there is not one man of sufficiently striking personality to enthuse the biographer. Some of the characters of the reign have had their apologists, notably Adam of Orleton[2]; not a single baron or bishop has been justified.

What added particular force to the transition from the reign of Edward I to that of Edward II was the new generation which succeeded among the barons, especially among the earls. The barons who had aided Edward I in his administrative work, or who had resolutely opposed it, had left the scene of their triumphs and reverses before the death of the king. The new generation of earls was young in age, immature in policy, weak in experience. Lancaster, Arundel, Warenne, Gloucester were new in their possessions. There were only two men who could assume the leadership of the barons, the earl of Lincoln and archbishop Winchelsey. Lincoln was by training and instinct a strong supporter of the royal position, almost a curialist; Winchelsey was worn out, and both lived only long enough to see the beginning of the troubles of the reign. The lead consequently went to the younger generation almost immediately.

Edward II's character was feeble rather in comparison with his immediate predecessor than judged by an absolute standard. Not the least of his misfortunes was the fact that he had to follow Edward I. It has been remarked that he was "the first king since the conquest who was not a man of business, well acquainted with the routine of government[3]." This is the essential fact in estimating his character and its influence upon the reign. It was the greatest possible misfortune that at a time when the administration of the country was

[1] Cf. Stubbs, *Constit. Hist.* vol. II, pp. 323, 385–6.

[2] *Registrum A. de Orleton* (Canterb. and York Soc.), 1317–27, ed. A. T. Bannister [1908], pp. xxix, xxxvi–xliv.

[3] Stubbs, *Constit. Hist.* vol. II, p. 328.

becoming increasingly dependent upon the king's personal character, ability and diligence and upon the character and skill of the officials he appointed—this as a necessary result of the growth of the personal system—that the king should be deficient in those very qualities which the situation demanded.

The first essential of an administrator is attention to detail. Edward II was a trifler. Business of government he neglected for petty considerations. Minstrelsy and acting were a frequent source of pleasure to him[1] and he is said to have been attracted to Walter Reynolds, on account of his skill in theatricals[2]. His wardrobe and chamber accounts contain innumerable payments to minstrels from all parts of England and Western Europe[3]. Next to his passion for amusement came his love of hunting and horses. He made frequent and lengthy stays in royal manors near his forests at Clarendon and Cowick and such places. He never hesitated to leave his duty for the sake of hunting. Even as prince he was interested in the rearing of horses and begged the archbishop of Canterbury to lend him a good stallion for the season[4]. Edward's traits were those of the country knight not of the monarch.

An administrator must possess endless activity in his office. Edward's activity took the form of strenuous hunting and employment in mechanical arts[5]. Words came to him far readier than deeds[6]. He could not keep that secrecy in counsel so necessary to personal government[7]. The power of initiative he either lacked or refused to use, relying more upon other men's counsel than upon his own[8]. His generosity sometimes took the form of prodigality[9]. He delighted in gorgeous array and feasts[10].

[1] *Ninth Rep. Dep. Keep. Rec.* App. II, pp. 246–9, contains a calendar of a portion of the roll of letters of Edward when prince of Wales, and throws interesting sidelights upon his character. The roll is now found Exch. Misc. 5/2. Writing to Walter Reynolds on 1 July, 1305, he directs him to provide for him in London for his players a pair of trumpets and kettle drums (p. 248).

[2] *Auct. Malm.* p. 197: "in ludis theatralibus principatum tenuit, et per hoc regis favorem optinuit."

[3] Cf. K. R. Acct. 379/7, f. 5. Stowe MS. 553, ff. 67, 68.

[4] *Ninth Rep. Dep. Keep. Rec.* App. II, p. 247.

[5] *Chron. Lanerc.* p. 222.

[6] *Auct. Bridl.* p. 91. *Chron. Knighton*, vol. I, p. 407: "ore promptus, opere varius."

[7] *Polychronicon Ran. Higden*, vol. VIII, p. 299: "he wolde lighliche telle out prive counseille."

[8] *Auct. Bridl.* p. 91: "magis alieno quam proprio consilio credens."

[9] Ibid. p. 91: "in dando prodigus." Cf. also *Chron. Knighton*, vol. I, p. 407.

[10] Ibid.

His barons appear to have had some cause of complaint, for he despised their counsel[1], and after his accession, failing to realise that a king had greater responsibilities than a prince, he still clung to the friends of his youth and acted by their advice[2]. Far more dangerous was his habit of becoming obsessed by one of his personal followers. The one who thus attracted his attention was courted, enriched, advanced and honoured[3]. The two classic examples of the king's infatuation are Gavaston and the younger Despenser. There were several other persons about the court whom the king honoured, considerably, though to less degree than his two chief favourites. This erection of one person into a position of supreme importance in the court was full of danger. The king's preference touched baronial pride, but there was a deeper significance to the baronial anger.

A far greater justification for their attitude is found in the fact that instead of associating with his barons he revelled in the company of actors, sailors, and labourers[4], with whom apparently he had much in common, partly due to his great muscular strength[5] and his intellectual qualities, for he was unlearned, and his official letters had to be translated from Latin into French for him[6]. His anger instead of being roused against his enemies raged at times most furiously against those who surrounded him.

The impression which the character of the king must have produced upon the minds of people, who from experience were accustomed to look for noble and high qualities in their rulers, explains the questionings whether the ruler could have been the true son of his great predecessor[7]. This accounts for the support obtained by the pretender[8] who appeared in 1318 at Oxford[9] and gives a touch of

[1] Trokelowe, *Annales*, p. 66. *Chron. Knighton*, vol. I, p. 408: "proceres suos parvipendit."

[2] *Ann. Paul.* p. 257: "statim spreto consilio senum, sicut Roboam, adhaesit consilio juvenum qui secum ab adolescentia fuerant conversati, et praecipue et super omnia consilio Petri de Gavestone."

[3] *Auct. Bridl.* p. 91: "ad unum aliquem familiarem ardenter adjectus, quem summe coloret, ditaret, praeferret, a cujus praesentia abesse non sustineret, ac prae ceteris honoraret." Cf. *Chron. Knighton*, vol. I, p. 407.

[4] *Auct. Bridl.* p. 91. *Chron. Knighton*, vol. I, p. 407. [5] Ibid.

[6] The pope thanked the archbishop of Canterbury for translating his letters to the king into French (*Cal. Pap. Letters*, 1304–42, pp. 430–1).

[7] The character and conduct of the king depicted in *Flores Hist.* vol. III, pp. 188, 214, 217, 227–8, which is adverse in the extreme, should be ignored. Robert of Reading is throughout the reign a bad authority for appreciation of the king. His bias is very definitely baronial. The vicious suggestions of *Chron. Mon. de Melsa*, vol. II, p. 355, are also unsubstantiated.

[8] *Ann. Paul.* pp. 282–3. *Auct. Bridl.* p. 55. [9] *Chron. Lanerc.* p. 222.

truth to the saying of Robert Bruce that he was more afraid of the bones of the dead king than of the living king[1].

It is difficult to determine how far Edward II had been trained by his father[2]. Exercise of severity appears to have been a chief instrument. The violent quarrel which broke out between them in 1305 illustrates the methods by which the father sought to get the son to amend his ways. The quarrel was due to words which had passed between the prince and Walter de Langton. The king was so enraged that he forbade the prince, or any of his entourage, to enter his house. The king's household and the exchequer were forbidden to give anything for the support of the prince's household[3]. Some weeks later the prince wrote that he dared not or could not make any request of the king[4]. The king's anger gradually relented to some extent, and soon after, writing to his sister the countess of Cornwall, he said that the king did not continue so harsh towards him, for he had commanded sufficient necessaries to be provided for him[5]. He was allowed to have two valets; but he longed for more company to lessen the anguish he had endured and still endured daily owing to the king's directions. The prince asked another sister, the countess of Holland, to beg his mother to ask the king to permit Gilbert de Clare and Peter Gavaston to live with him[6]. The king's permission had to be obtained before his sister could visit the prince[7] and even in so simple a matter as allowing a member of his household to go to Rome with the earl of Lincoln the prince could make no decision. The matter must be referred to the king[8].

Upon one of a sensitive nature, severity would have a prejudicial effect. Edward was given to brooding, and his enforced retirement into solitude would make him brood. He was moreover one who loved the company of his friends, and a more reasonable solution would have been the substitution of companions whose influence was prejudicial by others, a plan which was adopted in 1307, when Gavaston was banished[9]. The king's tendency to brood threw him into a sad mood after the death of Gavaston, from which however

[1] *Ann. Paul.* p. 265.

[2] His conduct as prince of Wales could not have been altogether bad, as his subsequent conduct as king is contrasted with it. *Auct. Malm.* p. 192: "O, qualis sperabatur adhuc princeps Wallie! Tota spes evanuit dum factus est rex Angliae."

[3] *Ninth Rep. Dep. Keep. Rec.* App. II, p. 247 (14 June, 1305), to the earl of Lincoln.

[4] Ibid. p. 248 (2 July, 1305), to the queen.

[5] Ibid. (21 July, 1305).

[6] Ibid. (4 August, 1305).

[7] Ibid. p. 249 (14 Sept. 1305).

[8] Ibid. (4 Oct. 1305).

[9] *Cal. Close Rolls*, 1302–7, pp. 526–7.

he was raised by the birth of his eldest son Edward[1], though the gloom was too heavy to be ended[2].

Misfortune must be numbered amongst the king's faults. During much of his reign he allowed events to take their course; when he did apply his hand, fate was pitted against him. His intermittent activity was as futile as his frequent inaction. He was not personally unpopular, evil in his designs or oppressive in his government. His people invested him with sanctity after his murder[3] and a chronicler[4] bestowed martyrdom upon him.

Many of the traits of his character might seem to be admirably suited to the working of the personal system of government. It might be suggested that his very withdrawal from government allowed the household officials to determine policy unimpeded by the interference of an inefficient king. Government by favourites or by household officials alone was not, however, a feature of the personal system. That system was based upon the king acting through the officials of his household. It was founded upon the ability of the king and the integrity of his household.

There is a danger of attaching too much importance to the personal character of the king in finding cause for the troubles of the reign. The personal factor may have accentuated or occasioned but did not cause them. Edward II allowed personal considerations to rule him at times, but there was something far more urgent and outstanding which supplied the background to the reign. Favourites came in but to complicate the constitutional struggle. Still the king's personal character is important inasmuch as it contributed considerably towards the conflict. It was one reason why the particular phase of conflict between royal authority as expressed in the personal system and baronial policy as expressed in the Ordinances occurred then rather than later.

The baronial position towards favourites and foreigners had changed considerably during the thirteenth century. In Henry III's reign the baronial opposition was concentrated, primarily, against foreigners. They stood between the king and his lawful advisers

[1] *Auct. Malm.* p. 188.

[2] *Chronicon Galfridi le Baker* (ed. E. M. Thompson), p. 6: "Hoc anno leticia nati filii et regine quam nimium dilexit et tenerrime confovit, ne quidquam molestie eis inferret, rex dissimulavit quam moleste gessit mortem Petri."

Edward in his joy gave the person who brought him the news of the birth £80 yearly from the farm of the city of London (cf. *Cal. Close Rolls*, 1318–23, p. 611).

[3] *Chron. Mon. de Melsa*, vol. II, p. 355.

[4] *Chron. Hemingburgh*, vol. II, p. 269.

Even in the time of Henry III the complaint against the foreigners was not made against them primarily as men of alien blood, but as those whose views of government were different from those of the English baronage. They were instruments of royal policy outside the common law of the land. They were irresponsible ministers from whom reckoning could not be taken[1]. By the time of Edward II the question of foreigners takes a secondary place. Some amount of the opposition to Gavaston was due to his foreign birth, though he was a Gascon by birth and name[2], and his father had served Edward I[3]. This opposition was but incidental to that raised by profounder causes. It was a source of complaint that the king should prefer a foreigner before all his magnates[4], and that the earldom of Cornwall should be given to an alien[5], the greater part of the barons objecting on this ground[6]. He returned to England from exile in 1311 bringing more foreigners with him[7]. Similar objection was taken to the count of Savoy and Otto de Grandison, on account of their foreign extraction[8].

Greater opposition was aroused against the favourites who prevented the barons from approaching the king and detracted from the barons' share in the government. The barons opposed the system, which allowed the favourites such power, more than the favourites. The exploitation of a system by the favourites showed the barons where the difficulty and danger lay. Under Edward II, it was no longer a revolt against foreign domination, or against the influence of favourites, but an attack upon a whole scheme of government.

One of the first acts of the king upon his accession had been the recall of Gavaston from the exile to which Edward I had sent him a few months earlier. Gavaston had been the friend of his

[1] *Chron. de Mailros* (Bannatyne Club), pp. 191–2, is useful on this point. The opposition is first against the queen and foreigners, then against John Maunsel. Cf. *Cal. Pat. Rolls*, 1258–66, pp. 269–270.

[2] Marin Dimitresco, *Pierre de Gavaston, sa Biographie et son Rôle*, pp. 17–18. *Arch. Journal* [1858], vol. XV, pp. 129–132.

[3] *Foedera*, vol. I, p. 689. Dimitresco, *Pierre de Gavaston*, pp. 18–19.

[4] Trokelowe, *Annal.* p. 66: "Rex alienigenam et ignobilem magnatibus praeposuit universis."

[5] *Auct. Bridl.* pp. 32–33.

[6] *Auct. Malm.* p. 155: "quia Petrus alienigena erat a Vasconia oriundus."

[7] Trokelowe, *Annal.* p. 69: "Et, assumptis secum alienigenis nequioribus se, Angliam repedavit." In January, 1312, a payment of £20 is made to Guilliou Arnaldi de Marsan, knight, the brother of Gavaston (Issue Roll, no. 159, m. 5), but he was no stranger to England as a payment of £200 was made to him in June, 1308 (Issue Roll, no. 143, m. 7).

[8] *Chron. Murimuth*, p. 11.

youth[1], and it was natural that when he assumed power a place should be found for him near the king. Gavaston had taken oath not to return, and Edward had sworn not to receive him without the king's permission[2], which oaths had been determined by the death of the king[3]. In less than a month Gavaston had become earl of Cornwall[4]. Previously the earldom had always been held by a scion of the royal family[5], and among other honours hitherto exclusively held thus and now given to him were the stannaries[6]. Almost immediately another proof of royal favour and regard was shown in the bestowal in marriage of the king's niece, Margaret de Clare, upon Gavaston[7]. From a needy squire Gavaston became the richest of earls[8]. When the king went to Boulogne for his marriage Gavaston was appointed keeper of England during his absence[9], specially wide powers being granted him[10]. In the king's coronation he carried the royal crown, immediately preceding the king in the procession[11]. All this unaccustomed wealth, honour and position had a most prejudicial influence upon Gavaston. He bore himself so arrogantly that the hatred and envy of the barons was aroused immediately[12] to such an extent that discord arose even at the coronation[13].

Had Gavaston borne himself prudently towards the barons[14], he

[1] Trokelowe, *Annal.* p. 64. Edward I had caused him to be educated with the prince for the services of his father. Vide also *Ann. Paul.* p. 255; *Chron. Hemingburgh*, vol. II, p. 272, story of request for Ponthieu for Gavaston.

[2] *Cal. Close Rolls*, 1302–7, pp. 526–7. The proceedings are also printed in Cobbett's *Complete Collection of State Trials*, vol. I [1809], p. 22.

[3] Cf. Brady, *A Contin. Compl. Hist. Engl.* p. 100. Walsingham, *Hist. Angl.* vol. I, p. 115, makes the final advice of Edward I to his son take the form of an oath not to recall Gavaston "sine commune favore," and on this ground says that in recalling him the king broke his sworn oath (ibid. p. 126).

[4] *Cal. Charter Rolls*, 1300–26, p. 108 (6 Aug. 1307). Cf. *Chron. Mon. de Melsa*, vol. II, p. 279: "cui absque mora dedit comitatum Cornubiae."

[5] *Flores Hist.* vol. III, p. 139. Trokelowe, *Annal.* p. 65: "qui specialiter spectat ad coronam."

[6] Holdsworth, *Hist. Engl. Law*, vol. I, p. 59.

[7] *Auct. Bridl.* p. 28. *Chron. Mon. de Melsa*, vol. II, p. 279.

[8] *Flores Hist.* vol. III, p. 139: "sicque de armigero inopi factus est comes locupletissimus."

[9] *Cal. Pat. Rolls*, 1307–13, p. 31 (26 Dec. 1307).

[10] Cf. ibid. p. 43 (18 Jan. 1308).

[11] *Cal. Close Rolls*, 1307–13, p. 53. *Ann. Paul.* p. 262, mentions the indignation on this account.

[12] *Chron. Murimuth*, p. 12.

[13] *Flores Hist.* vol. III, p. 331. Walsingham, *Hist. Angl.* vol. I, p. 121, reports a demand by the barons that Gavaston should be removed otherwise they would prevent the proceedings, and that the king made them a promise to do so in the next parliament. Vide also *Ann. Paul.* p. 260; *Chron. Lanerc.* p. 186.

[14] *Ann. Malm.* p. 168.

could possibly have overcome in time the prejudice of the lords to one of lower birth[1] than themselves and of foreign extraction[2], but his intolerable pride wrecked all hopes he had of ever reconciling them. The pride exhibited in his administration of Ireland[3] during his banishment was small and insignificant to that shown on every possible occasion in England. He insisted that he should no longer be called Peter but earl[4]. The earl of Cornwall wished to forget he had ever been a humble squire[5]. He was proud in action[6] and ultimately so swollen was he by his pride[7] that it overwhelmed him in death and it seemed just that one who was so puffed up[8] should be humbled to the dust.

His pride led Gavaston to despise and deride the magnates[9] and there was nothing which a sensitive baronage could stand worse than derision. His capacity of bestowing insulting epithets upon the barons was notorious[10]. By a word or phrase he caricatured traits of the great earls, holding them up to ridicule[11]. He did not consider any baron in the realm to be his peer[12]. The earls and barons he treated as his slaves[13] and they repaid insults by jealousy and hate[14]. They had envied him the gift of Cornwall[15], since which time they had had no reason to alter their feeling towards him. Frequently there occurred such disconcerting events as the Wallingford tournament of 1308 when Gavaston with a motley horde had overcome the great earls of England[16].

The gifts of land which the king made Gavaston were numerous and of great revenue and importance. Besides the earldom of Cornwall he obtained the custody of the lands of various heirs under age[17], large tracts of the duchy of Aquitaine, which brought him in a revenue of 3000 marks yearly[18], Wark in Tynedale[19], the castle of

[1] Gavaston was not of the low birth suggested in *Ann. Paul.* p. 258: "de pulvere elevatus." He was the younger son of a noble Gascon house. Vide Dimitresco, *Pierre de Gavaston*, pp. 17–19.

[2] *Auct. Malm.* p. 157.

[3] *Ann. Lond.* p. 156.

[4] Camd. Soc., *Political Songs*, p. 260: "vult hinc Comes et non Petrus dici per superbiam."

[5] *Auct. Malm.* p. 168.

[6] Ibid. p. 157.

[7] *Flores Hist.* vol. III, p. 142.

[8] Camd. Soc., *Political Songs*, p. 260.

[9] Walsingham, *Hist. Angl.* vol. I, p. 125. Trokelowe, *Annal.* p. 68.

[10] *Auct. Malm.* p. 161.

[11] Cf. Walsingham, *Hist. Angl.* vol. I, p. 115. Cf. *Chron. Lanerc.* p. 194.

[12] *Ann. Lond.* pp. 151–2.

[13] Ibid. p. 157.

[14] *Ann. Paul.* p. 269.

[15] *Auct. Malm.* p. 155.

[16] Trokelowe, *Annal.* p. 65. Walsingham, *Hist. Angl.* vol. I, p. 122. *Auct. Malm.* pp. 156–7.

[17] *Cal. Pat. Rolls*, 1307–13, pp. 17, 114.

[18] Ibid. pp. 74, 78.

[19] *Cal. Charter Rolls*, 1300–26, p. 181. *Cal. Doc. Scotl.* vol. III, p. 44.

Nottingham[1] and the town of Penrith[2] and rents in London[3]. The keepership of the office of the justice of the forests north of Trent was granted to him for life[4], and permission to hunt openly in the king's forests[5]. Grants of free warren[6], markets[7] and other liberties were widely given[8]. Lands resumed in the king's hands on the banishment of Gavaston were regranted with their issues during that period[9], and Scottish prisoners in castles granted to him were forthwith removed to relieve him of the charge[10].

The king's affection for Gavaston was shown in more ways than by the grant of lands and liberties. The king received him on his return in 1307 with the utmost joy[11], and his pleasure expressed itself in the way he honoured his friend by giving him even the wedding gifts sent by the king of France[12]. Gavaston immediately became the centre of the king's interests and the prime influence at court. He became the king's confidant and his closest personal servant[13]. Even in official correspondence the king called him his "dear brother and faithful Peter de Gavaston, earl of Cornwall[14]" and a reason given for Gavaston's banishment by Edward I was that the prince spoke of him openly as his brother[15]. Though the king called him his brother, it seemed to the chronicler that he more nearly resembled his idol[16]. After his marriage the king neglected his queen for Gavaston[17], and the affection which he should have bestowed upon his wife he showered on the favourite[18]. From youth Gavaston had held a pre-eminent position in the king's affections[19], and after his accession the affection changed into infatuation[20]. The king became so obsessed with the favourite that royal command materialised every passing fancy. The king's bounty extended even to those who served his favourite[21].

[1] *Cal. Fine Rolls*, 1307–19, p. 73. [2] Ibid. p. 76.
[3] *Cal. Letter Books, C*, pp. 65–66. [4] *Cal. Fine Rolls*, 1307–19, p. 73.
[5] *Cal. Pat. Rolls*, 1307–13, p. 211.
[6] *Cal. Charter Rolls*, 1300–26, pp. 110, 138.
[7] Ibid. p. 127. [8] Ibid. p. 139. [9] K. R. Mem. Roll, no. 83, mm. 11 d, 12 d.
[10] *Cal. Doc. Scotl.* vol. III, p. 11.
[11] *Flores Hist.* vol. III, p. 139. [12] *Ann. Paul.* p. 258.
[13] Ibid.: "secretarium et camerarium regni summum." Compare the pope's description of him in the bull annulling his excommunication—the king's "vassallum et familiarem" (Canterb. and York Soc.) *Registr. Ric. de Swinfield*, ed. W. W. Capes [1909], pp. 451–2.
[14] K. R. Mem. Roll, no. 81, m. 34 d, in a writ to the treasurer of 5 July, 1308.
[15] *Chron. Lanerc.* p. 184. [16] *Ann. Paul.* p. 259.
[17] Ibid. p. 262. Cf. *Flores Hist.* vol. III, p. 148, for queen and Gavaston.
[18] Trokelowe, *Annal.* p. 65. Walsingham, *Hist. Angl.* vol. I, p. 121.
[19] Trokelowe, *Annal.* pp. 64–65. [20] *Auct. Malm.* p. 168.
[21] *Cal. Pat. Rolls*, 1307–13, p. 177 (4 Nov. 1309). Grant for life of 10 marks

The king's love for Gavaston was not a temporary infatuation, but endured long after his death. His body was taken with great pomp to the Friars Preachers at Oxford where it remained unburied for a considerable time[1], the king charging the friars to say masses and other services over the body, making payment therefor[2], and sums were also paid from the exchequer to the king's clerk, Thomas de London, for expenses which he had incurred about the body when it was at Oxford[3]. The ceremonies at Oxford lasted a full month[4]. The body was then conveyed to Langley where it was buried with the greatest honour[5], and there the king founded a convent of Dominicans[6], endowing them from the treasury[7]. From his wardrobe the king paid for masses to be said for the soul of Gavaston in convents and churches throughout the land[8]. The borough of Oxford expended money on behalf of his soul[9] and the prior of Christchurch constantly ordered masses and services[10]. Years after the death of Gavaston the convent of Rewley could find no more effective opening to a petition to the king requesting confirmation of a charter than by praying for the grant for the soul of "Sir Peter de Gavaston formerly earl of Cornwall their avowee[11]."

The king also showed the depths of his feeling for Gavaston in more practical ways. Soon after his death provision was made for his widow by the grant of manors[12] and subsequently additional grants were made to her[13]. The king set about obtaining a suitable marriage

yearly payable at the exchequer to Henry Gonne of Guildford for good services to Gavaston.

1 *Ann. Lond.* p. 232. *Chron. Lanerc.* p. 203. 2 *Chron. Lanerc.* p. 203.

3 *Cal. Close Rolls*, 1313–18, p. 125. Issue Roll, no. 180, m. 3. The total expenses of Thomas de London in this matter were £144. 19*s.* 11½*d.* (K. R. Acct. 375/8, f. 18). Issue Roll, no. 172, mm. 5, 6, 9, also contains various expenses about the body of Gavaston.

4 Oxf. Hist. Soc. vol. XX [1891], A. G. Little, *Grey Friars at Oxford*, p. 27, note 9.

5 *Ann. Lond.* p. 232. King, bishop and clergy attended the removal of the body (Oxf. Hist. Soc. vol. XVII [1890], *Wood's City of Oxford*, vol. II, ed. A. Clark, p. 322).

6 *Ann. Lond.* p. 232. *Ann. Paul.* p. 273.

7 *Ann. Paul.* p. 273. Edward III still supported these friars in 1337 (Oxf. Hist. Soc., Little, *Grey Friars at Oxford*, p. 53, note 9).

8 E.g. "Friars Preachers of London, 20 marks, 16 July, 1314" (K. R. Acct. 375/8, f. 3).

9 Oxf. Hist. Soc., *Wood's City of Oxford*, vol. II, p. 339.

10 Camb. Univ. Lib. MS. Ee. v. 31, "Registrum Henr. Prioris," f. 120 (August, 1312).

11 Ancient Petition, no. 6801. Printed in Oxf. Hist. Soc., *Collectanea*, vol. III, p. 120.

12 *Cal. Pat. Rolls*, 1307–13, p. 497. 13 *Cal. Letter Books, E*, p. 75.

for Joan, the only child of Peter, his first effort proving unsuccessful through the marriage without licence of the heir selected by the king[1]. Subsequently Sir Thomas de Multon, lord of Egremont, entered into an agreement with the king for the marriage of his son and heir John, to Joan, the king promising to pay him £1000 for this[2], a third of which was paid almost forthwith[3].

Despite the king's liberal grants to Gavaston and the undue attentions which he paid him, the worst word that can be applied to the king's attitude is "ill-advised." There was no criminal intent in any of his conduct and there was no criminal result. They were all acts of folly which caused irritation and which provided no justification for the cruel death. Pride, ostentation and the love of fine clothes[4], these were the vices of Gavaston. By these, powerful interests were offended at every turn. Gavaston did not lack good qualities. He was courageous and proved his skill in warfare on the Scottish march[5]. His success in the administration of Ireland was no less definite. Rebel chiefs were killed and whole tribes subdued[6], and he impressed the Irish chronicler as being a very noble knight[7]. He was received there with state and glory[8]. His skill in tournament and his success in war but increased the intensity of the feelings of the barons towards him. They refused to see any virtue in one who though outside their caste exercised a predominant influence at the royal court, and overshadowed them in magnificence.

Not less in power, though of a different nature, was the influence exercised over the king and the administration by the Despensers. It will be necessary to consider the characters of father and son separately at first, and then, when each has been considered apart, to compare their characters and careers.

Hugh le Despenser, senior, was neither of an age nor a character to make himself the favourite of the young king, though he had cultivated him while prince[9]. He was an administrator trained in the school of Edward I. He had been employed in various offices by him and was one of the few men likely to prove indispensable to the young king on his accession. He had a tradition for administration

[1] *Cal. Pat. Rolls*, 1313–17, p. 553.
[2] *Cal. Close Rolls*, 1313–18, p. 468 (25 May, 1317).
[3] Issue Roll, no. 181, m. 3, payment 6 July, 1317.
[4] *Ann. Paul.* p. 262.
[5] Cf. *Ann. Lond.* p. 174; *Cal. Doc. Scott.* vol. III, pp. 20, 31, 33, 39–40.
[6] *Chartulary of St Mary's Abbey, Dublin*, vol. II, pp. 291, 293, 294.
[7] *Annals of Loch Cé*, vol. I, p. 545.
[8] *Chron. Lanerc.* p. 187.
[9] *Ninth Rep. Dep. Keep. Rec.* App. II, p. 249.

behind him, for he was the son of Hugh le Despenser, the justiciar of Simon de Montfort's government. When Edward II came to the throne Despenser held the office of justice of the forest south of Trent, but the first entry upon the fine roll of Edward II's reign appointed Payn Tibetot to that office[1]. This does not signify any loss of confidence as Despenser accompanied the king to France for his marriage[2], and the change of office was probably made to get him nearer the king. Moreover, in March, 1308, he was again appointed justice of the forest south of Trent[3], and in August, 1309, the grant was extended for life[4]. His administration there was probably efficient. Owing to the Ordinances he was superseded in December, 1312[5], but reappointed six months later[6].

During the early years of the reign he took a considerable part in administration. He acted as a frequent messenger between king and chancellor[7], and king and treasurer[8], he was a witness to most of the charters granted[9] and was present in the king's chamber when the seal and other surrenders were made[10]. Payments were made from the exchequer at his instance[11], and he acted as bearer of money for the household from the exchequer[12]. He was one of the few persons who supported the king and Gavaston and for that action drew upon himself the wrath of the barons[13]. During the years immediately following Gavaston's death he aided the earl of Pembroke in government[14], and jointly with the earl and the bishop of Worcester, chancellor, he summoned councils[15]. He was, in brief,

[1] *Cal. Fine Rolls*, 1307–19, p. 1 (18 Aug. 1307). Vide also *Rot. Parl.* vol. I, p. 321.

[2] Cf. *Cal. Fine Rolls*, 1307–19, p. 14.

[3] Ibid. p. 18 (16 Mar. 1308).

[4] *Cal. Pat. Rolls*, 1307–13, p. 183 (28 Aug. 1309). Vide also *Cal. Fine Rolls*, 1307–19, p. 187.

[5] *Cal. Fine Rolls*, 1307–19, p. 116 (2 Dec. 1312).

[6] *Cal. Pat. Rolls*, 1307–13, p. 464 (14 June, 1313).

[7] Vide *Cal. Close Rolls*, *Cal. Pat. Rolls* passim.

[8] Cf. K. R. Mem. Roll, no. 82, m. 15, Grants of Templars' lands: "Teste Johanne de Sandale per Regem nunciante Hugone le Despenser seniore" (14 May, 1309).

[9] Vide Charter Rolls for the reign passim. *Chartae, Privilegiae et Immunitates* (Irish Rec. Com.), pp. 42, 46, 49.

[10] E.g. *Cal. Fine Rolls*, 1307–19, p. 14. *Cal. Pat. Rolls*, 1307–13, p. 83. *Cal. Close Rolls*, 1307–13, pp. 67–68, 225.

[11] Issue Roll, no. 176, mm. 3 and 4 (3 Nov. and 6 Nov. 1315); no. 184, m. 3 (3 June, 1318); m. 8 (9 June, 1318).

[12] Ibid. no. 162, m. 6 (14 Sept. 1312): "£100 lib. eidem super expensis hospicii domini Regi per manus Hugonis le Despenser."

[13] *Auct. Malm.* p. 158. *Chron. Lanerc.* p. 187.

[14] The Pembroke administration 1312–16 will be treated below, pp. 322–330.

[15] Anc. Corresp. vol. XXXV, no. 102. Vide also below, pp. 325–8.

one of the select administrators of the personal system. He was employed as one of the king's representatives in the treaty between king and barons before the cardinal in 1312[1]. He acted with the treasurer at the exchequer[2], made himself responsible with Sandale for the king's debts[3], lent the king money[4] and went in solemn embassy to the king of Spain on the king's behalf[5]. On the king's behalf he allotted missions to officials[6].

During this period, too, Despenser's influence made itself felt outside the royal court. The mayor and bailiffs of London at his instance let the small balance of the weigh-house to a man he recommended[7], and the earl of Gloucester acted on his advice in the dispute between the citizens of Bristol and their constable[8]. The king for his good service made him grants of land and money. Payments were made to him from the exchequer[9]. Petitions which he requested the king to grant received the royal favour[10]. The grants of lands and privileges made to him were considerable. A marriage for the benefit of his daughter[11], custody of the castles of Striguil[12], Devizes[13] and Marlborough[14], lands forfeited by the Templars[15] and by Langton[16] and divers manors[17] were granted to him on favourable conditions. The privileges included extensive grants of free warren[18], the issues for all trespasses committed in parks[19], and licence to crenellate all his houses and chambers throughout the kingdom[20]. He was pardoned all trespasses committed by him in the king's forests, and

[1] *Foedera*, vol. II, p. 191. [2] L. T. R. Mem. Roll, no. 79, m. 91 d.

[3] *Cal. Pat. Rolls*, 1307–13, p. 120. [4] K. R. Acct. 375/1, f. 7.

[5] *Cal. Pat. Rolls*, 1317–21, p. 262.

[6] L. T. R. Mem. Roll, no. 78, m. 67, p. 5, to treas. (14 July, 1308): "Por ce qe nous voloms qe nostre cher et foial monsire Humfrei de Walden aille en noz busoignes solunc ce qe nostre cher et foial munsire Hugh le Despenser luy enchargera depar nous...."

[7] *Cal. Letter Books, C*, p. 155.

[8] H. Hall, *Customs Revenue*, vol. II, p. 15.

[9] Issue Roll, no. 164, m. 4, 27 Dec. 1312, payment of £100 by writ of liberate; of £200 on 19 Nov. 1312.

[10] Chan. Warr., File 64/609, writ of p.s. to chancellor enclosing petition at the request of H. le Despenser ordering letters under the great seal (19 July, 1309).

[11] *Cal. Pat. Rolls*, 1307–13, pp. 26–27 (14 Dec. 1307).

[12] *Cal. Fine Rolls*, 1307–19, p. 17 (12 Mar. 1308).

[13] *Cal. Pat. Rolls*, 1307–13, p. 51 (12 Mar. 1308). [14] Ibid. 1317–21, p. 578.

[15] K. R. Mem. Roll, no. 81, m. 8 d (15 March, 1308). L. T. R. Mem. Roll, no. 79, m. 9 d.

[16] K. R. Mem. Roll, no. 82, mm. 16 d, 43 (16 and 17 June, 1307). Vide also *Descr. Cat. Ancient Deeds*, vol. II, p. 167.

[17] *Cal. Charter Rolls*, 1300–26, p. 119. *Cal. Pat. Rolls*, 1307–13, p. 116.

[18] *Cal. Charter Rolls*, 1300–26, pp. 183, 334, 382.

[19] *Cal. Pat. Rolls*, 1307–13, p. 121. [20] Ibid. p. 394.

all accounts and reckonings which he ought to render the king for the various offices he had held[1]. Of the king's special grace he was allowed respite for all his debts to the exchequer[2]. It was not for himself alone that favours were obtained. Even his servants shared in the royal generosity, manors being granted them by exchequer writ[3].

Considerable sums were owing to Despenser the elder from Edward I and Edward II and these the king endeavoured to pay by assignments upon his revenue[4]. Despenser also aided the king by making him loans in his wardrobe and in 1312 a sum of 3000 marks was owing to him from this cause alone[5].

During the period after 1322 when his son held supreme power at court and had assumed virtual control of the administration[6], the position of the elder Despenser, though now earl of Winchester, appears to have suffered very little change. If there was any change, it was in the direction of less influence. The son entirely governed, the father rendered advice, but his voice was weak in comparison with that of his son. Some sidelights upon the father's influence are thrown by the letters which the pope and the prior of Christchurch, Canterbury, addressed to him. The prior sent the king a gift of 100 marks and by its bearer sent letters announcing it to the elder Despenser[7]. The prior appealed to Despenser for aid in a plea held against him[8] and in other letters he was asked to exercise his influence on behalf of the prior and his convent[9]. During the Despensers' exile the custody of the elder Hugh's lands were entrusted to Ingelram Berenger[10], his trusted servant and

[1] *Cal. Pat. Rolls*, 1307–13, pp. 558–9.

[2] K. R. Mem. Roll, no. 93, m. 24. L. T. R. Mem. Roll, no. 90, Brev. Pasch. m. 4.

[3] K. R. Mem. Roll, no. 82, mm. 13, 14 d (14 May, 1309).

[4] In May, 1308, a sum of £2544. 6*s*. 8*d*. was allotted to him of the receipts of the escheats on both sides Trent (*Cal. Pat. Rolls*, 1307–13, p. 74, 23 May, 1308), and it was ordered that no wardships or marriages were to be assigned away until he was satisfied of these debts (ibid. p. 76, 19 June, 1308). Some of these he obtained the same year (*Descr. Cat. Ancient Deeds*, vol. I, p. 9, 19 Nov. 1308), but many debts still ran for several years (vide *Cal. Pat. Rolls*, 1307–13, p. 512; 1313–17, p. 7; 1317–21, pp. 123–4).

[5] *Cal. Pat. Rolls*, 1307–13, p. 509.

[6] The administration of the younger Despenser, 1322–6, will be treated below, pp. 336–341.

[7] *Lit. Cantuar.* vol. I, pp. 60–61.

[8] Camb. Univ. Lib. MS. Ee. v. 31, f. 249.

[9] *Lit. Cantuar.* vol. I, pp. 100–1.

[10] As late as July, 1321, Despenser had put Ingelram Berenger in his place for the execution of all recognisances made to him in chancery (*Cal. Close Rolls*, 1318–23, p. 385). Berenger is almost always a witness to the charters and deeds

knight[1], and soon after Boroughbridge the object of the choice of custodian was made apparent when Berenger was ordered to deliver all the lands, goods and chattels with their issues to Despenser[2]. In addition to the lands he had held previously he obtained portions of the lands of Damory, Gifford, Badlesmere, Tyeys, Lancaster and others of the rebels of 1322[3]. Once more too he was granted the keeping of the forest south of Trent, following the earl of Pembroke in that office[4].

Hugh le Despenser the elder was certainly unpopular amongst the baronage. Anyone who aided or supported the king against them was bound to incur their anger and dislike. Apart from the support he gave the king and his action in opposition to their wishes, there was little ground upon which they could attack him. He was doubtless one of the foremost of the "curialists." His craft in his opposition to Lancaster is mentioned by a chronicler[5], but he offers no substantial ground for the charge. Lancaster and the elder Despenser were certainly not upon good terms. There was what almost amounted to a hereditary feud between them[6], and after the exile of Despenser, Lancaster immediately petitioned the king for lands which he claimed, Alice, countess of Lincoln, had alienated to Despenser in his disherison, as she held them only for life[7]. A few complaints were made against Despenser, especially concerning his severity, and the injustice of his forest administration[8], but it was difficult for anyone to hold a position like justice of the forest without prejudicing someone's right. Among the complaints the worst was the seizure of pasture into the king's hands without cause[9]. He was also charged with obtaining a certain manor in Ireland by fine by conspiracy between the seneschal of the manor and himself[10]. The evidence is inconclusive and if completely established little could be deduced from a solitary instance.

Whereas the father was from the first a staunch royalist, Hugh le Despenser, the son, opened his political career as a member of the

of the elder Despenser (vide *Descr. Cat. Ancient Deeds*, vol. I, pp. 23, 52, 55, 111; vol. II, p. 164, vol. IV, p. 555), and received money from the exchequer on his master's behalf (Issue Roll, no. 143, m. 5). Eleanor la Despenser wrote to John Inge on his behalf ordering respite for £24 which he owed him (Anc. Corresp. vol. XLIX, no. 142).

[1] K. R. Acct. 375/8, f. 10, 6.

[2] *Cal. Close Rolls*, 1318–23, p. 442 (7 May, 1322).

[3] *Cal. Charter Rolls*, 1300–26, pp. 442, 443–4, 448, 450, 463, 477.

[4] *Cal. Fine Rolls*, 1319–27, p. 287 (27 June, 1324).

[5] *Auct. Malm.* p. 240. [6] Cf. ibid. p. 195. [7] Ancient Petition, no. 2766.

[8] *Auct. Malm.* p. 260. [9] Oxf. Hist. Soc., *Collect.* vol. III, p. 110.

[10] Cole, *Doc. illustr. Eng. Hist. in 13th and 14th Cent.* p. 16.

baronial opposition[1], and in the story of his transition from strong opposition to royal favour, the influence of his wife Eleanor de Clare[2] is a factor of considerable importance, though his father's position as a trusted and valued royal servant, of considerable standing at court, is a consideration. Eleanor was the king's niece and either because she was attached to the queen's household or for other reasons, frequent payments were made for her expenses[3]. During the years 1308–10 she was a person of importance and influence at court. A hundred was granted[4] and a writ of privy seal issued at her request[5]. Her messenger conveyed to the king on her behalf news of such importance or value that he obtained a gift of 20 marks[6]. In 1313 frequent payments for her expenses were made to her husband from the exchequer[7].

During these opening years of the reign Despenser the younger was seldom mentioned. On 14 May, 1309, he obtained a grant of the Templars' manor of Sutton[8], a grant that may be attributed to his father's influence, for on the same day grants are made to two servants of the elder Despenser[9]. On 5 August of that year a grant was made at his instance[10]. But he soon fell into disfavour through disobedience of a royal order, Contrary to the king's prohibition he crossed the sea without licence and his lands were accordingly taken

[1] Stubbs suggests in his Introduction to the *Chronicles of Ed. I and Ed. II*, vol. II, p. liii, that in the early years of the reign Hugh the younger was under the influence of the earl of Warwick who was his mother's brother.

[2] The marriage took place in 1306 (*Chron. Pierre de Langtoft*, vol. II, p. 368), Edward I purchasing the marriage of Hugh from Hugh le Despenser the elder for a sum of 3000 marks (cf. Issue Roll, no. 143, m. 5). 500 marks of this were paid on 27 May, 1308.

[3] In 1308 she was staying in the castle of Rockingham, and on 1 April a grant of 20 marks was made to her for her expenses (Issue Roll, no. 141, m. 8). Later in the same year she left Rockingham to go to the king (ibid. no. 143, m. 2, 8 May, 1308, 10 marks for her expenses on the journey), and in a writ of privy seal of 19 June she is referred to as the "king's very dear niece" (L. T. R. Mem. Roll, no. 78, m. 65: "nostre tres chere niece"). In 1310 by the king's orders she journeyed from Northampton to Berwick-on-Tweed to the queen (Issue Roll, no. 155, m. 4, 28 Nov. 1310, 100 marks for her expenses and 20 marks "de dono Regis").

[4] L. T. R. Mem. Roll, no. 79, m. 51 (6 Feb. 1309).

[5] Chan. Warr., File 62/414 (7 March, 1309).

[6] Issue Roll, no. 155, m. 3 (21 Oct. 1310).

[7] Ibid. no. 167, m. 1 (10 Oct. 1313), £10; m. 2 (15 Oct.), £10; m. 4 (27 Oct.), £5 (29 Oct.). 5 marks; m. 5 (7 Nov.), £10; m. 6 (19 Nov.), 10 marks; m. 8 (11 Dec.), £4 and 1 mark; m. 9 (4 Feb. 1314), 5 marks.

[8] K. R. Mem. Roll, no. 82, mm. 14 d, 38 d. L. T. R. Mem. Roll, no. 79, m. 70 d.

[9] Vide above, p. 89, note 3.

[10] *Cal. Charter Rolls*, 1300–26, p. 130.

into the king's hands[1]. At the time of the Ordinances he was definitely of the baronial party, and a member of the king's retinue set out from the royal palace to attack him. The barons demanded in the additional ordinances[2] that those who perpetrated this offence should be removed from the king's household and retinue[3]. Despenser was sufficiently reinstated in the royal favour in September, 1312, to obtain a licence to hunt[4] and in the following year pardon was granted at his request[5] and custody of lands awarded him[6]. In 1314 he was engaged in the Scottish war[7] and shortly before the battle of Bannockburn obtained forfeited lands in Scotland by royal charter, some of them being granted jointly to himself and his wife[8].

The battle of Bannockburn was a decisive event in his career, for as a result he obtained a third of the great Gloucester inheritance. He was extremely anxious to obtain possession of this inheritance immediately. He seized forthwith the castle and manor of Tonbridge[9], and when the king's officials sought to enter into possession, Hugh's men defied the royal orders; and the council was ordered by the king to ordain a speedy remedy to such an outrage[10]. The pretended pregnancy[11] of the widow of earl Gilbert and the delay in partition which it involved caused him great annoyance, but his efforts to accelerate the division of the lands proved futile[12], and it was not until 15 November, 1317, that the delivery of the portions of the inheritance was ordered[13].

It was about this time or soon after that he commenced to incline towards the king. In 1317 he displayed signs of great activity. A petition of his to the king was sent to the chancellor, who was ordered to make suitable writs under the great seal[14]. He obtained grants of fine[15] and of wardship and marriage, the latter in payment

[1] *Cal. Fine Rolls*, 1307–19, p. 54 (9 Jan. 1310). Chan. Warr., File 66/864: "nous enrespoigne des issus a nostre Escheker tant quil en eit autre mandement de nous."

[2] For the discussion on these see below, pp. 382–6.

[3] *Ann. Lond.* p. 200.

[4] *Cal. Pat. Rolls*, 1307–13, p. 492 (8 Sept. 1312).

[5] Ibid. pp. 561, 571

[6] Ibid. 1313–17, p. 20.

[7] K. R. Mem. Roll, no. 87, m. 31 d. L. T. R. Mem. Roll, no. 84, Brev. dir. Pasch. m. 9 d.

[8] *Cal. Doc. Scotl.* vol. III, p. 69.

[9] *Cal. Fine Rolls*, 1307–19, p. 248.

[10] *Cal. Inq. P. M.* vol. V, pp. 351–2.

[11] Trokelowe, *Annal.* p. 86. The partition of the Gloucester inheritance is treated at length in a paper read in 1914 (November) before the Royal Hist. Soc. and published in their *Transactions*, vol. IX (1914–15), pp. 21–64.

[12] *Rot. Parl.* vol. I, pp. 353–5.

[13] *Cal. Fine Rolls*, 1307–19, p. 350.

[14] Chan. Warr., File 98/4050.

[15] *Cal. Pat. Rolls*, 1313–17, p. 634 (13 April, 1317).

of debts due to him for his service in the Scottish war[1]. A sum of 200 marks was paid him at the exchequer for staying in the king's company in Scotland[2]. Various manors forfeited by adherents of the Scots were granted to him[3] as well as the custody of Odiham castle[4], and on 18 November, 1317, the town and castle of Drysllwyn and Cantrev Mawr with knight's fees and all appurtenances were granted to him for life in satisfaction of 600 marks due to him for staying with the king[5].

This progress of Despenser's seems to have been made under the influence of the middle party and when its influence was strong in the parliament of York of 1318, he was nominated as king's chamberlain[6]. The chronicler's[7] statement that before this time he had been an object of hatred to the king is exaggerated, though the contrast between his attitude before and after 1318 is startling. He was now in a position to make the influence of his personality and policy felt upon the plastic mind of the king, and the result was soon seen. In less than three years it had gathered to a head in the Despenser war in Glamorgan and in the exile of the Despensers, father and son.

It had been agreed in the parliament of York that of the 600 marks of land which the king had granted Hugh for staying with him he should retain 300 marks and answer for the remainder at the exchequer, and he was to make surety that he would not ask for or take from the king estate in fee in those lands, or for the office of chamberlain any estate for term of life or in fee. The castle of Dynevor he was to have for the term of his life without rendering anything as the profits were all devoured by the charge of the castle[8]. In accordance with this decision letters patent were issued on 21 November, 1318[9].

The influence of Despenser in virtue of his office immediately became apparent. The day before he obtained his own letters patent, on his information, a grant of free warren was made to

[1] *Cal. Pat. Rolls*, 1313–17, p. 640 (20 April, 1317).

[2] Issue Roll, no. 180, m. 6 (31 May, 1317).

[3] *Cal. Pat. Rolls*, 1317–21, pp. 5–6, 10, 45. *Cal. Doc. Scotl.* vol. III, p. 109.

[4] *Cal. Pat. Rolls*, 1317–21, p. 46 (1 Nov. 1317).

[5] Ibid. p. 56 (18 Nov. 1317).

[6] Cole, *Doc. illustr. Eng. Hist. in 13th and 14th Cent.* p. 4. In the process of exile against him it is stated that "he was nominated and agreed upon as king's chamberlain in the parliament of York" (*Stat. of Realm*, vol. I, p. 181). J. de Cherleton was still chamberlain on 19 April, 1318 (*Cal. Pat. Rolls*, 1317–21, p. 133).

[7] *Chron. G. le Baker*, p. 6: "rex antea nedum minime dilexit immo odivit." The same chronicler makes him chamberlain in 1313.

[8] Cole, *Doc. illustr. Eng. Hist. in 13th and 14th Cent.* p. 9.

[9] *Cal. Pat. Rolls*, 1317–21, pp. 248, 255–6, 266.

Robert de Courtney, at Lancaster's instance[1]. For the moment Lancaster was working with the middle party. In December a grant of free warren to Ralph Camoys was made on his information[2]. In 1319 Despenser had writs issued to the various knights and others of the counties of York and Northumberland who were to be intendant to him[3] and his influence at court in that year appears in the grants which were made at his request[4]. The following year the number of grants made to him increased. The castles of Odiham, Porchester and Bristol fell into his custody[5]. He was granted respite from the payment of relief for the Gloucester property which he and his wife had inherited[6] and was appointed custodian of the forest of Windsor[7].

Then followed that sharp series of startling episodes in which the Despenser lands were ravaged and utterly devastated and which was the preliminary to the exile of the Despensers. The king appears to have realised that some action on his part was necessary. On 26 May, 1321, £500 was paid to the younger Hugh from the exchequer for his loans to the wardrobe[8], and four days later safe-conduct was granted to him until Michaelmas going beyond the seas on the king's business[9]. Perhaps the king thought a temporary honourable absence from England would right matters and decided to try this course. The plan was however given up as the writs were surrendered and vacated[10]. Before Boroughbridge had been fought, before even the episode of the castle of Leeds had taken place, the king was preparing for the return of the Despensers. On 13 November, 1321, the chancellor was ordered to issue no writ from the chancery concerning Despenser's lands which were in the king's hands[11], and next day the chancellor was ordered to send writs to the sheriff of Norfolk and Suffolk to make a bailiff come before the auditors assigned to audit the accounts of all bailiffs and ministers of those lands[12].

After the battle of Boroughbridge had been fought and the king's cause had vindicated itself on the battlefield, Despenser immediately

[1] *Cal. Charter Rolls*, 1300–26, p. 395 (20 Nov. 1318).
[2] Ibid. p. 397 (7 Dec. 1318). [3] *Rot. Scot.* vol. 1, p. 194.
[4] *Cal. Fine Rolls*, 1319–27, p. 2 (28 July, 1319).
[5] Ibid. pp. 18, 32, 33, 56–57.
[6] K. R. Mem. Roll, no. 94, m. 27. L. T. R. Mem. Roll, no. 91, Brev. Mich. m. 23 (30 Dec. 1320).
[7] *Cal. Pat. Rolls*, 1317–21, p. 530 (1 Dec. 1320).
[8] Issue Roll, no. 195, m. 2. The date is of great interest.
[9] *Cal. Pat. Rolls*, 1317–21, p. 591 (30 May, 1321).
[10] Ibid. [11] Chan. Warr., File 116/5890. Vide App. of Doc. no. 71.
[12] Chan. Warr., File 116/5896 (17 Nov. 1321).

obtained possession of all his lands, with the issues during his exile[1]. Then followed a profligate shower of grants to Despenser. The forfeited lands of the rebels, the issues of which might have placed the exchequer on a firm financial basis, were dissipated by lavish gifts to the favourite. The enrolments on the charter roll alone include thirty-nine charters of lands and honours to Despenser between 1322 and 1326[2]. The long list opens with a grant dated at Pontefract 24 March, 1322, in which a manor which belonged to Lancaster was bestowed upon the younger Despenser for his good service rendered and to be rendered[3]. Lands of Clifford, Tuchet, Badlesmere, Wylington, Mortimer, Mowbray and Gifford[4] all added to his already considerable inheritance.

The king now surrendered everything into the hands of Despenser who ruled entirely the king and government[5]. A petition addressed to the king by his chamberlain of South Wales touching the payment of fees to the constable of Drysllwyn and Dynevor during the period of the exile was sent to Hugh, whose advice concerning the remedy sought[6] was to be final. The relations between king and favourite were closer than ever. The king requested the pope to grant dispensation to intermarry to John, son of Thomas, earl of Kildare and Joan, Despenser's daughter[7]. The castle and barton of Bristol were regranted to him[8] and he became the keeper of the lordship of Brecon[9]. The issues of the Damory and D'Audley lands in Ireland became his[10]. He was respited £300 in the farm of the Brecon lands[11], and at this time he already owed the king nearly a thousand pounds[12]. The multitude of royal grants did not satisfy him and he obtained a grant of the New Temple in London from the Knights Hospitallers[13].

[1] Cf. *Cal. Pat. Rolls*, 1321–24, p. 115 (7 May, 1322).

[2] *Cal. Charter Rolls*, 1300–26, pp. 441–482 passim. Vide also *Descr. Cat. Ancient Deeds*, vol. I, p. 9; vol. III, pp. 112, 113, 116, 182.

[3] *Cal. Charter Rolls*, 1300–26, p. 441.

[4] Ibid. pp. 441–469 passim.

[5] The Despenser administration during this period will be treated below, pp. 336–341.

[6] Ancient Petition, no. 2749: "Soit maunde bref contenant la peticion a monsir Hugh le Despenser qil sauise des choses contenues face dreit et reson au Priour." Cf. Historical Soc. of West Wales, *Trans.* vol. I [1911], pp. 199–200.

[7] *Cal. Pap. Letters*, 1304–42, p. 231.

[8] *Cal. Fine Rolls*, 1319–27, p. 126 (3 May, 1322).

[9] Ibid. pp. 143, 179.

[10] *Cal. Close Rolls*, 1323–27, p. 9 (24 July, 1323).

[11] K. R. Mem. Roll, no. 97, Brev. dir. Pasch. m. 20 d (1 June, 1324).

[12] Chan. Warr., File 126/6854–6. On 6 April, 1324, Despenser owed the king £2243. 0*s*. 8*d*. and the king owed him £1325. 8*s*. 2*d*.

[13] *Descr. Cat. Ancient Deeds*, vol. I, p. 166. For further dealings in land, vide Chan. Misc., Bdles 86/14 (328), 88/1 (8).

All these grants, privileges and powers which Despenser obtained, illustrate the extent of the influence which he must have exercised over the mind of the king, as do the appeals made by persons to Despenser, to obtain favours from the king for them. John Inge, Despenser's sheriff of Glamorgan, desired the advancement of his brother, and Despenser undertook to find him a church. Despenser obtained a grant of a church from the king, but the church was of so little value that the chancellor had presented to it. He therefore promised Inge that he would procure from the king by all possible means that the brother should have the first good church the king could give[1]. Edmund Bacon, an official in Gascony with the earl of Kent, was guardian of his son-in-law, John de Brewosa, and wished to have his marriage. Bacon got the earl of Kent to write to Despenser on his behalf to advise the king to grant him the marriage[2], and himself wrote asking Despenser to further the request which the earl had made on his behalf[3]. In one letter which Despenser wrote to John Inge he stated that he was in high hopes of attaining his desire in a certain matter in which Inge had had a part, for to achieve the end the king was exerting all his power[4]. The matter which Despenser had so much at heart was the acquisition of the Island of Lundy. An assize had been held of which Inge had been one of the justices. Before the plea was held the king had made arrangements what to do. If the demandant won the assize the king, on Despenser's behalf, had arranged a bargain with him, and Despenser begged Inge to have the matter greatly at heart[5].

The accounts of the expenditure of the king's privy purse suggest in what intimate relations Despenser stood with the king. Even wax for Despenser's household was paid for out of the king's chamber[6], and the keeper of his horses was paid from the same source[7]. The king's gifts took the form of the extremest forms of necessities, including ballistas and stock[8]. The accounts of the expenses of Eleanor la Despenser during her stay at Cowick in 1323 were rendered

[1] Brit. Mus. Cotton MS. Vespasian F. vii, f. 6, a letter from Despenser to Inge (21 Sept. 1319).

[2] Anc. Corresp. vol. XLIX, no. 193: "vous prioms...especialment qe vous voillez mettre eide et conseil."

[3] Ibid. no. 112.

[4] Brit. Mus. Cotton MS. Nero C. iii, f. 181 (21 March, 1321): "Nous sumes en bon espoir qe nous ateindrioms biens et a ce faire le Roy y mettra tut son poer."

[5] Anc. Corresp. vol. XLIX, no. 144 (17 Feb. 1321).

[6] K. R. Acct. 379/7, f. 2 (20 Nov. 1322).

[7] Ibid. f. 2 (21 Nov. 1322).

[8] P. R. O. Pipe Roll, no. 171, m. 41, 1323, 17*s*. 6*d*. for five ballistas and £20. 2*s*. 8*d*. for stock.

by Despenser's clerk into the king's chamber, and payment of £100 was ordered out of it[1]. The expenses of Eleanor and her daughter Isabella were also paid out of the king's privy purse on other occasions[2], and when Eleanor was in child-bed in 1323 the king made her a present of £100 towards the additional expenses of the illness[3].

That long catalogue of charges which the barons in 1321 drew up against Despenser will be more profitably discussed elsewhere. There were however a number of personal complaints of individuals made against him, to which the objection of party malice or baronial policy cannot be brought. He had an overpowering greed for land and position. His cupidity for possessions is written indelibly on every page of the history of the last five years of the reign, especially in his grasping desire for the lands of the contrariants. It was useless for aggrieved persons to make complaint during the reign of Edward II. On the accession of Edward III complaints were welcome and they poured in. Actuated by cupidity Despenser accused persons of being adherents of the rebels in order to obtain their lands. The persons so charged were imprisoned until they enfeoffed him of their lands[4], a kind of coercion which was particularly mean and cowardly. Heirs were disherited[5]; their defenceless condition drew no pity from him. John de Lacheley was imprisoned at Colchester at the suit of John de Merk. Hugh took him from the sheriff and imprisoned him in his prison, keeping him until he released and quit-claimed to Hugh all the right he had in the manor of Lacheley. Hugh apparently failed to achieve his purpose, so handed him over to Bartholomew de Badlesmere, who imprisoned him until he had quit-claimed his right to him[6]. The natural result of this shameless proceeding was that in the crisis of 1322 John de Lacheley was found among the ranks of the contrariants[7]. Hugh was as greedy of money as of land and he hindered the letters patent restoring the manors of the bishopric of

[1] K. R. Acct. 379/17, f. 10 (2 Aug. 1323).

[2] Pipe Roll, no. 171, m. 41. For that and for articles bought for Hugh of the king's gift £53. 1*s.* 8*d.* was paid.

[3] Ibid. m. 41.

[4] Wm Salt. Soc., *Coll.* [1913], pp. 5–7.

[5] *Cal. Inq. P. M.* vol. VI, p. 172.

[6] Ancient Petition, nos. 2760–2: "et lui retynt en sa garde et en sa prison taunt qil auoit relesse et quiteclame au dit sire Hugh tut le droit qil auoit en le manoir auandit....Et pus le dit sire Hugh balya le manoir auandit sire Berthelmeu de Badlesmere et il baillia le dit Johan en la garde le dit sire Barthelmeu le quel lui retynt en sa garde et en sa prison taunt qil auoit tien reles de lui de tut son droit del manoir auandit" (Ancient Petition, no. 2760). Vide *Stat. of Realm*, vol. I, p. 184.

[7] Ancient Petition, no. 2759.

Rochester to the new bishop in 1319 until he had extorted ten pounds from him[1].

A comparison of father and son and their respective policies is suggestive. The father was first and foremost a minister of the household system. He had been trained in better traditions of government than the court of Edward II allowed the son to see in working order. He retained some of the qualities of the greater men of the previous generation and his first great fault in the eyes of the baronage was his loyalty to the king. His second fault was his paternal devotion[2]. Early in the reign father had been on one side and son on the other. From 1318 however they were both supporters and more than supporters of the king. Yet still their courses do not run in parallel lines. The younger Despenser became a royal favourite and sought to exploit the royal interest. The father, now introduced to the government by the son[3], never pursued that course of wanton and purely selfish aggrandizement which formed so striking a feature of the career of the younger Hugh. Contemporary opinion allotted the whole of the blame for the series of events which culminated in the exile of 1321 to the aggression of the son[4], and thought that the father fell a victim to his son's greed, and ambition[5]. The father was a very worthy knight, of great merit, prudent in counsel, strong in arms[6]. He was in fact one of the most eminent men of his time in ability and uprightness[7]. The son was of a most haughty spirit and drew down his father to death through his demerits[8]. Hugh the younger found an apologist in one chronicler who attributed even the crisis of 1321 to the father, who was of the utmost severity and was moved by greed. It seemed unfair to him that the son should

[1] H. Wharton, *Anglia Sacra*, vol. I [1691], Wm de Dene, *Historia Roffensis*, 1314–30, p. 361. For this he appears to have had some justification in the claim of the chamberlain to have a fee on such restoration. The chronicler says he demanded it "pro feodo suo contra omnem justitiam et consuetudinem per regnum Angliae prius usitatam."

[2] *Chron. G. le Baker*, pp. 6–7: "amor naturalis sed deordinatus quam visceribus paternis gessit erga predictum filium suum."

[3] *Stat. of Realm*, vol. I, p. 181. It was made a charge in the process of 1321 that though the elder Hugh had not been agreed to in the parliament of York as one who was to stay near the king, yet Hugh had drawn to him his father. In that very parliament Lancaster had refused to be reconciled with the elder Despenser.

[4] *Ann. Paul.* p. 292. Cf. *Trans. Royal Hist. Soc.* vol. IX (1914–15), 'The Despenser War in Glamorgan,' J. C. Davies, pp. 25–42.

[5] *Chron. G. le Baker*, pp. 6–7.

[6] Ibid. p. 6.

[7] *Auct. Bridl.* p. 87: "praeminens temporibus suis sensu et probitate pollens."

[8] *Chron. G. le Baker*, p. 7.

suffer for the sins of the father. His final conclusion however was that the malice of the son may have outweighed the severity of the father[1].

It is difficult to estimate precisely the respective culpability of father and son. During the concluding years of the reign the son was the dominant personality and, though the father doubtless aided the administration by his skill and experience, there is no trace of any grasping or illegality about his conduct. He was however too deeply involved and too intimately associated with his son to escape the fate of the other figures of the last years of the reign. In the plot which was designed to assassinate the king and his servants, both father and son were included amongst those to be destroyed[2]. The important distinction between the parts played by the father and son centres round the king's regard for the younger. He was a royal favourite, the elder Despenser was a royal servant devoted to the royal interests, obedient to the royal will and throughout loyal to his king. The younger Despenser joined the royal party when he conceived it in his interests to do so. Then by his schemes of personal aggrandizement he involved the king in that course which led to the tragedy of Berkeley Castle.

Before the discussion of the character and influences of the king and his favourites is ended there remains one important phase to be considered. There is a great contrast[3] in the position, character and influence of the two favourites, Gavaston and Despenser the younger. Those causes of antagonism which ranged the baronage in such violent opposition to Gavaston could not operate in Despenser's case. He was an Englishman of noble family and had been associated for a considerable time with the barons who opposed the royal policy. Yet the opposition which he aroused was far more intense and had a far greater and more substantial basis than the opposition which pursued Gavaston throughout his whole career.

Gavaston's influence upon the king was purely personal. He made no attempt to interfere in the government of the kingdom. He held no official position at court, for when the chroniclers said he was "secretarium et camerarium regni summum[4]" or "camerarius

[1] *Auct. Malm.* pp. 260–1. [2] *Parl. Writs*, vol. II, Pt i, p. 403.

[3] This contrast is discussed by Stubbs in his Introduction, *Chron. Ed. I and Ed. II*, vol. II, pp. xlix–li.

[4] *Ann. Paul.* p. 258. It is improbable that he was ever chamberlain, and it was by virtue of that office that Despenser exercised an overwhelming control on the administration. The point is discussed at length by Professor Tout, *The Place of Ed. II in Eng. Hist.* p. 12, note 2, where he inclines to the opinion that Gavaston was not chamberlain.

familiarissimus et valde dilectus[1]" they mean that he was the prime favourite and the person in power at court. His influence upon the administration was negative; he drew the king's mind away from his duty. He was the confidant of the king and his ruler[2]. He never became, as Despenser did, the ruler of king and kingdom. It was certainly a charge consistently made against him that he accumulated the royal treasure and jewels and sent them abroad by foreign merchants[3]. In a short time the king would have been utterly beggared by him[4]. Hemingburgh estimates the money which Gavaston obtained from the treasury of Edward I as £100,000 besides gold, precious stones and jewels[5], though of course Edward I died heavily in debt! Gavaston's banishments are said to be due partly to these financial reasons[6], though his banishments proved as costly as his presence[7]. Actually few payments appear to have been made to Gavaston out of the royal treasury. Some payments were ordered to be made of the royal gift in aid of his expenses[8] but they are comparatively few in number, and those from the exchequer are about equal to those in the wardrobe[9]. Repayment was made to him for a loan to the wardrobe[10] and payments for flour bought from him[11]. These however do not justify the charges made against him of exploiting and diverting the royal treasury. A more substantial ground was the complaint that he obtained lands which were thereby withdrawn from the integrity of the crown[12].

A certain number of writs under the privy[13] and the great seal[14] were issued at Gavaston's request or at his instance, but these were not many; some were of administrative effect[15], some personal favours. There is one instance of Gavaston acting with the earl of Lincoln in

[1] *Auct. Malm.* p. 155.

[2] *Chron. Murimuth,* p. 14: "fuit secretus regis et rector ipsius.

[3] Trokelowe, *Annal.* p. 64. *Ann. Lond.* p. 151. *Flores Hist.* vol. III, p. 142. *Chron. Mon. de Melsa,* vol. II, p. 280.

[4] Trokelowe, *Annal.* pp. 67–68.

[5] *Chron. Hemingburgh,* vol. II, p. 274.

[6] *Chron. Mon. de Melsa.*

[7] *Auct. Malm.* p. 160.

[8] Chan. Warr., File 60/249, 80 marks (June, 1308). Liberate Roll, no. 184, m. 2, 180 marks (10 June). Issue Roll, no. 143, m. 4, 1180 marks (10 June, 1308).

[9] K. R. Acct. 373/30, f. 14, £96. 13*s.* 4*d.* (19 June).

[10] Issue Roll, no. 141, m. 1, £500 (23 Oct. 1307).

[11] Ibid. no. 159, m. 3, £74. 0*s.* 6*d.* (18 Nov. 1311).

[12] *Chron. Mon. de Melsa,* vol. II, p. 280.

[13] L. T. R. Mem. Roll, no. 78, mm. 65 d, 68. K. R. Mem. Roll, no. 84, m. 6.

[14] *Cal. Pat. Rolls,* 1307–13, pp. 31, 60, 80, 83, 106, 137, 180, 181, 205, 206, 277.

[15] The sheriff of Cumberland at his request was granted allowance for the lack of revenue from his office, as he had been unable to collect the same on account of the Scottish war (K. R. Mem. Roll, no. 83, m. 16, 29 Jan. 1310).

the central administration. The earl was ordered to arrange between himself, Gavaston and others of the council at London certain letters of credence for messengers who were to go to the pope, and to inform the king about what was done[1].

The constitutional difficulty did enter in as far as the king did not consult the advice of his nobles but took that of Gavaston[2], though there is not a single instance of Gavaston's counsel being sought or given on a matter of administrative importance. His nearness to the king prevented other barons approaching him easily[3]. The close personal relation in which he stood to the king would account for the fact that there does not remain a single petition of Gavaston to the king or council[4]. He was in too constant attendance to need to urge his claims or redress his wrongs by the formal means of petition. There is however one letter to the chancellor requesting two writs[5].

The cause of complaint resolved itself into this, that he alone had grace in the king's sight so that his position seemed like that of a second king[6]. All the barons desired to have some share of royal grace; Peter alone succeeded in obtaining it[7]. If an earl or baron wished to have conference with the king, he entered the royal chamber only to find Gavaston already in possession, and when Peter was near, the king paid no attention to others[8]. The constitutional importance of Gavaston as expressed in the Ordinances of 1311[9] is of comparatively little note. It was charged against him that he had evilly led and counselled the king and induced him to commit various evil deeds. The charge of taking to his own uses and sending out of the realm the king's treasure was made though it contained little truth[10]. By making alliances of people to support him against all men he accroached royal power and dignity. A more substantial indictment was that he estranged the king's heart from his liege people; and a still stronger case could be based upon the lavish gifts he had accepted from the king. The other charges are all more or less incidental or complementary to these main ones; and taken as a whole they form no very strong indictment. No examples of his conduct were given; the barons preferred and considered it safer to rely on vague general

[1] K. R. Mem. Roll, no. 83, m. 11 d (23 Nov. 1309).

[2] *Chron. Murimuth*, p. 11: "et ipsius Petri consilio regebatur, spretis consiliis aliorum nobilium."

[3] *Chart. St Mary's Abbey, Dublin*, vol. II, *Annals of Ireland*, p. 340, s.a. 1311.

[4] P. R. O. Lists and Indexes, no. 1 [1892], *Index of Ancient Petitions*.

[5] Anc. Corresp. vol. XXXV, no. 56. Vide App. of Doc. no. 105.

[6] *Auct. Malm.* p. 155. [7] Ibid. p. 168. [8] Ibid.

[9] *Stat. of Realm*, vol. I, p. 162. Ordinance 20. [10] Vide above, p. 100.

charges, charges which might have been made against any of the royal favourites or partizans of the previous century.

Gavaston, apart from his vigorous personal attacks upon the dignity and self-esteem of the baronage, gave little cause to arouse a fierce constitutional opposition. There was a system in being which the barons opposed. Gavaston emphasised the importance of attack upon it, for he showed how and where by excess it could be made an instrument of royal tyranny. In their personal opposition to Gavaston the barons found a bond of union[1] which led them to create their great scheme of government as expressed in the Ordinances. With Gavaston removed the constitutional opposition subsided only to burst into fiercer and more angry flame at the conduct of the younger Despenser. It was only when the moderate men joined the irreconcilables that the baronial opposition became really dangerous to the king. Once the point was won the moderates drifted back to their old position of detachment, or even supported the king against the factiousness of the Lancastrians. That the moderates ever joined the extremists was due to the personal character and influence of Gavaston.

There are occasionally fierce denunciations of Despenser in the chroniclers, but Gavaston's was the figure that touched their imagination and inspired their eloquence. The personal character of the younger Despenser did not lend itself as easily to portrayal. There were no broad lines or strongly marked features upon which attention could be fixed. Despenser was less of a favourite than of an administrator. His influence was worked in a simple way. He was appointed king's chamberlain in the parliament of York in 1318[2]. His position meant constant attendance upon the king. The king was not fond of business and he soon found in his chamberlain one who was ready to conduct and control administration—at a price. That price was his own personal aggrandizement. The king was pleased to find one who would relieve him from the routine of business and so allowed him a free hand in the government.

The younger Despenser was by nature an administrator. He realised the importance of attention to details. In that remarkable series of letters which he wrote to John Inge, his sheriff of Glamorgan, in the years 1319 to 1321[3], he exhibited himself as a most painstaking

[1] Cf. *Auct. Malm.* p. 158. [2] Vide above, p. 93.

[3] Anc. Corresp. vol. XXXVII, no. 6. Brit. Mus. Cotton MS. Vesp. F. vii, f. 6. Cotton MS. Nero A. iv, f. 536. Anc. Corresp. vol. XLIX, nos. 143, 144; vol. XXXV, no. 8. Cotton MS. Nero C. iii, f. 181. Anc. Corresp. vol. LVIII, no. 10.

and prudent administrator. No detail was too small for his personal attention, and the most precise orders were issued for every conceivable emergency which could arise in his Glamorgan lands in that trying and troublous time. This personal supervision must have conduced to the efficient administration of his lands; and under more favourable circumstances the employment of such a capable minister would have been of great value to the king and kingdom. When the man in supreme power was actuated principally if not entirely by considerations of personal advancement and selfish aggrandizement, all the channels of administration were poisoned and ultimate disaster to administrator and administration was inevitable.

Besides having administrative ability, Despenser had definite constitutional principles. This was due, no doubt, partly to family tradition and partly to the association with the baronial opposition with which he had opened his career. He was the author or certainly a supporter of the distinction between the personal and political capacities and attributes of the king[1], a theory which found expression in a deed into which he sought to enter with John Gifford and others[2]. Nor did all his constitutional scruples leave him after he became the foremost of the royal supporters. When on 10 March, 1322, the armies of the king and the rebel barons stood facing each other near Burton-on-Trent, and the king desired to unfurl his standard, the younger Despenser most strongly and vehemently urged him not to fight against the nobles and liegemen of his realm[3]. Several of the grants made to him were conceded with the consent of parliament, instances being the grant of Drysllwyn and Cantrev Mawr[4] and the full grant of all royal and other liberties and free customs in his land of Glamorgan, as complete as any of his predecessors had ever held[5]. The town and barton of Bristol granted to him on 1 October, 1320[6], were on 28 October granted to him with the consent of the parliament of Westminster[7]. Despenser appeared to desire to make his grants doubly sure by obtaining the consent of parliament.

It can, then, be definitely said of the Despensers that they had a precise scheme of government, which had much in common with the household system of government. The younger Despenser proceeded

[1] This theory and its relation to the doctrine of capacities is discussed above in the Introduction, pp. 24–27.

[2] *Stat. of Realm*, vol. 1, p. 182, purports to give the text of this deed.

[3] *Auct. Bridl.* p. 75.

[4] *Cal. Pat. Rolls*, 1317–21, p. 248. Vide above, p. 93.

[5] *Cal. Charter Rolls*, 1300–26, p. 399 (21 Nov. 1318).

[6] *Cal. Fine Rolls*, 1319–27, p. 33.

[7] *Cal. Pat. Rolls*, 1317–21, p. 514.

on a preconceived plan, often with a considerable amount of constitutional theory behind it, though only too frequently theory was surrendered and the plan failed owing to the conflicts between his personal interests and public duty. Personal interests were always allowed to prevail. The administrative ability of the Despensers was undoubted, and in the eyes of the barons, next to their theory of personal government, their greatest crime was efficiency and ability, though the criminal taint was added by the selfish courses of the younger Hugh. This aroused fiercer and more permanent opposition than did all the sneers and gibes of Gavaston or his complete domination of the king. The process of exile drawn up against the Despensers in 1321 is more than a catalogue of their faults and a scheme of their administration. It is first and foremost an illustration of the working of the personal system and therefore its detailed treatment will come later[1]. The crux lies in the fact that Despenser was the king's private and confidential minister[2]. Entrenched in the royal chamber he maintained his position by keeping his enemies the whole time at bay. He refused to allow the magnates to approach the king[3]. At his own will he removed the officers of the household and appointed others in their place, and this without the counsel and consent of the barons[4]. He was in fact the right eye of the king and his chief adviser against the barons[5].

The chronicle says that Despenser the younger bore himself like a second king in the land[6], and the principal charges against Despenser in his process of exile deal with his accroachment of royal power[7]. In this indictment the barons do not content themsèlves with vague general charges. They give specific instances of wrongs committed.

The impression conveyed by this catalogue of charges[8] is that the Despensers had run the whole administration with the object of increasing their own revenue and estates. Whereas Gavaston had stood outside the administration, Despenser stood within exploiting the whole system of government, working through his own household office and through the officials he chose from his own personal

[1] Vide below, pp. 479–482.

[2] *Robt. de Avesbury*, p. 280: "sibi secretarium."

[3] *Stat. of Realm*, vol. I, p. 182.

[4] *Ann. Paul.* p. 292.

[5] *Chron. Lanerc.* (Maitland Club), p. 241, s.a. 1321: "quasi oculus dexter regis."

[6] *Robt. de Avesbury*, p. 280: "qui se gessit ut alter rex."

[7] *Stat. of Realm*, vol. I, pp. 181–4. The charge is stated in the preamble and in various counts.

[8] The recital and discussion of this process is postponed to pp. 479–482.

servants[1]. There was all the difference between a personal influence acting upon the mind or heart of the king and distracting his attention from his royal duties, and an influence at once personal and political, a personal influence combined with political principles and administrative ability, all of which was designedly and flagrantly directed to improve the position of the administrators. Both Gavaston and Despenser stood in close and intimate relation to the personal system of government. There was this distinction, the career of Gavaston showed it in its broad outlines, the career of Despenser showed the intricacies of the inner working and how those could be controlled by a master hand.

Of the few brief sketches of the character and position of the other actors in the drama of the reign which remain to be made, the queen is of importance. The minor position she occupied before 1326 has caused her character to be neglected until the last great crisis of the reign. The part she took in the administration was not considerable, though at times her influence is seen in the bestowal of grants and honours[2]. She was not, however, the colourless and innocent person she has been described as being up to the last years of the reign. She obtained a number of grants of land and honours including the castles, towns, boroughs and honours of Wallingford and St Valery with knight's fees, advowsons and all other appurtenances[3], the grant being subsequently enlarged to include all dues that could be or ought to be levied thereon for the use of the king and his heirs[4], and later adding all fines even in the chancery and exchequer[5].

In the election to the bishopric of Durham in 1317, the queen took a very independent course of action. The whole episode of the candidatures shows how the king and barons worked against each other in all matters. Lancaster desired the election of one of his clerks and his bidding included a promise to secure the bishopric against the Scots and the quieting of the king's wrath[6]. The king's candidate was Thomas de Cobham[7], then keeper of his privy

[1] The way in which Despenser obtained appointments both in the household and in the administration for his own servants will be discussed below, p. 340.

[2] Cf. K. R. Mem. Roll, no. 83, m. 7 (14 July, 1310).

[3] *Cal. Pat. Rolls*, 1313–17, p. 639 (4 April, 1317).

[4] Ibid. p. 642. *Descr. Cat. Ancient Deeds*, vol. I, p. 17 (22 April, 1317).

[5] *Cal. Pat. Rolls*, 1313–17, p. 668 (6 June, 1317).

[6] Surtees Soc. vol. IX [1839], *Hist. Dunelm. Scriptores Tres, Robt. de Graystanes*, p. 98.

[7] Thomas de Cobham had been elected to the archbishopric of Canterbury after the death of Winchelsey, but the king's influence had obtained it for

seal[1]. Hereford requested it for his clerk John Walwayn[2]. The queen tried to move the king on behalf of Lewis de Beaumont, whose sister, Isabel de Vescy, was one of her household[3]. The monks of Durham, however, took an independent line and chose Henry de Stanford, a monk. A host of magnates, Lancaster, Pembroke, Hereford, Henry de Beaumont with their followers waited the result of the election in the church, some threatening dire punishments if a monk were elected. The king would have admitted the elected bishop had it not been for the intervention of the queen. She implored him on her knees that her relative Lewis de Beaumont should have the bishopric. Yielding to her prayers the king refused to admit the bishop-elect[4]. He had written to the pope on behalf of Stanford[5], but now urged the necessities of the Scottish border in the favour of Beaumont[6], who eventually became bishop[7].

The independence of the queen and the way her will ultimately prevailed against that of the king shows her to have been a strong-minded woman. She took an equally strong attitude in the election to the see of Rochester in 1316. The king had written to the pope and the cardinals to hasten the election of the bishop-elect, Hamo de Heth. The queen wrote on behalf of her confessor and got the king of France to support her. The pope marvelled that the queen should have written in opposition to the request of her husband[8]. It was she who precipitated the great crisis of 1322 when she was refused admission to Leeds Castle[9]. On account of the insult done the queen, the king moved himself to punish Badlesmere[10], an effort which broadened into an endeavour to overthrow by force of arms the whole of the baronial opposition.

The precise cause of the disaffection which arose between the king

Reynolds. Contemporary opinion held him in high esteem. He was appointed to Worcester in 1317 (*Ann. Paul.* pp. 273–4, 280; *Auct. Malm.* pp. 196–7).

[1] Surtees Soc., *Hist. Dunelm. Script. Tres*, p. 98.

[2] Ibid.

[3] Cf. *Cal. Fine Rolls*, 1307–19, pp. 131–2. *Cal. Pat. Rolls*, 1313–17, p. 88. Isabel and her brother Henry de Beaumont were amongst those who accompanied the queen to France in 1314 (*Cal. Pat. Rolls*, 1313–17, pp. 85–86). The queen's uncle Charles of Valois projected coming to England with a force of 500 men to assist Edward II in his campaign against the barons in 1321 (*Eng. Hist. Rev.* vol. XXII [1907], p. 403).

[4] Surtees Soc., *Hist. Dunelm. Script. Tres*, p. 98.

[5] *Reg. Pal. Dunelm.* vol. IV, pp. 157–8.

[6] Surtees Soc., *Hist. Dunelm. Script. Tres*, p. 98. *Chron. Lanerc.* p. 217.

[7] Cf. *Ann. Paul.* p. 280; *Auct. Bridl.* p. 52.

[8] Wharton, *Angl. Sac.* vol. I [1691], Wm de Dene, *Hist. Roffens.* p. 358.

[9] *Ann. Paul.* pp. 298–9. *Chron. Murimuth*, p. 34.

[10] *Chron. G. le Baker*, p. 11.

and the queen is difficult to determine. Neglect of her in favour of the Despensers, and their treatment of her could easily have estranged husband and wife[1], and it is certain that the queen bore considerable hatred towards the younger Hugh, and gave her fear of him as a reason for her refusal to return to England[2]. On 18 September, 1324, the lands of the queen were taken into the king's hands on the threat of a French invasion[3], and this action did not tend to improve the relations of husband and wife.

The character of the queen as depicted in the awful tragedy of the close of the reign is that of one of the worst figures in history. Whatever justification the barons who supported her may have had, no such excuse can be alleged in her favour. She degraded her regal position, her marriage obligation and her womanly qualities in that awful vengeance which she pursued against her husband no less than in the adulterous connection she had established with Mortimer. Her interest in Mortimer was not of sudden growth and before she had left England she had addressed a letter to Norwich, treasurer, asking him to show Lady de Mortimer all the favour he could in what the king had granted her for sustenance[4].

Lancaster, who was until his death the rallying point of all discontent and opposition, had no qualifications to fit him for the place he filled except position and wealth. His contemporaries were much impressed by the splendid position he occupied in the kingdom. He was the king's cousin and the queen's uncle. He was the holder of five earldoms, Lancaster, Leicester, Lincoln, Salisbury, and Ferrars and Derby and had besides a great number of honours and much land and many castles in England and Wales[5]. His birth and his nobility no less than his wealth were impressive[6]. His mother was queen of Navarre, his sister, queen of France[7], and no duke or earl throughout the universe seemed so well provided with territory[8]. Yet in spite of all these advantages his whole career was a ghastly failure. Abundance of resources was useless without directive ability. Lancaster was factious, inclined to be envious, and was throughout indisposed or unable to take that personal direction of affairs which a successful opposition leader must on occasion take. As long as there were abuses to be attacked he rallied men to his side.

[1] Cf. *Chron. G. le Baker*, p. 17; cf. *Chron. Lanerc.* p. 249.

[2] *Cal. Pat. Rolls*, 1324–27, pp. 576–581. Vide also *Auct. Malm.* pp. 286–7.

[3] *Foedera*, vol. II, p. 569. *Cal. Fine Rolls*, 1319–27, pp. 300–1. Cf. *Cal. Close Rolls*, 1323–27, p. 223.

[4] Anc. Corresp. vol. XXXVII, no. 45. [5] *Chron. Mon. de Melsa*, vol. II, p. 344.

[6] *Chron. Lanerc.* p. 234. [7] *Auct. Malm.* p. 181. [8] Ibid.

When force of circumstances compelled the king to give him a deciding influence in administration he failed most hopelessly to answer the demands made upon him.

His importance was recognised in the letters which the prior and convent of Christchurch, Canterbury, sent asking his aid and influence in securing the canonisation of Winchelsey[1]. Winchelsey had been intimately associated with him in the demand for and the discussion of the Ordinances of 1311, and Lancaster was closely interested in the canonisation of such a pillar of baronial opposition[2]. In answer to his request a catalogue of the miracles of the archbishop was sent him[3] and he decided to send the account to Rome with all speed by one of his household[4]. The matter was still uncompleted when Lancaster died, and the prior made efforts to enlist the sympathies of his brother, Henry de Lancaster, in the project[5]. Lancaster attempted to thrust his clerk into the bishopric of Durham in 1317, and with remarkable assurance promised to quiet the anger of the king if his nominee were elected[6]! He also wrote to the convent of Durham on behalf of a clerk who desired sustenance there[7]. As the king tried to influence elections to bishoprics and obtain them for officials of his household, so Lancaster, with less show of reason, endeavoured to thrust members of his household into them; and as the king at the request of his friends sent old retainers and officials with letters under his privy seal to religious houses for sustenance and support, so also did the earl.

The political action of the earl is so closely interwoven with the theories upon which the barons acted, with the administrative and constitutional action by which the baronial opposition sought to secure a greater share in and control over the administration, and with the king's endeavours to meet these attempts, that it cannot be discussed apart from them. The failure of the earl as a practical statesman must be emphasised now. The failure depended partly upon his motives, partly upon his personal qualities; and on these two points there was the greatest divergence of opinion in his own time[8]. Some considered that he died a martyr to a noble cause, for

[1] Camb. Univ. MS. Ee, v. 31, f. 201 (13 May, 1318).

[2] Vide *Lit. Cantuar.* vol. III, App. pp. 398–9 (7 April, 1319).

[3] Camb. Univ. MS. Ee. v. 31, ff. 204–213 b.

[4] *Lit. Cantuar.* vol. I, pp. 50–53.

[5] Ibid. pp. 70–71.

[6] Vide above, p. 105. Surtees Soc., *Hist. Dunelm. Script. Tres*, p. 98: "promittens,...Regis indignacionem se sedaturum."

[7] Surtees Soc., *Hist. Dunelm. Script. Tres*, App. p. cxvi, no. xcvii.

[8] Cf. *Chron. Mon. de Melsa*, vol. II, p. 344; R. Higden, *Polychron.* vol. VIII, pp. 313–315.

the right of the church and kingdom[1], not forgetting the commons[2]. It was urged that he should be numbered among the saints because he was an almsgiver, because he honoured the religious and because he laboured for justice even to death[3]. On the other hand there were some who could not forget his marriage relations and how he had neglected his noble wife, and taking into consideration the manner of his life rather than the circumstances of his death, denied him sanctity[4]. The matter was decided for those who doubted by the miracles which report accredited to the virtue of Thomas of Lancaster. At his tomb at Pontefract all manner of miracles were performed, and also at places in London with which he had been associated[5]. So popular was his fame likely to become that the king forbade honours to be paid to his memory[6]. Offices were written to commemorate him[7], and his popularity was continually on the increase. As the king's government became more and more unpopular even those who had had no sympathy with his objects during his life rallied round his name as that of a good cause. A superstitious age noted that none who had participated in the earl's death came to any good: Arundel, the Despensers, the earl of Kent, Harclay, all died violent deaths[8]. The truth appears to be that a life which was marked by no virtue, rather by factiousness, selfishness, and licentiousness, was sanctified by its violent end and still more by the unpopularity of the administration of the remainder of the reign of Edward II. Lancaster's death was compared to that of Thomas of Canterbury; one died for the peace of the church, the other for the peace of England[9]. The point in which his career most closely resembled that of St Thomas[10] was that he also was more potent in death than he had ever been in life. Lancaster's opposition to the king had been fitful and inconsistent. His martyred name provided the war-cry for the revolution which hurled the king from his throne and sent royal favourites and faithful officials to their death.

[1] *Eulogium Hist.* vol. III, p. 196: "pro jure ecclesiae et regni." *Chron. Knighton*, vol. I, p. 426. Vide Brit. Mus. Cotton MS. Cleopatra C. iii, f. 302 b, Chron. Abb. de Mowbray: "pro defensione legium Angliae et matris nostrae ecclesiae."

[2] Camd. Soc., *Political Songs*, pp. 269–270. [3] *Chron. Mon. de Melsa*, vol. II, p. 344.

[4] Ibid. [5] *Flores Hist.* vol. III, pp. 213–214.

[6] Ibid. p. 214. *Chron. Knighton*, vol. I, p. 426. *Cal. Close Rolls*, 1318–23, p. 723 (28 June, 1323).

[7] Cf. Camd. Soc., *Political Songs*, pp. 268–272; ibid. vol. XXVI [1880], *Doc. illustr. Hist. of St Paul's*, W. S. Simpson, pp. 12–14. Cf. also *Arch. Journal*, vol. XXXVI, pp. 103, 104.

[8] *Chron. Knighton*, vol. I, pp. 427, 429. [9] Camd. Soc., *Political Songs*, p. 268.

[10] H. W. C. Davis, *England under the Normans and Angevins*, p. 222.

Judged from the mundane and mean facts of his life, little can be said in Lancaster's favour. He was useless as an opposition leader and worse than useless as an English baron. He let faction so rule his life that even in the great crisis of Bannockburn, instead of aiding the king to beat the Scots, and so obtain a little respite for the northern counties, he sulkily remained at Pontefract[1], urging a confirmation of the Ordinances even at that inopportune moment. He sent his service, but absented himself[2], yet he did not hesitate to reap the advantage which the victory of the Scots gave the baronial opposition. The barons were never stronger than in the period immediately following Bannockburn[3]. His dealings with the Scots[4] are an eternal stain upon his name and the rumours of such relations continually hampered the king's movements against the Scots, at no time more considerably than at the siege of Berwick in 1319[5]. Lancaster was as unscrupulous in his dealings about land as any of the king's supporters. He endeavoured to convert land held by socage into knight service[6]. On the dissolution of the Templars he took their lands irrespective of the rights of the donor[7]. His officials conducted purveyance more shamelessly than the most shameless royal purveyor without the least excuse or justification[8].

The one person in the reign of Edward II who has any claim to attractive features was Aymer de Valence, earl of Pembroke, the king's cousin. He was a statesman of considerable ability one of the moderate men who while they render satisfaction to neither extreme yet achieve a great deal of good. Pembroke was the man who acted least upon personal considerations. He was the king's sincere friend but was never degraded into a favourite. The king placed implicit trust in him. He said that he had always found his advice good and profitable and when he had important business in hand he always desired Pembroke's counsel[9]. He wished to do

[1] *Chron. Knighton*, vol. I, p. 410.

[2] *Flores Hist.* vol. III, p. 338. *Chron. Lanerc.* p. 206.

[3] The discussion of Lancaster's action in this period will come later. Vide pp. 394–400.

[4] *Cal. Close Rolls*, 1318–23, pp. 525–6. *Foedera*, vol. II, p. 474. *Rot. Parl.* vol. II, p. 4.

[5] *Auct. Bridl.* pp. 57–58. *Auct. Malm.* pp. 244–6. *Chron. Mon. de Melsa*, vol. II, p. 336. *Chron. Lanerc.* p. 226. The younger Despenser communicated the suspicions to Inge in a letter dated from the siege of Berwick (Brit. Mus. Cotton MS. Vesp. F. vii, f. 6).

[6] Ancient Petition, no. 4527.

[7] *Rot. Parl.* vol. I, p. 388.

[8] Ibid. p. 399.

[9] Anc. Corresp. vol. XLIX, no. 34 (11 May, 1316). Vide App. of Doc. no. 126: "por ce qe nous auons totes foitz trouez vostre conseil bon et profitable."

nothing without his advice[1]. The king moreover expressed, in a letter under his secret seal, the great affection which he entertained towards his cousin and assured him that he held all his quarrels as his own[2].

One of Edward's first acts on coming to the throne was to supersede Pembroke as keeper of Scotland[3], and in the opposition to Gavaston, he was definitely on the baronial side. On Gavaston's death, partly because his honour was involved[4], and partly because he thought that the barons were pursuing their course too far, he immediately became a whole-hearted supporter of the king, and then throughout the reign acted as a moderating influence in the royal counsels. His plan appears to have been to lead a moderate party which would restrain the baronage, and at the same time secure a better administration. It is in the crises of 1321 and 1322 that he stands out especially as a moderator. When in 1321, the barons, having devastated the Despenser property, endeavoured to exile them by petition in parliament, and the king refused to hear the matter, the earl advised the king to submit to the barons. Relying upon his loyalty, he urged this because of the great power of the barons, and his advice was followed[5]. Later in that year when the king was besieging the castle of Leeds, in company with the archbishop of Canterbury and the bishop of London he again endeavoured to mediate. When the barons were assembled at Kingston he visited them, but his efforts to keep the peace were in vain[6]. Early in the following year, at the request of Pembroke, Kent, Richmond, Arundel and Warenne, various safe conducts were issued to the Mortimers who were opposing the king in the middle march[7]. In the whole crisis however he supported the king[8], and acted as one of Lancaster's judges[9].

For several years after Gavaston's death he was the virtual head of the administration[10]. His chief employment throughout the reign was in foreign negotiations, a sphere for which his foreign ancestry

[1] Anc. Corresp. vol. XLIX, no. 49 (16 Aug. 1320).

[2] Ibid. vol. XLIX, no. 48 (8 May, 1320): "Car nous tenoms toutes voz quereles les noz."

[3] *Ann. Paul.* pp. 257–8.

[4] The earl of Pembroke's change of side is explained below, pp. 322–4.

[5] *Auct. Malm.* p. 259.

[6] *Chron. Murimuth*, p. 34.

[7] *Cal. Pat. Rolls*, 1321–24, pp. 48, 51, 70. Cf. *Chron. Murimuth*, pp. 35–36, where he states that the Mortimers were induced to surrender "per mediationem fraudulentam comitum Pembrokiae, etc."

[8] *Auct. Malm.* p. 263.

[9] *Auct. Bridl.* p. 77.

[10] The Pembroke administration will be treated at length below, pp. 322–330.

and interests specially adapted him. He was almost invariably a member of all solemn embassies, whether to the Roman court, Paris or elsewhere. In 1309 he was one of the mission to the pope to obtain a bull absolving Gavaston from excommunication[1]. In 1317 when returning from an embassy to Rome he was captured and detained in Germany[2], whence the king made every effort to ransom him[3]. His death in 1324 occurred when he was on a mission to the French court[4].

When Anthony Pessaign, who had been associated with Pembroke on many missions[5] and in administrative work in England[6], slandered him at the Roman court, stating that he was not only false to the king, but had suborned letters from the chancery, the king wrote to the pope asking him to believe no evil of Pembroke[7]. His devotion to the king's true interests was not of such a subservient nature as to make those who opposed or failed to see eye to eye with the king, regard him as an enemy. The queen also trusted him, and one of the king's greatest disasters was Pembroke's inopportune death. His knowledge of foreign affairs, his skill, his influence at the French court, would have either prevented or removed that state of tension and ultimate war, which existed between France and England from 1324 to 1326. Moreover his influence with the queen would have restrained her from that course of impetuous hatred and lust which drove her from one depth to another. On occasion he supported her wishes even in opposition to the king's plan, as in 1316 when he wrote to the pope on behalf of the queen's confessor for the see of Rochester[8]. As late as 27 June, 1324, Pembroke retained the queen's confidence and she wrote to Baldock, chancellor, desiring the appointment of the earl of Pembroke, William le Zouch of Ashby and others as justices of oyer and terminer for her forests of Havering[9].

The most attractive personality after Pembroke was Gilbert de Clare, the young earl of Gloucester. He had been Edward II's playfellow when prince[10], and immediately after his accession to the throne, though Gilbert was then but seventeen years of age[11], the king

[1] *Ann. Paul.* p. 267.

[2] *Chron. Murimuth*, pp. 25–26. *Chart. St Mary's Abbey, Dublin*, vol. II, *Annals of Ireland*, p. 355.

[3] *Cal. Close Rolls*, 1313–18, pp. 469–470. *Foedera*, vol. II, pp. 329–330.

[4] *Ann. Paul.* p. 307. Cf. also *Chron. Mon. de Melsa*, vol. II, pp. 347–8.

[5] E.g. he was a member of the embassy of 1317 (*Chron. Murimuth*, p. 26).

[6] Cf. Anc. Corresp. vol. XLIX, no. 33.

[7] *Reg. Pal. Dunelm.* vol. IV, p. lxiii.

[8] Wharton, *Angl. Sac.* vol. I [1691], Wm de Dene, *Hist. Roffens.* p. 359.

[9] Anc. Corresp. vol. XXXVI, no. 38.

[10] Vide above, p. 79.

[11] *Cal. Inq. P. M.* vol. IV, p. 311.

granted him all his father's lands on condition that certain payments were made, payments which were soon afterwards remitted[1]. In March, 1308, though still a minor, he was given licence to marry whomsoever he would[2], and in the same year he married Matilda, the daughter of the earl of Ulster[3]. Despite the close intimacy which existed between the king and Gilbert, no long list of liberal grants was made to him. He was given permission that all debts due by him to the exchequer should be charged upon his heirs, and his executors should have free administration of his goods and chattels[4]. Three of the king's manors in Norfolk and one in Suffolk were granted to him[5], and the issues of the bishopric of Down during vacancy[6].

His position in the early years of the reign was one of the utmost difficulty. He was bound to the king by ties of friendship and to Gavaston by ties of marriage. For a part of the time he adopted an attitude of neutrality. He could not support Peter without offending his peers, and he could not side with the barons since it was unbecoming to fight against his brother-in-law[7]. In the conspiracy which resulted in Gavaston's death, Gloucester had no part though he had promised to acquiesce[8]. At this time the king trusted him, and in 1309 he was appointed leader of the expedition against the Scots[9]. Notwithstanding his youth and inexperience, on the death of the earl of Lincoln in 1311, he was appointed to succeed him as keeper of the realm during the king's absence in Scotland[10], an appointment due, no doubt, to a feeling that there was no other to whom the king could trust such a responsible position. In 1309 the king granted him 3000 marks as a gift[11]; and in payment of a gift of 5000 marks, granted for his great expenses in the king's service in the Scottish war and elsewhere, he was to receive all custodies and marriages as they fell into the king's hand[12]. The king respected the advice which Gloucester gave him, and consulted him whether he should receive the cardinal and bishops in 1312, the earl advising that they should come to the

[1] *Cal. Pat. Rolls*, 1307–13, pp. 5, 21. *Cal. Close Rolls*, 1307–13, p. 10.

[2] *Cal. Pat. Rolls*, 1307–13, p. 50 (12 Mar. 1308).

[3] *Ann. Lond.* p. 156. *Chart. St Mary's Abbey, Dublin*, vol. II, *Annals of Ireland*, p. 338.

[4] *Cal. Pat. Rolls*, 1307–13, p. 107 (11 Mar. 1309).

[5] *Cal. Charter Rolls*, 1300–26, p. 130 (2 Oct. 1309).

[6] *Cal. Pat. Rolls*, 1313–17, p. 89 (14 Feb. 1314).

[7] *Auct. Malm.* p. 158.

[8] Ibid. p. 176.

[9] *Rot. Scot.* p. 74

[10] *Cal. Pat. Rolls*, 1307–13, p. 333 (4 March, 1311).

[11] Chan. Warr., File 66/824 (24 Nov. 1309). Liberate Roll, no. 86, m. 4. Issue Roll, no. 150, m. 5.

[12] *Cal. Pat. Rolls*, 1307–13, pp. 376, 387 (15 July, 1311).

king[1]. The death of the young, headstrong and impetuous earl in the first stages of the battle of Bannockburn[2] was a serious loss to the king. Even while so young he had displayed great promise, and the influence which his position as "the man of greatest inheritance and nobility and honour in all Saxon land[3]" gave him, would doubtless have exercised a salutary effect upon the other earls.

Of the earls who played an important part in the conflicts of the reign there remain Warwick, Hereford, Richmond, Warenne and Arundel. With the exception of Warwick, who maintained an attitude of resolute opposition to the king, even at the parliament of Stamford in 1309[4], in which all the other nobles had succumbed to royal influence, the other earls played an inconstant part. Hereford was for a time a member of the middle party led by Pembroke[5]. Richmond naturally belonged to the curialists rather than to the baronial faction. Warenne deserted the barons and had a very violent quarrel with Lancaster[6]. Arundel gradually veered towards the court, and before 1322[7] was a convinced royal supporter: after that year he was the faithful royal official, ruling Wales as justice[8] and being included among the victims of the revolution of 1326[9].

Warwick had been the man most deeply implicated in the murder of Gavaston[10], and he had the one merit of consistency in an age which was ruled solely by personal interest and knew not the meaning of consistency. Warwick was described as that most stern knight of Edward II[11], and there was a certain element of brutality and ferocity about him though he was noted for his wisdom, and was a discreet and learned man[12]. The rest of the baronage while also possessing a strong taint of brutality changed, with the alteration of personal advantage, from one side to the other. The earl of Warenne was lost to the king's party for a time out of anger at his defeat by Gavaston at the tournament of Wallingford[13]. The reasons for change were not usually as trivial as this, and generally had a far

[1] Anc. Corresp. vol. XLIX, no. 21. Vide App. of Doc. no. 124.

[2] *Auct. Malm.* pp. 203–4. *Chron. G. le Baker*, p. 8.

[3] *Annals of Loch Cé*, vol. I, p. 563.

[4] *Auct. Malm.* p. 160.

[5] Vide below, pp. 426–7, 435–9.

[6] Vide below, pp. 502–3.

[7] In that year he acted as one of the judges of the earl of Lancaster (*Ann. Paul.* p. 302; *Auct. Bridl.* p. 77).

[8] He was appointed to that office 5 Jan. 1322 (*Cal. Fine Rolls*, 1319–27, pp. 86–87).

[9] *Ann. Paul.* p. 321. *Auct. Bridl.* p. 87. *Auct. Malm.* p. 289.

[10] *Ann. Lond.* p. 207. *Ann. Paul.* p. 271. *Auct. Bridl.* p. 43. *Auct. Malm.* pp. 177–8.

[11] *Chron. Hemingburgh*, vol. II, pp. 295–6.

[12] Ibid. p. 236.

[13] *Auct. Malm.* p. 161.

deeper motive. There were some finer qualities about the earl of Hereford, and he was certainly a bold and able warrior[1], though gloomy and thoughtful[2]. He, like the other barons, pushed his own interests, and sought and obtained from the king a grant of a weekly market and fair for a manor of his cousin, Edmund de Bohun, also writing to the chancellor on the matter desiring him to order the necessary writs to be made[3].

Judged as a whole the barons were not a whit to be preferred to the favourites. Their characters appear to be all on about the same level, and in contrast to the opportunism of both baron and favourite the deep-rooted and lasting attachments of the king stand in a very favourable light. He, at least, did to a degree maintain a consistent policy to the end of the reign. He refused to give up the personal system of government. When the barons made onslaughts which proved successful, he immediately set about either a reconquest or a movement along a new line. The reign of Edward ended as it had begun with the personal system in power; and the government of Edward III was hardly less personal than that of his father. The failure of the barons is to be attributed in a great measure to their lack of sincerity and unity. The success of the king, for the system for which he stood prevailed though he fell, was due to the inherent strength and efficiency of that system.

The general nature of the household system of government demanded that the personal aspect of the reign should be treated at length. The character of the king had a potent influence upon the direction of baronial opposition, and the characters of the favourites must be considered in conjunction with that of the king. Though there is not so much strong and useful material upon which to base an appreciation of the characters of the outstanding figures in the baronial opposition, it is of importance that there should be some understanding of their motives, though their class consciousness and general theory is of equal importance. From a consideration of the personal aspect of the reign the transition to a detailed study of the various sources whence the household system drew its strength is natural. After this has been treated the importance of the personal aspect will be realised more fully.

[1] *Chron. G. le Baker*, p. 13.

[2] Cf. Cotton MS. Nero C. iii, f. 181: "De ce qe vous auez entendu qe le counte de Hereford est moreis pensifs plus qil ne soleit."

[3] Anc. Corresp. vol. XXXVI, no. 119.

CHAPTER IV

THE STRENGTH OF THE HOUSEHOLD SYSTEM

(i) *Control of Government*

The household was a little less personal than the chamber, and its officers were not in such direct and constant contact with the king. An accurate definition of the respective spheres and influence of household and chamber is difficult if not impossible. The household was the larger organisation of which the chamber was an essential and intricate part. The lesser was distinct from the greater, yet a part of it. Its tendencies towards independence were growing during the reign of Edward II, but there always remained a vital connection. The distinction between household and chamber is brought out in a letter concerning the countess of Warwick. The ladies and waiting-maids of her chamber and the men of her household had been arrested[1]. The chamber was officered by personal servants of the countess who stood in a very close relationship to her; the men of her household were also her personal servants, but while their dependence upon her was as complete as the servants of the chamber their relation was not as intimate. The great difference between chamber and household was the greater intimacy of the former with the head.

The household did not consist only of the officers of the various departments of the household. It can be fairly argued that the officers of the chancery and exchequer were considered to be of the king's household. In a writ of privy seal to the treasurer and barons of the exchequer, the king intimated his desire that Henry de Ludgershall, who had been a chamberlain of the exchequer and had served the king well and loyally in that and other offices when he was in the king's household, should be held discharged of his office on account of ill health[2]. The household also included all those who

[1] Anc. Corresp. vol. XXXIV, no. 107. Vide App. of Doc. no. 102: "les dames et les damoyseles de sa chambre et les gentz de son houstel."

[2] K. R. Mem. Roll, no. 85, m. 18: "qui ad este un de nous chaumberleyns de nostre dit Eschekier et qui bien et loiaument nous ad serui en cel office et en autres tant come il feust en nostre houstel."

lived near the king[1] or upon whom the king desired to extend those special privileges which members of the household enjoyed. One Roger de Flete begged the king's protection on the ground that he was of "hostiel le dite nostre seigneur le Roy et de sa meynee[2]," and Roger Damory had the sentence of death, passed upon him for his participation in the rebellion of 1322, pardoned because the king had loved him greatly "et fuistes de sa meigne et privez de luiy[3]." Damory had never held office in the household but had been one of the courtiers[4].

The connection between the household and the administration of the private and public functions of the king was not a mere growth from the inside, but was recognised by the king. Thus in 1301 Edward I expressed his wish that the earl of Hereford should henceforth be of his son's council and household[5], and when Edward II desired to honour a foreigner who had rendered him service at the Roman court, he appointed him to be of the council and household[6], or of the king's household and robes[7]. Though these appointments were mere formal honours, there was a real connection between the household and the "administrative" council[8] that carried out so much of the administration.

The present purpose is to insist upon the strength of the personal system as it affected the struggle between king and barons. Before proceeding to the different sources and manifestations of that strength its fundamental source must be stated, and the final origin of all the sources of strength of the household system is found in the ability and ease with which the king provided instruments to counteract the growing independence of administration and the increasing assaults of baronial opposition. The point will be more clear after one or two concrete instances have been given. The great seal was at first in direct association with the king. With the growth of business the chancery obtained a partial entity of its own and the king's control became less direct. Immediately the privy seal grew up to act as a warrant for the issue of the great seal. When that became formalised the secret seal and the signet grew up in the same way for the same purpose. The pipe roll of the exchequer was the first financial account, then came the wardrobe accounts, which in part almost

[1] Vide P. R. O. Parliamentary and Council Proceedings (Chancery), File 5/2.
[2] Chan. Warr., File 1706. [3] *Abbrev. Placit.* p. 351.
[4] For his part in the influence of the middle party, see below, pp. 431–2, 433–5.
[5] *Cal. Close Rolls*, 1296–1302, p. 487.
[6] *Cal. Pat. Rolls*, 1313–17, p. 79. [7] Ibid. 1317–21, pp. 50, 52
[8] For the "administrative" council see below, pp. 248–287.

superseded the pipe roll, and when the wardrobe accounts became too closely connected with the ordinary financial machinery and audit, the chamber accounts developed. The same thing is true in the evolution of the officials of the different departments. There was a succession of terraces each with protections of its own. The first terrace was the chamber, next came the household, and last came the great administrative offices of the chancery and the exchequer. This was the general principle which guided the course of the administrative history and development of the period, and it will be found to express itself in almost every phase of administration.

It can therefore be said that the strength of the household system depended upon its elasticity and upon the ease with which the king could provide vigorous substitutes for enervated instruments. Though the ultimate source of that strength depended upon what may be called the concentric fertility of the king's policy in this direction, the practical sources of the strength of the household system are no less important. The strength of the household system can be considered under the two broad heads that it controlled the government and was yet independent of it, having in all directions instruments and resources of its own. A precise division of the methods by which it controlled the government and of the methods by which it maintained its independence of the administrative departments is impossible. The two lines are interdependent and the two facts will have to be considered in co-ordination the whole time. The king's court was the parent of all the administrative offices and it retained its control after all those offices had obtained a separate existence, though with the course of time there was an increasing independence.

The great officers of state were appointed by the king. The chancellor was appointed by the king, the appointment not always being entered on the rolls of chancery, except in the form of memoranda[1]. Even when during the reign the barons possessed considerable influence the king conceded no more than to have a keeper of the great seal, and for some time Walter Reynolds, who was appointed chancellor in 1310[2], was styled keeper[3]. Reynolds was however

[1] Vide *Cal. Close Rolls*, 1307–27 passim.

[2] He first sealed writs on 7 July, 1310 (*Cal. Close Rolls*, 1307–13, p. 326).

[3] Professor Tout has worked out in detail the problems of Reynolds' position. (Tout, *The Place of Ed. II*, pp. 319–324.) This is generally his designation in and after 1312 though he is sometimes called chancellor during this period. Hugh le Despenser senior went to the exchequer on 6 Oct. 1312, and informed them of Reynolds' appointment as lieutenant of the chancellor (K. R. Mem. Roll, no. 86, m. 71). On the same day the great seal was restored to him (*Cal. Close Rolls*, 1307–13, p. 553).

virtually chancellor and performed all the functions of that office[1]. A very frequent expedient during the period of Reynolds' keepership and during the chancellorships of Sandale and Hothum, was the appointment of three or more keepers while the chancellor was ill or absent, and also during the periods when that office was vacant[2]. This was an expedient which could well be turned to the king's advantage in a crisis, as the keepers were king's clerks and were more dependent upon the king as they lacked the status and dignity of the chancellor. John, bishop of Norwich, chancellor from 6 January, 1320, to 5 June, 1323[3], the king "had nominated his chancellor in full Parliament[4]" though this nomination does not suggest any considerable pressure upon the king in his choice, as the middle party was still in power. When Robert de Baldock became chancellor in August, 1323[5], the appointment of keepers of the seal practically ceased. During his tenure of the office of chancellor only once, in November–December, 1324, were they appointed and then the chancellor wished to go to his home[6]. He was too intimately connected with the king and his household[7] to make such an expedient necessary as he was almost constantly resident at court. Moreover he had not the frequent calls upon his time, which their dioceses demanded from Sandale, Hothum and Salmon.

The chancery was the mainspring of the executive and it was of the utmost importance that complete control over the appointment and functions of the head of that great department should remain absolutely in the king's hands. The chancery was the official mouthpiece of the king and was the ultimate source of all formal administrative processes. The exchequer and judicature both had seals of their own and could put into operation stages of processes in their respective administrations. On occasion they even initiated processes; but the great bulk of the administration in all branches was originated by chancery writ.

The treasurer, who was the head of the exchequer, was likewise appointed by the king, and enrolments of his appointment by letters

[1] Vide Chan. Warr., Files 83–88 passim.
[2] Vide Tout, *The Place of Ed. II*, pp. 324–7.
[3] Ibid. p. 326.
[4] *Cal. Close Rolls*, 1318–23, pp. 219–220.
[5] Ibid. 1323–27, pp. 134–5.
[6] Ibid. p. 328.
[7] The relation in which Baldock as chancellor stood to the king and his household is illustrated by the fact that in August, 1324, the treasurer and chamberlains of the exchequer were ordered to send to the king £1300 for the expenses of his household in the company of the chancellor, the arrangements being made by agreement between Baldock, Despenser the younger and the exchequer officials (*Cal. Close Rolls*, 1323–27, p. 217).

patent appear on the chancery roll. It was in this way that Reynolds, Sandale, Langton, Walwayn, Stapleton, Melton and the other treasurers of the reign were appointed[1]. The king sent notification of the appointment to the chamberlains and barons of the exchequer[2], the writ being issued by warrant under the privy seal[3]. Though Melton, archbishop of York, was appointed by letters patent issued "by king[4]" a chronicler states that he obtained that office in the parliament of Westminster in 1325, against the will and argument of the archbishop of Canterbury[5]. Even if this statement is well founded it does not imply any choice, or even acquiescence in the royal choice, by parliament. Over the appointment of Langton to the office of treasurer in 1312[6] considerable troubles ensued, the appointment being resolutely opposed by the barons, an opposition which finally succeeded[7]. Frequently during the reign lieutenants were appointed to the office of treasurer. Sandale was thus elected on 4 October, 1312, on Pembroke's information[8], the exchequer being acquainted of the fact by the elder Despenser[9].

Walter de Norwich was on several occasions during the reign appointed lieutenant of the treasurer[10], these appointments being by letters patent[11]. At various other times also he was appointed to supply the place of the treasurer while the latter was absent from the exchequer on the king's business, these appointments being entered on the close roll[12]. The appointments by letters patent on the other hand were usually during the vacancy of the treasurership[13], though notification was sent to the barons by privy seal[14]. In 1314 Norwich was appointed treasurer, "by the king and council[15]," and the same formula was attached to Sandale's appointment in 1318[16]. Both

[1] *Cal. Pat. Rolls*, 1307–13, pp. 1, 234, 413; 1317–21, pp. 155, 417; 1324–27, p. 128.

[2] Cf. K. R. Mem. Roll, no. 81, m. 14. L. T. R. Mem. Roll, no. 78, m. 16.

[3] Ibid.

[4] *Cal. Pat. Rolls*, 1324–27 p. 128. Vide also *Auct. Malm.* p. 283.

[5] Wharton, *Angl. Sac.* vol. 1, Wm de Dene, *Hist. Roffens.* p. 365.

[6] *Cal. Pat. Rolls*, 1307–13, p. 413 (23 Jan. 1312).

[7] Vide below, pp. 389–392.

[8] *Cal. Pat. Rolls*, 1307–13, p. 501.

[9] K. R. Mem. Roll, no. 86, m. 71.

[10] Cf. Tout, *The Place of Ed. II*, pp. 332-3

[11] *Cal. Pat. Rolls*, 1307–13, pp. 369, 459; 1317–21, p. 417; 1321–24, p. 14.

[12] Vide *Cal. Close Rolls*, 1318–23, pp. 162, 613; 1323–27, pp. 116, 280.

[13] Cf. *Cal. Pat. Rolls*, 1307–13, p. 396; 1321–24, p. 14.

[14] Cf. P. R. O. Brevia Baronibus, 5 Ed. II. On 23 Oct. 1311, they were informed that the king had appointed Walter de Norwich to be lieutenant of the treasurer until the king had otherwise arranged for that office.

[15] *Cal. Pat. Rolls*, 1313–17, p. 178 (26 Sept. 1314).

[16] Ibid. 1317–21, p. 227 (16 Nov. 1318).

these appointments are important, as the first came during the period of Lancastrian domination following the defeat at Bannockburn[1] and the second after the parliament of York of 1318[2]. These two appointments contrast greatly with that of Norwich as lieutenant in 1321[3], which was made on the information of Roger de Northburgh, keeper of the king's wardrobe[4]. Besides the appointment by letters patent, the exchequer was acquainted with appointments by the king's writ under privy seal addressed to the barons[5]. Another check upon the office and officers was provided in the method of paying his fee. A writ of privy seal was addressed to the chancellor ordering him to issue letters under the great seal to the chamberlains of the exchequer to pay the fee of the treasurer[6].

All the justices of the two central bodies, the king's bench and common pleas, as well as those of assize, oyer and terminer and itinerant justices, were appointed by the king. During the reign of Edward I the council had assisted the king in the appointment of his justices, the appointment being made in the king's presence. On the first occasion mentioned on which justices were appointed in this manner, the appointments covered the whole of the king's bench and common pleas and justices in eyre for the north and south[7]. On the second occasion four sets of justices of assize were appointed[8]. During the reign of Edward II there is no evidence of justices being appointed in this way. At the opening of the reign the six old justices *de banco* were re-appointed by letters patent[9], and so throughout the reign there are various enrolments upon the patent roll of appointment of justices of the benches, the appointments being "by king[10]." Similarly discharge of justices was secured by royal writ[11], Hervy de Staunton succeeding Henry le Scrope as chief justice of king's bench in 1323[12] and Geoffrey le Scrope succeeding him the following year[13], the appointments being "by king."

The appointment of justices of assize, gaol delivery and oyer and terminer was somewhat different. On 16 April, 1317, it was agreed

[1] For this Lancastrian administration vide below, pp. 394–400.
[2] The parliament of York is discussed below, pp. 450–468.
[3] *Cal. Pat. Rolls*, 1321–24, p. 14 (25 Aug. 1321).
[4] Tout, *The Place of Ed. II*, p. 355.
[5] Cf. Madox, *Hist. of Exch.* vol. II, p. 60.
[6] Cf. Chan. Warr., File 59/180 (13 May, 1308).
[7] *Cal. Close Rolls*, 1272–79, pp. 503–4. [8] Ibid. 1288–96, pp. 519–520.
[9] *Cal. Pat. Rolls*, 1307–13, p. 2. Cf. also K. R. Mem. Roll, no. 81, m. 4 d. L. T. R. Mem. Roll, no. 78, m. 3.
[10] E.g. *Cal. Pat. Rolls*, 1313–17, p. 181; 1317–21, pp. 344, 508, 593.
[11] *Cal. Close Rolls*, 1318–23, p. 266. [12] Ibid. 1323–27, p. 2. [13] Ibid. p. 74.

by the king's council that no sheriff or coroner should be given a commission as justice in such cases because it was a part of their duty to be intendant to justices appointed for those purposes in their counties. If the king ordered the contrary, the chancellor was to inform him of the council's agreement before he did anything[1]. This restriction was dictated by reason and was not a limitation of the royal right of appointment. It was also usual for justices to be assigned in the chancery for various assizes and commissions of oyer and terminer. One who petitioned the king in a plea of trespass was informed that justices to hear and determine trespasses were assigned in the chancery[2], and one who asked for William Herle, Roger Beler and Roger de Boudon to take an assize of novel disseisin was told that justices ought to be assigned by the chancellor and treasurer and was advised to go before them[3]. It was quite usual for requests for assizes to be accompanied by the names of the justices desired[4], and similar requests were made for justices of oyer and terminer[5]. Despite the king's reply to these petitions, justices of assize were frequently assigned by him in writs of privy seal to the chancellor[6], and by other warrant[7].

Besides the method of appointment, there were two other means by which the king could influence the justices. They were paid from the exchequer, the payments being entered on the issue rolls[8], and sometimes made by writ of liberate from the chancery[9], the liberates being often issued by warrant of privy seal[10]. The justices also took their oath before persons delegated by the king, often in the exchequer[11].

The appointment of some of the subordinate officers of chancery and exchequer also rested with the king. The keepership of the rolls of chancery, a most responsible position, was granted by the king in 1316 to Sir William de Ayremynne, clerk of the chancery, though the

[1] *Cal. Close Rolls*, 1313–18, p. 463. *Foedera*, vol. II, p. 326.

[2] *Rot. Parl.* vol. I, 372.

[3] Ancient Petition, no. 3982: "Justicii assignari debent per Cancellarium et Thesaurarium Ideo coram eis."

[4] Anc. Corresp. vol. XXXVI, no. 5. This request was addressed to the chancellor.

[5] Ibid. no. 38. Vide above, p. 112.

[6] E.g. Ghan. Warr., Files 104/4635, 105/4704, 129/7174.

[7] Anc. Corresp. vol. XXXV, no. 68 A.

[8] Issue Rolls, nos. 141–220 passim.

[9] Ibid.

[10] Vide below, p. 143.

[11] K. R. Mem. Roll, no. 102, m. 134 a. Hervy de Staunton, chief justice of common pleas, took the oath on 24 July, 1326, before the archbishop of York, treasurer, the bishop of Exeter, the chancellor, the barons of the exchequer and the justices of the common bench.

appointment was made with the assent of Sandale, chancellor[1]. On 26 May, 1324, the appointment of Richard de Ayremynne to that office was made by the king at Westminster with the assent of Baldock, chancellor[2]. In July, 1325, Sir Henry de Clif was appointed by the king at Westminster in the presence of Baldock, chancellor, and others of the council[3], no mention being made of the chancellor's assent. Various clerks of chancery were also appointed by the king by his writ of privy seal addressed to the chancellor[4].

The organisation of the exchequer was a much more intricate matter than that of the chancery. It had been the first of the departments to obtain an administration of its own, and the nature of its business was complicated and required a more highly developed and varied organisation. The chief baron of the exchequer was appointed by the king, the writs of appointment being enrolled on the patent roll[5]. The other barons were similarly appointed[6]. The chancellor of the exchequer[7] and the king's remembrancer[8] owed their offices to royal appointment; the treasurer's remembrancer was sometimes appointed by that official, though his fee was paid from the exchequer[9]. The treasurer's remembrancer was not invariably his nominee. Walter de Norwich, remembrancer of Langton, Edward I's treasurer, was forced to follow his master into disgrace, the king being very angry with him[10]. The king then appointed Hugh de Nottingham to the office[11]. A little under two months afterwards Norwich[12] was received back into favour and re-appointed. The king ordered Walter Reynolds, treasurer, to receive him in that office, and this was done on 19 November, 1307[13]. On 23 November he was given the custody of various lands and hundreds in Norfolk by

[1] *Cal. Close Rolls*, 1313–18, pp. 427–8. *Regist. J. de Sandale* (Hampshire Record Society), p. 355.

[2] *Cal. Close Rolls*, 1323–27, p. 186 (26 May, 1324).

[3] Ibid. p. 386 (4 July, 1325).

[4] Chan. Warr., File 61/385. Vide also below, pp. 137–8.

[5] *Cal. Pat. Rolls*, 1307–13, pp. 7, 141, 265, 433, 437; 1313–17, pp. 179, 606, 655.

[6] E.g. ibid. 1307–13, pp. 7, 16, 22, 44, 100, 141, 265, 348, 385, 437, 526, etc.

[7] E.g. ibid. pp. 6, 72, 225, 515, etc.

[8] Ibid. pp. 220, 273, 392.

[9] Tout, *The Place of Ed. II*, p. 346.

[10] K. R. Mem. Roll, no. 81, m. 38 d.

[11] *Cal. Close Rolls*, 1307–13, p. 2 (26 Sept. 1307).

[12] Tout, *The Place of Ed. II*, p. 346, note 2, assumes that Norwich was treasurer's remembrancer from the accession of Edward II, and attributes his position to the fact that Reynolds objected to Edward's interference with his office by the appointment of Hugh de Nottingham, and so reinstated the old treasurer's remembrancer. The facts as recorded in the K. R. Mem. Roll (the entry however is not contained in the L. T. R. Mem. Roll) do not agree with these suggestions.

[13] K. R. Mem. Roll, no. 81, m. 38 d.

exchequer writ[1], grants which were tested by the treasurer and appear like an earnest of his return to favour. These two occasions were not the only ones upon which the king appointed to this office. On 30 June, 1323, he ordered the treasurer and barons of the exchequer by privy seal to receive John Travers to the office of treasurer's remembrancer in place of William de Fulbourn[2]. Of the chamberlains, one was appointed by the king[3], and the other, until his death in 1315, by the earl of Warwick, who held the office in fee[4]. After 1315, as the heir to the earldom was a minor, the king appointed to this office also[5].

While these appointments were made by letters patent, notification and order to admit were sent to the exchequer under the privy seal. The patent for the appointment of Ingelard de Warle was dated 29 December, 1316[6]. On the same day a writ of privy seal was sent to the exchequer[7] and on 14 January, 1317, he was admitted to his office[8]. Robert de Wodehouse who succeeded Warle was appointed on 24 July, 1318[9], and by privy seal the barons were ordered to admit him on 14 October, 1318[10]. This notification of the appointment and the direct order to admit under the king's privy seal provided an additional safeguard to the king. The same instrument of privy seal was used in January, 1319, to order a decrease in the number of barons if necessary. The treasurer was ordered to advise what number and which of them might be spared[11]. Though this seemed to leave a considerable amount of discretionary power in the hands of the treasurer it was natural that in matters affecting the administration of his departments he should be consulted. Moreover the king restricted his action by providing that Robert de Wodehouse and John de Okham should continue to be barons[12].

Some of the minor officers of the exchequer were appointed by the treasurer. In 1307 John Deuery became writer of the exchequer

[1] K. R. Mem. Roll, no. 81, m. 5 d. L. T. R. Mem. Roll, no. 78, m. 5. Vide also K. R. Mem. Roll, no. 82, mm. 12 d, 39; L. T. R. Mem. Roll, no. 79, mm. 16, 72.

[2] K. R. Mem. Roll, no. 96, m. 40 d.

[3] E.g. *Cal. Pat. Rolls*, 1307–13, pp. 7, 442, 447.

[4] For the chamberlain in fee see below, pp. 312–313.

[5] *Cal. Pat. Rolls*, 1313–17, p. 345; 1324–27, p. 212.

[6] Ibid. 1313–17, p. 406.

[7] K. R. Mem. Roll, no. 90, m. 22. L. T. R. Mem. Roll, no. 87, Brev. dir. Hill. m. 1.

[8] K. R. Mem. Roll, no. 90, m. 106.

[9] *Cal. Pat. Rolls*, 1317–21, p. 193.

[10] Madox, *Hist. of Exch.* vol. II, p. 60.

[11] Ibid. vol. II, pp. 60–61. This is also discussed below, pp. 455, 461.

[12] Madox, *Hist. of Exch.* vol. II, pp. 60–61.

tallies during the treasurer's pleasure[1]. The serjeants of the benches took their oaths at the exchequer and were on occasions appointed there. On 15 December, 1310, the treasurer and barons were ordered to take the oath of office of Edmund de Passelewe, serjeant of common bench and exchequer, and Geoffrey de Hartlepool, serjeant of king's bench[2]. On 27 December they were ordered to appoint another serjeant more sufficient than Hartlepool to be sworn at the exchequer[3].

The problem of the appointment of the chief of the local officials, the sheriff, is one of difficulty[4]. Throughout the reign, it can be fairly said that the appointment, or the principal part in the appointment, lay in the hands of the king. When the appointments were made in the exchequer the king influenced them by his writs of privy seal; and when others of the council were associated with the exchequer officials in the appointment the king still exerted his influence in the same way.

The subordinate officials of the local administration, the bailiffs of manors and lands, were appointed by writ of exchequer or chancery, in both cases the writ being often awarded by the king's request. The officials of the forest were appointed by writ of chancery and there was hardly an official of the local administration which the king could not appoint if he desired. That considerable measure of discretionary power which was left to chancery, exchequer and others was not always willingly exercised by them. The office of chamberlain of North Wales was vacant, and Roger Mortimer, justice, was ordered to appoint. He replied that there was no suitable man available and the treasurer wrote to the king on behalf of the council urging him to appoint immediately[5].

Sufficient has been said of the appointment of officials, central and local, chief and subordinate, to suggest that the control of the great departments of the administration, as far as the personnel of the officials went, was entirely in the king's hands. The way the king's choice of officials was dictated by the features of the household system and the influence of that system upon the administration will be treated more fully later.

Besides the appointment of officials the other great means of exercising control over the government was by regulating the issue of the great seal, the great instrument of administration. As long as the chancellor was a personal member of the king's court, writs under the great seal could be issued by direct verbal order. With

[1] Issue Roll, no. 141, m. 1. [2] K. R. Mem. Roll, no. 84, m 16
[3] Ibid. m. 19 d. [4] It will be fully discussed below, pp. 521–7.
[5] K. R. Mem. Roll, no. 85, m. 55 d.

the growth of business, the chancery with its corporation of clerks became an important and immobile department and the chancellor realised greater independence and discretion. The king could no longer exercise direct control over the issue of the great seal, so warrants under the privy seal were introduced. The issue of chancery warrants under the privy seal was a normal means of communicating the king's consent or desire for the issue of letters under the great seal[1].

Besides these direct royal warrants there were other warrants which were quite normal. Large numbers of writs were still issued on direct royal order[2] or by royal order conveyed by messenger[3]. When the king was abroad or in the Scottish war, and a lieutenant or guardian had been appointed, writs were addressed to the chancellor ordering the issue of writs under the great seal. These warrants of the regent were sealed with his own privy seal and had the force and effect of warrants under the king's privy seal. Warrants of this nature of the earl of Gloucester, who was regent after the death of the earl of Lincoln in 1311, survive ordering prohibition of a tournament[4] and an inquiry concerning a gathering[5].

A number of writs of June and July, 1313, were witnessed by John, bishop of Bath and Wells[6]. Two of these contain the addition "by council[7]," one the formula "by bishop of Worcester[8]." They are all concerned with the appointment of commissions of oyer and terminer and other judicial commissions, and the explanation seems that for a part of this time the seal was in the custody of Adam de Osgodby, Robert de Bardelby and William de Ayremynne[9], and during the whole of the time there was no chancellor, but Walter Reynolds was acting as keeper[10]. Writs are frequently issued by "petition of council[11]," sometimes "by council[12]" or by "king and council[13]." The council at times sought protection for their action in the formula "by council because it was sealed at another time by

[1] Cf. Chancery Warrants, Series 1; vide also Eugène Déprez, *Études de Diplomatique Anglaise, Le Sceau Privé, Le Sceau Sécret, Le Signet.*

[2] Verbal orders will be discussed below, pp. 166–174.

[3] Indirect verbal orders will be discussed below, pp. 167–9, 171–4.

[4] Anc. Corresp. vol. XXXV, no. 93. Vide App. of Doc. no. 107.

[5] Anc. Corresp. vol. XXXV, no. 94.

[6] *Cal. Pat. Rolls*, 1307–13, pp. 604–615. *Cal. Close Rolls*, 1307–13, p. 539; 1313–18, p. 66.

[7] *Cal. Pat. Rolls*, 1307–13, p. 605.

[8] Ibid. p. 604.

[9] 13 June, 1313 (*Cal. Close Rolls*, 1307–13, p. 583). 26 July, 1313 (ibid. 1313–18, p. 67).

[10] Vide above, pp. 118–119.

[11] E.g. *Cal. Close Rolls*, 1318–23, pp. 439, 448, 472.

[12] E.g. *Cal. Fine Rolls*, 1307–19, pp. 313, 314.

[13] Ibid. p. 318.

king[1]." Another curious instance of writs issued by council is "sealed at another time by king and council and renewed by privy seal[2]." The council's control over the issue of the great seal was not however vast. If it seemed to the council that the form of a writ was not drawn up according to the use and custom of the chancery, the writ could be recalled only after a conference between the king and the great council, in which the king ordered that full justice be done[3]. The council had in fact control over the great seal only with the king's consent. In the parliament of York, 1318, it was agreed by the king, prelates, earls and barons that the burgesses of Newcastle-on-Tyne should have pardon of their farm for two years, and accordingly it was ordered that command be made to the chancellor on the king's behalf to make a writ of great seal to them[4].

In addition to the constant normal check with which the king regulated the use of the great seal, there were a large number of expedients which he could use in times of stress and strain. The reign of Edward II illustrates the use of such expedients to counteract the growing influence of the baronial opposition. The easiest and most natural method was to take the great seal away from its custodian. A writ could then be written but could not receive driving force without the addition of the seal. Thus a writ was drawn up on 24 October, 1311, ordering the treasurer and barons of the exchequer to take the lands of Henry de Beaumont into the king's hands until the king had received from their issues the value of all sums received by Beaumont from lands, wardships and marriages granted to him after 16 March, 1310, contrary to the Ordinance. The writ had to be vacated because it was not sealed[5], for the seal was then in the king's possession[6]. When the king was in the north in May, 1312, endeavouring to protect Gavaston from the wrath of the barons, the seal was deposited in the wardrobe, in the custody of Edmund de Mauley, steward[7]. On frequent occasions the custodians of the seal

[1] *Cal. Close Rolls*, 1323–27, pp. 46, 48.

[2] *Cal. Fine Rolls*, 1319–27, pp. 59, 66.

[3] *Rot. Parl.* vol. I, p. 297.

[4] Cole, *Doc. illustr. Eng. Hist. in 13th and 14th Cent.* pp. 7–8: "et ensint fait la comaundement au Chanceller depar le Roi qe il les feust de ce aver bref du grant seal."

[5] *Cal. Fine Rolls*, 1307–19, p. 107.

[6] The seal was surrendered on 28 Sept. 1311 (*Cal. Close Rolls*, 1307–13, p. 438) and the keepers received it again on 9 Dec. 1311 (ibid. p. 433).

[7] *Cal. Close Rolls*, 1307–13, pp. 448, 459–460, 552. On 4 May Edmund de Mauley had the seal at Newcastle-on-Tyne and writs were sealed there. After the sealing of writs he took the seal with him and on the very same day Lancaster and other barons arrived at Newcastle, the king proceeding to Tynemouth and afterwards to Scarborough. The seal was returned to the keepers on 17 May (*Cal. Close Rolls*, 1307–13, pp. 459–460).

were summoned to come to the king with the seal, sometimes with the whole of the chancery office sometimes in person only[1]. Once, they were summoned to come to the king immediately with the great seal and the seal of the bishopric of Durham, and to bring with them Adam de Brom to receive the latter seal in the king's presence[2].

The crises of the years 1321 and 1322 are well marked in the history of the seal during that period. On 16 April, 1321, when the king had gone to Gloucester in anticipation of trouble between Despenser and the barons of the Welsh march[3], the chancellor delivered the seal to the king in his chamber and it was given to Roger de Northburgh to keep in the wardrobe[4]. When the king was besieging Leeds Castle later in the same year, he ordered the keepers of the great seal to come to him there on 3 November, and the whole chancery was to stay at Maidstone[5]. After the siege of Leeds the king made his way towards the western march[6] and the keepers of the great seal were ordered to proceed to Gloucester and there perform their office awaiting the coming of the king[7]. Indeed it can be said that from 5 November, 1321, to 24 January, 1322, one of the most critical periods in the whole reign, the great seal was in the king's possession when it was not in use[8], and again after 3 March, 1322, it was in his possession[9]. On occasion the king had difficulty in securing compliance with his orders. On 10 January, 1323, William de Ayremynne, Master Henry de Clif, William de Clif and William de Herlaston obtained the custody of the great seal[10]. Eight days afterwards they were ordered to leave everything and come to the king, with the whole chancery, with all possible haste[11]. On 28 January another writ of privy seal was despatched to the keepers marvelling greatly at their delay in carrying out the king's orders, and ordering hasty compliance[12]. Still the keepers did not go and a further order was necessitated on 28 February. They were to end all excuses, leave everything and appear before the king without delay[13]. By having the great seal and its keepers near him, the king could exercise a decisive

[1] E.g. Chan. Warr., File 95/3739, 3771. [2] Ibid. File 95/3752.

[3] The struggle did not actually break out until 4 May, 1321. Vide *Trans. R. Hist. Soc.* vol. IX [1914–15], J. C. Davies, 'Despenser War in Glamorgan,' p. 53.

[4] *Cal. Close Rolls*, 1318–23, p. 366.

[5] Chan. Warr., File 116/5884 (2 Nov. 1321). [6] *Auct. Malm.* p. 263.

[7] Chan. Warr., File 117/5942 (28 Jan 1322).

[8] *Cal. Close Rolls*, 1318–23, p. 478.

[9] Ibid. [10] Ibid. p. 689.

[11] Chan. Warr., File 121/6349 (18 Jan. 1323).

[12] Ibid. File 121/6370, Newark (27 Jan. 1323).

[13] Ibid. File 122/6429, Knaresborough.

influence upon its use, and the expedient of taking the seal from the custodian in time of danger and crisis was final.

An equally drastic and equally effective means of regulating the use of the great seal was the method of having writs sealed in the king's presence. On two occasions during the troubles between king and barons over Gavaston this was done. On the first banishment of Gavaston in 1308[1] the king appointed him his lieutenant in Ireland, letters patent to this effect being dated 16 June, 1308[2]. Letters to the king of France, asking his intervention on behalf of Gavaston, and to the pope and cardinals, asking them to suspend the sentence of excommunication made by Winchelsey against him, were also issued on the same day[3]. After the enrolment of these letters on the patent roll occurs the following note: "the above letters were read and sealed before the king, the king himself commanding them to be sealed in the presence of the earl of Richmond, Henry de Percy, Hugh le Despenser, William de Melton and Adam de Osgodby[4]." This record was probably made in order to safeguard the chancellor, though it is equally probable that he was unwilling to seal these writs in the formal way[5], though he was at that time at London and the king at Langley. The king ordered the chancellor to send him the seal, and it was returned the following day[6].

In the second instance, the chancellor was certainly an unwilling instrument, and the writs were sealed only under threat of forfeiture. Gavaston returned to England from exile at Christmas, 1311[7], and early in January the king proceeded north to join him[8]. Osgodby, Bardelby and Ayremynne, who had obtained the seal on 19 December, 1311[9], were summoned on 7 January, 1312, to bring the seal to the king at York[10]. On 18 January the king announced that Gavaston had been banished contrary to the law[11] and two days later his estates were restored to him[12]. It was these writs which the chancellor declined to seal and accordingly they were sealed in the king's presence

[1] Vide J. H. Ramsay, *The Genesis of Lancaster*, vol. I, pp. 13–15.
[2] *Cal. Pat. Rolls*, 1307–13, p. 83.
[3] *Foedera*, vol. II, pp. 49–50.
[4] *Cal. Pat. Rolls*, 1307–13, p. 83. Cf. *Parl. Writs*, vol. II, Pt ii, App. p. 15.
[5] Cf. Ramsay, *Genesis of Lancaster*, vol. I, p. 15.
[6] *Cal. Close Rolls*, 1307–13, p. 68.
[7] *Ann. Lond.* p. 202. *Auct. Bridl.* pp. 41–42. *Auct. Malm.* p. 174.
[8] *Auct. Malm.* p. 174.
[9] *Cal. Close Rolls*, 1307–13, p. 447. *Parl. Writs*, vol. II, Pt i, p. 77.
[10] *Cal. Close Rolls*, 1307–13, p. 448. *Parl. Writs*, vol. II, Pt i, p. 77.
[11] *Cal. Close Rolls*, 1307–13, pp. 448–9 (18 Jan. 1312). *Foedera*, vol. II, p. 153.
[12] *Cal.rClose Rolls*, 1307–13, p. 449 (20 Jan. 1312). *Foedera*, vol. II, p. 154.

and handed to him after being sealed. To the enrolment of the writ proclaiming Gavaston faithful the following memorandum was added:

"Fet a remember que la dite forme fu fete par le Roi meismes, et le seal et les breefs par lui livere a lespigurnel pur sealer le jour et le lieu contenuz es ditz breefs, et il tantost quant les breefs furent seales en sa presence, les prist en sa main, et les mist sur son lit[1]."

To the enrolment of the other writs the following note was added: "Memorandum, that these writs were made in the king's presence by his order under threats of grievous forfeiture, and that he retained them after they were sealed[2]."

An expedient closely akin to the sealing of writs in the king's presence was that of sending messengers to the chancery, before whom the form of the writ was determined and sealed. This plan was pursued in 1316, when the king's messengers were the earls of Pembroke and Hereford, Bartholomew de Badlesmere and Anthony Pessaign, and both the writs were in favour of Griffith de la Pole who had been a strenuous supporter of Lancaster in opposition to Sir John de Cherleton, lord of Powys and husband of Griffith's niece[3]. Both writs were dated 10 October, 1316. The first was a pardon at the instance of Lancaster for all trespasses committed by Griffith in his quarrel with Cherleton[4]; the second writ restored to Griffith his lands which had been taken into the king's hands, the restoration being made at Lancaster's request[5]. Both writs are described as issued "by king on information of the earls of Pembroke and Hereford, Bartholomew de Badlesmere and Anthony Pessaign in whose presence the said writ was read and agreed upon[6]." The form of writs under the exchequer seal was also determined in the presence of royal messengers, one to the sheriff of Kent about the Templars issued on 14 March, 1308, being agreed upon by the treasurer and barons in the presence of the count of Savoy and John de Drokensford[7].

[1] *Foedera*, vol. II, p. 153.

[2] *Cal. Close Rolls*, 1307–13, p. 449. *Foedera*, vol. II, p. 154.

[3] The disputed succession to Powys is a complicated problem involving the question of the Welsh and English laws of inheritance and the position of Powys as a marcher barony. It has been dealt with in detail in a thesis, *The history of Wales during the reign of Edward II*, J. C. Davies, which the Honourable Society of Cymmrodorion will publish shortly.

[4] *Cal. Pat. Rolls*, 1313–17, p. 548.

[5] *Cal. Close Rolls*, 1313–18, pp. 369–370.

[6] *Cal. Pat. Rolls*, 1313–17, p. 548. *Cal. Close Rolls*, 1313–18, pp. 369–370.

[7] L. T. R. Mem. Roll, no. 78, m. 81: "et memorandum quod forma huiusmodi mandati concordata fuit per Thesaurarium et Barones in presencia A. comitis Sabaudie et Johannis de Drokensford."

The chancellor was on occasion ordered to consider a matter and consult the king before letters under the great seal were issued. In 1326 a petition was sent to Baldock, chancellor, which touched the royal right and profit. He was to consider the petition but to execute no decision without first consulting the king[1]. A petition from Bristol was enclosed to the chancellor and treasurer, who were ordered to examine the petition and charters; the king expressed surprise that despite a previous prohibition they had granted so considerable a matter without first showing it to him. This might be held to infer that the writs which were to achieve the purpose of the petition were not to be granted before the king had previously seen them[2].

The issue of letters under the great seal might also be regulated by an agreement made between the king and his chancellor. Such an agreement had been made by Edward I with his chancellor, the bishop of Bath and Wells[3], though this was administrative in effect and was concerned with the ordinary routine of the chancery and not with special cases under extraordinary circumstances. In 1306 another expedient was used. Three writs which were directed to the pope and others of his court were not enrolled and transcripts of them were not delivered to the roll. The writs were delivered to the seal by the hands of Master John de Cadomo. Later the same day two further writs were sealed in the same matter, without enrolment or the delivery of transcripts and in this case Cadomo was warned and required by Osgodby, a chancery clerk, to deliver transcripts[4].

Very similar to this plan was that of sending writs to the chancery to be sealed only, the form being determined by the king or his advisers. On 19 January, 1309, the king sent to the bishop of Chichester, chancellor, procuratorial letters patent which he ordered to be sealed with the great seal and handed to the bearer[5]. In the Gavaston crisis of early 1312 a parliament which had been summoned for 13 February was countermanded[6], the writs being sent out on

[1] Chan. Warr., File 131/7386.

[2] Ibid. File 134/7571.

[3] The king ordered that the following writs should not pass his seal without his special order, writs of protection overt, of general attorney in all pleas, of safe conduct, of attorney "dedimus potestatem," of inquest of lands in the king's hands by wardship, escheat or otherwise, of inquest in order to amortize lands. The order was in an indented schedule, the bishop retaining one part and the other going into the king's wardrobe (*Cal. Close Rolls*, 1288–96, pp. 201–2).

[4] *Cal. Close Rolls*, 1302–7, p. 453.

[5] Chan. Warr., File 61/379.

[6] *Cal. Close Rolls*, 1307–13, p. 449. *Parl. Writs*, vol. II, Pt ii, p. 70.

the day that the great seal was in the king's possession and was being used in favour of Gavaston[1].

There were two other checks upon the use of the great seal which were of considerable importance—the use of the privy seal and the conveyance of verbal orders by the king himself or by his messengers. These two methods were in far greater use than the others and were most efficacious. Their detailed treatment will be more conveniently given below[2]. A single instance in which mention was made of both these checks is sufficient at present. On 26 October, 1319, the king ordered the bishop of Ely, chancellor, "not to make execution of any mandate under the king's seal on the information of any person whatever unless the king shall have told the chancellor his will concerning the same by word of mouth or shall send him a letter under his privy seal[3]."

The description of the various ways in which the household influenced and controlled the administration has not been exhausted, but sufficient has been said to lead to the detailed consideration of the manner in which the household, standing outside the administration and independent of it, was yet able to control it. It retained all the guidance and correction which a parent exercises, for it was the parent of the administrative departments. The appointment of officials, central and local, chief and minor, was almost entirely in the king's hands, and the way in which the personnel of the household obtained offices in the administration will be treated at length later. Hardly less important than the appointment of officials was the regulation of the great seal, the most potent instrument in administration. The completeness of the control of the government by the household will be more fully realised when its other sources of strength have been considered, for they were all interdependent.

[1] *Cal. Close Rolls*, 1307–13, p. 449. *Foedera*, vol. II, p. 154.

[2] For the use of the privy seal as a check upon the great seal and for the check by verbal orders see below, pp. 133–6, 166–170.

[3] *Cal. Close Rolls*, 1318–23, p. 211.

CHAPTER V

THE STRENGTH OF THE HOUSEHOLD SYSTEM (*cont.*)

(ii) *Executive*

The household system was independent of the government, and various spheres in which its independence was expressed and assured will now be discussed. It must not be supposed that the independence of the household system in these various directions, executive, finance, justice, personnel, meant that it was apart from the general administration. Its own departments were independent of the administrative departments. This independence is important because it assured the king freedom from outside control; but it is of far greater importance because by virtue of its independence it was able to exercise decisive influence upon the administrative departments.

The household had various instruments and offices. In the privy seal it had an instrument of executive authority which was also the final and most potent influence of the executive in the administrative departments. A study of the executive as formed and controlled by the household is of vital importance and leads from the consideration of ways in which it controlled the government to the consideration of the problems of the financial and judicial aspects of the household, aspects in which the independence of administration is of rather more importance than the control exercised over the administrative departments.

As the great seal and its office of the chancery was the normal executive instrument of the great departments, the privy seal with its office of keeper and clerks was the normal executive instrument of the household. The privy seal was not merely an instrument of the household. In various ways it interfered with the use of the great seal and acted as a check upon it. The great seal was the formal, the privy seal the effective instrument of the executive. The privy seal was not resorted to only on abnormal occasions and for very important matters. In normal times the privy seal was used as a normal warrant for the great seal and for matters of special grace and matters especially affecting the king; in abnormal times as warrant and prohibition it was the most effective instrument the king possessed.

Some indication of the number of writs issued under the privy seal can be obtained from the fact that between 18 July, 1310, and 13 February, 1311, payments for the delivery of 139 writs of privy seal were made in the wardrobe[1]. Besides warrants to the chancellor and treasurer, included in this number were many to the earls of Cornwall and Gloucester, Hugh le Despenser, the queen, the earl of Lincoln, Oliver de Bordeaux, Robert de Clifford and others, as well as many to various sheriffs and justices[2]. From 16 February, 1311, to 7 July, 1311, payments for the delivery of 157 writs of privy seal were made in the wardrobe[3]. These numbers represent but a portion of those issued during that time, as payments for the delivery of all writs of privy seal were not made there. Some were delivered directly at court to the persons to whom they were addressed. Others were delivered and payment to the messengers made out of the exchequer[4]. The frequent use of writs of privy seal is also illustrated by the notification which the king made to the sheriffs of London after he had lost his privy seal at Bannockburn[5]. He informed them of the loss and ordered proclamation to be made that no attention be paid to any command that might appear under it, without further order from the king, unless the order was to the king's profit and honour[6], a warning against forgery which was not unwarranted[7].

The ordinary check of the privy seal upon the issue of the great seal may be said to have taken the form of warrants to make a writ on a specific subject, and on occasion writs were made out only on such warrants. On 25 November, 1310, the chancellor or a chancery clerk writing to the chancery ordered that no business be done except such as instructed by himself, who had his orders under the privy seal[8].

There was also a negative method of checking the issue of writs by specifically prohibiting a writ on some matter, and this was a check used on several important occasions during the reign. In 1308 the king ordered the chancellor to do nothing in the warrant to him

[1] K. R. Acct. 374/7 passim.
[2] Ibid.
[3] Ibid. 373/30 passim.
[4] Issue Roll, no. 172, m. 9.
[5] Cf. *Eng. Hist. Rev.* vol. XXIII [1908], p. 558; *Cal. Doc. Scotl.* vol. III, p. 71. Cf. Chan. Warr., File 1328 passim. The king also lost his privy seal at Byland, 1322 (*Cal. Close Rolls*, 1318–23, p. 682; *Foedera*, vol. II, p. 498).
[6] Cf. *Foedera*, vol. II, p. 249; *Cal. Letter Books, E*, p. 36 (27 June, 1314); *Cal. Close Rolls*, 1313–18, p. 104.
[7] Cf. K. R. Mem. Roll, no. 81, m. 20; *Cal. Close Rolls*, 1307–13, p. 11.
[8] *Cal. Doc. Scotl.* vol. III, p. 33.

touching the liberation of two Scottish prisoners[1]. This countermanding of an order is not a very important example and greater importance attaches to warrants of prohibition addressed to the chancellor. In the triumph of the ordainers in 1311 baronial partizans sought to push their advantage in their personal or territorial disputes with royal supporters. Griffith de la Pole, who had a dispute with John de Cherleton, appeared before the council for a writ to inquire whether the lands of Powys which he claimed, were held by Welsh tenure or of the crown of England. The chancellor was strongly forbidden to make such a writ without special order from the king by word of mouth[2]. The reason given by the king was that the matter greatly touched the dignity of his crown which he was compelled to preserve[3]: but the fact that Griffith was a Lancastrian partizan[4] had some influence upon the royal action. Another instance of a writ of privy seal to the chancery has an interest from the endorsements which were made upon it. On 14 June, 1314, a merchant was pardoned for taking provisions and other goods to the Scots and otherwise communicating with them. This writ of privy seal remained inoperative as it was delivered into the chancery after the order that such writs should have no effect. The king however afterwards ordered it to have effect despite the endorsement[5].

The power of prohibiting a writ by privy seal was exercised in favour of the younger Despenser on at least two occasions in 1321. When the Despenser war in Glamorgan was imminent, the king ordered that no writ was to pass against the Welsh lands of Hugh the son without special order[6]. After the exile of the Despensers the interests of the son were safeguarded by a command that no writ touching the property of Eleanor la Despenser was to issue from the chancery[7]. The property was then in the king's hands[8], and, as long as it remained in his hands ungranted, its restitution would not be difficult. Such writs of prohibition were frequent and touched all sides of administration, though they generally did not possess the political importance

[1] *Cal. Doc. Scotl.* vol. III, p. 10.

[2] Chan. Warr., File 82/2430 (28 Oct. 1311): "vous mandoms et chargeoms fermement enioignantz qe vous ne facez faire nulle commission denquerre coment les dites terres sont tenues sanz especial mandement de nostre bouche."

[3] Ibid.: "Cele busoigne touche molt la dignete de nostre coroune a la quele garder nous sumes tenuz."

[4] *Ann. Lond.* p. 224. *Cal. Pat. Rolls*, 1307–13, p. 546. Vide also above, p. 130.

[5] *Cal. Doc. Scotl.* vol. III, p. 69.

[6] Chan. Warr., File 134/7546. Vide App. of Doc. no. 82 (4 April, 1321).

[7] Chan. Warr., File 116/5890. Vide App. of Doc. no. 71 (13 Nov. 1321).

[8] Ibid.

of these two instances. Warrant was not to be made for the delivery of a castle until the king had been advised[1]; fine was not to be taken without other order from a widow who had married without licence[2], protection was not to be made in a specific case without special order[3].

Besides checking the use of the great seal the privy seal could also be used as a substitute for it. The king's peace was proclaimed in London in 1307 by virtue of a writ of privy seal[4]. Gavaston's recall in January, 1312, was proclaimed in London by order of privy seal[5]; and about the same time a large number of writs under that seal were sent to the mayor and others in London touching the safeguarding of the city. The city was to be kept for the king's use and no armed force was to enter[6]. John de Gisors and other city magnates were urged to influence the citizens to undertake the defence so that it might be kept for the king[7]. Later, earls and barons who were unsuspected were to be allowed to enter provided they did not bring horses or arms[8]. This use of the privy seal in times of crisis in purely administrative orders was especially valuable to the king as it was not then of the greatest importance what action the chancellor was likely to take; as in the privy seal the king had a substitute for the great seal.

On one occasion during the reign the whole of the administration depended upon the privy seal. On 26 October, 1326, Edward, duke of Aquitaine, having been chosen keeper of the realm, commenced to exercise the rights under his privy seal because the great seal was still in the possession of his father[9]. Even summonses to parliament were then issued without the great seal[10].

The uses of the privy seal as a check upon, or rather as a prohibition to, and as a substitute for the great seal have been illustrated. At greater length will be treated the direct use of the privy seal as an independent warrant to the central departments of the chancery and exchequer, to the justices and the local administration.

The privy seal was used as a direct administrative warrant to the

[1] Chan. Warr., File 122/6464. Vide App. of Doc. no. 76.

[2] Chan. Warr., File 116/5832, 5857. App. of Doc. nos. 69, 70.

[3] Chan. Warr., File 115/5723. Vide also Files 60/293, 70/1213, 99/4173, 110/5283.

[4] *Cal. Letter Books, C*, p. 155.

[5] Camd. Soc. vol. XXXIV [1846], *De Antiquis Legibus Liber*, ed. T. Stapleton, App. p. 252. Vide also above, pp. 129–130.

[6] *Parl. Writs*, vol. II, Pt i, p. 77. *Cal. Letter Books, D*, p. 278.

[7] *Parl. Writs*, vol. II, Pt i, p. 78.

[8] *Cal. Letter Books, D*, p. 278.

[9] *Cal. Close Rolls*, 1323–27, p. 655.

[10] *Parl. Writs*, vol. II, Pt ii, p. 350.

chancery for other purposes than the issue of writs. Orders concerning the office of the chancery and its business were thus sent. When the king wished the chancellor or keeper of the great seal to come to him they were ordered in this way[1]. On 1 February, 1322, the king ordered William de Ayremynne to cease all other business on account of the great business which employed the king[2]. By means of the privy seal the king recommended matters which interested him to the chancery[3]. Orders which had been made previously were cancelled by privy seal, even such comparatively unimportant orders as protection and general attorney[4]. Information which the king desired was by writ of privy seal ordered to be sent to him. In 1323 the king wished to know whether Harclay, earl of Carlisle, had any commission under the great seal to treat with the Scots, and if so, for what term. William de Ayremynne was ordered to search the rolls of chancery to discover this and to send the answer by the bearer of the request[5]. Recognisances made before the king were sent under writ of privy seal to be enrolled in the chancery[6]. The chancellor was ordered "ne doignez nule foi ne neu facez rien" concerning inquests touching Wales made by the escheator south of Trent[7]. By another writ the chancery was forbidden without further order to give seisin to Lancaster of the castle of Denbigh which had belonged to the earl of Lincoln[8]. Though the usual way of obtaining writs and commissions was by application to the chancery, there are numerous instances of commissions of oyer and terminer[9], assizes of novel disseisin[10], and inquisitions *ad quod damnum*[11], being ordered by writ of privy seal. Some of these warrants under the privy seal had been enrolled on the chancery rolls during the reign of Edward I[12].

Officials of chancery were sometimes appointed by privy seal. In 1323 the king ordered Master Roger de Cliseby to have charge of the hanaper[13]. When the king greatly desired the promotion of a clerk

[1] Vide above, pp. 127–8.

[2] Chan. Warr., File 117/5948, 5949. Vide App. of Doc. no. 72.

[3] Keepers of the great seal were ordered to treat in as gracious and as favourable a manner as possible the business which Maud the widow of John Botetourte laid before them (Chan. Warr., File 128/7024, 30 Nov. 1324).

[4] Chan. Warr., File 104/4658 (25 April, 1318).

[5] *Cal. Doc. Scotl.* vol. III, p. 148 (13 Jan. 1323).

[6] *Cal. Close Rolls*, 1296–1302, p. 405.

[7] Chan. Warr., File 76/1857.

[8] Ibid. File 78/2047.

[9] Chan. Warr., Files 122/6432, 6484; 123/6518; 129/7170, 7175; 132/7406.

[10] Ibid. Files 106/4816; 110/5245; 111/5318; 114/5613; 119/6196; 120/6261.

[11] Ibid. Files 122/6431, 125/6755.

[12] *Cal. Close Rolls*, 1272–79, p. 395; 1279–88, p. 409.

[13] Chan. Warr., File 125/6778.

he wrote to one of the keepers of the seal to make the clerk a writer in chancery[1] or ordered that he should be received as a writer in chancery and enrolled among the other clerks of chancery[2]. A clerk was reinstated in the position he had previously occupied in the chancery[3], and the appointment of one clerk by privy seal was sometimes accompanied by the order to dismiss another to make room for him[4]. William de Ayremynne, who very frequently acted as a keeper of the seal, was by writ of privy seal, of the king's special grace, granted the same fee as the chancellor on occasions on which he held the household of the chancery[5].

Another important sphere in which the writ of privy seal touched the administration of the chancery was on its judicial side. Petitions were sent to the chancery by the king under the privy seal[6] with the injunction that award was to be made according to law and reason[7], or in as good a manner as possible[8]. Gavaston, when guardian of England, ordered the chancellor to hear the business of Sir Robert de Clavering a clerk, and arrange suitable remedy according to law and custom[9]. Petitions which had been considered by the council and endorsed, the endorsement being acceptable to the king, were sent to the chancellor under privy seal with the order to view the petition and to do what was necessary concerning that matter[10]. The privy seal entered in the initiation of processes in the chancery; and in subsequent stages. An inquisition concerning a manor was sent to the chancellor under privy seal who was commanded to view the muniments concerning the enfeoffment and do right[11].

The use of the privy seal in the exchequer[12] was as considerable as in the chancery, and as the writs addressed to the exchequer were both enrolled on the memoranda rolls of the king's and treasurer's remembrancers and filed—the writs addressed to the chancery being filed only[13]—the information is fuller and more accurate. The privy seal was used in all kinds of cases as a direct warrant to the treasurer.

[1] Anc. Corresp. vol. XLV, no. 205.
[2] Chan. Warr., File 122/6443.
[3] Ibid. File 123/6550.
[4] Ibid. File 121/6390.
[5] Stowe MS. 553, f. 116.
[6] Vide Chancery Warrants, passim; for Edward II's reign, Files 58–134.
[7] E.g. Chan. Warr., File 58/31.
[8] E.g. ibid. File 59/127.
[9] Anc. Corresp. vol. XXXV, no. 57: "Et ordeinz couenable dreiture solonc la lei et le usage du Roiaume."
[10] Chan. Warr., File 130/7220.
[11] *Cal. Inq. P. M.* vol. VI, p. 348.
[12] Cf. Madox, *Hist. of Exch.* vol. II, pp. 125–6, 144–5, 230.
[13] Cf. *Cal. Close Rolls*, 1296–1302, p. 136. Chan. Warr., File 1703: "par lettre de son priue seal que demoert en filez as Roulles eit grant sa protection."

Inquisitions were sent to the treasurer under the privy seal[1]. Warrants were sent ordering appointment to sheriffdoms[2]. The treasurer and chamberlains were ordered by privy seal to stay at their offices during the vacation in order to attend to urgent exchequer business[3]. When the king desired information from the exchequer it was ordered under privy seal. He might desire to know the value of a bailiwick. Search would be made in the exchequer and an official would send the information to the king in a letter[4]. The king might desire to know the nature of the tenure of certain lands[5], and this information the exchequer, as the revenue administration and as the treasury of records, could supply. When the king was dissatisfied with the conduct and business of the exchequer, that body was summoned to him by writ of privy seal to explain its conduct[6].

The privy seal was addressed to the exchequer in matters of grace to private individuals[7] as well as in official correspondence. Fines before justices of oyer and terminer were remitted and the exchequer ordered to acquit them[8]. The king wrote recommending the business which touched certain persons and asked that all possible favour, without offending right, should be shown them[9]. When land was requested the king wrote to the chancellor and treasurer to certify him as speedily as possible if the grant could be made without damage to the king[10], and subsequently the land was granted by writ of privy seal[11]. The king made great efforts to secure a better office at the exchequer for Richard de Luda. He wrote on 24 April, 1310, making that order[12], on 22 May[13], and again on 7 August[14], and eventually he was admitted to the office of marshal of the exchequer on 16 January, 1313, on the presentation of Nicholas de Segrave[15], then marshal. It is of interest to note that a royal nominee only succeeded in obtaining a better office on the presentation of one who held the office in fee.

[1] *Cal. Close Rolls*, 1288–96, p. 508.
[2] Vide below, pp. 521–7 for appointment of sheriffs.
[3] Madox, *Hist. of Exch.* vol. II, p. 6, note c.
[4] Anc. Corresp. vol. XXXV, no. 27. Vide App. of Doc. no. 103.
[5] Anc. Corresp. vol. XXXIII, no. 141.
[6] K. R. Mem. Roll, no. 83, m. 23 (12 May, 1310).
[7] Cf. K. R. Mem. Roll, no. 81, m. 3 d.
[8] K. R. Mem. Roll, no. 94, m. 54. L. T. R. Mem. Roll, no. 91, Brev. Trin. m. 4.
[9] L. T. R. Mem. Roll, no. 78, m. 63 d.
[10] K. R. Mem. Roll, no. 90, m. 37. L. T. R. Mem. Roll, no. 87, Brev. dir. Pasch. m. 7 (24 April, 1317).
[11] K. R. Mem. Roll, no. 90, m. 50 d. L. T. R. Mem. Roll, no. 87, Brev. dir. Trin. m. 13 d (13 June, 1317).
[12] K. R. Mem. Roll, no. 83, m. 20 d.
[13] Ibid. m. 25.
[14] Ibid. no. 84, m. 5 d.
[15] Ibid. no. 86, m. 75.

More important, from the consideration of the methods by which the king could meet or counteract the movements of baronial opposition, are the ways in which the privy seal could restrict the action of exchequer officials. The most frequent method was to command that nothing be done in a certain matter without the king's special order. The order would be general in its application and exception could only be made by direct warrant under the privy seal. On several occasions it was ordered that no payments or assignments be made to anyone without express mention of that order[1]. Special orders of this description were issued in favour of the Bardi in 1317[2]. Orders of this general nature were of importance as affecting the whole of exchequer administration, and memoranda of their enrolment were made in the Red Book of the Exchequer[3]. Such orders generally referred to debts due to the exchequer[4] and emphasise the financial chaos of the reign[5]. In returning the exchequer ordinances of 1321 to the exchequer, the king ordered that nothing was to be paid or allowed by these ordinances without the king's special order[6]. The barons of the exchequer were in like manner ordered not to grant attorney to any sheriff or other who had to make account at the exchequer without special order from the king[7], though the king subsequently permitted a sheriff to assign another to appear at the proffer, and he was not to be distressed for his failure to appear[8].

In a large number of specific cases also the exchequer was prohibited from acting without special order from the king. The most important class of writs of this nature are those which ordered the treasurer and barons not to remove sheriffs from their offices without another or special order[9]. The number of these writs of privy seal

[1] K. R. Mem. Roll, no. 90, m. 22. L. T. R. Mem. Roll, no. 87, Brev. dir. Hill. m. 1. K. R. Mem. Roll, no. 92, Brev. dir. Mich. m. 12. L. T. R. Mem. Roll, no. 89, m. 71 d.

[2] K. R. Mem. Roll, no. 91, Brev. dir. Mich. 1 d. L. T. R. Mem. Roll, no. 88, Brev. dir. Mich. m. 1 d.

[3] *Red Book of Exchequer*, ed. H. Hall, vol. III, pp. 840–1.

[4] Cf. K. R. Mem. Roll, no. 96, m. 35. Vide Madox, *Hist. of Exch.* vol. II, pp. 72–73.

[5] The financial state, and the reform of the exchequer which that necessitated, will be discussed below, pp. 527–533.

[6] K. R. Mem. Roll, no. 94, m. 34. L. T. R. Mem. Roll, no. 91, Brev. Hill. m. 4 d. Vide App. of Doc. no. 33.

[7] K. R. Mem. Roll, no. 88, m. 63. L. T. R. Mem. Roll, no. 85, Brev. dir. Trin. m. 5 (21 May, 1315).

[8] K. R. Mem. Roll, no. 91, Brev. dir. Mich. m. 1. L. T. R. Mem. Roll, no. 88, Brev. dir. Mich. m. 1 (19 Sept. 1317).

[9] Thomas de Swinford was made sheriff of Nottingham and Derby during pleasure and on 7 August, 1310, the treasurer and barons were forbidden to oust

is not considerable in the early years of the reign, when the king appeared to have a greater general control over the exchequer and when the exchequer took a greater part in general administration[1]. After the parliament of Lincoln and the statute of sheriffs of 1316[2] orders not to remove sheriffs without the special royal order became more frequent. Men by evil had tried to oust Walter le Gras, sheriff of Surrey and Sussex. It was the royal will that Walter remain in his office and he was not to be removed without special order[3]. When William de Beauchamp was appointed sheriff of Worcester, he was not to be removed without special order[4]. Sometimes a little more discretion was allowed the barons of the exchequer and the sheriff was not to be removed without special command as long as he bore himself well and faithfully[5], and Ingelram Berenger was to be suffered to remain in his office as sheriff Buckingham until the king had had consultation with the exchequer[6].

Other bailiwicks were also granted to men who were not to be removed without direct order from the king[7], though on occasion the bailiff could be removed without a special order if he committed a trespass for which he ought to be removed[8]. Similar restrictions were placed upon the granting of manors by the exchequer. The manor of Watlington which John de Knokyn held was not to be assigned to any other without special order from the king[9]. One who owed the king 1000 marks for marriage without licence was granted respite of the debt until another order was sent to the exchequer[10]. The Friscobaldi were not to be distressed or grieved in any way without special order[11]. No arrangement was to be made

him without the king's order, and John de Dene, sheriff of Leicester and Warwick who had well and faithfully performed his office was likewise not to be dismissed without special order. (K. R. Mem. Roll, no. 84, mm. 5, 24. Vide also K. R. Mem. Roll, no. 94, m. 50 d; L. T. R. Mem. Roll, no. 91, Brev. Trin. m. 7.)

[1] The relative positions of the exchequer and the chancery and the influence of the baronial opposition upon the exchequer will be discussed later, pp. 518–527.

[2] Vide below, pp. 524–5.

[3] K. R. Mem. Roll, no. 91, Brev. dir. m. 42. L. T. R. Mem. Roll, no. 88, Brev. dir. Pasch. m. 1 (25 April, 1318).

[4] K. R. Mem. Roll, no. 91, Brev. dir. Mich. m. 1. L. T. R. Mem. Roll, no. 88, Brev. dir. Mich. m. 1 d (20 Aug. 1317).

[5] K. R. Mem. Roll, no. 93, m. 10. L. T. R. Mem. Roll, no. 90, Brev. dir. Mich. m. 6 (16 Aug. 1319).

[6] K. R. Mem. Roll, no. 94, m. 50 d. L. T. R. Mem. Roll, no. 91, Brev. Trin. m. 1 (19 June, 1321).

[7] K. R. Mem. Roll, no. 84, m. 20 d.

[8] Ibid. no. 84, m. 5.

[9] Ibid. no. 86, m. 9.

[10] Ibid. no. 94, m. 7 d. L. T. R. Mem. Roll, no. 91, Brev. dir. Mich. m. 3 d.

[11] K. R. Mem. Roll, no. 84, m. 35 d.

concerning the castle of Cockermouth without further order from the king[1]. The farm of the town of Appleby was two years in arrears and it was the custom of the exchequer if a farm was a year in arrears to take it into the king's hands. The king ordered that Appleby should be taken into his hands and that it should not be placed out of his hands without another order from him[2]. When the exchequer took from Anthony Pessaign a custom which the king had assigned to him for debts, the king sent a strict order threatening punishment as an example to others for disobedience to the royal order[3]. Yet on occasion the treasurer and barons showed an unwillingness to act without this special order from the king though they could well have done so. They were unwilling to allow certain items in the account of Anthony Pessaign "saunz especial mandement du Roy[4]."

Besides letters of privy seal prohibiting action without the king's special order, there were other grounds upon which the king restricted the action of the exchequer officials. John de Crombwell, constable of the Tower of London, was appealed for the escape of a prisoner out of his guard. They were ordered to postpone the appeal until another order, because the king had reserved that matter to himself[5]. When the issues of the great seal were granted to Baldock, in 1326, Thomas de Sibthorp, keeper of the hanaper, was ordered to be intendant to him for the issues and the barons were forbidden by privy seal from grieving him against the form of the grant[6]. John Inge, who had been Despenser's sheriff of Glamorgan[7], was given the custody of that land during his master's exile to answer to the king for the issues[8]. When Hugh returned, restitution was made of them with the issues in the meantime[9]. Inge was distrained to come for audit to the exchequer to render account in the meantime, against the form of the restitution. The king ordered the treasurer and barons by writ of privy seal to make full discharge to him for the

[1] K. R. Mem. Roll, no. 83, m. 26. Vide App. of Doc. no. 12.

[2] Ibid. no. 85, m. 19 d (2 April, 1312): "sanz la mettre hors de nostre meyn tantqe vous euiez autre mandement de nous."

[3] L. T. R. Mem. Roll, no. 90, Rec. Hill. m. 4 d, Schedule. Vide App. of Doc. no. 32.

[4] K. R. Mem. Roll, no. 85, m. 24 d.

[5] K. R. Mem. Roll, no. 94, m. 33. L. T. R. Mem. Roll, no. 91, Brev. Hill. m. 3 d: "Tanqe vous eyez autre mandement de nous car nous auoms reseruez cele chose a nous meymes" (8 Jan. 1321).

[6] K. R. Mem. Roll, no. 102, m. 56 d (3 Feb. 1326).

[7] Vide *Trans. R. Hist. Soc.* vol. IX [1915], 'Desp. War in Glam.,' J. C. Davies, pp. 32, 35.

[8] K. R. Mem. Roll, no. 101, m. 26.

[9] Cf. *Cal. Pat. Rolls*, 1321–24, p. 115.

issues in the meantime[1]. Another restrictive use of the privy seal by the king was his veto on sheriffs who had been appointed, the instant removal of Patrick de Corewen, appointed sheriff of Westmorland in 1323, being ordered because he was a cousin of Harclay[2].

The power of the exchequer was also limited by grants which the king made. On 27 June, 1309, all the customs of wool in Scotland and Ireland were granted to the Friscobaldi, who were not to answer therefor except at the king's order under privy seal[3], and they were appointed receivers of money arising from customs on wines, cloths and spices and from old and new customs on wool on the same condition[4].

The privy seal was used as a warrant for payment at the exchequer. Writs of liberate were often issued by command under the privy seal[5], these writs ordering even such ordinary payments as fees of justices[6]. Other writs of liberate issued by warrant of privy seal ordered payment for the king's works at Westminster[7], of the armourer of the Tower of London[8], a gift of 3000 marks to the earl of Gloucester[9], and a yearly grant of 100 marks to one who had lost his lands in Scotland[10]. Payment by writ of liberate issued from the chancery on the warrant of a writ of privy seal was a formal method. Payments were also made out of the exchequer on direct warrant of privy seal[11]. Sometimes payments were made from the exchequer by writ of privy seal and by the king's command announced verbally[12].

In the early years of the reign a considerable number of grants of offices and lands were made by writ of exchequer[13], and many of these grants were made by the warranty of writs of privy seal[14]. The exchequer was in a fortunate position as it had in its hands the administration of the lands of the Templars and of Walter de Langton. Manors which had belonged to the Templars and to Langton[15] were

[1] K. R. Mem. Roll, no. 101, m. 26 (30 Sept. 1325).
[2] *Cal. Soc. Scotl.* vol. III, p. 152. Cf. also Anc. Corresp. vol. XLV, no. 202.
[3] *Cal. Fine Rolls*, 1307–19, p. 44
[4] Ibid.
[5] E.g. Chan. Warr., File 59/145 (5 April, 1308).
[6] Liberate Rolls, no. 85, m. 5; no. 86, m. 5; no. 87, m. 3.
[7] Ibid. no. 84, m. 3.
[8] Ibid. m. 4.
[9] Ibid. no. 86, m. 4 (24 Nov. 1309).
[10] *Cal. Doc. Scotl.* vol. III, p. 33. Liberate Roll, no. 87, m. 3.
[11] Issue Roll, no. 146, m. 2 (30 April, 1309). John de Weston knight received a sum of £50, of the king's gift on 30 April, 1309, by order of writ of privy seal.
[12] Issue Roll, no. 196, m. 7 (6 Oct. 1321).
[13] Vide *Commissiones* in K. R. Mem. Rolls, nos. 81–86; L. T. R. Mem. Rolls, nos. 78–83.
[14] E.g. K. R. Mem. Rolls, no. 82, mm. 4, 5 d, 6 d, 7 d, 9, 10, 10 d, 11, 12, 12 d, 13, 14 d, 16; no. 84, mm. 1 d, 2, 3 d, 4 d.
[15] Cf. K. R. Mem. Roll, no. 81, m. 5 d; L. T. R. Mem. Roll, no. 78, m. 5.

granted by warrant of privy seal[1]. Hundreds[2] and the castle and manor of Cockermouth[3] were granted in the same way. The appointment of sheriffs was also frequently by warrant of privy seal[4].

The influence of the privy seal was as considerable on the plea side of the exchequer as upon the financial. Its most frequent use was to order the barons to hold pleas of debts of various persons at the exchequer. Among those to whom this privilege was accorded were various foreign merchants[5], notably the Friscobaldi[6] and the Bardi[7], the executors of the late earl of Warenne[8], the earl of Pembroke[9], the executors of Langton[10], and Anthony Pessaign[11]. James de Ispannia, who was afterwards a chamberlain of the exchequer[12], also received permission to plead his debts there[13]. This privilege was sometimes granted for the good service which the person had rendered the king[14], or it was said to be granted of the king's special grace[15], or because the king desired to show all the favour he could[16]. On one occasion it was granted because the person by the king's command stayed in the queen's company, for which the king wished to show her favour[17].

The king ordered other pleas than those of debt to be tried at the exchequer. In 1310 by privy seal he ordered the treasurer and barons to hear the case of a groom of William de Melton who had been attacked in London, and this they were ordered to do of the king's special grace despite order to the contrary[18]. In the same year a writ of privy seal was issued in favour of the prior and friars preachers of London about grievances of purveyance. As the offenders could not be punished by common law they were allowed, of the king's special grace, to sue at the exchequer[19].

[1] E.g. K. R. Mem. Roll, no. 81, mm. 9, 11 d.
[2] K. R. Mem. Roll, no. 81, m. 4 d. L. T. R. Mem. Roll, no. 78, m. 3.
[3] K. R. Mem. Roll, no. 81, m. 7 d. [4] Vide below, pp. 522–6.
[5] K. R. Mem. Roll, no. 83, mm. 14 d, 32, 34; no. 84, m. 16; no. 87, mm. 18, 23. Vide also App. of Doc. no. 9. See also T. Madox, *Firma Burgi*, p. 96, note e.
[6] L. T. R. Mem. Roll, no. 79, m. 47.
[7] K. R. Mem. Roll, no. 96, m. 19. L. T. R. Mem. Roll, no. 93, m. 57 d.
[8] L. T. R. Mem. Roll, no. 79, m. 81. [9] Ibid. m. 28 d.
[10] K. R. Mem. Roll, no. 95, m. 25. L. T. R. Mem. Roll, no. 92, m. 56.
[11] K. R. Mem. Roll, no. 88, m. 6. L. T. R. Mem. Roll, no. 85, Brev. dir. Mich. m. 1.
[12] *Cal. Pat. Rolls*, 1313–17, p. 614.
[13] K. R. Mem. Roll, no. 83, m. 25. L. T. R. Mem. Roll, no. 78, m. 53.
[14] L. T. R. Mem. Roll, no. 79, m. 23.
[15] K. R. Mem. Roll, no. 83, m. 19; no. 84, m. 16.
[16] L. T. R. Mem. Roll, no. 78, m. 62. [17] K. R. Mem. Roll, no. 86, m. 6 d.
[18] Ibid. no. 83, m. 27. Vide App. of Doc. no. 13.
[19] Ibid. Vide App. of Doc. no. 14.

In addition to ordering cases to be tried in the exchequer court the king sent privy seals during the course of the plea. The barons were ordered to hasten the business[1] or the plea[2], to do immediate right in a case[3], or to allow respite until a fixed time[4]. They were ordered to render judgment in a plea in such a manner that nothing should be done in prejudice of the king because he had the business much to heart[5]. Proceedings in the exchequer of pleas were also stopped by writ of privy seal[6].

A constant source of difficulty to the exchequer was lack of revenue, and the king's frequent and urgent demands for money for his household. As early as March, 1308, the chancellor was ordered to go each day to the exchequer to arrange with the treasurer, chancellor and barons of the exchequer and others of the council how the king could most suitably and sufficiently be provided with money for the expenses of his household and other matters which touched him[7]. The exchequer had to provide the money for the wardrobe, or at least a portion of it[8], and it was sometimes paid to the wardrobe by order under privy seal. Thus between 8 July and 1 November, 1326, the keeper of the wardrobe received a sum of £4103. 5*s.* 0*d.* from the archbishop of York, treasurer, and the chamberlains of the exchequer by four writs of privy seal[9]. Money paid to individuals by the exchequer by writ of privy seal was sometimes entered on the wardrobe books[10]. By privy seal also the exchequer was ordered to allow in accounts presented before them sums that had been paid into the wardrobe[11].

The privy seal was similarly used on behalf of the chamber when the barons were ordered to do nothing concerning the account of Alexander de Compton, keeper of the Templars' manors in Leicester and Warwick, as the king wished him to account in his chamber[12].

[1] K. R. Mem. Roll, no. 81, m. 20. [2] Ibid. no. 83, m. 28 d.
[3] Ibid. no. 81, m. 17 d. [4] Exch. of Pleas, Plea Roll, no. 31, m. 13.
[5] K. R. Mem. Roll, no. 92, Brev. dir. Mich. m. 3. L. T. R. Mem. Roll, no. 89, m. 61: "Si auisement qe rien ne soit fait en preiudice de nous car nous auoms cele busoigne au cuer."
[6] Exch. of Pleas, Plea Roll, no. 31, m. 9. Vide App. of Doc. no. 50.
[7] Chan. Warr., File 59/120 (25 Mar. 1308).
[8] The wardrobe accounts will be treated below, pp. 181–192.
[9] P. R. O. Enrolment of Wardrobe Accts. Exch. L. T. R. Roll, no. 2, m. 26.
[10] Stowe MS. 553, f. 118. In 1323 the Carmelites gathered in Spain received 10 marks from the exchequer by writ of p. s., and the Carmelites and Augustines £10, the payments being entered in the wardrobe book in the king's charity.
[11] K. R. Mem. Roll, no. 86, m. 19 d (1 April, 1312).
[12] Ibid. no. 87, m. 27. L. T. R. Mem. Roll, no. 84, Brev. dir. Pasch. m. 4 d (20 April, 1314).

Accounts were ordered to be discharged because they had been answered in the chamber[1]. The treasurer and barons were ordered by privy seal to make writs under the exchequer seal directing the collectors of the tenth and eighteenth in Buckinghamshire not to levy the taxes from the tenants of the royal manors of Langley Mareys and Chippenham because the king wished to be answered for them in his chamber[2].

Payments to servants of the royal household were ordered out of the exchequer by writ of privy seal. A valet of the king's household had fifty marks, and another servant £30[3] as gifts from the king paid by the exchequer. In October, 1309, John de Sturmy, valet of the king's household, had a gift of ten marks, Roger de Knokyn ten marks, and William de la Beche, valet of the king's household, five pounds[4]. These facts give some indication of the way in which the privy seal served as an instrument of the household, and of the relation in which the exchequer stood to the organisations of the wardrobe and the chamber[5].

Writs of privy seal were frequently issued to the justices, though comparatively few remain on record or in original. Sometimes the use of the privy seal to justices can be seen in the wardrobe accounts from the expenses which their conveyance entailed, and there are references to writs being conveyed in this way to justices of the benches at London[6] and to justices of gaol delivery[7]. Early in the reign, in the parliament of Stamford, 1309, a chapter of the *Articuli super cartas*[8] had been re-enacted to the effect that "there shall no writ from henceforth that toucheth the common law go forth under the petty seal[9]." An Ordinance had been made to the same effect[10], and on 22 November, 1317, the justices of both benches and the barons of exchequer had been ordered "not to omit on account of any order directed or to be directed to them under the great seal or the privy seal to do justice for the king and others prosecuting their right before them not denying or delaying justice to anyone[11]." Despite these orders, writs of privy seal were still issued to the justices.

The privy seal was used to initiate a case before the justices.

[1] K. R. Mem. Roll, no. 98, Brev. dir. m. 1.

[2] K. R. Mem. Roll, no. 93, m. 43 d. L. T. R. Mem. Roll, no. 90, Brev. dir. Trin. m. 9 d.

[3] Issue Roll, no. 144, m. 5.

[4] Ibid. no. 150, mm. 1–2.

[5] Below, pp. 181–4, 192–6.

[6] Vide above, p. 134.

[7] K. R. Acct. 374/7, f. 22.

[8] *Stat. of Realm*, vol. 1, p. 139.

[9] Ibid. p. 156.

[10] Vide below, pp. 373–4.

[11] *Cal. Close Rolls*, 1313–18, p. 514. Vide also *Abbrev. Placit.* p. 329.

Certain information to the effect that the prior of Llanthony in Gloucestershire had aided the rebel barons in 1321 in various ways had been examined before the king[1]. The king sent the examination to Hervy de Staunton and the other justices of the king's bench, who were to proceed against the prior and the other accused according to the law and custom of the realm; but since clergy had informed the king of the matter, and had assisted in the examination, judgment of life or limb was not to be given[2]. The king by his privy seal ordered the hastening of the hearing of pleas[3]. In a plea concerning advowson which was before Roger le Brabazon and the justices of king's bench, the king wished no further delay and sent an order to that effect[4]. The king also issued privy seals to delay the hearing of pleas[5]. A writ of privy seal to a justice of assize might fix the date of the hearing. The archbishop of York commenced an assize of novel disseisin. The king wrote to John Inge, justice for that assize, and ordered it to be held on 11 March, though the king's parliament would then be in progress[6]. In a plea of advowson which belonged to the king through the minority of the heir, the king by privy seal, so that the royal rights might be preserved, ordered Bereford and his fellow justices for no procurement on that matter to proceed further until they had order from the king[7]. The following month the justices were ordered to render judgment in the same cause so that the presentation should not devolve upon the ordinary[8]. A request was made for a writ to Sir Edmund de Passelewe and his companions, justices assigned in Kent, to certify that one who was indicted with aiding Bartholomew de Badlesmere was actually at the taking of the castle of Leeds and in the king's Scottish war, and this was done so that the justices should not proceed against him[9]. Judgment upon Bartholomew de Badlesmere was ordered by writ of privy seal to be passed without delay[10].

Pardons under the privy seal addressed to the justices were also made. One who had been indicted in Stafford for an illegal distress and found guilty, and against whom 40*s.* damages had been awarded, was pardoned, and the fine and impost remitted to him[11]. Even the

[1] K. B. Misc., Class 138, no. 108, m. 277. Vide App. of Doc. no. 139.
[2] Ibid. Vide also *Parl. Writs*, vol. II, Pt i, p. 367.
[3] Anc. Corresp. vol. XXXII, no. 110. Vide App. of Doc. no. 97.
[4] Anc. Corresp. vol. XXXV, no. 102.
[5] *Cal. Close Rolls*, 1307–13, p. 418.
[6] Ancient Petition, no. 2273.
[7] Seld. Soc., *Year Bk* 4 *Ed. II*, p. 180.
[8] Ibid.
[9] Anc. Corresp. vol. XXXIII, no. 56.
[10] *Parl. Writs*, vol. II, Pt ii, App. p. 265, no. 45.
[11] Wm Salt Soc., *Coll.* vol. IX, p. 18.

strict session of the eyre[1] was interfered with by writs of privy seal. Edward I in 1279 notified his justices in eyre by privy seal that he had pardoned one who was charged with the trespass of erecting a gallows in his liberty without the royal licence. He was to be acquitted of the trespass, the liberty was to be restored to him and he was to be permitted to re-erect his gallows[2]. Edward II in 1321 ordered the chancellor to give Despenser the younger, of the king's special grace, letters of the great seal excusing him from attendance at the eyre of London[3].

The privy seal was used as a direct warrant to the officials of the local administration. These writs were sent to various kinds of officials, permanent and temporary. The leaders of the foot in English counties and in North and South Wales were ordered to hasten their levies[4]. By writ of privy seal the dean and chapter of York were ordered to maintain war against the Scots[5]. The constable of Skipton in Craven was ordered to fortify his castle with men and provisions[6], while a convent of Carmelite friars was sent to the constable of Windsor castle who was ordered to receive and sustain them out of the issues of his bailiwick[7]. The bailiffs of Colchester took premises into the king's hands for debts by order of writ of privy seal[8], and the bailiffs of Hereford took lands into his hands on the death of the owner[9].

Sheriffs were ordered by that seal to make payments from the issues of their bailiwicks[10], and to take lands into the king's hands after the death of the owner[11]. A sheriff was also prohibited from making distress for debt in a case[12]. The escheator was ordered by privy seal to assign dower[13], not to molest one who had entered a manor[14], and not to return an inquisition he had made of certain lands until the next parliament and then to return it before the king and his council[15]. A forester was ordered to allow a certain person to have six bucks of the king's gift[16]; Despenser senior, while forester of the forest south of Trent, was ordered by privy seal to deliver a manor and its members[17]. An inquest taken by writ of privy seal was

[1] Seld. Soc., *Eyre of Kent*, vol. I, pp. xvii–xx.
[2] *Cal. Close Rolls*, 1272–79, p. 518.
[3] Chan. Warr., File 113/5557.
[4] K. R. Acct. 373/30, f. 12.
[5] *Regist. J. de Halton*, vol. II (Canterb. and York Soc.), pp. 129–131.
[6] Anc. Corresp. vol. XLV, no. 206.
[7] K. R. Acct. 15/1.
[8] *Cal. Close Rolls*, 1296–1302, p. 366.
[9] *Cal. Inq. P. M.* vol. VI, p. 216.
[10] Stowe MS. 553, f. 119.
[11] *Cal. Inq. P. M.* vol. VI, p. 215.
[12] Anc. Corresp. vol. XLV, no. 146.
[13] *Cal. Close Rolls*, 1296–1302, pp. 83–84.
[14] *Cal. Inq. P. M.* vol. V, p. 185.
[15] Ibid. p. 75.
[16] *Cal. Close Rolls*, 1279–88, p. 324.
[17] *Descr. Cat. Ancient Deeds*, vol. II, p. 165.

delivered under the seal of the chancellor to a messenger to be taken to the king who was abroad[1], thus suggesting a very personal relation between the privy seal and the king.

The use of the privy seal in local administration was encouraged by the "administrative" council who recommended that while inquests of forfeited lands were being held the keeper should have order under the privy seal to find what demesne lands were certain, about which there could be no dispute and which it would be to the king's great profit to have in his hands[2]. The council also suggested that orders under the privy seal should be sent to the keepers for them to sell wool, crops, lead and other things in the manors for the king's profit[3].

Writs under the privy seal were sent to the seneschal of Gascony, concerning the payment of a large sum of money to Anthony de Lebret, for his service to Edward I[4], to the justice of Ireland to certify the king of the money arrested of the tenth of Ireland granted for the Holy Land[5], and to the chancellor of Scotland ordering him to send an inquisition made before him to the king[6]. The chamberlain of Carnarvon was ordered to collect debts wherewith to pay troops in the Scottish war[7], and the chamberlains of North and South Wales were ordered to pay the wages of the men of their districts going to that war[8]. Prisoners from the Isle of Man in Beaumaris castle were to be paid out of the issues of North Wales[9], and the chamberlain of Caermarthen was to account to Despenser the younger for the issues received from the land of Cantrev Mawr during his exile[10]. Writs were likewise addressed to the justices of West Wales[11], and to the lieutenant of the justices of North Wales[12]. Prohibition under the privy seal was sent to the justice and chamberlain of North Wales who were not without special order from the king to oust a Welshman who had received land from Edward I[13]. Writs of privy seal addressed to the mayor and sheriffs of London have been given[14]. There were also several relating to troops for the Scottish war from the city. The mayor and sheriffs were to arrest deserters from the king's army[15]. The king thanked them for military assistance[16]; and, for furnishing

[1] *Cal. Close Rolls*, 1296–1302, p. 195. [2] Chan. Warr., File 1705. [3] Ibid.
[4] Anc. Corresp. vol. XLV, no. 178. [5] *Cal. Close Rolls*, 1296–1302, p. 357.
[6] Anc. Corresp. vol. XLV, no. 145.
[7] Ibid. vol. XXXII, no. 76. Vide App. of Doc. no. 95.
[8] Stowe MS. 553, f. 25 b. K. R. Acct. 16/4. [9] K. R. Acct. 506/25.
[10] Ancient Petition, no. 2749. [11] *Cal. Inq. P. M.* vol. V, p. 32.
[12] K. R. Acct. 373/30, f. 4.
[13] Anc. Corresp. vol. XLV, no. 166. [14] Vide above, pp. 134, 136.
[15] *Cal. Letter Books, D*, pp. 222–3. [16] Ibid. *E*, pp. 98–99.

armour and military equipment to the value of £250, he ordered payment from the twelfth of the burgesses granted at the parliament of York[1].

The privy seal too may be considered as the particular instrument which expressed the personal will of the king. The whole use of the privy seal in interference with administration may be said to have been its use as the instrument of the king in administration, by means of which he retained his control over the departments after they had obtained organisations of their own, and tended to separate themselves more and more from the court. In its use as a prohibition the privy seal was in a special sense the instrument of the king's personal will. There is one aspect of the use of the privy seal in administration which has not been yet treated. This particular phase of the administration, while it was official in intent, was personal in its origin and purpose. Writs were addressed to local officials to acquaint the king of facts. Anthony de Lucy was ordered to certify the king at once of the men he had received into the king's peace who had adhered to the Scots, and of their names and conditions[2]. The chancellor was ordered by privy seal to send Hugh le Despenser, Geoffrey le Scrope and Robert de Aylleston, keeper of the privy seal, to Nottingham to demand, receive and report to the king answers to certain messages[3]. The chancellor was ordered to secure the arrest of a friar who had arrived with bulls. The friar was to be brought before the king and council according to the advice of Roger Beler, baron of the exchequer[4]. One who had come to England was forbidden to return abroad, without special order under the privy seal, until he had been to speak to the king in Scotland[5]. When Gilbert de Clare's lands were taken into the king's hands by Edward I[6], Walter Hakelut had the custody of them all by writ of privy seal[7]. The indentures of war made with barons for the safeguarding of the Scottish march were sealed by the king with his privy seal[8]. The privy seal was used in matters of grace, such as the grant of dower to widows[9], one grant being ordered although the husband had adhered to the rebels and his lands were in the king's hands[10].

[1] *Cal. Letter Books, E*, p. 106 (22 June, 1319).
[2] Anc. Corresp. vol. XLV, no. 209 (21 June, 1326).
[3] Chan. Warr., File 125/6744.
[4] Ibid. File 122/6433. Vide App. of Doc. no. 30.
[5] *Cal. Close Rolls*, 1296–1302, p. 363.
[6] Cf. *Cal. Chan. Rolls*, 1272–1326, pp. 334–349.
[7] *Cal. Close Rolls*, 1288–96, p. 437.
[8] K. R. Acct. 68/2, nos. 10, 17.
[9] Chan. Warr., File 120/6212.
[10] Ibid. File 121/6327

Another administrative use of the privy seal, which will be more fully discussed subsequently, was its employment as a warrant or communication to those who were in name or fact the real head of the administration. The earl of Gloucester, keeper of the realm, and the chancellor were ordered to examine an inquisition sent them and to do what seemed fitting[1]. When Pembroke was head of the administration the privy seal was the usual instrument of communication between king and earl[2]. Writs of privy seal were also issued to Pembroke in a dispute between him and Lancaster when he was the most prominent figure at court. Instead of writs under the great seal, those under the privy seal were sent ordering him to cease making assemblies and to settle the matter in the king's court according to the law and custom of the realm[3], and to prevent his men intimidating Lancaster's from attending before a commission of oyer and terminer that Lancaster had obtained[4].

The king used the privy seal in his private correspondence and especially in his negotiations with foreign powers. Foreign policy was entirely a matter for the king and his "administrative" council[5], and foreign correspondence was conducted under the privy seal. Edward wrote to Philip le Bel for a safe-conduct for Frederic, the son of Manfred, king of Sicily, who was returning from England to Italy[6]. Letters of protection for a merchant given under the great seal were returned endorsed with the request that he should have letters under the privy seal to the French king and a local French lord[7]. Letters under the privy seal were also sent to the king of France on business touching the duchy of Aquitaine[8]. The king wrote to Robert, count of Flanders, under that instrument, specially recommending one of his valets[9]. The king conducted his correspondence with his ambassadors or messengers to foreign powers under the same instrument[10]. The extent of its use in this way can be judged from the fact that there remain six such writs addressed to the bishops of Worcester and Carlisle, Badlesmere and the other

[1] *Cal. Inq. P. M.* vol. V, p. 172. [2] Vide below, pp. 324–8.

[3] Anc. Corresp. vol. XLIX, no. 24 (7 Feb. 1314). Vide below, p. 501.

[4] Anc. Corresp. vol. XLIX, no. 25 (28 Feb. 1314).

[5] J. F. Baldwin, *The King's Council* [1913], pp. 215–216.

[6] Brequigny's *Lettres du Roi*, vol. II, p. 33.

[7] Chan. Warr., File 1704.

[8] K. R. Acct. 375/8, f. 15 b.

[9] Anc. Corresp. vol. XLV, no. 144.

[10] Chan. Warr., File 125/6787 (11 Jan. 1324). Vide App. of Doc. no. 115. To Richard de Welles, Master John de Shoreditch and Master Richard de Gloucester, who were at Paris.

messengers who were in the north in February and March, 1321, treating with the Scots[1].

The writ that the king sent to the mayor and good men of London on 22 January, 1322, informing them of the progress of his campaign in the west march and the surrender of the Mortimers, and charging them to behave properly towards him, can well be classed amongst the king's private correspondence[2], as can also the writ which he sent to the bishop of Exeter on 10 February, 1321, touching the return of the Despensers[3].

The king sought favours by writs under his privy seal. A writ was sent to the abbess of Wilton ordering her to grant Roger de Northburgh a pension, which Ralph de Stokes had from the abbey by the gift of Edward I and for which the queen had previously made request[4]. Orders of this kind were not always obeyed, and after they had been ignored the king sometimes ordered writs under the great seal to the same effect[5]. The refusal to obey a writ to receive a man as a monk in a convent was followed by the order of a writ of privy seal[6]. The mayor, aldermen and sheriffs of London were desired to grant the small balance of the weigh-house to a nominee of the queen[7], a request which was fulfilled[8], though a subsequent request did not prove successful[9].

The privy seal was used in royal mandates which required secrecy. The sheriff of Lincoln was ordered to arrest certain men in his bailiwick, and he was ordered to do so in such a secret and careful manner that the suspects should not be frightened and thus escape, for should that happen the king would blame him[10]. It was used for a similar reason in 1326 when the king sent a roll under his privy seal to the treasurer and barons touching the garniture of the royal castles, which was to be examined and amended as they thought necessary[11].

Closely related to the use of the privy seal in matters of grace and favour was its use in matters touching the royal prerogative. Sir Thomas de Mandeville had been taken prisoner by the Scots at Bannockburn and part of his ransom consisted of a debt of £94 which Robert de Bruce owed to Nicholas de Banton, who had formerly been steward of his lands in Essex. He had purchased cloth and

[1] Anc. Corresp. vol. XLV, nos. 197, 198; vol. XXXII, no. 87; vol. XLV, nos. 199, 200, 201.

[2] *Parl. Writs*, vol. II, Pt i, p. 273.

[3] *Regist. W. de Stapleton*, 1307–26, pp. 442–3.

[4] Anc. Corresp. vol. XLIX, no. 57.

[5] Chan. Warr., File 130/7208.

[6] Anc. Corresp. vol. XXXVI, no. 145.

[7] *Cal. Letter Books, D*, p. 227.

[8] Ibid. p. 228.

[9] Ibid. *E*, pp. 61–62.

[10] Anc. Corresp. vol. XLV, no. 208.

[11] K. R. Mem. Roll, no. 102, m. 47 d.

other things for Bruce for which he had not been paid. Before Nicholas received the debt he obtained permission from the king by writ of privy seal to send an acquittance for the amount to Bruce, who had undertaken to pay that sum to the person to whom the ransom was due[1]. A plea in the court Christian was prohibited by writ of privy seal on the ground that it was a plea of lay fee[2]. Writs under privy seal were sent to Brabazon and the justices of king's bench, the chancellor, and Despenser touching a delay of justice in a plea of advowson, saving to the king the right of his prerogative and to the other party his right according to common law; for it was not the king's intention to damage anyone by his prerogative but to save to each his right[3]. Licences to alienate were ordered to be granted by writ of privy seal, and the king was petitioned to order a writ of attaint[4] to be issued by warrant of privy seal[5].

The privy seal was used by the king for the general administration of the government as well as for personal matters, in other words it was becoming a formal executive instrument. In general administration it was also used by the "administrative" council[6] which carried out so much of the business of government during the reign. Roger de Northburgh, keeper of the king's privy seal, remained in London at the king's council for the king's business with the privy seal and three clerks from 18 September to 30 October, 1312[7], the expenses for that period being entered on the wardrobe accounts[8]. He also remained in London early in 1313 with four clerks by the royal order with the privy seal to write and seal various letters according to the arrangements or decisions of the king's council[9], and subsequently in that year by royal command he was in London from 25 February to 15 May with two clerks with the privy seal for the sealing of letters and other matters enjoined upon him by the king's council[10]. Matters ordained in the council in August, 1308, relating to the government of Scotland were ordered to be put into effect by privy seal[11]. It was agreed, for instance, that order should be made by the king to the chamberlain of Scotland to view and counsel

[1] Writ printed in *Arch. Journal*, vol. XXI [1864], p. 161.

[2] Anc. Corresp. vol. XXXII, no. 91. Vide App. of Doc. no. 96.

[3] Anc. Corresp. vol. XXXV, no. 102: "Sauuant a nous nostre droit de nostre prerogatiue et auxint au dit William son droit solonc la lei commune. Kar nostre entenet nest pas a fer...a nulli par nostre prerogatiue mes sauuer chescun y droit."

[4] Vide Pollock and Maitland, *Hist. Engl. Law*, vol. II, p. 665.

[5] Chan. Warr., File 109/5110.

[6] For the "administrative" council, vide below, pp. 248–287.

[7] K. R. Acct. 375/8, f. 6. [8] Ibid. [9] Ibid, f. 8. [10] Ibid. f. 11 b.

[11] Chan. Misc., Bdle 22/12 (26). Vide App. of Doc. no. 52.

concerning the faults of the castle of Dundee, and order to this effect was made by writ of privy seal[1]. It was also agreed that order should be made to the keeper of victuals at Berwick to provision the castle; and this was done by writ of privy seal[2].

Besides these warrants issued on the recommendation of the council, writs of privy seal were also made to the exchequer by the council. A writ to the treasurer and barons of the exchequer, ordering them to search the rolls for the debts a citizen of London owed Edward I which were to be levied for the king's aid, was endorsed "per consilium[3]," and a writ was addressed to the exchequer by the assent of the king's council pardoning John Paynel the sum of £20[4]. Payments were also made in the exchequer by privy seal and the assent of the council[5]. It can fairly be said that the privy seal was used as an instrument of the council.

In considering writs of privy seal directed to the exchequer it was seen that they sometimes had reference to the financial position of the wardrobe and chamber[6]. Before various minor miscellaneous points concerned with the privy seal are discussed, a little more must be said of its relations to the household. The influence of the privy seal on the finance of the household will be considered later[7], as well as its office and officers[8]. The privy seal as the personal instrument of the king and the essential relation between the privy seal and the household must be emphasised. When the king had not the privy seal by him he once sealed a writ, which had the same virtue, with the seal of Oliver de Bordeaux[9], a household official, who was valet of his chamber. When a writ under privy seal was incorrect it was returned to the king for emendation[10]. More often, however, the entry of its return for correction was made in this formula:

"Postea hoc breue remittitur garderobe ad emendandum[11]."

Sometimes too, writs were vacated because they were returned to the

[1] Chan. Misc., Bdle 22/12 (26). Vide App. of Doc. no. 52.

[2] Ibid. [3] Brev. Baron. 5 Ed. II.

[4] K. R. Mem. Roll, no. 89, m. 52. L. T. R. Mem. Roll, no. 86, m. 110.

[5] Issue Roll, no. 164, m. 1 (6 Oct. 1312). J. de Mowbray received 100 marks "per mandatum regis de priuato sigillo tenenti locum Thesaurarii Baronibus et Camerariis directum in custodia Camerariorum remanendum et per assensum domini Adomari de Valencia et tocius consilii domini Regis."

[6] Vide above, pp. 145–6. [7] Vide below, pp. 155–6. [8] Vide below, pp. 224–9.

[9] Chan. Warr., File 1328/97: "Et pur ce qe nous nauioms mie nostre priue seal pres de nous quant ceste lettre fu faite si auoms mis le seal nostre cher vallet Oliver de Burdeux."

[10] K. R. Mem. Roll, no. 82, m. 42 d: "Postea hoc breue remittitur domino Regi ad emendandum etcetera."

[11] Ibid. mm. 34, 36 d.

wardrobe[1]. It must be remembered that it was in the wardrobe that the writs of privy seal originated, and this fact explains the source of the influence the household exercised over the executive.

The privy seal was used also as the instrument of the wardrobe in the administration of its own household duties. Payments were made out of the wardrobe on the warrant of privy seal[2], and also into and on behalf of that department. Payments of £20 of fines were ordered to be made by the mayor of Lincoln to Ralph de Stokes, keeper of the great wardrobe, for that office[3], and the sheriff of Lincoln was directed to purchase parchment in Lincoln for the books, rolls and memoranda of the wardrobe[4]. Delivery of a wardrobe book was ordered to be made in the wardrobe[5], and certain letters and muniments were ordered to be brought to the wardrobe[6]. Letters of acquittance of receipt under privy seal were made to the keeper of the wardrobe for what the king received therefrom[7]. Anthony Pessaign was ordered by writ of privy seal to pay Oliver de Bordeaux, who had a bill of the wardrobe, £62. 3*s*. 6*d*. owing to him for restoration of horses, and he was to have allowance in the customs of London at the wardrobe[8]. Writs of privy seal were addressed to the chancellor to make writs of liberate to the treasurer and chamberlains to deliver to Robert de Wodehouse, keeper of the wardrobe, £200 for the expenses of the household[9], and to the guardian of the temporalities of York, who was to pay all sums levied from those temporalities into the wardrobe with all haste for the expenses of the household[10].

The wardrobe, as the department which financed the Scottish wars, used the privy seal in summoning men to serve there, and among those thus summoned were Roger Mortimer, justice of Wales[11], the constable of Nasserton[12] and the king's bachelor, John de Belhouse[13]. The prior of Holy Trinity, Canterbury, was ordered to supply provisions for the war through the sheriff of Kent[14], and cattle and corn supplied for the king's expedition of 1310 by the Yorkshire monasteries were acknowledged by letters under the privy seal[15]. A payment for a person's equipment for Scotland was ordered by the same seal[16].

[1] K. R. Mem. Roll, no. 83, m. 11 d: "Vacatur quia breue remittitur garderobe."
[2] Stowe MS. 553, f. 69.
[3] K. R. Acct. 377/10.
[4] Ibid. 375/8, f. 6 b.
[5] Anc. Corresp. vol. L, no. 117.
[6] Ibid. vol. XXXII, no. 140. Vide App. of Doc. no. 99.
[7] K. R. Acct. 375/8, f. 7.
[8] Anc. Corresp. vol. XLV, no. 168.
[9] Chan. Warr., File 126/6898.
[10] Anc. Corresp. vol. XLIX, no. 4.
[11] Chan. Warr., File 1703.
[12] Anc. Corresp. vol. XLV, no. 150.
[13] Ibid. no. 147.
[14] Ibid. no. 148.
[15] Surtees Soc. vol. LXVII [1876], *Fountains Abbey*, vol. II, Pt i, p. 22, note 1.
[16] Anc. Corresp. vol. XLIX, no. 140.

The keepers of the king's stores of victuals at various places were ordered to deliver portions of those stores to various persons nominated by the king by writ of privy seal. The keeper at Carlisle was ordered to deliver flour and wine to Master John Walwayn for the use of the earl of Hereford, a prisoner with the Scots[1], and to the executors of Sir Robert de Clifford for the interment of his body[2]. The keeper of victuals at Newcastle-on-Tyne was ordered by various writs to give corn of the king's charity[3], and the Dominicans of Carlisle received gifts of flour[4].

The privy seal was used in mandates to servants of the royal household. By its order the king's baker was commanded to take flour from Kingston-on-Hull to Pickering for provision against the coming of the king to those parts[5], the clerk of the king's pantry and buttery to hand various things to various sheriffs and others[6], and the clerk of the king's kitchen to give 200 stock-fish to Lady la Despenser[7]. By the same instrument the sheriff of Nottingham and Derby was assigned to receive two horses of the king and keep them[8]. By writ of privy seal Edward de Balliol was assigned to stay in the household of Thomas and Edmund the king's brothers[9]. The evidence shows that there was a vital connection between the privy seal and the wardrobe.

There remain to be considered a number of miscellaneous uses of the privy seal among which its use as a writ of summons is important. Orleton, bishop of Hereford, was summoned to come to the king at London with all haste to give his counsel and advice which the king desired upon certain weighty and important matters touching the estate of the realm[10]. William fitz William was similarly ordered to come to the king, who desired to speak to him on weighty matters[11]. Thomas Wake, though he had received frequent letters of privy seal ordering him to come to treat of certain of the king's affairs, ignored the royal commands, so a writ under the great seal was made ordering him to appear[12]. The clergy were similarly ordered to attend with other prelates and magnates of the realm to have counsel and treaty[13]. The dean and chapter of York in 1316 were ordered to assemble the clergy of that province to grant an aid to the king for his Scottish

[1] *Cal. Doc. Scotl.* vol. III, p. 74.
[2] Ibid. [3] Stowe MS. 553, f. 123. [4] Ibid. f. 124.
[5] Ibid. f. 119 b. [6] Ibid. f. 122. [7] Ibid. f. 122 b.
[8] K. R. Acct. 375/8, f. 10. [9] Ibid. f. 6.
[10] Canterb. and York Soc., *Reg. A. de Orleton*, p. 50.
[11] Anc. Corresp. vol. XLIX, no. 5.
[12] *Cal. Close Rolls*, 1323–27, p. 549. [13] *Parl. Writs*, vol. II, Pt ii, p. 349.

expedition[1]. Master John de Shoreditch was ordered, by writ of privy seal, to come from York to Nottingham, to the king's council[2]. Richard de Ayremynne and Adam his brother were frequently ordered to appear before the king's council to answer certain things charged against them[3]. Even summonses to parliaments were made by writ of privy seal. In 1297 Edward I so ordered the earl of Warwick to come to the parliament which was to be held at London[4], and in 1318 Edward II ordered the archbishop of Canterbury, despite his excuse, to appear because he held the archbishop's presence necessary for carrying out the great and weighty affairs which were to be discussed and enacted[5]. Master John de Shoreditch was in like manner summoned to come from London to York to the parliament which the king held there in May, 1322[6].

To be distinguished clearly from warrants and writs under the privy seal are letters patent under the privy seal. Letters patent under the privy seal were sent to local officials[7]. Various abbeys, priories and other religious houses in Suffolk, Essex, Hertford, Bedford, Buckingham, Kent, Surrey, Sussex and Southampton were requested by such letters to say masses for the soul of Gavaston[8]. Grants of money were made by letters patent under the privy seal, the grant of the issues of the great seal to Baldock being made in this form[9]. In 1306 Edward I promised to provide the brother of the count of Bar, by letters patent sealed with the privy seal, with 500 marks yearly of land in Scotland[10], and Edward II issued similar letters concerning the payment of £20,000 tournois to Amadeo de Libret of the king's gift[11]. Letters patent under the privy seal were also used to acknowledge the receipt of money and to assign sources for its repayment[12].

In addition to the formal warrant under privy seal there was a warrant which was informal and yet sealed by the privy seal. This was not like the informal warrants which will be treated subsequently, as it had to go through the hands of the keeper of the privy seal or one of his clerks. The warrant was not written in the office of the privy seal, but was an administrative warrant, written in some

[1] Surtees Soc., *Rec. of Northern Convocat.* pp. 67–68.
[2] Stowe MS. 553, f. 119.
[3] *Cal. Close Rolls*, 1323–27, pp. 554–5.
[4] Ibid. 1296–1302, p. 130.
[5] *Lit. Cantuar.* vol. I, pp. 38–41.
[6] Stowe MS. 553, f. 29.
[7] K. R. Acct. 374/7, m. 11, to the justice of Chester. Ibid. 373/30, f. 4, to the lieutenant of the justice of Wales.
[8] Ibid. 375/8, f. 15.
[9] K. R. Mem. Roll, no. 102, m. 56 d.
[10] *Cal. Close Rolls*, 1302–7, p. 520.
[11] Anc. Corresp. vol. XLV, no. 178.
[12] Ancient Petition, no. 4426. Vide App. of Doc. no. 136.

department, which derived its force from the seal. Writs were frequently issued in the chancery on the warrant of these bills of privy seal, including writs of liberate. The debts and issues of the lands of Langton, of the Templars and of the arrears of the papal tenth granted to Edward I were assigned to John de Benstede, late keeper of the king's wardrobe[1], to pay debtors of the wardrobe[2]: John de Drokensford, late keeper of the wardrobe obtained a *liberate* on a similar warrant for the same purpose[3]. Ordinary liberate writs to the wardrobe were made on a similar warrant, Ingelard de Warle receiving one for 10,000 marks on 10 December, 1311[4]. Grants of land and offices entered on the close and patent rolls were made on a warrant of a bill under privy seal[5].

An instrument more private than the privy seal, and used sometimes as a substitute for it, and sometimes as a substitute for verbal orders[6], was the secret seal. The secret seal had been necessitated by the same reason as the privy seal,—the formularising of the more private of the king's instruments,—and its functions were to be the same as the privy seal in its early stages. Its use was not restricted therefore to purely private matters of the king and his household. It was used in all spheres of administration to make the king's personal will felt. In writs under this seal personal statements about the royal health frequently mingle with official instructions. The secret seal and writs under it were personal in their origin but sometimes they were official and administrative in their effect, though the purely personal element was seldom entirely absent. The king wrote a letter to Pembroke on 26 January, 1313, under the secret seal which is characteristic of such writs. The earl had advised, and had the support of the earl of Gloucester in his opinion, that the king should summon the cardinal and the bishop of Poitiers to be with him on 29 January at Sheen. The king answered that he could not himself make any such order as he was practically unattended, only two squires being with him. He asked the earl to send the message by the bishop of Worcester or another on the king's behalf, that they

[1] Liberate Roll, no. 84, m. 2. [2] Ibid. no. 85, m. 6.

[3] Ibid. m. 5. Note also payments to the count of Savoy and to clerks of the works at the palace of Westminster.

[4] Ibid. no. 88, m. 2.

[5] Vide *Cal. Close Rolls* and *Cal. Pat. Rolls* passim, e.g. at the queen's request the king granted the office of marshal of the justices of common bench to Robert de Snodhill, by bill of privy seal (Chan. Warr., File 909; vide App. of Doc. no. 83), a writ issuing in the form of letters patent on this warrant (*Cal. Pat. Rolls*, 1307–13, p. 393).

[6] Vide below, pp. 166–174.

should be there on that day[1]. Immediately after this business of state came the reply to a personal request by the earl concerning the wardship and marriage of the heir of Sir John de Benstede, which he had begged. The king willingly granted this and only regretted that it was so small[2].

When Pembroke controlled the administration[3] various writs under the secret seal were addressed to him, including mandates to make suitable letters for a grant which he had recommended[4]; to treat about a Gascon matter and decide according to right and reason with all possible haste[5]; to consider and to hear what the bearer had to say, and with the council to ordain a suitable remedy[6]. By secret seal, too, he was ordered to give credence to William de Cusance, king's clerk, whom the king was sending to report certain things to him[7]. Under writ of secret seal a letter touching the right of the chapel of Tickhill was sent to Norwich, treasurer, in 1315 with the order to ordain concerning it in the best way to save the king's right and honour[8].

The secret seal was used as a warrant to the chancery, the exchequer, the justices and the local administration. The use as a chancery warrant was not extensive when compared with the use of the privy seal, though there remain among the chancery warrants more than two hundred writs under the secret seal[9]. Its use coincided with the periods of the reign when the barons were hard pressing the king, and generally the writs of secret seal were in favour of royal favourites, such as grants to Cherleton[10], Damory[11] and Despenser the elder[12]. On 26 August, 1321, various keepers were ordered to discover by inquisition and other means what goods and chattels were in Despenser's castles, manors, towns, hundreds and lands on 14 August, as his property ought to be taken into the king's hands. They were also ordered to ascertain what goods had been eloigned from the castles and lands and to inquire in whose hands they were, the king to be

[1] Anc. Corresp. vol. XLIX, no. 21. Vide App. of Doc. no. 124.
[2] Ibid.
[3] For the Pembroke administration, see below, pp. 322–330.
[4] Anc. Corresp. vol. XLV, no. 176. Vide App. of Doc. no. 119.
[5] Anc. Corresp. vol. XLV, no. 177.
[6] Ibid. no. 207 (12 Feb. 1323). Vide App. of Doc. no. 122.
[7] Anc. Corresp. vol. XLIX, no. 51. Vide App. of Doc. no. 127.
[8] Anc. Corresp. vol. XLV, no. 188. Vide App. of Doc. no. 121.
[9] Vide Chan. Warr., Files 1328 and 1329 passim.
[10] *Cal. Fine Rolls*, 1307–19, p. 205 (3 Aug. 1314).
[11] *Cal. Pat. Rolls*, 1317–21, p. 76 (3 Feb. 1318). The writ was "vacated because surrendered and cancelled and otherwise on Fine Roll."
[12] *Cal. Close Rolls*, 1318–23, pp. 394–5.

notified of the results. Seven writs of this nature were issued by warrant of the secret seal[1]. When danger from France and the queen's revolution were threatening in August, 1325, the constable of Dover was ordered not to permit any messenger from the queen or the king's envoys to show letters or recount news until they had been to the king, the order having its warrant in a writ of secret seal[2]. In a writ of secret seal to the bishop of Norwich, chancellor, and the bishop of Exeter, treasurer, the king expressed great surprise that they had not certified him of the business concerning the church of Winchester as he had charged them. They were to call the council, have good advisement and decide according to reason[3]. In corresponding with the king the chancellor sent him letters under his secret seal[4] and the comparison between royal writ under secret seal directed to the chancellor and the chancellor's letters under secret seal sent to the king is interesting. The secret seal was essentially a private instrument.

The use of the secret seal as a warrant for payment from the exchequer was frequent. Sometimes the payment was made by the king's command by privy and secret seal[5]. Almost invariably the payments ordered by writ of secret seal have reference to the wardrobe or household, and the charges of conveying such writs fell upon the wardrobe[6]. Payments for horses bought of the earl of Richmond for the king[7], for the purchases from a London saddler[8], for cloth purchased for the king's use, were ordered by the secret seal[9]. The payments from the exchequer direct to the wardrobe were sometimes made by warrant of the secret seal though writs of liberate and privy seal predominate[10]. A loan of £300 which the burgesses of Shrewsbury had made to the wardrobe on 20 January, 1322[11], and a loan by the Bardi[12] were repaid from the exchequer by order of secret seal. Wages owing in the wardrobe were paid by writ of secret seal in the

[1] Chan. Warr., File 1328/14.
[2] *Cal. Close Rolls*, 1323–27, p. 361.
[3] Anc. Corresp. vol. XXXVI, no. 6.
[4] Issue Roll, no. 206, m. 6. Four were sent to the king at Beverley, Jan. 1323.
[5] Ibid. no. 186, m. 7: "per mandatum domini Regis de priuato et secreto sigillo." Ibid. no. 196, m. 4: "in custodia camerarii per duo mandata domini Regis unum de priuato sigillo et alterum de secreto sigillo remanentes inter mandata de termino presenti."
[6] Stowe MS. 553, ff. 129, 130.
[7] Issue Roll, no. 186, m. 7.
[8] Ibid. no. 180, m. 4.
[9] Ibid. no. 183, mm. 5, 6.
[10] Enrolm. of Wardr. Accts. Exch. L. T. R. Roll, no. 2, m. 24. £18,512. 4*s*. 9*d*. was paid out of the treasury by seven writs of liberate, six of privy seal and one of secret seal. Such payments were made on 11 Dec. 1321 (Issue Roll, no. 196, m. 4), and 18 May, 1325 (ibid. no. 213, m. 1).
[11] Issue Roll, no. 198, m. 3.
[12] Ibid. no. 202, m. 11; no. 206, m. 7.

exchequer[1]. Payments for good service to the king[2], to the king's valets for purchases made[3], and business carried out by them[4], were made by the exchequer by warrant of secret seal. Forty pounds, the expenses incurred by Mary, the king's sister, and Lady de Burgh in going to and returning from Canterbury, were paid to Henry de Shirokes, a clerk of the wardrobe, by the king's order under secret seal[5]. The frequency of the use of the secret seal in ordering payments from the exchequer is suggested by the fact that a clerk succeeded in obtaining ten marks from the exchequer on the warrant of a forged writ of secret seal[6].

In the administration of the exchequer as well as in payments therefrom the secret seal was employed by the king. Under that seal a writ concerning the administration of the lands of those who had been killed at Bannockburn was sent to the treasurer and barons on 13 July, 1314[7]. On 27 November, 1323, a long writ under the secret seal relating to the administration of the exchequer and its accounts and debts was sent to the barons[8], and on 19 February, 1324, the barons were ordered under the same warrant to search without delay the receipts, payments and issues in the exchequer of the lands of Langton, of the Templars, and of the tenth of the clergy, the king to be certified before the end of the next parliament[9]. The king stated that he had written under the secret seal because he had the business much at heart[10]. Under the secret seal too, the king advised the keeper of the office of treasurer and the barons of the exchequer of the progress of his campaign in the Welsh march in 1322 and sent the Mortimers to them for safe keeping[11]. Writs under the secret seal to the exchequer ordered respite of debts for Richard Damory, steward of the household[12], and for William de Montague[13]; and John de Weston was ordered to have quittance for fifty marks for which he was impleaded and which he had paid into the wardrobe[14].

[1] Issue Roll, no. 172, m. 5.
[2] Ibid. no. 180, m. 5.
[3] Ibid. m. 3.
[4] Ibid. m. 5.
[5] Ibid. mm. 4–5.
[6] Ibid. no. 167, m. 1.
[7] K. R. Mem. Roll, no. 87, m. 43 d. L. T. R. Mem. Roll, no. 84, Brev. dir. Trin. m. 11 d.
[8] K. R. Mem. Roll, no. 97, Brev. dir. Mich. m. 14 d.
[9] Ibid. Brev. dir. Hill. m. 11 d.
[10] Ibid.: "Et qe vous sachez qe nous auoms ceste busoigne a cuer nous vous escriuoms souz nostre secre seal."
[11] K. R. Mem. Roll, no. 95, m. 17 d. L. T. R. Mem. Roll, no. 92, m. 48 d (22 Jan. 1322).
[12] K. R. Mem. Roll, no. 97, Brev. dir. Trin. m. 9.
[13] Ibid. Brev. dir. Pasch. m. 2.
[14] Ibid. no. 98, Brev. dir. m. 2 d.

Writs under the secret seal were addressed to the exchequer in its wider sphere in its relation to the "administrative" council. The lieutenant of the treasurer and barons were ordered by secret seal to summon the justices of both benches and other good men to consider the petition of the archbishop of Canterbury[1], and a similar writ was addressed to Despenser, the son, the bishop of Exeter, treasurer, and Baldock, chancellor, on 3 April, 1324, about a charter of Henry de Lancaster[2].

Little evidence now remains of interference with the course of justice by writ under the secret seal. John Inge was ordered, as a justice of assize, to hear a plea of novel disseisin despite the fact that parliament was being held. The disseisor secured a writ of secret seal, which he took to Inge, summoning him to the parliament at Westminster the same day, although the thing was impossible. The demandant naturally regarded the intrusion of this writ with ill-favour and claimed that it was to the great damage of other people who had obtained assizes[3]. While the eyre of London was in progress the king announced to the chancellor, under the secret seal, that he had sent under that seal to the justice of eyre concerning the alliances of Londoners[4].

The only use of the secret seal which has been noted in the local administration was as a receipt for payments made to the household. The citizens of York made payments totalling £89 to various clerks of the king by order of the king under his secret seal[5]. William, archbishop of York, for fine for his service in the Scottish war in the seventh year of the king, paid into the wardrobe 500 marks, for which he had the king's letter under the secret seal[6].

The use of the secret seal as an instrument of the wardrobe has been discussed[7]; the king also used it as a receipt for what he received from the wardrobe. In the last few weeks of his actual reign £2000 which was paid out of the wardrobe to him was acknowledged by a letter patent sealed with the secret seal[8].

There remains to be treated the use of the secret seal as a means of private correspondence. The king used the secret seal to send letters

[1] K. R. Mem. Roll, no. 88, m. 17 d (27 July, 1314).

[2] Ibid. no. 97. Brev. dir. Pasch. m. 2. Vide App. of Doc. no. 37.

[3] Ancient Petition, no. 2273.

[4] Chan. Warr., File 1329/26. The chancellor was to make writs with the great seal according to the tenor of the secret seal if he considered it advisable (14 Jan. 1321).

[5] Issue Roll, no. 172, m. 4.

[6] Ibid. no. 170, m. 7.

[7] Vide above, pp. 160–1.

[8] Enrolm. of Wardr. Accts. Exch. L. T. R. Roll, no. 2, m. 26.

to the queen and to lady la Despenser[1]. He wrote under it to the earl of Pembroke on business touching his nephew the earl of Arundel[2], to the pope and cardinals on behalf of Baldock[3], and on other business[4]. The letter which the king addressed to William de Ayremynne from Westminster on 1 March, 1321, and which was sealed with the secret seal, may be regarded as a private communication, though Ayremynne was a keeper of the great seal. The king expressed great satisfaction at the diligence shown in his business and besought him to continue diligent. If news reached him that the king was going towards Gloucester he was to pay no attention to it. For the king had no news of those parts and he only went to see the country and to ride through his land as was agreed before his departure[5].

Besides the warrants under the privy and secret seals there was a class of informal warrants which had no official or formal connection with the king except that they expressed his will. These warrants were written by official or unofficial persons about the king. They were administrative but were not authenticated by any of the royal seals. The informal warrants frequently started with the phrase "le Roy voet" and such writs as those of protection[6] were ordered by them. A writ to Henry de Percy to certify the king if he had arrested John de Dalton was ordered in this way[7], and writs for licence to cut timber in a forest[8], to the bailiffs of Hartlepool to supply the king with a ship with sixty men, allowance for which was to be taken out of the maltolt[9], to the taxors of the twentieth and fifteenth to pay £100, to the poulterer of the king's household[10], to Robert de Holand, justice of Chester, concerning the gathering of men at arms[11]. The king wished Bernard Feranto to become the provost of La Réole and, by informal warrant, a writ to this effect was ordered to be made to the seneschal of Gascony[12]. Petitions were enclosed in informal letters to the chancellor, who was ordered to do justice according to reason[13]. Orders prohibiting writs were sent to the chancery in this informal way. The bishop of Norwich, chancellor, wrote to Ayremynne,

[1] Stowe MS. 553, f. 67 b.
[2] Anc. Corresp. vol. XLIX, no. 48.
[3] Stowe MS. 553, f. 130.
[4] Anc. Corresp. vol. XXXV, no. 89.
[5] Ibid. vol. XXXVI, no. 209. Vide App. of Doc. no. 112.
[6] Chan. Warr., File 1705. Vide App. of Doc. no. 89.
[7] Ibid.
[8] Ibid. File 1704. Vide App. of Doc. no. 88.
[9] Chan. Warr., File 1704. Vide App. of Doc. no. 88.
[10] Ibid. File 1703. Vide App of Doc. no. 87.
[11] Anc. Corresp. vol. XXXVI, no. 154.
[12] Ibid. vol. XXXV, no. 100. The address of this is similar to a writ under the privy seal but it has no testing clause and no seal.
[13] Ibid. vol. XXXII, no. 138.

Bardelby and Clif, keepers of the great seal, giving the king's will that, after the receipt of that letter, they were to seal no writ with the seal which was in their keeping but to remain in peace[1]. If there was any urgent business the writs were to be sent to the chancellor under the keepers' seals and if not they were to await the chancellor's arrival[2]. It was his will that the couriers of the pope should have letters of safe-conduct to go safely throughout all his power in the form which those of his council wished, and this message was made known to the responsible person in a private letter from a member of the king's court[3].

Payments from the exchequer were made on the warrant of these informal commands, 2000 marks being ordered to be paid to the Friscobaldi in this way[4]. Sometimes the name of the source of the informal warrant appears. On 26 January, 1322, payment of £15 was made to one of the king's valets for the passage of certain great horses from abroad to England and thence on to the king in the marches of Wales, the money being raised by the collectors of customs in the port of London, by order of Walter de Norwich, keeper of the office of treasurer, by letter of the younger Despenser[5]. In a like manner the treasurer and the council were ordered to examine the faults which Robert de Wodehouse, viewer of the various castles in North Wales, found the last time he was there and they were ordered to ordain hasty remedy for each one[6]. An informal warrant was sent to the justices ordering the release of a prisoner indicted before them as he had made fine before the king[7], and the sheriff of Kent was ordered to secure 100 men from the town of Sandwich for the king's war[8].

Informal warrants were also used in communication between various officials of the administration. The class which will be specially noticed here will be communications between officials of the household and the departments of the administration, which include the household warrants. The treasurer wrote to the chamberlains

[1] Anc. Corresp. vol. XXXVI, no. 19: "Et nous vous mandoms qe la volunte nostre seigneur le Roi est qe del houre qe ceste lettre vous ieit aunne qe vous ne facez sealer nul bref du seal qest en vostre garde mes qe vous la place demorez en pees."

[2] Ibid.: "Et si les bosoignes demandent haste nous enuiez les brefs desuth voz seaux et si noun les retenez vers vo...a nostre venue."

[3] Ibid. vol. XXXVII, no. 104.

[4] Ibid. vol. L, no. 114. Vide App. of Doc. no. 132.

[5] Issue Roll, no. 196, m. 5.

[6] Parl. and Council Proc. (Chan.), File 5/6.

[7] Anc. Corresp. vol. XXXVI, no. 155. Vide App. of Doc. no. 109.

[8] Chan. Warr., File 1705. Vide App. of Doc. no. 89.

of the exchequer that the king and council ordained that Gilbert Perch should have immediate payment of the debt of £100 which the king owed him for the store of a castle[1]. The treasurer used an equally informal warrant when, on behalf of the king, he ordered them to pay Ingelard de Warle, keeper of the wardrobe, 1000 marks[2].

The steward of the household made warrant to the chancellor for writs of protection for those who were going in the king's company to the Scottish war, or in his service in the company of others[3]. Edmund de Mauley, when steward, made warrant for king's serjeants[4], John de Crombwell for two knights in the king's service in Cherleton's company[5]. Some of the warrants contained a long list of names and were certified by the testimony of the steward[6]. Sometimes the protection by the steward was particular and not general. Badlesmere made warrant for one going for the fortification of Carlisle[7]. Crombwell made testimony for one going in the company of his brother Ralph to stay in Beaumont's company, in the Scottish march[8]. The lieutenant of the steward made similar warrants[9]. The steward also wrote to the chancellor for one who being in the king's service was impleaded in a plea of land before the justices of the bench. He asked for warrant for his absence[10]. Richard Damory, when steward, requested the bishop of Exeter, treasurer, to make writs to the sheriffs of Derby and Lancaster to cease demands of the debts of one who was in the king's service in Gascony as long as he was thus employed[11].

Warrant for protection for one going to Scotland with the king was issued to the chancellor by the keeper of the wardrobe[12]. That official, by the king's orders, wrote acquainting the chancellor that the prior of Holy Trinity, London, had come to court to present himself to the king[13]. This instance of the keeper of the wardrobe acting as the king's private secretary is valuable and throws light upon his importance in administration.

The household warrants are mainly concerned with requests for writs for the purveyance of necessaries for the household offices. The keeper of the wardrobe requested writs to obtain wax, ink and

[1] Anc. Corresp. vol. L, no. 26.
[2] Ibid. no. 115.
[3] Vide Chan. Warr., Files 1703–5 passim, 1648, nos. 25 a, 30 c.
[4] Ibid. File 1703. Vide App. of Doc. no. 87 b.
[5] Ibid. File 1704.
[6] Ibid.
[7] Ibid. File 1705.
[8] Anc. Corresp. vol. XXXV, no. 1444.
[9] Chan. Warr., File 1705, protection by Robert de Haustede.
[10] Anc. Corresp. vol. XXXVI, no. 135: "nostre seigneur le Roi veut qe le dit Johan eye son garant por sa absence."
[11] Ibid. vol. XXXVII, no. 1.
[12] Chan. Warr., File 1706.
[13] Anc. Corresp. vol. XXXVI, no. 55.

other things for his office[1]. Warrants for purveyance were made, especially for provisions for the royal household, payment being ordered on the wardrobe[2], and for the appointment of purveyors[3]. Similar warrants were made for the mariners of the king's ships to provide men for the ships[4], and for commissions for divers offices of the queen's household[5].

Almost as important as the orders conveyed by warrant, formal and informal, were those made by word of mouth, directly by the king, or indirectly by his messengers. Writs under privy seal were little less personal than royal orders, and Edward I in a writ to the treasurer and barons of the exchequer ordered them to grant respite until he should give them order by word of mouth or under his privy seal[6], a juxtaposition which is important when the nature and effect of the two methods are considered. The evidence in the records concerning the use of the verbal order is no measure of its use to convey commands. The essence of the verbal order was its personal nature and its possibilities of secrecy. The verbal order was used far more in the household offices than in the chancery and exchequer, and of the household offices there is less evidence of its use in the wardrobe than in the chamber accounts. With the growth of the idea of the responsibility of ministers there was an increasing use of the written warrant, though the verbal order is throughout important.

The verbal order was extensively used as the warrant for chancery writs and to the exchequer and wardrobe for payments. A large number of writs on the various chancery rolls were tested and the note "by the king himself" added[7]. Sometimes the privy seal was used in confirmation or extension of such direct verbal orders from the king to the chancellor. The chancellor was ordered thus to make the commission for Robert de Aylleston, keeper of the privy seal, and John de Stonore, with which he was charged on his departure from the king[8]. Margaret, the queen of Edward I, wrote to the archbishop of Canterbury, who held the great seal, for letters under that instrument

[1] Chan. Warr., File 1648/59. [2] Ibid. no. 1 a.

[3] Ibid. nos. 6 a, 50 b; File 1703 passim.

[4] Ibid. File 1649/93 a: "pur prendre leur mene pur leur niefs."

[5] Ibid. File 1650/217 a. [6] *Cal. Close Rolls*, 1288–96, p. 347.

[7] Vide *Cal. Close Rolls, Cal. Pat. Rolls, Cal. Fine Rolls* passim. The enrolments are not always a safe index on this point, as the words "per ipsum Regem" are sometimes omitted in the roll when they are found in the writ. Cf. writ to J. de Benstede, 4 August, 1312 (*Cal. Pat. Rolls*, 1307–13, pp. 489–490; *Foedera*, vol. II, p. 175). The enrolments omit "per ipsum Regem" whereas the writ (K. R. Acct. 309/18) has these words.

[8] Chan. Warr., File 125/6752. Vide App. of Doc. no. 79.

on the grounds that Edward II had previously specially recommended the queen and her business to him at St Alban's, in Margaret's presence[1]. When the king was in an extremity he ordered the chancellor not to proceed in a certain matter without special order by word of mouth from himself[2].

Writs of liberate were made on direct verbal warrant from the king. A writ of liberate was made to Master William de Testa concerning the archbishopric and mint of Canterbury, which had been granted out by Edward I, the writ being issued by command of the king made to the chancellor and treasurer[3]. Such writs to the prior and convent of Langley for the sustenance of fifty-five friars[4], to the Bardi for £2000 in recompense of losses and by reason of delay in the payment of debts[5], and to the queen[6] and Stephen de Mauley[7] for repayment of loans in the wardrobe, were made by the king himself.

A few instances of the use of the direct verbal order to the wardrobe and chamber will suffice here. By the king's order by word of mouth the keeper of the wardrobe was ordered to pay £40 to John de Crescak, banneret of Ireland, and twenty marks to John de Beauchamp of Somerset[8]. In the account of William de Langley, clerk of the king's chamber, audited early in Edward III's reign, he reported various expenses and payments made by command of the king himself by word of mouth[9].

Verbal orders as warrants for writs and payments were also made by royal messengers, sometimes by the officials of the administrative offices, but more often by household officials. Chancery writs were issued on the announcement of the treasurer[10], a justice[11], Melton[12], Warle[13], Mauley[14] Writs of liberate were issued on the announcement of the treasurer[15], and Norwich[16], and by such court officials as

[1] Anc. Corresp. vol. XXXV, no. 131.

[2] Chan. Warr., File 82/2430. Vide App. of Doc. no. 56.

[3] Liberate Roll, no. 87, m. 2: "Per preceptum Regis factum Cancellario et Thesaurario."

[4] Ibid. no. 89, m. 3.

[5] Ibid. m. 2.

[6] Ibid. no. 88, m. 2.

[7] Ibid. m. 1.

[8] Stowe MS. 553, f. 136.

[9] Pipe Roll, no. 171, m. 41: "Et diuersas expensas et liberaciones faciendum per preceptum ipsius Regis oretenus."

[10] E.g. *Rot. Scot.* p. 61.

[11] E.g. *Cal. Close Rolls*, 1307–13, pp. 13, 15, 17 (15 Dec. 1307). *Rot. Scot.* p. 153.

[12] E.g. *Cal. Fine Rolls*, 1307–19, p. 121. *Rot. Scot.* pp. 58, 108.

[13] E.g. *Cal. Close Rolls*, 1307–13, p. 417.

[14] E.g. ibid. pp. 464, 488; *Cal. Pat. Rolls*, 1307–13, pp. 427, 469; *Rot. Scot.* p. 109.

[15] Liberate Roll, no. 87, m. 3.

[16] Ibid. no. 89, m. 4.

Warle, keeper of the wardrobe[1], and Mauley, steward of the household[2].

Information conveyed by privy seal to the chancellor was sometimes extended by verbal orders. A commission of novel disseisin was thus ordered in April, 1318, the chancellor to be more fully informed by Oliver de Ingham[3], a household servant. On 1 May, 1317, the chancellor was ordered by privy seal to make good and suitable letters under the great seal, for the purpose of the matters which Richard de Ayremynne and Master John de Hildesle, the king's clerks, would tell him by word of mouth[4].

Grants under the exchequer seal were made by the king's verbal order conveyed by a messenger. Sometimes the messenger was the treasurer or his lieutenant[5] or a royal confidant like Melton[6] or Baldock[7]. Administrative writs also issued from the exchequer on the king's order by the announcement of some official such as the lieutenant of the treasurer[8] or John de Okham[9], the cofferer of the wardrobe. A petition which had come before a council in the exchequer was returned by the king to the exchequer by Melton, controller of the wardrobe[10]. Another petition which the king had considered, Sandale, chancellor of the exchequer, was ordered to expound to the treasurer and barons on the king's behalf[11].

Payments were made from the exchequer by the king's command conveyed by various persons, generally a person around the royal court, though sometimes by such a trusty official as Walter de Norwich[12], the treasurer[13], the chancellor[14], or Pembroke[15]. Among those who ordered payments from the exchequer on the king's behalf were Warle[16], Thomas de Useflet[17], clerk of the king's chamber[18], and

[1] Liberate Roll, no. 89, m. 4 (15 Oct. 1312).

[2] Ibid. (3 Aug. 1312). The number of writs of liberate issued in 6 Ed. II by the announcement of various persons is greater than usual, a probable result of the Ordinances of 1311. Vide Liberate Roll, no. 89.

[3] Ibid. Files 104/4635 d, 125/6748: "vous dirra plus pleinement de þouche."

[4] Ibid. File 99/4190.

[5] K. R. Mem. Roll, no. 82, m. 15 d.

[6] Ibid. m. 4; no. 85, m. 3.

[7] K. R. Mem. Roll, no. 97, m. 5 d. L. T. R. Mem. Roll, no. 93, m. 1.

[8] K. R. Mem. Roll, no. 85, m. 98.

[9] Ibid.

[10] Ibid. no. 81, m. 52.

[11] Ibid. m. 39.

[12] Issue Roll, no. 189, mm. 1, 2.

[13] Ibid. no. 145, m. 2 (9 May, 1308): "per preceptum domini Regis et ordinacionem eiusdem nunciante Thesaurario"; no. 157, m. 3.

[14] Ibid. no. 189, m. 2.

[15] Ibid.

[16] Ibid. no. 146, m. 2.

[17] Vide below, p. 232.

[18] Issue Roll, no. 196, m. 7 (6 Oct. 1321). This was in confirmation of a privy seal to the same effect: "per mandatum domini Regis de priuato sigillo et per

Baldock[1]. In 1315 a payment for debts due to the recipient in the wardrobe was announced on the king's behalf by Oliver de Ingham and Hugh D'Audley[2], junior, who was then finding a place in the royal favour and was to help to establish the sway of the middle party[3].

The connection between the administration and the household is suggested by the fact that the persons who conveyed the king's order in these instances were in many cases household officers, and also by the fact that the same person was the king's messenger to the exchequer and wardrobe. Thus payments were made in the wardrobe in 1322 on the announcement of Baldock[4]. Amongst others upon whose announcement payment was made in the wardrobe were Oliver de Bordeaux, Richard Damory, king's steward, and Thomas de Weston[5].

Besides the officials of administration and household, various magnates and others conveyed the king's orders to the different departments. Writs of chancery were frequently issued on the information of Pembroke[6], and the elder Despenser[7]. A writ of liberate was issued on their joint announcement and another of a gift of £50 to Walter de Norwich, lieutenant of the treasurer, in aid of expenses in that office, on Pembroke's information[8]. A commission, under the exchequer seal, of the office of weigher of receipt was conveyed to the treasurer by the bishop of Worcester, chancellor, who had lately received the order from the king at Woodstock[9]. Orders delivered by messenger in this way were not always accredited. The king's will had been reported to the archbishop of York, treasurer, by various persons, that he should fortify the Tower of London. He was unwilling to do this on such information alone, as the king had ordered him not to expend anything out of the treasury without special order[10].

The potency of the verbal order was as great in the routine of administration and in emergency measures as in the issue of writs and the payment of money; for instance, the chancellor might be

preceptum domini Regis nunciante Thome de Ouseflete clerico dicti domini Regis."

[1] Issue Rolls, no. 198, m. 1; no. 200, m. 1.

[2] Ibid. no. 174, m. 2.

[3] Vide below, pp. 432–3.

[4] Stowe MS. 553, ff. 67b–8.

[5] Ibid. f. 67.

[6] *Cal. Fine Rolls*, 1307–19, p. 140. *Cal. Pat. Rolls*, 1307–13, pp. 483, 486, 491, 497, 503, 524. *Cal. Close Rolls*, 1307–13, pp. 481, 506, 566.

[7] *Cal. Pat. Rolls*, 1307–13, p. 491. *Cal. Close Rolls*, 1323–27, p. 240.

[8] Liberate Roll, no. 89, m. 4.

[9] K. R. Mem. Roll, no. 84, m. 4 d (22 June, 1311).

[10] Anc. Corresp. vol. XLIX, no. 83.

ordered by word of mouth to send the king the great seal[1]. The barons of the exchequer were forbidden by writ of privy seal to make any assignment or payment to anyone whatsoever out of the money of the tenth that came there, unless the king commanded them to do so by word of mouth[2]. The treasurer was ordered by word of mouth to make arrangements and decision concerning the position of one Sir Adam de Gourdoun, and on his failure to do so a writ under the privy seal was addressed to him[3]. A command that one of the barons should go outside the exchequer on its business was given to Walter de Norwich by word of mouth[4].

Verbal orders by the king were also made to the justices. When some defendant before the king's bench put himself upon the country, the king by word of mouth ordered Henry Spigurnel to associate with him a knight of Stafford and try the case at Stafford[5]. Verbal orders to proceed were also given by the king to his justices[6].

The verbal orders made to local officials of which evidence remains all had reference to expenditure, notably to expenditure upon repairs to castles. The sheriff of Nottingham was ordered, by command from the king's mouth, to pay for certain works done in the castle[7]. By similar order the sheriff of Cumberland was commanded to keep men at arms in the castle of Carlisle[8], and the sheriff of Nottingham and Derby to pay the wages of certain carpenters and workmen repairing the peel in the royal park at Clipston[9]. Walter de Beauchamp, constable of Warwick, was ordered by the king by word of mouth to keep ten men-at-arms and thirty cross-bow men in the castle for its safe-guarding[10], and to repair its mills and walls[11]. Pembroke, constable of Rockingham, was ordered to undertake certain works

[1] *Cal. Close Roll*, 1307–13, p 68. Vide also above, pp. 127–8.

[2] K. R. Mem. Roll, no. 93, m. 53 d. L. T. R. Mem. Roll, no. 90, Brev. dir. Trin. m. 13.

[3] K. R. Mem. Roll, no. 83, m. 15.

[4] K. R. Mem. Roll, no. 95, m. 16 d. L. T. R. Mem. Roll, no. 92, m. 47 d (10 Dec. 1321).

[5] Wm Salt Soc., *Coll.* vol. x, pp. 18–19.

[6] *Year Bk* 15 *Ed. III* [Rolls Series], p. 142.

[7] K. R. Mem. Roll, no. 92, Brev. dir. m. 43 d. L. T. R. Mem. Roll, no. 89, m. 108 d.

[8] Liberate Roll, no. 89, m. 4.

[9] K. R. Mem. Roll, no. 92, Brev. dir. 43 d. L. T. R. Mem. Roll, no. 89, m. 108 d.

[10] K. R. Mem. Roll, no. 92. Brev. dir. m. 37 d. L. T. R. Mem. Roll, no. 89, m. 102 d. K. R. Mem. Roll, no. 93, m. 17. L. T. R. Mem. Roll, no. 90, Brev. dir. Hill. m. 3 d.

[11] K. R. Mem. Roll, no. 93, m. 15 d. L. T. R. Mem. Roll, no. 90, Brev. dir. Hill. m. 1 d.

there by similar command[1], and the constable of Northampton castle to execute repairs[2]. In association with these direct verbal orders to the local administration must be considered an order made to the merchants of the company of the Bardi who acted as the royal financial agents. They were ordered, and obeyed the order, to pay Pembroke a sum of 500 marks, though they had no stronger warrant at the time of payment than the king's verbal order. A writ of great seal was however ordered subsequently[3].

Direct orders were given by the king to the officials of his household. The clerk of the marshalsea of the household was ordered by word of mouth by the king to give eighteen quarters of oats to certain men who had charge of some of the king's horses[4]. Thomas de Useflet, clerk of the great wardrobe, was ordered verbally to provide certain necessaries for the king's need[5]. An instance of the way in which the verbal order was used in the household is provided by a summons which was issued to attend a meeting of the council. The king gave the order verbally to Despenser who in haste passed it on to the official who sent out the summons[6].

Verbal orders were also conveyed to the administration, local and central, indirectly by messengers. Walter, bishop elect of Worcester, treasurer, ordered the chancellor in 1308 by special order of the king made to him by word of mouth, to send the great seal to the king at Windsor, the message being delivered by the treasurer in the presence of the steward of the household[7]. On 5 October, 1312, Pembroke and the elder Despenser on the king's behalf ordered Osgodby, Ayremynne, and Bardelby, clerks of chancery, to seal the great seal with their seals in the presence of the chancellor[8]. The appointments of the bishop of Worcester as lieutenant of the chancellor, and of Sandale as lieutenant of the treasurer, were announced in the exchequer by Despenser on the king's behalf on 6 October, 1312[9].

In the exchequer, too, royal messengers bore the king's will to the officials. On 23 October, 1311, the bishop of Worcester, chancellor, went to the exchequer, and when the barons and chamberlains were

[1] K. R. Mem. Roll, no. 94, m. 49 d. L. T. R. Mem. Roll, no. 91, Brev. dir. Pasch. m. 5 d.

[2] K. R. Mem. Roll. no. 92, Brev. dir. m. 34 d. L. T. R. Mem. Roll, no. 89, m. 100.

[3] Chan. Warr., File 134/7551.

[4] Stowe MS. 553, f. 122 b.

[5] Issue Roll, no. 219, m. 3.

[6] Anc. Corresp. vol. XXXVII, no. 88. Vide App. of Doc. no. 113.

[7] *Cal. Close Rolls*, 1307–13, p. 68.

[8] Ibid. pp. 552–3 (5 Oct. 1312).

[9] K. R. Mem. Roll, no. 86, m. 71.

summoned he announced to them on behalf of the king that for certain reasons it was not the king's will that Sandale, treasurer, should act any longer in that office until further orders, and said that he had announced that to him by the king's command[1]. The chancellor likewise informed Norwich, lieutenant of the treasurer, on 20 December, 1311, on the king's behalf, that it was his will that the horses and armour of Peter de Friscobaldi, taken into his hands by virtue of the Ordinance, should be restored[2]. Orders to the exchequer were carried there in 1319 by the two great officials of the household, Despenser, chamberlain, and Badlesmere, steward[3]. The king, who was sending Adam de Lymbergh to Gascony to survey victuals in 1324, sent him to the exchequer to speak the king's intention, as the king had charged him to do fully by word of mouth[4]. The treasurer and barons of the exchequer in 1297 had been told fully by the bishop of Ely by word of mouth on the king's behalf to hand over a prisoner charged with the forgery of writs to the bishop of London, in accordance with the privilege of the clergy[5]. Sandale, chancellor of the exchequer, handed to the exchequer a certain petition. The petition had been presented to the king in parliament and there endorsed, and Sandale, who had been present, was enjoined by the king by word of mouth to explain the matter to the treasurer and barons on his behalf[6].

Royal messengers also appeared in the courts of justice, and on the royal behalf superseded writs of great seal. An abbot had secured a writ, ordering the justices to proceed to an inquisition to be made by the country; Pembroke and Despenser, holding the place of the king, on his behalf ordered the justices, on the announcement of Henry Spigurnel, that, notwithstanding the order under the great seal, they should supersede the taking of the inquisition and place it in respite until the octave of St Hilary[7].

The king communicated with the "administrative" council by

[1] K. R. Mem. Roll, no. 85, m. 41. L. T. R. Mem. Roll, no. 82, m. 18: "conuocatis Baronibus et Camerariis nunciauit eisdem ex parte Regis quod certis de causis non est voluntatis Regis ad presens quod Johannes de Sandale Thesaurarius Regis se intromittat amplius de eodem donec Rex alias inde etcetera asserens se habere mandatum ad hoc quod ipse nunciaret hoc eidem Johanni ex parte Regis." Vide Madox, *Hist. of Exch.* vol. II, pp. 47–48.

[2] K. R. Mem. Roll, no. 85, m. 45 d.

[3] Ibid. no. 92, Brev. dir. m. 25 d. L. T. R. Mem. Roll, no. 89, m. 88.

[4] K. R. Mem. Roll, no. 100, Brev. dir. Mich. m. 7 d.

[5] *Cal. Close Rolls*, 1296–1302, p. 56.

[6] K. R. Mem. Roll, no. 81, m. 39.

[7] *Abbrev. Placit.* p. 313.

means of a messenger. It was ordered to cause the process against Henry de Beaumont to be drawn up and enrolled on the roll of the benches, as Geoffrey le Scrope was to tell them more fully on the king's behalf[1]. A mainprise of certain men to keep the peace in the city of London was made before the bishop of Worcester, Pembroke, Despenser, Sandale and other of the king's council, provided it was agreeable to the king. It was submitted to the king, and Pembroke notified the council of his assent[2]. The king and the members of his council who were with him sent a messenger to the archbishop of Canterbury and others of the council at London in 1316 that they were to hear what he should explain to them by word of mouth[3]. Similar to the use of the messenger as a means of communication between king and council was the employment of William de Cusance to report certain things to the earl of Pembroke[4].

Royal messengers were employed on more than one occasion to wait upon provincial councils. The messengers appeared as a solemn deputation. In March, 1312, the archbishop of Canterbury and the bishops of that province who were about to assemble with certain earls and barons at London were ordered to give credence to certain knights and clerks whom the king was sending to explain to them certain matters touching the Ordinances made by them and the same earls and barons[5]. A similar though smaller deputation was sent by the king to the provincial council which was being held at London in November, 1321. The council was ordered to give credence to what the earls of Richmond and Arundel and Master Robert de Baldock would explain to them verbally touching the king's affairs[6]. The object which the king sought to attain was the opinion of the provincial council upon the exile of the Despensers[7]. The king sent messengers to the pope who were to expound certain matters to him, and others who were to inform him more fully verbally of matters about which he had already written to him[8]. He also

[1] Chan. Warr., File 123/6542. Vide App. of Doc. no. 77.

[2] *Cal. Close Rolls*, 1307–13, p. 484.

[3] Cf. *Cal. Close Rolls*, 1313–18, p. 429.

[4] Anc. Corresp. vol. XLIX, no. 51. Vide App. of Doc. no. 127.

[5] *Cal. Close Rolls*, 1307–13, p. 451. They were the bishop of Norwich, Guy Ferre, John de Crombwell, Hugh D'Audley, William Deyncourt, Henry Spigurnel, Henry le Scrope, knights, and Master Thomas de Cobham, Robert de Pickering, Walter de Thorp, Gilbert de Middleton, John Francis and Andrew de Burges, king's clerks.

[6] Ibid. 1318–23, p. 410. *Cal. Pat. Rolls*, 1321–24, p. 38 (30 Mar. 1321).

[7] Cf. *Chron. Murimuth*, p. 35.

[8] *Cal. Doc. Scotl.* vol. III, p. 56. *Foedera*, vol. II, pp. 175–6 (6 Aug. 1312).

sent a clerk and counsellor of his who were to relate certain matters to the pope on the royal behalf[1].

Verbal orders by messenger in the local administration are difficult to trace. A keeper of manors which had belonged to the Templars gave corn, stock and other goods and chattels to a yeoman of the king's chamber at his request for the king's use, without the king's writ[2]. A more important instance was the deputation which, on 20 September, 1312, went to the Guildhall. The deputation consisted of Pembroke, Despenser, Mauley, steward of the household, Nicholas de Segrave, marshal, and John de Crombwell, constable of the Tower, who proposed many things on the king's behalf and for the security of the city. They were unable, however, to show any commission made to them by the king. A great tumult therefore arose and they hardly escaped without danger to life[3].

There were also various other matters which the king could and did effect by word of mouth. Roger de Northburgh was appointed keeper of the wardrobe by the king by word of mouth[4]. The king sought to exert his influence to obtain the bishopric of Winchester for Sandale and verbally asked the prior and monks of St Swithin's to assist him[5]. Robert Poun, an adherent of the earl of Hereford in 1321–2, was pardoned by the king by word of mouth[6].

In various ways the king sought to exert his personal influence. In the parliament of Northampton in 1309 Gavaston was confirmed in his earldom of Cornwall, a result which the chronicler attributed to the privy procurement of the king beforehand[7]. In 1312, after Gavaston's murder, the king appeared in London and personally appealed to the citizens to assist him and to undertake the defence of the city in his cause. The king's speech had the desired effect and the citizens promised to do this[8].

Requests were made to the king in person by word of mouth. Bartholomew de Badlesmere begged the king in this way to grant the bishopric of Winchester to Henry de Burghersh his nephew[9]. Another begged the king to show grace and favour to one of his valets in what John de Benstede would tell him verbally[10]. As the king sent messengers with verbal orders to the council so the council

[1] Anc. Corresp. vol. XXXII, no. 120. Vide App. of Doc. no. 98.

[2] *Cal. Close Rolls*, 1313–18, p. 497.

[3] *Ann. Lond.* pp. 215–216. *Ann. Paul.* p. 272.

[4] Enrolm. of Wardr. Accts. Exch. L. T. R. Roll, no. 2, m. 1.

[5] Anc. Corresp. vol. XLIX, no. 35.

[6] Chan. Warr., File 132/7431.

[7] *Chron. Lanerc.* p. 189.

[8] *Ann. Lond.* pp. 208–9.

[9] Anc. Corresp. vol. XXXIII, no. 10.

[10] *Cal. Doc. Scotl.* vol. III, p. 22.

sent messengers to the king. A petition which came before the council was ordered to be delivered to Sir Richard de Sturmy who was to show it to the king that he might state his will regarding it[1]. The treasurer assembled the council to consider certain bulls touching the king's profit which had been found in the exchequer. Transcripts were sent to the king by Master William de Maldon who was to inform him more fully by word of mouth of the council's advice[2]. The messenger who was to convey information from the exchequer was sometimes appointed by the king. In August, 1326, the king desired to have information about the Tower of London, the array of the exchequer, the names of the auditors, and other ministers of the exchequer, and the treasurer and barons were to supply it without delay and to send Adam de Lymbergh to inform the king fully of these matters[3].

The different ways in which the king, notwithstanding the increased bulk and intricacy of business, could exercise almost complete control of the administration, were but varied forms of one central fact, that the executive was still entirely in the hands of the king and the household. The instruments of the executive, the privy seal, the secret seal, informal warrants and verbal orders, entered into every phase of the administration and exerted their powerful influence. The completeness of the king's control over the executive was in part dependent upon the financial freedom of the wardrobe and chamber from the administration; in part that financial freedom was a result of the strength of the executive.

In addition to the complete power which the king had over the executive and which, working through the instruments of the executive, he had over the whole administration, there were one or two ways in which the king's presence and advice made themselves felt in the administration. At times he sat in the chancery. The earl of Warenne acknowledged in chancery before the king at Lincoln that he owed him £1000[4]. Recognisances were made by Despenser and Badlesmere in the king's presence[5].

The ways in which the great seal was bestowed and returned in the king's chamber in his presence have been stated previously[6]. In

[1] Ancient Petition, no. 2481: "soit ceste peticion liuere a sire Richard de Sturmy et il la face monstrer a nostre seigneur le Roi a dire ent sa volente."

[2] K. R. Mem. Roll, no. 85, m. 55 d. Vide App. of Doc. no. 17.

[3] K. R. Mem. Roll, no. 102, m. 74.

[4] *Cal. Close Rolls*, 1313–18, p. 325 (23 Feb. 1316).

[5] Ibid. 1318–23, p. 225. A recognisance was made before Edward I in 1300 (*Cal. Close Rolls*, 1296–1302, pp. 405–6) and sent to the chancery by writ of privy seal.

[6] Above, pp. 68–69.

the king's presence Adam de Brom was to receive the seal of the bishopric of Durham in 1316 during its vacancy[1]. Hamo de Chigwell, mayor of London, was deposed from the mayoralty at Westminster in 1323 in the king's presence, and Nicholas de Faringdon was elected mayor by the king and was sworn in chancery[2]. The mayor of London was presented to the king in his palace of Westminster[3]. Sir Thomas de Grey, constable of Norham, undertook in the king's presence to provide for the defence of that castle[4]. An indenture between the king and the burgesses of Berwick about the safe keeping of the castle and town was sealed in 1317 in the presence of the king and the prelates, earls, barons and others of his council[5]. In the king's presence, at the Tower of London, Norwich was instructed to search the rolls and memoranda of the exchequer for certain particulars concerning the castle of Tintagel[6]. The treasurer and barons of the exchequer and others of the king's council were ordered to place in respite the king's butler, who was impleaded before them, as he was to be tried in the king's presence[7]. Badlesmere, who was loth to give up the custody of the castle and barton of Bristol, was ordered to do so without delay or to come before the king to certify why he had not done so and to receive judgment[8].

It was constantly necessary for the administration to consult the king to discover his will on various points. Petitions to the king and council were referred to him that he might state his will[9]. A letter of the count of Hainault was sent to the bishop of Exeter, treasurer, and Norwich, chief baron of the exchequer. They were ordered to call the council, and if perchance there was any point which they could not decide without advisement of the king, they were to make it known to him clearly[10]. By another petition, enclosed to the treasurer and barons, they were ordered to do right and reason, and if

[1] Chan. Warr., File 95/3752. [2] *Cal. Letter Books, D*, p. 32.

[3] K. R. Mem. Roll, no. 91, Pres. Mich. m. 3. L. T. R. Mem. Roll, no. 88, Pres. Mich. m. 3. K. R. Mem. Roll, no. 94, m. 125. L. T. R. Mem. Roll, no. 91, Pres. Mich. m. 2 d.

[4] *Cal. Doc. Scott.* vol. III, pp. 143–4.

[5] K. R. Mem. Roll, no. 90, m. 118. L. T. R. Mem. Roll, no. 87, Rec. Trin. m. 4.

[6] Anc. Corresp. vol. XXXIV, no. 148.

[7] K. R. Mem. Roll, no. 91, Brev. dir. m. 37. L. T. R. Mem. Roll, no. 88, Brev. dir. Hill. m. 13 d. Vide App. of Doc. no. 23.

[8] *Cal. Pat. Rolls*, 1307–13, p. 452. [9] *Rot. Parl.* vol. I, p. 418.

[10] K. R. Mem. Roll, no. 94, m. 47. L. T. R. Mem. Roll, no. 91, Brev. dir. Pasch. m. 2: "Et si par cas y eit nul point qe vous ne puissetz deliuerer saunz auisement de nous le nous facetz sauoir distinctement et apertement ensemblement od voz auys."

there was any cause by which they could not proceed without the king's advice they were to acquaint him with the fact under the exchequer seal and ask his will[1]. In no account of the keeper of the wardrobe or others rendered before them were they to make allowance for the delivery of any money to the king by anyone, who had not warrant of the king's seals, until the king had been sent details and he had returned his will[2]. Certain petitions from the king's council of Ireland were sent to the treasurer and barons. They were to ordain the remedy, which they could from their office, and if there was any matter which they could not do without the king's advice or special order they were to certify him fully without delay[3].

The king's position in the administrative machinery was fundamental and concentric. Every department was subject to his influence, and, following closely his influence, was the influence of the household officials and the king's personal advisers, whether drawn from the great earls like Pembroke, the baronage, as the Despensers, the lesser baronage, as Badlesmere, or the official class, as Melton and Baldock. What supplied a considerable amount of independence to the household or personal system of government was the organisation of its two financial departments of the wardrobe and the chamber.

[1] K. R. Mem. Roll, no. 100, Brev. dir. Hill. m. 1 d.
[2] Ibid. Brev. dir. Pasch. m. 3 d.
[3] Ibid. no. 102, m. 51 d.

CHAPTER VI

THE STRENGTH OF THE HOUSEHOLD SYSTEM (*cont.*)

(iii) *Finance*

The wardrobe as a department was divided into two, the great wardrobe and the wardrobe of the household, both rendering separate accounts to the exchequer[1]. The business of the great wardrobe was mainly official. The essential of the wardrobe of the household was its personal character and the personal relation in which it stood to the king. It was the "special mouthpiece of the personal will of the king[2]." The organisation of the wardrobe was complex, and the ways in which it was related to the administration were many and varied. The great seal was regularly deposited there. When the chancellor did not surrender the seal in the king's presence[3] it was sent to the wardrobe by him[4], and when in 1292 Robert Burnell the chancellor died, the seal was delivered into the wardrobe by one of the late chancellor's clerks who continued after that date to seal writs with it[5]. The wardrobe influenced the use of the great seal, by restricting its issue by the privy seal and by verbal orders carried by wardrobe officials[6].

The wardrobe was a frequent place for the deposit of various documents, the deposit being sometimes ordered by writ of privy seal. Robert de Leycet in September, 1307, was ordered by privy seal to send charters, writings and other muniments with all haste to the wardrobe[7]. Letters were thus deposited, a memorandum of their delivery being sometimes made on the close roll[8] or an enrolment being made there and the letters subsequently delivered to the

[1] K. R. Mem. Roll, no. 100, Brev. dir. Hill. m. 7 d: "totes acountes de Garderobe auxi bien de la grant garderobe come de la garderobe de nostre houstel."

[2] *Eng. Hist. Rev.* vol. XXIV [1909], 'The Chief Officers of the Wardrobe down to 1399,' T. F. Tout, p. 496.

[3] Vide above, pp. 68–69.

[4] *Cal. Close Rolls*, 1279–88, pp. 77, 147, 444; 1288–96, p. 71.

[5] Ibid. 1288–96, p. 243.

[6] Vide above, pp. 68–69.

[7] Anc. Corresp. vol. XXXII, no. 140. Vide App. of Doc. no. 99.

[8] *Cal. Close Rolls*, 1279–88, pp. 122–3.

wardrobe[1]. Deeds granting lands to the king[2], including one by the earl of Lancaster to Edward II of the manor of Melburn[3], of release of right in an earldom[4] and of acknowledgment of debt[5], were delivered into the wardrobe. The escheator was ordered to purchase land and the advowson and to send the charter to be deposited in the wardrobe[6]. Charters effecting the change of advowson when the king was a party, and the charter by which Roger Bigod, earl of Norfolk, granted manors and castles to Edward I[7], were ordered to be kept in the wardrobe[8]. A final concord in which the king was a party was ordered to be kept with other fines in the wardrobe[9].

A good number of these documents would seem to be purely personal, and therefore their deposit in the wardrobe does not cause surprise. Instruments which were much more public in their nature were similarly deposited there. A papal bull was delivered there, a memorandum of the fact being entered on the close roll[10], and also the acknowledgment by the papal nuncio of 4000 marks, the payment of cess for four years[11]. An indenture concerning writs of protection and others between the king and chancellor were made in triplicate, one being deposited in the chancery, another in the exchequer, and the third in the wardrobe[12]. The indentures of war made between the king and magnates for the protection of the Scottish march were sealed under the king's privy seal and were to remain in the king's wardrobe[13].

Rolls were temporarily delivered in the wardrobe by the chancellor for some specific purpose. In the king's wardrobe at St Alban's the chancellor delivered four rolls to one who was going as the king's messenger to treat for peace and truce with the king of France, three relating to the truce between the kings of France and Aragon and the last relating to the truce between Henry III and the king of France[14]. In 1305 a transcript of a plea in parliament concerning

[1] *Cal. Close Rolls*, 1288–96, p. 142; 1307–13, p. 254. The letters concerned a grant from the king to the count of Foix (ibid. 1288–96, p. 142), a procuration under the seals of the *consules* of certain Gascon towns that they might buy and sell salt wherever they wished (ibid. 1279–88, pp. 122–3), a letter of Alexander de Baliol touching his son Alexander (ibid. 1307–13, p. 254), which was in effect a mainprise (*Cal. Pat. Rolls*, 1307–13, p. 202).

[2] *Cal. Close Rolls*, 1272–79, p. 513; 1296–1302, p. 295.

[3] Ibid. 1307–13, p. 42 (30 Sept. 1907).

[4] Ibid. 1272–79, p. 511.

[5] Ibid. p. 425.

[6] Ibid. p. 175.

[7] Ibid. 1288–96, p. 201.

[8] Ibid. 1279–88, p. 284.

[9] Ibid. p. 46.

[10] Ibid. 1288–96, p. 51.

[11] Ibid. 1279–88, pp. 189–190.

[12] Ibid. 1296–1302, p. 304. *Stat. of Realm*, vol. I. p. 131.

[13] K. R. Acct. 68/2, no. 10. Vide App. of Doc. no. 46.

[14] *Cal. Close Rolls*, 1288–96, p. 505.

Nicholas de Segrave was delivered to the keeper of the wardrobe to be kept there[1]. In 1298 Edward I made provision of the first prebend of the value of 100 marks or more which should become vacant in England or Ireland for Master John Lovel and after he had been satisfied Sandale was to have the next prebend of that value. The king ordered that this memorandum should be registered in his wardrobe[2].

Recognisance of a debt was made before the cofferer and clerks of the wardrobe, the debt to be paid out of the next money due to the debtor from the wardrobe[3]. Information from the local administration was returned to the wardrobe. The sheriffs were ordered to require all in their bailiwicks who had £40 or more of yearly rent to come to the king at Carlisle at Midsummer 1300. They were to certify the king in his wardrobe before Whitsunday of the names of those whom they thought would come and also of those who would not come[4]. The sheriffs were also to make proclamation that those who ought to receive knighthood should present themselves at the wardrobe to receive their gear[5]. An inquest trying the loyalty of the earl of Stratherne was returned to the wardrobe[6].

In Edward I's reign the wardrobe rolls were used as a substitute for the chancery rolls in matters which the king desired to keep secret. A memorandum was entered on the close roll in 1290 to the effect that "certain letters concerning the matter of Norway were sealed secretly at London in the presence of R. bishop of Bath and Wells, the Chancellor, so that they were not enrolled on the rolls of chancery but were forthwith carried by William de Bliburgh to the king's wardrobe to be enrolled on the rolls of the same[7]." Letters sent to the Roman court in 1295 were taken to the chancellor to be sealed, the royal envoys receiving them sealed together with two letters sent to the king of Sicily. The transcripts were enrolled in the king's wardrobe and not in the chancery[8].

The wardrobe also claimed the appointment of the measurers of cloths at fairs. Letters patent from the clerk of the king's great wardrobe ordered that the bearer should be admitted by the keepers of the fair of St Ives to measure woollen and other cloths made in England. The fair belonged to the abbot of Ramsay who held that this writ was contrary to his charter, so the steward was ordered not

[1] *Cal. Close Rolls*, 1302–7, pp. 334–5.
[2] Ibid. 1296–1302, p. 224. [3] K. R. Acct. 373/30, inside cover of book.
[4] *Cal. Close Rolls*, 1296–1302, p. 395. [5] Ibid. 1302–7, pp. 434, 520.
[6] *Cal. Doc. Scotl.* vol. III, p. 22. [7] *Cal. Close Rolls*, 1288–96, p. 149.
[8] Ibid. p. 443.

to admit unless the letters patent were surrendered. This the bearer did and craved special grace, and at the instance of the merchants he was admitted temporarily[1]. The wardrobe also appointed the clerks who were to take prises in fairs[2]. The wardrobe was closely connected with the military and naval expenses of the king, payments for which were made in the wardrobe. The keeper of the wardrobe was also employed to provide ships for the king's need[3].

The connection between the wardrobe and the exchequer was close. It was from the exchequer that the wardrobe received the bulk of its resources. The wardrobe accounted to the exchequer[4], the accounts being rendered there before the chancellor, treasurer, chancellor and barons of the exchequer and others of the council[5]. There is at least one curious instance in which the chancery had some cognisance of those accounts. One part of the indenture of the final account of Langton, keeper of the wardrobe, for the twenty-second and twenty-third years of Edward I was delivered by the king's council to Osgodby, keeper of the rolls of chancery, to be kept in the chancery in testimony of the rendering of the account[6].

In certain external matters the exchequer and wardrobe would seem to be parallel departments. A form of truce made between the king and the communities of the towns of Ghent, Bruges, and Ypres in 1325, with certain letters touching the business, was delivered by the council to the treasurer and chamberlain of the exchequer to keep, and a similar form was handed to the wardrobe[7].

In inter-relations the wardrobe always appears as the favoured partner. Debts due by the king in his wardrobe were ordered to be allowed to the creditors in the sums they owed at the exchequer[8]. Debts due to the king in the exchequer were paid into the wardrobe. An acknowledgment of debt by the king was vacated because it had been paid to the keeper of the wardrobe, who ought to answer for

[1] Seld. Soc. vol. XXIII [1908], *Select Cases on the Law Merchant*, ed. C. Gross, p. 42.

[2] Ibid. p. 76.

[3] *Cal. Close Rolls*, 1296–1302, p. 196. John de Drokensford, keeper of the wardrobe, was ordered to provide eighty ships from the ships of the Cinque Ports, to be at Sluys in Flanders for his speedy passage.

[4] This applied also to the wardrobe of the prince, for when a grant of 1000 marks was made to the household of prince Edward in 1306 the steward, treasurer and controller of his household were ordered to certify the treasurer and barons of the exchequer of the particulars of the expenses, but they were also ordered to certify the keeper of the king's wardrobe (*Cal. Close Rolls*, 1302–7, p. 392).

[5] K. R. Mem. Roll, no. 83, m. 58 d.

[6] *Cal. Close Rolls*, 1296–1302, p. 403.

[7] Issue Roll, no. 213, m. 1.

[8] *Cal. Close Rolls*, 1302–7, pp. 355, 369.

it to the exchequer[1]. The sheriff of Norfolk and Suffolk paid £20 to the wardrobe which ought to have been paid to the exchequer, and the treasurer and barons were ordered to acquit his son of that amount[2]. For sums due to the exchequer, which were thus paid into the wardrobe, letter of recognisance was made by the keeper of the wardrobe to the treasurer and chamberlains of the exchequer[3]. The exchequer sometimes distrained for payments made out of the wardrobe, though the wardrobe did not permit this invasion of its independence to be effective[4].

The liberate writs issued in favour of the wardrobe, averaged three in the regnal year, the average amount being between fifty and sixty thousand pounds[5]. The great majority of these writs were issued "by bill of wardrobe[6]" though bill[7] and writ of privy seal were also employed[8]. These warrants of liberate were not always operative, and payments to the wardrobe were ordered by the treasurer to the chamberlains by informal warrant[9]. For the wardrobe received the money from the exchequer in small amounts or by assignments made upon the exchequer. When the money was actually paid to the keeper of the wardrobe, he received it by the hands of an official of the wardrobe or exchequer, or by one of those about the court, such as Pembroke, Badlesmere or Brother Lenham, king's confessor[10]. To pay the debts incurred by John de Benstede when he was keeper of the wardrobe, the extra sources of revenue which Edward II possessed on his accession were assigned by bill of privy seal, the extra sources being the debts and issues of the lands of Langton and the Templars, and the arrears of the papal tenth granted for three years to Edward I[11]. Loans which had been made to the wardrobe were repaid by writ of liberate. William le Latimer

[1] *Cal. Close Rolls*, 1288–96, p. 140. [2] Ibid. p. 174.

[3] Anc. Corresp. vol. XXXVII, no. 67.

[4] Hugh D'Audley received £50 out of the wardrobe, on going to the Gascon war, for armour and other things. That sum was demanded by summons of the exchequer and he was distrained by the sheriffs in all counties in which he held land. On his petition the king ordered that he should be quit (Ancient Petition, no. 414), and a writ to this effect was issued (*Cal. Close Rolls*, 1302–7, p. 303). It had been respited until further order on 12 April, 1300 (ibid. 1296–1302, p. 346).

[5] Liberate Rolls, nos. 84–103 passim.

[6] Ibid. no. 84, m. 4; no. 85, mm. 2, 5, 6; no. 86, mm. 1, 2; no. 87, mm. 1, 3, 4; no. 89, mm. 1, 3, 4; no. 90, mm. 2, 3.

[7] Ibid. no. 84, m. 3; no. 88, m. 2.

[8] Ibid. no. 84, m. 4; no. 89, m. 2. Chan. Warr., File 84/2692.

[9] Anc. Corresp. vol. L, nos. 38, 39. Vide App. of Doc. nos. 129, 130. K. R. Mem. Roll, no. 82, m. 33. [10] Issue Roll, no. 1325.

[11] Liberate Roll, no. 84, m. 2 (24 Jan. 1308). Vide below, p. 192 and pp. 192–3, note 3.

had made a loan of 200 marks to the king, and it was ordered that he should be paid this from the first sums of money from the revenues of the kingdom that should come to the exchequer[1]. A writ of liberate *per ipsum Regem et consilium* was issued for fish to the value of 27*s*. 6*d*. for the king's need[2]. Payments were also ordered to be made from the exchequer for expenses undergone in the king's service in Scotland, which were to be charged to the king's wardrobe[3].

The receipts from the exchequer formed but a portion of the revenue of the wardrobe. In the receipt books of the wardrobe these payments are always placed first, but they are followed by various sums received from foreign accounts. The receipt book for the third year of Edward II[4] is worthy of analysis. After the receipts from the exchequer[5] come the foreign receipts[6], which included £400 paid to the wardrobe by the sheriff of York from the revenues of that county, a fine from the bishop of St Asaph for the confirmation of the liberties of his church and fines for charters, fines for licences to appropriate lay fees, payments by sheriffs from the issues of their bailiwicks, by the chamberlain of North Wales and bailiffs of various manors, the farm of Hull and of manors and of abbey lands in the king's hands. Such payments into the wardrobe were quite usual, and this receipt book is not exceptional. Edward I had received the farm of Lincoln[7], the tallage of the Jews[8], money found in Jews' houses[9], payments from sheriffs[10], issues from lands of Glastonbury abbey during vacancy[11], and revenues derived from forests[12], as payments into his wardrobe. Fines for trespasses committed[13], for the wardship of lands[14], fines for freedom from distraint of knighthood[15] and the fines made by religious for the custody of their lands during vacancy[16] were paid into the wardrobe. Receipts of this nature were also attached to the queen's wardrobe, as she was seised of the issues of *amobr* in North Wales[17].

Receipts from administrative officers inside and outside England formed a regular and considerable source of revenue. In a receipt book covering a part of the eighth and ninth years of Edward II,

[1] Liberate Roll, no. 88, m. 2 (28 Jan. 1312).
[2] Ibid. no. 101, m. 6 (20 Aug. 1324).
[3] *Cal. Close Rolls*, 1307–13, p. 396
[4] K. R. Acct. 506/16.
[5] Ibid. f. 1: "Recepta de anno tercio de scaccario."
[6] Ibid. ff. 2, 2 b, 6: "Recepta forissaca."
[7] *Cal. Close Rolls*, 1272–79, pp. 538–9.
[8] Ibid. p. 106.
[9] Ibid. p. 535.
[10] Ibid. p. 108.
[11] Ibid. p. 143.
[12] Ibid. 1279–88, pp. 315, 329.
[13] Ibid. 1272–79, p. 384; 1296–1302, p. 506.
[14] Ibid. 1279–88, p. 320.
[15] Ibid. pp. 397–8.
[16] Ibid. 1272–79, p. 87.
[17] P. R. O. Ministers' Account, no. 1287/1.

£309. 5*s*. 3½*d*. was acknowledged from the constable of Alnwick, £120 from the chamberlain of North Wales and £101 from the treasurer of Ireland[1]. In the seventeenth year 500 marks were obtained from the chamberlain of North Wales[2]. Revenues were derived from the lands of sees that were vacant[3]; and from lands held in chief after the death of the baron[4]. Among other foreign receipts was £200 paid by the dean and chapter of St Paul's in fine for having the vacancy of the bishopric of London[5].

The king in securing the payment of these foreign receipts into his wardrobe did not do so without the knowledge of the exchequer. So complete was his control over that department that he could order them to grant land and order the receipts to be paid to the wardrobe. A tenant-in-chief had died and his heir was under age. The treasurer and barons were ordered to sell the wardship at once to the highest bidder and send the receipts to the wardrobe[6]. If those who made such payments had to render accounts in the exchequer, the king intervened on their behalf. Reasonable allowance was ordered to be made in the account of the keeper of the alnage throughout England for all the things he could show by good and sufficient indenture made between him and Ralph de Stokes, clerk of the great wardrobe, that he had delivered for the king's need[7].

The next rubric in the receipt book of the wardrobe acknowledged receipts of the papal tenth granted for three years. The abbot and convent of St Mary's, York, sub-collectors, paid in £400, the abbot and convent of Selby £300, the dean and chapter of Hereford £100. Twenty-two separate payments were made in all under this head[8]. The king sent notification, that he received sums from the papal tenth, to the treasurer and chamberlains of the exchequer[9]

The collectors of the twenty-fifth sometimes paid in their receipts to the wardrobe, though this does not appear to have been done frequently. In the third year of Edward II only four such payments are recorded[10]. Edward I is found receiving payments of the fifteenth into his wardrobe[11].

[1] K. R. Acct. 376/11, f. 8.

[2] Enrolm. of Wardr. Accts. Exch. L. T. R. Roll, no. 2, m. 22.

[3] Ibid. m. 1. [4] Ibid. [5] K. R. Acct. 375/1, f. 3.

[6] K. R. Mem. Roll, no. 92, Brev. dir. Mich. m. 13. L. T. R. Mem. Roll, no. 89, m. 75.

[7] K. R. Mem. Roll, no. 86, m. 19 d.

[8] K. R. Acct. 506/16, f. 3: "De Decima." [9] Anc. Corresp. vol. XXXVII, no. 67.

[10] K. R. Acct. 506/16, ff. 3 b, 6: "De vicesima quinta." Oxford £85; Wiltshire £250; Cumberland £100; Stafford £20.

[11] *Cal. Close Rolls*, 1279–88, p. 8.

The next section of the receipts was the loans made to the king by various persons, including the Friscobaldi, Sandale and Henry de Percy[1]. The king's financial position was frequently such that he had to borrow money from those about him[2]. The loans were not repaid out of a replenished wardrobe but were made a direct charge upon the exchequer. In 1309 Henry de Lacy advanced the keeper of the wardrobe 600 marks for which he had a bond of repayment[3], and which a few months later was paid to the earl out of the exchequer[4]. In 1310 he again lent the king 2000 marks for the war in Scotland which were delivered to Ingelard de Warle, keeper of the wardrobe[5]. Less than a month afterwards he had payment of that sum out of the exchequer[6]. The citizens of London made a loan to the king's wardrobe of 1000 marks, which they remitted and pardoned the king in return for a confirmation of their charters[7].

The issues of the great seal generally formed a source of revenue for the wardrobe, the money being paid into the wardrobe by the keeper of the hanaper. The money derived from this source was considerable. In the third year of Edward II it amounted to nearly £900[8]. For the eighth, ninth and tenth years of that reign the proceeds reached the total of £3223. 17*s.* 2*d.*[9], and in the eleventh year £909. 5*s.* 2*d.*[10] The sum generally was about £900, which may be taken as a fair average of this source of revenue. The money was paid into the wardrobe in small amounts of £10 or £20[11]. The keeper of the hanaper was on occasion ordered by the keeper of the wardrobe to make payment of debts due by the wardrobe. Warle, keeper of the wardrobe, ordered William de Thorntoft, keeper of the hanaper, on 1 April, 1310, to pay William de Ayremynne eleven and a half marks due to him in the wardrobe[12], a payment which was made on 5 April[13]. The keeper of the hanaper was likewise ordered to give a person his charter, and the 20*s.* would be allowed him in the first money he paid into the wardrobe[14].

[1] K. R. Acct. 506/16, f. 4: "De mutuo."
[2] Cf. *Cal. Close Rolls*, 1272–79, p. 284; 1279–88, p. 97.
[3] *Cal. Pat. Rolls*, 1307–13, p. 123 (4 July, 1309).
[4] Issue Roll, no. 150, m. 8 (10 Oct. 1309).
[5] *Cal. Pat. Rolls*, 1307–13, p. 286 (23 Oct. 1310).
[6] Issue Roll, no. 155, m. 4 (19 Nov. 1310).
[7] *Munim. Gildh. Lond.* vol. II, Pt i, pp. 255–273.
[8] K. R. Acct. 506/16, f. 4 b: "De exitibus magni sigilli Regis de anno iij. £892. 13*s.* 2*d.*"
[9] Enrolm. of Wardr. Accts. Exch. L. T. R. Roll, no. 2, m. 1.
[10] Ibid.
[11] K. R. Acct. 211/6, nos. 3, 4, 5, 9, 10–21.
[12] Ibid. no. 7.
[13] Ibid. no. 6.
[14] Ibid. no. 8.

The whole of the revenue from the use of the great seal did not pass into the wardrobe, as the expenses of the clerks of chancery were also paid therefrom[1]. The bishop of Winchester, chancellor, received this source of revenue in 1317 for the support of his household and the chancery, and his successor, the bishop of Ely, also received the grant, which was confirmed by the parliament of York in 1318. The bishop of Ely held this source of revenue until his resignation early in 1320. In 1326 the issues of the great seal were bestowed upon Baldock, to assist him to support his position[2]. On several occasions the wardrobe was thus deprived of a substantial source of revenue.

A source of revenue invariably paid into the wardrobe was the issues of markets. This revenue was partly derived from fines for trespass of measure[3] or of mill[4], for breaking the assize of bread and ale[5], or for contempt[6], and provided a small and regular amount.

A considerable source of revenue was the sale of victuals and this formed the next rubric[7]. The account of the third year from this source included such large sums as £934. 10*s*. 4*d*. received from the receiver of victuals at Carlisle and £584. 13*s*. 4*d*. received from Walter Waldeshef, king's butler[8]. Various smaller sums were received from sheriffs[9]. Between 18 July, 1321, and 30 April, 1322, £3734. 5*s*. 2*d*. was received from Stephen de Abingdon, chamberlain of the king's wines, from the sale of wines of the *recta prisa* and the king's store[10]. In the sixth year of Edward II £1026. 6*s*. 3½*d*. was paid into the wardrobe from the sale of victuals at Berwick[11], and in the same year £1024 from the sale of wines of the *recta prisa*[12]. The revenue derived from this source was considerable, though liable to variation.

The fines which were levied in the court of the marshalsea[13] formed an inconsiderable but constant source of revenue to the

[1] K. R. Acct. 211/6, nos. 1 and 2.

[2] Tout, *The Place of Ed. II*, pp. 181–3.

[3] K. R. Acct. 506/16, f. 5: "De exitibus mercati de anno iii." "De villata de Toucestre de fine in commune pro transgressione mensurarum et aliis. C.s."

[4] Ibid. 375/1, f. 5: "De priore de Rossa pro transgressione molendini sui et aliis transgressionibus xl. s."

[5] Ibid. f. 5: "De hominibus ville de Charringe pro assisa fracta xl. s."

[6] Ibid.: "De Willelmo Bate de fine pro contemptu...dimidia marca."

[7] Ibid. 506/16, f. 6 b: "Victualia vendita."

[8] Ibid.

[9] Ibid. Cf. £8. 10*s*. from the sheriff of Somerset and Dorset, £9. 4*s*. 10*d*. from the sheriff of Norfolk and Suffolk.

[10] Enrolm. of Wardr. Accts. Exch. L. T. R. Roll, no. 2, m. 1 d: "de precio diuersorum vinorum tam de recta prisa quam de stauro Regis."

[11] K. R. Acct. 375/1, f. 3 b.

[12] Ibid. f. 3.

[13] The court of marshalsea will be treated below, pp. 199–203.

wardrobe. In the third year these fines amounted to £60. 14*s.* 10*d.*[1], but this amount was considerably above the average from this source, though in some years it was even greater[2].

The next rubric contained money paid out of the wardrobe and restored[3]. Brother John de Lenham, king's confessor, restored to the wardrobe in this manner on 2 July, 1310, 33*s.* 8*d.* from a sum he had received for his expenses outside the court[4].

The receipt book of the wardrobe for the third year of Edward II closed with a few small sums of money received from the sale of wood, hides, and various small accounts[5]. In the sixth year three separate sums of £133. 6*s.* 8*d.*, £66. 13*s.* 4*d.* and £100 were paid into the wardrobe from the money derived from the sale of wood and underwood in the Templars' woods in the county of Lincoln[6].

While the analysis of this receipt book gives a general idea of the nature of the sources of the wardrobe revenue, no complete appreciation can be obtained without a fuller study of several of the headings of these accounts. The receipts from the great seal, the pleas of the hall, and from the market are comparatively constant. The amount derived from the sale of victuals varied considerably, while the items which might contribute to the omnibus title of foreign receipts had an infinite variety. There are moreover one or two ways of obtaining money or its equivalent from other sources which do not occur in this receipt book, especially that of the payment of scutage into the wardrobe. The close rolls of Edward I contain frequent orders to the treasurer and barons of the exchequer to acquit a certain tenant-in-chief who had paid his scutage into the king's wardrobe[7], and those of Edward II also contain a number of such orders[8]. In the tenth year of Edward II £20 was paid into the wardrobe by the collectors of scutage in York[9]. A payment closely akin to this was a sum of £1871. 15*s.*, 4*d.*, received from the bishop of Bath and Wells and others, given to the king in aid of the war with the barons in 1321–2[10].

[1] K. R. Acct. 506/16, ff. 7–7 b: "De exitibus Placitorum Aule."

[2] Enrolm. of Wardr. Accts. Exch. L. T. R. Roll, no. 2, mm. 1–1 d; 10 Ed. II £74. 12*s.* 2*d.*; 11 Ed. II £10. 13*s.* 8*d.*; 12 Ed. II £27. 13*s.* 4*d.*; 13 Ed. II £5. 19*s.* 6*d.*; 14 Ed. II £29. 10*s.* 9*d.*; 15 Ed. II £67. 2*s.* 3*d.*

[3] K. R. Acct. 506/16, f. 8: "Denarii restituti."

[4] Ibid. [5] Ibid. f. 8 b. [6] Ibid. 375/1, f. 3.

[7] *Cal. Close Rolls*, 1279–88, pp. 92, 101, 104, 152, 164, 169, 174, 199, 318, 382, 383, 447, 460, 499, 515, 518, 520; 1288–96, pp. 159, 207, 212, 280, 281, 287, 288, 340, 343, 348; 1296–1302, pp. 29, 32, 67, 275, 336, 570; 1302–7, pp. 125, 149, 296, 418.

[8] Ibid. 1307–13, p. 21.

[9] Enrolm. of Wardr. Accts. Exch. L. T. R. Roll, no. 2, m. 1.

[10] Ibid. m. 1 d.

Small sums of money from fines in the household[1] were occasionally paid into the wardrobe[2], and the clerk of the great wardrobe also paid money there[3]. Gifts were sometimes made to the king in his wardrobe, especially by ecclesiastical bodies. The prior of Christ Church, Twyneham, made a gift of £5 to the king in aid of carriage towards Scotland and the prior of Merton gave 10 marks and the prior of Leeds £5 for the same object[4]. A sum of £157. 3*s.* 2*d.* was granted as an aid to the king in his fifteenth year by the men of Colchester, John Ispanes and the communities of Westmorland and Cumberland[5]. In the same period a sum of £867. 2*s.* 8*d.* was received from the keeper of the castle and town of Carlisle, being the proceeds of goods and chattels of Harclay[6]. After Boroughbridge the issues of some of the forfeited lands, and fines for the saving of the lives of rebels who participated in that campaign[7] were paid into the wardrobe[8]. A source of revenue to the wardrobe was the chamber[9].

Before concluding with the subject of payments to the wardrobe, a summary of the receipts as contained in the wardrobe book[10] and entered in the enrolments of wardrobe accounts[11] for the period 1 May, 15 Edward II, to 8 July, 17 Edward II, will be given:

Receipts from the exchequer[12]:
1st liberate[13]
2nd liberate[14]
3rd liberate[15]
4th liberate[16]
Total ... ... £45,405. 12*s.* 3½*d.*

	£	*s.*	*d.*
Issues of pleas of the hall[17]	31	3	4
Issues of markets[18]	157	4	7
Issues of great seal[19]	1319	1	0
Sale of jewels[20]	75	1	4
From sheriff of Lincoln received by Hugh, son of Hugh le Despenser, junior[21]	11	5	4½
Sale of cloth of gold and other things touching great wardrobe[22]	1242	4	2

[1] Household fines will be discussed below, pp. 205–6.
[2] K. R. Acct. 376/11, f. 3: "Denarii recepti de penis compoti, xxviii. s. iii. d."
[3] Ibid. f. 3 b.
[4] Enrolm. of Wardr. Accts. Exch. L. T. R. Roll, no. 2, m. 1.
[5] Ibid. no. 2, m. 20.
[6] Ibid.
[7] Ibid. m. 22.
[8] Ibid. mm. 20, 22.
[9] Vide below, pp. 196–7.
[10] Stowe MS. 553.
[11] Enrolm. of Wardr. Accts. Exch. L. T. R. Roll, no. 2, m. 20.
[12] Stowe MS. 553, f.
[13] Ibid. f. 8 b.
[14] Ibid. ff. 8 b–9 b.
[15] Ibid. ff. 9 b–11.
[16] Ibid. ff. 11–12.
[17] Ibid. ff. 12–13.
[18] Ibid. ff. 13–13 b.
[19] Ibid. ff. 13 b.
[20] Ibid.
[21] Ibid.
[22] Ibid. f. 14.

	£	s.	d.
Owing to wardrobe by grant 15th year[1]	82	16	8
Remission made to king by John Botetourte[2] ...	22	9	0
Sale of victuals[3]	13908	2	8
From Roger de Northburgh, late keeper of wardrobe[4]	1583	4	11
From the king's chamber[5]	11133	6	8
From goods and chattels of Andrew de Harclay[6] ...	867	2	8
From various bailiffs, constables and small sales[7] ...	1232	8	9½

Total of the foreign receipts[8] £31,565. 11*s.* 2*d.*
Sum total of all receipts[9] £76,971. 3*s.* 5½*d.*

While the greater part of the revenue of the wardrobe was obtained from the exchequer, either directly, or by assignments upon it made to pay debts due to the wardrobe, the amount derived from foreign sources was considerable and was quite sufficient to give it the independence of control essential to a household office. Moreover the king had the necessary power and ample opportunity to interfere with the exchequer and its administration, especially upon the financial side, whenever he desired. An essential point in an assault upon the household system would be an attack upon the independence of the wardrobe and a control of the sources of its revenues. This was an integral part of the baronial scheme of reform in 1311[10]. The issue of the wardrobe is worthy of attention, though not of the importance of the receipts to the present purpose. The chief charges upon the wardrobe funds were the expenses of the royal household, the payment of the household officials, gifts made by the king, and other personal expenses. But besides these there were a number of considerable amounts paid from the wardrobe for extra-personal expenses, the chief being the expenses of war. The payment of troops and the expenses incurred by war, such as the restoration of horses, provisioning of the troops, and victualling of castles, were always charged upon the wardrobe accounts. This connection between the household and payments for war is illustrated by the fact that when Edward I made a payment of 1000 marks into the wardrobe of prince Edward in 1306, he allocated the payment for the expenses of the household in going to Scotland. He ordered the officials of the prince's household to receive the money and to keep it for the necessary expenses of the household and for the wages of the footmen who were setting out with the prince. The money was to be expended in necessary expenses and wages and not to be diverted to any other purpose[11].

[1] Stowe MS. 553, f. 14. [2] Ibid. [3] Ibid. ff. 14 b–18. [4] Ibid. f. 18 b.
[5] Ibid. [6] Ibid. f. 18 b. [7] Ibid. f. 19. [8] Ibid. f. 19 b.
[9] Enrolm. of Wardr. Accts. Exch. L. T. R. Roll, no. 2, m. 20.
[10] Vide below, p. 373. [11] *Cal. Close Rolls*, 1302–7, p. 372.

In 1321–2 the expenses of the siege of Leeds Castle and the pursuit of Lancaster were entered in the wardrobe accounts. The expenses included fees of various earls, bannerets, and knights for staying with the king in war, and in payment of their wages, and of various horse and foot staying in the company of the king in the siege and in the pursuit of Lancaster and his adherents, and of the wages of various sailors on the sea and elsewhere in the king's business. These expenses amount to £9287. 16*s.* 1*d.*[1] The expenses of the Scottish campaign of 1322, including the payment of the wages of the barons engaged therein, of the Welsh levies, and of the English foot, occupy a considerable portion of the wardrobe book of that period[2] and absorb a considerable part of the wardrobe revenue. Roger de Cliseby, king's clerk, was sent to Gascony in 1324–5 to pay the wages of the horse and foot engaged in the war with France, a sum of 5250 marks being paid him from the wardrobe[3].

Among the expenses of the wardrobe were payments made by the keeper of the hanaper for the fees of the chancellor and others of the office of the chancery[4]. The ambassadors who went so frequently to the French court, the clerks and lawyers who went to the parlement of Paris[5], the envoys to the papal court[6] and messengers to other courts in Europe[7], received their expenses in the wardrobe. John de Benstede, who in 1312 acted as a royal messenger to the earls of Lancaster, Hereford and Warwick, received his expenses in the wardrobe[8].

The wardrobe acted as a place of audit for all accounts which it paid, and some view of the nature of the payments will be secured from a consideration of the nature of these accounts. Petitions for payments of money long due from the wardrobe were referred by the king to that office, which apparently had an organisation for dealing with such requests[9]. For accounts rendered into the wardrobe, letters were issued out of chancery ordering the treasurer and barons to acquit[10]. On other occasions after the reckoning had been made in the wardrobe, if the king owed as a result of the account the

[1] Enrolm. of Wardr. Accts. Exch. L. T. R. Rolls, no. 2, m. 2.

[2] Stowe MS. 553 passim.

[3] Enrolm. of Wardr. Accts. Exch. L. T. R. Rolls, no. 2, m. 24.

[4] Ibid. no. 2, m. 1 d. These amounted to £2431. 5*s* 1½*d.* for 8, 9, and 10 Ed. II, £984. 11*s.* 7*d.* for 11 Ed. II., and £847. 13*s.* 8*d.* for 12 Ed. II.

[5] K. R. Acct. 375/8, ff. 9, 10 b, 11 b, 12 b, 16, 17 b, 18 a.

[6] Ibid. f. 9 b.

[7] Ibid. f. 7 b.

[8] Ibid. f. 7; 309/18.

[9] Ancient Petition, no. 5694: "E de ceo qe homme lui doit en Garderobe seuwe de vers ceaux de la Garderobe."

[10] E.g. *Cal. Close Rolls*, 1279–88, pp. 225–6, 337.

exchequer was ordered to allow the person that sum in his debts there[1].

In a list of accounts of money and victuals to be accounted at the wardrobe for receipts from the twelfth to the fifteenth years of Edward II, when Northburgh was keeper of the wardrobe, the most important referred to various officers of the household like Stephen de Abingdon, butler, Ralph de Stokes, clerk of the great wardrobe[2], and Brother Philip de Baston, king's almoner[3]. These were heads of separate departments of the household and their accounts necessarily appeared in the wardrobe books. Various accounts concerned with the details of expenditure for the food-supply of the household were also so presented, such as that of Peter de Paye for wines received for the expenses of the king's household and of others for wines received in Gascony, the porter of the wardrobe for carriage, or another for the carriage of the king's victuals. A large number of the accounts were concerned with the expenses of war. William de Garderobe, valet of the king's chamber, had to account for the money received by him for his expenses in staying at York to repair armour; Pembroke for the money and victuals received for certain of his men, and wages in war and other expenses; the king's armourer for money received for the manufacture of armour; Sir Theobald de Goldington for the price of ballistas, quarrels, arrows, cords, baldricks, given to him to take to the king at Leeds; Sir Griffith Llwyd for the money received by him for wages for himself and his men-at-arms in the king's war. Others referred to the care and custody of castles, the victualling of Alnwick, Oxford, Warkworth, for the fortification of the priory of Tynemouth and repairs to the castles of York and Carlisle, and for the custody of Bamburgh. Sir Peter de Montfort had to account for the money received for the custody of the city of Worcester and the bailiff of the peel of Clipston for the seed received for sowing that manor. Messengers to the Roman court, the earl of Ulster for the money received for coming to England at the king's command, Sir Geoffrey de Say for his expenses in staying with the king and Master Simon de Birye for the expenses of the king's scholars at Cambridge, accounted there. Among the other miscellaneous accounts rendered there were some relating to the repair of the royal ships, and the expenses of the royal horses and dogs[4].

In the wardrobe the king's influence was personal and supreme and royal policy could not be controlled without controlling the

[1] E.g. *Cal. Close Rolls*, 1296–1302, p. 444.
[2] K. R. Acct. 377/17, m. 1.
[3] Ibid. m. 2.
[4] Ibid. mm. 1–2.

wardrobe. It recognised no authority but the royal will and the royal will expressed itself there on personal matters and upon matters seriously affecting the administration of the realm. There is an instance of the king's council ordering a payment out of the wardrobe, but its significance is not great. A whale had been stranded upon land which belonged to the bishop of London, but it had come into the king's hand. It was agreed by the king's council that if the bishop could not have restitution, he should be paid the value of the whale out of the king's wardrobe[1]. This case supplied no real interference with the king's position, as the body which made the order was the king's "administrative" council[2], and it concerned no important matter of policy.

The strength of the royal position was increased and its continuance assured by the development of yet another financial body inside the royal household, the financial administration of the chamber. The baronial assaults upon the wardrobe would be comparatively fruitless as long as there was an inner financial organisation upon which the household could lean when necessary. The development of the financial position of the chamber is but another instance of that tendency to substitute a more personal organisation for one which had become or was becoming formalised.

It was during the reign of Edward II that this development of the financial side of the chamber became apparent. Payments had previously been described as being made *in camera regis*, these payments being made from the exchequer and entered upon the issue roll of that department. During the reign of Edward II the chamber has independent sources of revenue and there are frequent references to lands assigned to the chamber.

Before considering the receipt, issue and organisation of the chamber there are a number of facts and suggestions which should be borne in mind. Among these not the least in importance are the financial disorder and serious debts which Edward I left his son. Edward II however failed to realise the opportunities afforded him to alleviate the financial distress. The revenue which he might have derived by skilful application of the issues of the lands of Langton and of the Templars was dissipated by grants. Had he retained them all in his own hands and applied the revenue to his household or the exchequer[3] a partial remedy might have been afforded.

[1] *Cal. Close Rolls*, 1307–13, p. 117. [2] Vide below, pp. 253–261.

[3] In the single year 1308, even after lavish grants, the following sums were received in the exchequer from the following extraordinary sources of revenue:

Already the king was dealing with mighty and wealthy subjects. The wealth and territorial position of Lancaster, for instance, was proverbial. The opulence of some of these subjects stood in strong contrast to the financial embarrassment of the king. Moreover the baronial attitude towards taxation of all kinds was well summed up in the demand that the king should live of his own, and they extended their demands that the king's sons and brothers should be sufficiently provided with lands that they should not be a burden to the kingdom[1]. In addition to these two important considerations there was a third factor which tended to the same result. The barons were assailing the independence and influence of the wardrobe and insisting that that department should be accountable to and dependent upon the exchequer. Though the demand by the barons that the king should live of his own, and the demand that his wardrobe should be subordinate to and dependent on the great departments of government appear inconsistent, since the wardrobe was as much a department of the administration as it was of the household, there was reason in the baronial policy.

It was necessary therefore for the king to obtain fresh sources of revenue and a new department to administer them and such of the old as could be drawn to it. It was the traditional method to create a new instrument or department to take the place of that which was being superseded. The chamber was therefore given new functions to substitute the wardrobe. Lands were assigned to it. It appeared to be an anticipation of the policy later advocated by Fortescue who had postulated that the king should not be allowed to alienate "ffor sellynge off a kynges livehod is propirly callid delapidacion

Langton's lands	£2421. 18*s*. 4*d*.
Templars' lands	£ 978. 7*s*. 3*d*.
Arrears of papal tenth	£ 215. 16*s*. 2*d*.

(P. R. O. Receipt Roll, no. 173). By a *liberate* of January, 1308, the revenue from these sources was granted to John de Benstede, who had been keeper of Edward I's wardrobe, and sums amounting to over £600 were paid him (Issue Roll, no. 1323). The money derived from these sources was accounted independently of the ordinary revenue and had independent receipt (cf. Receipt Rolls, nos. 173, 1772) and issue rolls (cf. Issue Roll, no. 1323).

[1] This is brought out by the petition in the first year of Edward III. "Et pur ceo qe le Roialme est power, et chescun home est besoignes de Sey trover il covendra qe les Fuitz de Reys, et les Freres de Reys vivent solonc lour Estat: Prions qe lestat Monsire Johan de Eltham soit ordinee, qil puisse vivre come fitz de Roy, de les Eschetes qe resonablement devient demorent au Roy, saunz prendre en la Terre, sinoun pur ses deners" (*Rot. Parl.* vol. II, p. 9).

It was also petitioned that the intention of Edward I with regard to the grants to the earls of Kent and Norfolk should be fulfilled, "issint qil neyent escheson de rien prendre en la Terre, sinoun pur lour deners."

off his crowne and therefore is a gret infame[1]," and therefore the crown should be endowed by resumptions. Though Edward II was a great sinner in this respect, for he failed to use the opportunity given by Langton and the Templars and gave great sources of revenue like Cornwall as grants, he appears partly to have realised his mistake, and when after 1322 he had another opportunity he endeavoured to retrieve his past errors, though it is possible that the reform after 1322 was due to the inspiration of the Despensers or the other able administrators who then surrounded the king. Moreover there was a scarcity of money at hand[2] and the chamber could remedy this.

Before the development of the chamber as a financial department the king had groped in various directions for a substitute, and his negotiations with some of the foreign financiers had this object in view. On 29 December, 1312, the king acknowledged a sum of £5000 from Anthony Pessaign "pro priuatis expensis camere sue[3]."

Whatever may be the relative weight which must be attached to the causes which operated to start the development of the chamber, it seems as if the aim of the barons towards the wardrobe as expressed in the Ordinances[4] provided a culminating cause, and the victory of the king in 1322 an excellent occasion, for an accelerated development. For though it was only after the battle of Boroughbridge that the chamber is found with a full organisation and records, there are traces of a chamber organisation from the beginning of the reign. It is most probable that before 1322 the organisation was immature and the result of tentative experiments on the king's part. The forfeitures made by the rebels in 1321–2, which the king ordered to be paid into his chamber[5], may have necessitated the developed organisation; or the power which the king's victory then gave him may have provided the opportunity to develop and strengthen what had been undeveloped and feeble before. For as early as November, 1312, the king received 40 marks into his chamber from the keeper of the Templars' manors in Leicester and Warwick and he informed

[1] Fortescue, *Governance of England*, ed. Plummer, p. 134.

[2] Cf. Anc. Corresp. vol. XLV, no. 171.

[3] K. R. Acct. 375/8, f. 7.

[4] Vide below, p. 373.

[5] The organisation of the chamber with its sources of revenue has been treated in an article in the October number of the *English Historical Review*, vol. XXX [1915], 'The First Chamber Journal of Edward II,' J. C. Davies, pp. 662–673, together with a considerable portion of the text of that journal (ibid. pp. 673–680). A summary of that article will be given here without references, the references and further information will be found there. When new or additional matter is incorporated references will of course be given.

the treasurer and barons of the exchequer that the keeper was to render his account into the chamber and not elsewhere. In November, 1315, the escheator was ordered to seize the lands of a traitor in Ireland, and deliver them to the messenger "a garder a nostre oeps sicome nous lui auoms chargez." The lands were to be extended, and the extent was to be sent into the king's chamber[1]. In 1316 the mayor and citizens of London were ordered to pay into the chamber 400 marks of a fine levied from them for pulling down a wall near the Tower.

The first accounts of the chamber are those of Master James de Ispannia, receiver of the issues of lands and manors assigned to the chamber. These accounts, which are only concerned with one side of chamber revenue, start on 8 November, 1320, and run continuously until 24 May, 1323. The completest accounts of the chamber which remain are a series of chamber journals running continuously from 4 October, 1322, to 21 May, 1325[2], which contain the various receipts from chamber lands and foreign sources, and an account of the daily expenditure of the chamber. The accounts of the chamber follow those of the wardrobe very closely in form, but there is one important difference. The accounts of the wardrobe were written in the formal Latin of the exchequer, those of the chamber in the French of the court. This fact is interesting, as it emphasises the more personal nature of the latter. The accounts of these two financial organisations also differed in their audit. The chamber accounts were not rendered before the exchequer. They were rendered before special auditors assigned by the king.

Before the receipt and issue of the chamber are analysed something must be said of the lands which were assigned to the chamber. Among the lands which accounted to the chamber were the manors of Brustwick, Byfleet, Chippenham, Langley, Chiltern Langley, Gravesend and Thunderley, Holderness, the town of Rockingham and the town and castle of Hadleigh. The administration of these lands was the king's in a special sense. They were withdrawn from the ordinary administration of chancery and exchequer. The functions of the escheator too were superseded by the official of the chamber, and the taxes, which were payable to the exchequer for other parts of the kingdom, were here payable to the chamber.

In analysing the sources whence the chamber drew its revenue it is important to notice that it received no money from the exchequer.

[1] Chan. Misc. 138. (An unsorted bundle.)
[2] K. R. Acct. 380/4, f. 27.

One of the most considerable sources of its revenue was the issue of the chamber lands. Though there was an official definitely appointed to receive the issues of chamber lands, it was only a portion of the issues from those lands that was paid into the chamber by the receiver. The bailiffs of some of the manors paid in their issues directly to the clerk of the chamber. During the five months covered by the first chamber journal the total revenue from land was £689. 6*s*. 8*d*.

In contradistinction to this definite source of revenue, must be considered the foreign receipts of the chamber, which were composed of sums from the sale of the goods and chattels of rebels, from the sale of provisions, for freightage of the king's ships and repayments of loans. In the same five months the revenue from this source was £728. 11*s*. 0½*d*. The average revenue of the chamber from the issues of the lands assigned thereto and from the foreign receipts appears to have been a little below £2000.

The payments made from the chamber were especially concerned with the king's private expenditure. The arrangement of the issue portion of the account was simple. The payments were entered daily, and when no payments were made on any day this fact was noted and recorded. The payments included some for work done for the king in his manors and parks, wages for his servants and payments for his pleasures and luxuries, charity, and gifts for members of his household and frequent payments on behalf of Despenser. Though most of the payments were of a personal nature sometimes there is an administrative significance. Of this nature are payments for the delivery of writs of secret seal and to royal officials engaged in administrative or partially administrative missions. There is indeed one instance in which money was paid out of the chamber to the treasurer.

The personal nature of the chamber is also emphasised by the frequency with which payments were made out of it *par comande le Roi*, by the king's word of mouth; sometimes the order being given in his bedchamber. If the king did not order the payment it was made on the announcement of some such official as John Harsik, squire of the chamber, Sir John de Sturmy, steward of the chamber, Peter Bernard, usher, Thomas de Useflet, controller, or Oliver de Bordeaux, squire.

A point of interest in a consideration of the chamber accounts is the connection between the chamber and the wardrobe. In the first place sums of money were paid out of the chamber to the wardrobe for the king's expenses, and this was especially the case in 1322 when in a period of two months sums totalling £10,960 were thus paid, the king being then on a Scottish expedition. A department able to pay a sum of that magnitude to the wardrobe in so short a period must have possessed considerable sources of revenue. In the second place payments were made from the wardrobe to the chamber, though not with the frequency or in such magnitude as those made by the chamber into the wardrobe. To sum up, "the chamber was the most personal organisation of the king. It was the direct expression of his will. After 1322 it had a complete system and organisation. It had a separate staff of officials, clerical and lay, who were constantly about the king and were his personal servants. It had independent sources of revenue and could subsidize the other departments of the household, which had become more closely associated with the administrative departments and more formalized. It accounted before specially appointed auditors. In all directions its independence was considerable, and as an instrument of the royal will it was in a position to be of much service[1]."

Before passing from the financial organisation of the household to its judicial side, there are two points which bring out the personal character of the organisation, especially of the chamber, which demand notice. Payments were sometimes made to the king; thus on 19 January, 1311, a sum of 100 marks was paid to the king out of the wardrobe by the hand of Griffith Llwyd, valet of his chamber[2], and on the following 14 February a further sum of £100 by the hand of Reginald de Warle[3]. The king also received payments direct from the treasurer. There is notice of an account of payments to the king by the hand of Sir John de Shadworth in the months of January and February, 1313, which ought to be borne by the wardrobe. One item consisted of £200 paid to the king in the park of Windsor on 12 February by the hand of James D'Audley[4]. In the crisis of 1326 a sum of £2000 was paid to the king out of his wardrobe by order of letters patent under the secret seal[5].

A curious instance of payment to the king is found in a memorandum upon a wardrobe book. It records that on 26 May, 1325, in the abbey of Chertsey in the king's chamber, in the presence of the bishop of Exeter, treasurer, Baldock, chancellor, Sir Geoffrey le

[1] *Eng. Hist. Rev.* vol. XXX [1915], p. 673.

[2] K. R. Acct. 374/7, f. 29.

[3] Ibid. f. 32. Reginald de Warle was probably a brother of Ingelard de Warle, then keeper of the wardrobe.

[4] Ibid. 375/6.

[5] Enrolm. Wardr. Accts. Exch. L. T. R. Roll, no. 2, m. 26.

Scrope, chief justice of king's bench, Norwich and Beler, barons of the exchequer and others, at the request of Roger de Waltham, the king acknowledged that he had received £100 on that day and at that place from Waltham, keeper of his wardrobe, and he had made his will that the sum should not go by the hand of any clerk of his chamber or other who ought to make reckoning[1]. In the second class of payments which it is desired to notice are those made in the king's presence. It was in the chamber especially that payments were made in the king's presence[2].

Considerable strength accrued to the household system in its financial aspect. The wardrobe was an administrative department connected not with finance only. It was not solely dependent upon the exchequer for its revenues. Its subsidiary sources of revenue from the foreign receipts, the issues of the great seal, the market and the pleas of the hall, gave it a position of considerable independence. On the issue side the wardrobe was concerned with matters which were connected with the administrative and personal sides of the king's court. The personal side monopolised the accounts of the chamber much more than it did the wardrobe. Although the expenditure in the chamber was mostly of a purely personal nature, it was of considerable importance that it should be financially independent of outside control. As long as the personal system prevailed, it was important that the personal expenditure of the king, as well as the administrative departments, should be free from the control of opposition forces. Pressure exerted upon the source and use of the personal expenditure of the king might be made a fruitful instrument of coercion, and it was essential that conditions should make this pressure impossible. The sources of the chamber revenue were entirely independent. The greater portion was derived from the issues of lands assigned to the chamber, lands which did not come under the control of the administrative departments in any detail. The foreign receipts provided a useful if not considerable amount. From the king's point of view there was this special virtue in the chamber, that if encroachments and restrictions were effected in the wardrobe, the chamber could be substituted for its more personal and intimate functions.

[1] Stowe MS. 553, f. 33.
[2] *Eng. Hist. Rev.* vol. XXX [1915], pp. 678–9.

CHAPTER VII

THE STRENGTH OF THE HOUSEHOLD SYSTEM (*cont.*)

(iv) *Justice*

The household also had a court, that of the marshal and steward of the household, known as the court of the verge or hall. The king's servants and officials, though for most ordinary purposes under the common law, were in certain matters privileged, the privilege extending to the right to plead in courts not open to the ordinary man, and immunity from being impleaded in certain actions when on royal service. Summary justice was also meted out to the officials of the household who attended to the supply and keeping of provisions for the royal need, by a system of household fines.

Among the various courts mentioned by *Fleta* was that of the steward of the household, which was concerned with all actions against the peace of the king within the bounds of his household[1]. There had been a tendency for this household court to usurp the functions of the common law courts, and in the *Articuli super cartas* of 1301 pleas of debt, covenant, contract between common people were forbidden to be held there. The court was to confine itself to pleas of trespass within the household and within the verge, and those of contracts and covenants between members of the household[2]. The time limit within which such cases should be tried was defined. The case was to be pleaded and determined before the king's departure from the limits of that verge, otherwise the case was to come before the common law[3]. This definition of the sphere and functions of the steward's court was re-enacted in the parliament of Stamford in 1309[4] and formed one of the Ordinances of 1311[5].

In the reign of Edward II the court of the steward if it had not its former power was still an instrument which was of considerable

[1] *Fleta*, ed. Selden, p. 6: "cujus vices gerit in parte idem seneschallus hospitii Regis, cujus interest de omnibus actionibus contra pacem Regis infra metas hospicii."

[2] *Stat. of Realm*, vol. 1, p. 138. [3] Ibid. [4] Ibid. pp. 155–6.

[5] Vide below, pp. 376–7. Ordinance 26.

use to the personal system of government, and gave an added status to the household. The importance of the steward's court here lies not in its encroachments upon common law but in the fact that the members of the king's household and offences committed in the household were tried in a special court, a fact that conduced to the independence of the household system.

The plea roll of the steward's court for the reign of Edward II[1] is mostly concerned with petty trespasses committed in the household or in its verge. The defendant did not generally attend the court, and distraint was ordered to be made upon his chattels. The amounts distrained were all small[2]. Many of the fines were exacted from pledges because the accused was not present; a few were fined for a false plea[3]. The amounts of the fines varied with the social status of the accused. Jurors and bailiffs who did not attend were fined, and the sheriff of York was fined as much as £40 for contempt[4].

A more significant class of case was that concerned with contempt. No one in the realm was allowed to exercise the office of gauger of wines without special commission from the king under the great seal. A burgess had exercised the office in Northampton in contempt of the king and he was attached[5]. When the king resided anywhere all other jurisdiction was suspended in favour of the steward's court. The prior of Merton was attached for contempt done to the king in holding his court in the verge without warrant, thus usurping royal power and the office of the steward and marshal[6]. Another plea of contempt consisted of the usurpation of the office of the steward and marshal in imprisoning one indicted for the death of a man[7].

The jurisdiction of the steward's court sometimes came into conflict with that of corporations and persons to whom special privileges had been granted, thus in the eleventh year of Edward II such collisions took place between the steward's court and the burgesses of Wallingford who pleaded their charter[8], and the abbot of Reading who pleaded liberties that had been granted him by the king and his predecessors[9]. When complaint was made in parliament it was answered:

Bene licet hujusmodi ministris exercere officium suum in presencia

[1] P. R. O. Marshalsea Court, Plea Roll, no. 3 passim. An example of the amounts of fines is given in K. R. Accts. 375/1, f. 6, and 256/1.
[2] Marshalsea Court, Plea Roll, no. 3 passim.
[3] K. R. Acct. 256/1 passim. [4] Ibid.
[5] Marshalsea Court, Plea Roll, no. 3, m. 1. [6] Ibid. m. 23.
[7] Ibid. m. 32. [8] Ibid. m. 38. [9] Ibid. m. 38 d.

Regis non obstante aliqua carta generali de libertatibus hujusmodi nisi carta inde expressam faciat mencionem[1].

It was with the citizens of London that such conflicts were most frequent. The citizens were jealous of their liberties, and the king's household often resided there. A writ was issued to the steward and marshal of the king's household in 1315 ordering them not to draw any citizen out of the city to plead, but to observe the terms of the charters granted to the citizens[2]. When, a little later in the same year, such a plea was before that court the mayor of London appeared and urged that it should not be held because of a charter of Edward I and that writ. When the charter and writ had been examined the franchise was allowed[3]. The matter arose again in the parliament of York, 1318. The citizens claimed that no citizen other than the king's moneyers and officers should be impleaded outside the city, except in pleas touching land held outside. This claim the steward and marshal of the household had frequently ignored. When the representatives of the city at the parliament were told to substantiate their claim by the production of charters they were unable to do so. The chancellor, treasurer and barons of the exchequer were ordered to inquire into the claim[4].

Attachments of persons indicted for trespass before the steward were made within the city by serjeants of the city of London[5]. Serjeants of the city were also deputed to accompany the clerk of the king's marshalsea into the suburbs for the delivery of hostels for the use of the king's household, as he was about to come to Westminster[6]. Sheriffs were also employed in pursuing and arresting men, to be brought to the king under safe conduct, to be delivered to his steward and marshals[7].

The cases which came before the steward's court all had a strong personal reference to the king and his household. The essential point is contained in the fiction upon which the cases proceeded. All trespasses committed in the verge were said to have been committed "in the presence of the king himself and in his verge[8]." This fiction that all these petty trespasses were committed in the king's presence

[1] Cole, *Doc. illustr. Eng. Hist. in 13th and 14th Cent.* p. 36. Cf. *Cal. Close Rolls*, 1307–13, p. 185.

[2] *Cal. Letter Books, E*, p. 45 (9 Mar. 1315).

[3] Ibid. p. 49.

[4] Ibid. p. 99.

[5] P. R. O. Exchequer K. R. Bills, Bdle 1, no. 5.

[6] *Cal. Letter Books, E*, p. 80.

[7] E.g. *Cal. Close Rolls*, 1318–23, p. 549.

[8] Marshalsea Court, Plea Roll, no. 3 passim: "in presencia ipsius domini regis et infra virgam suam."

and hence were a personal matter to him supplied the origin and the justification for the court. Although the court was a personal one held by one of the most intimate personal officials of the king its procedure had much in common with that of the other courts. Inquests were held and juries were called in to decide on points of fact. There was seldom need of such a process in insignificant cases like those of trespass in the verge. In the plea of contempt against the burgess of Nottingham cited above, a jury was summoned to give evidence[1]. Juries were also employed to assess damages[2]. Even in pleas of trespass the defendant could place himself upon the country[3].

Those who committed trespasses in the verge and other offences were imprisoned in the prison of the marshalsea. Those who, pretending to be of the king's household or of the households of various magnates, went and seized provisions and carried them away, were to be placed in the marshalsea prison[4]. Those guilty of homicide in the verge were imprisoned there until the king should order otherwise[5], and persons were imprisoned there for debt[6]. After the Boroughbridge campaign there are instances of men surrendering themselves at the prison of the marshalsea so that their names might be cleared of suspicion. One whose lands had been seized by the sheriff on suspicion that he was against the king, was found not guilty[7]. A similar course was adopted in various cases of felony presented *coram Rege* in Staffordshire. Subsequently suspects came and surrendered themselves. Prisoners were committed to the marshalsea, and Richard Damory, steward of the king's household, and others testified that they were of good faith[8]. The pretender at Oxford in 1318 was brought before the king's steward sitting in judgment[9]. The office of marshal was during the reign of Edward II taken into the king's hand for the escape of prisoners committed to him[10].

The money derived from the multitude of small fines in the steward's court went into the wardrobe and formed a regular source

[1] Marshalsea Court, Plea Roll, no. 3, m. 5 d.
[2] Ibid. mm. 1 d, 14 d.
[3] Ibid. m. 5 d.
[4] *Cal. Pat. Rolls*, 1313–17, p. 534.
[5] Chan. Misc., Bdle 64/7 (196).
[6] Anc. Corresp. vol. XLIX, no. 161.
[7] *Cal. Inq. P. M.* vol. VI, p. 351. Cf. *Cal. Close Rolls*, 1302–7, p. 1, where one who had been put in exigent appeared before the king and found mainprise before the steward.
[8] Wm Salt Soc., *Coll.* vol. X, p. 45.
[9] *Chron. Lanerc.* p. 222.
[10] *Abbrev. Placit.* p. 347.

of revenue to it[1], though estreats of the pleas were towards the end of the reign handed in to the exchequer, perhaps as a result of the recent exchequer and household ordinances[2].

These sums were sometimes paid directly into the wardrobe. Acknowledgments were made in the wardrobe accounts of the receipts of such sums by the hands of William de Rockingham[3], and of Simon le Croiser, coroner of the king's household[4]. At other times the issues were paid to various men of the royal household by William de Rockingham, by bill of Warle, keeper of the wardrobe, and of John de Okham, cofferer of the wardrobe[5]. Officials of the household too figure in many of the cases which came before the steward's court. Assaults in the verge were often committed upon household officials[6]. Recognitions between various officials were entered on the plea rolls of the marshalsea[7].

The independence of the household was further increased by the privileged position of the officials in certain directions. They had access to courts which were denied to ordinary subjects. They could plead their debts at the exchequer[8], and there is even an instance of a case of assault upon a servant of William de Melton, king's clerk, being ordered to be tried there[9]. A citizen of London was likewise ordered to answer a servant of Sandale, then lieutenant of the treasurer, at the exchequer, for a plea of detention of his chattels[10]. Moreover when the king allowed other persons to plead their debts in the exchequer it was sometimes stated that they were allowed to do so because they were of his household. This fiction was used by Edward II on behalf of foreign merchants. The Friscobaldi[11], and the Bellardi[12] were to be allowed to plead at the exchequer because they were of the king's household. When a Gascon community desired to have special favour from the king they asked for the

[1] Cf. Stowe MS. 553, ff. 12–13: "De finibus amerciamentis et catallis foris factis diuersorum hominum et villatorum amerciatorum et conuictorum coram senescallo et marescaliis domini Regis ad placita aula inter primum diem maij quintodecimo et xix diem Octobris anno xvii^mo: Summe totale Recepte de exitibus placitorum aule. £31. 3*s*. 4*d*." Vide also above, pp. 186–7.

[2] K. R. Mem. Roll, no. 102, m. 111. L. T. R. Mem. Roll, no. 98, Hill. Rec. m. 6, under the rubric "De extractis placitorum hospicij Regis liberatis." K. R. Acct. 256/1, end of last m.

[3] Enrolm. of Wardr. Accts. Exch. L. T. R. Roll, no. 2, m. 22.

[4] Ibid. m. 24.

[5] K. R. Acct. 375/1, f. 6.

[6] Marshalsea Court Plea Roll, no. 3 passim.

[7] Ibid.

[8] The jurisdiction of the exchequer will be discussed below, pp. 242–5.

[9] Vide above, p. 144.

[10] Exch. Misc. 2/40.

[11] L. T. R. Mem. Roll, no. 78, m. 20 d: "Par la reson qil sont de nostre hostel."

[12] Ibid. no. 79, m. 23.

privileges Bordeaux enjoyed, for the king in a writ to the chancellor said they were "souz nostre protection et deffense especial come ceux de nostre chaumbre[1]."

The interesting point arises as to whether the officials of the king's household were under a special law, consisting of various privileges due to their position as royal servants, a special law which might stand comparison with what is known as "administrative law"; and there is a certain amount of evidence worthy of consideration. The most considerable evidence is a clause in the Articles of the Clergy of 1316. The barons of the exchequer claimed as a privilege that they ought not to answer any complainant outside that place. They extended the same privilege to clerks staying there, who were called to orders or residence, so that ordinaries should not in any way or for any reason call them to judgment as long as they were in the exchequer or in the king's service. The king in 1316 allowed the ordinary the right to correct any clerks that attended in his service if they offended, but they were not to be compelled to keep residence in their churches as long as they were occupied about the exchequer; for it was customary that clerks employed in royal service should not be compelled to keep residence as long as they were thus engaged, for such things as were considered necessary for the king and the common good ought not to be said to be prejudicial to the liberty of the church[2].

This formed little more than a statement or definition of existing custom. The king by privy seal wrote to the chapter or suitable ecclesiastical official asking and almost ordering him to excuse a clerk from the duties attaching to his ecclesiastical office. He wrote in this way to the chapter of Beverley in 1309 on behalf of Melton, controller of his wardrobe[3]. The king informed the chapter that Melton was with him by his order, and asked them to excuse his attending the chapter of Beverley as provost, as he had been summoned to do[4]. Sometimes the king ordered the chancellor to issue letters under the great seal for the same purpose. In 1325 Baldock was ordered to issue letters under the great seal to the bishop of

[1] Chan. Warr., File 99/4117.

[2] *Stat. of Realm*, vol. I, p. 172. *Articuli Cleri*, § 8.

[3] Tout, *The Place of Ed. II*, p. 355.

[4] Surtees Soc. vol. XCVIII [1897], *Beverley Chapter Act Book*, vol. I, p. 229, 23 January, 1309: "vous prioms cherement que vous li tiegnez pour excusez de ceo que par reson de notre dit servise il ne porra venir a votre chapitre a Beverlee de vous faire serment pour meisme la Provostee au iour auant dit." Vide also pp. 286–7.

Chichester to allow the holder of a benefice in his diocese to be quit of residence, because he was in royal service, as the king had heard that the bishop distressed him to make residence[1]. A request for a writ under the great seal for a similar purpose was made by Bereford, chief justice of the common bench to the bishop of Chichester when he was chancellor. He wrote on behalf of a clerk sworn in the bench, who was oppressed by the archdeacon of Buckingham to come in his proper person[2]. Edward I had ordered the archbishop of Canterbury and other ecclesiastics not to compel the king's clerks to take orders or to make personal residence in their benefices while they were engaged in his service, or to be molested or disquieted in any way, as the king and his ancestors had always used the privilege or liberty for their clerks from time out of mind[3].

Though this evidence is not considerable in amount, it is sufficient to warrant the suggestion that there were a number of rules and privileges which affected the officials of the king, which may be regarded as approaching "administrative law." The protections issued for those who went to Scotland in the king's service[4], protections often issued on the warrant of the steward of the household[5], are related to this special body of regulations. Demands for debts from persons in the king's service in Gascony were to cease as long as they were so employed.

Fines were exacted in the household from various officials of the buttery, pantry, and other officers of the household proper. These fines consisted of a number of pains or penalties taken for defects in purchases or accounts. When a few instances have been given the nature of the fines will be better appreciated. The rolls of the fines thus incurred were headed "Rotulus de penis compoti[6]." On 23 November, 1311, the clerk of the pantry paid 12*s*. 5*d*. for bread wrongly spent in the hall[7]. On 21 January, 1312, a penalty of 4*s*. 5½*d*. was made against one William de Pirie for 33 gallons of beer and 5 gallons of wine wrongly expended in the hall[8]. The larderer,

[1] Chan. Warr., File 130/7230 (30 Oct. 1325).

[2] Anc. Corresp. vol. xxxv, no. 160.

[3] *Cal. Close Rolls*, 1302–7, pp. 88, 193, 411.

[4] Chan. Warr., Files 1703–6 passim. Vide above, p. 165.

[5] Ibid.

[6] K. R. Accts. 374/12, 375/4.

[7] K. R. Acct. 374/12, m. 1: "Memorandum quod xxiii die Novembris ponuntur super clericum panetarie pro pane male expendendo in aula. xii s. v d."

[8] Ibid. m. 2: "Item quod die veneris xxi die Januarie ponebantur super Wilhelmo de Pirie pro xxxiii lagenis ceruisie precio lagene, i d. et v lagenis vini precio lagene iiii d. male expendendis in aula. iiii s. v d. ob."

poulterer and the official in charge of the wines were likewise fined[1]. Besides these fines there was a more drastic method of punishment within the household. On 16 February, 1312, Master Richard and Master John, officers of the king's kitchen, were placed outside the wages of the king, at the will of the steward and the treasurer of the wardrobe, for contempt made in their account[2]. In March of the same year the clerk of the pantry and buttery was placed outside wages for fourteen days, because he was not present to account before the steward and treasurer of the wardrobe[3].

It is thus seen that the accounts of the officers of the household pertaining to the supply of the royal table and the hall were rendered before the steward of the household and the keeper of the wardrobe. These had full powers to dismiss or suspend an official who did not render a satisfactory account of his office. This extreme method was sometimes adopted, but the more normal course was to fine or to disallow items in the account. Though this system was but a number of disciplinary measures reduced to order, its significance is sufficiently important to demand a reference. The fines and rejection of items in these household accounts were entered in the receipt book of the wardrobe. In the receipt book for 8–9 Edward II 28*s.* 3*d.* was acknowledged as money received from penalties of account[4]. The details of this sum were for wrong purchases of bread, wine and other materials for the kitchen, and the fines were levied by view of the steward and keeper of the wardrobe[5].

The position of the household and its officials in justice was secure, and even had the king not retained control of the common law courts little or no pressure could have been exerted upon them by that means. For grave offences officials of the household could claim no special privilege, but even here the royal favour could work on their side. In minor matters they were independent, and the independence of the household courts and the privileges of the officers were sufficient to be effective in resisting attacks.

[1] K. R. Acct. 375/4.

[2] Ibid. 374/12, m. 2: "xvi die februarie ponebantur extra vadiis Regis Magister Ricardus Salsarius et Magister Johannes Salsarius Regis ad voluntatem senescalli et Thesaurarii pro contemptu facto in compoto."

[3] Ibid.: "Die Jouis xvi die marcii Stephanus de Suthee clericus panetarie et Butarie positus fuit extra vadiis per xiiii dies proximos sequentes quia non fuit ad compotum coram senescallo et Thesaurario garderobe."

[4] Ibid. 376/11, f. 3: "Denarii recepti de penis compoti. xxviii s. iii d."

[5] Ibid.: "per consideracionem senescalli et custodis garderobe."

CHAPTER VIII

THE STRENGTH OF THE HOUSEHOLD SYSTEM (*cont.*)

(v) *The Chief Officers*

Before the complete strength of the household system can be realised it is necessary to have some knowledge of the officers who directed and worked it. The far reaching influence and efficiency of the executive, the independence and power of its financial resources, the privileged position of its officers and its partial independence in justice were all dependent for their efficacy upon the officials responsible for the administration of the household. A consideration of the household offices and their personnel, both superior and inferior, is of the utmost importance, and that consideration will lead naturally on to an appreciation of their place in and influence upon the administration of the kingdom.

It is not necessary to make more than a passing reference to the way in which in feudal states the officers of the king's household became great officers with a share in the government of the country. Here the way in which the king circumvented the difficulty which arose as a result is more important. When the office of the king's steward became hereditary in a great house the primary functions of that official were transferred to a subordinate official[1]. The steward of England was a mighty baron, the bearer of an empty title. The steward of the household was a minor person, always near the king, in almost complete control of the organisation of the household and a person of considerable if not outstanding importance.

By the time of Edward II the household had its own marshal, its own steward and its own chamberlain. Lancaster who was the steward of England made endeavours to add executive functions to that office, but it was the steward of the household who had a decisive voice in the household and exercised some power in the administration. The chamberlainship was held by the earls of Oxford[2], but

[1] Round, *King's Serjeants*, p. 69. Harcourt, *His Grace the Steward*, p. 128.

[2] Harcourt, *His Grace the Steward*, pp. 178–9.

the chamberlain of the household, at one period of the reign the most potent figure in the kingdom, was the important official. The case of the marshal is somewhat different. The marshal of the household does not figure as prominently as the steward or chamberlain, and this may be attributed to the fact that the marshal of England was not a mere figure-head but an official with definite functions, and a place in the administration.

The marshalship of England was still in the king's hands when Edward II ascended the throne, and on 3 September, 1307, Robert de Clifford was appointed to the office during pleasure[1]. His tenure of the office was short, as in the following March, Nicholas de Segrave was appointed[2]. As long as the appointment was thus in the king's hands and he could appoint whomsoever he would the necessity for an independent and important marshal of the household did not arise. Segrave's appointment was not acceptable to the barons and, in a council held at Northampton in August, they forced the king to dismiss him from the court[3], though he still retained his office.

The grants of the office of marshal to Clifford and Segrave had been made without the lands pertaining to that office. An interval of more than three years elapsed between the grant of the lands of the late earl of Norfolk[4] and the office of marshal of England[5] to Thomas de Brotherton, the king's brother. These two facts suggest that the tenurial element about the great offices was becoming generally weakened and that this office, which retained some administrative function, was not in the same category as the offices of the steward and chamberlain of England. The marshal still had a place in the personal system, and the tenurial character of the office was to some extent controlled by this fact. The marshal of the household was not an independent official, he was the deputy of the earl marshal, and references to him run: "lieutenant le conte Marschal en nostre houstel[6]." Walter de Beauchamp, lieutenant of the earl marshal in the king's household, for the later portion of the reign, was a faithful royal servant who before he had that office had been entrusted with various important administrative work[7]. In his official capacity

[1] *Cal. Pat. Rolls*, 1307–13, p. 6.
[2] Ibid. p. 51. *Parl. Writs*, vol. II, Pt ii, App. p. 11 (12 March, 1308).
[3] *Ann. Paul.* p. 264.
[4] *Cal. Charter Rolls*, 1300–26, pp. 205–6 (16 Dec. 1312).
[5] Ibid. p. 304 (18 March, 1316).
[6] K. R. Mem. Roll, no. 99, m. 27.
[7] Cf. *Cal. Pat. Rolls*, 1321–24, pp. 24, 30. *Cal. Fine Rolls*, 1319–27, p 72.

he made an indenture with the sheriffs of London on 3 April, 1324, giving to their charge the bodies of two men to keep them safely, the one until the king should express his will and the other until he was released by the law of the land[1]. Beauchamp was also described in judicial records as the king's marshal when he attached Stephen de Segrave, constable of the Tower, for the escape of Roger de Mortimer from his custody. After the preliminary hearing the prisoner was again delivered to the king's marshal[2].

In the organisation of the household the steward was the most important official. His activity was general and his independence of outside control complete. He was directly responsible to the king and to the king alone. The relation in which the steward stood to the king is well expressed in the sentence passed upon Badlesmere, who was appointed steward of the king's household in the parliament of York, 1318[3], and was still acting on 14 June, 1321[4]. He was to be drawn for his treason, hanged for his robberies and homicides, and beheaded for his flight, "and in as much as he was the king's seneschal it was the king's will that his head be spiked upon the gate of the city of Canterbury as a warning to others not to commit such acts of treason and wickedness[5]."

Richard Damory, steward of the household between July, 1322, and April, 1325[6], and brother of Roger Damory[7], a member of the middle party[8], who had married one of the heiresses of the Gloucester estates[9], was more than a mere personal servant of the king. Before his appointment as steward he had held various administrative positions. He had been sheriff of Oxford and Berkshire[10], and guardian of the young prince Edward[11]. When he was steward he was ranked as a banneret of the household, a position which the younger Despenser also held at that time[12]. Though his administrative training made him suitable for the office and may have weighed

[1] K. B. Misc., Class 138, no. 108, m. 33: "monsire Wauter de Beauchampe lieutenant le counte mareschall en lostel nostre dit seigneur le Roi."

[2] *Abbrev. Placit.* p. 343. Wm Salt Soc. *Coll.* vol. x, p. 44.

[3] Cole, *Doc. illustr. Eng. Hist in 13th and 14th Cent.* p. 3.

[4] Tout, *The Place of Ed. II*, p. 354. *Chron. Mon. de Melsa*, vol. II, p. 339, says that the king besieged the castle of Ledes "quod fuit B. de Badlesmere senescalli regis." There seems to be no ground to suppose that Badlesmere "ab officio seneschalliae contra regis affectum recesserat" (*Flores Hist.* vol. III, p. 199).

[5] Parl. Writs, vol. II, Pt i, pp. 293–4. *Abbrev. Placit.* p. 351.

[6] Tout, *The Place of Ed. II*, p. 354.

[7] Ancient Petition, no. 2053.

[8] Vide below, pp. 431–2, 433–5.

[9] *Flores Hist.* vol. III, p. 194.

[10] P. R. O. List and Indexes, no. 9 [1898], *List of Sheriffs*, p. 107.

[11] Chan. Warr., File 104/4629.

[12] Stowe MS. 553, f. 65.

with the king in making the appointment, it is probable that his appointment was inspired by the Despensers. Richard Damory seems to have been associated with the elder Despenser, for he was a frequent witness to grants made by him[1], one of the grants being made to such a personal follower of Despenser as John de Handlo[2]. The very fact that he should have held this important office for nearly three years when Despenser was in complete control of the administration supports this view, and the fact that he was a skilled administrator justifies it.

The king frequently made grants to those who held the office of steward of his household. On 15 February, 1317, he made a grant for life to William de Montague, steward of the household, of 200 marks a year to be received at the exchequer until he was provided with lands or rents to that value; the grant being made that Montague might maintain himself more fittingly in the king's service[3], and by the writ of liberate which was issued on the same day he received 100 marks by the hand of John de Wengrave, mayor of London[4]. In the same year he obtained the grant of wardship of lands of a minor[5], the grant of lands forfeited by a Scottish rebel[6], and a grant of free warren in his desmesne lands[7]. The grant of the lands of the rebel was regranted the following year with the assent of the prelates, earls, barons and other magnates in the parliament of York[8].

Badlesmere, when he was steward, likewise received various grants. At the parliament of York, 1318, when he was appointed to that office, it was agreed that for good service rendered and to be rendered he should have a grant of 500 marks until he should have lands to the value of 500 marks[9]. In October, 1319, payments amounting to over £1300 were made to him[10]. The castle of Dover and the Cinque Ports were granted to him by the assent of the parliament of Westminster in 1320[11], and in 1321 the castle of Tonbridge, forfeited by Hugh D'Audley, was committed to him[12].

Besides grants of lands and money, the stewards were in a position to obtain special favours from the king. The treasurer and barons of the exchequer were ordered to search the rolls and remembrances

[1] *Descr. Cat. Ancient Deeds*, vol. I, pp. 6, 159; vol. V, p. 44
[2] Ibid. vol. II, p. 166. [3] *Cal. Pat. Rolls*, 1313–17, p. 609.
[4] Issue Roll, no. 180, m. 3 (29 April, 1317).
[5] *Cal. Fine Rolls*, 1307–19, p. 337 (2 Aug. 1317).
[6] *Cal. Charter Rolls*, 1300–26, p. 361. [7] Ibid. p. 366. [8] Ibid. p. 403.
[9] Cole, *Doc. illustr. Eng. Hist. in 13th and 14th Cent.* p. 9.
[10] Issue Roll, no. 189, m. 1. [11] *Cal. Fine Rolls*, 1319–27, p. 38 (30 Oct. 1320).
[12] Ibid. p. 57 (17 May, 1321).

for all debts demanded from Richard Damory and to certify the king immediately. The demands for such debts were to be stopped until they heard the royal will. If any distress had been made it was to be released without delay[1]. The following year, by writ of secret seal, he was allowed a respite from debts[2]. Similar respite was granted to Thomas le Blount, steward in 1326[3].

For the present purpose the most important point about the steward is the influence he exercised on the administration. Merely as a personal servant of the king or as the head of the royal household organisation, his importance was limited, but as the personal servant of the king, acting as a royal instrument in the policy of controlling and restricting the administrative machinery, and as the head of the household organisation, which touched the whole administrative system at every point, the importance of the steward of the household was considerable. Edmund de Mauley, steward during the Gavaston and Ordinance crisis of 1310–12[4], was used by the king as the bearer of the great seal[5]. Mauley was custodian as well as bearer of the great seal. On 8 October, 1312, by the king's order, he delivered the great seal, which was in his custody, to the bishop of Worcester at the exchequer[6]. In a letter of privy seal to the bishop of Worcester commanding him to receive and keep the great seal, the king informed him that he was sending Mauley to deliver to him the great seal which had been in his keeping[7].

It was natural that the steward should act frequently as messenger between king and chancellor, with verbal orders to issue writs under the great seal. The steward was employed thus with more than usual frequency in the year 1312[8]. Some of the writs issued on Mauley's information in 1312 are significant. The letters patent re-appointing Despenser, senior, justice of the forest south of Trent, resumed in compliance with the Ordinances, were made on his information on 14 June, 1312[9], and a writ of 26 June, 1312, concerning the fortification of the Tower, was issued on a similar warrant[10]. These two matters were of considerable importance, and the employment of

[1] K. R. Mem. Roll. no. 97, Brev. dir. Mich. m. 3; Brev. dir. Hill. m. 18 (2 Aug. 1323).

[2] Ibid. Brev. dir. Trin. m. 9 (1 July, 1324).

[3] Ibid. no. 102, m. 60 (5 June, 1326).

[4] Tout, *The Place of Ed. II*, p. 353.

[5] Vide above, p. 127, note 7.

[6] *Cal. Close Rolls*, 1307–13, pp. 552–3.

[7] Ibid. *Parl. Writs*, vol. II, App. ii, p. 56 (5 Oct. 1312).

[8] *Rot. Scot.* vol. I, p. 109. *Cal. Close Rolls*, 1307–13, pp. 427, 465, 469. *Cal. Pat. Rolls*, 1307–13, p. 485.

[9] *Cal. Pat. Rolls*, 1307–13, p. 464.

[10] *Cal. Close Rolls*, 1307–13, p. 427.

the steward in them would suggest that he was used because the secrecy and importance of the matter demanded a trusty messenger. Payments from the exchequer were also made on the announcement of the steward[1]. Five hundred marks were paid for horses purchased for the king in France, the payment being made by the king's order announced by Sir William de Montague, steward[2]. The steward also carried orders to the wardrobe ordering payment therefrom. Mauley was the bearer of the royal order to the wardrobe for the payments for horses which he had bought[3], and orders for payment were announced by Richard Damory when he was steward[4].

The steward of the household was almost invariably a witness to the charters granted by the king, whether dealing with grants of lands or of liberties, and the charter rolls supply the surest record of the terms of office of the various stewards. Badlesmere was a witness as steward to the confirmation of the liberties of London granted in 1319[5] and Montague as steward witnessed a deed of Badlesmere's in 1318[6].

The influence of the stewards with the king is apparent in the number of grants of writs which were made at their request or on their instance[7]. Their influence also extended to the administrative offices. A day was given to a person at the exchequer at the instance of Robert fitz Payn[8], steward 1308–10[9]. A payment from the exchequer was endorsed by the treasurer at Badlesmere's instance in 1320[10]. The sheriff of Salop and Stafford was appointed by exchequer writ by the treasurer himself witnessed by Robert fitz Payn[11].

The steward was employed in various other administrative duties. Henry de Shirokes, clerk of the wardrobe, received from the exchequer in 1317 a sum of £40 for the expenses of Mary, the king's sister, and Lady de Burgh going to and returning from Canterbury. Henry de Shirokes received that sum by the view and assent of Montague, steward[12]. Robert fitz Payn, when steward, was a member of an embassy to Rome[13]. John de Crombwell, knight and steward of the

[1] Issue Roll, no. 189, m. 1. [2] Ibid. no. 181, m. 3.
[3] K. R. Acct. 375/8, f. 13 b. [4] Stowe MS. 553, f. 67 b.
[5] *Munim. Gildh. Lond.* vol. II, Pt i, p. 268.
[6] *Cal. Close Rolls*, 1313–18, p. 607.
[7] E.g. *Cal. Pat. Rolls*, 1317–21, pp. 269, 433, 509.
[8] K. R. Mem. Roll, no. 86, m. 108 d.
[9] Tout, *The Place of Ed. II*, p. 353. [10] Issue Roll, no. 193, m. 2.
[11] K. R. Mem. Roll, no. 82, m. 5. L. T. R. Mem. Roll, no. 79, m. 5 d: "Teste Waltero Wygorniense Episcopo per ipsum Thesaurarium testante Roberto filii Pagani."
[12] Issue Roll, no. 180, m. 5. [13] *Regist. Pal. Dunelm.* vol. IV, p. xlix.

household, was sent by the king and his council to Welshpool to quiet and pacify disturbances which had arisen between Griffith de la Pole and John de Cherleton, and received payment of £10 from the exchequer for his expenses[1]. Richard Damory, when steward, held an inquest at Castle Barnard in company with Master Robert de Aylleston, keeper of the privy seal, touching the account of the constable of that castle, the inquest being subsequently sent by the king to the bishop of Exeter, treasurer[2]. There does not occur during the reign of Edward II such a direct and formal instance of administrative participation as in the reign of Edward I when an acknowledgment was made in chancery before the chancellor and the steward of the household[3].

The steward of the household was a member of the king's "administrative" council. The mayor and commonalty of London were asked in 1319 by the treasurer and barons of the exchequer, and by the king's steward and others of the council, to grant a loan to the king to assist him in his war[4]. In 1320 Badlesmere was continually among those of the king's council[5]. In an agreement made by the council in 5 Edward II the name of Mauley, steward, followed those of Pembroke, Despenser, Sandale, and preceded those of the lieutenant of the treasurer, and barons of the exchequer[6].

The control which the steward exercised over those who were employed in the royal service was considerable. Those who had been in the king's service petitioned the steward to show their estate to the king[7]. Petitions addressed to the king by men who were in the royal service were referred to the steward and other officials of the household. The petitioner was told to sue before the steward, the keeper of the wardrobe and the king's confessor[8]. To another petitioner for reward for long service, the reply was made that he should sue before the steward of the household and the king's confessor, show them his service and they would inform the king[9].

The accounts of the officials of the household were rendered before the steward and the keeper of the wardrobe[10], and it was ordained in

[1] Issue Roll, no. 176, m. 11.
[2] K. R. Mem. Roll, no. 97, Brev. dir. Mich. m. 1.
[3] *Cal. Close Rolls*, 1279–88, p. 352. [4] *Parl. Writs*, vol. II, Pt i, p. 224.
[5] Cf. *Cal. Close Rolls*, 1318–23, pp. 234, 334–8. *Parl. Writs*, vol. II, Pt i, p. 241.
[6] K. R. Mem. Roll, no. 85 d.
[7] Chan. Warr., File 129/7114. Vide App. of Doc. no. 80.
[8] Ancient Petition, no. 4717. Vide App. of Doc. no. 137. Vide also Ancient Petitions, nos. 4720, 4730.
[9] *Cal. Doc. Scotl.* vol. III, p. 130.
[10] Vide above, p. 206. *Cal. Close Rolls*, 1279–88, p. 145.

the household ordinances of 1318, that "le seneschall et le tresorer oient en garderobe checun iour la counte de lostell soiorne[1]." They had the power to dismiss the official who presented an unsatisfactory account, to suspend him or to fine him[2]. There is a memorandum in one of the wardrobe accounts of the admission of a simple knight to the household before Mauley, steward, and Warle, keeper of the wardrobe[3]. The steward by an endorsement on a petition was ordered to give the petitioner a suitable office[4]. Even in that part of the administration which had a definite relation to the wardrobe, the steward had a part. The bishop of Winchester, treasurer, sent a sum of 2500 marks for the king to Badlesmere, steward of the household, and to Northburgh, keeper of the wardrobe[5].

The importance of the office of the steward of the household would appear to be threefold. His control of the household was complete and excluded all outside influence either of the administrative departments or of the baronial opposition. Though outside the control of the administration he was yet a member of the "administrative" council and participated in a considerable number of administrative processes and could make the weight of his influence felt in the administration in various directions. He also stood in a close personal relation to the king. He was appointed by royal favour, and after his appointment was in a position to use and extend his personal influence over the king. He was in a position even to abuse that influence, and the odium which some of the stewards drew upon themselves from the baronial opposition[6] would give some slight credence to this suggestion.

Great as were the possibilities of the exercise of personal influence by the steward of the household upon the king, his first importance was administrative, and in this he might be contrasted with the king's chamberlain. There is evidence only of two men holding the office of chamberlain during the reign. John de Cherleton held that office until 1318, and on 20 October[7] of that year, Despenser

[1] Tout, *The Place of Ed. II*, App. I, p. 306.

[2] K. R. Acct. 374/12, m. 2. Vide above, p. 206.

[3] K. R. Acct. 375/8, f. 5.

[4] Ancient Petition, no. 5694.

[5] Anc. Corresp. vol. L, no. 41. Vide App. of Doc. no. 131.

[6] In 1312 Edmund de Mauley, knight and steward of the household, was charged with forgery of the privy seal, but he cleared himself before the king's justices at Westminster (*Ann. Paul.* pp. 272–3). Cf. also the part which the baronial partizan Robert of Reading says he took at Bannockburn (*Flores Hist.* vol. III, p. 159).

[7] *Cal. Pat. Rolls*, 1317–21, p. 133. He was still acting on 19 April, 1318.

was appointed chamberlain by the parliament of York[1]. Cherleton owed his office solely to the position which he held in the royal favour, and if the younger Despenser was thrust into that office against the king's will by the middle party, with the Lancastrian influence, perhaps, added, he became a devoted royal partizan after his appointment and soon became the chief object of the royal affection. There is little trace of any administrative functions inside or outside the household being attached to that office, though, as a mouthpiece of the royal will, the chamberlain often interfered with the normal course of administration. Subsequent to the time of Edward II the chamberlain appears to have acquired a number of functions which had administrative significance. He was the organ through which the royal will was communicated to parliament and the council. Often too he was appointed to assist the triers of petitions and to aid the execution of ordinances made by the council[2]. It was the chamberlain also that endorsed, with the king's will, the petitions presented to the king[3].

The date when Cherleton first acted as chamberlain is uncertain. The first reference to him in that capacity is found on 16 April, 1313[4], though for several years previously he had been well established in the royal favour. In 1301 he had gone to the Scottish war as the constable of fifty-nine archers from the county of Stafford[5]. He had been a member of the prince's household[6]. In a grant of free warren in his demesne lands in Charlton and Pontesbury in September, 1307, he was styled king's yeoman[7], and a little later he was styled knight[8]. In January, 1308, Cherleton accompanied the king to France for his marriage[9], and in June of that year again left England on royal business[10]. Already he was a frequent messenger between king and great seal[11], and was in a position to obtain exemptions from various duties and services for himself and his friends[12]. Writs of the great seal[13] and the privy seal[14] were issued at his request.

[1] Cole, *Doc. illustr. Eng. Hist. in 13th and 14th Cent.* p. 4.

[2] W. J. Thoms, *The Book of the Court* [1838], p. 318. [3] Ibid.

[4] Brit. Mus. Cotton MS. Nero C. viii, ff. 91 d, 93. In June, 1313, the pope gave J. de Cherleton faculty to have a portable altar (*Cal. Pap. Letters*, 1304–42, p. 115).

[5] *Arch. Jour.* vol. XXXIV [1877], p. 447, J. Bain, original doc. in P. R. O.

[6] Vide above, pp. 53–54. [7] *Cal. Charter Rolls*, 1300–26, p. 107 (18 Sept. 1307).

[8] Eyton, *Antiq. of Shropshire*, vol. IX, p. 32.

[9] *Cal. Pat. Rolls*, 1307–13, p. 44. [10] Ibid. p. 80.

[11] Cf. *Cal. Pat. Rolls*, 1307–13, p. 57. [12] Ibid. pp. 84, 197.

[13] *Cal. Close Rolls*, 1307–13, p. 488. *Cal. Pat. Rolls*, 1307–13, pp. 57, 388, 497.

[14] K. R. Mem. Roll, no. 86, m. 15 d (21 Oct. 1312): "a la requeste nostre cher bacheler monsire Johan de Charleton." Chan. Warr., File 70/1240 (18 Sept. 1310).

On 20 March, 1309, he obtained a grant of the manor of Pontesbury which Edward II had received from Rees ap Howel to be held by the service of a fortieth part of a knight's fee[1].

Already in the third and fourth years of Edward II he received the wages of a banneret of the household[2]. Whether he was chamberlain in 1311 or not—and the presumption is strongly that he was—he had sufficiently incurred the dislike of the barons for them to petition for his removal from his office, whatever that may have been, and from court[3]. If he did not hold the office of chamberlain he was always attending on the king. On 23 February, 1310, a payment of £60 was made to Cherleton, who was then either a knight of the king's chamber or chamberlain[4]. In the year 1314 frequent grants were made to him. The castle of Builth was committed to Cherleton, chamberlain, at the usual rent[5], and the chamberlains of Carmarthen and Carnarvon were ordered to allow or pay him a sum of £336. 12*s*. 4*d*. due to him for wages of men in the Scottish war[6]. This latter grant was made by warrant of secret seal, a fact which is explained by its date, 13 August, 1314, after the king's defeat at Bannockburn, when Lancaster temporarily secured a hold upon the administration[7]. On 29 March of that year a grant of 100 marks was made to him for his work in Scotland[8]. In the last three years of his office numerous writs were granted at his instance[9] or his information[10], payments were made to him from the exchequer[11] and he was released from the payment of money there[12], and grants were made to him of lands[13], the last reference to him as chamberlain being contained in a writ granting to him a messuage and tenements without Newgate in the suburb of London[14].

It was however in the struggle for the land of Powys that the king's favour of Cherleton found its strongest expression. Griffith de la Pole, relying upon Welsh law and custom, claimed the inheritance of the lordship against his niece Hawys, the daughter of his

[1] *Cal. Charter Rolls*, 1300–26, p. 127 (10 March, 1309).

[2] Cotton MS. Nero C. viii, f. 36.

[3] *Ann. Lond*. p. 200.

[4] Issue Roll, no. 150, m.: "domino Johanne de Cherleton milite (q. camere *or* camerario) Regis."

[5] *Cal. Fine Rolls*, 1307–19, p. 188.

[6] Ibid. p. 205.

[7] Vide below, pp. 394–400.

[8] Issue Roll, no. 167, m. 9: "militi camerario domini Regis."

[9] *Cal. Charter Rolls*, 1300–26, pp. 305, 367.

[10] Ibid. pp. 370, 378.

[11] Issue Roll, no. 180, m. 3.

[12] K. R. Mem. Roll, no. 91, Brev. dir. m. 40. L. T. R. Mem. Roll, no. 88, Brev. dir. Hil. m. 16 d.

[13] *Cal. Fine Rolls*, 1307–19, p. 317.

[14] *Cal. Pat. Rolls*, 1317–21, p. 133 (19 April 1318).

eldest brother. Hawys was married to John de Cherleton and the king threw the whole weight of his influence in her favour. Griffith, the brother of Hawys and therefore the nephew of the elder Griffith de la Pole, died in June, 1309, in the king's ward. On 25 June, 1309, the justice of Wales was ordered to take the inheritance into the king's hand[1]. The inquisition was held forthwith and Hawys was returned as heir[2]. No time was lost in the delivery of the land. On 9 August, 1309, the chancellor was ordered, by writ of privy seal, to give Hawys immediate seisin[3] and on the 29th the escheator was ordered to deliver the lands to John de Cherleton and Hawys his wife[4]. The other claimant of the Powys' lands naturally allied himself with the baronial opposition, and with their triumph in 1311 his opportunity came. Griffith besought the council for a commission from chancery to inquire if the land of Powys was held by Welshery or of the crown of England[5]. The king immediately forbad the chancellor to make such a commission without special verbal order from him[6]. When the constitutional method failed him Griffith proceeded to force, and the whole machinery of the royal power was put into operation to rescue the castle of Welshpool from him[7].

One chronicler states that in the parliament of York in 1318, the chamberlain and other officials were removed[8]. Whether this is so or not is doubtful, but it is certain that Despenser the younger was appointed chamberlain in that parliament on 20 October[9]. It is equally certain that Cherleton did not lose his office through royal disfavour. He continued to be employed by the king in a personal capacity. He took the king's letter to the city of London on 20 December, 1318, which promised that the expense of the military aid which the city had borne should not be a precedent[10].

Despenser's tenure of the office of chamberlain may be divided into two periods, the first ending with his exile in August, 1321, and the second dating from his return later in that year to his death in 1326. During the first of these periods he so cruelly abused the

[1] *Cal. Fine Rolls*, 1307–19, p. 43.
[2] *Cal. Inq. P. M.* vol. v, pp. 90, 114
[3] Chan. Warr., File 64/642.
[4] *Cal. Fine Rolls*, 1307–19, p. 48.
[5] Chan. Warr., File 82/2430.
[6] Ibid. Vide App. of Doc. no. 56. Vide also above, pp. 130, 135.
[7] *Cal. Close Rolls*, 1307–13, pp. 417, 419, 424, 457, 459.
[8] *Auct. Bridl.* p. 56.
[9] Cole, *Doc. illustr. Eng. Hist. in 13th and 14th Cent.* p. 4. *Chron. Mon. de Melsa*, vol. II, p. 332, and *Chron. G. le Baker*, p. 6, both date Despenser's appointment in 1314.
[10] *Cal. Letter Books, E*, pp. 98–99.

office that gradually he alienated the whole of the baronage. The process of exile drawn up by the barons against him was one long catalogue of ways in which, relying on his position, he and his father had accroached the royal prerogative[1].

In view of the part Despenser took in administration there was some amount of justification in the baronial charges. As chamberlain, together with the steward, he conveyed the king's message to the treasurer on 6 February, 1319[2], and his influence and place at court as well as his methods are well illustrated in his treatment of the bishop of Rochester in that year. The bishop of Rochester, having done fealty for certain manors before the clerks of chancery, had letters patent to the escheator south of Trent to hand over his temporalities. Despenser as chamberlain hindered the delivery of the letters until he had received from the bishop, by extortion, £10 as his fee[3]. The Rochester chronicler condemns his action as being contrary to all justice and custom observed in the kingdom of England before[4]. This was perhaps not an altogether fair criticism, as there is evidence that it was customary for the chamberlain to receive a sum of £10 as his fee when an earl did fealty. When John de Baliol did homage for the kingdom of Scotland to Edward I the chamberlain was told to be content with £20 as his fee[5] Despenser probably demanded the sum as a payment from the bishop on his adoption of baronial status.

After the Boroughbridge campaign Hugh was again chamberlain, and then completely dominated the whole administration, a phase which will be treated later[6]. The present purpose is but to point to the fact that the office of chamberlain was a source of strength to the personal system, and the officer one of the foremost and most important of the officials of that system. It is curious to note what comparatively small acts were done in Despenser's presence and at which his presence was recorded. During the Boroughbridge campaign goods of rebels had been left at the priory of Tutbury, including a barrel of sturgeon valued at 60*s*. On the arrival of the king there the prior showed him the barrel of sturgeon, and the king out of his kindness gave it to the prior in Despenser's presence[7]. Payments

[1] *Stat. of Realm*, vol. I, pp. 181–4. Vide below, pp. 336–341.

[2] K. R. Mem. Roll, no. 92, Brev. dir. m. 25 d. L. T. R. Mem. Roll, no. 89, m. 88.

[3] Wharton, *Angl. Sac*. vol. I [1691], Wm de Dene, *Hist. Roffens*. p. 361.

[4] Ibid.: "pro feodo suo contra omnem justiciam et consuetudinem per regnum Angliae prius usitatam."

[5] *Cal. Close Rolls*, 1288–96, p. 317.

[6] Vide below, pp. 336–341.

[7] Wm Salt. Soc., *Coll*. vol. IX, p. 98.

out of the chamber were frequently made in the presence of the king and Despenser[1], though this considering his office was but natural.

The chief officials of the household are all found exercising some amount of influence on the conduct of the government, and their influence is apparent in chancery and exchequer and local administration. Though they could interfere with the administration they were independent of it. They were appointed by the king, by word of mouth, held their offices during the royal pleasure and could be dismissed at will. They were constantly the instruments of the royal policy, and at times its directors. The administration within the household fell principally upon the steward, who acted with the keeper of the wardrobe. The importance of the administration of the household and the character and work of its officials were considerable inasmuch as all executive power emanated from the household.

[1] *Eng. Hist. Rev.* vol. XXX [1915], p. 678.

CHAPTER IX

THE STRENGTH OF THE HOUSEHOLD SYSTEM (*cont.*)

(vi) *The Minor Officers and the Clerical Staff*

In dignity and position the minor officers and the clerical staff of the various departments of the household were inferior to the chamberlain, steward and marshal. While the latter were characterised by their power and position, the essential feature about the former was their ability. The separation of the administrative departments from the royal court had not robbed it of its capacity as a training ground for officials. There was no more certain way of attaining high office in the administrative departments and in the church than through the household. The household therefore continued to attract ability and train it; and in view of the intricacy of household organisation and its administrative influence it was of vital importance that its staff should be well trained and possess ability.

There were attached to the household a number of officials whose significance was mainly military. Of these the chief were the bannerets and knights of the household. There were three bannerets generally in residence at court, two of them holding the offices of chamberlain and steward. Thus in the eighth year of the reign the bannerets *in curia* were John de Crombwell, Cherleton and William de Ferrars[1]; in the sixteenth year, Despenser, Richard Damory, and Robert de Insula[2]. Few in number, living in close and constant contact with the king, noble and of the rank of baron, their attendance added dignity to the king's court and person. Much of the preparation for war fell upon the household; and it was necessary on various occasions that the king should be surrounded by a large body of barons. These held the rank of bannerets *extra curiam*[3], not being bound to residence. The bannerets *in curia* received a fee

[1] K. R. Acct. 378/6. [2] Stowe MS. 553, f. 65.
[3] K.R. Acct. 378/6.

of ten marks the half year and robes[1]; the bannerets who were *extra curiam* generally did not receive a fee, though some received robes[2]. A number of them were Gascons and received fees and robes when they were beyond sea[3]. The list of bannerets for the eighth year is interesting, and contained at its head the name of Robert fitz Payn, who had been steward, though he did not long retain the position of banneret[4]. Next came the royal favourite and friend Guy Ferre and barons like Nicholas de Segrave, William le Latimer, Richard de Grey, Theobald de Verdon, John de Mowbray, and John de Somery[5]. Despenser, junior, also figured amongst them[6] as early as this. Additions were constantly being made to the list, and amongst the additions of the following year were the earl of Angus, William de Ros and Simon Warde[7].

Below the bannerets came the simple knights who were more in number and composed of people standing lower in the social scale. They were probably more useful servants and could be more readily and easily employed upon administrative work and as royal messengers. The number of simple knights maintained was considerable, and the list of any given year contains the names of many who were subsequently to distinguish themselves as barons or officials of the royal household[8]. All the simple knights were not in residence. They were scattered throughout the country, usefully employed in administration or defence. Hugh D'Audley, father and son, William de Montague, Robert de Kendale, Robert de Sapy, Edmund Bacon, Warin de Insula, Oliver de Ingham, Alan de Cherleton, Roger Damory, were included in the long list of simple knights of the household in the eighth year of the reign[9]. Some like John de Foxle and Henry le Scrope received robes only, because they acted as justices[10]. William Inge, though a justice of the bench, was also a simple knight of the household[11]. Others were garrisoning Berwick at the king's wages, Andrew de Harclay and Robert de Leyburn were at the king's wages at Carlisle; John de Wysham and John de Felton were outside the court on the king's business; some were in Scotland. Certain Gascon and Welsh knights, because they were in their own districts,

[1] Stowe MS. 553, f. 65. The same three were bannerets the following year (ibid. f. 126 b).

[2] K. R. Acct. 378/6. [3] Ibid. [4] Ibid.

[5] Ibid. Cf. K. R. Acct. 375/8, f. 33. [6] K. R. Acct. 378/6. [7] Ibid.

[8] Ibid. 375/8, ff. 34, 36, contains in the list Robert de Sapy, John de la Beche, Adam Swynbourn, Edmund Bacon, William de Montague, John de Weston, John de Wysham, Thomas le Blount, William de Vescy, Warin de Insula, Hugh D'Audley.

[9] Ibid. 378/6. [10] Ibid. [11] Ibid.

had no fees. Thomas le Blount, who was in the king's service at Drysllwyn, and Edmund Hakelut at Dynevor had robes[1]. Among the new admissions of the following year were William de Beauchamp and Walter le Gras[2].

Among the simple knights for the thirteenth year were Robert de Haustede, Roger de Felton, Robert de Sapy, John de Weston, William de la Beche, Humphrey de Walden, and John de Dene[3]. Their fee was five marks the half year[4], but they generally held other offices or were employed on local or temporary administration. Humphrey de Walden was steward of the chamber lands[5], and the other simple knights were employed after Boroughbridge as keepers of forfeited lands, constables of castles or similar employment. Memoranda of the admissions of simple knights to the fees and robes of the king were made upon the wardrobe accounts, the admissions being made on the announcement of household officials like Mauley, steward, Warle, keeper of the wardrobe, or Oliver de Bordeaux[6].

Lower in position than the simple knights came the squires who in the household list of the eighth year are classified with the clerks. Of the squires Oliver de Bordeaux[7] was throughout the reign the most prominent, and a few details of his career will serve as symptomatic of the position and possibilities of the squires of the household. At the beginning of the reign he was a valet of the king's chamber[8] and possessed some influence with the king. A writ of privy seal to the treasurer was issued at his request as early as 19 August, 1310[9]. On 4 March, 1311[10], and 26 April, 1311[11], gifts of 100 marks made to him by the king were paid at the exchequer. As squire of the king's household he obtained twenty marks as a gift on 6 September, 1322[12]. Donald de Mar[13] was another squire whose career is of interest, an interest especially springing from the fact that the king employed him to raise troops in the last stage of the crisis of 1326[14]. Among others who held the same position then were John de Knokyn, Simon de Dryby, who became steward of the household for a brief period in 1322[15], Robert Lewer, Rees ap Griffith, and John de Sturmy, who became a knight at this time[16].

[1] K. R. Acct. 378/6. [2] Ibid.
[3] Stowe MS. 553, f. 102. [4] Ibid. f. 126 b. [5] Ibid. f. 29 b.
[6] K. R. Acct. 375/8, ff. 5, 32. [7] Ibid. 378/6, dorse. Stowe MS. 553, f. 104.
[8] Issue Roll, no. 141, m. 4.
[9] K. R. Mem. Roll, no. 83, m. 35 d. [10] Issue Roll, no. 155, m 8.
[11] Ibid. no. 157, m. 1. [12] Stowe MS. 553, f. 67 b. [13] Ibid.
[14] *Cal. Pat. Rolls*, 1324–27, pp. 284, 352. *Cal. Fine Rolls*, 1319–27, p. 421.
[15] Tout, *The Place of Ed. II*, p. 354. [16] K. R. Acct. 378/6 d.

There were also serjeants of the king's household, who performed more menial duties but in common with all military officials of the household also took a share in the administration. They were considerable in number and included a fair proportion of foreigners[1]. None of them became persons of importance though they were perhaps the most faithful and useful section of the household. An inquiry into the conduct of John de Gisburn, bailiff of the manor of Faxfleet in the king's hand, and answering in the chamber, by reason of the forfeiture of John de Mowbray, concerning ships, was taken before Thomas de Burgh, escheator north of Trent, and Roger atte Water, serjeant-at-arms of the household[2]. King's yeomen also took a considerable part in local administration. A few instances will suffice. Rees ap Griffith, king's yeoman, was appointed to levy all forces horse and foot of West and South Wales in November, 1321, to suppress any insurrection in those parts[3]. In 1322 William de Aune, king's yeoman, was appointed to arrest all disturbers of the peace preventing merchants passing with provisions to Nottingham. He was also to arrest all persons passing to aid the rebels besieging Tickhill, and to seize the lands of John de Mowbray in the Isle of Axholm[4]. A king's yeoman was also the conductor of the wives and children of certain rebels to the Tower in 1322[5].

A study of the details of the crises of 1321–2 and of the instruments the king used to overcome the greatest attempt of the barons to control him by force of arms, proves how useful the military members of the king's household could be. Against the martial force of the powerful barons the king employed the organising skill, fidelity and efficiency of the household. The preparations for the overthrow of the barons were undertaken by such men as John de Beauchamp, Andrew de Harclay, Simon Warde, Ralph Basset, Oliver de Ingham, Robert Lewer, and the Welsh leaders Rees ap Griffith and Griffith Llwyd[6]. The overthrow of the barons was due in no small measure to their efforts and was a well-deserved tribute to the use of what might be regarded as the spectacular rather than the utility side of the household.

Considerable as was the part taken in administration by the military officers this was small when compared with the importance of the administrative officers of the household, of the executive and its

[1] K. R. Acct. 378/6. [2] Anc. Corresp. vol. XXXIII, no. 83.
[3] *Cal. Pat. Rolls*, 1321–24, p. 35 (15 Nov. 1321).
[4] Ibid p. 47 (10 Jan. 1322). [5] Ibid. p. 75.
[6] Cf. *Cal. Close Rolls*, 1318–23, pp. 506–7.

instrument the privy seal, and of the financial department, the wardrobe, with its reserve of the chamber behind it. Among those who are found in the list of clerks in the household list of the eighth year, some already holding important and responsible positions, others not yet promoted to offices, were Roger de Northburgh, Robert de Wodehouse, Richard de Blebury, William de Maldon, John de Ispannia, Richard de Luda, Richard de Ayremynne, John de Carleton, and Reginald de Warle[1].

The secretariat of the household, the office of the privy seal with its keeper and clerks, demand first attention. The importance of the influence of the privy seal as an instrument of government rendered the personal character of its keeper of vast moment. The custody of the privy seal was in the hands of the controller of the wardrobe, and William de Melton, controller, had its custody until the Ordinances of 1311 ordered that the two offices should be separated[2]. Northburgh was appointed keeper of the privy seal, and acted until he became keeper of the wardrobe in 1316[3]. The keepership of the privy seal and the controllership of the wardrobe were again combined by Northburgh's successor, Master Thomas de Cherleton, and also by Baldock who was appointed keeper of the privy seal in 1320, and held the office of controller of the wardrobe, though he was the last person to combine the two offices.

Whether as the result of the Ordinances or not, it seems that during the reign of Edward II the office of the privy seal became separated from the wardrobe; and the appointment of Northburgh as the first independent keeper is important if not decisive. His stay as keeper of the privy seal in London with four clerks to put into execution the orders of the king's council has been noticed, though a little more emphasis may now be placed upon the organisation of the office. It is interesting to note that at this time the four clerks who remained with Northburgh were not described as clerks of the privy seal but as clerks of the wardrobe[4].

There was a development in the functions of the keeper as well as in the organisation of the office of the privy seal during the reign. Robert de Aylleston, keeper of the privy seal in 1323–4, took an active part in administration, especially in the administration of justice. Inquests relating to contempts and trespass committed in forfeited castles, honours, farms and manors were held in 1323 before

[1] K. R. Acct. 378/6 d.
[2] Ordinance 14.
[3] Tout, *The Place of Ed. II*, pp. 98–99, 162–8, 356.
[4] K. R. Acct. 375/8, f. 8.

Aylleston, keeper of the privy seal[1]. In the same year inquests were taken before him and Robert de Holden, controller of the wardrobe[2], touching the king's manor of Skipton in Craven and various trespasses[3]. In company with Despenser, who was then assuming complete control of the administration, and of Geoffrey le Scrope, then a justice of the common bench[4], and shortly after to become chief justice of the king's bench[5], Aylleston, keeper of the privy seal, was sent to Nottingham to demand, receive and report to the king, answers to certain messages[6]. Elias de Johnston was ordered to hand over the processes relating to Gascony to Master Roger Staunford, in the presence of the treasurer of the exchequer or of the keeper of the privy seal[7]. An inquisition, which the chancellor ordered the escheator to take by writ of great seal issued on the warrant of a writ of privy seal, was returned to the chancery and thence to the keeper of the privy seal. Although the inquisition found that the petitioners had right to the lands which they claimed, the matter remained in the wardrobe unexecuted[8].

Aylleston was employed as the royal messenger to the justices who were at Wigan in Michaelmas term 17 Edward II with certain articles which they were to inquire in the counties of Lancaster, Derby and Stafford touching the gatherings with Lancaster against the king at Burton the previous year[9]. On 10 January, 1324, Hervy de Staunton, Henry Spigurnel, John de Stonore, Robert de Malberthorp and Aylleston received a commission as justices to make inquisition in Salop, Staffordshire, Gloucester. Worcester and Hereford and to take fines and ransoms[10]. The association of a clerk of the household, though he held the office of keeper of the privy seal, with such a commission of professional judges—for Staunton, Spigurnel, Stonore and Malberthorp were all justices of repute and experience[11]—is strange. Though in May, 1324, Aylleston was appointed a baron of the exchequer[12], at the time of his commission to act with these judges he held only the office of keeper of the privy seal. On 16 March, 1324, Aylleston went to the king's court at Westminster

[1] *Cal. Close Rolls*, 1323–27, p. 46.

[2] Tout, *The Place of Ed. II*, p. 355.

[3] Chan. Warr., File 124/6699. Vide App. of Doc. no. 78. Vide also Chan. Warr., File 125/6776.

[4] *Cal. Pat. Rolls*, 1317–21, p. 340.

[5] Ibid. 1321–24, p. 409.

[6] Chan. Warr., File 125/6744. Vide *Cal. Close Rolls*, 1323–27, p. 147.

[7] Anc. Corresp. vol. XXXII, no. 112.

[8] *Cal. Inq. P. M.* vol. VII, p. 442.

[9] *Abbrev. Placit.* p. 343.

[10] *Cal. Fine Rolls*, 1319–27, pp. 253–4.

[11] Cf. Foss, *Judges of England* [1851], vol. III, pp. 303–5, 510–512, 301–3, 459–460.

[12] *Cal. Pat. Rolls*, 1321–24, p. 415.

and handed to Staunton and his fellow justices of the king's bench, certain schedules relating to a conspiracy made by some partizans of Roger de Mortimer for the murder of the chief persons about the court—the earls of Winchester and Arundel, Despenser junior, Baldock and Geoffrey le Scrope[1].

References to the clerks of the privy seal are few, and little is known about them, besides the fact that they were four in number[2]. In the sixteenth year of Edward II, Sir Richard de Ayremynne, John de Barton, John de Carleton and William de Colby were the four clerks of the privy seal[3]. Richard de Ayremynne was a chancery clerk who in 1324 acted as one of the keepers of the great seal[4] and was appointed keeper of the rolls of chancery on 26 May, 1324[5], and held the king's seal for a period[6]. William de Colby was controller of the king's chamber from 8 July, 1323, the commencement of the seventeenth year[7].

The number of writs issued under the privy seal has already been noticed[8] and the number of clerks would not seem to be in excess of the requirements of the office. The clerks were also used in direct administrative work. On occasion the nature of the work hardly suited a person of such status. John de Carleton, clerk of the privy seal, was appointed to go to Wales with men-at-arms and foot to pursue Robert Lewer, the king's enemy and rebel, his expenses being paid out of the royal chamber[9].

The chroniclers of the reign of Edward II sometimes refer to certain persons as being the king's secretaries. It is difficult to suppose that any definite office was meant. The secretaries of the king were probably those servants or supporters who dwelt in his household and to whom he gave his confidence[10]. Gavaston on his return from exile was in 1312 referred to as the king's secretary[11], and with Gavaston, Beaumont, Mauley, steward, and other secretaries, the king went to Scarborough with Lancaster and the barons pursuing him[12]. Despenser, John de Crombwell and others are referred to as the king's secretaries in 1322[13]. Robert Lewer, who had

[1] *Parl. Writs*, vol. II, Pt ii, App. p. 244.
[2] K. R. Acct. 375/8, ff. 8, 11 b.
[3] Stowe MS. 553, f. 108.
[4] *Cal. Close Rolls*, 1323–27, p. 628.
[5] Ibid. p. 186.
[6] Vide above.
[7] K. R. Accts. 379/11, 379/17, f. 1.
[8] Vide above, p. 134.
[9] Pipe Rolls, no. 171, m. 41 d. Vide also *Eng. Hist. Rev.* vol. XXV [1910], p. 430.
[10] Cf. *Eng. Hist. Rev.* vol. XXV, p. 430, 'Secretaries in 13th and 14th Centuries,' L. B. Dibben, p. 430.
[11] *Auct. Bridl.* p. 42
[12] Ibid.: "et alii secretarii.
[13] Ibid. p. 79.

been brought up in the king's court[1], and who was sufficiently in the royal grace for his dismissal to be demanded by the ordainers in 1311[2] and who held the position of king's yeoman in 1321, threatened the king's secretaries with injury to life and limb, wherever he should find them, whether within or without the royal presence[3]. Whomever the threat was made against, it was the elder Despenser whose manors he pillaged and whom he attacked and besieged in the castle of Windsor[4].

In all these instances the persons to whom the term secretary was applied were those men who were in constant personal attendance upon the king, who were favourites or personal friends and advisers. In 1323 Despenser, lord of Glamorgan, chamberlain, Geoffrey le Scrope, justice of the bench, and Aylleston, keeper of the privy seal, were referred to in a writ of great seal as "the king's secretaries to whom the king had committed and communicated his secret affairs[5]," the matter in reference being an interview they had held with Master John de Shoreditch who had gone to Rome as the king's envoy[6]. The term secretary is definitely used in this instance referring to those who were the king's confidants, and who were engaged in the king's private and secret business, "in matters which specially touched the king" being defined as "secret matters[7]."

Already in the reign of Edward II the word secretary had acquired another shade of meaning. Badlesmere, when steward of the household, wrote to a cardinal requesting favour for William de Ayremynne, the king's special clerk and secretary of the chancery[8], and at the same time Edward II writing to a cardinal referred to William de Ayremynne as secretary of the chancery[9]. The official positions which Ayremynne then held in the chancery were keeper of the rolls of chancery[10] and keeper of the *domus conversorum*[11]. During this time also, in company with Bardelby and other clerks of chancery, he frequently acted as keeper of the great seal[12]. He was unofficially referred to as chief clerk of the chancery[13], and vice-chancellor[14].

[1] *Auct. Malm.* p. 273.
[2] *Ann. Lond.* p. 199.
[3] *Cal. Pat. Rolls*, 1317–21, p. 596.
[4] *Auct. Malm.* p. 272.
[5] *Cal. Close Rolls*, 1323–27, p. 147.
[6] Ibid.
[7] Vide *Eng. Hist. Rev.* vol. XXIII [1910], p. 437. *Cal. Close Rolls*, 1346–49, p. 238.
[8] *Reg. Pal. Dunelm.* vol. IV, p. lvi.
[9] Ibid. p. lvii.
[10] He is found acting on 26 Aug. 1316 (*Cal. Close Rolls*, 1313–18, p. 430) and he surrendered the office on 26 May, 1324 (ibid. 1323–27, p. 186).
[11] He was appointed on 20 Aug. 1316 (*Cal. Pat. Rolls*, 1313–17, p. 534).
[12] Vide Tout, *The Place of Ed. II*, pp. 324–7.
[13] Camd. Soc. N.S. vol. XXVI [1880], *Doc. illust. Hist. of St Paul's*, p. 49.
[14] *Flores Hist.* vol. III, p. 189: "vicecancellarius Angliae."

All these were purely administrative positions; and it would seem as if the word secretary was applied to him as keeper of the rolls of chancery or as keeper of the great seal. Whether it was applied to him in either or both of these capacities or as a clerk of chancery, the word cannot have entire reference to him as a person concerned with secret matters relating to the king, and it is doubtful if as applied to him it has any such meaning.

Gradually there was being evolved an office of secretary. The chancellor had been in origin a kind of royal secretary, but the development of administration and the separation of the chancery from the court had robbed him of that position. The privy seal was designed to replace the personal use of the great seal after its issue had been formalised, so the keeper of the privy seal can be regarded as fulfilling the place of the royal secretary. During Edward II's reign the keeper of the privy seal was still frequently also the controller of the wardrobe[1], and it is amongst the controllers of the wardrobe that we find the officials referred to as king's secretaries. Before pursuing that point it is useful to remember that the secret seal had by this time sprung up to fulfil the functions of the privy seal, as the latter was becoming more and more used as an instrument of administration[2].

It is impossible to say who had the custody of the secret seal during the reign of Edward II; there is a suggestion that the person who was called the king's secretary, though he may have been at the same time keeper of the privy seal, also administered the secret seal. In 1299 John de Benstede, then controller of the wardrobe and keeper of the privy seal[3], was specifically called "secretarius" in a list of witnesses to a deed[4]. Elsewhere too he was referred to as secretary; and his work was to write the king's letters under the privy seal[5]. An entry on the close roll dated 15 March, 1308, states that Sir William de Melton, secretary of the king, delivered a small seal at the exchequer at Westminster to Norwich, remembrancer of the exchequer[6]. Melton had been a clerk to Edward when prince of Wales[7] and was one of the few men who displayed a consistent loyalty throughout all the crises of the reign, and although he was one of the king's courtiers he led a religious and honourable life[8].

[1] Vide above, p. 224. [2] Vide above, p. 153.

[3] *Liber Quotidianus Contrarotul. Garderobe*, 28 *Ed. I*, pp. 78, 313, 326.

[4] *Foedera*, vol. I, p. 916.

[5] *Liber Quotidianus Contrarotul. Garderobe*, p. 83.

[6] *Cal. Close Rolls*, 1307–13, pp. 57–58. [7] Vide above, p. 53.

[8] *Chron. de Lanerc.* p. 217. *Auct. Malm.* pp. 283–4. *Historians of the Church*

Immediately on Edward's accession he became controller of the wardrobe[1] and in October, 1307, he is found acting as keeper of the privy seal[2]. Thomas de Cherleton, who was keeper of the privy seal, was called the king's "secretary" in letters the king wrote to the pope on his behalf[3]. Though the king's secretary eventually became distinguishable from the keeper of the privy seal, in the reign of Edward II, the two offices were held by the same person, or perhaps it would be more correct to say that the controller of the wardrobe acted as keeper of the privy seal, though at times the two offices were distinct, and that the keeper of the privy seal acted as the royal secretary. In order to avoid confusion it would be better to consider the secretariat of the household as a whole, and to define it as being composed of the keeper of the privy seal, who sometimes acted as, or was named, the king's secretary, and the clerks of the privy seal. Besides having charge of the great instrument of the executive these officials sometimes acted in administrative capacities outside the household; and it can be fairly said that the freedom from control of the secretariat and its efficiency were a considerable source of strength to the household system.

The question of the custody of the secret seal remains. The secret seal may be described as the instrument of the chamber and was nearer the king than the privy seal. The same person cannot have been the custodian of both instruments, as writs under the secret seal were addressed in May, 1318, to Master Thomas de Cherleton, keeper of the privy seal, ordering him to make a writ under the privy seal[4]. The secret seal was probably in the custody of a clerk or official of the chamber, though as it was a new instrument it may have changed its custodian frequently.

As the office of the privy seal was the chancery of the household, with the keeper as chancellor, so the wardrobe was the exchequer of the household with the keeper as treasurer, and indeed the keeper of the wardrobe was often called the treasurer. The keeper or treasurer of the wardrobe then was in charge of the revenue of the household. The various subsidiary departments rendered their accounts before him. The wardrobe books supply the finished record of his work. He was also engaged in other than financial matters within the household, sometimes acting with the steward, as in the

of York, vol. II, pp. 416–417. Twysden, *Hist. Anglic. Script. Decem* [1652], c. 1731.

[1] Tout, *The Place of Ed. II*, p. 355. [2] *Cal. Close Rolls*, 1307–13, p. 42.

[3] *Reg. Pal. Dunelm.* vol. IV, pp. xlv, xlvii.

[4] Chan. Warr., File 1328/126 (13 May, 1318).

audit of accounts. The steward was the chief lay official of the household, and the keeper of the wardrobe the chief clerical officer. The sheriff of Southampton was ordered to choose fifty carpenters in his bailiwick and to cause them to go to Westminster to do what the keeper of the wardrobe and the steward of the household or one of them should direct[1].

In the administration of the government as opposed to the administration of the household the keeper of the wardrobe had a share. He acted as a messenger between king and great seal[2]. Grants of land were made by the king at the request of Warle, keeper of the wardrobe[3]. Accounts of foreign merchants at the exchequer were rendered before the chancellor, the keeper of the wardrobe and others appointed by the king to audit their accounts[4]. The keeper of the wardrobe witnessed a surrender to the king[5]. He also acted as a royal messenger. The constable of the Tower of London, the mayor, sheriffs and aldermen of the city were ordered to act concerning the outrages committed on Gascons coming to the city as Warle, keeper of the wardrobe, would command them on the king's behalf[6]. The keeper of the wardrobe went to the city bearing this writ of privy seal and declared the king's command that no one should injure the Gascons coming into the city, by word or deed[7]. In company with Sandale, lieutenant of the treasurer, Warle was in 1313 appointed to go to St Alban's to receive the horses and effects which Lancaster and other barons had taken from the king in the north in their campaign against Gavaston early in 1312, and which had to be returned according to the form of the treaty of December, 1312[8].

The keeper of the wardrobe was frequently present at the exchequer among those of the council assisting the treasurer and barons. John de Benstede, Edward II's first keeper[9], acted in this way[10]. A writ under the exchequer sent to the taxors and collectors in Kent on behalf of John Vanne was tested by the treasurer himself with the bishop of Chichester, chancellor of England, Sandale, chancellor

[1] *Cal. Close Rolls*, 1302–7, p. 377.

[2] E.g. *Cal. Close Rolls*, 1307–13, p. 417; 1318–23, p. 377. *Cal. Pat. Rolls*, 1321–24, p. 14. *Rot. Scot.* vol. I, pp. 155, 166, 188. *Cal. Fine Rolls*, 1319–27, pp. 53, 57.

[3] K. R. Mem. Roll, no. 84, m. 4.

[4] *Cal. Close Rolls*, 1279–88, p. 32.

[5] Ibid. 1288–96, p. 403.

[6] *Cal. Letter Books, D*, p. 228.

[7] Ibid.

[8] Chan. Warr., File 83/2572 a. Cf. *Cal. Close Rolls*, 1307–13, p. 574. *Foedera*, vol. II, pp. 191–2.

[9] Tout, *The Place of Ed. II*, p. 355

[10] Madox, *Hist. of Exch.* vol. II, pp. 29–30.

of the exchequer, Benstede, keeper of the wardrobe, and certain barons of the exchequer assisting him[1]. Benstede was also among those of the council sitting at the exchequer with the treasurer and barons when a petition was considered by them[2]. A petition was sent under the privy seal to the chancellor, John de Drokensford, keeper of the wardrobe, and Sandale, lieutenant of the treasurer[3].

Two crowns were handed to the treasurer by the Baldi in the presence of Northburgh, keeper of the wardrobe[4]. The keeper also sat as a member of the council when it acted elsewhere than at the exchequer. Geoffrey de Hartlepool took his oath as serjeant of the king's bench before the keeper of the wardrobe, Walter de Gloucester, escheator, and others of the king's council[5]. The keeper sat with the chancellor, justices and clerks of chancery in the chancery, when a manor, which had previously been held in chief of the king, was surrendered to him[6]. Northburgh, keeper, was sent from the council at Westminster to the king at Windsor with certain letters addressed to Roger Mortimer of Wigmore, justice of Ireland, touching pardons. The letters were sent in duplicate so that the king might send them with or without a certain condition as he should think fit. A month later Northburgh returned to the chancery with the letters containing the condition which were cancelled, saying that the letters without the clause were sent by the king[7]. This instance shows the keeper acting on the council as a person closely associated with the king, and moreover gives a characteristic instance of the king's employment of the keeper in administration.

Though the part that the keepers of the wardrobe, as indeed of all the officials of the household, took in the administration was designed to maintain and increase the king's control over it, on occasion their action was not acceptable to the king or was discountenanced from motives of policy. An ordinance had been made for the arresting of wool for the king's use, but the wool of native merchants was not to be so arrested. It was afterwards agreed and provided by Despenser, Drokensford, keeper of the wardrobe, and others of the king's council sitting at the exchequer, because the sum of wool provided could not be obtained by the ordinance, that the wool of wealthy native merchants should be arrested for the king's use. The king disclaimed any knowledge of such an

[1] L. T. R. Mem. Roll, no. 78, m. 82.
[2] K. R. Mem. Roll, no. 81, m. 52.
[3] Chan. Warr., File 63/513 (13 June, 1309).
[4] Ibid. no. 93, m. 77.
[5] *Cal. Close Rolls*, 1296–1302, p. 594.
[6] Ibid. 1302–7, p. 540.
[7] Ibid. 1313–18, p. 405.

arrangement and the treasurer and barons of the exchequer were ordered to cause the wool to be restored to the native merchants[1].

Subordinate to the keeper of the wardrobe was the controller. A number of those who held this office succeeded later to the higher, and some of them became great officers of state. Melton, who became controller on the king's accession, held that office until 30 November, 1314, when he became keeper[2]. He subsequently became archbishop of York and treasurer of England. Baldock, who held the office 1320–3[3], surrendered it to become chancellor of England. Robert de Wodehouse, who held it twice, first from 1314–16 and again July–October, 1323, surrendered it on the second occasion to become keeper[4]. The controllers influenced the king and the administration in the same manner as the other household officials. Robert de Wodehouse, when controller, obtained a grant of the office of escheator in Ireland for his brother Richard[5]. The king sent to the treasurer and barons of the exchequer a petition he had received, employing Melton, controller of the wardrobe, as his messenger[6].

The personnel of the chamber, both in its financial and general activities, has a peculiar importance on account of the specially personal relation in which those offices stood to the king. The head of the chamber organisation was the clerk of the chamber, a position which William de Langley held during the reign of Edward II[7]. There was also a controller of the chamber, the most prominent of the men who held this position being Thomas de Useflet[8]. These were the chief administrative officers who resided in the chamber. There were in addition a number of administrative officers whose duties carried them outside, including a receiver of the issues of chamber lands[9] and a steward of chamber lands[10], the former office being held by James de Ispannia and the latter by Sir Humphrey de Walden. The majority of the officers of the chamber were personal attendants of the king. Sir Robert de Grendon, who was a simple knight of the household[11], was marshal of the king's hall[12], Sir Giles de Beauchamp was a knight of the chamber[13], John de Sturmy was steward of the chamber[14], Peter Bernard usher of the chamber[15], Rees ap Griffith[16] was referred to as a privy squire of

[1] *Cal. Close Rolls*, 1296–1302, p. 111.
[2] Tout, *The Place of Ed. II*, App. II, p. 355. [3] Ibid. [4] Ibid.
[5] Chan. Warr., File 94/3675. [6] K. R. Mem. Roll, no. 81, m. 52.
[7] *Eng. Hist. Rev.* vol. XXX [1915], p. 673. K. R. Accts. 379/11, 379/17, f. 1.
[8] *Eng. Hist. Rev.* vol. XXX [1915], p. 673. [9] Pipe Roll, no. 171, m. 42 d.
[10] Stowe MS. 553, f. 29 b. [11] Ibid. ff. 105, 126 b.
[12] K. R. Acct. 380/4, f. 60. [13] Ibid. 379/17, f. 4.
[14] *Eng. Hist. Rev.* vol. XXX [1915], p. 678. [15] Ibid. [16] Ibid.

the chamber, and Oliver de Bordeaux[1] and John Harsik[2] as squires of the chamber. Below these there were several valets of the chamber[3]. William Warde, a valet of the chamber for a considerable portion of the reign, received a regular sum of money at the exchequer, assigned to him for keeping a certain secret of the king in the palace of Westminster[4].

A request was made to the chancellor for a protection by William de Sengham: "qui demoert en le seruice le Roi en sa chambre qui viet en Escoce en le seruice le Roi[5]." After the battle of Boroughbridge the king sent orders to the prior of Tutbury to deliver all jewels and other goods which had been left in the priory by the rebels to John de Sturmy and Giles de Ispannia[6]. The officials of the chamber frequently received sums of money from the king, Oliver de Bordeaux being especially favoured[7].

The number and variety of officers in the household were enormous. The buttery, the chandlery, the kitchen, the larder, the marshalsea, the pantry, the scullery, all had their subsidiary offices and various officers[8]. Most of the departments had little to do with administration, but when the officers of the chamber, the wardrobe, the great wardrobe and the privy seal are taken and that omnibus title of king's clerk, the influence exercised upon the various departments of the administration was considerable. Something has already been said of the administrative influence of these officials. There remain one or two points of interest to be dealt with in this particular subject. In the sixth year of Edward II a payment was made to Robert de Elton for his wage for boats for the treasurer, cofferer and the clerks of the wardrobe staying on the king's business in London going and returning between London and Westminster to the king's council[9]. The keeper of the wardrobe was certainly a member of the "administrative" council[10], though up to the present no other instance of the cofferer or clerks of the wardrobe as members has been discovered. This attendance upon, if not in, the king's council which is suggested here is of some interest and supplies another instance of the place of the wardrobe in administration.

[1] K. R. Acct. 380/4, f. 64. [2] Ibid. 379/17, f. 2.

[3] *Eng. Hist. Rev.* vol. XXX [1915], pp. 675–6.

[4] Issue Rolls, no. 176, mm. 8, 12; no. 180, m. 3; no. 183, m. 2; no. 187, m. 4; no. 191, m. 2; no. 195, m. 1.

[5] Chan. Warr., File 1703. [6] Wm Salt Soc., *Coll.* vol. IX, p. 98.

[7] K. R. Accts. 379/17, ff. 3, 4; 380/4, f. 64.

[8] Vide the household ordinances of 1318 and 1322 printed by Tout in his *The Place of Ed. II*, App. I, pp. 270–318.

[9] K. R. Acct. 375/8, f. 7 b. [10] Vide above, pp. 230–1.

Sometimes the household and chancery officials worked together. In 1317, by royal writ, John de Croseby, chancery clerk, and Stephen le Blount, king's clerk, were sent to bring chronicles, which illustrated claims to land, to the chancery[1]. In 1324 the treasurer and chamberlain of the exchequer were ordered by the king to pay expenses to the king's clerks who had been sent to divers parts of the realm on his affairs[2]. The earl of Warenne, in accordance with the king's letters, did fealty to Henry de Thrapston, king's clerk, for certain manors which he held for life, the reversion of which had been granted to the king[3]. In January, 1322, safe conduct for one year was granted to Robert de Baldock the younger, clerk of the king's household, who was going beyond seas on the king's affairs[4]. On 15 March, 1308, Melton, controller of the wardrobe, took to the exchequer the seal which had been used in England when the king was abroad[5], the seal being under the privy seal of the bishop of Chichester, chancellor[6].

Various grants of lands and money were often made to officials of the household, among those who received such grants in 1316–18 being the apothecary of queen Isabel, the ushers of her hall and her chamber, and the steward of the household[7]. After the surrender of Leeds Castle in 1321 the keeping of the lands, goods and chattels of the rebels who had defended the castle was given to Richard de Potesgrave, the king's chaplain[8]. Master Robert de Aylleston, king's clerk, who had a few days before been appointed a baron of the exchequer[9], was on 26 May, 1324, appointed keeper of certain lands in Westminster and in the county of Middlesex[10].

The most common way in which the king rewarded his officials and clerks was by ecclesiastical preferment. Sandale, when a clerk in the king's service, held no fewer than two dignities, eight prebendal stalls, and ten rectories[11]. John de Euerdon, who became a baron of the exchequer in 1307[12], was successively chancellor of Exeter, dean of Wolverhampton and dean of St Paul's[13]. A royal official succeeded

[1] Surtees Soc. vol. CXVII [1909], *Percy Cartulary*, p. 224.
[2] *Cal. Close Rolls*, 1323–27, p. 225.
[3] *Descr. Cat. Ancient Deeds*, vol. III, p. 109. [4] *Cal. Pat. Rolls*, 1321–24, p. 47.
[5] K. R. Mem. Roll, no. 81, m. 43 d. L. T. R. Mem. Roll, no. 78, m. 40 d.
[6] Ibid.
[7] *Cal. Fine Rolls*, 1307–19, pp. 284, 268, 275, 351. [8] Ibid. 1319–27, p. 77.
[9] *Cal. Pat. Rolls*, 1321–24, p. 415 (21 May, 1324).
[10] *Cal. Fine Rolls*, 1319–27, p. 279.
[11] Seld. Soc., *Year Bk 3–4 Ed. II*, p. xix. [12] *Cal. Pat. Rolls*, 1307–13, p. 22.
[13] Surtees Soc. vol. LXXVIII [1884], *Memorials of Ripon*, vol. II, p. 200. *Ann. Paul*, p. 306. Camd. Soc. N.S. vol. XXVI, *Doc. illustr. Hist. of St Paul's*, p. 50.

a royal official in a prebend. When Benstede resigned his prebend of Studley Magna John de Merkingfeld was collated to it[1], Merkingfeld being successively king's remembrancer and chancellor of the exchequer[2]. The holding of prebends by royal clerks and officials was not without considerable advantage to the ecclesiastical communities. They could and did use them to further their interests at the administrative departments. The chapter of Beverley wrote to Sandale and Melton, both of whom held office in the chapter, asking them to aid their attorney in the king's bench[3].

These minor preferments were but preliminary to the greater dignities to which the king raised his clerks. The chapter of Beverley noted that two of their canons were elected to greater office at the same time, Melton to the archbishopric of York, and Sandale to the bishopric of Winchester[4]. Drokensford, keeper of the wardrobe in 1308–9, and previously chancellor of the exchequer[5], became bishop of Bath and Wells. Northburgh, who had been keeper of the privy seal and subsequently keeper of the wardrobe[6], became bishop of Coventry and Lichfield, the pope providing him to that see at the king's request[7]. The provision of Reynolds, treasurer, to the see of Worcester and his subsequent translation to the archbishopric of Canterbury, the provision of Thomas de Cobham, king's clerk, to Worcester, and other appointments to bishoprics, were cases of promotion of royal officials at the king's desire. The promotion of William de Ayremynne, keeper of the rolls of chancery, to the bishopric of Norwich, if done against the king's will, was nevertheless an outstanding instance of the promotion of a hard-working and diligent official.

The officials of the king's household were frequently appointed to positions in the great offices of the administration; thus the household, while it had given birth to those departments, still, by a transfer of personal influence, affected even their normal course and progress. The keepers of the wardrobe invariably obtained promotion; Benstede became a justice of the common bench, Drokensford, chancellor of the exchequer, Warle, a baron and chief baron of the exchequer, and Robert de Wodehouse, baron of the exchequer Baldock, from controller of the wardrobe and keeper of the privy seal, became chancellor of England[8]. Robert de Holden, controller of the wardrobe,

1 Surtees Soc., *Memorials of Ripon*, vol. II, p. 185.
2 Tout, *The Place of Ed. II*, pp. 348, 345.
3 Surtees Soc. vol. XCVIII [1897], *Beverley Chapter Act Book*, vol. I, p. 301.
4 Ibid. pp. 338–9.
5 Tout, *The Place of Ed. II*, pp. 355, 345.
6 Vide above, pp. 224, 231.
7 *Cal. Pap. Letters*, 1304–42, p. 337.
8 Vide above, p. 224.

during his tenure of that office was appointed keeper of the *domus conversorum*[1] and held the two offices together. John de Okham, twice cofferer of the wardrobe[2], became a baron of the exchequer. In the same way many of the officials who took a prominent part in the local administration had received their training in the king's household. This ability to promote officials to positions in the general administrative systems was an instrument of value in the direction and control of the departments of government.

It has been seen how the king acting through his household controlled the government. The appointment of the great officers of government and the minor officers of the administration, local and central, gave the king an all-important control over the whole of the administrative machinery and enabled him to transfer suitable officers from his household into administrative positions. The various ways in which the king was able to regulate the use of the great seal, which was the instrument of government, was equally vital. In the privy seal the king had an instrument of great efficacy by which he could interfere with every department of government in every detail of administration. The influence of the secret seal, of informal warrants and verbal orders was similar. While the king exercised such a complete control over the government, his household, whence that control sprang, was itself independent of outside interference. It had a completeness of organisation which rendered attempts at outside interference improbable of success. Its finance organisation in the wardrobe, supplemented by that of the chamber, its system of justice and privilege, the position and powers of its chief officers and the ability of its clerical staff all combined to render it almost impregnable. There were two possibilities open to the baronial opposition. The barons might seek to obtain a measure of control over the government in matters of appointment and administration, and they might also endeavour to assault the impregnability of the household system by a direct attack, with a view to lessening its independence and reforming its organisation. It will be seen hereafter that the baronial opposition to Edward II followed both these lines of policy, though they found the system they attacked too strong to be overcome at the first or any subsequent assault. They accordingly modified their policy, so that it came more into relation with the personal system. At times the baronial opposition seemed desirous of becoming curialist itself, and there were certainly tendencies in that direction.

[1] *Cal. Pat. Rolls*, 1324–27, p. 176.

[2] Tout, *The Place of Ed. II*, p. 356.

CHAPTER X

THE INFLUENCE OF THE HOUSEHOLD SYSTEM UPON THE ADMINISTRATION

(i) *Chancery and Exchequer*

The various sources of strength of the household system have been considered from within that system; and the administration only in so far as it illustrated those sources of strength. The present series of chapters may be regarded as explaining and emphasising, from another point of view, the ways in which the independent household system controlled, guided and checked the administration. In other words it may be said that hitherto the problem of the relations between the household and the administration has been regarded from the interior of the household and that now the problem will be viewed from the exterior. That statement of the purpose of the present series of chapters would be partial, for it would not cover the whole case. Besides that of viewing the problem from a new standpoint, which, if it were alone, would run the danger of constant repetition, there are other purposes. The aim is supplementary as well as complementary. The great departments of the chancery and exchequer, the executive, meaning by executive now the "administrative" council, and the formal assemblies of the great council and parliament, will be considered in broad outline, and the way in which the king could exert his influence over them irrespective of the control of the household system or of its independence. Moreover a number of instances will be afforded in which the household officials took part in general administration, and in which the various sources of strength of the household system were operative to practical ends. Though these considerations supply the primary purpose of the detailed consideration of the influence of the household system upon the administration they are not exhaustive. As a secondary purpose of considerable importance the opportunity will be afforded of discovering the strength and weakness of the administrative departments, of the executive and of the formal assemblies, and the abuses which were prevalent in them. For the household system concerns the present purpose only in so far as it interprets the baronial opposition to Edward II and dictates its policy and character. The consideration of the administration, especially in so far as the household influenced it, is important for the same purpose. It may aid to explain the direction which baronial opposition took and suggest or supply the reasons.

The pre-eminent position which the chancery occupied among the administrative departments, and its functions as the source of formal executive power to the other departments suggest an amount of final authority which it had not. Though there was a growing tendency towards independence on the part of the officials of chancery, the king had well maintained his position as the source of executive authority. The powers of chancery were still very limited. The great seal itself could be completely regulated by the king[1]; and by the use of the privy and secret seals, informal warrants and verbal orders the normal and formalised use of the great seal was dictated or checked.

Assignment of dower was made in the chancery[2] but frequently on the warrant of writs of privy seal[3]. Inquests relating to land were returned into chancery, and those who complained of them had to challenge them there[4], but in this matter the king could interfere both in initiation and in subsequent processes. Lieges in chancery were sometimes ordered to inquire into the truth of statements made in petitions[5], but this was only after the petition had been considered by the council. The chancellor was already extending his jurisdiction in this direction, and in 21 Edward I, petitions which concerned the great seal or asked for matters of grace were assigned to the chancellor[6]. Before the end of the reign of Edward II a petition was directed to the chancellor asking him to proceed with a matter referred to him by parliament[7], and during the reign petitions on wardships of infants, dower, partition, goods of felons and similar matters were referred to the chancellor who was to act alone or jointly with justices[8].

Early in 1326 the king enclosed a petition under the privy seal to Baldock, chancellor, ordering him to examine it and make decision

[1] Vide above, pp. 116–132, 133–177. [2] Chan. Warr., Files 62, 68/414, 68/1010–1.
[3] Seld. Soc., *Year Bk* 3 *Ed. II*, p. 63. *Cal. Inq. P. M.* vol. v, pp. 144–5.
[4] *Cal. Inq. P. M.* vol. v, p. 308. [5] *Cal. Doc. Scotl.* vol. III, p. 135.
[6] *Cal. Close Rolls*, 1288–96, p. 289.
[7] *Rot. Parl.* vol. I, p. 437. Vide Kerly, *Equity* [1890], p. 29.
[8] Campbell, *Lives of Lord Chancellors*, vol. I, pp. 206–9.

by the advisement of Geoffrey le Scrope. The petition was examined, and the sheriff of Norfolk was ordered to have certain people in the chancery on a given date, when they appeared before the chancellor, Scrope and others of the council at Norwich and an inquisition was taken[1]. This instance supplies a good example of the judicial activity of the chancery. Though this power was increasing, the decisions were still subject to the king's approval or acquiescence; and he had instruments at his hand to enforce his will. Boroughs pleading for a confirmation of their charters were told to go to the chancery and plead before the chancellor to have the desired confirmation[2]. The burgesses of Newborough petitioning thus were told to go before the chancellor and treasurer, show their charter, and make fine[3].

The jurisdiction of the chancery on matters other than petitions was also increasing. Those who had omitted to take the degree of knighthood were in 1326 ordered to appear in chancery to answer for their contempt and failure to obey the ordinance and proclamation and to do what should then be decided[4]. Pleas concerning recognisances made in chancery were held there sometimes, the matter being pleaded before the chancellor at a parliament[5], and the earl of Gloucester was given a day in chancery in a plea of *quo waranto* which was proceeding against him[6]. It was recognised in the thirteenth century that the chancellor, by virtue of his office, might confer all benefices in the king's gift of less value than 20 marks[7] and this right was exercised under Edward II[8]. Yet the clerks of chancery sent the king a long list of Scottish benefices which they requested might be granted to them[9]! A fine of £10 imposed upon a sheriff for an insufficient return was remitted by the chancellor[10], but the exercise of power of this kind was exceptional. The power of chancery was limited, and even its most formal and routine business could be, and was, regulated and checked by the king.

Its jurisdiction was growing but there were well-defined limits, and pleas commenced in chancery had sometimes to be adjourned to the court of king's bench because according to the custom of England such pleas could not be decided by the chancellor[11]. The justices moreover tended to usurp a number of the functions of

[1] P. R. O. Placita in Cancellaria, File 1/2 (3). [2] Ancient Petition, no. 7778.
[3] Ibid. no. 1320. [4] *Parl. Writs*, vol. II, Pt i, p. 444.
[5] Anc. Corresp. vol. XXXV, no. 41. [6] Chan. Misc., Bdle 64/3 (77).
[7] *Cal. Pat. Rolls*, 1334–38, pp. 61, 196. Seld. Soc., *Year Bk* 3–4 *Ed. II*, p. xix.
[8] Brit. Mus. Cotton MS. Vespasian F. vii, f. 6.
[9] Anc. Corresp. vol. XXXV, no. 31.
[10] Wm Salt Soc., *Coll.* vol. VI, Pt i, p. 107. [11] *Abbrev. Placit.* p. 336.

chancery by an extension of the use of judicial writs. The chief justice could by his own writ, for instance, grant an attaint of the jurors of all assizes that came before the eyre and in the same way he could grant a writ for disseisin made during the eyre[1]. There was no necessity of suing a writ out of the chancery in such matters[2]

The wider question of the council at the exchequer will be more fully discussed subsequently; but it is important to notice the association of the chancellor with the treasurer and barons of the exchequer in the work of that department. The bishop of Worcester, chancellor, sat with the treasurer at the exchequer[3]. The lieutenant of the treasurer and the barons were ordered not to sell any escheats in the king's land to anyone without his presence[4]. When, by virtue of the royal order, a member of the Friscobaldi was arrested, he was brought before the bishop of Worcester, the lieutenant of the treasurer and the barons[5]. Warle, the late keeper of the wardrobe, appeared in matters relating to his accounts before the treasurer and barons, Sandale, chancellor of England sitting with them[6], and Roger de Waltham, keeper[7] of the wardrobe, likewise appeared before the chancellor and exchequer officials.

Besides this active interference in exchequer business by the council, the exchequer proceeded considerably upon the warrant of writs under the great seal. The justices had no power to send writs to the exchequer on administrative matters. When Willoughby asked Bereford, chief justice of common pleas, for a bill to the chamberlains to cause a record to come out of the treasury, he was told to sue a writ out of the chancery to the treasurer and chamberlains to send him the record[8]. Arising from this influence which the chancery possessed over the exchequer the influence which the king and the personal system exercised over the exchequer would depend largely upon his influence upon the chancery.

The importance with which the king of France invested the chancellor of England in the style in which he addressed him[9] and

[1] Seld. Soc., *Eyre of Kent*, vol. I, p. 158. [2] Ibid.

[3] K. R. Mem. Roll, no. 83, m. 56 d.

[4] Ibid. no. 85, m. 11 d (25 Nov. 1311). [5] Ibid. m. 44.

[6] Ibid, no. 88, m. 154 d. L. T. R. Mem. Roll, no. 85, Rec. Trin. m. 1 d.

[7] K. R. Mem. Roll, no. 97, Rec. Hill. m. 2 d.

[8] Seld. Soc., *Year Bk 4 Ed. II*, p. 133.

[9] Anc. Corresp. vol. XXXV, no. 53: "cancellario ac ceteris gentibus...ad tenendum post instans pascha proximum parlamentum anglie apud Londonium a Rege eodem deputatis." Ibid. nos. 106, 107: "discreto viro nobis dilecto Regni Anglie Cancellario et omnibus justiciariis carissimi filij nostri Regis Anglie per Angliam constitutis."

in the matters upon which he wrote to him[1], was to a great extent exaggerated and suggests a misconception of his functions and a misunderstanding of his position. The chancellor, in his original position as one of the personal system, had not developed into an independent official with a control over the whole administration. The development of his office had been hampered by its origin and by the strength which this personal system had maintained after the departments of administration had been separated from it.

The household as the stronghold of the executive, with its instruments and means of regulation and prohibition[2], with the promotion of officers from the household to the administration[3], and with the use of household officers in administration[4], exercised a decisive influence upon the chancery. At least one important phase of the exercise of this influence will be sketched in detail in the treatment of the personal system in action[5]. There were also other means by which the interference with the chancery was extended.

Even in such chancery matters as the issue of letters the chancellor was sometimes ordered to act in concert with other persons named by the king. Letters under the great seal to the pope and cardinals, opposing the restoration of the bishop of Glasgow to his office or his country, were to be drawn up by the chancellor with the co-operation of the earl of Lincoln, king's lieutenant, and the treasurer of Scotland[6]. The king sent an order jointly to the bishop of Worcester, chancellor, and Despenser to assemble the chancery clerks, and on their advice made a writ of great seal to certain justices, in the way used in the time of the king's ancestors, to make a fine in a certain plea without delay[7]. In the matter touching the commission of the king's valet John Pecok, Sandale, chancellor, was to act according to the counsel and advice of Norwich, treasurer, and William Inge, justice[8]. Inquests sent into chancery were sometimes taken by officials of the household and not by order of chancery or by chancery officials. Thus the inquest taken before Aylleston, keeper of the privy seal, and Holden, controller of the wardrobe[9], was sent into the chancery; and the chancellor was ordered to summon before him those concerned to hear and determine the matters contained therein[10].

[1] Anc. Corresp. vol. XXXV, nos. 53, 106, 107.
[2] Vide above, pp. 116–132, 133–177.
[3] Vide above, pp. 235–236.
[4] Vide above, pp. 221–234.
[5] Vide below, pp. 321–2.
[6] *Cal. Doc. Scotl.* vol. III, p. 38 (Jan. 1311).
[7] Anc. Corresp. vol. XXXV, no. 102.
[8] Chan. Warr., File 94/3603 (2 Mar. 1316).
[9] Vide above, p. 225.
[10] Chan. Warr., Files 124/6699, 125/6776.

On some occasions when the chancellor was associated with the justices his position was of but secondary importance. In the process which was being drawn up against William de Ayremynne between the chancellor, Geoffrey le Scrope, chief justice of the king's bench, and his companions, the predominant position was assumed by the chief justice[1], who was at this time well established in the royal favour[2]. In the two last years of the reign Baldock, chancellor, was ordered to take Scrope's advice on matters of every nature. He was to be called in to consider petitions[3] and matters were to be considered with full advice before him[4]. The chancellor and chief justice acted jointly in a matter touching Yarmouth[5]; and in other matters the chancellor was ordered to act on the advice of the chief justice[6]. On one occasion, if he were not in town, Roger Beler was to act in his stead[7]. This part which Scrope assumed he did not exercise by virtue of his office. It was as one of the personal advisers and confidants of the king that he acted a part very similar to that played by Beler with whom he sometimes acted[8].

The few facts recorded here cannot adequately suggest the all-powerful influence which the king could exercise upon the chancellor and his department whenever he so desired; the ways were multifarious. The easiest and surest means to employ was to use the instrument which lay most ready to his hand—the household system. The first essential therefore in baronial aims should be not to reform the chancery but to break, reform, or control the household system. There was one important manner in which the personal system affected the exchequer to a degree unknown to the chancery. This influence, which was of an indirect nature, consisted in the important part which the council took in exchequer administration[9].

The description of the exchequer contained in the *Mirror of Justices* noticed its dual capacity, firstly as a court of justice and secondly as a financial organisation[10]. The exchequer was originated

[1] Anc. Corresp. vol. XLIX, no. 95.

[2] Stowe MS. 553, f. 128. In going to the tournament of Northampton in 1323 a payment of £26. 13*s*. 4*d*. was made him from the wardrobe in aid of his expenses.

[3] Chan. Warr., File 129/7130 (1 June, 1325), and File 131/7302 (27 Jan. 1326).

[4] Ibid. File 129/7193 (22 Sept. 1325). [5] Ibid. File 130/7294 (25 Jan. 1326)

[6] Ibid. File 131/7408 (30 Jan. 1326). [7] Ibid. File 130/7216 (5 Oct. 1325).

[8] Ibid. File 130/7225 (20 Oct. 1325).

[9] The activities of the council and the influence which the personal system exercised on its composition and functions will be treated in the next chapter, the subject of the council and the exchequer on pp. 261–278.

[10] Seld. Soc., *Mirror of Justices*, p. 36.

as the king's financial department; and great as was its importance in this capacity, here the judicial activity is almost as important as the administrative, since it provided a fruitful source of grievance. The administration of the finance of the kingdom in part involved the judicial functions of the exchequer. The extension of these functions outside the province of finance and its administration, and the use of the court of exchequer as a court of common law, promoted opposition.

The financial organisation of the household exercised an important influence upon the exchequer[1]. The money which the exchequer paid to the wardrobe was a constant drain upon its resources. Often the only warrant that the exchequer had for such payments was a bill of the wardrobe[2]. Besides the normal issue of money to the wardrobe from the exchequer, loans made to the wardrobe were paid by the exchequer. A payment of 100 marks was made to the mayor of Newcastle-on-Tyne from the exchequer by the assent of the treasurer and the keeper of the wardrobe[3], an interesting and instructive instance of the influence of the household upon the administration.

It was natural that such matters as amercements concerning the execution of writs should come before the barons of the exchequer[4]. It was less obvious, however, why one whose conduct at the parliament of Lincoln in 1306 had displeased the king should be sent to the exchequer and thence to the Tower for safe custody[5]. In the reign of Edward II several people were indicted on various occasions before the exchequer for slandering the king[6]. A royal ordinance had been made that bearers of false news should be kept in prison at the king's will; one Hugh de Croxton was brought before the exchequer court, charged with falsely relating in public that James Douglas and other Scots had entered England, and was imprisoned[7]. A plea was brought to the exchequer by the poor burgesses of Scarborough against the rich burgesses of that town[8] and a similar plea was successfully pleaded by the poor burgesses of Newcastle against the rest of the burgesses and the merchant gild there[9]. Actions for trespass were held there[10]; actions for the recovery of debt were of

[1] Vide above, pp. 181–4.
[2] Issue Rolls, nos. 141–220 passim. [3] Issue Roll, no. 202, m. 2.
[4] K. R. Acct. 1142. [5] Madox, *Hist. of Exch.* vol. II, p. 108.
[6] Ibid. pp. 84–85. K. R. Mem. Roll, no. 89, m. 100. L. T. R. Mem. Roll, no. 86, m. 93.
[7] K. R. Mem. Roll, no. 102, m. 138.
[8] Madox, *Firma Burgi*, p. 96. [9] Ibid.
[10] Ibid. Wm Salt Soc., *Coll.* vol. VII, p. 156.

great frequency[1] though they were prohibited[2]. The king overcame the difficulty by ordering the exchequer by privy seal to entertain such pleas[3]. The hearing of pleas at the exchequer interfered with the hearing of accounts and on 12 May, 1310, on this score the king had prohibited the hearing of all pleas except those that touched him[4].

In the judicial work of the exchequer the barons were sometimes assisted by one of the king's justices. In the proceedings which took place in the exchequer court in the early years of Edward II on the debts owed to Langton, whose lands were in the king's hands, Bereford, who was then a justice of the common bench, frequently sat with the barons[5]. In 1310 the treasurer and barons of the exchequer and the justices of king's bench were ordered to inquire into the king's right in the matter of certain lands held of the king in chief, of which Henry fitz Hugh claimed the guardianship[6], and another case touching the king's right in lands was discussed by the barons and the king's justices of both benches[7]. The exchequer was unwilling to allow the justices too great a part in its administration. The oath which sheriffs took on their appointment at the exchequer had included an undertaking not to receive writs of any justice except justices in eyre. The council in 1303 agreed that sheriffs should receive also the writs of justices of gaol delivery[8].

The king frequently sent petitions to the exchequer for consideration. A petition to the king from the apprentices of the common bench was ordered to be shown to the treasurer and Bereford[9]. A petition to the king and council at parliament from the merchants of Ireland was sent to the treasurer with the endorsement that the petitioners should go to the treasurer, who was to call before him the person of whom complaint was made and do them justice[10]. Another petition was sent to the treasurer because the king wished to place the matter in his discretion[11]. Petitions which Gavaston had handed

[1] Vide Madox, *Firma Burgi*, pp. 96–97.
[2] Holdsworth, *Hist. Engl. Law*, vol. 1, p. 101.
[3] See writs directed to the exchequer in K. R. Mem. Rolls, nos. 81–103 passim.
[4] K. R. Mem. Roll, no. 83, m. 22 d. Vide App. of Doc. no. 11. Cf. *Cal. Close Rolls*, 1302–7, p. 91.
[5] Exch. of Pleas, Plea Roll, no. 31, mm. 44 d. 20, 34, 48.
[6] K. R. Mem. Roll, no. 83, m. 27 d.
[7] L. T. R. Mem. Roll, no. 85, Rec. Hill. m. 4 d.
[8] *Cal. Close Rolls*, 1302–7, p. 44.
[9] Seld. Soc., *Year Bk* 3–4 *Ed. II*, pp. xli–xlii.
[10] K. R. Mem. Roll, no. 82, m. 60. L. T. R. Mem. Roll, no. 79, m. 58
[11] K. R. Mem. Roll, no. 83, m. 12.

to the treasurer, the chancellor and treasurer were ordered to cause to be examined before the council[1].

The extension of the judicial business of the exchequer, while it tended to increase its administrative importance, also acted as an additional source of strength to the king, as it prevented the judicial courts obtaining a monopoly of justice. The desire of the baronial opposition to prohibit this jurisdiction of the exchequer court[2] was partly due to a wish to lessen the king's power, though the main object was to promote the financial efficiency of the exchequer. As the exchequer acted as a substitute for the judicial courts, so the exchequer seal may be said to have acted as a substitute for the chancery seal. Commissions of lands and custodies were made under the seal of the exchequer[3], the writs being frequently issued by order of writs of privy seal[4]. The treasurer and barons were ordered to allow the wife of a tenant-in-chief to have licence to marry whomsoever she would, the licence to be given by letters patent under the exchequer seal[5]. In 1325 the king ordered the treasurer and barons to commit to farm for seven years all lands and monies in the king's hands by forfeiture of rebels or other causes by letters under the exchequer seal[6]. In the issue of writs under the exchequer seal the chancellor sometimes assisted the treasurer, the writs to the taxors of the tenth and fifteenth in Kent being an instance[7]. The exchequer seal tested by the treasurer, or one of the barons of the exchequer, was very widely used in the normal administration of that department to summon persons to present account, to give power of attorney, to give a day for appearance and various similar processes involved in its administration[8]. It was also used to convey to the king information which he desired from the exchequer[9].

There are a number of interesting points about the exchequer and its functions which must be noted briefly. Ordinances[10] were made in the exchequer. It was by virtue of an ordinance made at

[1] Chan. Warr., File 59/127. [2] Vide below, p. 376.

[3] Vide *Commissiones* in K. R. Mem. Rolls, nos. 81–103 passim.

[4] K. R. Mem. Rolls, nos. 81–103 passim.

[5] *Cal. Close Rolls*, 1288–96, p. 493. [6] Ibid. 1323–27, p. 417.

[7] L. T. R. Mem. Roll, no. 78, m. 82.

[8] E.g. K. R. Mem. Roll, no. 81, m. 13. L. T. R. Mem. Roll, no. 78, m. 15: "De castris et maneriis Regis superintendendis et inquisitionibus faciendis super diuersis articulis per singulos comitatus Anglie" (24 July, 1308).

[9] E.g. *Cal. Close Rolls*, 1272–79, p. 265. K. R. Mem. Rolls, nos. 81–103 passim.

[10] The meaning and use of the word "ordinance" will be discussed below, pp. 257–8.

the exchequer that alien churchmen in England had their temporalities taken into the king's hands during war between the kings of England and France[1]. Payments to its officials were made "by ordinance of the treasurer and barons of the exchequer[2]." The exchequer was used as a treasury for the records of the various administrative departments and the king's seals were also deposited there[3].

It was almost as important for the king to retain influence over the exchequer as it was that he should remain in absolute control of the chancery. The financial department was nearly as important as the formal executive department of the administration. There was little tendency to independence of action in the chancery; but there appears still less in the exchequer: often, on what appear to be formal and routine matters, the exchequer would not proceed without consultation with or orders from the king. Even when baronial power was at its height and the opposition to the treasurership of Langton was being successfully maintained, the exchequer officials would do nothing without the king. Sandale, who had a little previously vacated the office of treasurer, appeared in the exchequer and stated that the king had been informed he was dead and that therefore his lands had been taken into the king's hands. He asked for the possession of them. The exchequer refused to give possession because they did not know the causes of the seizure and they asked the king's will in the matter[4]. It was to the king's greater advantage that he should exercise his influence at the exchequer through both chancery and household. On both the financial and judicial sides the king's influence upon the exchequer was complete. Indeed his interference with the routine administration of the exchequer appeared to be greater than in the chancery. It was partly because the king's influence was greater in the exchequer and partly because there was more need of drastic change and overhauling in its administration that the barons concentrated upon the exchequer in their scheme of reform. The need of reform in the exchequer was due largely to its complex processes and its ever increasing business together with the heavy arrears.

In both great departments baronial attack would be useless because ineffective. However much control they had in formal business

[1] *Cal. Close Rolls*, 1302–7, p. 18.

[2] Issue Rolls, no. 172, m. 9; no. 198, m. 6.

[3] E.g. *Cal. Close Rolls*, 1307–13, pp. 57–58.

[4] K. R. Mem. Roll, no. 85, m. 52. L. T. R. Plea Roll, no. 82, m. 45. Vide App. of Doc. no. 16.

they were permitted to exercise it only by the king's pleasure. The king had retained in his own hand complete executive power. Besides the executive reserve of the king there were other sources of great strength to him in the administrative tendency of the departments to exercise competing and overlapping jurisdictions, processes and instruments. It would be useful if on occasion the king could employ the organisation of the exchequer as a substitute for that of the chancery. The tendency in medieval administration for each department to encroach upon the domain of others, and for all to exercise a certain number of general administrative functions in addition to their specialised work aided this. A grant of custody of land could be made under the seal of the chancery or exchequer. Certain cases might be tried in the courts of common law or in the exchequer, while petitions could be considered in the chancery, in the exchequer, in any body of men drawn from those departments, the benches, the household or elsewhere, as the king chose to direct. Duplication of function was completely to the king's advantage.

CHAPTER XI

THE INFLUENCE OF THE HOUSEHOLD SYSTEM UPON THE ADMINISTRATION (*cont.*)

(ii) *Council*

The connection between the great departments and the council was close, for the council was the source whence those departments drew a considerable amount of authority. The council, and here by council is meant that manifestation which will hereafter be defined as "administrative," was in fact the executive instrument of the administration. As the king, the source of all executive authority, worked through his clerks, with the office of the privy seal as the mouthpiece of his executive power, and the wardrobe as its financial support, so the council was the source of formal executive power, with the chancery as the mouthpiece of its executive power and with the exchequer as the counterpart of the wardrobe. In a scheme of complete differentiation one might be the executive of the household and the other of the administration, but that time was not yet. The king's executive authority was omnipotent over household and administration. The executive authority of the "administrative" council was derived from and answerable to the king. The "administrative" council had authority because the king had chosen to delegate powers to it. The king asked a number of men to advise him on particular occasions for particular purposes. Thus when Edward I was abroad the business of the realm was done by "Edward the king's son supplying the king's place in England and by the king's council with him[1]." The composition of the body was not fixed: it had no fixed place of meeting. Apart from the king it had no authority, but it was a slightly more formal executive body than was contained in the household, and in it there were great potentialities for development as an important and intricate part in the machinery of administration. Already by the time of Edward II there were a number of routine matters in administration which came under its cognizance.

[1] *Cal. Close Rolls*, 1296–1302, p. 61 and passim.

Various phases of the council will therefore be considered and their functions stated, and then the relation between the council and the great departments will be treated in detail, and finally the influence of the king and the household upon the council will be stated.

The reign of Edward I had seen an increased organisation of the permanent council[1]. The council was a body which manifested itself in various ways, different manifestations differing in composition and functions. "Council" was at that time indefinitely applied to various committees acting in the administration, varying in size from a few to many. Henry de Beaumont was said to be sworn of the king's great and secret councils[2]. The king's great and secret councils have not been regarded as two distinct bodies but as two manifestations of the same. The council was concerned with matters of general administration. It stood in a peculiar relation to the exchequer. It rendered advice to the king and took an active part in judicial matters. In addition to the manifestations of the council that conducted this business, the term council was applied to embassies and deputations from the king. The commission which treated of peace with Bruce in 1323, composed of Pembroke, Despenser the younger and Baldock, is called "consilium nostrum" in that truce[3].

Though all these manifestations of the council may have originated from the same body, yet there is one point of distinction which it is necessary to emphasise. In one aspect the council was a household body, in another governmental. It is important to labour this immediately because it was the king's endeavours to develop the council as a household body at the expense of its governmental aspect that produced much of the baronial opposition. The official and household elements in the council were increased at the expense of the baronial, a process which was commenced by Henry III[4] and extended by Edward I[5]. The administration of the kingdom, in so far as it was conducted by the council, was carried out by a manifestation which may be described as "ministerial" or in its most general phase as the "administrative council." The council in its "ministerial" manifestation will be noticed in three phases, (i) the "privy" council, (ii) "special" councils, and (iii) the "administrative" council. These three phases were but different aspects of one manifestation and that manifestation was but one form of the council.

[1] Baldwin, *King's Council*, p. 69. Vide also Stubbs, *Constit. Hist.* vol. II, p. 271.

[2] *Cal. Close Rolls*, 1318–23, p. 717. *Abbrev. Placit.* p. 342.

[3] *Chron. H. de Blaneford*, p. 134.

[4] Baldwin, *King's Council*, pp. 24–29.

[5] Ibid. pp. 72–73, 79.

A precise and clear separation into classes dependent upon different phases of one manifestation is not possible, but that a certain phase of the "ministerial" council was called the "privy" or "secret" council can be established and that another phase of that "ministerial" council may fairly be called "special" from the considerations which dictated its composition, and a third phase may, from its composition, functions and the work it performed, be equally fairly called "administrative," it is hoped will be supported with sufficient evidence.

When Edward II desired to recall Gavaston he was said to have had communication on this matter with "suis privatis consilio[1]." In the time of the great scarcity he was said to have made the ordinance of prices "per suum privatum concilium, absque majorum consensu[2]," though another source states that the ordinance was made by "plusours de son prive counseill saunz assent du Roi et des grantz de la terre[3]." In the course of the campaign of 1321–2, after the capture of the Mortimers, the king proceeded to Gloucester and there he held his "consilium secretum[4]." Bishop Stratford after his disgrace was received back into the royal favour and "restitutum de consilio suo privato juratum[5]."

Nor is it only in the chronicles that the use of the term "privy" or "secret" council is found. During the reign *secretum consilium* and *privatum consilium* appear on the regular rolls[6] and later French equivalents like *le prive conseil, les prives de conseil* and *les plus secretz* appear[7]. In a petition from the clerks of the common bench for their fees it was recorded that a previous attempt to obtain them had been made; and as the rolls of the wardrobe which contained evidence of their right had been lost at Stirling it was then answered and ordained that the petition should come before the king and his privy council at the next parliament[8]. This petition, coming from Bereford, chief justice of the court of common pleas, with its reference to the privy council, is important though difficult to interpret. It points to the council which considered petitions in parliament though it may be used to distinguish the council referred to from the meeting of the "great" council. By writ of privy seal of 16 November, 1307, the bishop of Chichester, chancellor, and Reynolds, treasurer, were

[1] Walsingham, *Hist. Angl.* vol. I, p. 125.

[2] *Chron. Mon. de Melsa*, vol. II, p. 332.

[3] Camb. Univ. MS. Mm. i. 33.

[4] *Flores Hist.* vol. III, p. 346.

[5] *Chron. H. de Blaneford*, pp. 48–49.

[6] Baldwin, *King's Council*, p. 105.

[7] Ibid.

[8] Ancient Petition, no. 4051: "par quei fu donqe respondu et ordene qe ceste peticion fust mie deuant le Roi et son priue conseil au prochein parlement."

ordered to summon those they wished of the king's council at London, to hear and examine secretly the petitions and requests of the bearer of the letters which referred to the customs of Bordeaux[1]. It is difficult to decide whether this selected council which was to hear and examine in secret could be called a "privy" council.

When the king travelled about the country a number of advisers accompanied him, and these advisers were members of his council. In 1316 the king sent to the archbishop of Canterbury and others of his council at London certain memoranda touching the Friscobaldi; and they were ordered "to inspect the advisement of the king and certain of his council now assisting him," which was contained in a schedule amongst the memoranda[2]. In 1322 at Pontefract the king decided with "the common counsel and assent of the magnates of the realm who are with him, to proceed against the Scots by land and sea[3]," and shortly afterwards writs for levies were issued, "the king by the common counsel of the earls, barons and others attending him" having ordained and proposed to be at Newcastle at a certain date[4]. Certain occasions on which those with the king acted in this manner might perhaps be described as action by the "privy" council; though frequently it was too formal a body to be so termed.

The personnel of the "privy" council is a difficult problem. In 1316 Roger le Brabazon, who through age and ill health resigned the office of chief justice of king's bench, was retained as one of the privy council for the remainder of his life[5], and when Norwich was relieved of the treasurership at his own request in 1317 the king desiring to retain him in his service made him chief baron of the exchequer, wishing that he should be present when he could at the king's council, both secret and others[6]. In October, 1326, Hamo de Chigwell, mayor, the sheriffs and other important men of the city of London, were chosen to be present before Geoffrey le Scrope, Norwich, Staunton and others of the king's privy council at the Friars Preachers to have an important conference[7]. This would suggest a very official character to the "privy" council. Scrope was chief justice of king's bench, Norwich, chief baron of the exchequer and acting treasurer[8], and Staunton, chief justice of common bench. A more probable suggestion

[1] Chan. Warr., File 58/39: "oiez et examinez priueement les peticions et les requestes maistre Jordan Gaufray de Bordeaux porteur de ces lettres."

[2] *Cal. Close Rolls*, 1313–18, p. 429. [3] *Cal. Pat. Rolls*, 1321–24, p. 95.

[4] *Cal. Fine Rolls*, 1319–27, p. 124.

[5] *Cal. Pat. Rolls*, 1313–17, p. 437 (23 Feb. 1316). [6] Ibid. p. 655.

[7] Camb. Univ. MS. Gg. i. 15, f. 80.

[8] Tout, *The Place of Ed. II*, p. 333.

is that the members of the "privy" council were a selection of the more intimate and personal advisers of the king, though those advisers might hold high official positions. Indeed at this time Scrope was one of the most intimate advisers of the king, high in the royal favour, and took a prominent part in the direction of royal policy, while Norwich was more than a diligent official of long experience. The conditions which caused a particular phase of the "ministerial" council to be called "privy" cannot be decided by a knowledge of those present alone. Importance must also be attached to the matters discussed. It would seem that those were meetings of the "privy" council which demanded secrecy or were concerned with matters intimately personal to the king, the members attending which were most probably his most trusted and personal advisers. The functions were similar to those of the "administrative" council, and it would be difficult to draw a precise difference between them.

In sending a Gascon petition to the chancellor and treasurer in 1307 the king ordered them to summon to them Master Richard de Havering, constable of Bordeaux, and those of the king's council whom they wished to summon to consider it[1]. This plan of associating with the council people whose special knowledge might aid the discussion of the matter before them was frequently adopted. In 1310 the bishop of London, Master Robert de Pickering, Master Walter de Thorp, Master Gilbert de Middleton and four other clerks were ordered to be at London on a given date, to take counsel concerning the king's affairs, with the earl of Lincoln, king's lieutenant, the bishop of Worcester, chancellor, Sandale, treasurer, and others of the king's council[2]. These clerks, and the others who were engaged in diplomatic negotiations with France, were on very frequent occasions summoned to the council when French or Gascon matters were under consideration[3]. Their position may be regarded as that of experts who were called in for consultation.

"Special" councils, which were in effect committees of the council, were also appointed by the king for various specific purposes. In this class might be included the committees chosen in parliament to consider the petitions from the various dominions ruled by the king of England, Wales, Scotland, Ireland and Gascony[4]. In 1324 prelates and magnates were chosen to treat on the passage of the king to

[1] Chan. Warr., File 58/48. [2] *Cal. Close Rolls*, 1307–13, p. 338.

[3] Chan. Warr., File 97/3974. Gilbert de Middleton, Walter de Thorp, Robert de Baldock and John de Stratford.

[4] For examples of such committees vide below, pp. 409–410, 451–2.

Gascony, the reply being given to the king at Mortlake on 1 November. It seemed to them that 1000 men-at-arms, and 10,000 foot, 6000 English and 4000 Welsh, should be furnished for the army[1]. Hugh de Courtney's claims to the lands of the countess of Albemarle were examined in the presence of Langton, the earls of Lincoln, and Warenne, John de Berwick, Roger le Brabazon, John de Metingham, John de Drokensford and Gilbert le Roubiry[2]. This was almost entirely a judicial and official committee. The bishop had been Edward I's treasurer, Berwick had acted as itinerant justice[3], Brabazon was chief justice of king's bench. Metingham was at the head of the common pleas[4], Roubiry was a justice of king's bench[5], while Drokensford was keeper of the wardrobe[6]. In 1312 a council was summoned to meet at York expressly to confer on the affairs of Aquitaine[7]. Councils summoned for special purposes of this nature had need of more expert or full knowledge than the average member possessed, and it is not without purpose to note a distinction and certain characteristics in these meetings.

The "administrative" council was the body concerned with the general administration of the realm; and this is by far the most important phase of the "ministerial" council. Before its functions are considered it is necessary to note its composition. Its personnel varied with time and circumstances and also with the business which it had to consider and administer. The council as described in the *Modus tenendi Parliamentum* consisted of "the chancellor of England, the treasurer, the chamberlain, the barons of the exchequer, the justices, all the king's clerks and knights, together with the serjeants-at-law[8]." Though this account is not contemporary, and although scarcely any knights are found in the councils of Edward II's time[9] it does broadly summarise the chief members. Meetings of the council

[1] Anc. Corresp. vol. XLIX, no. 89: "y semble sire as Prelatz Countes et Barons queux vous auez chargez a parler le dit array."

[2] *Rot. Parl.* vol. I, p. 335. Cf. ibid. p. 298, when a petition of the abbot of Rufford was considered at the Friars Preachers by the archbishop of Canterbury, the earls of Hereford and Warenne, Badlesmere, Sandale, chancellor, Norwich, treasurer, and Masters Walwayn, Barton, Osgodby, Bardelby and Ayremynne.

[3] Foss, *Judges of England*, vol. III, pp. 237–8.

[4] Ibid. pp. 131–2.

[5] Ibid. pp. 293–4.

[6] Ibid. pp. 86–87.

[7] *Parl. Writs*, vol. II, Pt ii, pp. 70–71.

[8] Stubbs, *Select Charters*, 9th edit. p. 503.

[9] Baldwin, *King's Council*, p. 87. The "tres milites de consilio domini regis" who on the king's behalf presented certain prohibitions in writing in the provincial council at St Paul's in 1309 (Wilkins, *Concilia*, vol. II, p. 312) were probably not knights of the council in the sense in which that term was afterwards used. It is probably used here to suggest lay members as opposed to clerical.

were normally summoned by the chancellor alone or jointly with the treasurer[1]; and those two important officials are generally found present. Sometimes however the headship was taken by unofficial persons like the earl of Pembroke or the archbishop of Canterbury[2]. The justices of both benches and the barons of the exchequer were almost invariably present[3]. These officials were generally the last definitely mentioned on the list, though afterwards followed the indefinite words "and others of the king's council[4]." Sometimes a suggestion is made as to whom these others might include. Gilbert de Clare, when the king's lieutenant, was ordered to call the chancellor, treasurer, justices of both benches, barons of the exchequer, clerks of chancery and others of the council[5]. The persons included in the phrase "others of the council" were probably those holding subordinate offices like the chancery clerks, king's clerks, king's serjeants, and perhaps some of the lower officials of the exchequer and household. Various barons, generally associated with the king, were often present. A council of 1320 included, besides the chancellor and the other officials, the archbishop of Canterbury, the two Despensers and Badlesmere, steward of the household[6]. An indenture of war was made in the presence of the archbishop of Canterbury, the earls of Richmond, Pembroke and Hereford, the chancellor, treasurer and others of the council[7]. A meeting at York in the fifth year of Edward II, on a treaty concerning Flanders, consisted of Langton, Mauley, steward, William Inge, who was then closely associated with the council[8], Osgodby, Bardelby and Ayremynne, keepers of the great seal, and others of the council[9]. In a writ of 1315 the chancellor and treasurer were ordered to summon to them the justices and serjeants of both benches and others of the council to ordain concerning certain grievances[10]; and in 1321 a bill from a merchant was sent to the keepers of the great seal who were ordered to call to them Geoffrey le Scrope and John de Denum[11], two of the king's serjeants[12].

[1] Vide Chan. Warr., Files 58–134 passim. [2] Vide below, pp. 324–330, 331–6.

[3] E.g. *Cal. Close Rolls*, 1318–23, pp. 334–5; Anc. Corresp. vol. XLV, no. 163; K. R. Acct. 68/2, no. 10. The official and judicial nature of the councils of Edward I are instanced. *Cal. Close Rolls*, 1278–88, p. 519; 1296–1302, pp. 484–5; 1302–7, p. 216.

[4] Anc. Corresp. vol. XLV, no 149. [5] Ibid. no. 163 (5 June, 1311).

[6] *Cal. Close Rolls*, 1318–23, pp. 334–5.

[7] K. R. Acct. 68/2, no. 10. Vide App. of Doc. no. 46.

[8] Vide above, p. 68, note 4. [9] *Rot. Parl.* vol. I, p. 357.

[10] Chan. Warr., File 91/3364 (20 June, 1315).

[11] Ibid. File 117/5909 (4 Dec. 1321).

[12] Foss, *Judges of England*, vol. III, pp. 422–3, 494–5.

Among the barons frequently associated with the chancellor and treasurer in the council were the earl of Richmond[1], the elder Despenser[2], and the earls of Lincoln[3] and Gloucester[4], who succeeded each other as keeper of the realm. There were many other barons including the Mortimers who were sworn of the king's council[5]. When Griffith de la Pole made complaint to the king and his council, two cardinals, those sent by the pope in 1312[6] to make peace between king and barons, were present[7], and amongst those staying near the king in his council was Sir Henry de Sully, a banneret from France[8]. There is much valuable evidence even in these few instances to suggest how the king was increasing the official element and how royal influence could be exercised over the council through its personnel[9].

The "administrative" council was in the first place an advisory body. The king sought its advice on various matters, and he did this of his own free will because an advisory body dependent on the king's will was a useful instrument in administration. The council was ordered to consider and advise upon petitions sent to the king. To the petition of one who had been at the battle in which Edward Bruce was killed in Ireland, it seemed to the council that he and his heirs should have fifty marks of forfeited lands[10]. A petition concerning certain lands was accompanied by a copy of an inquisition. The council was advised that the king should remove his hand from those lands[11]. On the petition of the widow of the earl of Gloucester concerning certain manors, it seemed to the council that, if it was pleasing to the king, charters or copies should be given to her so that she could have allowance according to reason[12]. The abbot of Gloucester petitioned to hold a certain hundred at farm. The petition reached the council who, after examining all the evidence submitted by the chancery and exchequer, advised that under conditions the request should be granted notwithstanding the statute[13]. The council's advice on these petitions was always subject to the will of the king.

[1] Chan. Warr., Files 60/277, 69/1164. [2] Ibid. Files 60/277, 63/507.

[3] Ibid. File 63/507. Anc. Corresp. vol. XLV, no. 149. Vide App. of Doc. no. 116.

[4] Chan. Warr., File 73/1981.

[5] Exch. Misc. 24/12: "jurree du counsail nostre seigneur le Roi." Vide App. of Doc. no. 44.

[6] Ancient Petition, no. 13027. [7] Vide *Foedera*, vol. II, pp. 191–2.

[8] Stowe MS. 553, f. 65. [9] Vide below, pp. 281–4.

[10] *Cal. Doc. Scotl.* vol. III, p. 121. [11] *Cal. Inq. P. M.* vol. VI, pp. 352–3.

[12] Parl. and Council Proceedings (Chan.), File 33/14: "il semble a counseil sil plet au Roi qil est bien qe le chartres soient liuerez a la dame ou qe copie de y celes soit enuoiez en ses places issint qele puisse auoir allouance solunc reson."

[13] Chan. Misc., Bdle 59/3 (71).

The king sent transcripts of letters to the council asking their advice thereon[1]. The archbishop of Canterbury, the chancellor and treasurer and the council were to consider certain financial matters with a Florentine merchant[2]. The archbishop, the earl of Hereford, the chancellor and treasurer were ordered to call the council to consider great outrages concerning the castle of Norwich, which the king was sending John Walwayn to show them[3]. A petition and transcript of letters patent were sent to the chancellor, Despenser and the lieutenant of the treasurer, who were to call the council to examine the petition and transcript well and diligently and certify the king what he should do[4]. The hospices of the city of London taken by the king's marshal for the lodging of the barons for the king's coronation were redelivered to the owners by consideration of the king and council[5].

Besides giving advice in matters affecting general administration there were two problems during the reign on which the king constantly required the advice of the council—Gascony and Scotland. After having conferred with his council and certain loyal Scottish barons, the king requested Pembroke to meet him at Berwick on a certain day to march against the Scots[6]. In 1316 the king sent one of his valets to the chancellor and treasurer with transcripts of letters from Ireland and Scotland and letters to William Inge of the great plight of his people at Berwick. He asked that their advice be sent with all haste by his messenger, in especial, how the Irish letters should be answered. They were to show the copy to the council and advise them accordingly[7]. In the same year Baldock who had been attending to the king's business in the north was sent to show more fully the event of that business to the council. The archbishop of Canterbury, the bishop of Winchester, chancellor, Pembroke and the other good men of the council were ordered to give advice on the matter[8].

Articles relating to Gascony were submitted to the council, who expressed opinions upon them[9]. Two great rolls touching the dispute with the king of France about Aquitaine were sent to the earl of Gloucester, the chancellor and the treasurer, who were to charge the

[1] Chan. Warr., File 93/3594. Vide App. of Doc. no. 64.

[2] Chan. Warr., File 95/3717 (21 Aug. 1316).

[3] Ibid. File 93/3515 (20 Oct. 1315).

[4] Ibid. File 63/505 (4 June, 1309): "bien et diligeaument examinez les ditz peticion et transcript nous certifiez de ceo qe nous emporrons faire en bone manere."

[5] *Parl. Writs*, vol. II, Pt i, p. 15.

[6] *Cal. Doc. Scotl.* p. 18 (16 June, 1309).

[7] Ibid. p. 90 (26 Feb. 1316).

[8] Chan. Warr., File 96/3819 (4 Dec. 1316).

[9] Chan. Misc., Bdle 25/2 (11).

justices and others of the council to consider the matter and place in it all the good counsel that they could[1]. A roll touching certain of the Gascon notables was sent to the council for them to examine, the writ being addressed to the archbishop, the chancellor and the treasurer[2]. The lieutenant of the treasurer and the keepers of the great seal were ordered to consider and decide, concerning certain transcripts of letters patent of the king of France, by the counsel and advice of the archbishop and others of the council[3]. Acting on the advice of his council, the king ordered the seneschal of Gascony and the constable of Bordeaux to remove all officials, other than those appointed for term of life, and to appoint others[4].

More important than the advice which the council gave the king, when requested to do so by writ of privy seal, was the actual part it took in the working of the administration, that is, its executive functions as opposed to its advisory. One of the ways in which the council took its part in administration, was by ordaining a matter or making an ordinance. The primary meaning of an "ordinance" was an arrangement or rule[5] or order and its general use in the English records confirms this. Payments were made in the exchequer "per preceptum et ordinacionem Thesaurarii[6]" or "per ordinacionem[7]." The clerk who wrote the summons of the exchequer received £10 a year as his fee "per ordinacionem eorundem Thesaurarii et Baronum[8]." A payment was made to certain clerks for writing certain ordinances touching the state of Gascony[9]. It was ordained by the treasurer and barons that a tally should be made to a certain man[10]. Despenser in a letter to his sheriff of Glamorgan in 1319 ordered him that he should place "en vostre ordenaunce" the business which touched Sir William de Brewosa and all others which touched Despenser[11]. The sheriff was also ordered to see that £2000 were safely carried to the treasury at Tewkesbury and put into safeguard "et ceo par bone ordynaunce[12]." It was with arrangements of this nature that the

[1] Chan. Warr., File 77/1929 (18 April, 1311).

[2] Ibid. File 91/3346 (11 June, 1315).

[3] Ibid. File 87/2949 (22 April, 1314). [4] *Reg. Pal. Dunelm.* vol. IV, p. lxviii.

[5] J. P. Migne, *Lexicon Manuale ad Scriptores mediae et infimae Latinitatis*, s.v. ordinatio. Care must be taken not to confuse an ordinance of the council or exchequer with a judicial ordinance, which was "a decision given after consultation with the great officers of state, based not upon precedent or analogy, but upon the broad lines of practical convenience" (Seld. Soc. vol. XIII [1899], *Select Pleas of Forest*, ed. G. Turner, Introd. p. xi).

[6] Issue Roll, no. 143, m. 2. [7] Ibid. no. 144, m. 4. [8] Ibid. no. 218, m. 13.

[9] Ibid. no. 152, m. 2: "quasdam ordinaciones statum Ducatus Aquitanie tangentes."

[10] Ibid. no. 210, m. 1. [11] Cotton MS. Vesp. F. vii, f. 6. [12] Ibid.

council was primarily concerned, though some of the ordinances of the council, owing to the important matters with which they were concerned, became a part of the law of the land. Yet even these were probably designed as temporary arrangements to meet particular circumstances.

In the fourth year of Edward II the council at London ordained concerning the sale of wines in London, the rubric of the ordinance running "forma ordinata consilium Regis de vinis vendendis in Londinio[1]." The previous year the bishop of Worcester, treasurer, and the earl of Lincoln had been ordered to summon the justices and others of the council and make ordinance concerning the carrying of money out of the realm[2]. In 1314 the council at London was ordered by writ of privy seal to ordain a remedy in maintenance of the peace of the people on account of prevailing turbulence[3]. It was recorded that it was ordained that Sir Robert de Clifford and Sir John de Segrave should be wardens of Scotland[4]. In addition to the redress of grievances and the appointment of officials the exchequer reforms which are such a prominent feature of the later years of Edward II's reign were made by ordinance of the king and council[5]. In the later portion of the reign too, many executive acts were done by the council. It was agreed in 1324 that the queen's castles and lands should be seized into the king's hands[6], and this "the king and council having ordained and agreed" upon, orders were issued to the sheriffs of the various counties[7]. It was similarly ordained by the king and council that the lands, goods, and chattels of alien priories should be taken into the king's hands[8]. It was ordained by the king's council that considerable numbers of springals and quarrels should be made by a certain time in various places[9].

It was an easy transition for the council to translate its advice into ordinance. In 1308 it was agreed, if it pleased the king, to have a parliament at Westminster in three weeks after Michaelmas[10]. The

[1] K. R. Mem. Roll, no. 84, m. 60. The ordinance then ran: "fiat a remembre qe ceo est le fourme ordine par Henri de Lacy counte de Nicole tenaunt le lieu nostre seigneur le Rei en Engleterre...Johan de Sandale Tresorer Roger de Brabazoun et autres du conseil nostre seignor le Rey de achat et de vende de vyns."

[2] Ibid. no. 83, m. 11.

[3] Anc. Corresp. vol. XLV, no. 185 (4 Dec. 1314).

[4] *Cal. Doc. Scotl.* vol. III, p. 21 (20 Dec. 1309), pp. 26–27 (10 April, 1310).

[5] *Red Book of Exchequer*, vol. III, pp. 848, 908, 930. Vide also below, pp. 531–2.

[6] *Cal. Fine Rolls*, 1319–27, p. 300.

[7] Ibid. pp. 300–1.

[8] Ibid. p. 320.

[9] *Cal. Close Rolls*, 1323–27, pp. 247–8.

[10] *Cal. Doc. Scotl.* vol. III, p. 9.

council was not, however, always so careful of the king's pleasure, and in 1317 a gentle remonstrance was provided in cases where the king should act against an arrangement they had made, for "it was agreed by the whole of the king's council at Westminster that no sheriff or coroner should be made a justice to take assizes, deliver gaols, of oyer and terminer or to do any other office of justice because they ought to be intendant to other justices appointed in their county, and if it happen that the king order the contrary, the chancellor shall inform him of this agreement of the council before he do anything[1]."

From an ordinance to direct administrative action was an easy stage. The council assisted the king's lieutenants in administration. In 1311 the provincial council at London was ordered to examine certain articles of subjects of the king of France concerning the status of the king in the duchy of Aquitaine, and to advise the earl of Gloucester, keeper of the realm and king's lieutenant, the chancellor and treasurer and such of the king's council as were in London, what should be best done in that matter for the information of the embassy in the duchy on the king's business[2]. A commission for alleged defamation of John de Somery was made on 18 May, 1308, to Bereford and others. On 18 June the commission was superseded by the king's lieutenant and his council[3]. Here the council is seen assisting the king's lieutenant in executive matters. Writs were sealed by the council[4]; and when its advice was sent to the chancery, writs were sometimes issued on that advice, the issue being on one occasion "per ipsum Regem et rotulum de consilio[5]."

In various other general ways the council acted as an executive authority, sometimes with the king, at other times alone. In 1321 Mortimer, justice of Wales, was ordered to come before the king at Cirencester to inform him and his council about the state of Wales[6]. It was agreed before the archbishop of Canterbury and the king's council that a certain castle and manor should be re-extended[7]. The treasurer and barons of the exchequer and others of the king's council asked the citizens of London for a loan[8]. In 1316 the archbishop, Pembroke, the chancellor and treasurer were ordered to call the council and make arrangements concerning the victuals of Berwick

[1] *Cal. Close Rolls*, 1313–18, p. 463.
[2] *Cal. Pat. Rolls*, 1307–13, p. 338 (18 April, 1311).
[3] Ibid. p. 369.
[4] Brev. Baron. 5 Ed. II.
[5] K. R. Mem. Roll, no. 85, m. 5 d.
[6] *Cal. Close Rolls*, 1318–23, p. 506.
[7] *Cal. Inq. P. M.* vol. VI, pp. 40–41.
[8] *Cal. Letter Books, E*, pp. 37–38 (21 Mar. 1319).

and the treasury of Ireland[1]. The fees of the clerks of the common bench were fixed in a certain agreement made and granted by the king and his council, the council on this occasion consisting of the archbishop and Despenser acting in the name of the king[2].

The council also sent and instructed royal messengers and deputations for various purposes. The bishop of Worcester, chancellor, was ordered to be at Westminster together with the earl of Lincoln, keeper of England and king's lieutenant, the treasurer and barons of the exchequer, the justices of the common bench and certain others of the king's council to ordain the message which Henry Spigurnel and John de Benstede were to take to the pope[3]. William Herle and Geoffrey le Scrope were sent by the king and his council at London to Newcastle-on-Tyne to treat there with the Scots for a truce[4]. The earl of Warenne made his journey to Gascony in 1325 "ex ordinatione consilii domini regis[5]." Despenser and other lords were sent from Newark to Scotland by the king and his council as hostages for the bishop of St Andrews and others coming to treat with the king and council[6]. The king and council, or the council only, also sent a clerk outside the court for the munition of castles[7], for the purchase of victuals[8], and in matters concerning ships[9], and Aquitaine[10]. Certain clerks were assigned by the treasurer and others of the king's council to search, array and collect muniments at the castles of Pontefract, Tutbury, Tonbridge, the Tower and the Friars Preachers[11].

Foreign relations were an important sphere in which the activity of the council manifested itself[12], both in giving advice and in its execution. The general functions of the council, the advisory and the executive, have been treated in a wide manner, and it will have been noticed that the king could without exertion maintain his control of both these functions.

The relations of the council with the great departments will have to be considered next. The "council," hardly less than the "household," stood in its relation with the administrative departments in

[1] Chan. Warr., File 94/3604 (3 Mar. 1316).

[2] Ancient Petitions, nos. 4051–2. The position of the archbishop and Despenser as revealed here is interesting: "de certein couenaunt a li taillez et grauntiez par nostre seigneur le Roi et par son conseil cest asauoir par Lerceuesqe de Cauntirbire qi ore est et par sire Hugh Despenser le pere en noun du Roi."

[3] Chan. Warr., File 73/1579 (17 Dec. 1310).

[4] Stowe MS. 553, f. 26 b.

[5] *Ann. Paul.* p. 308.

[6] Stowe MS. 553, f. 27.

[7] Ibid. ff. 29 b, 30.

[8] Ibid. ff. 31 b, 32, 32 b, 33.

[9] Ibid. f. 32.

[10] Ibid. f. 32 b.

[11] Stowe MS. 553, f. 33.

[12] Baldwin, *King's Council*, pp. 215–216.

the place of a parent, and its influence directed by the household upon the various departments remained considerable. In the case of the chancery there is not much of great interest. The chancery in the fourteenth century, it has been said, "was made the principal organ of the king's council in matters both administrative and judicial[1]." The chancellor was the normal person to summon the council[2] and he was generally left some amount of discretion in the choice of those to be summoned[3]. Chancery clerks were used as messengers by the council. One was sent by the council to the counties of Cambridge and Huntingdon to superintend the provision of victuals[4]. A chancery clerk and a clerk of the king were sent by royal writ to obtain from the abbots of Malton and Alnwick certain chronicles which had details touching a case then before the king's council[5]. The evidence moreover was to be taken into the chancery[6]. The great seal was recorded as being delivered to the chancellor in the presence of the king's council at Westminster[7]. Charters which the king had granted to Beaumont and which did not seem to him to be sufficient, the chancellor was ordered to amend as was best recommended between him and those of the king's council[8].

Persons were sometimes summoned before the council in chancery. The sheriff of Berkshire was ordered to take into the king's hand in 1313 those who had attended a tournament against the king's prohibition. He was to appear in person before the council in chancery to certify the council of his action in the matter and of the names of those who were guilty[9]. In 1325 Master John Walwayn was ordered to appear before the king's council in chancery, leaving all other matters, to inform the king about certain affairs which would be more fully explained to him there[10].

Of greater importance was the part taken in exchequer administration by the council. In the first place, the council took a part in the financial side of the exchequer. With the assent of his council, the king granted an allowance to his wife of eight marks a day for the expenses of her household and 1000 marks for all necessary expenses to be paid at the exchequer[11]. The queen previously had

[1] Baldwin, *King's Council*, p. 236. [2] Chan. Warr., Files 58–134 passim.
[3] Ibid. File 91/3364: "appellez a vous noz Justices et seriaintez del un Baunk et del autre et autres de nostre conseil qe vous verrez qe a apeller y facent."
[4] Stowe MS. 553, f. 29 b. [5] Surtees Soc., *Percy Cartulary*, p. 224. [6] Ibid.
[7] *Cal. Close Rolls*, 1302–7, p. 235. [8] Chan. Warr., File 73/1600 (28 Dec. 1310).
[9] *Cal. Fine Rolls*, 1307–19, p. 167 (1 April, 1313).
[10] *Cal. Close Rolls*, 1323–27, p. 493 (18 July, 1325).
[11] Issue Roll, no. 210, m. 14: "Isabelle Regine Anglie cui Rex de assensu consilij sui certis decausis concessit."

11,000 marks annually for the expenses of her household and other things which the king had granted to her with assent of his council[1]. With his council the king granted a pension of 100 marks a year to one who had lost his Scottish lands[2]. Payments were also made directly from the exchequer by the assent of the council. A payment of £20 was made to the archbishop of Dublin in 1317, for his expenses when sent to the earl of Lancaster to state various business on the king's behalf, by the assent of the archbishop of Canterbury and the whole of the king's council staying at Westminster[3]. A payment was made to a messenger, who bore a letter from the archbishop of Canterbury in the name of the whole council, by the assent of the archbishop and the whole of the king's council at Westminster[4]. Adam de Lymbergh, king's clerk, was paid his expenses, for staying at the parliament of York[5] on the king's business, by writ of *mandamus* and by assent of the treasurer and others of the king's council[6], and a payment was made to Thomas de Useflet, clerk of the great wardrobe, for his office, by the assent of the king's council[7].

Payments were also made in the exchequer which were the result of agreements made by the council. In 1310 a payment was made to Master John de St Quentin, clerk, for wages assigned to him for collecting the clerical tenth on the king's behalf; for it had been agreed by the bishop of Worcester, chancellor, Sandale, treasurer, and others of the king's council that he should have fifty marks yearly for his wages and six marks for robes[8]. A sum of £60 was paid Henry Spigurnel in 1311 for going to the Roman court, for according to the agreement made by the chancellor, treasurer and others of the council he was to have 20*s*. a day for his expenses[9]. A tally for £250 on the collectors of the wool custom in Boston was made to one John de la Tour for the king's debts to him for wine. Although the custom had been otherwise assigned it was agreed in the presence of the treasurer

[1] *Cal. Close Rolls*, 1313–18, p. 380. Issue Roll, no. 180, m. 7.

[2] Liberate Roll, no. 87, m. 3.

[3] Issue Roll, no. 183, m. 3: "per assensum domini Archiepiscopi Cantuariensis et tocius consilii domini Regis apud Westmonasterium existentis."

[4] Ibid. no. 180, m. 10 (18 Sept. 1316).

[5] Vide below, pp. 450–460.

[6] Issue Roll, no. 186, m. 9.

[7] Ibid. no. 219, m. 3.

[8] Ibid. no. 155, m. 4 (13 Nov. 1310): "Et memorandum quod concordatum est per venerabilem patrem Walterum Wygorniensem Episcopum cancellarium Anglie et Johannem de Sandale Thesaurarium et alios de consilio domini Regis quod idem magister Johannes habeat per annum pro vadiis suis l marcas et pro robis suis vi marcas."

[9] Ibid. no. 155, m. 7 (12 Feb. 1311): "Et memorandum quod concordatum est per Cancellarium et Thesaurarium et alios de consilio domini Regis quod idem Henricus habeat per diem pro expensis suis xx solidos."

and others of the council that he should have first payment[1]. Sometimes the payment was the result of an agreement entered into by the council with the creditor. A payment was made to Gilbert Coteman, master mariner, for the conveyance of wine from Hull to London, by an agreement made with him by the bishop of Exeter, treasurer, and Baldock and others of the king's council[2].

There are also instances of payments made by ordinance of the council. On 12 February, 1308, a part payment of 800 marks was made as was ordained by the council[3]. A payment of £150 made to the king's butler on 24 July, 1312, for the purchase of fifty skins of wine for the approaching parliament at London, was made by the assent and ordinance of the council on the announcement of Norwich[4]. In 1316 a payment of £4 was made to the countess of Warenne, in part payment of 250 marks for expenses in going abroad, by writ of privy seal, and by ordinance and assent of the archbishop of Canterbury and the whole of the king's council staying at Westminster[5].

Payments were made in the exchequer of expenses assigned by the king's council, Master John de St Quentin, notary public, receiving a payment of his expenses for prosecuting a certain matter for the king against Master William de Testa[6], and Richard de Plumstok receiving his expenses for following a matter between the kings of England and France[7].

Payments and acknowledgments were made sometimes with the addition of the brief note "per consilium" or "per Thesaurarium et consilium" after the entry. A sum was allowed to the prior of Carmarthen, chamberlain of South Wales, in one tally made to him "per Thesaurarium et consilium[8]." In 1324 various clerks of chancery

[1] Issue Roll, no. 183, m. 7: "concordatum fuit in presencia Thesaurarii et aliorum de consilio domini Regis."

[2] Ibid. no. 202, m. 5: "per conuencionem super hoc factam cum eodem Willelmo per dominum Walterum Exoniensem Episcopum Thesaurarium et Magistrum Robertum de Baldok et alios de consilio domini Regis."

[3] Ibid. no. 141, m. 7: "Memorandum quod persolvuntur de viii marcis secundum quod ordinatum fuit per consilium Regis."

[4] Ibid. no. 162, m. 6: "per assensum et ordinacionem consilii domini Regis nunciante domino Waltero de Norweyco."

[5] Ibid. no. 180, m. 10: "per mandatum ipsius domini Regis sub priuato sigillo et eciam per ordinacionem et assensum domini Archiepiscopi Cantuariensis et tocius consilij domini Regis apud Westmonasterium existentis."

[6] Ibid. no. 150, m. 6: "de prestito super expensis suis assignato per consilium domini Regis."

[7] Ibid. no. 152, m. 1: "super expensis suis assignatis per consilium domini Regis ad prosequendum inter Reges Anglie et Francie."

[8] Ibid. no. 193, m. 2. Vide also no. 187, mm. 2, 7, 10, 11, 12.

were paid their expenses in superintending alien priories, inquiring the amount of their stock and crops and certifying the exchequer thereof, the payments being made "per consilium[1]." Master Elias de Johnston, clerk, received £6 in 1321 for all debts due to him in the wardrobe, the payment being made by the council because he was poor[2]. Master William de Maldon, chamberlain of the exchequer, in 1319 received ten marks in payment of his expenses going to London to do there certain business of the king's, by the advice of Norwich by the king himself and his council[3].

Still more important than these payments made at the exchequer by the grant, assent, agreement, ordinance, or assignment of the council was its activity within the exchequer department. In making these payments it was exercising its executive function from a distance. In its activity in the exchequer administration it was exercising its influence directly and internally. The exact position which the council occupied when it was at the exchequer it is difficult to decide, and before attempting to do so certain considerations must be stated.

The treasurer was frequently ordered by writ of privy seal to summon the council. The purposes for which these councils were summoned by the treasurer were sometimes connected with exchequer business; though sometimes any apparent connection is not readily found. He was ordered in a matter touching dower to call to him the justices and others he wished of the king's council at London, and to examine and ordain on the case[4]. This matter would equally well have come before the chancery, as the memoranda and evidences touching it were there and the chancellor was ordered to send them under his seal to the treasurer[5]. On 30 May, 1310, the treasurer was ordered to summon "ceux de nostre conseil a Londres qe vous verrez" to consider the grievances of Robert de Waynflet who called himself abbot of Bardney[6]. The treasurer and barons were ordered in July, 1314, to summon the justices of both benches and other good men of the king's council to consider a petition of the archbishop of Canterbury, the order being sent under the secret seal[7].

[1] Issue Roll, no. 210, m. 7. Vide also no. 187, m. 5.

[2] Ibid. no. 195, m. 3: "per consilium quia pauper est."

[3] Ibid. no. 189, m. 3: "per auisamentum domini Walteri de Norwyco per ipsum Regem et consilium."

[4] K. R. Mem. Roll, no. 83, m. 15: "appellez a vous noz Justices et autres de nostre conseill a Londres qui vous verrez qe y facent a appeller" (1 Jan. 1310).

[5] Ibid.

[6] Ibid. m. 27 d.

[7] Ibid. no. 88, m. 17 d (27 July, 1314).

On another occasion the treasurer was ordered to summon before him and the chancellor, the bishop of Exeter, Geoffrey le Scrope and others of the council to consider certain exchequer business[1]. In 1317 the treasurer and barons were ordered by letters under the great seal to summon such of the king's council as they should think fit to consider and provide a remedy for the introduction of clipped and counterfeit money into the realm[2]. In reply to a petition presented to the king and council the treasurer was ordered by chancery writ,

> quod assumptis secum quibusdam Justiciariis et aliis de Concilio Regis, prout viderit expedire, audiant omnes peticiones et querelas tangentes processus habitos in scaccario, in quibus asseritur error intervenisse, ac injustas oneraciones factas ibidem ut dicitur, et eas ibi terminent et faciant prosequentibus Justiciam competentem[3].

Writs were also issued to the treasurer jointly with others of the council. A writ of privy seal was sent to the bishop of Worcester, treasurer, the earl of Lincoln "et as autres de nostre conseil a Londres" ordering them to aid in every way the messengers going to the pope and to France, as was previously ordained at York by those of the council who were there[4]. In the dispute pending before them between the king and Henry fitz Hugh about the wardship of certain lands and marriage, the treasurer and others of the king's council at London were ordered to have every regard for the king's right, so that he should lose nothing[5]. A transcript of an indenture made between Harclay, earl of Carlisle, and Bruce was sent with a writ of privy seal to the treasurer and his lieutenant and to the barons of the exchequer and others of the king's council at York[6]. Besides this association of the treasurer with the council, petitions were also presented to the treasurer and the council, one who had formerly been the controller of the society of the Friscobaldi in the mines of Devon petitioning the treasurer and the council at the exchequer[7]. The treaty on the matter was made in the presence of the earl of Lincoln[8].

The treasurer therefore held a position of considerable importance

[1] K. R. Mem. Roll, no. 102, m. 36 d.

[2] *Cal. Close Rolls*, 1318–23, p. 198 (18 June, 1319). It is interesting to note that this writ was issued "by king and council."

[3] *Rot. Parl.* vol. I, p. 274.

[4] K. R. Mem. Roll, no. 83, m. 10.

[5] Ibid. no. 84, m. 7 (7 Sept. 1310).

[6] Ibid. no. 96, m. 19 d. L. T. R. Mem. Roll, no. 93, m. 58.

[7] K. R. Mem. Roll, no. 83, m. 49 d: "supplicauit Thesaurario et consilio *hic* per peticionem suam."

[8] Ibid: "Et habito super hoc tractatu in presencia Henrici de Lacy, comitis Lincolnie."

in the council. Petitions were addressed to him and enclosed under privy seal to him for consideration[1]. When one who had been assigned by the council failed to carry out his mission, the treasurer was ordered by the king to assign another and efficient person[2]. A petition requesting land was enclosed with the statement, "Et Thesaurarius per Consilium Regis faciat quod viderit ad commodum Regis[3]." The treasurer also acted as the mouthpiece of the council. A letter sent to the chancellor and the lieutenant of the treasurer concerning the disturbances at Bristol was answered by the lieutenant of the treasurer, with the assent of the council at Westminster[4]. The importance of the treasurer in the "administrative" council was small compared to the large part that body took in the exchequer.

Meetings of the council were held at the exchequer. These meetings may or may not have been concerned with exchequer business, or the council may have used the exchequer building as a convenient place of meeting. For there was at this time a place in the exchequer which was usually used for holding councils[5]. A matter concerning the release of prisoners by mainprise was treated by the treasurer, "coram consilio Regis existente hic in scaccario[6]." In 1309 the earl of Lincoln was ordered to go to the exchequer as soon as possible and by the advice and counsel of Bereford and Spigurnel, who had been at York when a certain arrangement was made, and who were to advise him more fully on the matter, and others of the council whom the earl might summon, letters of credence for certain embassies were to be arranged[7]. The king had requested Despenser the elder to concern himself with the conclusion of peace with the king of France. Transcripts of the reply were enclosed to the chancellor and treasurer, and they were informed that Despenser would be at the exchequer at the octave of St Michaelmas to discuss the matter with the council[8]. Two of these meetings of

[1] K. R. Mem. Roll, no. 81, m. 15. L. T. R. Mem. Roll, no. 78, m. 17 d.

[2] K. R. Mem. Roll, no. 83, m. 11. [3] Oxf. Hist. Soc., *Collect.* vol. III, p. 110.

[4] *Rot. Parl.* vol. I, p. 475. K. R. Mem. Roll, no. 86, m. 43 d: "Responsio facta ad literas predictas per Johannem de Sandale tenentem locum Thesaurarii de assensu consilii Regis existentis apud Westmonasterium."

[5] *Eng. Hist. Rev.* vol. XXI [1906], 'The exchequer chamber under Edward II,' Johnson, pp. 726–7, instances a meeting of the council held "in loco de scaccario pro consiliis habendis consueto." Prof. Tout (*The Place of Ed. II*, pp. 56–57) explains in this way the instances given by Madox (*Hist. of Exch.* vol. II, pp. 26–32) of the king's council sitting at the exchequer.

[6] K. R. Mem. Roll, no. 82, m. 61 d.

[7] Ibid. no. 83, m. 11 d: "vous maundoms enpriaunt qe vous approchetz a nostre Excheqier au plus tost qe vous porrez bonement" (4 Nov. 1309).

[8] Chan. Warr., File 92/3458 (21 Sept. 1315).

the council at the exchequer do not appear to be connected with exchequer business, while the other one might be so construed. References to the council at the exchequer may therefore concern meetings of the council held in the exchequer which dealt with matters of general administration or executive, or which dealt with exchequer business.

In addition to sitting *at* the exchequer, the council is also found sitting *with* the exchequer. In the second year of Edward II, for instance, a person came before the barons, the chancellor of England and certain others of the king's council, the justices of both benches and others, sitting with them[1]. In the same regnal year, one Roger de Ryvers came to the exchequer before Sandale, lieutenant of the treasurer, and the barons, Brabazon, Bereford, Spigurnel, justices of the king and others of the council sitting with them and showed certain letters close to the lieutenant of the treasurer[2]. It can be fairly assumed that in the references in which the council is said to sit with the exchequer, exchequer business was generally under consideration.

In dealing with the relations of the exchequer and council, the two phases of the council *at* the exchequer and sitting *with* the exchequer will be treated separately. A precise and definite separation cannot be made. When the council sat at the exchequer, the business might or might not be exchequer; when it sat with the exchequer the probability was that it was treating exchequer business. The distinction will therefore be observed for the purposes of simplification, though it must not be pressed too far.

The council sitting at the exchequer took a part in the internal administration of that department. On 1 March, 1308, Walter de Bedwynd, king's remembrancer, took his oath before the treasurer, barons and others of the king's council in the exchequer[3]. Walter de Norwich, treasurer, was in 1322 ordered to summon those of the council he desired to ordain about the transfer of the exchequer to York, and by virtue of these letters the archbishop of Canterbury, Staunton, chancellor of the exchequer, Henry le Scrope and Spigurnel, justices of the king's bench, Bereford and Herle, justices of common

[1] K. R. Mem. Roll, no. 82, m. 61 d: "coram Baronibus assidentibus eis in scaccario Cancellario Anglie quibusdam aliis de consilio Regis tam justiciariis de utroque Banco quam etcetera."

[2] Ibid. m. 65 d. L. T. R. Mem. Roll, no. 79, m. 89. Vide App. of Doc. no. 6.

[3] L. T. R. Mem. Roll, no. 78, m. 40: "coram Thesaurario et Baronibus et aliis de consilio Regis in eodem scaccario presentibus."

pleas and others of the king's council were summoned for this purpose[1].

It also took a part in the general administration of the exchequer. The treasurer and barons and others of the king's council allocated certain wages to the master and brethren of the Temple for their maintenance[2]. Subsequently it was agreed, by the treasurer and barons and others of the council in the presence of the count of Savoy, that the allowance should be increased[3]. A clerk was assigned by Norwich, keeper of the office of treasurer, and others of the king's council at London, to ordain concerning the expenses of the children of a number of the rebels of 1322[4]. The mayor and certain important citizens of London, present at the exchequer before the council, were addressed about a previous injunction made to them concerning the crimes perpetrated in the city[5]. When the king left the Tower for the last time, in 1326, he ordered Norwich, lieutenant of the treasurer, and Geoffrey le Scrope, chief justice of king's bench, to send 700 armed foot to him. On 9 October it was agreed at the exchequer by the barons and others of the council what the rate of wages of the men should be[6]; and the leaders of the men who were to conduct them to the king were similarly ordained by the assent of the council[7]. The treasurer and barons of the exchequer were ordered to assign a rent to Robert de Waynflet, who claimed to be abbot of Bardney, and to the monks of that abbey going to Rome. The grant was made before the bishop of Chichester, chancellor, the treasurer and barons, the earl of Richmond, Despenser, and others of the council[8]. The time for rendering the Gascon accounts was agreed in the presence of the bishop of Chichester, chancellor, the treasurer, the earls of Lincoln and Richmond, the barons of the exchequer and others of the council[9].

As so much of the work of the exchequer was financial, a clear

[1] K. R. Mem. Roll, no. 95, m. 69 d. L. T. R. Mem. Roll, no. 92, m. 17. Cf. P. R. O. Sheriffs' Acct. 49/8.

[2] K. R. Mem. Roll, no. 81, m. 43 d. L. T. R. Mem. Roll, no. 78, m. 40 d (17 Feb. 1308).

[3] K. R. Mem. Roll, no. 81, m. 43 d. L. T. R. Mem. Roll, no. 78, m. 40 d: "Postea, xiiii die marcii concordatum est per prefatos Thesaurarium et Barones et alios de consilio etcetera presente Amadeo comite Sabaudie."

[4] Issue Roll, no. 196, m. 6.

[5] K. R. Mem. Roll, no. 87, m. 92: "presentes hic modo coram consilio Regis."

[6] Ibid. no. 103, m. 115: "concordatum est hic eodem die per Barones et alios de consilio Regis quod vadia."

[7] Issue Roll, no. 219, m. 3.

[8] K. R. Mem. Roll, no. 82, m. 56 d. L. T. R. Mem. Roll, no. 79, m. 55.

[9] K. R. Mem. Roll, no. 83, m. 50.

distinction between the interference of the council in the administrative and financial work of the exchequer is impossible. It is important to make some distinction, inasmuch as the exchequer often appeared to act as a general administrative department, while its financial work was somewhat definite. A deliberation concerning the accounts of the wardrobe was held in the little exchequer on 22 July, 1311, in the presence of the bishop of Worcester, chancellor, Sandale, treasurer, the barons, remembrancers and chamberlains of the exchequer and other good men of the king's council[1]. For the apportionment between all his lands of the debts Alan de Lovel owed at his death, the treasurer was ordered to call to him the justices of both benches and the others of the council whom he wished[2]. An agreement was made between the archbishop of York, treasurer, the bishop of Exeter, Baldock, chancellor, and others of the king's council and Roger, the king's master moneyer, on a certain new coinage to be made for Gascony[3]. An inquest concerning the account of Anthony Pessaign was delayed on account of the absence of the treasurer and certain others of the council[4].

The council at the exchequer was also summoned to give advice upon certain matters. The treasurer notified the king that he had assembled Master Walter de Thorp, Master Gilbert de Middleton and others of the council at London, justices and clerks to counsel on certain bulls touching the king's profit which had been found in the royal treasury[5]. Certain requests made by Pessaign were to be ordained by the exchequer officials, Norwich, and the others of the council[6]. On 7 December, 1310, Sandale, treasurer, acquainted the king that he had assembled at the exchequer Brabazon, Roubiry, Benstede, Staunton, Master Walter de Thorp, Master Gilbert de Middleton, Master Thomas de Cobham and Master Richard de Plumstok, before whom and his companions and himself certain notes and transcripts touching Gascony were considered[7].

Exchequer writs were sometimes issued by the council. A writ of 12 December, 1308, to the collectors of new customs at Lincoln was

[1] K. R. Mem. Roll, no. 83, m. 58 d

[2] Ibid. no. 97, Brev. dir. Trin. m. 10.

[3] Ibid. no. 102, m. 128.

[4] Ibid. no. 88, m. 136 d. L. T. R. Mem. Roll, no. 85, Rec. St Mich. m. 3 d: "Et inquisicio capit dilacionem propter absenciam Thesaurarii et quorundam aliorum de consilio etcetera."

[5] K. R. Mem. Roll, no. 85, m. 55 d.

[6] Ibid. no. 91, Brev. dir. m. 1 d. L. T. R. Mem. Roll, no. 88, Brev. dir. Mich m. 1 d.

[7] Anc. Corresp. vol. XXXV, no. 134.

issued *per consilium*[1]. These writs were however recalled by the council and were not sealed[2]. Exchequer writs ordering an inquisition into the lands of a late sheriff[3], about provisions for the Scottish war[4], summoning various persons to the exchequer to answer what should be objected against them[5] about the drainage near the Thames[6], and the trespass of an official[7] were issued *per consilium*. An exchequer writ of 27 March, 1308, to Badlesmere, constable of Bristol, issued by warrant of privy seal, was handed to the messenger, in the presence of the treasurer and barons and others of the council[8], to convey to the constable, and writs relating to the grants of the twelfth and eighteenth at the parliament of York were handed to those assigned to tax, before the council at Westminster in the presence of the treasurer and barons[9].

The council at the exchequer sometimes had a preponderating voice in administration there, and if the king could control the council and decide the occasion when it sat there, it would prove the most effective check upon the growth of independence within the exchequer or of other than royal interference there.

The council interfered in the exchequer with work which was more or less judicial in character. In 1313 sheriffs who were not present to account were amerced before the bishop of Worcester, lieutenant of the chancellor, Pembroke, Despenser and other faithful subjects[10]. Men were summoned to be before the treasurer, barons and others of the council in the exchequer court by a writ, the cause of the summons not being stated[11]. The abbot of Glastonbury was ordered, early in

[1] L. T. R. Mem. Roll, no. 79, mm. 116 d, 117.

[2] Ibid: "Hec breuia reuocata fuerunt per consilium et non consignantur. Ideo vacantur."

[3] K. R. Mem. Roll, no. 83, m. 5 d.

[4] Ibid. no. 84, m. 96 d.

[5] Ibid. no. 86, m. 140. Vide App. of Doc. no. 20.

[6] K. R. Mem. Roll, no. 89, m. 6 d. L. T. R. Mem. Roll, no. 86, m. 7 d.

[7] Ibid. no. 84, m. 97 d.

[8] L. T. R. Mem. Roll, no. 78, m. 82.

[9] K. R. Mem. Roll, no. 92, Rec. Trin. m. 1 d. L. T. R. Mem. Roll, no. 89, m. 30: "coram consilio Regis apud Westmonasterium in xv sancti Johannis Baptiste liberantur in presencia Thesaurarii et Baronum."

[10] K. R. Mem Roll, no. 86, m. 71. L. T. R. Mem. Roll, no. 83, Rec. Mich. m. 1.

[11] This writ has a resemblance to the chancery writ of *subpoena* which according to Baldwin, *King's Council*, p. 227, was devised in the reign of Edward III and in the case of which the procedure of the exchequer followed that of the chancery. "The most radical departure lay...in the initial words: 'for certain causes' whereby a defendant was given no warning or hint of the charges to be made against him" (ibid. p. 289). Though the analogy is not full, it is sufficient to warrant a comparison. In these writs of the exchequer the cause of summons was not given.

the reign of Edward II[1], to be "hic coram Thesaurario et Baronibus et aliis de consilio Regis audiendum et faciendum quod iidem Thesaurarius Barones et consilium sibi exponerent ex parte Regis[2]." The abbot appeared, was heard and examined by the king's council[3]. Writs which were very similar were sent to the bishop of Exeter and the abbots of St Alban's and Waltham, in the first year of Edward II, who were summoned "coram Thesaurario et Baronibus et aliis de consilio Regis hic...ad audiendum et faciendum quod per eosdem Thesaurarium et Barones et alios de consilio predicto sibi hic iniungetur ex parte Regis[4]."

The pleas of the exchequer were frequently heard before the council. Henry de Gisors was impleaded "devant le conseil le Roi en le dit Escheker" at the suit of one who was not a minister of the exchequer[5]. A schedule charging a person with slander of the king was shown to the council at the exchequer[6]. In 1315 Gerard de Salveyn was present in the exchequer court before the treasurer, barons and others of the king's council, charged with speaking unbecomingly of the king and to his contempt[7]. In the nineteenth year of Edward II a process was recited, and after discussion a unanimous agreement was arrived at, by Baldock, chancellor, Geoffrey le Scrope, justice of king's bench and his associates, and Bereford, justice of the bench and his associates, together with the treasurer and barons of the exchequer[8]. For the consideration of a dispute about the miners of the king's mines in Devon in 1308, there assembled the bishop of Chichester, chancellor, the bishop of Worcester, treasurer, Brabazon, justice of king's bench, Drokensford, chancellor of the

[1] The pleas concern the debts of Walter de Langton, bishop of Coventry and Lichfield, and this writ standing early in the roll would probably date 1 Ed. II.

[2] Exch. of Pleas, Plea Roll, no. 31, m. 4.

[3] Ibid. The subject of the examination was whether he and his convent owed the bishop of Coventry and Lichfield a certain sum of money.

[4] K. R. Mem. Roll, no. 81, m. 79. Note also ibid. no. 86, m. 140, where John de Hothum, escheator north of Trent, and others, were ordered to come to the exchequer at Westminster "ad audiendum et faciendum quod tenens locum Thesaurarii et Barones de eodem scaccario et alij de consilio Regis ibidem ei iniungent ex parte Regis." With these writs should be compared an exchequer writ of 13 October, 1312, to a sheriff. He was ordered to come with all speed to the exchequer at Westminster "ad respondendum Regi super quibusdam sibi ex parte Regis ibidem obiciendis" (ibid.). There again no indication is given as to the nature of the charges which would be made. Vide above, p. 270, note 11.

[5] Chan. Warr., File 106/4808–9.

[6] K. R. Mem. Roll, no. 89, m. 89 d.

[7] Ibid. no. 88, m. 158 d. (2 July, 1315). L. T. R. Mem. Roll, no. 86, Rec. Trin. m. 6 d.

[8] K. R. Mem. Roll, no. 102, m. 90.

exchequer, Benstede, keeper of the wardrobe, William de Carlton, Roger de Hengham, Master Richard de Abingdon and Master John de Euerdon, barons of the exchequer, and Bereford, justice of the bench[1]. This imposing array of officials, composed exclusively of that class, shows the "administrative" council in a perfect light, though the addition of a small non-official element closely associated with the king would show the council in an equally characteristic phase. Other cases that came before the council were concerned with the subtraction of service from the army[2], the examination of idiots[3], and the application by a wife for goods and belongings forfeited by one exiled for felony[4]. In one case a person was recorded as coming before the council at the exchequer and showing a certain sealed inquisition to them[5]. The state of the Hospital of St Catherine outside the Tower of London was considered before the treasurer and barons, justices of both benches and others of the council[6].

Petitions addressed to the king and council were frequently sent to the treasurer; and he was ordered to summon certain of the king's council to consider them. On 19 November, 1307, Reynolds, treasurer, was ordered to call to him Sandale, chancellor of the exchequer, and William Inge, and between them to receive the petition which a merchant of Bayonne sent[7]. William Servat, a London citizen, came before the earl of Lincoln, king's lieutenant in England, before the treasurer and barons, the justices of both benches and others of the king's council and showed certain petitions touching appeals to the pope by William de Testa[8]. A petition of the city of York was handed to the exchequer by the bishop of Norwich, chancellor, and the mayor and commonalty sought justice there before the treasurer, barons and others of the council[9]. The bishop of Bath and Wells, who had been keeper of the wardrobe to Edward I, petitioned

[1] K. R. Mem. Roll, no. 81, m. 53. L. T. R. Mem. Roll, no. 78, m. 69.

[2] K. R. Mem. Roll, no. 84, m. 54. Before the earl of Lincoln, the king's lieutenant, the bishop of Worcester, chancellor, John de Sandale, treasurer, the barons and others of the council.

[3] Ibid. no. 83, m. 57. Before John de Merkingfeld, the chancellor of the exchequer, lieutenant of the treasurer, Master Richard de Abingdon and Master John de Euerdon, barons, and Walter de Gloucester, escheator south of Trent.

[4] Ibid. m. 38 d. Before the bishop of Worcester, treasurer, the earl of Lincoln, the barons of the exchequer, certain justices and others of the council.

[5] Ibid. no. 88, m. 150. L. T. R. Mem. Roll, no. 85, Rec. Pasch. m. 5 and schedule, m. 2.

[6] K. R. Mem. Roll, no. 91, Rec. Trin. mm. 3, 3 d. L. T. R. Mem. Roll, no. 88, Rec. Trin. mm. 2 d, 3 d.

[7] L. T. R. Mem. Roll, no. 78, m. 20.

[8] K. R. Mem. Roll, no. 84 , m. 57.

[9] Ibid. no. 96, m. 68. L. T. R. Mem. Roll, no. 93, m. 15.

the archbishop of Canterbury, the treasurer and barons of the exchequer to be allowed to account by deputy. This was granted to him by the archbishop, treasurer, barons and the others of the council[1].

Mainprises in the exchequer were often made before the council. Walter de Bedwynd came before the treasurer, barons and others of the council to be mainprised[2]. Sometimes the mainprise to be before the council was made before the treasurer alone, sometimes before the council. Mainprise was made in 1315 before Norwich, treasurer, to have the body of Stephen de Preston before the king's council at the exchequer[3]. A Kent mainprise was made before the treasurer, barons and others of the council to have a certain man before the same council at the exchequer and before the king to do and receive what the court should decide[4]. Where indications of the personnel of the council are given, the same body of officials and barons as have been seen acting in the council at the exchequer are found to be present, though the importance of the matter concerned is now very much less. A mainprise was made in 1309 at the exchequer before the bishop of Chichester, chancellor, the earl of Lincoln, Despenser, Sandale, lieutenant of the treasurer, the barons of the exchequer and others of the council[5]. In 1311 a mainprise for debts was made before the barons in the presence of the bishop of Bath and Wells, Pembroke, Despenser, Benstede, the justices and others of the king's council[6]. A mainprise in 1315 was made before the archbishop of Canterbury, Sandale, chancellor, Norwich, treasurer, and others of the king's council at the Friars Preachers, the mainprise being to have a certain clerk "coram consilio domini Regis hic ad scaccarium" at a certain time[7].

Though there can be little doubt that in a great many cases in which the council sat at the exchequer it was concerned with business wholly or partly exchequer, in its origin and intent, the plan of treating that aspect of the council apart from the manifestation of the council sitting with the exchequer is justified. The exact position of those who sat with the exchequer, or in whose presence exchequer business was said to be transacted, it is difficult to state with precision.

[1] K. R. Mem. Roll, no. 90, m. 101.
[2] Ibid. no. 88, m. 166 (3 June, 1315).
[3] Ibid. m. 167. L. T. R. Mem. Roll, no. 85, Manuc. Trin. m. 1.
[4] K. R. Mem. Roll, no. 90, m. 127.
[5] L. T. R. Mem. Roll, no. 79, m. 91 (12 June, 1309).
[6] K. R. Mem. Roll, no. 85, m. 69.
[7] Ibid. no. 88, m. 162 d. L. T. R. Mem. Roll, no. 85, Manuc. Hill. m. 3.

They appear to have been a strengthening of official and administrative wisdom called in to advise and counsel the exchequer in certain of its business. The return to a writ sent to the exchequer on 12 March, 1319, showing the calling of Bereford and stating the object for which he was called, illustrates the position and duty of those who sat with the exchequer: "Pretextu huius mandati prefati Thesaurarius et Barones presente Willelmo de Bereford capitale Justiciario de Banco per informacionem et auisamentum eiusdem habita plenius consideracione ad premissa concordauerunt quod predictus Willelmus de Cestrefeld percipiat de Rege pro labore suo et expensis per ipsum appositis in forma predicta decem libros[1]."

The council sat with the exchequer for administrative business which may be roughly classified as internal. The bishop of Worcester, treasurer, handed three papal bulls to a clerk of the bishop of London, in the presence of the bishop of Chichester, chancellor, Sandale, chancellor of the exchequer, Drokensford, William Inge and others of the council[2]. The auditors of accounts were appointed before the treasurer and barons, the earl of Lincoln, king's lieutenant, and others of the council sitting with them[3]. An indenture dated 21 November, 1314, between the treasurer and chamberlain and Anthony Pessaign, was made in the presence of the chancellor and the barons of the exchequer and others of the king's council[4]. William de Ros of Hamelak had a certain bill of the wardrobe under the seal of Northburgh for £181. 16*s*. 5½*d*. owing to him in the wardrobe for his wages and those of his men-at-arms. On 30 November, 1322, Ros came to the exchequer before the treasurer and barons in the presence of Northburgh, then bishop of Coventry and Lichfield, who sat with them[5]. This association of Northburgh with the exchequer on a matter of which he had the best information lends support to the suggestion that some of those who sat with the exchequer had special knowledge on the particular subject or point raised. The process touching the bishop of Worcester when he was keeper of the prince's wardrobe was recited in full exchequer before Sandale, chancellor of the exchequer, Abingdon and Euerdon, barons, and certain others of

[1] K. R. Mem. Roll, no. 92, Rec. Pasch. m. 2 d. L. T. R. Mem. Roll, no. 89, m. 27 d.

[2] K. R. Mem. Roll, no. 81, m. 54 d. L. T. R. Mem. Roll, no. 78, m. 71 d.

[3] K. R. Mem. Roll, no. 84, m. 54. L. T. R. Mem. Roll, no. 81, Rec. Mich. m. 3 d: "coram Thesaurario et Baronibus hic assidente eis Henrico de Lacy comite Lincolnie tenente locum domini Regis in Anglia et aliis de consilio."

[4] K. R. Mem. Roll, no. 88, m. 137 d. L. T. R. Mem. Roll, no. 85, Rec. Mich. m. 4 d.

[5] K. R. Mem. Roll, no. 96, m. 57.

the king's council sitting with them[1]. It was decided by the chancellor and barons that the process should be fully transcribed and sealed with the exchequer seal[2]. Norwich was replaced in his office of treasurer's remembrancer[3] at the exchequer, before the barons of the exchequer, William Inge, William Howard, Bereford and several others of the council sitting with them[4]. Two crowns were handed to the treasurer by the Bardi in the presence of the bishop of Exeter, treasurer, the bishop of Hereford, Pembroke, Northburgh, keeper of the wardrobe, and Norwich, baron of the exchequer[5].

The council sat with the exchequer also in its general administrative work. An ordinance relating to the mines of Devon was made by the bishop of Worcester, treasurer, in the presence of Sandale, chancellor of the exchequer, Sir William de Carlton, Thomas de Cambridge, Sir Roger de Hengham, Master Richard de Abingdon, Master John de Euerdon, barons of the exchequer "et plusours autres del consail de dist nostre seigneur le Roi en son parlement le terme de saint Michel lan de son regne secund[6]." On 17 February, 1312, Norwich called before him the lieutenant of the keeper of the palace of Westminster and the two porters of the exchequer about the safe keeping of the palace, in the presence of Merkingfeld, chancellor of the exchequer, Abingdon, Euerdon, barons of the exchequer, and others of the king's council sitting with him[7].

In various pleas at the exchequer the council sat with the exchequer officials; those of the council who sat usually included a number of justices among them. On 18 September, 1307, certain men came before the treasurer and barons, Guy Ferre, Brabazon, Roubiry, and John de Bakewell[8] and others of the king's council sitting with them[9]. A dispute about the custody of an abbey during vacancy and the letters of the bishop of Lincoln thereon were treated by the treasurer, Brabazon, Roubiry, Bakewell and Ralph de Sandwich, constable of the Tower, and others of the king's council assisting them[10]. Another

[1] K. R. Mem. Roll, no. 82, m. 57: "et quibusdam aliis de consilio Regis eis assidentibus."

[2] Ibid. m. 57: "concordarunt ipsi Cancellarius et Barones quod idem processus plenarie transcribatur et sigillo scaccarii consignatur...."

[3] Vide above, p. 123.

[4] K. R. Mem. Roll, no. 81, m. 38 d.

[5] Ibid. no. 93, m. 77 (22 Feb. 1320).

[6] Ibid. no. 82, m. 55. L. T. R. Mem. Roll, no. 79, m. 41.

[7] K. R. Mem. Roll, no. 85, m. 49.

[8] He was appointed a baron of the exchequer on 10 Nov. 1307, his previous administrative posts including the seneschalship of Ponthieu, 1299–1305 (Tout, *The Place of Ed II*, p. 341).

[9] K. R. Mem. Roll, no. 81, m. 40 d.

[10] Ibid. m. 36.

person came before the treasurer and barons on 27 May, 1308, when the bishop of Chichester, chancellor, Brabazon, justice of king's bench, Hengham, justice of the common bench, Benstede, keeper of the wardrobe, and others of the council were sitting with them, and at the same time Nicholas de Warwick, king's serjeant was present[1]. When the abbot of Evesham sought to make fine with the king, the matter was treated by the treasurer and barons with the bishop of Chichester, chancellor, and others of the council sitting with them[2]. The archbishop of Dublin and others were summoned, concerning various trespasses, before the treasurer and barons with John de Hothum, bishop of Ely, Baldock, chancellor, and Geoffrey le Scrope, justice of the king's bench, sitting with them[3]. The petition of the abbot of Cluny against the ordinance that no money should be taken out of the kingdom by foreigners was examined before the treasurer and barons, William Inge and others of the council sitting with them[4]. A matter was commenced by a writ which Peter de Friscobaldi brought into the exchequer in presence of Merkingfeld, chancellor of the exchequer, and Euerdon, baron of the exchequer, Lambert de Trickingham and Benstede, justices of the bench, sitting with them, Crombwell, keeper of the Tower, also being present[5]. A disturbance in London against the Lombards was brought to the notice of the treasurer, barons and others of the council. The mayor and others were summoned and appeared at the exchequer before the treasurer and barons in the presence of the archbishop of Canterbury, the bishop of Exeter, the earl of Hereford, Walwayn, Mutford, Baldock, Master Richard de Burton and others of the council sitting with them[6]. William Paynel, who had exercised certain liberties to the disinheritance of the crown in William de Brewosa's honour of Brembre, was ordered to come to the exchequer to show what rights he had to hold the liberties so that the treasurer and barons of the exchequer, in the presence of the others of the king's council they might call, should examine the matter and do justice[7].

The council sitting with the exchequer was in composition the same as the council sitting at the exchequer, and they were both but

[1] K. R. Mem. Roll, no. 81, m. 52.

[2] Ibid. no. 82, m. 56 d. L. T. R. Mem. Roll, no. 79, m. 54 d.

[3] K. R. Mem. Roll, no. 102, m. 89. [4] Ibid. no. 81, m. 36.

[5] Ibid. no. 85, m. 50.

[6] L. T. R. Mem. Roll, no. 89, m. 31 d (28 June, 1319).

[7] Ancient Petition, no. 559, Endorsement: "quod Thesaurarius et Barones de Scaccario in presencia illorum de consilio Regis qui vocandi fuerint examinent negocium illud et faciant inde iusticiam."

phases of the "administrative" council, which was itself but one manifestation of the council. Any definite division of functions between the council sitting with the exchequer and the council sitting at the exchequer would be impossible. It is possible that the council may be described as sitting at or with the exchequer according to the caprice or preference of the scribe, though inasmuch as when the council is described as sitting at the exchequer in the king's remembrancer's memoranda roll, it is also so described in the lord treasurer's remembrancer's roll[1], and when the council is described as sitting with the exchequer in the lord treasurer's remembrancer's roll it is so described in the king's remembrancer's[2] roll, this is improbable. It is unlikely that in all these instances the council was merely using exchequer premises for its meetings and was on occasion called in to consult with and advise the exchequer officials because it happened to be near. Too much importance can be attached to the convenience of exchequer premises, for the council also met at the exchequer at York[3] where that body had no fixed or definite premises[4]. Moreover exchequer business was transacted before "the king and council[5]" or before "the treasurer, barons and others of the king's council[6]" elsewhere than at the exchequer, at Windsor or the Friars Preachers, so that the question of premises or local convenience was not the essential reason why the council was called in. Again, in consideration of the bulk of the king's remembrancer's and treasurer's remembrancer's rolls at this time, it is unlikely that the officials responsible for them, or their clerks, would burden their rolls by giving the record of the innumerable occasions on which councils merely occupied exchequer premises, even if some of the exchequer officials were present at those meetings. The position therefore would seem to be this; the council frequently occupied a room at the exchequer for the transaction of business concerned with the general affairs of the realm. When formal proceedings of importance were taking place in the exchequer, a number of members of that council selected by the treasurer or his lieutenant were invited to take their place with the purely exchequer officials to witness them. When a matter

[1] Vide references above, p. 268, nn. 1–3, 8; p. 269, n. 4.

[2] Ibid. p. 274, nn. 2–4; p. 275, n. 6.

[3] One was ordered to be "at the exchequer at York to treat with the king's council" (*Cal. Close Rolls*, 1302–7, p. 87), and another was ordered to be at "York at the king's exchequer before his council" (ibid. 1296–1302, p. 291).

[4] The king ordered the houses without York castle and other houses to be repaired for the exchequer and the bench which were to be transferred to York (*Cal. Close Rolls*, 1318–23, p. 76).

[5] K. R. Mem. Roll, no. 86, m. 104 d.

[6] Ibid. no. 84, m. 68 d.

which proved difficult was being discussed at the exchequer, the justices of the benches and others of the council would be introduced to give expert legal advice[1] or to form an official stiffening. It comes out quite clearly that the council was called by the treasurer and barons. Yet when the council was called in to sit with or assist its position was different and far nearer that of the ordinary exchequer officials, for sometimes the chancellor and barons of the exchequer are included amongst those who sat with the treasurer or his lieutenant much in the same way as the elected members of the council sat with them. Finally it may perhaps be said that the question of the relative position of the council when it sat at and with the exchequer, really resolves itself into one of degree. When the council sat with the exchequer the probability that it was concerned with the exchequer business was greater than when it sat at the exchequer. In the latter case the council might, on frequent occasions, merely be using exchequer premises.

The judicial work of the council at this time must be noted in passing. A certain amount of this work might claim to be discussed under the chancery, and reference has been made to the judicial work of the council in the exchequer. Pleas were heard before the king's council at Westminster[2], and there are in various collections membranes headed "Placita coram consilio Regis[3]." An exchequer bill addressed to the treasurer and barons of the exchequer, complaining of the mayor of London, was endorsed "apud fratres predicatores in presencia Archiepiscopi Rogeri Brabazon et aliorum consilii[4]."

The greatest part of the judicial work of the council was the result of petitions addressed to the king, or the king and council. Such petitions were sent to the chancellor under writ of privy seal with order to call others of the council and examine them[5]. Sometimes the persons to be summoned were named, a bill of the mayor and bailiffs of London being sent to the bishop of Norwich, chancellor, who was to summon the bishop of Exeter, treasurer, Bereford, chief justice of common bench, Norwich, baron of the exchequer, Staunton, chief justice of the eyre[6], and William de Ayremynne, to consider,

[1] K. R. Mem. Roll, no. 91, m. 3, Rec. Trin.: "pretextu cuius breuis conuocatis justiciariis de utroque Banco et aliis de consilio Regis in curia existentibus."

[2] *Cal. Doc. Scotl.* vol. III, pp. 106–7.

[3] Cf. K. R. Mem. Roll, no. 91, Rec. Pasch. dorse of last membrane; no. 93, m. 103 d. Cf. also P. R. O. Parliamentary and Council Proceedings (Exchequer), Roll no. 17.

[4] Exch. K. R. Bills, 1/6.

[5] E.g. Chan. Warr., File 63/515.

[6] An eyre was held in London early in 1321. Vide *Mun. Gildh. Lond.* vol. II, Pt i, pp. 285–384.

discuss and ordain on the matter in such a manner as not to disturb the eyre or be in prejudice to the crown[1]. On a petition by the abbot of Osney, the chancellor was ordered to call the justices to him to examine the matters which were contained therein and to do what could be done by the royal grace without offending right or the royal jurisdiction[2]. A petition which Edward II received from Margaret, countess of Foix, he referred to the archbishop of Canterbury and the council[3].

The council also examined persons who were alleged to be idiots[4]. A man, who had charged a clerk of chancery with taking gifts from men of London and others for hindering the king's right, was attached to appear before the king and council, and upon failing to substantiate his charges was committed to Newgate to remain there during the king's will[5]. Matters which proved difficult to the lower courts were referred to the king and his council, an adjournment of this nature being made even from the eyre of London of 1321[6].

The treatment of the council undertaken here is justified by the importance of that body as an instrument of royal policy, an importance that is amply proved by the attention which the baronial opposition paid to the control of the council in their schemes of reform and, in practice, when they were powerful enough to coerce the king[7]. It has been suggested that "had the plans of Edward I been carried out to their logical conclusion, there is reason to believe that the council in all its functions would have become entirely, or at least mainly, a professional body[8]." That this result did not occur was due to the opposition of the barons, who considered that the increasing professional element in the council was usurping their rights. It was not in the royal administration alone that this movement was taking place. The increase of the official element was a feature of the council of the palatinate of Durham during the thirteenth century which went on increasing in the fourteenth century. The legal and clerical element increased at the expense of the noble or feudal[9].

As an introduction to the study of the household influence upon the

[1] Chan. Warr., File 113/5555 (7 Jan. 1321). [2] Ibid. File 63/518.

[3] Chan. Misc., Bdle 25/2 (12): "Le Roi voet qe Lerceuesqe de Cantebire et les autres de son consail a Londres deliure ceste peticion et lautre procheine siuant selonc ce qil verrent qe mielz force a faire."

[4] *Cal. Close Rolls*, 1307–13, p. 367; 1323–27, p. 54.

[5] Ibid. 1307–13, p. 563. [6] *Mun. Gildh. Lond.* vol. II, Pt i, pp. 352–3.

[7] Vide below, pp. 412–413, 448–451. [8] Baldwin, *King's Council*, pp. 74–75.

[9] Lapsley, *Pal. of Durham*, p. 140, 144–7, 155.

council its relations with the wardrobe must be considered. Payments in the wardrobe were frequently made by ordinance, or agreement of the council. This was partly due to the position the wardrobe occupied in general administration. It was more than the king's private financial department, or rather the whole of the financial administration was the king's private concern. In theory, the exchequer was as much a royal department as the wardrobe, and theory and ancient practice held good to this extent, that though there may have been specialisation of functions, that specialisation did not interfere with the general practice. The result was that though the wardrobe was becoming increasingly the private and personal finance department of the household, it still retained an important part in payments for public activities, for example the expenses of war[1]. Ambassadors and messengers also were paid there. The interference of the council, especially of that particular manifestation of the council which has been called "administrative," therefore can be readily accounted for. It came within its functions as the body which considered and dealt with foreign affairs to send ambassadors, and it was natural that the rate of payment of those ambassadors and messengers should be fixed by their ordinance, or as the result of agreement between ambassadors and council. Moreover the fact must not be overlooked that the council was still in one phase essentially a personal body, a part of the personal system.

Master Thomas de Cobham, who was sent by the king to France together with Pembroke and Henry de Beaumont, received payment of 15*s*. a day "per ordinacionem consilii Regis" in the name of expenses[2]. Robert Sturmy, who went to Flanders on the king's business, received half a mark a day "iuxta ordinacionem consilii Regis[3]." Sometimes payments were made to notable messengers "per ordinacionem ipsius Regis et consilii sui." The earl of Pembroke received 100*s*. a day by such ordinance[4] when sent by the king to France, and Alexander de Abernythy, going to the Roman court, received 20*s*. a day similarly[5]. On occasion too the names of the chief members of the council making the ordinance were included in the account of the payment. Beaumont, going to Paris to prepare for the king's arrival, received payment of £400 by ordinance of Reynolds, elect-confirmed of Canterbury, Pembroke, Sandale and others of the council[6]. John de Shoreditch, going to France, received payment of half a mark by ordinance of the bishop of Exeter, treasurer, and others of the council[7], and Master

[1] Vide above, pp. 189–190. [2] K. R. Acct. 375/8, f. 76. [3] Ibid.
[4] Ibid. ff. 9, 15 b. [5] Ibid. f. 9 b. [6] Ibid. f. 15. [7] Stowe MS. 553, f. 119.

John de Weston, going to France with Pembroke, had 10*s*. a day by ordinance of the treasurer and others of the council[1]. Nor was it only for payments for messengers going abroad that an ordinance was made. Sir William de Montague, staying in London about two ships for the king, by ordinance of the king and council, received payment from the wardrobe[2]. Roger de Waltham, keeper of the wardrobe, and clerks assisting him to array his accounts received 5*s*. a day by ordinance of the treasurer and barons of the exchequer[3], while the fee of Edward de Balliol was fixed by ordinance of the chancellor and treasurer[4]. All of these payments by ordinance of the council were made out of the wardrobe.

Payment was also made out of the wardrobe by an agreement between the council and the creditor. William de Dene, sent to France on the king's business, received 10*s*. a day "per conuencionem secum factam per consilium ipsius Regis[5]." Master Raymond de Suburiano, staying in England for the king's business, received 20*s*. a day for his expenses by a certain agreement made by the king's council with him[6]. When Master Richard de Burton was sent with the bishop of Exeter to France, receiving 10*s*. a day, the agreement was made by Sandale and others of the king's council[7]. By agreement made with the earl of Richmond by Pembroke and others of the king's council, he received 106*s*. 8*d*. a day for going to France with the king[8]. The bishop of Exeter, going in the king's company to France, received a payment of £333. 6*s*. 8*d*. for all his expenses, by agreement made with him by the king, Reynolds, bishop of Worcester, Pembroke, Despenser, Lenham, king's confessor, and others of the king's council[9].

By virtue of the influence which the king could exercise upon the composition[10] of the council and upon its personnel, the "administrative" council was almost a household body. The more important officers of the household had places in it. The keeper of the wardrobe was sometimes present[11] and *Fleta* says that he was sworn of the council and because of this oath was exempted from taking any other oath when rendering accounts[12]. On 13 June, 1309, a writ enclosing a petition, which was to be considered by the council, was addressed to the bishop of Chichester, chancellor, Drokensford, elect-confirmed

[1] K. R. Acct. 375/8, f. 18 A. [2] Ibid. 375/8, f. 6.
[3] Brit. Mus. Stowe MS. 553 Liber Garder Ed. II. f. 121.
[4] K. R. Acct. 375/8, f. 6. [5] Ibid. f. 7 b. [6] Ibid. f. 10.
[7] Ibid. ff. 11 b, 16. [8] Ibid. f. 11 b. [9] Ibid f 12 b.
[10] Vide the names present at councils given in Madox, *Hist. of Exch.* vol. II, pp. 29–32.
[11] Vide above, pp. 230–1. [12] Selden, *Fleta* (Bk II, § 14), pp. 78–79.

of Bath and Wells, keeper of the wardrobe, and Sandale, lieutenant of the treasurer[1]. The steward of the household, too, acted on the council[2]. In 1319 he accompanied the treasurer and barons of the exchequer and others of the council and requested the mayor and city of London to contribute a loan towards the king's war expenses[3]. The controller of the wardrobe and other king's clerks acted on the council[4]; and the king's chamberlain, though his status as a baron might rule him out of the official class, had a place on the council by virtue of his office in the household rather than by virtue of his baronial position. Among other household officials who are found acting upon the council was the king's confessor[5].

In addition to those members who were purely household officials, there was a second class who were a regular section of the "administrative" council. These can be said to have been partly household, partly official, also in part independent of either household or official ties. This class was composed of those barons and bishops who, on account of administrative ability, power or personal friendship, the king desired should act upon his council. One of this class at times assumed the complete direction of the council, and by virtue of the royal confidence temporarily superseded the chancellor and the other officials in a considerable part of their functions. The archbishop of Canterbury sometimes assumed the headship[6], and it has been seen that his presence was frequent and important[7]. At one period Pembroke was the decisive figure on the council[8]. The frequent attendance of the elder Despenser in the council[9] supplies another instance of this class of counsellor who though baronial in status was royalist in policy and was content to take a useful part in administration. Various other barons and bishops at times acted on the council, and in this class the king had a useful if not servile support.

Lastly there was the official class. The chancellor and the clerks of his department, the treasurer, the chancellor and barons of the exchequer, together with some of the minor officials of that department, such as the chamberlains and the remembrancers, the justices of king's bench and common pleas, the king's serjeants, and at times local officials like the escheator, these were all at various times called to take part in the work of the council. Though the officials

[1] Chan. Warr., File 63/513.
[2] Vide above, pp. 213–214.
[3] *Parl. Writs*, vol. II, Pt i, p. 224.
[4] *Memoranda de Parliamento*, 1305, ed. F. W. Maitland, p. xliii.
[5] K. R. Acct. 375/8, f. 12 b.
[6] Vide below, pp. 331–6.
[7] Vide above, pp. 254–280.
[8] Vide below, pp. 320–330.
[9] Vide above, pp. 268–281.

undoubtedly had tendencies towards independence, the control of the king was so complete over their appointment and administration that such tendencies were kept well in check. Moreover in struggles between king and barons the official classes supported the king. That strange mixture of conservatism and radicalism which characterised the baronial policy found little or no support among the officials. It was not that they followed the king blindly on every occasion. Administrative reform and development they desired, but they saw the only hope of such reform in royal and not in baronial action. The particular officials to serve on the "administrative" council on any given occasion could be selected by the king; and since those officials held their positions by royal appointment, the king's control upon the official element in the council was complete.

Arising out of the king's control of the composition of the council was the influence which he could exercise upon the personnel. The household officials were bound to the royal policy by interest and position. They could be trusted on all occasions to act as the king desired or directed. A word from the king would be sufficient to make them fulfil his will. Even if no express order were given their knowledge of the king's desires would be sufficient to influence their actions. They would be as solicitous of the royal interest as of the royal will.

The class of baronial and episcopal members of the council, though not as a whole as amenable to royal influence, could be trusted on every occasion to consider the true royal interest. Some members of this class stood almost in the position of royal favourites. Since their interests were bound up with those of the king, reliance could confidently be placed upon them. Some of them were men bound to the king by nobler motives than self-interest. The revolutionary tendencies of the baronage, seconded by their self-interested motives, made these men firm and consistent supporters of the personal system, though they were fully aware of its faults. These bishops and barons, who formed an element in the "administrative" council, even if they were not courtiers were, to some extent, absorbed into the household system. There was no mid-way between baronial opposition and the personal system. It will be seen hereafter that the middle party exerted its influence through the household system[1], and that even the barons were forced to adapt their policy to suit the necessities of the time[2], an adaptation which acknowledged the household system. Since these bishops and barons

[1] Vide below, pp. 425–436, 442–3.

[2] Vide below, pp. 451–7.

were at least unofficial members of the royal household, who came into frequent personal contact with the king, the king had opportunity to exercise his influence over them.

The purely official or administrative class were equally susceptible to the king's influence. The lower officials looked to him for ecclesiastical preferment, and advancement in office. The higher officials had also much to gain by supporting the king—advancement, grants and favours. There were also higher motives to urge the officials to allow the royal influence to have its effect. The spirit of obedience and official brotherhood, the love of order and administration, interest in and enthusiasm for their work, all combined to this end.

The method of summoning the council also allowed the influence of the king and the personal system full power. The council was summoned by letters of privy seal addressed to the chancellor or treasurer or both those officials, ordering them to call together the council. The orders sometimes specifically mentioned those who were to be so called. Sometimes the writ of privy seal was sent to one of those unofficial bishops or barons who were ordered to summon the council. On occasion the council was summoned by letters under the great seal. The chancellor or treasurer was in 1323 ordered to make such letters for a council at York[1], and writs of summons appear on the close rolls[2]. Besides these writs of privy seal, the council was also summoned by informal warrants or by verbal orders through the chancery, exchequer, or individuals.

There were also a number of safeguards which the king could exercise upon the conduct of council business. The decisions of the council were subject to the royal will and pleasure. This is especially noticeable in the endorsements of petitions which the council considered. The reply was frequently "il semble au conseil sil plest au Roi[3]" or "videtur consilio si placeat Regi[4]." Such an endorsement only had force after the addition at the king's command of some such formula as "il plest au Roi[5]" or "le Roi veut[6]." When the council considered a matter they were ordered to certify the king of the result[7]. On 21 October, 1315, a letter of the king of France was sent to the archbishop of Canterbury, Sandale, chancellor, and Norwich, treasurer. They were ordered to consider the matter referred to therein and to

[1] Chan. Warr., File 123/6534 (21 May, 1323).

[2] E.g. *Cal. Close Rolls*, 1307–13, p. 317; 1313–18, p. 459; 1323–27, p. 334.

[3] *Rot. Parl.* vol. 1, p. 438.

[4] Cole, *Doc. illustr. Eng. Hist. in 13th and 14th Cent.* p. 53.

[5] *Rot. Parl.* vol. 1, p. 438. Parl. and Council Proc. (Chan.), File 4/19.

[6] Ancient Petition, no. 4913, Endorsement.

[7] Chan. Warr., File 63/505.

certify the king what seemed best to them should be done[1]. The decision of the council was not final. Its duty was to express its opinion to the king. In the first year of Edward II's reign the council gave its opinion about the restoration of franchises of the bishop of Durham, the opinions in the various points running "auys est au consail qe le Roi[2]." In the dispute of Griffith de la Pole and Cherleton, orders were issued that the council were to do nothing in this business without the king's order[3]. At the suit of Oliver de Bordeaux, a valet of the king, it was agreed in the presence of the treasurer and others of the council that the custom of the port of Boston, which had been assigned to one person should be allowed to another[4]—a characteristic example of royal interference with the work of the council. Another instance of interference is found in a grant of £200 made to the bishop of Norwich in 1317. The bishop had been to Rome as a royal ambassador, the council assigning him a fixed daily sum for the expenses of his household. The king ordered the treasurer and chamberlains to pay him £200 in addition to his daily allowance[5].

The king's excuse for referring a matter to the council was sometimes that he had not such counsel near him as the business demanded. Edward I had on occasion delayed an inconvenient matter on this plea[6]. In 1316, Baldock, on behalf of the prelates and clergy of the province of Canterbury, took a roll to the king containing certain requests. Because the king had not such counsel near him as was necessary for the decision of so weighty a matter, he sent the roll to the archbishop of Canterbury, the chancellor and treasurer, who were to decide[7]. Such actions did not detract from but rather increased the influence of the king over the council. It was a method employed only when the king desired and the decision of the matter was subject to his approval. The king sometimes acted with or in the presence of his council. Edward I pardoned a fine in the presence of his council[8]. After the king's departure, the proceedings of the council were sent after him. A council was held at Lincoln in 1315 after the king's departure. A roll was sent to him by Northburgh and the king returned the roll on 8 September, 1315, under privy seal with his assent to the matters contained therein[9]. Communication of this

[1] Anc. Corresp. vol. XXXV, no. 124. [2] Parl. and Council Proc. (Chan.). File 4/3.
[3] Anc. Corresp. vol. XLIX, no. 66. [4] Issue Roll, no. 183, m. 7.
[5] *Cal. Close Rolls*, 1313–18, p. 420. [6] Ibid. 1288–96, p. 526.
[7] Chan. Warr., File 96/3822: "Et pur qe nous nauiens tieu consail pres de nous come couendroit a deliuerer si grosse busoigne."
[8] *Cal. Close Rolls*, 1272–79, p. 484.
[9] Chan. Warr., File 92/3443. Vide App. of Doc. no. 61.

nature between the king and council was frequent. On 20 January, 1319, Adam de Lymbergh, clerk, received 60s. for his expenses in going to and from the king to acquaint him from the treasurer and others of the council of certain business[1]. When the king was in Paris the same clerk was sent to him with a letter from the bishops of Worcester and Bath and Wells, the earl of Gloucester and others of the king's council staying in England[2]. The king sent to the council two friars from Ireland, with whom it was to treat about the state of that country, so that the council could fully inform the king of its advice and counsel on coming to him[3]. The king sometimes summoned the council to be before him[4]. So careful was it not to infringe the king's authority that it sought justification for issuing a writ of purely administrative bearing and not of great importance in the formula "by council because it was sealed at another time by the king[5]."

Though the king did not exploit his personal will and desires to excess in the control of the council, such requests as to provide a good and quick remedy without offence of law to a certain petition "car nous auoms la busoigne molt a cuer[6]" could not have been without effect. The king's influence in the council was in fact greater than in the administrative departments. The "administrative" council was a body which was but slowly realising its importance and cohesion. Its composition had not the permanency of that of the administrative departments. It had no recognised head[7], no organised system, no specialised clerks, no great rolls or records. Its ever changing composition, due to royal policy or caprice, was a factor which acted against the growth of such formalism and officialism as the great departments had. This also tended to make it more dependent upon the will of the king. There was, however, growing up in the council a professional spirit, which manifested itself against the king in the addition of a professional judge to those he suggested to hear and determine the complaints against John de Segrave, justice of the

[1] Issue Roll, no. 186, m. 5.
[2] K. R. Acct. 375/8, f. 18 A.
[3] Chan. Warr., File 128/7081 (28 Mar. 1325).
[4] Ibid. File 61/346.
[5] *Cal. Close Rolls*, 1323–27, p. 48 (6 Dec. 1323).
[6] Chan. Warr., File 112/5424 (7 Sept. 1320).
[7] In Ireland the chancellor could already call himself "vostre chaunceller qest le secunde de vostre conseil es dites parties" (Ancient Corresp. vol. XXXV, no. 24), the justice being first, and though in England things were tending to the recognition of the chancellor as the head of the council there was competition between the treasurer and an unofficial head like the archbishop of Canterbury or the earl of Pembroke.

forest; but this in baronial crises would support and strengthen the king's position against the baronial[1].

In a discussion of the personal system and the "administrative" council it is of the utmost importance to notice its great activity in the exchequer and the importance of the exchequer as a general administrative body, as a place whence the royal influence could radiate in all directions even if the chancery were captured by the baronial opposition. A duplication of functions by the chancery and the exchequer would act entirely in the royal favour. That this was seen is apparent in the strenuous opposition which the barons offered to the exchequer. Even as the great financial department the exchequer was vital. As a general department interposing in the work of the chancery by its commissions under the exchequer seal, in the local administration by the appointment of sheriffs, in justice by the extension of exchequer pleas, the importance of the exchequer was too great; and its limitation in certain directions was an essential part of the baronial scheme of reform. The constant association of the council with the exchequer had a twofold importance. In the first place it extended its administration and jurisdiction and gave it added prestige and power. Its second result was not less important. Over the exchequer and over its increasing functions and power, the king, through the "administrative" council, was able to exercise and maintain his control. The council, in its phase as a part of the household system, was of the utmost importance not in the exchequer alone, but throughout the whole of the administration.

[1] Parl. and Council Proc. (Chan.), File 4/13.

CHAPTER XII

THE INFLUENCE OF THE HOUSEHOLD SYSTEM UPON THE ADMINISTRATION (*cont.*)

(iii) *The Great Council and Parliament*

The great departments were the instruments of the royal administration; the "administrative" council was one phase of the royal executive; the great council and parliament were the formal assemblies which were royal and something more. The great council and parliament were formal assemblies where the earls and barons as such had a place. It was in part by virtue of the place they held in these bodies that they claimed that participation in the royal administration which the king was so opposed to granting them and it was in part through these bodies that they had to work in their assaults upon the royal position.

The definition of "great council" and "parliament is a matter of much difficulty and the first consideration must be an endeavour to distinguish them. The problem of differentiating between the great council and parliament is mainly one of time—to fix the date when the distinctions and differences were sufficiently marked for the name great council to be applied to one assembly and the name parliament to another. Both institutions sprang from a single stem[1]. By a gradual process the original body was divided into two[2]. Close inter-relations existed between council and parliament in the reign of Edward I[3]; and during the fourteenth century "the great councils which antedated the constitutional formation of parliament continued to be brought together in the old way[4]." After the relations between the great council and parliament, as they are made apparent in the reign of Edward II, have been discussed, the great council and parliament will be treated separately, in the light of future development rather than as a description of their state at the beginning of the fourteenth century.

[1] Baldwin, *King's Council*, p. 507.
[2] Ibid. note 1.
[3] Ibid. p. 507.
[4] Ibid. p. 106.

It was only as parliament was given definite form that the council differed from it; and this definite form can hardly be said to have been established by the reign of Edward II. A parliament met at Westminster at Easter, 1309, in which certain articles, agreed upon by the earls and barons for the profit of the kingdom and of the king, were proposed[1]. Also in the third year of Edward II enactments in "full parliament" were spoken of although no deputies to it had been summoned, and in the following year a "full parliament" was spoken of after the representatives of the shires and towns had been dismissed[2].

During this reign parliament frequently used for its enactments the same phraseology as the council used. The term "ordinance[3]" was used by the great council for decisions arrived at or arrangements made by that body. A petition to the king and council relating to measures at Oxford was heard "Coram Rege et Magno Consilio." The endorsement ran: "Respondu est par la commune ordenaunce. Respondu est par comun acord et assent de parlement[4]," an illustration of the close connection between the great council and parliament which would account for the similar phraseology for acts of like intent. The *Statutum de Escaetoribus* of Edward I was made at the king's parliament at Lincoln, where it was agreed upon by the king's council. In its enrolment on the dorse of the close roll for that year it was called "quedam ordinacio facta per Regem et concilium suum[5]." In a fourteenth century collection of the statutes it is called *Statutum Lincolnie*[6]. The royal writ enclosing the Statute of Stamford to the sheriffs in 1309 stated that a certain ordinance of Edward I having been discussed at the parliament at Stamford and recited before the king and his council, the king willed that from henceforth the said ordinance should be firmly observed[7]. It was ordained by unanimous assent in the parliament of York in 1319 that the king and all magnates should take a journey towards Scotland on a given date[8]. At a parliament held at the Tower of London in 1324, it was ordained concerning the estate of the queen that all the French and foreigners should be expelled from the court, and that her lands and those of the earl of Chester should be taken into the king's hands[9]. At Westminster earlier in that year, it was ordained in a parliament

[1] *Ann. Lond.* p. 157.
[2] *Report on Dignity of Peer*, vol. I, pp. 257–294.
[3] Vide above, pp. 257–8.
[4] Oxf. Hist. Soc., *Collect.* vol. III, p. 117.
[5] *Stat. of Realm*, vol. I, p. 142.
[6] Camb. Univ. Additional MS. 3129, f. 54 b.
[7] *Stat. of Realm*, vol. I, p. 156.
[8] *Auct. Bridl.* p. 56: "ordinatum fuit."
[9] *Le Livere de Reis de Brit.* p. 350.

that all the rebel barons whose bodies remained on the gallows should be taken down and buried; and that Henry de Lancaster should have the earldom of Leicester[1].

During the reign of Edward II it has been suggested "uncertainty and confusion arises: parliament and council are becoming distinct organisms[2]." The uncertainty and confusion are apparent: any distinct division it is hard to find. The same body is called at different times by different names, now parliament, now council. On Edward III's accession petitions by the adherents of the earl of Lancaster were presented to him. On 3 February, 1327, these petitions "furent mostrez en Parlement adonqes tenu a Westminster[3]." To one petition the reply ran in these words: "a quele peticion fust respondu par comune assent de tot le Parlement qe...[4]"; to another it was answered "mes nest pas lentencion du conseil, qe ceux...[5]." As long as such loose usage was observed in the records of parliament itself, distinct differentiation was impossible. In the first year of Edward II the bishop of Ely and other prelates were ordered by exchequer writ to be in person to hear and do what the treasurer, barons and others of the council should enjoin upon them on the king's behalf. The bishop stated that he had received a writ of privy seal to certify the king on the premises and that he would be in person at the next parliament at Northampton sufficiently instructed to certify him and his council according to the tenor of that writ[6]. A day was given him by the council[7]. The same confusion occurs in the preamble of the *Statutum de Terris Templariorum* of 17 Edward II. A conference was held in the *parliament* at Westminster before the king in the presence of the prelates, earls, barons, nobles and great men of the realm and others there present as to whether the lords could with safe conscience retain the lands of the Templars, by the law of the land. The greater part of the king's *council* having assembled, as well justices as other lay persons, the justices stated that this might be done, but because the lands were given for religious purposes it seemed good to the king, noblemen and others assembled in that *parliament* that the lands should be given to religious. "Thereupon in the same *parliament* it was agreed, ordained and established for law to continue for ever" that no one should retain possession[8].

[1] *Ann. Paul.* p. 306.

[2] Harcourt, *His Grace the Steward*, p. 308. [3] *Rot. Parl.* vol. II, p. 5.

[4] Ibid. [5] Ibid. p. 6. [6] K. R. Mem. Roll, no. 81, m. 35.

[7] Ibid. The abbot of St Alban's had a day given him by the treasurer, barons and council.

[8] *Stat. of Realm*, vol. I, pp. 194–6.

Another curious combination of council and parliament is found in the writ enclosing the *Articuli cleri* in 1316 to the sheriffs. The writ was issued "per ipsum Regem et consilium" and ran thus: "of late in our *parliament* held at Lincoln in the 9th year of our reign we caused the articles under-written with certain answers made to some of them heretofore, to be rehearsed before our council and made certain answers to be corrected, and to the residue of the articles under-written answers were made by us and our *council*...[1]." Of one who was summoned to a parliament at York the king stated that he had "caused him to be summoned as others of his Council were" to that parliament[2].

It cannot be maintained that in all these instances the council referred to was the great council. In some, at least, it can equally well be the "administrative" council, for they were but two manifestations of the same body. It is frequently difficult to determine which manifestation of the council is referred to in a given instance. On 8 October, 1301, orders were issued: "to do further in this matter what has been more fully ordained by the king's council as it has been unanimously agreed by the council of the earls, barons and other magnates and subjects of the king in his company and in that of his son in his expedition to Scotland that three or four knights or others shall be elected in each county by the communities of the counties in order to assess tax and collect the said 15th[3]." Two manifestations of the council might be referred to here. The great council or such part of it or substitute for it as the king had with him may be said to have agreed to the matter upon which the "administrative council" ordained. On the other hand the agreement and the ordinance may both have been made by the great council.

Besides similarity of phraseology and formation, the composition and personnel of the great council was not dissimilar from that of parliament, with the exception of course of the borough representatives and the knights of the shire. The council which met at Bishopsthorp on 30 May, 1323, will be taken as a characteristic meeting of the great council. The king was at Bishopsthorp in May and caused the archbishop of York, the bishop of Norwich, chancellor, the bishop of Exeter, treasurer, the earls of Kent, Pembroke, Winchester and Athol, Despenser the younger, William de Ros and other barons of the realm, the justices of both benches, the barons of the

[1] *Stat. of Realm*, vol. I, pp. 171–4.
[2] *Cal. Pat. Rolls*, 1313–17, p. 238 (8 Oct. 1314).
[3] *Cal. Close Rolls*, 1296–1302, p. 499.

exchequer and others of his council, to be before him in his council to treat of confirming or refusing a truce with Bruce[1]. A complete list of those present at this council has survived[2], and an added interest is given to the council by the dramatic refusal of Henry de Beaumont, who was "sworn of the king's great and secret council," to give the king advice when it was asked, and by the insult he flung at the king when ordered to leave[3]. An analysis of the list of those present at the council is interesting. The archbishop of York headed the list, the other ecclesiastics and barons running as above, with the omission of the chancellor and a marginal insertion of the abbot of Selby. Before the list of barons the names of the dean of York and the Seigneur de Sully appear. The list of barons is on the whole colourless; several of them were royalists like Sir Simon Warde and Sir Oliver de Ingham[4]. Immediately after the barons came the mayors of York and Newcastle-on-Tyne. In the list there is a break between the baronial and the official members of the great council. At the head of the officials comes the name of Norwich, then chief baron of the exchequer, followed by those of the chief justices of the two benches, and Staunton, chancellor of the exchequer, and they are followed by chancery clerks like Ayremynne, barons of the exchequer like Beler, justices like Malberthorp, king's serjeants like Geoffrey le Scrope, the king's confessor, and knights of the household like Giles de Beauchamp and John de Sturmy[5]. A comparison of this list with that of the great council, before which the process against Llewelyn, prince of Wales, was recited in 1276, is interesting[6]. The most notable point of difference is the larger number of ecclesiastics, earls and barons which that earlier list contained. This is in part, doubtless, due to the occasion and purpose of the earlier meeting, which was purely feudal. In part, too, it is to be attributed to the fact that the instance which has been taken from the reign of Edward II occurred after the earls and barons had rebelled against the king and after the battle of Boroughbridge and its consequences.

[1] *Cal. Close Rolls*, 1318–23, p. 717. Vide also *Foedera*, vol. II, p. 520; *Parl. Writs*, vol. II, Pt ii, p. 285; *Abbrev. Placit.* p. 342.

[2] Parl. and Council Proc. (Chan.), File 45/13. Vide App. of Doc. no. 94.

[3] *Cal. Close Rolls*, 1318–23, p. 717. *Le Livere de Reis de Brit.* p. 354, states that Beaumont was attached "pur ceo quil ne voleit faire le serment au roi e a sire Hugh Despensers le fiuz destre oues enus a vivere e a morier."

[4] Oliver de Ingham acted as justice of Chester from 1 November, 1322 to 14 November, 1323, and was appointed seneschal of Gascony on 10 March, 1326 (Tout, *The Place of Ed. II*, pp. 380, 396).

[5] Parl. and Council Proc. (Chan.), File 45/13. Vide App. of Doc. no. 94.

[6] *Cal. Close Rolls*, 1272–79, p. 360.

Compared with a parliament of the same period, the difference is not so startling. The parliament has a larger number of ecclesiastics summoned and a larger number of barons[1]. But the council list of 1323 is a record of those who were actually present; and a considerable portion of those summoned to parliament did not attend in person. On the other hand the officials summoned to parliament were more likely to attend, and the list of those summoned is very similar. While the instances of the composition of the great council which have been cited suggest rather a close resemblance to parliament, other meetings of the great council suggest comparison with the "administrative" council. It is, in fact, impossible to decide in many cases which phase of the council is concerned, and the difficulty is complicated by a royal definition of the great council. The earl of Lincoln, acting as king's lieutenant, was ordered to call "nostre grant consail" to consider a roll treating of Gascon affairs, the king proceeding to define those he meant by great council—the chancellor, treasurer, justices, barons of the exchequer and others of the king's council[2].

The functions of the great council may be roughly classified into formal, advisory and judicial. At present only the normal use of these functions will be dealt with; their use under the pressure of baronial opposition will be treated subsequently when the nature and methods of that opposition come to be discussed. Little need be said of the formal functions of the great council, as they are similar to the advisory, since those had no force of execution behind them. On 1 February, 1317, the king, to fulfil a vow he had made when in danger, granted, with the assent of the prelates and magnates of the council, certain property in Oxford to the Carmelite Friars there[3]. The assent of the prelates and magnates on this occasion was purely formal, a fact which is emphasised as the writ was issued by the royal order on the information of William de Montague, steward[4]. The treaty with the Scots on 30 May, 1323, was made by the king's council on the one part and certain Scottish messengers on the other, by the assent of the archbishops, bishops, earls, barons and magnates of the realm[5].

The functions of the advisory council are no less uncertain. The king demanded their counsel and advice. A writ sent to the justiciary, chancellor and treasurer of Ireland in 1316 ordering a

[1] *Parl. Writs*, vol. II, Pt ii, pp. 1–3, 20–21, 136–8.

[2] Anc. Corresp. vol. XLV, no. 149. Vide App. of Doc. no. 123.

[3] *Cal. Pat. Rolls*, 1317–21, p. 75.

[4] Ibid.

[5] *Chron. H. de Blaneford*, p. 134.

meeting of the great council of Ireland, which was based upon that of England, and with which the analogy, if not complete, is reasonable, is instructive. They were "to convoke the archbishops, bishops, abbots, priors, earls, barons and community of Ireland as speedily as possible, and to take their counsel and advice if they can agree, or if not, having asked separately by the king's writ the counsel of the prelates and magnates, if they cannot conveniently assemble, concerning the peace of the land and by what law the people shall be treated, to certify the king of their proceedings so that ordinance may be made by his council concerning the grievances contained in the petition of the people of Ireland before the king and his council[1]." This suggested a limited power. Certain matters relating to Flanders were treated before a council which consisted of the archbishop of Canterbury, the bishop of Norwich and Chichester, the earls of Lancaster, Pembroke and Richmond, Sandale, chancellor, Norwich, treasurer, and certain justices of both benches, Badlesmere and other barons and faithful called to treat on certain matters touching the king and kingdom[2]. In 1316 the king, in his writs ordering military service, stated that it had been agreed, by the counsels of the prelates, earls, barons and other magnates with the king, that the lands and chattels of those who failed to obey the summons should be taken into the king's hands[3]. Proclamation was made in 1317 that the king with the proceres and magnates of the realm and others of his council would cause punishment to be inflicted upon those who had attacked the cardinals within the palatinate of Durham[4]. Writing to the earl of Pembroke in 1316, the king said that he wished Sir Alexander de Abernythy and other Scottish subjects to be before the prelates, earls, and barons of the realm and others of the council at Westminster on 16 June, who were to advise the king how and in what manner he could place best counsel in his Scottish business[5]. A petition of the archbishops, bishops, earls and barons, asking that the prices of food might be fixed, was considered by the great council, who were to ordain a remedy and fix prices. Their decision was couched in the form "il semble au conseil..." and concluded "et si ceste chose soit assentu, soit livere au Chaunceler de maunder par

[1] *Cal. Close Rolls*, 1313–18, pp. 358–9 (8 Aug. 1316).

[2] *Rot. Parl.* vol. I, p. 359. [3] *Cal. Close Rolls*, 1313–18, p. 430 (20 Aug. 1316).

[4] Ibid. p. 568 (20 Sept. 1317).

[5] Anc. Corresp. vol. XLIX, no. 6. These Scottish nobles are found obtaining payments for their expenses "moranti in parliamento pro negociis Regis terram scocie tangentibus per mandatum Regis de priuato sigillo" (Issue Roll, no. 159, m. 4; vide also *Cal. Doc. Scotl.* vol. III, p. 59).

tot le Roiaume a touz Viscontes qil le facent fermement garder en lur baillies[1]." The matter was shown to the king, who assented to it, and accordingly writs were issued to all sheriffs[2]. A great council was held on 26 June, 1325, at Westminster concerning his passage to France to do homage for the duchy of Gascony[3], and on 29 July the constable of Dover was ordered to provide ships as by the counsel of the magnates and proceres of the realm[4] the king intended to cross the sea. The earl of Kent was sent to Gascony in 1325 by the king and the magnates of the land[5]; and it was after the matter had been treated with the magnates of the land that the earl of Chester was sent to France to his mother[6]. Some of these acts may be called administrative rather than advisory, but as no precise distinction is attempted, the latter general term is as suitable as the former.

The judicial activity was greatly concerned with petitions. Petitions were frequently endorsed "Coram Rege et Magno Consilio[7]," or "Coram Magno Consilio[8]." The bishop of St David's asked for licence to alienate lands to the value of £30[9]. The petition came before the king and the great council and he was ordered to come before the chancellor and treasurer and make fine[10], the endorsement also including the statement "Il plest au roi par fyn[11]." A petition which involved an interpretation of the Statute of Gloucester and which came before the great council was not decided there. It was shown to the magnates and then an explanation made[12]. A complaint of the commonalty of England showing the non-observance of the Statute of Lincoln came before the great council, a writ being ordered to the treasurer and barons of the exchequer on the Statute of Lincoln commanding them to enforce it at the suit of those who wished to complain[13].

The great council considered and amended or recalled writs issued from the royal chancery. The matter of a writ of election of a prior was "acorde par Lerceuesqes Leseuesqes Countes e touz les autres du counsail le Roi[14]." In the eighth year of Edward II it was agreed by

[1] *Rot. Parl.* vol. I, p. 295. [2] Ibid. [3] *Ann. Paul.* pp. 308–9.
[4] *Cal. Close Rolls*, 1323–27, p. 496. [5] *Auct. Bridl.* p. 85.
[6] Ibid. [7] *Rot. Parl.* vol. I, p. 420. [8] Ibid. p. 336.
[9] Ancient Petition, n. 2062.
[10] Ibid. dorse: "Veniat coram cancellario et thesaurario faciat finem."
[11] Ibid.
[12] *Rot. Parl.* vol. I, p. 336: "Quia petitio ista non potest finaliter expedire sine explanacione statuti predicti ideo ostendatur coram Majoribus et fiat inde explanatio."
[13] Parl. and Council Proc. (Chan.), File 4/20. Vide App. of Doc. no. 92.
[14] Anc. Corresp. vol. XXXVII, no. 95.

the council that the accustomed writ of escheat should not be changed and that the word "suspensus" should have a place in all cases where anyone suffered death for a felony committed by him, whether he was beheaded or died in any other manner. This agreement was to be entered in the rolls of chancery and before the justices of common bench[1]. In 1315 a number of writs relating to the church of Axminster were considered before the great council. A part of one writ appeared to be prejudicial to ecclesiastical right and liberty. Another seemed to be against ecclesiastical liberty and the accustomed style of the chancery, another was new and not before seen or heard and plainly against ecclesiastical liberty[2]. A writ of prohibition sent to the bishop of Exeter touching the jurisdiction in the church of Bosham, the form of which did not seem to the council to be drawn up according to the usage and custom of the chancery, was recalled after the king had been consulted[3].

When the more active judicial functions of the great council are considered, a new description is found applied to it at times—"the council in parliament." A petition was presented by a rector about frauds committed by a pretended king's minister. A day was given him "coram domino Rege et consilio ad parliamentum apud Westmonasterium[4]." The rolls of Parliament frequently contain *placita coram Magno Consilio in parliamento*[5], or *responsiones facte coram Rege et Magno Consilio in parliamento*[6]. "The council in parliament," the body which considered these judicial matters, was composed, at the time of Edward II, of the prelates and barons, with a considerable number of justices. Gradually the independent functions of the justices were absorbed by the prelates and lords; and ultimately the "council in parliament" meant nothing less than the house of lords[7]. The great council also heard such judicial matters as the examination of the bishop of Hereford for treason[8], "coram Rege et cunctis regni proceribus," though the intervention of the ecclesiastical authority prevented their proceeding[9]. Some of the wider judicial power of the great council arose out of petitions. A petition to the king and

[1] *Rot. Parl.* vol. I, p. 293: "Concordatum est per concilium."

[2] Parl. and Council Proc. (Exch.), File 2/4: "Et videtur quod ista brevia sint noua et prius non visa nec audita et manifeste contra ecclesiastica libertate."

[3] *Rot. Parl.* vol. I, p. 297.

[4] Parl. and Council Proc. (Chan.), File 45/15. Vide also *Cal. Inq. P. M.* vol. v, p. 225.

[5] *Rot. Parl.* vol. I, pp. 287, 288.

[6] Ibid. pp. 289, 294.

[7] Baldwin, *King's Council*, p. 318.

[8] *Chron. H. de Blaneford*, pp. 140–1.

[9] *Chron. Murimuth*, pp. 42–43. *Chron. G. le Baker*, p. 16.

council asking that a woman might be put to take her action at common law, was referred to the great council, "because the petition intends to exclude the said Joan from her petition of dower, the whole process must come before the great council[1]."

Though apart from the king the great council had not much authority in normal times, it was important that it also should be and remain a working part of the personal system, and that the king's personal influence over it should be the decisive factor. If any body had remained or was successful in working itself outside the influences of that system there would be an immediate tendency, and soon a conscious endeavour, to extend and develop that independence and the functions of that body. The great council did not, however, obtain that independence. The king could in the first place, determine largely the composition of that body. "The peers gained a *right* to be summoned to parliaments, but no such right was acknowledged in regard to councils. That the king was free to summon 'whom he wills' to his councils was a statement of general acceptation[2]." This power of selecting who should be called was a valuable asset to the king, and was one which he could still further increase in value by the influence which he could exercise on the individual members thus summoned. A considerable portion of the great council during the reign of Edward II was composed of justices and officials of the administrative departments. The king could easily make his influence felt upon them by either personal or administrative means. Moreover, they would almost inevitably take the royal side in a struggle with the barons, either in the great council or in parliament. Those officials of the household and chamber were bound still more closely to the king though their numerical inferiority left the decisive power in the hands of the official class. Even over the prelates and barons the king's influence was considerable. A fair proportion of the bishops were old royal officials, and this would influence their judgments and opinions unconsciously. The extent to which the king could rely upon the support of the bishops is well illustrated in the attitude of the provincial council of 1322, which gave the opinion that the exile of the Despensers was not according to law[3]. To those bishops not present the king wrote asking their opinion[4]. Drokensford, bishop of Bath and Wells, who had held the keepership of the wardrobe and other offices, replied expressly approving the answer the council had given, and adhering to the protest the bishops had

[1] *Cal. Inq. P. M.* vol. VI, p. 456.
[2] Baldwin, *King's Council*, p. 106.
[3] *Cal. Close Rolls*, 1318–23, pp. 510–511.
[4] Ibid.

made in parliament against the exile of the Despensers[1]. Walter de Stapleton, bishop of Exeter, who had already held the office of treasurer for a short period, and was soon again to be re-appointed[2] was not so ready to acquiesce. His constitutional principles urged that as the exile was made in parliament it would be safer if the revocation was also made there, rather than elsewhere[3]. This did not satisfy the king, and a writ of privy seal was sent to the bishop ordering another answer which was to be more specific[4]. To this the bishop sent a reply in which he reiterated his principle that the final revocation, although the parliament that exiled them did so without the consent and presence of the prelates, would be more honourably, usefully and safely done in parliament than elsewhere[5]. The fact that the exile had been made unjustly and in error was no reason why its revocation should bear the same taint[6]. Independence of view of this nature in a bishop would not ultimately result in weakness to the royal cause. Less than three months after his second letter was written the bishop was re-appointed treasurer, and for the remainder of the reign was one of the dominant personalities. Influence on the barons summoned was not so easy to exercise; yet even in the stress of the opposition which Gavaston produced on every hand, the king was able by the exercise of his private influence to render the barons amenable to his will.

Even without this influence upon the composition and personnel of the great council, there was one means at once complete and final, by which the king could in normal times exercise an iron control over the activities of the great council. They could deliberate, advise, ordain and decide as much as they wished, but it would all come to naught. The execution of all their decisions had to be made through the administrative departments of the chancery and the exchequer, and over these the king's control was entire. As long as the king had control of the executive it was difficult to make him concede a point anywhere; and a point when conceded was valueless. Once loosen his grasp on the executive, and the baronial opposition would rush in

[1] *Regist. J. de Drokensford*, 1309-1329, p. 200. [2] Vide below, p. 529.

[3] *Regist. W. de Stapleton*, 1307–1326, pp. 441–2. Vide also Wilkins, *Concilia*, vol. II, pp. 509–510.

[4] *Regist. W. de Stapleton*, 1307–1326, pp. 442–3.

[5] Ibid. pp. 443–4: "quod finalis revocacio consideracionis predicte, que tempore Parliamenti licet absque consensu et presencia Prelatorum facta extitit, honorificencius, utilius, et securius in Parliamento fieri poterit quam alibi."

[6] Ibid.: "Consideracio predicta per injusticiam facta fuerit in errorem, non tamen videtur expediens quod injusticia seu error aliquis interveniat in revocacione ipsius quomodolibet facienda."

and take possession in all directions. The king's control of the executive depended in part upon the household system, hence that was the objective of baronial attacks. The king could prevent the execution of an endorsement of a petition made before the great council by prohibiting the chancellor to issue a writ to that effect or by forbidding the treasurer to act as instructed. Had he so desired his executive power could at two stages have prevented the endorsement of the petition concerning sheriffs[1] from taking effect. The chancellor might have been forbidden to issue the writ to the treasurer and barons, or the treasurer and barons might have been ordered not to obey the writ sent to them from chancery. Writs under the great seal were seldom issued "by the council[2]" though on frequent occasions they are issued "by the king and council[3]." A writ was issued in 1315 "by king and council" which illustrates the executive power. The king had ordered Brabazon and the other justices of the king's bench to do nothing until parliament met concerning the ancient fines pending in discussion before them. In the parliament held at Westminster in that year, it was agreed that execution should be made of fines levied before and after the late issue of the Statute of Fines, and the justices were by this writ ordered to proceed[4]. Even if the council succeeded in getting writs issued from the chancery, the whole system of privy seal, verbal order and other methods remained to the king to frustrate them. In the relation of the "administrative" to the great council the king found another instrument of effect[5].

The functions of parliament at the beginning of the fourteenth century were as varied as those of any department of the adminis-

[1] Vide above, p. 295.

[2] It is difficult to determine when the council is really the manifestation which has been called above the "administrative" council and when it is the great council. In the *Rot. Scot.* passim, for instance, there are a considerable number of protections "per consilium." These should refer to the "administrative" council. On the other hand, in March, 1318, several writs were issued "per consilium" (*Rot. Scot.* pp. 179–181; for Oct. 1318, vide p. 188). This might refer again to the "administrative" council or the great council, as in 1318 the power of the king was not altogether normal (vide below, pp. 448–459). Writs were sometimes issued "by petition of the great council" (*Cal. Close Rolls*, 1313–18, p. 184, June, 1315).

[3] E.g. *Rot. Scot.* p. 165, 6 Oct. 1316: "per ipsum Regem et consilium nunciante Magistro Thoma de Charleton"; to some extent the difficulty mentioned in the revious note is visible here also. The king generally allowed the "administrative" council to consider questions without his presence, while he was frequently present at the great council.

[4] *Cal. Close Rolls*, 1313–18, p. 173 (1 May, 1315).

[5] Vide below, pp. 304–7.

tration. In the parliaments of this time Professor Maitland saw the whole governmental force of England brought into a focus and the actions of the different administrative bodies brought under review[1]. Besides the supervision of administration, a considerable part of the business was "judicial[2]." More important than its law-making was its declaring of the law[3]. The justices were ordered to hasten the more weighty matters before them, so that they could be at the king's parliament[4], though no indication of any "judicial" function at the parliament was conveyed in the writ of summons[5].

Parliament obtained its opportunity to declare the law through petitions; the most important of which were referred to it. A petition relating to the attaint of jurors of assizes seemed to the council to require greater deliberation and that in full parliament[6]. Another petition the council sent to the justice of Wales who was to inspect it, inform himself of its contents and of all circumstances touching it and to certify the king in the next parliament[7]. Langton wished that a petition complaining that he had been summoned to judgment "contre forme de la ley de la terre e en contre les poyntz de la grant Chartre," should be read before the prelates, earls and barons in full parliament[8]. In the same way parliament would interfere in the course of proceedings in the lower courts. On complaint, parliament ordered the record to be produced and itself settled the case, or ordered the lower court how it should be settled. This was especially done when the king's interests were affected[9]. In 1324, Staunton and his fellow justices of king's bench were ordered "to attermine until the next parliament at Westminster all matters touching the king against Master John de Stratford pending before them, giving day to be there then to do and receive what shall be considered in the premises in the said parliament[10]." A plea concerning the advowson of a church was adjourned to the next parliament[11]; and claims of various persons to be heirs of a tenant-in-chief

[1] *Mem. de Parl.* 1305, ed. Maitland, pp. lxxi–lxxii.

[2] C. H. McIlwain, *The High Court of Parliament and its Supremacy*, pp. 25, 109–116.

[3] Ibid. pp. 109–110.

[4] *Cal. Close Rolls*, 1313–18, p. 320.

[5] *Parl. Writs*, vol. II, Pt ii, pp. 153–4.

[6] Cole, *Doc. illustr. Eng. Hist. in 13th and 14th Cent.* p. 26: "Videtur consilio quod...requiritur inde maxima deliberacio et hoc in pleno parliamento."

[7] Ancient Petition, no. 3813.

[8] Cole, *Doc. illustr. Eng. Hist. in 13th and 14th Cent.* pp. 4–5.

[9] Holdsworth, *Hist. Engl. Law*, vol. I, p. 182.

[10] *Cal. Close Rolls*, 1323–27, p. 154 (15 Jan. 1324).

[11] Wm Salt Soc., *Coll.* vol. VI, Pt i, p. 243.

who had died were likewise to be decided in parliament[1]. A *quo warranto* case between the king and Badlesmere was, by king's writ to the itinerant justices, summoned to parliament, a day being given Badlesmere in the next parliament[2]. A request for an inquisition *ad quod damnum* which should be before the king in his next parliament was made to the bishop of Worcester, chancellor, by one who held of the king a certain serjeanty in fee in Somerset, and who wished to demise it to his relative for life[3].

There were various miscellaneous functions which arose out of the petitions and "judicial" work of parliament. A commission was appointed in parliament to hear and determine all complaints against John de Segrave and his ministers by reason of his custody of the forest beyond Trent[4]. By common assent of parliament William Inge, John de Freshingfeld, William de Dene and John de Wyston were assigned justices to hear and determine various complaints on conspiracies and other trespasses committed in Norfolk and Suffolk[5]. The king nominated the bishop of Norwich, his chancellor, in full parliament[6]. In a parliament held at Westminster in 1324, the barons of the realm having treated for the use of the kingdom, and especially for the salvation of the duchy of Aquitaine, the bishops of Winchester and Norwich and the earl of Richmond were chosen as solemn messengers to be sent for the making of peace between France and England[7].

The petitions which were presented to parliament produced "legislative" as well as "judicial" results. The Articles of the Clergy of 1316 were the result of petitions[8]. This "legislation" was not always formal, but was contained in the reply to a petition in some such form as "accorde est et assentu par Erceuesqes, Evesqes, Abbes, Priours, Contes, et Barons et autres du Roialme, en le Parlement nostre Seigneur le Roi[9]." A petition presented by the king's liegemen relating to the Charter of the Forests was granted in parliament at Westminster in 1325 with the assent of the prelates, earls, barons and others then in that parliament[10].

The king's influence on parliament could not be exercised in the

[1] *Cal. Inq. P. M.* vol. V, p. 311.
[2] Chan. Misc., Bdle 64/3 (78).
[3] Anc. Corresp. vol. XXXV, no. 118.
[4] *Rot. Parl.* vol. I, p. 325.
[5] Anc. Corresp. vol. XLV, no. 187.
[6] *Cal. Close Rolls*, 1318–23, pp. 219–220.
[7] *Chron. H. de Blaneford*, p. 152.
[8] *Stat. of Realm*, vol. I, pp. 171–4.
[9] *Rot. Parl.* vol. I, p. 298. This is the opening of an agreement that no fines should be demanded or taken from freemen for entering lands and tenements which were of their fee.
[10] *Cal. Close Rolls*, 1323–27, pp. 539–540.

same manner as upon the great council and the administrative departments. In the first place he did not have the same control over its composition, and its numbers were so considerable that it was difficult to influence sufficient of the individual members. Inasmuch, however, as the composition was not fixed there was still some room for royal intervention. This took the form of increasing the number of justices and clerks summoned, and though not altogether effective it was a useful expedient. In the parliament of Northampton in 1307, the justices and clerks summoned numbered thirty[1], a number which was fairly constant during the reign. Even the composition was subject to alteration, as the abbot of St James without Northampton was in 1319 discharged from attendance in parliament by proceedings in chancery[2]. Moreover the king could and did bring his personal influence to bear even on the barons[3].

In the selection of those committees in parliament which were to answer petitions, the king could exercise his influence. In the Westminster parliament of 1320, the king--the archbishop of Canterbury, the bishop of Norwich, chancellor, the bishop of Exeter, treasurer, the bishops of London, Ely, and Coventry and Lichfield, the earl of Pembroke and Edmund de Woodstock, the king's brother, and certain other magnates and barons of the realm sitting with him—ordained concerning the method of receiving and hastening petitions in that parliament[4]. In the presence of the prelates and magnates and others, the king ordained and ordered that Adam de Lymbergh[5] and William de Herlaston[6] should be the receivers of all petitions of England and Wales in that parliament[7]. The appointment of the receivers of the petitions from Gascony, Ireland and the Isles was made by the king; Master Edmund de London and Master Henry de Canterbury, being chosen[8]. It was of value to the king that the appointment of these officials should rest in his hand. It was still more important that he should have a decisive part in the appointment of the auditors of the petitions. In the same parliament the appointment of the bishops of London, Coventry and Lichfield and

[1] *Cal. Close Rolls*, 1307–13, p. 41. *Parl. Writs*, vol. II, Pt ii, pp. 2–3.

[2] Selden, *Titles of Honour* [1672], pp. 614–616. *Parl. Writs*, vol. II, Pt i, p. 223.

[3] Cf. *Chron. Lanerc.* p. 188.

[4] *Rot. Parl.* vol. I, p. 365.

[5] Adam de Lymbergh was king's remembrancer from 1311 to 1322, in which latter year he was appointed constable of Bordeaux (Tout, *The Place of Ed. II*, pp. 348, 397).

[6] William de Herlaston was a clerk of the chancery, and acted as keeper of the great seal and also as keeper of the privy seal, 1325–6 (Tout, *The Place of Ed. II*, pp. 327, 357).

[7] *Rot. Parl.* vol. I, p. 365.

[8] Ibid.

Chichester, the abbot of St Alban's, John de Somery[1], Richard de Grey, William Herle, John de Stonore, Robert de Bardelby, Master Henry de Clif and Geoffrey le Scrope to be auditors of petitions for England and Wales, was made by the king[2]. This committee was to all intents and purposes a meeting of the "administrative" council. Some of the bishops had been royal officials; the barons were unimportant, and there were the justices, chancery clerks, and king's serjeant to make the composition complete. The auditors of the petitions of Gascony and Ireland were to be the bishops of Bath and Wells, Worcester and Hereford, the abbot of Ramsay, Hugh de Courtney[3], William Martin[4], Guy Ferre[5], Walter de Friskeney, Master Jordan Moraunt, Master Richard de Burton and Gilbert de Toudeby[6], another committee of official bishops, barons, not over factious, a justice, clerks and a king's serjeant. The king's ability to retain the appointment of these auditors even in 1320 is important, for the auditors not only heard but sometimes endorsed the petitions with a formula opening "videtur auditoribus peticionum quod[7]." Those appointed were mainly tried officials and barons connected with the household[8]. William de Ayremynne, keeper of the rolls of chancery, also acted as clerk of parliament; and letters from boroughs appointing their representatives to parliament were addressed to him[9]. Petitions of Henry de Lancaster in the parliament of York in 1319 were handed to William de Ayremynne to make search in the rolls of chancery on the matters contained therein[10].

There are a few references to attempts of the king to interfere with the deliberation of parliament. The king was said to have held a *secretum parliamentum* at York in October, 1309, to which the earls of Lancaster, Lincoln, Warwick, Oxford and Arundel refused to go

[1] John de Somery was a member of the standing council of 1318. Vide below, p. 451.

[2] *Rot. Parl.* vol. I, p. 365.

[3] Hugh de Courtney was an ordainer and a member of the standing council of 1318. Vide below, pp. 361, 448.

[4] He was an ordainer and a member of the council of 1318. Vide below, pp. 361, 451.

[5] As early as 1298 he was "staying continually in the company of the king's son" (*Cal. Close Rolls*, 1288–96, p. 502). In 1314 with other representatives he had been charged with ordering the king's affairs in Gascony, and before that had acted as seneschal in Gascony (Tout, *The Place of Ed. II*, p. 394).

[6] *Rot. Parl.* vol. I, p. 265.

[7] Ibid. vol. I, p. 291.

[8] Compare the barons who acted thus with those who were bannerets of the household. Vide above, pp. 220–1.

[9] *Parl. Writs*, vol. II, Pt ii, p. 252.

[10] Cole, *Doc. illustr. Eng. Hist. in 13th and 14th Cent.* p. 54.

on account of Gavaston[1]. In January, 1320, the king had summoned his barons to York to treat of the state of his kingdom. The earl of Lancaster though urgently summoned did not come, his excuse being—"non enim decebat habere parliamentum in cameris ut dixit[2]."

Though the power of parliament was increasing the king still retained his control in a safe manner. The citizens of London were beginning to look to parliament for a remedy for the king's contravention of their charters and liberties, the matter of tallage in 1313–14[3] being an instance, and in the parliament of Lincoln the mayor and sheriffs of London appealed from the terms of the king's writ appointing the alnager of cloth, as the form of the writ was different from previous ones, and was held to be prejudicial to the liberties of the city, the chancellor and treasurer having refused redress[4]. As long as the king retained the control of the executive machinery, by means of which the stàtutes and decisions of parliament and its endorsements of petitions would have to be put into operation, such an increased power was apparent, not real. It was agreed at the parliament of York in 1318 by the king, prelates, earls and barons that the burgesses of Newcastle-on-Tyne, for the injuries they had suffered, should be pardoned their farm for two years "et ensint fait la commaundement au Chanceller depar le Roi qe il les feust de ce auer bref du grant seal etcetera[5]." This agreement only had force after a writ under great seal had been issued, and during the reign a few writs were issued "by king and parliament[6]."

Finally the relations between the great council and parliament on the one hand and the "administrative" council on the other must be considered. On occasion it is difficult to distinguish between what was done by the great council and what was done by the "administrative" council, but in the following instances the distinction is clear. The "administrative" council sometimes referred matters to the consideration of the great council. In the seventeenth year of Edward II the council gave its opinion on certain articles relating to Gascony. In the ninth article it was advised that a matter should be done but that it should be shown to the king and his great council, and that the king by his great council should say his will on that matter[7]. The treasurer, barons, justices and other of the council in

[1] *Chron. Hemingburgh*, vol. II, p. 275.
[2] *Auct. Malm.* p. 250.
[3] *Cal. Letter Books, D*, pp. 305–6.
[4] Ibid. *E*, pp. 58–59.
[5] Cole, *Doc. illustr. Eng. Hist. in 13th and 14th Cent.* pp. 7–8.
[6] *Cal. Pat. Rolls*, 1321–24, p. 409.
[7] Chan. Misc., Bdle 25/2 (11): "Item a ix article il est auis qil fait a fere mes

the exchequer, who were considering the state of the House of St Catherine without the Tower of London, advised the king that a final decision of the matter should be secured "per magnatos de consilio Regis in presencia consilij domine Isabelle Regine[1]" and subsequently when the king referred the matter back to them they advised "habeat auisamentum per prelatos et magnatos[2]." This reference of matters to parliament or the great council as to a superior tribunal must not be supposed to involve any interference on the part of those bodies with the "administrative" council. The "administrative" council owned no inferiority. On the contrary it interfered with the business of the great council and of parliament at two stages, in preliminary negotiation and in execution.

The business which was to come before parliament was frequently treated first of all in a meeting of the council. The king informed the earl of Lincoln on 4 November, 1309, that a great parliament was shortly to be summoned at York to treat of the affairs of Scotland and various other matters, according to the advice the king had received from him and others of the council. The earl was ordered to call the treasurer and others of the council whom he wished, to advise in what manner the king could carry through this parliament. He was to advise the king of the results of the deliberation without delay[3]. On 28 August, 1313, the earl of Pembroke was summoned to a preliminary meeting of the king's privy council before parliament, "sur les besoignes qe se deuerent treter et faire a meisme nostre parlement[4]." In the disturbances between the constable and borough of Bristol[5], Badlesmere, constable of the castle and keeper of the town and barton, was ordered not to meddle with the custody of the town and barton as the king had committed it to the mayor, bailiffs and commonalty, upon hearing that they were oppressed by the constable. In the next parliament the king would ordain as seemed best to him concerning such acts of oppression and the custody of the town. The

soyt ceste chose mostre au Roy et a son graund counsail et que le Roy par cel counsail dit sour ceo sa volunte."

[1] K. R. Mem. Roll, no. 91, Rec. Trin. mm. 3, 3 a. L. T. R. Mem. Roll, no. 88, Rec. Trin. mm. 2 a, 3.

[2] L. T. R. Mem. Roll, no. 88, Rec. Trin. m. 3 a.

[3] K. R. Mem. Roll, no. 83, m. 10 d. Vide App. of Doc. no. 7.

[4] Anc. Corresp. vol. XLIX, no. 23. Vide App. of Doc. no. 125.

[5] A short account of these disturbances is found in H. Hall, *Custom Revenues*, vol. II, pp. 12–15. The close and patent rolls contain very frequent references to them. There are references in various other sources, including the treaty made by the earl of Warwick and John de Sandale in Ancient Correspondence, vol. XXXV, nos. 135, 135 A.

writ was issued "by king and council," a fact which is significant in consideration of the remedy which was to be provided in the next parliament[1]. In 1325 the treasurer was ordered to call the council about the ordinance which had been made concerning the levy of scutages, in such a way "qe nous puissoms sur ce prendre auisement et assent si mestre soit des grantz de nostre terre auant lour departir de nostre parlement[2]." These preliminary meetings of the privy or "administrative" council before the meeting of parliament, and this preliminary discussion would result in a strengthening of the king's position and influence. For, when parliament met, the king and his friends and advisers would have a definite and concerted policy upon which to proceed, and a unity of purpose which would go far.

The "administrative" council also acted in capacities which might be called executive to the great council. In 1324 the chancellor was ordered to summon Henry le Scrope and William de Bereford, the heads respectively of king's bench and common pleas, and others of the council to put in suitable form the process formerly made before the king and his council at Bishopsthorp against Henry de Beaumont[3]. On 27 July, 1322, the bishop of Norwich, chancellor, was ordered to call justices of both benches for advice on a certain process to be made against the fugitives at the Roman court as was ordained "par comun conseil," and also that the things which were ordained and accorded at the king's last parliament should be put in statute form[4]. The earl of Gloucester, as keeper of the realm with the chancellor and treasurer, was ordered to summon the council to consider and treat on certain matters concerned with France, which had been treated at London, so that the matters should be in good state for hasty termination when the king came to London[5]. The council in the exchequer was similarly used. A petition of the city of London was referred from parliament:

> coram Cancellario, Thesaurario et Baronibus de Scaccario ut illi vocatis ad eos justiciariis de utroque Banco et aliis de concilio Regis[6].

A record upon the exchequer rolls concerning a gathering of merchants made for the purpose of lending money to the king, illustrates the same point. The king by the assent of the prelates, earls, barons and

[1] *Cal. Pat. Rolls*, 1307–13, p. 485 (12 Aug. 1312).
[2] K. R. Mem. Roll, no. 99, m. 64.
[3] Chan. Warr., File 123/6542. Vide App. of Doc. no. 77.
[4] Chan. Warr., File 119/6121. [5] Ibid. File 79/2138.
[6] Cole, *Doc. illustr. Eng. Hist. in 13th and 14th Cent.* p. 31.

other faithful of his kingdom was to set out for Scotland in 1319, on which matter a treaty was had with the king's council at the exchequer. It was agreed by the council that the foreign merchants staying in the city of London should be gathered together. In the presence of the sheriff of London they came before the treasurer and others of the king's council at the Friars Preachers. The treasurer was to go to the king's parliament at York to certify the king of the answers of the merchants[1].

The relation of the "administrative" council to the great council and parliament was advantageous to the king. In the discussions of that smaller body which sometimes preceded the meeting of the formal assemblies, and in the completion and execution of the decisions of those assemblies, opportunity was given to the king to exercise his influence and the "administrative" council was largely, in one phase, a household body.

The baronial opposition could not have been interpreted fully until the household offices and their influences on the administration had been stated. It was necessary that the administrative departments, the executive body of the government, and the formal assemblies should be considered. The discussion of the whole of the administrative machinery in the relation of the various parts to each other was important. It was especially important that the relations between the administration and the household should be considered from the side of the administration. That task has now been completed, and the chancery and exchequer, the various phases of the "ministerial" council, the great council and parliament have been seen in various characteristic phases of their work.

The influence which the personal or household system was able to exercise over the great administrative departments and the council and parliament was considerable. This was due, to some extent, to the origin of those institutions in the *curia regis*. The decisive factor in that influence was the strength of the household system. That strength did not depend so much upon the king's prerogative as upon his executive power. The centre of the whole system was the king as the final executive authority; as the source from which a certain amount of executive power was delegated to the various administrative departments and the other bodies, the source always maintaining its position as the ultimate power. The strength of the household system was in part itself maintained by the influence which it was

[1] K. R. Mem. Roll, no. 92, Rec. Pasch. m. 3. L. T. R. Mem. Roll, no. 89, m. 28 d.

able to exert upon those institutions which it had itself created. By that influence it prevented them from erecting themselves as superior to their origin, and hence gave itself a new lease of life. A considerable factor in the maintenance of the strength of the household system was the conservatism of official custom and usage. The administrative departments formalised their processes, which became formalised at a time when baronial opposition was still feudal in essence. The result was that when the barons came into opposition with the household they found themselves in conflict, not with the strength and resources of that system alone, but with the officialdom and usage of the administrative departments. More important perhaps than this conservatism was the way in which the king was constantly able to add supports to his system from beneath. As his control in one direction became diminished, he compensated himself by a new device. As the use of one instrument became formalised another more personal grew into use. This capacity, by which new safeguards gradually grew up under the old, was of the greatest value and provides one of the most interesting studies in medieval administrative history.

CHAPTER XIII

THE WEAKNESS OF THE HOUSEHOLD SYSTEM

The strength of the household system was almost overwhelming, and its influence over the administration well-nigh complete. The strength was so apparent that its defects escaped notice. There were, however, inherent in the household system a number of weaknesses. Though these weaknesses do not to any degree counterbalance its great strength, they did act as contributory causes to such success as the baronial opposition achieved.

The first causes of weakness may be described generally as personal. It has been suggested[1] that the causes which precipitated the crisis under Edward II were in part personal. In the household system the king was no mere figurehead; he was the centre whence radiated all the functions of government. His was the brain that had to conceive a plan; and his was the arm that was to execute it. The system was likely to run with perfect smoothness as long as the hand behind it was strong, and the mind which controlled it was powerful. Unfortunately an hereditary monarchy cannot provide a continuous succession of men of above the average ability; and to rule the household system more than average ability was required. In all systems of government the personal factor is important; in the household system the personal factor was supreme. The system was becoming increasingly organised, but there was still a good deal of an indefinite character about it. This rendered its efficiency all the more dependent upon the king. The extent to which the household system of government was dependent upon one person was a potential source of considerable weakness, a source of weakness which realised itself in the reign of Edward II.

The human element also entered into the household system of government as a source of weakness, in the officials employed. The smooth running of the machinery depended upon the instruments of the system. The appointments of officials depended in the first instance upon the character and ability of the king and in the second

[1] Vide above, pp. 72–73.

upon the character and ability of the officials appointed. A bad king, or a good king who was a bad judge of character and ability, would be likely to appoint officials who were incapable if not utterly bad. Even a king who was himself a good administrator might fail to surround himself with suitable men. Good officials might degenerate, but as long as they retained the confidence or favour of the king they would retain their offices.

While it is true that the king's court was a training ground of administrators and was generally most efficiently worked, the human element had too great a place in the success of that work. A system which in one generation might be a complete success owing to able and trustworthy officials might in the next be an utter failure for no other reason than that it was badly worked by incapable or colourless officials. The household system was too dependent upon the personal capacity of the officials, and was liable to gross abuse. The offices could be exploited for selfish ends by the officials themselves or by persons who nominated them. The officials were so dependent upon the king that they might be forced to actions which were opposed to the interests of the country and of the household system itself. Incapacity might often lead to grosser abuse than actual conscious misdeeds.

Incapable and bad as the officials might be there was no means of removing them without the king's will. They were responsible to no authority but the king, and as long as his interests were protected and his policy was pursued there was little danger that they would be removed from their posts. The position practically amounted to this. All those potential sources of weakness might also be sources of the utmost strength. In an established system controlling such important matters, the supreme and ultimate causes of success and failure should not depend upon the human element. It was difficult to provide for times of weakness, since in times of strength the potentialities towards weakness were not visible. When the times of weakness came they were all the more startling in contrast and dangerous in result. It was not that the results were internally dangerous to the household system, but rather that the victims of the abuse were irritated and at times excited to acts of rebellion. The system of government which the barons desired to see established was aided in its progress by the opportunities which the king's character provided, and herein lies the importance of the personal causes of the weakness of the household system.

Another cause of weakness was one which was present always, but which was more apparent and likely to prove dangerous when the king was incapable. This weakness arose from divided control—a relic of the period before the full development of the personal system and a result of feudal government. The barons appointed a number of the officers of the administration. The right of appointment, however, if valuable was not decisive and it was not so widespread as to interfere appreciably with the royal control of administration. In the first place a number of sheriffdoms were held in fee. Earls appointed sheriffs of certain counties. The earl of Lancaster appointed the sheriff of Lancaster, notifying the treasurer and barons of the exchequer by letter of the appointment. The person so named was admitted for the present by favour of the court, on condition that the earl came to present, as others, in his own person[1]. The earl of Warwick, who held the office of sheriff of Worcester, including the amercements and profits of the county[2], went to the exchequer and before the treasurer and barons presented his nominee to that office[3]. According to one chronicle, it was acting on the king's writ to all the sheriffs of England ordering them to take exiled Gavaston wherever he could be found in England, an order which had not been revoked, that he took Gavaston and put him to death[4]. Margaret, countess of Cornwall, had the sheriffdom of Rutland for life[5], holding it in dower and presenting the sheriff at the exchequer[6]. Later in the reign, Edmund, earl of Kent, the king's brother, was sheriff in fee of Rutland; and the person appointed by him was duly admitted[7]. The office of sheriff in the county of Westmorland belonged in fee to Robert de Clifford[8], and he duly presented his nominee, who was admitted[9], and in like manner did his son Roger after his death[10]. Edward II by his gift granted the sheriffdom of Cornwall to queen Isabella for the term of her life. She duly signified to Norwich, baron of the exchequer, that she had appointed a sheriff, and he was admitted[11].

[1] K. R. Mem. Roll, no. 88, m. 182 d. L. T. R. Mem. Roll, no. 85, Pres. Trin. m. 5 d: "admissus est ad presens de gratia curie Ita tamen quod dictus comes cum aliis presentare voluerit veniat in propria persona sua etcetera." Vide also K. R. Mem. Rolls, no. 90, m. 139 d; no. 94, m. 125; L. T. R. Mem. Rolls, no. 87, Pres. Trin. m. 1; no. 91, Pres. Mich. m. 24; no. 78, m. 29.

[2] *Cal. Inq. P. M.* vol. V, p. 410. [3] K. R. Mem. Roll, no. 84, m. 72 d.

[4] *Chron. Mon. de Melsa*, vol. II, p. 328.

[5] K. R. Mem. Roll, no. 84, m. 72 d. [6] L. T. R. Mem. Roll, no. 78, m. 45.

[7] K. R. Mem. Roll, no. 97, Mich. Pres. m. 3. L. T. R. Mem. Roll, no. 94, Mich. Pres. m. 2.

[8] L. T. R. Mem. Roll, no. 79, m. 40 d. [9] Ibid. m. 46 d.

[10] K. R. Mem. Roll, no. 94, m. 124. L. T. R. Mem. Roll, no. 91, Pres. Mich. m. 1 d.

[11] K. R. Mem. Rolls, no. 96, m. 102; no. 97, Hill. Pres. m. 5. L. T. R. Mem. Rolls, no. 93, m. 45 d; no. 94, Hill. Pres. m. 2.

The results of the divided control in the appointment of sheriffs were not serious to the king. When a sheriff of Worcester was convicted of conspiracy in the county of Salop, a writ under the exchequer seal was sent to the earl of Warwick ordering him to remove the sheriff, and he appointed another in his place[1]. On death without heirs or upon escheat the sheriffdom reverted to the king's hands. On the death of the earl of Warwick, his heirs being under age, the king appointed the sheriff of Worcester[2].

Other local appointments were held by magnates. They appointed the bailiffs of hundreds held by them. Magnates held in this way almost all the hundreds of Devon as their liberties[3]. The administration by those officials appointed by the baronage was not as efficient or popular as royal administration, and complaints were frequent. The community and sheriff of Devon complained that the bailiffs placed by the magnates in the hundreds of that county were insufficient, and the sheriff could not answer for the money which those bailiffs levied within their liberties[4].

A number of offices in the central administration were held in fee. The marshal of England appointed the marshal of the court of king's bench[5]. Nicholas de Segrave, whom the king had appointed marshal of England, appointed the marshal of the exchequer[6], though he did not hold the office in fee. Thomas de Brotherton, earl of Norfolk, the king's brother, afterwards held the office of marshal in fee, and before the treasurer and barons at the exchequer presented one to perform his office in the exchequer[7]. When Nicholas de Segrave was marshal the king succeeded in inducing him to appoint Richard de Luda, whom the king had on several occasions unsuccessfully asked the treasurer and barons to provide with a suitable office[8], as deputy at the exchequer, and he was admitted on 15 January, 1313[9]. Earlier the marshal of the exchequer died when Segrave was in Scotland and accordingly the office was taken into the king's hand until his return, the treasurer and barons on the king's behalf deputing a clerk to that office[10]

A more important administrative officer than the marshal—the

[1] L. T. R. Mem. Roll, no. 79, m. 63.

[2] K. R. Mem. Roll, no. 89, m. 94 d. L. T. R. Mem. Roll, no. 86, m. 53 d.

[3] *Rot. Parl.* vol. I, p. 381.

[4] Ibid.

[5] *Cal. Close Rolls*, 1323–27, pp. 44–46.

[6] Madox, *Hist. of Exch.* vol. II, p. 287.

[7] K. R. Mem. Roll, no. 89, m. 99. L. T. R. Mem. Roll, no. 86, n. 91. Vide Madox, *Hist. of Exch.* vol. II, p. 287.

[8] Vide above, p. 139.

[9] K. R. Mem. Roll, no. 86, m. 75.

[10] Ibid. no. 84, m. 52.

chamberlain—was appointed by a baron. Originally the two chamberlains of the exchequer had been magnates, who held the office in fee, appointing deputies to discharge their duties. One of these chamberlainships had lapsed to the crown in 1293[1]. The other chamberlainship was still hereditary. The office was associated with the tenure of certain estates[2]. The earl of Warwick, who held the office of chamberlain[3], by letter to the exchequer required his nominee to be received. He was admitted and took the oath to conceal the secrets of the king[4]. He was admitted provided the earl came thereafter in person to present his chamberlain[5]. Subsequently when another chamberlain came to be appointed the earl presented him at the exchequer[6]. Though the normal appointment lay outside the influence of the crown opportunities were frequently given the king to appoint. Thus in 1315 after the death of the earl this chamberlain of the receipt was appointed by the king[7]. If the clerk appointed by the earl committed a trespass in the exchequer the office was taken into the king's hand. In 1278 it was restored to the earl, the king having remitted the trespass, provided that he appointed a suitable clerk to execute the office in his place[8].

The appointment to the office of constable of the exchequer was made by the earl of Hereford, who wrote to the treasurer and the barons signifying his appointment[9]. An usher of the receipt of the exchequer was appointed by the earl of Warwick[10]. John Dymmok, an usher of the exchequer, who held the office of John de Dagworth, an usher of the exchequer in fee[11], sought that his son should perform the office as often as he was absent[12]. Subsequently, as he had absented himself without licence, the office was taken into the king's hand—but afterwards restored[13]. A purparty of another serjeanty of the

[1] Tout, *The Place of Ed. II*, p. 349.

[2] J. H. Round, *The Commune of London* [1899], pp. 82–84.

[3] K. R. Mem. Roll, no. 81, m. 43 d. L. T. R. Mem. Roll, no. 78, m. 40 d.

[4] L. T. R. Mem. Roll, no. 79, m. 76.

[5] Madox, *Hist. of Exch.* vol. II, p. 299.

[6] K. R. Mem. Roll, no. 84, m. 72 d.

[7] Ibid. no. 89, m. 89. L. T. R. Mem. Roll, no. 86, m. 30. Vide Madox, *Hist. of Exch.* vol. II, p. 301.

[8] *Cal. Close Rolls*, 1272–79, p. 486.

[9] K. R. Mem. Rolls, no. 86, m. 30; no. 87, m. 24; no. 93, m. 86. L. T. R. Mem. Rolls, no. 84, Brev. dir. Pasch. m. 1; no. 90, Rec. Pasch. m. 2 d.

[10] K. R. Mem. Roll, no. 89, m. 89. L. T. R. Mem. Roll, no. 86, m. 32 d. Vide Madox, *Hist. of Exch.* vol. II, p. 302.

[11] L. T. R. Mem. Roll, no. 89, m. 15 d.

[12] K. R. Mem. Roll, no. 87, m. 120. L. T. R. Mem. Roll, no. 84, Pres. Hill. m. 2 d.

[13] L. T. R. Mem. Roll, no. 89, m. 15 d.

ushership of the exchequer was held by a woman[1]. Another office to which the appointment lay with the earl of Warwick was that of the keeper of tallies in the exchequer[2]. With the other offices of the earl this came into the king's hands on his death, and the king appointed[3].

The local and administrative offices which the barons held in fee, if inconsiderable in comparison with the number and importance of the other offices, still had a special importance of their own. They served as a reminder to the baronage of past influence and part in administration. In themselves a relic of earlier feudal times, of tenure by serjeanty, their real importance consisted in the fact that though a survival of the past they were yet in perfect harmony with the present aims of the barons. If of little practical importance they suggested and strengthened a policy inevitably tending in directions somewhat similar.

The local influence of some of the barons gave them a position in local government which was a source of weakness to the household and general administrative system. The earl of Warwick by virtue of his local influence wrote suggesting the names of taxors in the counties of Warwick and Worcester, and the council advised acquiescence to the demand[4]. Local lords were sometimes asked to take the oaths of sheriffs from distant counties. This plan saved time and a long journey, but it was dangerous. Hugh de Courtney certified that he had taken the oath of the sheriff of Devon[5], and one Robert de Barton was ordered to take the oath of the sheriff of Westmorland and returned that he had done so[6]. Another lord, probably Badlesmere, sought that the commission to receive the oath of the sheriff of Cambridge, who had been found sufficient by inquest, might be made to him, urging in support of the request that he had seen several oaths of this nature taken outside the court[7]. Local nobilities received commission to take the fealty of various people, and to take oaths not to marry without licence[8]. The oaths

[1] Exch. K. R. Bills, 1/7. Vide above, p. 51.

[2] K. R. Mem. Rolls, no. 89, m. 89; no. 90, m. 112. L. T. R. Mem. Rolls, no. 86, m. 30; no. 87, Rec. Pasch. m. 1.

[3] Ibid.

[4] Anc. Corresp. vol. xxxv, no. 46. Vide App. of Doc. no. 104.

[5] Anc. Corresp. vol. xxxv, no. 177.

[6] P. R. O. Chancery Files (under arrangement), C, File 12.

[7] Anc. Corresp. vol. xxxv, no. 172: "et qe la commission de son sairement receuoir soit faite a nous selonc ce qe nous prions ensement a nostre seigneur le Roy par nos lettres. Kar tint soit ce qe communs viscomtes douient iurer a Leschequer nous veoms et auons veu plusours faire leur sairementz hors de court a autres a ce deputitz par commissions Roials." Vide also ibid. no. 181.

[8] Chan. Files (under arrangement), C, Files 9–12 passim.

of taxors were similarly taken, though generally by ecclesiastics[1]; and the chancellor of St Paul's took the oath of Norwich as treasurer at the exchequer[2].

Another source of weakness closely resembling divided control was the association of royal officials with barons. The clerks and knights of barons sometimes secured positions in the administrative departments. John de Langton, who is described as the familiar clerk of Walter de Langton[3], became a chamberlain of the exchequer[4]. John Abel, who was twice a baron of the exchequer and was also escheator south of Trent[5], was a bachelor of Margaret the widow of Edward I[6]. Even Sandale, who attained to the two highest offices in the administration, those of chancellor and treasurer, was a clerk of the earl of Lincoln as well as of the king and acted as one by his executors[7]. In these cases of divided allegiance or divided obligation there was a source of potential weakness though the remedy lay entirely in the king's hands. Divided control between barons and the household system was insufficient to endanger the permanence of the household system. Its importance lay rather in the powers of suggestion than in its actual weight.

Another cause of weakness which might be classed as due to divided control, was the conflict between the governmental or administrative and the executive. Despite all the checks, as time went on, there was inevitably an increasing tendency to independence in the administrative departments which would begin as soon as they had obtained a definite organisation and staff of officers. The more highly organised the departments became the more indirect became the king's control. Before the separation the king's control had been direct and personal. Separation necessitated a written instead of a verbal warrant. Though in decisive matters the control of the king was still final, it was quite impossible for him to control the ordinary routine of administration. The ordinary administrative processes were therefore left entirely in the hands of the head and staff of the departments. As business increased, formalism in phraseology and in the course of processes crept in. The great seal, when the work of the chancery was still a part of the work of the *curia regis*, was almost a personal instrument of the king, but when the chancery obtained an identity of its own it became the instrument of an administrative

[1] Chan. Files (under arrangement), C, File 12.

[2] K. R. Mem. Roll, no. 98, m. 134.

[3] Exch. of Pleas, Plea Roll, no. 31, m. 34.

[4] Tout, *The Place of Ed. II*, I. 351.

[5] Ibid. p. 342.

[6] Anc. Corresp. vol. XXXV, no. 70.

[7] Cf. *Regist. J. de Sandale*, p. XXV.

department. The issue of writs under the great seal became formalised. It was only in exceptional cases that the king interfered directly with the issue. The danger from formalised use of this nature would have been considerable had not the king had the happy faculty of providing substitutes for the formalised instrument, department or process.

There was another danger in the departments arising from the growth of a corporate spirit within them. Already the chancery and exchequer were highly developed. They had a highly developed organisation, a large staff of officers, intricate processes in administration, which the lay mind could not appreciate or understand; the oath taken on admission to office bound them together, they had certain definite and well-established privileges. All these factors combined to promote the growth of a corporate spirit. They were masters of an art and needed combination of effort as much as any trade-gild. The clerks of chancery were an organised body, and formed "the household of the chancery" which was presided over by the chancellor or, in his absence, by the keeper of the chancery rolls[1]. During the reign of Edward II the keeper of the rolls of chancery also acted as keeper of the *domus conversorum*[2]. Adam de Osgodby, who had been appointed keeper of the rolls of chancery in 1295[3], was on 7 November, 1307, appointed keeper of the *domus conversorum*[4]. He was succeeded in both positions by William de Ayremynne in August, 1316[5]. Under this regime the *domus conversorum* was used to accommodate the "household of the chancery" on occasion, and was used so freely by Adam de Osgodby as to draw a protest from the chaplains and converts in 1315. They complained that he had made them all homeless and had harboured the chancery clerks there. The matter was decided by the chancellor against the chaplains and converts[6].

If the exchequer officials had not been formed into a corporation, each baron and high officer appears to have had a number of clerks in his household and there were manifest dangers arising therefrom.

[1] Stowe MS. 553, p. 116.

[2] The *domus conversorum* was a religious foundation for the reception of Jewish converts and their chaplains. It was situated on the site now occupied by the Public Record Office in Chancery Lane. The house of converts is noticed in *Middlesex and Hertfordshire Notes and Queries*, vol. II [1896], pp. 49–68, W. J. Hardy.

[3] *Cal. Close Rolls*, 1288–96, p. 454.

[4] *Cal. Pat. Rolls*, 1307–13, p. 15.

[5] *Cal. Close Rolls*, 1313–18, p. 430. *Cal. Pat. Rolls*, 1313–17, p. 534.

[6] *Cal. Close Rolls*, 1313–18, pp. 228–9.

By 1310 the danger had become so apparent as to necessitate a writ to the treasurer and barons who were ordered "not to admit any person of their household or of the household of any other minister of the exchequer as attorney of any prelates or other, to challenge, prosecute and defend any liberties in the exchequer or to win or lose in any suits whatsoever there, receiving, however, other fit persons[1]." The treasurer, too, was assuming some amount of independent authority. In the first year of Edward II, John Deuery took oath before the treasurer and council to write the tallies of the exchequer and to do what belonged to that office "ad voluntatem Thesaurarii[2]," and another was admitted by the treasurer's order to the office of accounter in the exchequer[3]. The independence which the treasurer might exercise is illustrated very forcibly in the list of memoranda drawn up against Langton[4]. The corporate feeling of the exchequer is also evidenced by the unwillingness of the barons to arrive at a decision in certain cases on account of the absence of the treasurer[5] or of important barons like Norwich[6] or others[7]. From the households of the departments there sprang two dangers, firstly, an increased independence due to the community of purpose, and secondly the danger of abuses by the improper use of the households.

There was competition within the administrative departments. Their functions and spheres of influence had not been defined, and there was a tendency for each department to act as a general administrative department in addition to performing its own specialised functions. This led to confusion. The competition was at once a source of strength and weakness to the personal system, of strength as the king could use them as alternatives and if foiled in one department could try the other, of weakness inasmuch as it tended to confusion and abuses. The divided control between administration and executive and between department and department was not a source of serious weakness to the household system; for in the face of baronial opposition, internal strife and competition ended, and a united front was generally presented.

A more considerable source of opposition was caused by the relations of the household system to the people. The reasons why the people should look with disfavour upon the household system

[1] *Cal. Close Rolls*, 1307–13, p. 292. [2] Issue Roll, no. 141, m. 1.

[3] Ibid. [4] Exch. of Pleas, Plea Roll, no. 31, m. 21.

[5] K. R. Mem. Roll, no. 81, m. 42. L. T. R. Mem. Rolls, no. 78, mm. 38, 56; no. 84, Rec. Mich. m. 5.

[6] L. T. R. Mem. Roll, no. 84, Rec. Mich. m. 5.

[7] K. R. Mem. Roll, no. 81, m. 42. L. T. R. Mem. Roll, no. 78, m. 38.

were mostly connected with finance and the more general administrative work of some of the household departments. It was the wardrobe which was the great spending department. The expenses of the Scottish and Gascon wars were paid out of the wardrobe, and they were a serious drain upon the resources of the country. However carefully arranged expenditure is, the department which conducts it becomes unpopular.

Still more unpopularity was aroused by the purveyance which the wardrobe conducted. It conducted purveyance for the Scottish war. The campaigns were so frequent and the numbers engaged so considerable that the strain upon the counties was great. Purveyance was also conducted by the wardrobe for the royal household. In November, 1309, when the king and queen and the earl of Cornwall left York for the south, one about the court writing to his lord said that the king had done much harm in the country, taking corn and cattle and exempting no one but the person to whom the letter was written[1]. In August, 1312, sheriffs in several counties were ordered to purvey great quantities of corn and animals for the king's household, "the king being unable at present on account of divers arduous business to pay for the many kinds of victuals needed by him[2]." Some of the sheriffs were ordered to purvey "to the greatest advantage of the king and the least damage to the men of those parts[3]." Sheriffs of counties also made purveyance on their own behalf. It was complained against Simon Warde, sheriff of York, that he had taken twenty quarters of charcoal and paid nothing for it. The petitioner was ordered to await the coming of the justice of assize or prosecute the matter at the exchequer[4].

The complaints of the people against purveyance were so great that frequent remedies had to be ordered. On 11 June, 1309, writs were issued to the sheriffs on petitions by the people reciting the provisions in the Statute of Westminster I, concerning the taking of unjust prices from ecclesiastics and others, and proclamation was ordered[5]. In the parliament of Stamford certain clauses of the *Articuli super Cartas* defining what purveyors should take, how payment should be made, touching the showing of their warrants, ordering that no more than was needful should be taken, ordering

[1] *Cal. Doc. Scotl.* vol. III, p. 20.
[2] *Cal. Fine Rolls*, 1307–19, pp. 142–4. Cf. also *Cal. Close Rolls*, 1307–13, p. 18.
[3] Ibid. p. 143.
[4] Cole, *Doc. illustr. Eng. Hist. in 13th and 14th Cent.* p. 36.
[5] *Stat. of Realm*, vol. I, pp. 153–4.

answer to be made for the things taken, ordering punishment for undue purveyance, making purveyance without warrant a felony, were recited[1] and embodied in the Statute of Stamford, the whole being the result of petitions[2]. In 1310 sheriffs were forbidden to take victuals against the will of the owners[3]. The Ordinances attacked the abuse[4], and after the parliament of 1315 writs were again issued reciting the relative provision of Statute of Westminster I[5], complaint having been made to the king on the abuses of purveyance and forced labour[6]. In April, 1316, sheriffs were ordered to make proclamation against demanding prisage and purveyance of ecclesiastics under the penalty prescribed by the Statute of Westminster and for the strict observance of the Ordinance lately made on the subject[7]. Proclamation against the seizure of goods, against the wishes of the owners without payment, was ordered to be made in November, 1317[8], and in April, 1322, the suitable provisions of the *Articuli super Cartas* were ordered to be published every market-day[9]. All this shows the widespread character of purveyance and the complaints it produced among the people. The purveyors of the king's household were impleaded at the exchequer for abuses but the king stepped in and intervened. If the keeper of the wardrobe, by reference to the records of his office, was satisfied that the purveyances complained of were for the household the purveyors were to be quit, otherwise the cases were to proceed[10]. Purveyance brought home one of the abuses of the household system to the people in the most personal manner. The great offices of the chancery and the exchequer may have had their abuses but they were distant and did not touch their material comfort.

Through purveyance the wardrobe seemed to enter into the daily life of the people. It touched them so nearly and personally that the irritation produced by inconvenience was intensified. Closely allied to the work of purveyance, was the duty of providing lodging for the king and his household and also for parliaments, a burden from which the city of London claimed immunity[11]. Through these functions the whole of the household system was brought into contact with the

[1] *Stat. of Realm*, vol. I, pp. 154–6. [2] Ibid.
[3] *Rot. Scot.* vol. I, p. 96. *Cal. Letter Books, D*, p. 254.
[4] Vide below, p. 379.
[5] *Cal. Close Rolls*, 1313–18, p. 235.
[6] *Ann. Lond.* pp. 234–6. [7] *Cal. Letter Books, E*, p. 63.
[8] Ibid. p. 79. [9] *Cal. Close Rolls*, 1318–23, p. 532.
[10] K. R. Mem. Roll, no. 100, Brev. dir. Pasch. m. 5.
[11] *Mun. Gildh. Lond., Liber Albus*, p. 303.

people. The purveyance was sometimes conducted by sheriffs[1], but often by the officials of the household[2]. As a result of the frequent complaints which had reached the king of the purveyors of the household who had commissions to make various purveyances for the expenses of the household and of the other ministers whom the king had ordered on occasion to aid them, that the purveyances were made in such an outrageous manner that they were not to the king's need or profit, and that others who were out of the king's household without commission had made purveyances in the king's name, commissions of oyer and terminer were ordered to be made for such trespasses[3]. It was difficult to obtain redress from a member of the household, because he had no chattels[4].

Even the grievances with which the personal system afflicted the people were not sufficient to promote an uprising which would imperil its safety. The importance of these causes of weakness was that they aided a movement against the household system which had its origin elsewhere. The weaknesses of the household system were not considerable in amount. There was little probability of that system being overthrown, at this time, by inherent or developed weaknesses. Its strength and resources were far too great for it to be affected appreciably by such minor considerations. These minor considerations aided a movement which sprang from other causes. They were partly in harmony with those other tendencies, but in other phases they had nothing in common. They provided vulnerable points which the baronial opposition might attack, but it will be found that the strength of that system was too secure for it to fall before even frontal assaults.

[1] E.g. *Cal. Fine Rolls*, 1307–19, pp. 142–4.
[2] Vide Chan. Warr., Files 1648–51 passim. *Cal. Pat. Rolls*, 1307–13, pp. 1, 11, 13, 15, 58, 450, etc.
[3] Chan. Warr., File 80/2244 (12 July, 1311).
[4] Wm Salt Soc., *Coll.* vol. VI, Pt i, pp. 273–4.

CHAPTER XIV

THE HOUSEHOLD SYSTEM IN ACTION

Before the various experiments by which the baronial opposition sought to overcome the strength of the household system are examined, a description of the way in which certain prominent royal supporters assumed an unofficial yet decisive part in the administration must be given. For a description of the household system in action is complementary to the previous study which has been made of that system and its influence. The description will illustrate the sources of strength and weakness and show the household system acting upon the administration. The study of the household system in action supplies a fitting conclusion to the study of the administrative and household machinery, and a suitable preparation to the study of the practical problems which confronted the baronial opposition and the measures with which they endeavoured to face those problems.

In the three instances of the household system in action that will be taken there will be one important common factor They were all instances of the administration being undertaken by persons who held no official position. They show how the sources of strength which were inherent in the household and its organisation enabled the king to work the machinery of government, not by the chief officers of great departments but by persons really outside the normal administrative system. The first instance of the personal system in action is found in the administration of the earl of Pembroke after Gavaston's death, the second in the part played in the administration by Walter Reynolds, archbishop of Canterbury, during periods when he held no official position. For some reasons the third—the administration of Hugh le Despenser the son, from the battle of Boroughbridge till the end of the reign, is the most perfect instance. Inasmuch as this was partly based upon his position as a royal favourite, and as favouritism was not essential to the working of the personal system, the control of the government by Pembroke has a special importance.

It is important to emphasise that not one of them was the head of any of the great departments of government when he controlled the administration. Pembroke never held any important office in the central administration, though he took charge of the Scottish march[1] and acted as justice of the forest[2]. The archbishop of Canterbury before his translation to the primacy had been treasurer, chancellor and keeper of the great seal[3]. Despenser the son held no official position during the reign though he was the king's chamberlain after 1318[4]. This brings out a strong contrast between Edward II's policy and his father's. In the first place, Edward I took a greater personal part in the administration, and those who administered under his guidance were the great officials. First Robert Burnell, chancellor, was the prominent figure and after his death Walter de Langton, treasurer, became the dominant official.

It was after the death of Gavaston in June, 1312[5], that the earl of Pembroke first completely dissociated himself from the baronial opposition. He had been one of the ordainers of 1311[6] and had been amongst those who had besieged Gavaston in Scarborough Castle[7]. Gavaston surrendered to the earls of Pembroke and Warenne and Henry de Percy upon conditions, and letters patent were issued by them from Scarborough on 19 May, 1312[8]. The way in which the earl of Warwick and his confederates seized Gavaston and, notwithstanding the plighted word of Pembroke and his associates, had executed him summarily roused Pembroke and Warenne. Both felt that their honour was at stake and they immediately joined the king's party[9]. Pembroke was greatly moved. He appealed to the earl of Gloucester to intervene and then stated his case before the University of Oxford[10]. Henry de Percy, who had also received the surrender of Gavaston and had gone security for his safety, did not leave the baronial side, and a writ ordering his arrest was issued by the king on Pembroke's information[11].

The earl of Pembroke now assumed the predominant position in the royal counsels, and became the real head of the administration. Before 1312 as a supporter of the baronial opposition few grants or favours had been made him. Lands of his in Scotland which had been seized by the king were restored[12] and the castle and town of

[1] *Foedera*, vol. II, pp. 4, 245–6. [2] *Cal. Fine Rolls*, 1319–27, pp. 23, 35.
[3] Vide below, pp. 331–3. [4] Vide above, pp. 217–219.
[5] *Auct. Bridl.* p. 44. [6] *Ann. Lond.* p. 172. *Auct. Bridl.* p. 37.
[7] *Ann. Lond.* p. 204. *Auct. Bridl.* p. 42. *Auct. Malm.* p. 177.
[8] The letters patent are printed in *Ann. Lond.* pp. 204–6. *Lit. Cantuar.* vol. III, App. pp. 388–393.
[9] *Ann. Lond.* p. 208. *Chron. Lanerc.* pp. 198–9.
[10] *Auct. Malm.* pp. 178–9. [11] *Cal. Pat. Rolls*, 1307–13, p. 486.
[12] *Cal. Close Rolls*, 1307–13, p. 13.

Haverfordwest were granted for life[1], otherwise little had gone his way. Before 1312 as an opponent of the royal policy he had had but a small part in administration. As early as 9 October, 1308, a grant of lands, by writ of the exchequer, had been made by the treasurer at his instance[2]. In company with the earl of Richmond in 1309 he had gone to the papal court as a royal messenger[3]. In July, 1310, he had been ordered by privy seal to be at Leicester to speak with the bishop of London, the earls of Lincoln and Richmond, and Robert de Clifford whom the king had charged to say his will on certain business, and Pembroke was enjoined to listen and do what they told him on the royal behalf[4]. Now he assumed supreme power.

During the period July, 1312, to July, 1317, which was covered by the first phase of the Pembroke administration, the number of grants made to the earl, if not great compared with the grants made previously to Gavaston and subsequently to the younger Despenser, may fairly be called considerable. In September, 1312, he was granted the custody of forfeited lands[5], and in November lands were assigned in part payment of the king's debts to him[6]. In December the New Temple was granted to him and his heirs[7], followed a few days later by a grant of all the goods and chattels therein[8]. From that time onward grants of lands, custodies and favours were frequent. He was appointed custodian of the castle of Rockingham and keeper of the forest between Oxford and Stamford[9]. Manors in Gloucester[10], wardship of the lands of minors[11], licences to crenellate[12], return of the king's writ within certain of the lands[13], free administration of his will by his executors[14], and pardon for acquiring lands in fee without licence[15] were all granted him.

The position in the administration which he obtained in 1312 was given him by the deliberate policy of the king. The king expressed high appreciation of his services[16] and that splendid series of writs under the privy and secret seal preserved in the *Ancient Correspondence*[17] which the king sent him, shows in detail how the king relied

[1] *Cal. Pat. Rolls*, 1307–13, p. 145.
[2] K. R. Mem. Roll, no. 82, m. 4. L. T. R. Mem. Roll, no. 79, m. 4.
[3] *Ann. Paul.* p. 267. *Cal. Pat. Rolls*, 1307–13, p. 103.
[4] Anc. Corresp. vol. XLIX, no. 7.
[5] *Cal. Pat. Rolls*, 1307–13, p. 493.
[6] Ibid. p. 513.
[7] *Cal. Charter Rolls*, 1300–26, p. 202.
[8] Chan. Warr., File 83/2564. *Cal. Charter Rolls*, 1300–26, p. 203.
[9] *Cal. Pat. Rolls*, 1313–17, p. 85.
[10] Ibid. p. 106.
[11] *Cal. Fine Rolls*, 1307–19, p. 211.
[12] *Cal. Pat. Rolls*, 1313–17, p. 278.
[13] *Cal. Charter Rolls*, 1300–26, p. 235.
[14] *Cal. Pat. Rolls*, 1313–17, p. 282.
[15] Ibid. p. 607.
[16] Vide above, pp. 110–111.
[17] Anc. Corresp. vols. XLV, XLIX passim.

upon his advice and opinion in every phase of the administration. Gavaston had died in June and by the middle of July Pembroke was taking a part in the administration[1], and until the middle of 1314 he was supreme. After the battle of Bannockburn his supremacy was challenged by the increased importance of Lancaster[2], but Pembroke maintained much of his power and he may be regarded as one of the moving figures until July, 1317. Then began a disposition of forces which increased rather than diminished his influence[3].

Pembroke's position in administration necessitated frequent interviews with the king. On 4 January, 1313, the king wished the earl to know that on the following Sunday he could be found at the castle of Windsor whatever time he desired to see him[4]. On 16 January Pembroke was summoned to Windsor for the following Wednesday to hear various news the king had received[5]. Letters received by the king containing news from Scotland were sent to the earl[6], and the proposed itineraries and sojourns of the king were communicated to the earl to enable him to send news as frequently and speedily as possible[7]. These conferences were sometimes held for the king to acquaint the earl of his will in certain matters[8]. Sometimes Pembroke was summoned to discuss matters with the king[9]; sometimes because the king desired to have his advice and then he was ordered to go with all speed, neglecting everything else[10]. On one occasion the earl was asked to come because the king desired his counsel and advice on certain weighty matters[11]. He was enjoined to put all the good counsel he could into the king's business and the king was most insistent that news which reached the earl should be sent as often as possible[12]. The store he placed upon that news may be estimated by the fact that Pembroke's messenger received 40*s*. from the exchequer by writ of secret seal[13]. On 28 August, 1313, Pembroke was summoned to a

[1] *Cal. Fine Rolls*, 1307–13, p. 140 (20 July, 1312). Liberate Roll, no. 89, m. 4 (22 July, 1312).

[2] Vide below for the power of Lancaster and his share in the administration after the battle of Bannockburn, pp. 394–400.

[3] Vide below, pp. 394–400, for the rise of the middle party.

[4] Anc. Corresp. vol. XLIX, no. 19: "nous vous fesoms asauoir qe vous nous trouerez iceo dimenge prochein au nostre chastel de Wyndesore quele heure qe vous vendriez."

[5] Ibid. no. 20: "por diuerse nouele qe nous auoms oiz."

[6] Ibid. no. 10. [7] Ibid nos. 10, 11. [8] Ibid. no. 12.

[9] Ibid. no. 22. [10] Ibid. no. 43.

[11] Ibid. no. 37: "por aucunes grosses busoignes qe nous touchent es quieux nous voudriens auoir counseil et auisement de vous."

[12] Ibid. vol. XLVII, no. 27.

[13] Issue Roll, no. 174, m. 6.

meeting of the "secretaries" of the king's council which was to be held before the approaching parliament[1].

The king's writs to Pembroke do not assume the formal note of his communications with the administrative officials. The writs contain informal matter[2] and questions about the earl's health and estate mingle with matters touching the machinery of government[3]. They help to emphasise his unofficial position. He was a person acting on the king's behalf, less than a regent in some matters and more than an official in all. He made constant endeavours to settle the troublesome dispute between the town and constable of Bristol[4]. The king and he had decided at Clipston that Anthony Pessaign, whom the king styles "nostre cher Bachiler," should proceed immediately to France upon the earl's business, but the king kept Pessaign near him for certain weighty matters. Their nature the king would inform the earl more fully on his arrival[5]. Pessaign made a loan to the king of 800 florins and Pembroke's valet conveyed the money to the king[6]. The earl acted even as a buyer of horses for the king[7].

During the period 1312–17, especially for the first few years, Pembroke often acted as head of the executive. Petitions were addressed to him[8]. The chancellor and treasurer were subordinate to him; in all departments his influence was supreme, the king referring to him for consideration matters concerning chancery, exchequer, and council. Writs affecting all departments were sent to him and any ordered arrangement of his influence and work is very difficult. A number of the writs are too general to be classed as relating to the work of any one department. They are in effect writs under the privy seal to Pembroke as head of the executive to do in certain matters what the king himself or one of his great officials might do or cause to be done. Pembroke and Henry de Beaumont were ordered to recommend specially one Gerard Dauro to the king of France[9]. The association of Beaumont with Pembroke was merely incidental; Despenser the elder on the other hand acted with him frequently. Despenser was an administrator of ability and value and was constantly associated with Pembroke in the writs. They were jointly ordered to make letters of acquittance for money paid into

[1] Anc. Corresp. vol. XLIX, no. 23: "priuez de nostre conseil." Vide App. of Doc. no. 125.

[2] Vide above, p. 151.

[3] Anc. Corresp. vol. XLIX, no. 40.

[4] *Cal. of Pat. Rolls*, 1307–13, pp. 483, 491, 524.

[5] Anc. Corresp. vol. XLIX, no. 33.

[6] K. R. Acct. 375/5, m. 6.

[7] Ibid. 375/8, f. 13.

[8] Ancient Petition, no. 3819.

[9] Anc. Corresp. vol. XLIX, no. 9.

the king's chamber[1]. With the association of Sandale, treasurer, they were ordered on 17 November, 1312, to consider and ordain how the king's household could be better sustained[2]. On 13 January, 1313, Pembroke and Despenser were ordered to send a keeper into the county of Cornwall and the moor of Devon until a seneschal was appointed, ordering him on the king's behalf to make inquiry from all the poor people of Cornwall how John de Bedwynd bore himself in the stannary[3]. A ship had been taken, the goods in it seized and the men imprisoned. Pembroke was ordered to amend and redress the trespass. An inquiry was to be held in the parts where the trespass had been committed, so that remedy could be made according to law and reason[4]. Pembroke was ordered to aid and counsel by all the ways possible what the king's cousin and clerk, Master Boniface de Saluce, had before him, as was best for the king's honour[5]. With Badlesmere, Pembroke was jointly ordered to advise the king how the march of Scotland could then be guarded best[6]. It was Pembroke also who was sent by the king to the monks of the chapter of Winchester to try to influence them to elect Sandale to that see. The king had previously ordered him to do this by word of mouth and on 10 July, 1316, Pembroke was ordered by privy seal to go to Winchester without delay[7]. In all directions Pembroke's was the hand that moved and it was through Pembroke that the king made his personal wishes felt and effective.

Besides this general administrative control, writs ordering the issue of the great seal were also sent to Pembroke. By letters of secret seal on 7 May, 1313, he was ordered to make letters granting a close[8]. Pembroke and Despenser were ordered to make Pessaign keeper of the mine of Cornwall[9]. As head of the executive the earl's superiority to the chancellor was marked. Beaumont required a favour from the king for a dependent and wrote to the king on that behalf. The king enclosed the letter under privy seal to Pembroke and ordered him "qe vous comaundez au chaunceler e au clers de la chauncelerye qe ses bosoignes seyent fetes e ke vous memes veyez ke la chose soit fete si ke il ne soit plus delaye[10]." Beaumont was a person well established at court and likely to be well informed and

[1] Anc. Corresp. vol. XLV, no. 171. Vide App. of Doc. no. 118.
[2] Anc. Corresp. vol. XLIX, no. 15. Vide App. of Doc. no. 123.
[3] Anc. Corresp. vol. XLV, no. 174. [4] Ibid. no. 173.
[5] Ibid. vol. XLIX, no. 17. [6] Ibid. no. 32.
[7] Ibid. nos. 35, 36. [8] Ibid. vol. XLV, no. 176. App. of Doc. no. 119.
[9] Anc. Corresp. vol. XLIX, no. 14.
[10] Chan. Misc., Bdle 138 (unsorted bundle).

his letter to the king requested this procedure in words almost verbatim with the royal writ[1].

Similar orders affecting exchequer business were sent to Pembroke alone or jointly with the elder Despenser. He was ordered to appoint a suitable man on the king's behalf to be collector of the customs of Bordeaux[2]. The king had granted £300 to be paid to certain persons by assignment on wardships and marriages. The assignment was no longer available and Pembroke and Despenser were ordered to let them have the money by other assignments[3]. Pembroke was ordered to make assignments on the customs of wool in Kingston-on-Hull to pay 1000 marks which the king owed Sandale[4]. The debts which the wardrobe owed, Pembroke and Despenser were ordered to assign out of the first money that could be levied[5].

Pembroke also acted as head of the council. Petitions were sent to him and Despenser, under writ of privy seal, to provide a remedy[6]. The business of a Gascon subject was recommended to Pembroke who was ordered to dispose of it according to right and reason, the king desiring him to show grace in the matter[7]. A messenger from Gaston, count of Foix, to Edward II with letters of credence was sent to Pembroke and Despenser who were to listen to what he had to say and to provide a suitable reply, and hasten the business as much as possible[8]. The conduct of Nicholas D'Audley towards the king had been faulty. His wife wished to give her lands to James de Perers, who had married her daughter. The king approved of this if he was not thereby prejudiced, Pembroke was to advise with others of the council if this result would happen, otherwise the earl was to give licence[9].

The administrative authority with which the warrants under the privy and secret seals vested Pembroke was final. Subject to the king's approval there was no authority which could dispute or deny the earl's power. The lack of checks upon the royal power in administration allowed the king to delegate his duty to a person elected by him and allowed that person to draw to himself the functions of the chief officers of the great administrative departments of exchequer and chancery. Pembroke also actively intervened in the general administration of those departments and of the realm in general in other ways. Pembroke, Despenser and Nicholas de Segrave were the king's

[1] Chan. Misc., Bdle 138 (unsorted bundle).
[2] Anc. Corresp. vol. XLV, no. 175.
[3] Ibid. no. 169.
[4] Ibid. no. 170.
[5] Ibid. no. 174.
[6] Ibid. vol. XLIX, no. 16.
[7] Ibid. vol. XLV, no. 177.
[8] Ibid. vol. XLIX, no. 18.
[9] Ibid. vol. XLV, no. 172.

representatives in the treaty which was made between king and barons before the cardinals in 1312[1]. In September, 1314, Pembroke, with the bishops of Exeter and Worcester, was given power to open the parliament about to assemble at York and to conduct it until the king's arrival[2], and again Pembroke and Richmond and the bishops of Exeter and Norwich were appointed to be the king's lieutenants in the parliament of Lincoln in 1316, during the king's absence until the arrival of the earl of Lancaster[3]. In February, 1313, safe conduct was granted him going beyond seas on the king's service[4].

He frequently acted in matters touching the seal and its issue. Pembroke and Despenser on 5 October, 1312, on the king's behalf enjoined Osgodby, Ayremynne and Bardelby to seal with their seals the great seal in the keeping of the chancellor[5], a protective measure against its issue. Pembroke also issued warrants to the chancellor. Writing on the king's behalf to the bishop of Worcester, chancellor, he ordered a writ of liberate to be made to the treasurer for twenty marks assigned by the king[6]. On frequent occasions Pembroke acted as messenger between king and great seal. A petition was endorsed with the statement that the king granted it on the announcement of the earl of Pembroke[7]. Writs of liberate were issued on his announcement[8] and also on the joint announcement of Pembroke and Despenser[9]. Chancery writs entered on the close, patent and fine rolls were similarly issued. The grant of the forest of High Peak and other land to the earl of Warenne was made on Pembroke's information[10]. Writs touching the appointment of Badlesmere as constable of Bristol[11], appointing Sandale treasurer[12], ordering the mayor and sheriffs of London not to admit the earl of Hereford and the barons into the city[13], concerning the victualling of St John's, Perth[14], ordering respite for Roger Mortimer of Wigmore[15], and many others[16] were all issued on the information of the earl of Pembroke. Grants under the

[1] *Foedera*, vol. II, p. 191.
[2] *Cal. Pat. Rolls*, 1313–17, p. 169.
[3] *Parl. Writs*, vol. II, Pt i, p. 169. *Rot. Parl.* vol. I, p. 350.
[4] *Cal. Pat. Rolls*, 1307–13, pp. 525, 576.
[5] *Cal. Close Rolls*, 1307–13, pp. 552–3.
[6] Anc. Corresp. vol. XXXV, no. 168.
[7] Ancient Petition, no. 5459.
[8] Liberate Roll, no. 89, m. 4.
[9] Ibid.
[10] *Cal. Fine Rolls*, 1307–19, p. 140 (25, 26 July, 1312).
[11] *Cal. Pat. Rolls*, 1307–13, p. 483 (30 July, 1312).
[12] Ibid. p. 501 (4 Oct. 1312).
[13] *Cal. Close Rolls*, 1307–13, p. 481 (5 Oct. 1312).
[14] *Cal. Pat. Rolls*, 1307–13, p. 503 (8 Oct. 1312).
[15] Ibid. p. 566 (4 Febr. 1313).
[16] Cf. *Cal. Close Rolls*, 1307–13, pp. 491, 506, 524. *Cal. Pat. Rolls*, 1307–13, pp. 491, 497, 524; 1313–17, pp. 548, 563, 602.

great seal were often made on his instance or at his request[1] and licences[2] and pardons[3] were similarly issued.

He took part in the ordinary routine of exchequer business. Respites were granted there at his instance[4]. Pembroke went to the exchequer and, on the king's behalf, announced to the lieutenant of the treasurer and the barons that they should search the rolls and memoranda for the debts which the king owed Despenser[5]. On 21 December, 1312, John de Gisors, mayor of London, was presented to the king by Pembroke and Sandale[6]. Pembroke was amongst those of the council who sat at the exchequer. He was present there amongst the council when, on 14 May, 1313, the great seal which had been used in England during the king's absence was handed to the bishop of Worcester, chancellor[7]. The last entry among the *recorda* of Trinity term 5 Edward II shows Pembroke heading the council[8]. In the presence of Pembroke and others of the council, John de Bedwynd was charged at the exchequer by Anthony Pessaign with speaking words in contempt of the king and council concerning evil counsellors, and with saying that the gift of the stannary of Cornwall to Pessaign was ill-considered[9]. Pembroke testified before the treasurer, barons and others of the council that the king accepted the person who had been elected mayor of Oxford by the bailiffs and commonalty and wished him to take oath before the treasurer and barons[10].

In the council in its other phases Pembroke had a leading part. A payment was made from the exchequer on 6 October, 1312, by the assent of Pembroke and the whole of the king's council[11]. The earl of Richmond received money for expenses he had undertaken on the royal behalf by agreement made with him by Pembroke and others of the king's council[12]. When on 30 December, 1312, the mayor appeared before the council about the tallage of the city of London, the earl was among the council[13]. Writs intended for the council were addressed to him. On 21 October, 1312, with others of the

[1] Cf. *Cal. Pat. Rolls*, 1307–13, p. 131. *Cal. Close Rolls*, 1313–18, p. 343.

[2] Cf. *Cal. Pat. Rolls*, 1307–13, p. 37; 1313–17, p. 615.

[3] Cf. ibid. 1307–13, p. 44; 1313–17, p. 332.

[4] K. R. Mem. Roll, no. 86, mm. 99, 107.

[5] Ibid. m. 73. L. T. R. Mem. Roll, no. 83, Rec. Mich. m. 3.

[6] *Cal. Letter Books, D*, p. 21.

[7] L. T. R Mem. Roll, no. 78, m. 40 d.

[8] K. R. Mem. Roll, no. 85, m. 61.

[9] Ibid. no. 86, m. 76 d. L. T. R. Mem. Roll, no. 83, Rec. Hill. m. 1 d.

[10] K. R. Mem. Roll, no. 86, m. 100.

[11] Issue Roll, no. 164, m. 1.

[12] K. R. Acct. 375/8, f. 11 b.

[13] *Parl. Writs*, vol. II, Pt i, p. 131.

council at London he was ordered to consider how the king could grieve and damage Griffith de la Pole according to the law and usage of the realm because he had disobeyed royal orders and assembled men-at-arms[1]. On 21 December, 1316, a writ of privy seal was directed to the archbishop of Canterbury, Pembroke and others of the council[2].

Everywhere Pembroke's influence as director of the administration was felt, and the way in which this great magnate worked in the interests of the kingdom, with no thought or endeavour to promote purely personal or class ends, shows how the personal system could and did attract and use men of ability. The period when Pembroke controlled the administration was one of comparative calm. The battle of Bannockburn complicated matters and gave an increased stimulus to the action of the Lancastrian faction, though that did not remain such a cohesive body as before. The period also saw another phase of baronial opposition in the work of the parliament of Lincoln of 1316. Judged as a whole, however, the years 1312–17 were not a period of violent convulsion. The administrative machinery was working quietly and under the supervision of Pembroke no violent cause for radical reform was offered.

The period 1317–22 is taken up largely by the activities of the middle party[3]. Pembroke did not cease to take an active part in administration, but under pressure of circumstances he found it necessary to adapt his methods; and in the intricate relations between the members of the middle party individually and collectively with the king on the one hand, and the Lancastrian faction on the other, the same consistency of administrative policy on Pembroke's part could no longer be expected. The battle of Boroughbridge crushed the baronial opposition and with its destruction ended both the necessity and the practicability of the middle party. Pembroke, for the remainder of his life, was a consistent supporter of the king and if during the period 1322–4 his importance was eclipsed by that of Despenser the son, the fact that he was willing and was allowed to take an active part in the administration shows at once his single-mindedness and the virtue of a system that could simultaneously embrace a Despenser and a Pembroke.

During this period Pembroke's activity was less apparent at home

[1] Anc. Corresp. vol. XLIX, no. 13.

[2] Ibid. vol. XLV, no. 192.

[3] The whole subject of the growth and influence of the middle party 1317–22 will be reviewed below, pp. 425–443.

than abroad[1]. At home it took the form of the shadow of his previous administration. After Boroughbridge some small amount of the land of the rebels fell to him. The castle and manor of Thorpwaterville and Higham Ferrers in Northampton were granted to him in fee tail[2] and also the New Temple in London[3]. His advice was still earnestly sought. In April, 1324, the king desired his counsel on certain weighty matters and he was to be at London at a certain time to confer with the king and others of the council[4]. In the previous month the king had sent him a letter which he was going to send to the king of Bohemia, together with a transcript, and the earl was to advise the king on the letter and transcript when he came to him in the course of a few days[5]. His influence was still felt, at times, in the chancery. The king wrote to the keepers of the great seal on 31 March, 1322, informing them that the previous day he had received a letter from the mayor of Newcastle containing the news of the Scottish invasion. A transcript of the letter had been sent to Pembroke and he had replied by letter. The king sent the letter to the keeper of the great seal, who was ordered to cause writs to be drawn up as the earl advised[6]. His influence in the council remained considerable and at times predominant. He still acted as its head on occasion. On 12 February, 1323, the king under his secret seal sent Pembroke a letter which he was to consider and to hear more fully on the matter from the bearer. He was to ordain with the king's council such remedy as he considered suitable according to right and reason[7].

The position which Walter Reynolds, archbishop of Canterbury, held and his activity after his erection to the primacy, it is difficult to define or appreciate. He held no official position yet appeared to act as head of the council. At one period he was the king's lieutenant in England and it was quite natural that he should then assume the chief position in the council[8], but it will be seen that he consistently led the council.

In estimating the position which he occupied it is important to notice the relation in which he stood to the king. Reynolds had been keeper of the wardrobe of Edward while prince of Wales[9] and

[1] For his embassies see above, pp. 111–112.

[2] *Cal. Pat. Rolls*, 1321–24, p. 87 (15 March, 1322). The charter was ordered to be renewed on 30 March, 1322 (Chan. Warr., File 117/5963).

[3] *Cal. Charter Rolls*, 1300–26, p. 441 (23 March, 1321).

[4] Anc. Corresp. vol. XLIX, no. 56.

[5] Ibid. no. 55.

[6] Chan. Warr., File 117/5964. Vide *Cal. Doc. Scotl.* vol. III, p. 140.

[7] Anc. Corresp. vol. XLV, no. 207. Vide App. of Doc. no. 122.

[8] K. R. Mem. Roll, no. 87, m. 100.

[9] Brit. Mus. Additional MS. 22,923, f. 2 b and passim.

immediately upon the latter's accession to the throne he became treasurer, a position which he held until his appointment as chancellor in 1310. The king also procured ecclesiastical promotion for him. In 1308 he was elected and provided, by the royal influence, to the see of Worcester[1] and, at the king's request, the pope allowed him to delay his consecration[2]. When, on Winchelsey's death, the see of Canterbury fell vacant the king made every endeavour to secure him the primacy. The pope declared void the election of Thomas de Cobham, canon of York, and translated the bishop of Worcester to the see[3]. This provision was without doubt the result of the king's endeavours. Without accepting the chronicler's description of Reynolds as an illiterate man without dignity or learning[4], it can be well conceded that in piety as well as intellectual attainments he was inferior to Cobham[5] and his appointment was stated to be due to the bribes of the king[6].

It was after his appointment as archbishop that he began to take the important unofficial part in the administration. His influence with the king during this period is shown in the grants of lands and custodies made to him. Between February, 1314, and October, 1315, the grants were particularly numerous. Weekly markets and fairs[7], the wardship of lands[8], the custody of manors[9] were granted and out of special affection the king allowed him to have the fines of all his men and tenants of the archbishopric and the issues of all forfeitures wherever they might arise[10].

Reynolds' tenure of office in the chancery was very chequered. For the first two years of his appointment he was always styled chancellor[11]. After April, 1312, his usual title was keeper of the great seal[12], and on 4 October there was a formal recognition of his lowered status when the elder Despenser announced at the exchequer that the king had appointed him the lieutenant of the chancellor[13], just as Sandale was at the same time appointed lieutenant of the treasurer[14]. Two days later the great seal which had been in the

[1] *Cal. Pap. Letters*, 1304–42, p. 34. [2] Ibid. p. 41. [3] Ibid. p. 115.
[4] *Chron. Lanerc.* pp. 202–3. *Flores Hist.* vol. III, pp. 155–6.
[5] *Chron. Mon. de Melsa*, vol. II, p. 329.
[6] *Auct. Malm.* pp. 196–7. *Chron. Mon. de Melsa*, vol. II, p. 329.
[7] *Cal. Charter Rolls*, 1300–26, pp. 235, 271, 274, 289.
[8] *Cal. Fine Rolls*, 1307–19, pp. 214, 237. [9] Ibid. pp. 224, 259.
[10] *Cal. Charter Rolls*, 1300–26, p. 236.
[11] Vide Chan. Warr., Files 68–82 passim.
[12] Ibid. Files 85–88 passim. [13] K. R. Mem. Roll, no. 86, m. 73.
[14] Vide above, p. 120. For Sandale's appointment letters patent also were issued.

custody of Osgodby, Bardelby and Ayremynne was restored to him[1]. Even after his elevation to the primacy the more dignified title of chancellor was still denied him. On 31 March, 1314, the three chancery clerks, Osgodby, Bardelby, and Ayremynne received the great seal from the archbishop and from the 5th of April they acted as independent keepers, the warrants for the issue of the great seal being addressed to them. After 31 March, 1314, Reynolds held no official position. It was after that date however that he took an important position in general administration, especially in the work of the council.

As early as 20 April Reynolds commenced to act in his unofficial capacity. The king ordered the keepers of the great seal to make writs by the counsel and advice of the archbishop who was ordered to give them advice and counsel[2], and subsequently warrants were addressed to the archbishop of Canterbury and the keepers of the great seal[3]. Moreover, on occasion, he was ordered to perform such official acts as make writs, arrange for the purveyance of carts for the Scottish campaign and receive petitions[4]. In May, 1314, he issued writs of liberate, one being issued by the king and council on the command of the archbishop of Canterbury[5] and another by the archbishop of Canterbury[6]. A writ of 7 June, 1314, entered on the Scottish roll, was issued by the archbishop and the council[7], and in September a release was ordered at his request[8].

Grants under the exchequer seal were similarly made by the lieutenant of the treasurer in 1314[9] and by Norwich, treasurer, in 1316[10] at the archbishop's instance. In November, 1316, the archbishop and the treasurer received the fealty of a prior[11]. Though it was at Lambeth that the letters patent of the king were exhibited in the presence of the archbishop and the treasurer, the matter really concerned the exchequer and a record of it was made on the roll of

[1] Tout, *The Place of Ed. II*, pp. 320–4, treats the subject at length, but the appointment as lieutenant has escaped Professor Tout.

[2] Chan. Warr., File 87/2941–2. Cf. File 1328/59.

[3] Ibid. File 87/2976 (9 May, 1314). Cf. no. 2984.

[4] Ibid. File 88/3015, 3021, 3033–4, 3037.

[5] Liberate Roll, no. 90, m. 2: "per ipsum Regem et consilium precipiente Archiepiscopo Cantuariense" (26 May).

[6] Ibid. (27 May). [7] *Rot. Scot.* p. 127: "per Archiepiscopum et consilium."

[8] *Cal. Close Rolls*, 1313–18, pp. 114–115.

[9] K. R. Mem. Roll, no. 87, m. 4. L. T. R. Mem. Roll, no. 84, m. 5 (16 July, 1314).

[10] L. T. R. Mem. Roll, no. 86, m. 7 (5 July, 1316).

[11] K. R. Mem. Roll, no. 90, m. 105. L. T. R. Mem. Roll, no. 87, Rec. Mich. m. 4 d.

that department[1]. The archbishop was then probably acting as one of the unofficial members of the king's council, owing his place not to his ecclesiastical position but to his position as a friend and confidant of the king, one who had been an official member of the household system and was still an unofficial or personal member.

There is ample evidence of the important position the archbishop held in the king's council. A writ of privy seal, enclosing letters of the duke and duchess of Brabant, which were to be considered by the council, was addressed to the archbishop, the chancellor, treasurer and others of the council[2], and another writ concerning the appointment of Adam de Orleton to the see of Hereford was similarly addressed to the archbishop, the bishop of Winchester, chancellor, and others of the council[3]. A letter sent by certain Gascon officials to Edward II and dated at Bordeaux on 20 March, 1314, has the curious endorsement that the "archbishop of Canterbury brought this letter here on 28 May, 1315[4]." Writs were frequently directed to the archbishop ordering him to summon the council. As early as 23 April, 1314, he was ordered to call the council to examine the charters of Battle Abbey[5]. Within the next few months he was ordered to summon councils to consider the petition of the countess of Foix[6], the king's endorsement to the petition specifically referring the matter to him[7]. He was also ordered to call the council to consider the question of the waste of Templar lands granted to the Hospitallers[8], to decide the right of the advowson of Hameldon which Badlesmere and the king claimed[9], and to examine the business pending in the king's bench between the king and John Gifford at the suit of Thomas de Berkley in the right of the manor of King's Stanley[10]. "Lerceuesqe et les autres bones gentz de vostre consail" made a return to the king in a certain matter[11]. These writs were all addressed individually to the archbishop and establish the fact that he was the working head of the council. The pre-eminence of his position there is also proved by the fact that business was transacted at Lambeth. In addition to the incident connected with exchequer administration which took place at Lambeth[12], petitioners appeared

[1] K. R. Mem. Roll, no. 90, m. 105. L. T. R. Mem. Roll, no. 87, Rec. Mich. m. 4 d.

[2] Chan. Warr., File 96/3820 (4 Dec. 1316).

[3] Ibid. File 99/4194 (2 May, 1317).

[4] Anc. Corresp. vol. XLIX, no. 82.

[5] Ibid. vol. XLV, no. 179.

[6] Ibid. no. 180 (22 May, 1314).

[7] Chan. Misc., Bdle 25/2 (12).

[8] Anc. Corresp. vol. XLV, no. 181 (30 May, 1314).

[9] Ibid. no. 182 (14 June, 1314).

[10] Ibid. no. 183 (18 June, 1314).

[11] Chan. Warr., File 90/3215.

[12] Vide above, p. 333.

at Lambeth before the archbishop and others of the king's council and there it was decided that a new extent of certain lands be made[1].

Sometimes the letters were addressed to the archbishop and the other good men of the council, the king writing in this form on 18 May, 1315, about the stopping of commissions of oyer and terminer in divers complaints of conspiracy in Norfolk and Suffolk. The king greatly marvelled at the stopping of them, and if it was found that they were stopped without good reason, the archbishop and council were to ordain that they should proceed without delay[2]. In the years 1315 and 1316, other persons were generally associated with the archbishop in writs ordering the summons of the council. The archbishop and Sandale, chancellor, were ordered to summon the council to consider and reply to a letter of the king of France[3], and in the writ of summons of a council that was to consider a certain wrong, Norwich, treasurer, was associated with them[4], and the same three were to call the council to consider a roll of articles touching Guienne[5]. Even after the parliament of Lincoln in 1316, when Lancaster had been appointed chief of the king's council[6], the archbishop did not lose his place of importance there. A writ of privy seal of 15 March, 1316, enclosing letters received from the constable of France to be considered and answered by the council, was addressed to the archbishop, Lancaster and others of the king's council at London[7]. In December of the same year the archbishop, the bishop of Winchester, chancellor, and Pembroke were ordered to summon a council to consider certain transcripts of letters which the king sent them, and to make remedy under the great seal[8].

The archbishop's position during the years 1314–16, if not as imposing or complete as that held by the earl of Pembroke in 1312–14 or by Hugh le Despenser the son in 1322–6[9], was important and effective. His influence seems to have been concentrated upon the administration of the council. Here he displaced the chancellor and was able to maintain his position even against Lancaster after the latter had been appointed chief counsellor. His position was due to the royal will and his place in the king's esteem, rather than to his ecclesiastical dignity; and the place he occupied in the council

[1] Wm Salt Soc., *Hist. Coll. Staff.* [1911], pp. 342–4.

[2] Anc. Corresp. vol. XLV, no. 187.

[3] Ibid. vol. XXXV, no. 123 (9 Sept. 1315).

[4] Ibid. no. 124 (21 Oct. 1315).

[5] Ibid. no. 124 (21 Oct. 1315).

[6] Vide below, pp. 412–413 et seq

[7] Anc. Corresp. vol. XXXV, no. 126. Vide App. of Doc. no. 108.

[8] Anc. Corresp. no. 128.

[9] Vide below, pp. 336–341.

over-riding the chancellor, the official head, provides an excellent instance of the personal system in action.

Considerably more complete than the part played by the archbishop, and more complete than even the Pembroke administration, was the part taken in the whole control of the government after 1322 by Hugh le Despenser the son. However important a figure he may have been in the political history between 1318 and his exile in 1321, it was after the battle of Boroughbridge that his influence throughout the whole administration became predominant. A chronicler writing after the event saw a gradual decline in the fortunes of the younger Despenser and a weakening of the condition of England[1], but judged by administrative standards the period of rule by him was one of efficiency if not popularity. In 1323, the condition of the king was better than it had been in 1322, for in that year, by the truce with Scotland, he freed himself from an enemy more powerful than even the baronial opposition. As a mark of his strength in that year the king perambulated the towns of the Welsh march. All the disturbers of the peace and the oppressors of the country-side were punished, old wrongs were done away with and the king ordered the law of the land to be observed in all places[2]. There was opportunity for a strong and effective administration and the young Despenser had considerable administrative ability. But there was a fatal flaw in his policy. It was too much designed for the promotion of self and the petty though constant oppression of individuals under his administration roused a greater storm of opposition than real vice or fierce oppression would have done. Those administrative reforms which were introduced during this period and with which the name of Stapleton, bishop of Exeter, was so closely associated, evoked the unpopularity which a strict and efficient financial system often produces.

Despenser exercised a strong influence over the king. His position as royal chamberlain and the intimate relations which existed between master and servant combined to make him the greatest power in the land. Nor was his influence hidden from the public eye. The control which he exercised over the king was notorious. Those who desired grace or favour from the king first approached Despenser. The prior of Christchurch, Canterbury, wrote to one about the king's court begging him to speak to and beseech Despenser the younger, or someone else about the court, to explain a matter which troubled him to

[1] *Chron. Mon. de Melsa*, vol. II, pp. 344–5.

[2] *Chron. H. de Blaneford*, p. 139.

the king and ascertain his wishes[1]. Shortly after, the prior wrote to Despenser requesting him to discover the king's will on a matter[2], the letters being sent to John de Dene, who was to hand them to Despenser at a convenient time and place, since he was fully occupied with other affairs[3]. The king had requested the prior to let him know how many pensions he paid to royal clerks and to what amount. The prior informed the king[4] and simultaneously wrote to Despenser asking him to arrange that no further pensions were demanded of him[5]. The pope, too, frequently sent Despenser letters. He was enjoined to be watchful in the king's service[6], to use his influence with the king to remove the causes of difference between the pope and king[7], to cause the bishop of Winchester to be received with favour[8], and to see that the king ceased his demands for the deposition of the bishops of Winchester, Lincoln, and Bath and Wells[9]. The bishop of Winchester subsequently acknowledged to the pope that his restoration was effected by the efforts of the bishops of Norwich and Exeter, and Despenser[10]. In 1326 in the critical months preceding the invasion of the queen, the pope made strong endeavours to promote peace. In March he wrote to Despenser suggesting that, since his participation in the government was given by the queen as the reason why she could not return to the king without danger, he should retire and devise means by which the queen might no longer fear to return to her husband[11]. A letter written in May contained a note of impatience. Instead of provoking enmities and causing grievances to prelates and princes he was enjoined to study to promote friendships[12]. Later in that month the cause of the papal irritation appears to have ended and Despenser was desired to continue his good offices in the promotion of agreement between the king and queen[13].

These letters testify to the fact that during the years 1322–6, the decisive influence at court was that of the younger Despenser. In fact, he conducted the administration on the king's behalf. He was the king's agent in all matters of business[14]. In 1324 the bishop of Exeter, treasurer, was in the north negotiating concerning the Scottish peace. Thence he wrote to Despenser about letters which the king had previously ordered from the chancery, the king obtaining

[1] *Lit. Cantuar.* vol. I, pp. 164–7.
[2] Ibid. pp. 168–171.
[3] Ibid. pp. 170–1.
[4] Camb. Univ. MS. Ee. v. 31, f. 235.
[5] Ibid.
[6] *Cal. Pap. Letters*, 1304–42, p. 444.
[7] Ibid. p. 457.
[8] Ibid. p. 459.
[9] Ibid. p. 457.
[10] Ibid. p. 460.
[11] Ibid. p. 475.
[12] Ibid. p. 477.
[13] Ibid. p. 478.
[14] *Chron. Lanerc.* p. 249.

his information of the matter from the treasurer's letter to Despenser[1]. News from royal servants concerning the Scottish march was sent not to the king but to Despenser[2]. He headed the royal deputation that went to Nottingham to interview a recalcitrant royal envoy to the papal court[3]. Henry de Clif and Adam de Brom, two chancery clerks who were guardians of the priory of Bermondsey, had a dispute with the prior. They begged the king that he would be pleased to charge the chancellor or the treasurer, Despenser or Baldock, to come to Bermondsey personally to survey the condition of the priory and to examine their actions and ordain according to the condition of the house[4]. The chancellor and the treasurer were appointed to go[5].

Despenser's power was not always used to the best ends. Adam de Murimuth, who had considerable knowledge of foreign affairs, relates an abortive attempt by Despenser and Baldock to prevent the king from receiving certain messages from the king of France[6]. In 1327 a petitioner complained of ejectment from his lands by the malice of Sir William de Clif, who informed Despenser and Baldock, chancellor, until a fine of 200 marks had been made[7].

It was in the administration of Gascony in the troubled years 1324–5 that Despenser's methods are seen in their most characteristic light. The correspondence with the officials in Gascony was conducted by Despenser[8]. He was more than the king's secretary or adviser; he directed Gascon affairs. The officials corresponded with him[9] and took their orders from him. He wrote to Adam de Lymbergh, constable of Bordeaux, informing him that the king and all his council were very pleased with his conduct of the king's business to which he had attended so diligently[10]. To the same official he wrote stating that the treasurer and seneschal at their coming to the court had informed the king of his good behaviour and his diligence on the king's business which had caused him great pleasure[11]. He wrote to the archbishop of Dublin and Master William de Weston informing them that Arnald Caillou would tell them by word of mouth all the things concerning his wishes and the arrangements for the parts in which he was[12]. Ralph Basset, John de Wysham and Adam de

[1] Chan. Warr., File 128/7027.
[2] Anc. Corresp. vol. XLIX, no. 58.
[3] Chan. Warr., File 125/6744.
[4] Ancient Petition, no. 1944.
[5] Ibid.
[6] *Chron. Murimuth*, pp. 39, 40.
[7] *Cal. Inq. P. M.* vol. VI, pp. 228–9.
[8] Anc. Corresp. vol. XLIX, no. 152; vol. LIV, nos. 3 a, 4, 7, 9, 10.
[9] Ibid. vol. XLIX, nos. 114–115; vol. L, no. 36; vol. LIV, no. 6; vol. LVIII, no. 1.
[10] Ibid. vol. LIV, no. 9.
[11] Ibid. no. 10.
[12] Ibid. no. 4: "Et Arnald Caillou vous soet direr assez pleinement totes choses de bouche des noz voluntez et des noz arraiz des parties en nous sumes."

Lymbergh sent under their seal to Despenser a transcript of a letter which they were sending to the king[1]. Hugh ordered two officials to hold a certain matter touching the affairs of Gascony in the strictest secrecy in order that the king's estate and honour might be maintained[2]. The bishop of Norwich writing from Gascony begged Hugh that the treasurer should be ordered to send money if the king wished him to stay abroad, because of the great expense thereby entailed[3].

The men who carried out the Gascon policy were almost without exception Despenser's friends or dependents and whether friends and dependents or not they all looked to him as their superior officer. Ralph Basset, deputy of the earl of Kent, as seneschal[4] had been closely associated with Despenser and in July, 1322, had witnessed a charter made to him[5]. Oliver de Ingham who became seneschal in March, 1326[6], had served under Hugh as one of his knights in the Scottish war[7], while Robert de Waterville[8] and others had been identified with the Despenser interest.

In every detail of Gascon administration Despenser's hand was found and at times his conduct of Gascon affairs appears to justify the charge made against him of erecting himself to be a second king. In some of his correspondence there appears to be an assumption of regality. He constantly refers to the king and himself in the correspondence with the Gascon officials. Robert de Swynbourn was informed that the king and Despenser held him in especial good grace and was asked to inform the king and Despenser as often, fully and definitely as possible on all matters concerning the duchy[9]. Oliver de Ingham gave orders to Ralph Basset on behalf of the king and on behalf of Hugh[10] and Basset stated that he had remained in Gascony to his great danger and peril at the wish of the king and Hugh[11]. A draft of a letter from Despenser to Robert de Waterville is still

[1] Anc. Corresp. vol. LVIII, no. 1.
[2] Ibid. vol. LIV, no. 3 a.
[3] Ibid. vol. L, no. 36.
[4] Tout, *The Place of Ed. II*, p. 396.
[5] *Descr. Cat. Ancient Deeds*, vol. I, p. 21.
[6] Tout, *The Place of Ed. II*, p. 396.
[7] Stowe MS. 553, p. 61.
[8] *Descr. Cat. Ancient Deeds*, vol. I, p. 110.
[9] Anc. Corresp. vol. LIV, no. 7: "et vous fesoms sauoir qe nostre seigneur le Roi et nous vous en sauoms especialment bon gre...facez sauoir a nostre dit seigneur et a nous distinctement et pleinement totes les choses touchauntes sa Deuschee."
[10] Ibid. vol. L, no. 74: "La entencion de mon seigneur Rauf Basset si est qe par ceo qe monsire Oliver Dengham le dist depart le Roi et depart monsire Hugh qil demorast en Gascoyne."
[11] Ibid.: "et il a la volunte du Roy et de monsire Hugh est demore a grant damage et peril de lui."

more illuminating. Despenser stated he had learnt Waterville's request from his letters which he had shown the king and his council as desired. The first draft continued: "it seems to our lord the king and to us that you have acted wisely and advisedly done what you state in your letter." This was subsequently amended and the words "et a nous" were cancelled[1]. Another phrase replaced by a more suitable one ran "which excuse our said lord and ourself hold as true[2]." Despenser had an exalted view of his own importance.

Despenser, Stapleton and Baldock dominated everything. They worked together in close sympathy for they had a common administrative ability to bind them together. The bishop of Exeter and Baldock were the two important witnesses to the grant of Striguil to Hugh[3]. Under their direction administrative form was closely observed. Writs under the great seal were, after 1322, generally issued on the information of Baldock, chancellor, Stapleton, treasurer, or clerks like William de Ayremynne[4]. It was but seldom that the Despensers obtruded themselves. King, favourite and officials worked together with a common purpose, unimpeded by external pressure. The heads of the administration were reformers like Despenser, and he saw to it that the subordinates were recruited from among his own clerks. It had always been a part of Despenser's policy to be on good terms with the officials and justices. In 1318 when D'Audley thought to obtain Spigurnel's support against Despenser, the latter was quite confident that the justice would do nothing against him[5]. William de Cusance, who had been a personal clerk of Despenser and was still his clerk in 1319 though then receiving the king's wages[6], in 1320 was made keeper of the great wardrobe[7]. Another of Despenser's clerks, William de Clif, became a chancery clerk[8]. The policy was so prevalent that it was made a charge against him in 1321[9], but it was after 1322 that it was most general. It was natural that he should use his own instruments to fulfil such a sway of personal domination.

Despenser also interfered directly with the administration of the great departments. In April, 1322, the king sent to the chancellor

[1] Anc. Corresp. vol. XLIX, no. 152: "Et semble a nostre dit seigneur (et a nous) qe vous auez molt sagement et auisement face de ce qe vous lui auez si aparti par voz lettres."

[2] Ibid.: "quele excusacion nostre dit seigneur et nous tenoms par verroie."

[3] *Descr. Cat. Ancient Deeds*, vol. III, p. 116.

[4] Vide *Cal. Close Rolls*, 1323–27; *Cal. Pat. Rolls*, 1321–24, 1324–27; *Cal. Fine Rolls*, 1319–27 passim.

[5] Cotton MS. Nero C. iii, f. 181. [6] Tout, *The Place of Edward II*, p. 136.

[7] Ibid. p. 357. [8] Ibid. p. 136. [9] Vide below, p. 480.

a bill containing the substance of certain commissions and letters to be made to such persons as Despenser would inform him on the royal behalf[1]. Payments in the wardrobe were made on his announcement[2]. His position in the council was important. The eschevins and council of Ghent and the burgomaster and eschevins and council of Bruges in a letter to Despenser in 1323 described him as the privy counsellor of the king[3]. In a letter the earl of Kent stated that he sent a certain messenger to the king, Despenser and others of the council[4]. In 1324 a writ under the secret seal was addressed to Despenser, the bishop of Exeter, treasurer, and Baldock, chancellor, stating that the king had heard what they had done about a certain charter[5].

The Pembroke administration, the administrative action of the archbishop of Canterbury, and the Despenser administration all illustrate certain phases of the personal system in action. The Pembroke administration appears to have been effective and did not rouse opposition. The archbishop of Canterbury did not command such an imposing place but his work on the council was useful. The administration of the young Despenser partly from internal causes and in part from external, ended in revolution and bloodshed. That the personal system was able to make use of three men so diverse in qualifications, aims and policy was a proof of its inherent strength. The complete control which these three unofficial persons exercised, by virtue of the royal will, upon the administration both in general policy and in interference with all the departments, shows to what a great extent administration was still even in its formal processes vested in the king, and how little the consciousness of the rights and position of officials had developed. The personal system with its organisation of the household was the decisive fact in administration.

The peculiar importance attaching to the reign of Edward II was described as being connected with the beginning of a differentiation of the functions and offices of the administration and the household. The king's household was considered, historically and practically, as the source of all administrative authority, and the system of government which obtained was shown to be extremely personal. Great importance therefore attached to the character of the king and of the

[1] Chan. Warr., File 117/5995. Vide App. of Doc. no. 73.

[2] Stowe MS. 553, f. 67 b.

[3] Anc. Corresp. vol. XXXVII, no. 35: "priuie conseil."

[4] Ibid. vol. XLIX, no. 190: "a nostre seigneur le Roi et vous seigneur et as autres du conseil."

[5] K. R. Mem. Roll, no. 97, Brev. dir. Pasch. m. 2. Vide App. of Doc. no. 37.

other chief figures in the reign, especially to the personalities of the king's favourites. The inherent strength of the household system and the way in which it exercised its influence upon the government demanded a paramount place. The administrative departments had not shaken themselves free of household control, for the household and administration were barely distinguishable parts of the king's court. There was a nascent differentiation but for practical purposes it was hampered by the control which the household system exercised by the appointment of officials and its complete check upon the great seal. The strength of the household was dual, it controlled the government and was independent of it. The effective executive lay in the household, with its instruments of the privy and secret seals, with its informal warrants and verbal orders. In the wardrobe and the chamber the household had independent and potent financial departments. In the marshalsea court and in various household privileges it had a certain independence in justice. The officials of the household, chief and minor and the clerical staff, were another source of strength. The "administrative" council, an executive body controlled by the household and yet outside it, was able to exert a decisive influence on the great departments of the chancery and exchequer and also upon the formal assemblies of the great council and parliament. Upon the administrative, executive and formal bodies the household system, independent of all accessories, could dictate policy and exercise a dominant control. Against the overpowering strength of the household system such minor weaknesses as were present are negligible. All these features of the household system were exemplified in the instances which were taken of the household system in action. Still more did they stand out in the struggles between king and barons during the reign of Edward II. That struggle in its origin, course and results can only be interpreted by an appreciation of the intricacies and influence of the household system, and this statement will be more clear after the successive expedients by which the barons endeavoured to put their plans into operation have been considered.

PART II

THE CONSTITUTIONAL AND ADMINISTRATIVE ACTION OF THE BARONIAL OPPOSITION

CHAPTER I

RESTRAINT UPON THE KING

Against the great strength of the household system there stood a baronial opposition resting on a principle which was in direct contradiction to that upon which the household system worked. It was a clash of opposing theories; a conflict in which both sides could claim to rest upon conservatism, though actually both contained revolutionary ideas. Ever since the Conquest baronial opposition to the monarchy had existed in England. There had been a number of barons who, acting upon the principle of baronial privilege or upon an exaggerated view of their own position and functions, had withstood the king and his policy by force and sought to substitute for the royal a baronial policy. For the first century after the Conquest the opposition of the barons was based upon feudal theories. Their object was to obtain more local independence in development of the separatist tendencies of feudalism. The strong centralised organisation built up by Henry II ended all hopes of ultimate success in this direction. The main motive of the baronial opposition altered. Under the stress of circumstances they were compelled to surrender their ideas of feudal local independence and to concentrate their efforts upon obtaining a voice in the new central organisation which was developing. From the time of Magna Carta the purely feudal policy was no longer the main motive. Baronial opposition demanded a wider definition. From a demand for local independence it was expanding to an insistent demand for complete or part control of the central administration. The barons in the reign of Edward II were still under the influence of the new baronial opposition, the principle and action of which was first exemplified in Magna Carta. The increased mechanism of administration which the thirteenth century had produced necessitated certain changes in the machinery, but fundamentally the underlying principle of the opposition was the same. This new baronial opposition was still based upon feudalism. The aims of the policy were not constitutional, they were to a considerable extent personal, which was but another way of stating that they were oligarchical. Nor was the baronial opposition of Edward II the last phase of this particular policy. It continued until the Wars of the Roses. The barons had by that time obtained power to use the council and all other administrative organs for their own ends. The organisation of government was directed to baronial objects[1].

Though the objects of the baronial policy were new, they claimed to be demanding their rights. They acted upon a theory of baronial rights, which they claimed to exercise. Their plea during the reign of Edward II was that the king had usurped their rights, and the object of their opposition claimed to be but an endeavour to regain what had been usurped. However untrustworthy may be the *Mirror of Justices*, in one passage in which it deals with the king and the barons, it seems to summarise the problem fairly in its broad outlines:

> And whereas ordinances ought to be made by the common consent of the king and his earls, they are now made by the king and his clerks and by aliens and others who dare not oppose the king but desire to please him and to counsel him for his profit, albeit their counsel is not for the good of the community of the people, and this without any summons of the earls or any observance of the rules of right, so that divers ordinances are now founded rather upon will than upon right[2].

The precedents of opposition upon which the barons of the reign of Edward II acted were fully recognised. Especially was the opposition of Simon de Montfort to Henry III noted[3]. It was the latest and most serious attempt to control the king and its power as an example was great. Baronial respect for previous leaders of opposition was emphasised in the requests made to the pope for the canonisation of Thomas de Cantelupe, bishop of Hereford[4].

The baronial policy which the barons pursued from Magna Carta onwards was one of restraint exercised upon the king. The nature, the degree, the method of restraint varied, but restraint was the

[1] Fortescue, *Governance of England*, ed. C. Plummer, § xv, pp. 145–9.
[2] Seld. Soc., *Mirror of Justices*, pp. 155–6.
[3] *Auct. Malm.* p. 196.
[4] *Reg. Pal. Dunelm.* vol. iv, p. xxxi. *Cal. Pap. Letters*, 1304–42, p. 199.

underlying principle. The king was still to exercise the functions of government, subject to baronial restraint which would be exercised, or attempted, whenever the king acted in direct contradiction to baronial wishes. Employment or threatened employment of physical force was the only means of exercising restraint. When in a campaign in 1240 Henry III's desire to defend a town in Gascony meant envelopment and consequently surrender and annihilation, Montfort opposed him. He told the council, "As for the king, treat him like Charles the Simple; there are iron-bound rooms in Windsor well adapted for his residence[1]." The discovery of machinery to bring pressure to bear upon the king was a difficult and lengthy process. There was no easy compromise between leaving the king with complete discretionary powers, and placing the royal power in commission[2]. The employment of physical or quasi-physical restraint inevitably led to a complete suspension of royal power.

The various stages of the history of restraint upon the king have to be examined, and the development of the machinery traced. That history may be said to commence with Magna Carta. The executive clause of Magna Carta[3] provided for the appointment of a committee of twenty-five barons to observe, hold and make to be observed the liberties which the king had granted. If the king or any officials failed in any detail of the obligations, the matter should be shown to a sub-committee of four who were to go to the king, or if he were abroad to his justiciar, and demand the correction of the fault without delay. If in forty days the error were not redressed, the matter was to be referred to the remainder of the twenty-five. The twenty-five barons with the whole community of the land[4] should then distress and grieve the king in every way in their power, by taking his castles, lands and possessions and in other ways, until the king had made amends according to their will. Whoever wished to swear to the barons was to be allowed to do so. This committee of twenty-five barons has been variously called a committee of rebellion, for it was given a legal right to organise rebellion[5], a committee of remonstrance and constraint and a "permanent organisation for making war against the king[6]." But it was more than this. The

[1] Bémont, *Simon de Montfort*, Appendix no. 36, p. 341.

[2] This was the effect of the Provisions of Oxford. Vide below, pp. 347–8.

[3] Cf. Magna Carta, § 61 (Stubbs, *Select Charters*, 9th edit. pp. 301–2); McKechnie, *Magna Carta*, pp. 465–477.

[4] "Cum communa totius terrae."

[5] McKechnie, *Magna Carta*, p. 468.

[6] S. R. Gardiner, *Short History of England*, p. 184.

commentary of a contemporary chronicler upon the clause is suggestive. "Over and above all this they desired that twenty-five barons should be chosen, and by the judgment of these twenty-five the king should govern them in all things, and through them redress all the wrongs that he should do to them, and they also, on the other hand, would through them redress all the wrongs that they should do to him. *Also they further desired, along with all this, that the king should never have power to appoint a bailiff in his lands except through the twenty-five*[1]." Whether or not this was a correct description of the powers possessed by the committee of twenty-five barons, the extract certainly shows that the idea of a committee of barons, not as a mere temporary expedient for the fulfilment of a specific purpose, but as a part of the ordinary system of government, was prevalent at that time. The great complaint to be made against this scheme was that it rested upon the feudal idea of private war, which was the remedy for a grievance[2]. It contained no constructive statesmanship[3]. It did not provide an effective executive; it provided means to punish a bad executive. Even with this faulty machinery more power than was subsequently granted to similar schemes was given in 1215.

In 1244, when owing to various causes, domestic and foreign, there was a growing feeling of opposition against the king, Henry III asked for a subsidy[4]. The council considered the matter and a committee of twelve, four prelates, four earls and four barons, was appointed[5]. A paper constitution was drawn up, which illustrated the advances which had been made since Magna Carta. All liberties which had been bought, granted or confirmed by the king's charter were to be observed in future and for greater security a new charter was to be made[6]. The proposed constitution suggested the appointment, by common assent, of four magnates of the more discrete of the whole kingdom, to be of the king's council and to swear to treat the business of the king and kingdom faithfully, and do justice to all without exception of person. They were to follow the king, at least two of them were always to be present to hear complaints. They were to supervise the treasury and expenditure and to be conservators of liberties. Since they were to be chosen by the assent

[1] *Histoire des ducs*, ed. F. Michel [1840], p. 150. Cf. McKechnie, *Magna Carta*, p. 468, note 2.

[2] Pollock and Maitland, *Hist. of Engl. Law*, vol. II, pp. 505–6. Holdsworth, *Hist. of Engl. Law*, vol. II, p. 167.

[3] McKechnie, *Magna Carta*, p. 74.

[4] J. H. Ramsay, *The Dawn of the Constitution*, p. 108.

[5] Matt. Paris, *Chron. Maj.* vol. IV, pp. 362–3.

[6] Ibid. p. 366.

of all, not one of them was to be removed without common assent. Writs made against the king and custom of the kingdom were to be recalled immediately. The justiciar and the chancellor, who were to be constantly with the king, and the itinerant justices were to be chosen by the council. Various matters touching the use of the seal, the appointment of other officials and kindred matters were likewise stated[1]. If the king removed the seal from the chancellor, whatever was sealed in the interval was null and void[2]. The constitution was an attempt to redress past grievances, and to provide a machinery of government for the future. A baronial committee was to restrain and control the king's actions. It was an important step towards the baronial opposition to Edward II. It is unlikely that the scheme was ever presented to the king[3], much less carried out[4], but its importance lies in its conception and in the developing policy of the barons.

In 1248, in a meeting of the great council, the barons again protested against the king continuing to govern without a justiciar, chancellor or treasurer approved by the council. As long as officials like John Maunsel held important positions in the administration, the barons could accomplish nothing[5]. A responsible official or a baron or prelate holding office would suit their purpose. The great council in 1255 renewed its demands for the appointment of a justiciar, a chancellor and a treasurer acceptable to itself, but again no success attended the demand[6].

In the Provisions of Oxford in 1258 another important advance was made. The scheme may have been complicated and impracticable, and its machinery cumbrous and contradictory, yet as an endeavour to exercise restraint it has great importance. There was an advance in political theory. The Provisions of Oxford contained a crude expedient to constrain royal officials to keep the law. An oath of office to be taken by all ministers was provided[7]. A commission of twenty-four members, half appointed by the barons, and half by the king, was appointed to redress grievances and draw up a new scheme of government. This commission of reform proceeded to provide for the appointment of a standing council of fifteen, who were

[1] Matt. Paris, *Chron. Maj.* vol. IV, pp. 366–8.

[2] Ibid. p. 367. Cf. *Eng. Hist. Rev.* vol. XXVII [1912], 'Chancellors and Keepers of the Seal under Henry III,' Miss L. B. Dibben, pp. 45–46.

[3] G. W. Prothero, *Simon de Montfort* [1877], p. 72.

[4] T. F. Tout, *Political History*, 1216–1377, p. 66.

[5] Ramsay, *Dawn of Constit.* p. 122. Prothero, *Simon de Montfort*, p. 33.

[6] Ramsay, *Dawn of Constit.* p. 152.

[7] McKechnie, *Magna Carta*, p. 433.

to attend all parliaments. The council of fifteen was to be elected by a complicated system of cross election. The king was to rule in future by the advice and consent of this council. Grants to the crown were to be made by another council of twenty-four, while the original council of twenty-four was still to arrange for the reform of the royal household. Three times a year a further council of twelve, elected by the barons, was to consult with the standing council of fifteen[1]. Various officers of state were to be appointed and to be responsible to the king and council. The king's action in almost every direction was restrained and controlled by the baronial committees, especially by the standing committee of fifteen. The effect would have been the establishment of an oligarchy, in which the control rested in the hands of the council of fifteen. The scheme did not endure, and it was soon followed by the battle of Lewes and the subsequent triumph of the barons in 1264.

The triumph of Montfort in 1264 produced a new endeavour to impose restraint. Three persons called electors were to be appointed who were, on the king's behalf, to elect or nominate nine counsellors. All business of administration, including appointment of officials, was to be conducted by the counsel of these nine, three of whom were to be always with the king. If any official, great or small, transgressed, the king was to depose him at once by the counsel of the nine, and by the same counsel appoint another. A member of the council of nine could only be displaced with the advice of the three electors, who would substitute another. If the council of nine could not agree, the matter was to be referred to the electors, the voice of two of whom was to prevail. If the whole body of prelates and barons considered that any one of the electors should be removed, the king should appoint another in his place on their advice[2]. Besides the negative merits of being less complicated than the scheme in the Provisions of Oxford, there was a distinct advance in the scheme by the introduction of new principles which were of far-reaching importance and great influence in the future development of the constitution[3].

[1] *Ann. Monast.* vol. 1, *Annales de Burton*, pp. 438–453. Ramsay, *Dawn of Constit.* pp. 166–174. Tout, *Polit. Hist.* 1216–1377, pp. 98–101. Prothero, *Simon de Montfort*, pp. 186, 202.

[2] For discussion on the scheme vide Prothero, *Simon de Montfort*, pp. 288–9; Ramsay, *Dawn of Constit.* p. 229; Tout, *Polit. Hist.* 1216–1377, pp. 119–120. The documents relating to the new constitution are printed in Stubbs, *Select Charters*, 9th edit. pp. 399–404; *Foedera*, vol. 1, pp. 443–4.

[3] Prothero, *Simon de Montfort*, pp. 289–293.

The final example of the exercise of restraint to be considered is the committee of twelve barons set up by the Scottish parliament in 1294 to advise the king of Scotland in all matters[1]. It has been said that this committee "though established professedly on the model of the twelve peers of France had a nearer prototype in the fifteen appointed under the Provisions of Oxford[2]." The composition of this committee of four bishops, four earls and four barons would suggest a resemblance to the committee which drew up the paper constitution of 1244[3]. Whatever was its model or prototype, its effect was to make the king a puppet in the hands of the barons.

From the time of Magna Carta it may be said fairly that the barons had realised that their best policy was to use the royal administrative machinery and the royal officials to control the king. Control was taking the place of supersession. This was the important fact which Magna Carta suggested and the history of the thirteenth century brought into relief. Under Edward II baronial control endeavoured to work its way into all departments of the administration, and all phases of those departments.

There was a continual series of attempts to exercise restraint. In the opening of the reign in the stringent coronation oath exacted from the new king[4], there was a slight element of compulsion, though in comparison with subsequent actions that effort was inconsiderable. From one point of view, the most complete instance of restraint is found in the Ordinances of 1311, when restraint was imposed even in the use of the privy seal[5]. Another phase of restraint came out strongly in the parliament of Lincoln of 1316, when Lancaster became the king's chief counsellor[6]. The extent to which the reign was a struggle between the barons seeking to impose restraint and the king resisting the imposition is brought out in the revocation of the Ordinances in 1322. The Ordinances were revoked because "by the matters so ordained the royal power of our said lord king was restrained in divers things, contrary to what ought to be, to the blemishing of his royal sovereignty, and against the estate of the crown[7]." It was not sufficient for the king to revoke the results

[1] Lang, *Hist. of Scotl.* vol. I, p. 177. Ramsay, *Dawn of Constit.* p. 417. Tout, *Polit. Hist.* 1236–1377, p. 194.

[2] Tout, *Polit. Hist.* 1216–1377, p. 194.

[3] Vide above, pp. 346–7.

[4] Cf. Stubbs, *Constit. Hist.* vol. II, pp. 331–2. Gneist, *Constit. Hist.* vol. II, pp. 21–22. *Stat. of Realm*, vol. I, p. 168, gives the text of the new coronation oath.

[5] *Stat. of Realm*, vol. I, p. 165. Ordinance 32.

[6] *Rot. Parl.* vol. I, pp. 351–2. *Parl. Writs*, vol. II, Pt i, pp. 169–170.

[7] *Stat. of Realm*, vol. I, p. 189.

of successful efforts to exercise restraint. Adequate safeguards had to be made for the future. It was accordingly provided:

> That for ever hereafter, all manner of ordinances, or provisions made by the subjects of our lord the king or his heirs, by any power or authority whatsoever, concerning the royal power of our lord the king or of his heirs, or against the estate of our said lord the king or his heirs, or against the estate of the crown shall be void and of no avail or force whatever[1].

In all these attempts to exercise restraint, before and during the reign of Edward II, certain well-defined objects in baronial policy made themselves apparent. The primary object of the baronial opposition was to break down the system of government which has been called the household or the personal system. The key to that system was the executive, and before any successful attack could be made it was essential for the barons to obtain some control over the executive or provide an alternative body. Whether the executive consisted of household officials or the "administrative" council this control was vital to baronial success. The first essential was the executive, and the executive body was the council. The activity and composition of the effective phases of the council were dependent upon the household and chamber. The barons concentrated against the household and council but the dual policy was inextricably interwoven. They sought to re-organise the council and by a reformed council with themselves in complete command to influence the king and control the administration; but the household was too powerful. There were two ways in which the strength of the household system could be attacked. In the first place the barons might lessen its control of the government by obtaining a greater share in administration themselves. In addition to that secondary method there was a primary method, an attempt to weaken the sources of strength of the household system and to decrease its independence—in the direction of executive, finance, justice and officials. Baronial policy touched all these lines and there were many various ways in which it sought to achieve the given end.

The barons therefore made it one of their objects to obtain the appointment or at least some control over the appointment of officials. Montfort had acted upon the idea of the baronial control of officials and when in dispute with Henry III over the government of Gascony declared himself ready to resign his governorship, provided it was the will of the prelates, magnates and counsellors of the king[2]. In

[1] *Stat. of Realm*, vol. I, p. 189.

[2] Cf. Bémont, *Simon de Montfort*, p. 46. *Eng. Hist. Rev.* vol. I [1886], p. 161.

1264 Master Thomas de Cantelupe was "elected" to the chancery by the king and the magnates who were of his council[1]. The writ making the appointment was sealed by the king in the presence of Hugh le Despenser, the justiciar and other barons[2]. Edward II never became so powerless as to be humiliated thus[3]. The idea of baronial participation in the appointment of an administrative official was repugnant to the king. When an effort was made to interfere with Edward I's officials, he said that they might as well take away his kingdom as interfere with his choice of servants[4]. Early in the reign of Edward II the barons endeavoured to interfere with the positions of officials. In the parliament at Northampton in 1308 the king and the earls agreed that the king should remove from his council and presence Despenser, Segrave, Bereford, William Inge and two others[5]. The claim to assist in, or control, the appointment of officials was made several times during the reign. The chronicler noted that when Walter Reynolds was made chancellor "communitate tamen Angliae non consentiente[6]." In the arrangements made during the reign of Edward I for the Scottish king's household[7] the appointment of officials was given great prominence. "Good and sufficient ministers to serve the king both within and without (the household)" were to be appointed by the counsel and consent of all the baronage[8]. The chancellor was to be appointed in this manner[9]. The magnates were to appoint suitable justices[10]; and sheriffs were to be elected by the advice and election of the good people of the county[11].

Whatever claims the barons may have had to appoint or participate in the appointment of administrative officials, they were certainly trespassing very seriously upon the king's personal rights

[1] Madox, *Hist. of Exch.* vol. I, p. 76: "per nos et magnates nostros qui sunt de concilio nostro electus sit, in cancellarium regni nostri."

[2] Ibid. [3] Cf. Harcourt, *His Grace the Steward*, pp. 128–137.

[4] *Rishanger Chron.* p. 460. *Chron. P. de Langtoft*, vol. II, pp. 328–331.

[5] *Ann. Paul.* p. 264. [6] Ibid. pp. 268–9.

[7] A transcript of a portion of Corpus Christi Coll. MS. no. 37 was made by Miss Mary Bateson and was published in the *Juridical Review*, Dec. 1901, and March, 1902. It has since been reprinted with an introduction in Scottish Hist. Soc. vol. XLIV [1904], *Miscellany*, vol. II, pp. 3–44. The MS. is a collection of miscellaneous matter relating to household and administration, and this particular portion has been set down by Miss Bateson as ordinances made for the administration of Scotland either by Edward I or the Scottish barons. Madox, *Bar. Angl.* p. 164, interprets these ordinances as referring to the administration of England.

[8] Scot. Hist. Soc., *Miscellany*, vol. II, p. 38. [9] Ibid.

[10] Ibid. p. 43. [11] Ibid.

when they demanded a similar part in the appointment of officials of his household. Yet in an assault upon the household system it was of the utmost importance that the barons should obtain a predominant control over the choice of the household officials. This right the Ordinances claimed[1], and in the parliament of 1318 the chronicler announces the removal of the king's steward, treasurer, chamberlain and all sheriffs[2]. The arrangements for the Scottish king's household had provided that the chamberlain should be appointed by the great men[3], but since this chamberlain had "to guide and govern the burghs and demesne lands of the king[4]," his office had more administrative functions than the king's chamberlain in England, the baronial interference can be more easily justified. It was not until the reign of Richard II that any such drastic proposal was made in England[5], though in 1341 the chamberlain of the king's household with other officers was ordered to be sworn on appointment to keep and maintain the laws of the land and the articles of Magna Carta as well as other statutes[6].

Another baronial method was the association of administrative officials with household officials in their work. The coroners of the district, for instance, were associated with the king's coroner, in the conduct of inquests[7], or the royal coroner took inquests subsequently to the local coroner[8]. Efforts were also made to make the household departments dependent upon the administrative. Even the steward of the household was to return estreats to the exchequer[9].

The barons endeavoured to obtain control over the council, especially over the council in its "administrative" phase In a matter of favour the main question might be decided by the king, details being left to the "administrative" council[10]. This system in its working left a great deal of power in the hands of the "administrative" council. Despenser during the period when he controlled the administration worked through this small body with its great power[11] It was against this body that the opposition of the barons was ranged largely, and against this system that their efforts of reform and alteration were directed.

[1] Vide below, pp. 371–2. [2] *Auct. Bridl.* p. 56.
[3] Scot. Hist. Soc., *Miscellany*, vol. II, p. 38. [4] Ibid.
[5] Cf. *Liber Niger Domus Regis Ed. IV* (Soc. of Antiq., 1790), p. 81.
[6] Thoms, *Book of the Court*, p. 319. [7] Seld. Soc., *Select Coroners' Rolls*, p. 85.
[8] Seld. Soc., *Eyre of Kent*, vol. I, p. 132.
[9] *Stat. of Realm*, vol. I, p. 191. [10] Anc. Corresp. vol. XXXVII, no. 104.
[11] Vide above, pp. 340–1. Cf. also Anc. Corresp. vol. XXXVII, no. 88. Vide App. of Doc. no. 113.

It was to the personnel and composition of the council rather than to its power that the barons objected. The official element was too considerable, and the non-official element was nominated by the king. In 1224 the peers of France had protested against the chancellor, butler, chamberlain, and constable of France—the principal officers of the royal household—being with them to do justice as peers of France. The household officers however claimed use and custom and the matter was decided in their favour[1]. The baronial opposition in England based their dislike of the official element upon the same grounds. The official element supported the king, and their preponderance prevented the barons exercising their just rights. The baronial attempt to control the council came out more strongly after the Ordinances, especially in the parliament of Lincoln in 1316[2] and of York in 1318[3]. Immediately after the Ordinances, however, the king found it necessary to prohibit the mayor and bailiffs of Bristol from appearing before an assembly of barons. They had given the earl of Gloucester security to appear before him and the prelates, earls and barons about to assemble there, to answer for certain contempts. The king ordered them not to appear because he considered it might prejudice him and his royal dignity[4].

The barons also endeavoured to restrict and control the use of the great seal. As an important instrument of the executive and the origin of most administrative processes it was a vital object of the baronial opposition to control its issue. The appointment of the chancellor would have given them this in part, but there were various other ways which they endeavoured to use.

The importance of the exchequer as an administrative department was too great for the barons not to make it one of the objects of their attack. They attacked it as a court because it heard pleas of debts other than those of the king and his officials[5]. The *Mirror of Justices* gives a long list of abuses in the exchequer[6]. It was however with the exchequer as a financial institution supplying the king's personal needs that the barons were primarily concerned, and it was its functions in this direction that they tried to define and control. Without revenue the barons imagined that the king could be brought to his knees. After the restoration of Gavaston in 1312 the barons

[1] C. V. Langlois, *Textes Relatifs à l'Histoire du Parlement* [1888], pp. 35–36. Viollet, *Institutions Politiques*, vol. III, pp. 301–2.

[2] Vide below, pp. 412–413, 416–423. [3] Vide below, pp. 444–468.

[4] *Cal. Close Rolls*, 1307–13, p. 450 (8 March, 1312).

[5] Madox, *Hist. of Exch.* vol. II, pp. 74–78. Cf. also *Cal. Close Rolls*, 1279–88, pp. 194, 296. [6] Seld. Soc., *Mirror of Justices*, p. 158.

decided that "the king who would not agree with his lieges in anything, should not receive from his exchequer so much as a halfpenny or a farthing[1]."

The methods by which the barons sought to attain their ends must be outlined. While the barons were united in their objects, there was a great divergence of opinion concerning the method to employ. This difference was not the result of mere questions of tactics or expediency. The barons differed about the degree of restraint to be imposed. One party seemed desirous of pushing their opposition to extremity; another party of steering a middle course.

Throughout the reign Bishop Stubbs[2] sees three parties in the country. There was the royal party, a group of bishops and barons supported by officials. The other two parties mark the great division amongst the barons. There was the Lancaster faction, acting under the direction of Thomas, earl of Lancaster. The party was strong in wealth and possessions and included the majority of the baronage. It had the traditions of Montfort behind it, but it lacked leaders of constructive ability. Its leaders required the elements of statesmanship. There was the middle party, acting under Pembroke's direction. Though this middle or mediating party was not in existence throughout the reign as an organised body, yet the principles which underlay its action were always operative. Though it could not compare with the Lancaster faction in dignity and wealth, it had a tremendous advantage over it in one particular. The earl of Pembroke was a leader of consummate ability and if the party which he guided was not strong in numbers or influence, what it lacked in these respects it made up in others. On the Ordinances the barons were at one, but in the subsequent schemes of the Lancaster faction, Pembroke and his followers did not take an active part and at times supported the king against the baronage. They never sought to humiliate the king to the dust and the king consequently did not regard them with the dislike which he exhibited towards certain of the Lancaster connection. Moreover the middle party remained personally faithful to the king, and sought to work through him rather than in opposition.

The methods employed by the baronial opposition varied with the power of the two parties. The methods may be divided roughly into direct and indirect action. The most outstanding of the direct were the efforts made to reform the household, the chief of which were the Ordinances of 1311. This was a direct attempt to impose a new scheme upon the king against his will. No less direct were the

[1] *Chron. Lanerc.* p. 196.

[2] Vide Stubbs, *Introd. to Chron. Ed. I and Ed. II*, vol. 1, pp. cxiii–cxv.

various schemes to make the king govern by the counsel and advice of a permanent council appointed by the barons. The very directness of these methods proved their undoing. The nature and operation of the restraint was so palpable that it brought the baronial opposition into too sharp and clear conflict with the king. Consequently the direct method had to give way to the indirect.

The indirect action was less visible but more insidious, and therefore had more possibilities of success. On the other hand, however, the objects attainable by this method were not so considerable. The indirect method took the form of an effort to become a part of the personal system. This was the means employed by the middle party between 1316–21. The policy of the Lancastrian party also developed from the direct to the indirect method. There were various ways in which the barons could influence the administration, and so control the government indirectly. The indirect method in effect only strengthened the household system, for it was through its organisation that the action was felt. The barons sought to obtain the favour of the king. The members of the middle party, Badlesmere, Damory, D'Audley employed this means and the earl of Hereford was also found in close association with the king, though at times he was as extreme as Lancaster himself. A parliament held in October, 1313, granted the king a twenty-fifth, other matters being postponed until the next parliament. After the parliament the earl of Hereford remained of the king's household, while the other earls went home[1].

There was also a more impersonal way of indirect action. The barons sought and obtained offices for their dependents. The clerks of barons sometimes obtained the highest offices in the administration. John Walwayn, who was twice escheator south of Trent, and for a brief period treasurer[2], was a clerk of the earl of Hereford[3]. Even after he was in the royal employment Walwayn still acted for the earl[4]. These facts suggest that Walwayn owed his position to the

[1] *Auct. Malm.* p. 196: "et comes Herfordire remansit de regis familia, ceteri vero comites reversi sunt ad propria."

[2] Tout, *The Place of Ed. II*, pp. 363, 332.

[3] In 1308 a payment of £200 for services in the Scottish war was made to Hereford by the hand of Master John Walwayn (Issue Roll, no. 144, m. 3). When Hereford was a prisoner in Scotland after Bannockburn, stores were handed to Walwayn for Hereford (*Cal. Doc. Scotl.* vol. III, p. 74). In the treaty made in December, 1312, by the cardinals, between king and barons, Walwayn acted on behalf of his master (*Foedera*, vol. II, p. 192), and when the see of Durham was vacant the earl endeavoured to secure the election of his clerk (Surtees Soc., *Hist. Dunelm. Script. Tres, Robt. de Graystanes*, p. 98).

[4] On 6 March, 1319, he received payments on the earl's behalf for his expenses

influence of Hereford, and by this means the barons had a certain, if indirect, method of influencing the administration. In the crisis of 1322, however, Walwayn, then escheator south of Trent, remained loyal to the king, and was considered faithful enough to be employed in administrative work even in the midst of the disaffected area of the Welsh march[1], when he was even ordered to destroy the castle of Brecon which had been in Hereford's hands[2]. Walwayn was not the only high official associated with a baron. John de Sandale, who became treasurer and afterwards chancellor, acted as one of the executors of the earl of Lincoln[3]. William de Ayremynne, who held offices in the chancery, acted as attorney for Eleanor, the widow of Henry de Percy[4], when a royal official, and was in correspondence with Sir Hugh D'Audley[5].

It now remains to trace the objects of the barons through the series of experiments by which they endeavoured to attain their ends. A single line of treatment in the discussion of such complex experiments as the Ordinances of 1311 is almost impossible. A policy develops and changes under the pressure of external circumstances. During the reign of Edward II there are two lines of policy running concurrently, followed by two different baronial parties. The policy of one of these parties, the Lancaster faction, altered during the reign. Its first object was to break down the household system. The futility of this endeavour caused a modification of plan. It sought to become a part of the household system—to work itself within and then exercise the control there was no possibility of obtaining outside. In the discussion of the various experiments these considerations will have to be remembered. The main purpose of all these experiments too will have to be borne in mind. They were all designed to exercise restraint over king and administration. With that object in view the barons sought to secure the appointment of officials, to control the council, to regulate the use of the seal and to check expenditure. They used diverse methods to attain these objects. They endeavoured to reform the household, to saddle the king with committees, to obtain a share in the household system itself. These experiments illustrated some or all of these objects and methods.

in going to Hainault as a royal ambassador (Issue Roll, no. 186, m. 7), and in Hereford's will made on 11 August, 1319, he was made an executor (*Arch. Journal*, vol. II [1846], p. 347), and various gifts were bequeathed to him (ibid. p. 346).

[1] Cf. *Cal. Fine Rolls*, 1319–27; *Cal. Pat. Rolls*, 1321–24, p. 75; *Cal. Close Rolls*, 1318–23, p. 438.

[2] *Cal. Pat. Rolls*, 1321–24, p. 75.

[3] Ibid. 1307–13, p. 326.

[4] *Descr. Cat. Ancient Deeds*, vol. IV, p. 45.

[5] *Cal. Inq. P. M.* vol. VI, p. 32.

CHAPTER II

THE EXPERIMENTS

(i) *The Ordinances of* 1311

Of all the experiments in the constitution made during the reign the Ordinances of 1311 were the most important. They were a serious attempt at constructive statesmanship on the part of the barons. They were at once a definition of baronial objects and a program of reform. All subsequent attempts to restrain the king were based upon them or drew a considerable amount of inspiration from them. The unanimity with which the barons applied themselves to their task on this occasion is a sufficient proof of their value. The earl of Pembroke joined hands with the earl of Lancaster for a common purpose. Though the Ordinances were the work of a united baronage the reason which prompted a chronicler to call them "the ordinances of the earl of Lancaster" is apparent[1]. Even when they were first mooted Lancaster took a leading part in the movement. When they were published he placed a commemoration tablet in St Paul's[2]. Lancaster had been in almost consistent opposition since the beginning of the reign. When Lincoln, Gloucester and the other earls had temporized with the king and Gavaston, Lancaster with the earl of Warwick had stood aside. Still it was in the light of Lancaster's attitude after the publication of the Ordinances that they could be so called. His constant complaint was that the Ordinances were not observed and his constant demand was that they should be confirmed and kept.

The principle of restraint was expressed in the Ordinances in the movement which ended in the appointment of the ordainers, in the method of that appointment and most of all in the results of their work. In all three directions the barons were influenced by previous efforts made to achieve similar objects. The Ordinances are called in one chronicler "les ordinances de Sir Simon de Mountford, vont

[1] *Le Livere de Reis de Brit.* p. 344: "les ordinances le dit counte de Lancastre."
[2] Camb. Univ. MS. Gg. i. 15, f. 756.

establir en son temps[1]." Precedents guided the ordainers throughout but they did not follow precedent slavishly. That elaborate system of councils and committees to which the Provisions of Oxford were to give birth was absent from the Ordinances. In fact no permanent council was intended. The ordainers were a temporary committee appointed for a specific purpose and for a limited time. No machinery was provided for the execution of the Ordinances. It was apparently considered that restrictive principles coming in the form of ordinances, the work of a body appointed by the whole baronage, the appointment being freely allowed by the king, the avowed object of the ordinances being reform of the royal household, would commend themselves sufficiently. The event was to prove that the restraint could only be supported and maintained by coercion.

The causes for the appointment of ordainers in 1310 are found in the conflict of two opposing theories of government and of clashing principles. The baronial and the royal theories and policies were irreconcilable. The disputes about Gavaston were the occasion rather than the cause. The baronial attempt in the Westminster parliament of 1309 to secure from the king certain articles, which were postponed[2] to the parliament at Stamford in the same year and then granted[3], was a slight foreshadowing of the demands. The great council which had been summoned for 8 February, 1310[4], gave the barons an opportunity. Lancaster made preparations to appear in arms. The king ordered him and others not to appear in parliament in arms as the king's safe conduct would protect them and the earls of Gloucester, Lincoln, Surrey and Richmond had been appointed to keep peace and order in London[5]. Despite the prohibition Lancaster and the others persisted. The council commenced its sittings on 27 February, and they lasted until 12 April[6].

The barons immediately presented a petition[7], stating the great losses and perils to the crown and realm unless immediate remedy was ordained by the prelates, earls and barons and the wisest of the kingdom. Though the king was bound by oath to maintain peace,

[1] Camb. Univ. MS. Ii. vi. 8, f. 121. Cf. Caxton, *Chronicle* [1440], p. 92.

[2] Cf. *Ann. Paul.* p. 267. [3] *Stat. of Realm*, vol. I, pp. 154–6.

[4] *Cal. Close Rolls*, 1307–13, p. 237. *Parl. Writs*, vol. II, Pt i, pp. 40–41.

[5] *Cal. Pat. Rolls*, 1307–13, pp. 206–7 (7 Feb. 1310). *Foedera*, vol. II, p. 103. Arrangements were made in London for the safeguarding of the city gates and the citizens were enjoined not to harbour strangers unless they were prepared to be responsible for them (*Cal. Letter Books, D*, pp. 213–214).

[6] *Ann. Lond.* pp. 167–8.

[7] This petition is printed *Ann. Lond.* p. 168; *Mun. Gildh. Lond.* vol. II, Pt i, pp. 198–9.

by unsuitable and evil counsel he had brought great shame upon the land. He had so impoverished the land and treasure that he could neither defend it nor maintain his household, except by the extortions of his officials who took the goods of the church and the poor people without paying anything therefor, which was against the form of the Great Charter which they prayed might be held and maintained in its force. Edward I had left him whole the crown of England, Ireland and the most of Scotland in good peace. By unsuitable and evil counsel he had lost the whole land of Scotland and the crown was seriously dismembered in England and Ireland without the assent of the barons and without reason. The twentieth of moveables which the commonalty had granted to the king in aid of the Scottish war, and the twenty-fifth for the release of prises and grievances were still levied, and by bad counsel the money was foolishly spent and wasted, for the war was not advanced and the people were not freed from fines and grievances, but day by day were more grieved than before. After this recital of grievances the barons came to the important and operative part of their petition:

> Par quei, Sire, voz bons gentz vous prient umblement, pur savacion de vous et de eux, e de la corone, la quele il sunt tenuz a meyntir pur lour ligeaunce qe vous voillez assentir a eux, qe ceux perilz et autres peussent estre oustez et redresces par ordynance de vostre Barnage[1].

As a result of this petition the king, on 16 March, 1310, issued his letters patent[2] allowing the appointment of ordainers. He granted of his own free will[3] to the prelates, earls and barons that they should choose certain persons from the prelates, earls and barons and others who should seem to them sufficient with power to last until Michaelmas, 1311, to ordain and establish the estate of his household and realm according to right and reason. The powers granted were complete:

> Nous grantons, par ceste noz lettres, a ceux qui deyvent estre esluz, queux quil soient, par les ditz prelatz, contes, et barons, plein poair de

[1] *Mun. Gildh. Lond.* vol. II, Pt i, p. 199. Cf. *Ann. Lond.* p. 169.

[2] Canterbury Cathedral Library MS. K. 11 is a roll containing a copy of the Ordinances under the title "Ceux sunt les noveles ordenaunces faites a Lundres lan du Regne nostre seigniur Rei Edward filz Edward Quynt et par le Rei confermes et desouz seon graunt seal enseallees. Et desouz mesme se seal dites ordenaunces et le confermement sunt en la Tresorie de ceste Eglise en garde." A transcript of the letter from the patent roll is in *Foedera*, vol. II, p. 105. Cf. *Cal. Pat. Rolls*, 1307–13, p. 215; *Ann. Lond.* pp. 169–170 and also *Auct. Bridl.* pp. 35–37.

[3] "De nostre fraunche volunte."

ordener lestat de nostre hostel, et de nostre roiaume desusditz, en tieu manere que leur ordenances soient faites al honur de Dieu et al honur e au profit de seinte eglise, et al honur de nous et a nostre profit et au profit de nostre people, solonc droit et reson, et le serment que nous feismes a nostre corounement. Et voloms que les esluz, et touz ceux qui sont de nostre seignurie et de nostre ligeance, les ordenaunces que faites serront par les prelatz, contes, et barons qui a ce serront esluz, et autres par eux, a ce appelez, teignent et gardent en touz leur pointz, et quil se puissent a ce asseurer; lier et entreiurer sanz chalenge de nous, ou de noz[1].

If any of the persons chosen were prevented by death, illness or other reasonable excuse the ordainers had power to call others to fill the vacancy[2].

The next day the prelates, earls and barons sent their letters to the king promising that the concessions should not be turned to his prejudice or disadvantage[3]. The list of persons issuing these letters is interesting. At their head stood Winchelsey, archbishop of Canterbury, with the bishops of London, Lincoln, Salisbury, Winchester, Norwich, Bath and Wells, Chichester, Worcester, Exeter and St David's[4]. Almost the whole body of earls was included, the earls of Gloucester, Lancaster, Lincoln, Hereford, Richmond, Pembroke, Warwick and Arundel[5], the exceptions being the earls of Warenne and Oxford. The list of barons, if small, was representative and included the most important. They were, Henry de Lancaster, Henry de Percy, Hugh de Veer, Robert de Clifford, Robert fitz Payn, William le Marshal, John Lovel, Ralph fitz William, Payn Tibetot, John Botetourte, Bartholomew de Badlesmere, John de Grey, and John de Crombwell[6]. The royal grant was recited in these letters and was followed by the baronial declaration.

Nous grantoms et promettoms, pur nous et pur noz successors et noz heirs, qe le grant qe nostre dist Seignor ad fait en le manere dessusdite ne soit autrefoiz tret en custome ne en usage, ne ne tourne en prejudice du dist nostre Seignor le Roi ne ses heirs, ne de nous, ne de noz successors, ne de noz eglises, ne de noz heirs, ne a damage de nulli, contre droit et reson, sicom est dedusit; ne qe le graunt avauntdist peusse en autre manere estre entendue, fosqe proprement de sa curtoisie et de sa fraunche volunte. E qe le poair des ditz, Ordynours quaunt as ordynances faire, ne dure outre le terme auantdist[7].

On 20 March they proceeded to the election of the ordainers.

[1] *Foedera*, vol. II, Pt i, p. 105. [2] Ibid.

[3] This letter of the barons is found in Cant. Cath. MS. K. 11, m. 2 d; *Mun. Gildh. Lond.* vol. II, Pt i, pp. 200–2; *Ann. Lond.* pp. 170–1. Cf. *Cal. Close Rolls*, 1307–13, p. 253, where the letters were enrolled.

[4] *Mun. Gildh. Lond.* vol. II, Pt i, p. 200. *Cal. Close Rolls*, 1307–13, pp. 251–3.

[5] Ibid. [6] Ibid. [7] Ibid. pp. 201–2.

The archbishop of Canterbury and the bishops present elected two earls—Lincoln and Pembroke. The earls elected two bishops—those of London and Salisbury. These four then proceeded to elect two barons, Hugh de Veer and William le Marshal. This preliminary cross election of two of each order was made so that the six so elected should act as the electors of the remainder of the ordainers. They proceeded to elect fifteen other ordainers to whom they were associated. The fifteen were composed of five prelates, six earls and four barons[1]. The twenty-one ordainers were the archbishop of Canterbury, the bishops of London, Salisbury, Chichester, Norwich, St David's and Llandaff representing the prelates; all the earls present at the meeting, Gloucester, Lancaster, Hereford, Lincoln, Pembroke, Richmond, Warwick and Arundel, and representing the barons, Hugh de Veer, William le Marshal, Robert fitz Roger, Hugh de Courtney, William Martin and John de Grey[2]. On the very day of the election an oath was taken by the ordainers. They swore that they would make such ordinances as should be to the honour and profit of Holy Church, the honour of the king and to his advantage and that of his people according to right and reason and the oath the king had sworn at his coronation. They would not omit this for any man rich or poor, for love or for hate nor for anything[3]. The bishop of Chichester, who was still chancellor[4], received the oath of the archbishop and the other ordainers and the archbishop then received his oath[5]. This ceremony took place in the painted chamber at Westminster[6].

Although the whole course of the proceedings leading up to the appointment of the ordainers was extremely orderly and normal, the chroniclers who suggested the appointment was due to coercion were not far wrong. It was by the exercise of pressure that the king was forced to submit to the baronial demands, though even when the compulsion under which the king acted was recognised one chronicler stated that the commission was granted to the barons

[1] The form of the election is found in *Parl. Writs*, vol. II, Pt i, p. 43, a transcript of Brit. Mus. Cotton MS. Claudius D. ii, f. 276, and in Cant. Cath. MS. K. ii, m. 2 d.

[2] Cant. Cath. MS. K. II, m. 2 d. *Ann. Lond.* p. 172. *Mun. Gildh. Lond.* vol. II, Pt i, p. 202. *Auct. Bridl.* p. 37.

[3] *Parl. Writs*, vol. II, Pt i, p. 43; Pt ii, App. p. 27. Cant. Cath. MS. K. II, m. 2 d.

[4] He did not remain chancellor for long after his association with the ordainers. On 11 May, 1310, he surrendered the seal (*Cal. Close Rolls*, 1307–13, p. 258).

[5] *Parl. Writs*, vol. II, Pt i, p. 43. Cant. Cath. MS. K. II, m. 2 d.

[6] Ibid.

freely[1]. The barons certainly appeared in London in arms[2], and they had the means to compel the king to concede their demands[3]. When the king seemed unwilling to grant their requests they took a high hand. They withstood the king unanimously, several saying that if their petitions were not granted they would not have him as king nor keep the oath they had sworn to him, since he would not keep his coronation oath. If one side could break faith so could the other[4]. In the face of these arguments the king was forced to acquiesce.

The first result of the grant of power to the barons was the issue of a number of interim ordinances on 19 March[5], the day previous to the appointment of the ordainers. The Ordinances were not however confirmed by the king until 2 August, when the sheriffs were ordered to publish and enforce them[6]. As these seven preliminary ordinances were subsequently embodied in the final issue of 1311 they can be treated better in the light of the whole. A part of one of these ordinances was purely temporary in its effect and it can be dealt with immediately. In order to secure the disinterestedness of the ordainers it was ordained that no grant of any sort should be made to any of them as long as the power granted to them by the king endured. Nor was any grant to be made to anyone without the counsel and assent of the ordainers or the majority, or at least six, of them. All sources of revenue were to be used to the king's advantage until the state of his finances was retrieved[7]. A manuscript collection of statutes in Cambridge University Library[8] before proceeding to relate the Ordinances, gives under the rubric "La primere ordinance" an ordinance which was purely temporary in character and appears to be requests sent to the king to make orders.

Ordyne est qe les gentz qi sunt esluz e assignez par le roy e par la comunaute de la terre pur lostel le Roy e lestat du realme ordyner e tryer ou peoent plus couenablement demorer quaillurs pur diuerses resuns. Cest assauoyr pur cunsail des Justices e de autres sages plus prestement auoyr la qaillurs e pur les remambrances de la chancelerye e de lescheker e autres auisementz plus prestement trouer la qe aillurs e sur ce seit mande

[1] *Chron. Mon. de Melsa*, vol. II, p. 280.

[2] *Chron. Hemingb.* vol. II, p. 276. Vide above p. 358, note 5. *Cal. Pat. Rolls*, 1307–13, pp. 206–7.

[3] *Chron. Hemingb.* vol. II, p. 276.

[4] *Auct. Malm.* p. 163.

[5] *Ann. Lond.* pp. 172–3.

[6] *Foedera*, vol. II, p. 113. *Rot. Parl.* vol. I, p. 446. *Cal. Pat. Rolls*, 1307–13, p. 274. Cf. *Cal. Close Rolls*, 1307–13, p. 175.

[7] Ordinance 3. *Stat. of Realm*, vol. I, p. 158.

[8] Camb. Univ. MS. Dd. vii. 14, f. 12.

par le Roy al Meyr e as Aldremantz de la dite cyte qeux les facent sy sauuement garder qe mal ne dampmage ne desturbance nauiegne e ditz ordynurs ne a lurs durant le temps de lur ordynances.

Effect was certainly given to the second part of this ordinance. On 29 May, when the first ordinances had been promulgated and approved[1], the mayor, sheriffs and aldermen of London were ordered to cause the city to be safely guarded in such a way that no evil or hurt should be done to the ordainers or to any residing in the city[2].

By August, 1311, the work of the ordainers was at an end and they presented the results of their labour to the king for confirmation[3]. The king's attitude after the appointment had not been reassuring. The bishop of Chichester, chancellor, one of the ordainers, had to surrender the seal on 11 May, 1310[4], only a few months after the appointment of the ordainers, and on 7 July, Walter Reynolds, bishop of Worcester, who had previously been treasurer, sealed writs under the great seal[5]. The king also made arrangements to leave London and devote his energies to the Scottish expedition. A meeting of the council was called in June to arrange for the government of the kingdom when the king was in Scotland. In this council the influence of the ordainers was supreme. The earl of Pembroke was amongst those summoned to counsel the king with the prelates and other earls[6]. The work of the council shows the importance of the ordainers in it. A commission was to be made to the earl of Lincoln appointing him keeper and lieutenant of the king while he was in Scotland and writs were to be issued to all sheriffs in England ordering them to obey him[7]. The Ordinances made by the ordainers[8] were to be sent to the chancellor who was to make writs ordering them to be kept in all points[9].

The magnates of England were ordered to meet the king at Northampton in August and proceed with him against Bruce[10]. The earls

[1] *Ann. Lond.* pp. 173–4.

[2] *Mun. Gildh. Lond.* vol. II, Pt i, p. 202. *Cal. Letter Books, D*, p. 225. *Ann. Lond.* p. 174.

[3] The Ordinances are printed in the *Statutes of the Realm*, vol. I, pp. 157–167; *Rot. Parl.* vol. I, pp. 281–6; other texts are found in Cant. Cath. MS. K. 11; P. R. O. Statute Roll, no. 2.

[4] *Cal. Close Rolls*, 1307–13, p. 258.

[5] *Foedera*, vol. II, p. 110.

[6] Anc. Corresp. vol. XLIX, no. 6 (6 June, 1310).

[7] Parl. and Council Proc. (Chan.), File 4/9. Vide App. of Doc. no. 90. Vide also for the commission *Cal. Pat. Rolls*, 1307–13, p. 277; *Foedera*, vol. II, p. 116.

[8] This must refer to the seven preliminary ordinances.

[9] Parl. and Council Proc. (Chan.), File 4/9. Vide App. of Doc. no. 90. Vide for the commission to the sheriffs *Cal. Pat. Rolls*, 1307–13, p. 274 (2 Aug. 1310).

[10] *Ann. Lond.* p. 174. *Chron. Hemingb.* vol. II, p. 277.

of Lancaster, Pembroke, Hereford, Warwick and Arundel failed to appear[1] though they sent their due and accustomed services[2]. They were engaged about the business of the Ordinances at London[3]. Others of the ordainers put patriotism before class advantage and accompanied the king. Among these was the earl of Gloucester[4], who appeared to have had little sympathy with the baronial opposition, and Henry de Percy[5], whose subsequent conduct makes it difficult to place him. The earl of Surrey[6], who had held aloof from and been ignored by the ordainers, and Gavaston, again earl of Cornwall[7], also accompanied the king. When the barons were passing Ordinances against them, both Gavaston and Beaumont[8] were acquitting themselves creditably in the Scottish war.

The earls were not wholly united over the Ordinances. Gloucester, Lincoln, Richmond, Arundel and Warenne appear to have had strong leanings towards the king. Their conduct when the ordainers were sitting suggests this for they supported the king on several occasions though they possibly saw the need for some degree of reform. On 24 May the king gave Gloucester, Lincoln, Richmond and Arundel authority to guarantee to Pembroke, Hereford and Warwick that they could safely go to Kennington to treat with the king[9]. This gives some insight into the different relation in which the two sections of earls stood to the king.

The earl of Lincoln's position as keeper of the realm was a difficult one. The ordainers were disturbed and angered at the king's actions, for the king ordered the exchequer and benches to be removed to York by Easter[10]. The king either anticipated trouble over the Ordinances or desired the removal for purely administrative purposes. The ordainers however feared the worst. Each had gone to his own district having privately arranged to return together[11]. Lincoln was opposed to the removal, informed the king to this effect and told him that he would no longer act as his lieutenant or keep the peace. It seemed however to those about the king that the earl and the king

[1] *Ann. Lond.* p. 174. *Auct. Malm.* p. 164. *Chron. Hemingb.* vol. II, p. 277.
[2] *Ann. Lond.* p. 174.
[3] Ibid. *Auct. Malm.* p. 164. *Chron. Hemingb.* vol. II, p. 278.
[4] *Ann. Lond.* p. 174. *Auct. Malm.* p. 164. *Chron. Hemingb.* vol. II, p. 277.
[5] *Chron. Hemingb.* vol. II, p. 277.
[6] *Ann. Lond.* p. 174. *Auct. Malm.* p. 164. *Chron. Hemingb.* vol. II, p. 277.
[7] Ibid.
[8] Cf. *Cal. Doc. Scotl.* vol. III, pp. 31, 40. *Cal. Close Rolls*, 1307–13, p. 324.
[9] *Cal. Pat. Rolls*, 1307–13, p. 228.
[10] *Cal. Doc. Scotl.* vol. III. p. 33, a letter of 25 Nov. 1310, from York.
[11] Ibid.

understood each other[1]. When Lincoln died in February, 1311[2], the king lost a good friend, but the barons gained no advantage as Gloucester was appointed keeper and lieutenant in his stead[3].

Gloucester assumed the keepership at a critical time. Lancaster, Hereford, Pembroke and Warwick were at London, and it was unknown what their business there was at that time[4]. The chancellor had urged the king to send his lieutenant to London and Gloucester was ordered to go there immediately after his appointment[5]. He had however trusty advisers in William de Bereford and Henry le Scrope, the justices whom the king had ordered to advise him[6]. Their advice would be weighty as only a few weeks before they had been summoned to Berwick-on-Tweed for conferences with the king[7]. The king had probably imparted detailed instructions to the justices as Gloucester was to consult with the justices alone and other advisers[8]. On a matter which was pending concerning the archbishop of York the king ordered his lieutenant to call his council which was to consist of the chancellor, two bishops, Sandale, Robert fitz Payn, the two justices and the household of the earl, that is to say Badlesmere, Botetourte and John de Ferers[9]. At the end of March the king was almost unattended at Berwick and it was considered by those who were with him that Despenser the elder and other great lords should be sent to him without delay[10].

The king remained in the north as long as possible. A close observer writing from the north early in April said that he was yet in no mood for a parliament, but thought that when Gloucester and the council met at London he would be forced to accede to their wishes[11]. Nor was the king reconciling opposition but issued commands which even members of his household considered "marvellous[12]."

As the Ordinances were being completed pressure was brought to bear upon him and on 16 June, 1311, writs were issued summoning a parliament for 8 August[13]. It was not fear of the Ordinances alone that kept the king in the north. He was aware of the feelings of the barons towards Gavaston and had the king needed any confirmation

[1] *Cal. Doc. Scotl.* vol. III, p. 33, a letter of 25 Nov. 1310, from York

[2] *Ann. Lond.* p. 175. *Ann. Paul.* p. 269.

[3] *Cal. Pat. Rolls*, 1307–13, p. 333. *Foedera*, vol. II, p. 129.

[4] *Cal. Doc. Scotl.* vol. III, p. 50.

[5] Chan. Misc., Bdle 22/10 (8 a).

[6] Ibid. Bdle 22/10 (8) contains the letter partly calendared in *Cal. Doc. Scotl.* p. 40, no. 201.

[7] Chan. Misc., Bdle 22/6 (6). Cf. also Issue Roll, no. 155, m. 7.

[8] Chan. Misc., Bdle 22/10 (8).

[9] Ibid.

[10] Ibid.

[11] *Cal. Doc. Scotl.* vol. III, p. 40.

[12] Cf. ibid. p. 41.

[13] *Parl. Writs*, vol. II, Pt ii, p. 44.

of this Lancaster's conduct towards him when he appeared near Berwick to do homage for the earldoms of Lincoln and Salisbury[1] after the death of the earl of Lincoln would have provided it. The king remained in the north to keep and protect Gavaston[2]. It was a matter of the greatest urgency that the king should be induced to meet his barons and confirm the Ordinances, as the power of the ordainers expired at Michaelmas[3]. Eventually at the end of July the king left the north. On 3 August, a copy of the Ordinances was sent to him[4]. The king arrived at London and took up his residence at the Blackfriars[5]. The victory of the ordainers was not yet won. The king still endeavoured to temporize and delay. The Ordinance against Gavaston was especially distasteful to him[6]. The barons were however resolute and unanimous on this point[7]. The king's advisers saw to what straits matters had come and urged him to yield[8]. Eventually prudence prevailed and the Ordinances were accepted.

Disturbances at the parliament had been anticipated and preparations made by the authorities of the city of London. On 14 August the king was at Westminster and the magnates in and about the city in preparation for the parliament in which the Ordinances were to be completed and confirmed. On that day the mayor and aldermen of London made ordinance for the safe keeping of the city. Guards were chosen for the gates and the hour at which they were to be closed was appointed[9].

The parliament met on 16 August, and there were present the archbishop of Canterbury, many bishops, earls and barons. All the magnates, the chancellor, treasurer, justices, barons of the exchequer[10], the knights of the shire, the mayor and aldermen of London and the worthiest citizens were sworn to keep and maintain all the Ordinances made in that parliament[11]. On 27 September, two days before the power of the ordainers expired, and in the churchyard of St Paul's, the bishop of Salisbury, acting as the lieutenant of the archbishop of Canterbury, published the Ordinances in the presence of several

[1] Vide *Chron. Lanerc.* p. 192.

[2] *Auct. Malm.* p. 167. [3] Ibid. pp. 169–170.

[4] Anc. Corresp. vol. XXXVII, no. 110. Vide App. of Doc. no. 114.

[5] *Auct. Malm.* p. 170. [6] Ibid. [7] Ibid. pp. 170–1. [8] Ibid. p. 171.

[9] *Cal. Letter Books, D*, pp. 286–7. *Parl. Writs*, vol. II, Pt i, p. 69.

[10] This was an attempt to carry out one of the executive clauses of the Ordinances. Vide Ordinance 39; below, p. 380.

[11] An excellent account of the publication of the Ordinances is found in Camd. Soc., *De Antiquis Legibus Liber*, ed. T. Stapleton, App. pp. 251–2. The other accounts do little to supplement this.

bishops, the earls of Lancaster, Pembroke, Warwick, Hereford, Oxford and Arundel and several barons[1]. On 5 October, Gloucester, Henry de Percy, Despenser, Robert fitz Payn, Payn Tibetot, the chancellor, treasurer and other lords of the king's council, announced the Ordinances to all the people, at the cross in the churchyard of St Paul's, by the king's grant and goodwill to be maintained throughout all his realm[2]. On 11 October, the Ordinances were sealed with the king's great seal and sent under writs to all the counties in England to be published and confirmed[3]. All this while the king had been at London. On the very day on which the writs were issued he left for Windsor[4].

It was on 5 October, the day upon which the Ordinances were announced to the people, that the first writs were issued. On that day the mayor and sheriffs of London received the Ordinances under the king's seal. They were ordered to publish the Ordinances in the city and to make them be observed inviolably in every article. After they had been published the Ordinances were to be deposited in a safe place in the city under the seal of the mayor and sheriffs and four of the worthiest men[5]. The writs to the sheriffs were dated October 10[6]. The Ordinances were long and the transcription of thirty or forty copies could not be done in a day.

Before the Ordinances are discussed in detail, a comparison of the Ordinances with Magna Carta may be useful. Though the true parent of the Ordinances was the Provisions of Oxford, the former have so much in common in purpose, form and machinery with Magna Carta that a comparison will stand. Magna Carta was the result of a petition presented by the barons. Though the petition which secured the appointment of the ordainers was less full and not so formidable as a catalogue of abuses, the comparison is interesting. Both Magna Carta and the Ordinances open with a confirmation of the franchises to Holy Church[7]. However similar in outward form there was however a vital difference between these two great constitutional documents. The aim of Magna Carta was the declaration of existing law. That such declaration should be made was a new principle, but the

[1] Camd. Soc., *De Antiq. Leg. Lib.* App. p. 251. Vide also *Stat. of Realm*, vol I, p. 167. Cant. Cath. MS. K. 11, m. 4. Cf. *Chron. Trokelowe*, p. 67; *Flores Hist.* vol. III, p. 334; *Ann. Paul.* p. 270.

[2] Camd. Soc., *De Ant. Leg. Lib.* App. p. 251.

[3] Ibid. pp. 251–2.

[4] Ibid. p. 252.

[5] *Mun. Gildh. Lond.* vol. II, Pt i, p. 203.

[6] *Cal. Close Rolls*, 1307–13, p. 439. *Foedera*, vol. II, p. 146. Cf. also *Auct. Malm.* p. 171. *Chron. Murimuth*, p. 15.

[7] Magna Carta, § 1 (Stubbs, *Select Charters*, 9th edit. pp. 292–3). Ordinance 1 (*Stat. of Realm*, vol. I, p. 158).

law so declared was merely the old feudal code. The Ordinances could not pretend merely to be a declaration of existing law or even a return to ancient custom. There were new laws and principles embodied in them. The ordainers sought by compulsion to extort from the king changes in administration and a new code of government. The Ordinances sought to introduce a new system of government in which the barons should have an added control. They would effect a declaration of existing law and a declaration of what the barons conceived to be the king's rights, and an assertion of what they conceived to be their rights in administration. While Magna Carta was essentially a definition of existing law and a catalogue of grievances the result of "unlawful" acts by the king, the Ordinances were primarily a series of administrative reforms. This fact marks the progress that had been made between the reigns of John and Edward II in the development of the administrative system. The very name which was applied to this program of reform is suggestive. The reforms were neither couched in the form of a charter nor a statute. They were ordinances, administrative arrangements made by a "council" for the conduct of the administrative departments. The essential difference between them and other "ordinances" was their source. The baronial "council" took the place of the king's "administrative" council and ordained in its stead for the administrative departments. The source of the Ordinances was, of course, all important. Instead of being the ordinances of the executive with the whole force of the executive machinery behind them they were ordinances imposed upon an unwilling executive. For in the Ordinances as in subsequent experiments the barons failed to secure any firm hold upon the executive. Law was secondary in the Ordinances. The barons wished to secure control over the administration, and the surest way of obtaining that was by administrative reform. The Ordinances therefore took the form of a program of administrative reform with the object of securing to the baronage a greater share in administration.

A detailed study of the Ordinances, arranged in various groups, is both desirable and necessary. For after the manner of all medieval schemes of reform, the work was confused and ill-arranged. The Ordinances opened with a formal confirmation to the church of her franchises[1] and with the statement that the king's peace should be

[1] Ordinance 1. The Ordinances are printed and translated in *Statutes of Realm*, vol. 1, pp. 157–167. The references will in all cases be to the Ordinances as numbered and arranged there.

kept throughout the land so that everyone might go, come and stay with safety according to the law and custom of the land[1]. No less formal was the Ordinance which ordained that Magna Carta should be kept in all points[2], though this clause received importance on account of the ordainers' claim to declare doubtful or obscure points[3]. The confirmation of the Great Charter and the Charter of Forests[4] which complemented this Ordinance, was likewise formal, its importance being derived from the baronial claim to explain it[5]. As well as these two great bulwarks of franchises all the statutes made in amendment of the law and to the profit of the people by the king's ancestors were to be maintained, if not contrary to Magna Carta, the Charter of the Forests or the Ordinances[6].

What seemed to contemporary opinion, and not without some cause, the most important clauses of the Ordinances were those dealing with personal matters, directed against those the barons regarded as the king's favourites and "evil counsellors." It is upon the clauses directed against Gavaston, the Beaumonts and the Friscobaldi that the chroniclers lay the emphasis[7], and it is doubtful indeed whether a majority of the barons would not have placed them first in importance. For the favourites and "evil counsellors" were symptomatic of the whole ground of the baronial opposition to the king and the household system.

There was a long catalogue of charges against Gavaston. He had evilly led and counselled the king. The royal treasure had been sent abroad by him. He had accroached royal power and dignity by making alliances and by lording it over the king and crown. He had estranged the king's heart and made him despise the council of his lieges. He had interfered in the administration by removing good ministers, replacing them by servants of his own who would obey him rather than do right. The royal possessions had been diminished by grants to him and others. He had carried the king to hostile lands without the assent of the baronage. He had induced the king to grant him blank charters under the great seal. Exiled by Edward I, he had returned without the common assent of the barons, only by the assent of certain of them. Accordingly as the open enemy of the king and of his people he was to be exiled for ever from all the king's dominions. The day by which he was to go and the port of his

[1] Ordinance 2. [2] Ordinance 6. [3] Vide below, p. 375.
[4] Ordinance 38. [5] Vide below, p. 375. [6] Ordinance 31.
[7] *Auct. Bridl.* pp. 40–41. *Chron. Lanerc.* pp. 193–4. *Auct. Malm.* pp. 172–3. *Chron. Mon. de Melsa*, vol. II, p. 326. *Le Livere de Reis de Brit.* p. 328.

departure was fixed and penalties for disobedience ordered[1]. There was some amount of reasonable cause for the baronial dislike of Gavaston. Their constitutional opposition to him was quite reasonable, though their list of charges was open to grave questionings. There was throughout serious exaggeration and at times gross misrepresentation. It is well to remember that the Ordinances were the statement of a party case and in no section did party feeling run higher than in the personal clauses.

The Ordinances against Henry de Beaumont and his sister Lady de Vescy were not as severe as that against Gavaston. They were less powerful sinners. Since the appointment of the ordainers, Beaumont had accepted from the king the realm of Man and other lands, offices and franchises[2] and had procured similar grants for others. Because he had evilly counselled the king contrary to his oath, he was to be put out of the king's counsel and presence for ever. He was never to approach the king except in "parliament or in wartime[3]." His lands were to be taken into the king's hands and retained until the issues he had received contrary to the Ordinance were recovered. If he disobeyed he was to be disinherited[4]. The ordainers discovered that the grants to Beaumont had been made at the instigation of Lady de Vescy. At her instance writs of privy seal had been issued against the law[5]. She was therefore to be removed from court, never returning to stay there. The castle of Bamburgh, which she held, belonged to the crown and it was to be recovered[6]. Beaumont and his sister were associated with the queen rather than with the king[7], and the opposition to them would have been made against anyone holding a position at court bringing them into contact with the king and hence liable to exert an influence over him. Apart from the Ordinances approved by the king there were a number of additional ordinances dealing specifically with the royal household, but as they were not an integral part of the Ordinances as published they will be treated separately[8].

The Ordinance directed against Emery and others of the company of the Friscobaldi was not purely personal in intent, there were the usual baronial dislike of foreigners and the dissatisfaction produced by the financial functions of the company. They were to render account

[1] Ordinance 20

[2] *Cal. Charter Rolls*, 1300–26, pp. 107, 153, 224, give a few grants to Beaumont.

[3] This was subject to the assent of the barons. Note below, p. 371.

[4] Ordinance 22.

[5] For an instance of a privy seal issued at her request Chan. Warr., File 80/2259

[6] Ordinance 23. [7] Vide above, p. 106. [8] Vide below, pp. 382–6.

by a certain date in the manner which had been decided and published. Meanwhile, they were to be arrested and their goods and lands seized. If Emery did not come at the appointed day he was to be banished and held as an enemy[1].

The personal clauses, if severe, were not actuated solely by personal motives. Their importance is that they were but special applications of the general policy which directed the barons in their opposition. In other words the personal clauses form one phase of the policy of restraint as expressed in the Ordinances. The barons claimed and exercised the right, under exceptional circumstances it is true, for the ordainers claimed to act by virtue of the king's commission[2], to interfere with those whom the king kept around him. Gavaston was exiled the land. Beaumont was put out of the king's counsel for ever and was not to approach the king, except at the common summons to parliament or in war if the king wished to have him, "unless it be by common assent of the archbishops, bishops, earls and barons and that in full parliament[3]." The expulsion from court of Lady de Vescy was a still more flagrant instance of the right claimed by the barons to decide who should be near the king. Because the king had been evilly guided and counselled, all evil counsellors were to be removed and other fitter people put in their places. In like manner the servants of such counsellors were to be removed, and also those in the king's household who were unfit[4].

Connected with this claim to interfere with the king's household and remove his friends from his presence was the claim of the ordainers to participate in the appointment of officials. This claim appeared to be more reasonable than their endeavours to dismiss and remove the king's personal friends and officials. The ordainers insisted that the collectors of the customs of the realm should be natives and not aliens[5]. This however was small in comparison with the other demands. It was ordained that the king should appoint the chancellor, the chief justices of both benches, the treasurer, chancellor and chief baron of the exchequer, the steward of the household, the keeper and controller of the wardrobe, a suitable clerk as keeper of the privy seal, chief keepers of the forest north and south of Trent, escheators north and south of Trent and the chief clerk of the common bench by the counsel and assent of his baronage in parliament[6]. If it was found necessary to appoint any of these officers

[1] Ordinance 21.
[2] *Stat. of Realm*, vol. I, p. 158.
[3] Ordinance 22.
[4] Ordinance 13.
[5] Ordinances 4, 8.
[6] Ordinance 14.

before parliament should meet the king should make an interim appointment by the good counsel he had near him until that time[1]. The chief wardens of ports and castles upon the coast were to be similarly appointed[2] and officers for Gascony, Ireland and Scotland were to be likewise provided[3].

The completeness of the demands of these articles and the restraint with which they could have been exercised had it been possible to give them full effect it is difficult to realise fully. It was claimed that the officials of the great administrative departments, chancery and exchequer, of the judiciary, some of the local officials and the officials of the foreign possessions should be appointed by the baronage. Complete mastery over the administration was not sufficient for the barons, they desired to encroach upon the king's household and to secure a share in the appointment of such purely household officials as the steward. The vast power which participation in all these appointments would have given the barons would have placed practically the whole control of the administration in their hands. The king would have been well-nigh powerless. He could no longer have played off the household against the administrative departments. The wardrobe would have been as much an administrative department as the exchequer. The keeper of the privy seal would have been as dependent upon and therefore as obedient to the barons as the chancellor would have been. A baronial nominee in the position of steward could have checked and reported upon every act of the king.

The temporary check placed upon the king's power of granting gifts, liberties and offices in the preliminary ordinances in 1310[4] was expanded. The crown had been abased and dismembered by gifts. All gifts made in England, Gascony, Ireland, Scotland and Wales were repealed as having been given without common consent in parliament. Any gifts or releases given henceforth without the assent of the baronage in parliament, until the king's debts were paid and his state relieved, were to be held as naught and whosoever received such gifts was to be punished in parliament by the award of the baronage[5]. This was a serious restriction upon the king's power, partly justified by the financial chaos of the time. Its duration was specifically limited until the royal finances were in a healthier state. It was however a part of the general policy of restraint which the barons pursued and its motives must be judged along with the other instances of its application.

[1] Ordinance 14. [2] Ordinance 15. [3] Ordinance 16.
[4] Ordinance 3. Vide above, p. 362. [5] Ordinance 7.

The barons also sought to restrain the king's movements. He was not to go to war against anyone nor to go out of the realm without the common consent of his baronage in parliament. If he went out with that consent given in due form and it was necessary to appoint a keeper of the realm, the king was to appoint him with the common assent of his baronage in parliament. If the king disobeyed and undertook any such enterprise without the assent of his baronage, the summons issued for service was to be of no effect[1]. This was more than a straightforward attempt to exercise restraint upon the king. It was coercive in its effect and it deprived the king of all means of resisting coercion. If maintained, it would have legalised rebellion; for it made repression of rebellion impossible if not illegal. Obedience to it would have made the king the permanent slave of the oligarchy.

The customs of the realm, which the king regarded as a purely personal source of revenue, collected and administered outside the exchequer, were to be drawn within the ordinary financial machinery. The revenue was still to go to maintain the household, but it was to be collected by natives and paid into the exchequer like the other issues of the realm and thence paid by the treasurer and chamberlains to the household[2]. The object of the clause was to diminish the financial independence of the wardrobe and to increase its dependence upon the exchequer. An attack upon the sources of the household revenue was a feasible means of reducing the whole power of that system and was therefore an insidious and indirect effort to impose restraint upon the king's action. In the same category may be placed the baronial demand that, when the king wished to make an exchange of money, inasmuch as the people were greatly aggrieved in many ways thereby, the exchange was to be made by the common counsel of the baronage in parliament.

The effort to limit the use of the privy seal was another attempt to impose restraint. Henceforth the law of the land and common right were not to be delayed or disturbed by letters under the privy seal. Such letters against right or the law, issued to any court of justice were to be of no avail[3]. The effect of royal protections issued to those who were or claimed to be in the royal service was also restricted. If a party in a lawsuit, after appearance, urged a royal protection and his opponent could prove that he was not at

[1] Ordinance 9. [2] Ordinances 4, 8.

[3] Ordinance 32. It was re-enacted in the Statute of Northampton, 2 Ed. III, § viii (*Stat. of Realm*, vol. I, p. 259).

that time actually in the royal service the cause should go against him by default. If the protection was urged before appearance and the other party could prove that he was not in the royal service the day the suit was delayed by the protection, damages should be awarded to the party so delayed and the other party should be committed to prison[1]. The issue of the king's charters of pardon was also restricted. It seemed to the ordainers that the king by evil advice gave such charters too lightly. In future no felon or fugitive should be protected or defended from any felony by virtue of the king's charter of peace granted to him, except in a case where the king could give grace according to his oath and that by process of law and by the custom of the realm. Any charter granted otherwise should be of no avail[2]. Thus two of the king's rights, the rights of issuing protection and pardon, were limited.

The Ordinance ordering one or two parliaments to meet each year[3] restricted the royal as opposed to the baronial power to do justice. Parties in the royal courts were delayed because the other parties alleged that answers ought not to be made without the king. Others were aggrieved by the king's officials against right and such grievances could not be redressed without a common parliament. On these accounts parliaments were to be held once or twice annually. In these parliaments such pleas, as well as pleas on which the justices were divided, and bills delivered to parliament were to be decided[4]. *The Mirror of Justices* had advocated parliaments twice a year "for the salvation of the souls of trespassers" and had complained that parliaments were then "held but rarely and at the king's will for the purpose of obtaining aids and collection of treasure[5]." A few years before the Ordinances, two parliaments a year had been the ideal in France[6]. The baronial desire for these parliaments was in part due to the increased power it gave them and the consequent diminished freedom of action it gave the king.

Several of these efforts to impose restraint were also in effect attacks upon the royal prerogative. The Ordinance which prohibited the king going out of his kingdom[7] was of this nature, though it was an idea that was also expressed in a contemporary political song which went to the effect that "a king ought not to go out of his kingdom to make war unless the commons of his land consent...let

[1] Ordinance 37. [2] Ordinance 28. [3] Ordinance 29.
[4] Ibid. Vide below, p. 388. [5] Seld. Soc., *Mirror of Justices*, p. 155.
[6] Langlois, *Textes Relat. à l'Hist. du Parl.* pp. 161, 178.
[7] Vide above, p. 373.

not the king go out of his kingdom without counsel[1]." The restriction of the king's rights to make grants[2], to issue letters, protections and charters[3] was also an attack upon the prerogative. A more serious and important attack upon the prerogative was the baronial claim to interpret Magna Carta and the Charter of the Forests[4]. It was ordained that, for the duration of the commission of the ordainers, any obscure or doubtful point in the Great Charter should be declared by them and others whom they wished to call for that purpose[5]. Such a position might have been tolerated for the period when the ordainers were in power and the authority of the king was temporarily in commission. It was intolerable that such a right should be further vested in the baronage and this would seem to be the effect of another clause in the Ordinances[6]:

> Likewise we do ordain, that the Great Charter of Franchises and the Charter of the Forest which king Henry the son of king John made, be holden in all their points, and that the points which are doubtful in the said Charters of Franchises be explained, in the next parliament after this, by the advice of the Baronage, and of the justices and of other sage persons of the law. And this thing shall be done, because we have it not in our power to do the same in our time.

When a royal charter was called into question the matter could not be decided even by the royal judges until the king had granted them power to do so[7]. What the king could claim for a charter concerning the merest grant of land the barons sought to deny him in such an important matter as grants of franchises, and the excuse they gave did little to mitigate the seriousness of the claim.

Many of the Ordinances which have been treated in the class of those which definitely exercised restraint were also legislative and administrative in their effect. The Ordinance which restricted the power of royal protections[8] was of this nature. Indeed its object was probably legislative rather than restrictive. The effect of the Ordinance ordering one or possibly two parliaments each year[9] was likewise perhaps intended to be administrative and judicial and restrictive. Other Ordinances were however more purely and strictly legislative or administrative in their aim, though since the whole Ordinances as a scheme had one primary object, an endeavour to capture and control the executive and hence the administration any division of

[1] Camd. Soc., *Political Songs*, p. 182.
[2] Vide above, p. 372.
[3] Vide above, pp. 373–4.
[4] Ordinances 6, 38. Vide above, p. 369.
[5] Ordinance 6.
[6] Ordinance 38.
[7] Vide above, p. 10.
[8] Ordinance 37. Vide above, pp. 373–4.
[9] Ordinance 29. Vide above, p. 374.

the clauses into classes must be incomplete or overlapping. Amongst the legislative and administrative clauses was one relating to the appointment of sheriffs[1]. Henceforth the sheriff was to be appointed by the chancellor, treasurer and others of the council present. If the chancellor was not present, the treasurer and barons of the exchequer with the justices were to appoint and those appointed were to have lands and tenements whereof they could answer to the king their deeds. They were to have their commissions under the great seal[2]. The Ordinance seemed to convey a suggestion of lessening the power of the exchequer.

The exchequer was also the object of other Ordinances. When the sheriff or other royal official, who ought to render account there, presented his account the tallies, writs and quittances he had of sums of money paid to him were to be allowed so that the people should not henceforth be aggrieved by exchequer summons for debts which had been paid and for which they had acquittance by tally, writ or other quittance[3]. This was a matter which concerned merely the efficiency of administration and as far as can be seen no ulterior motive can be assigned to this Ordinance. Another Ordinance prohibited the holding of pleas in the court of the exchequer, except pleas touching the king and his officials, who were answerable in the exchequer by reason of their offices, and the officers of the exchequer and their attendants and servants[4]. If anyone was impleaded in the exchequer court against this Ordinance he was to have remedy in parliament[5]. The hearing of pleas at the exchequer had long been a grievance and previous efforts had been made to check it[6]. The ordainers stated that common merchants and many other people were received at the exchequer court in pleas of debt and trespass because such pleas were acknowledged by the officials of that court more readily than they ought to be[7]. The reason which they gave for limiting the pleas held at that court was twofold. By the hearing of these pleas the accounts and other things touching the king were the more delayed and many of the people aggrieved[8]. This was all the more serious because of the disordered state prevailing in the exchequer.

Ordinances were also made touching the administration of the household court of the marshalsea. One Ordinance dealt with the holding of pleas in the marshalsea. Pleas were held by the steward

[1] Vide below, pp. 521–7.
[2] Ordinance 17.
[3] Ordinance 24.
[4] Ordinance 25.
[5] Ibid.
[6] Vide above, p. 245.
[7] Ordinance 25.
[8] Ibid.

and marshal which did not belong to their office. Henceforth pleas of freehold, debt, covenant, contract or any common plea concerning the common people were not to be held there. The court was to concern itself with the trespasses of those of the household and with trespasses committed within the verge. Contracts and covenants made between members of the same household in that household were also to be tried in the marshalsea court. No plea of trespass was to be tried by the steward and marshal other than those which were attached by them before the king departed from the verge where the trespass was committed. The case was to be heard speedily so that it could be pleaded and determined before the king left the verge. Otherwise it would cease and the plaintiff sue by common law. Henceforth too, they were to receive attorneys for defendants as well as for plaintiffs. If the steward and marshal did anything against this Ordinance, their action should have no effect and the person aggrieved should have a chancery writ pleadable in the king's bench to recover damages against them and they should never henceforth be employed in the king's service[1]. This Ordinance was designed to prevent the marshalsea court encroaching upon the domains of the common law courts, for it was a prerogative court attached to the household. Similar interference was made with the office of coroner within the verge. The coroner of the county or franchise where a homicide was committed was associated with the coroner of the household to hold the inquest. The coroner of the county or franchise thus had cognisance of the homicide and entered it on his roll. If the steward could not then determine the plea, because the felon could not be attached or found, the coroner of the county was to show the process in eyre as he did of other felonies committed out of the verge[2]. The reason given for the reform was that many felonies had heretofore gone unpunished because the coroner of the county had not been authorised to inquire into felonies committed in the verge[3].

A number of Ordinances were concerned with reform in justice. The application of the Statute of Merchants was restricted to cases between merchants and merchants and of merchandises made between them and the method of making and sealing recognisances made in this matter was defined[4]. Persons of good fame, appealed by those who of right ought not to have any voice, if able to find good mainprise to be at the next gaol delivery to do law and acquit themselves of the charge, were not to be put in prison. Nothing was to be taken from them for being led to mainprise and if the gaol

[1] Ordinance 26. [2] Ordinance 27. [3] Ibid. [4] Ordinance 33.

delivery was delayed by the absence of the justices they were to be left at the same mainprise or they were to find other sufficient security until the coming of the justices[1]. The design of this Ordinance was to prevent sheriffs and others abusing their positions and grieving people by false appeals[2]. Persons appealed through malice of felonies in counties where they did not have lands or tenements and outlawed, were not to be put to death or disinherited, if they rendered themselves to the king's prison and could acquit themselves by the counties in which they were outlawed of these felonies or trespasses. Persons outlawed, because the sheriff testified they could not be found and had not lands by which they could be distrained, though they had lands in other counties were not to be put to death or disinherited, if they rendered themselves to the king's prison and acquitted themselves[3]. Appeals of felonies were not henceforth to be abated when the appellor gave details of the alleged felony, for the result of abating appeals for too slight causes and of imprisoning and ransoming the appellors had been to encourage crime. On the other hand, if the persons appealed were able to acquit themselves of the felonies, provided they were not indicted of them by solemn inquest, they were to have recovery from the appellors[4]. These Ordinances appear to have been real and sincere efforts to improve the administration of justice and attempts to redress pressing grievances. They help to redeem the Ordinances from being a barren party instrument.

In the same class can be placed the Ordinances which dealt with the forest. On account of the grievances which the people had suffered from the forest officials, it was ordained that the offices of all wardens, bailiffs and officers of the forest, those held for life no less than those held during pleasure, should be taken into the king's hands. Sufficient justices were to be assigned to inquire into and hear and determine all complaints made against such officers, the matter to be settled before the following Easter. Those found guilty were to be removed for ever and the others reinstated[5]. Persons had been disinherited and destroyed by the chief wardens and other officers of the forest north and south of Trent, against the form of the Charter of the Forest and against the form of the Ordinance of the Forest. Such officers were prohibited for the future from taking or imprisoning anyone except in certain cases. In these specific cases the person was to be mainprised until the eyre

[1] Ordinance 34. [2] Ibid. [3] Ordinance 35.
[4] Ordinance 36. [5] Ordinance 18.

of the forest without anything being taken for his deliverance. Should the warden refuse to do this he was to be ordered to do so by writ and eventually, if he persisted in his refusal, to be ousted from the king's service. The fines, amercements and ransoms unlawfully levied were to be accounted for at the exchequer[1].

The clauses of the Ordinances primarily concerned with finance were an important part of the baronial scheme. The ordainers were not satisfied with laying down as a rule for the future that the customs should be paid into the exchequer[2]; they were determined to make it retrospective. The alien merchants, who had received the customs of the realm and other things belonging to the king, were to be arrested with all their goods until they had rendered reasonable account of their collections since the accession of the king, before the treasurer and barons of the exchequer and others joined to them by the ordainers[3]. This association of persons by the ordainers with the exchequer officials in the administrative work of that department furnishes another instance of the baronial endeavours to influence administration. The Ordinance concerning the payment of customs to the exchequer had formed one of the seven preliminary ordinances issued in 1310. The ordainers found that it was not observed[4] and it was repeated in the issue of 1311. The customs together with all the issues of the realm were to be received and kept by natives and delivered into the exchequer. Other financial Ordinances dealt with prises and the new customs. All prises were to cease, except the ancient prises which were the king's right and due. Anyone acting contrary and making purveyance, without paying immediately for the goods taken to their full value, unless the seller freely gave respite, was to be taken to the nearest gaol and tried at common law as a thief and a robber, notwithstanding any commission which he had[5].

Great importance attached to the Ordinance abolishing the new customs[6]. All customs and imposts "levied since the coronation of Edward I" were entirely repealed for ever[7]; and this despite the charter Edward I had made to the foreign merchants, because that charter was made contrary to Magna Carta and the franchise of the city of London and without the assent of the baronage. Anyone who levied anything beyond the ancient customs was to pay damages, be put

[1] Ordinance 19.
[2] Ordinance 4. Vide above, p. 373.
[3] Ordinance 5.
[4] Ordinance 8.
[5] Ordinance 10.
[6] Cf. Dowell, *Hist. of Taxation*, vol. 1, pp. 78–81.
[7] An exception was made of the *Antiqua* or *Magna Custuma* granted to Edward I in 1275.

into prison and removed from the king's service for ever. The customs on wool, wool fells and leather the king was still to have and foreign merchants were to be subject to these alone[1]. The barons had previously induced the king at the parliament of Stamford in 1309 to suspend the new customs. This he promised to do for a limited period to see its effect[2]. On 2 August, 1310, however, the king again ordered the new customs to be collected "it being now clear that no utility resulted to the king and people[3]." Serious as was the unrest which the new customs caused amongst the merchant class in England and especially in London, it can hardly be said that "in 1311 a temporary community of economic and political interests resulted in an alliance between the English merchants and the English baronage, whose combined efforts forced the 'Ordinances' upon Edward II...[4]." This Ordinance may have been a concession to the merchant classes but to speak of an alliance and of combined effort is to exaggerate the influence of the merchants and to depreciate seriously the power of the barons.

The effect of the operative clauses which touched such important themes as interference with the personal element around the king, the exercise of restraint upon him, encroachment upon his prerogative, legislative and administrative reform, and financial considerations, the effect of all these was to depend upon the machinery which the ordainers provided for their maintenance and enforcement. A consideration of the executive clauses of the Ordinances is of as great importance as the operative. No adequate machinery was provided to give even temporary effect to the Ordinances. It could not be supplied in the circumstances. To ensure that the Ordinances would be kept by the administrative officers it was ordained that the chancellor, treasurer, chief justices of both benches, the chancellor of the exchequer, the treasurer of the wardrobe, the steward of the king's household, all the justices, sheriffs, escheators, constables, holders of inquests for all purposes and all other royal bailiffs and officers should be sworn, when they received their offices, to keep all the Ordinances without contravening them in any point[5]. As long as there was no authority to enforce the observance of this oath the taking of the oath itself was quite valueless. This objection was met. In each parliament one bishop, two earls and two barons were to be assigned to hear and determine all the complaints made against

[1] Ordinance 11. [2] *Cal. Close Rolls*, 1307–13, p. 170 (20 Aug. 1309).
[3] *Cal. Fine Rolls*, 1307–19, pp. 68, 70. *Cal. Close Rolls*, 1307–13, p. 275.
[4] McKechnie, *Magna Carta*, p. 406. [5] Ordinance 39.

whatever officer or officers of the king contravened the Ordinances. If all the five could not attend or should be hindered from hearing and determining the complaints, then three or two of them should do so. Those found to have contravened the Ordinances were to be punished both as against the king and as against those who made complaint according to the discretion of the committee of five[1].

This committee could remain effective only as long as the king's power remained a cipher or the barons were in a position to exercise continual coercion upon him. Great as were the defects of the executive clause of Magna Carta with its right of legalised rebellion, it did at least recognise fact. The executive machinery of the Ordinances was dependent for its efficiency upon external factors. The rebellion in this case would not have been legalised. There was no element of permanency in the machinery. The Ordinances provided that parliament should meet at least once if not twice a year. This committee was therefore to be appointed at least once a year. Its smallness in size need not have been necessarily a defect, and for a normal judicial body five would have been an ample number. But for a commission which was to try such important persons as the chancellor, the chief justice and the treasurer, the body was small and insignificant, especially when there would be one power in perpetual opposition. It was unlikely that the king would ever become reconciled to the principles of the Ordinances or that he would ever submit tamely to their operation. It was only by the exercise of coercion that he had granted the ordainers their commission and accepted the results of their labour. There were limits to the efficacy of coercion and to the opportunities for exercising it.

It was ordained that the Ordinances should be maintained and kept in all their points and that the king should cause them to be put under his great seal and sent into every county in England to be published, held and firmly kept[2]. The ordainers to all outward appearance had won a complete victory. That victory was however apparent rather than real. It is true that they had forced upon the king reform of his household and administration. They had succeeded in putting into practice some part of their theories of administration. The king had been forced to accept and confirm principles which were repugnant to him and subversive of the household system of government. But the barons had no guarantee that the king would abide by his confirmation. Moreover, apart from coercion by force of arms, they had no means of securing observance. The

[1] Ordinance 40. [2] Ordinance 41.

executive machinery they had designed was weak, almost futile. It could not stand against a king determined to resist to the utmost the operation of the Ordinances.

The problem of the additional ordinances has still to be considered. Three copies are known. One is embodied in the *Annales Londonienses*[1], the second is contained in the *Liber Custumarum* of the city of London[2], and the third is found on the dorse of the copy of the Ordinances in the Cathedral Library at Canterbury[3]. The question of their source and origin is one of difficulty. The rubric of the Canterbury manuscript—"Declaraciones quorundam articulorum ordinationum infrascriptorum[4]"—would suggest that they were an explanation or enlargement of certain doubtful points in the Ordinances. The Guildhall copy supports this suggestion. There they are under the title "Ces sunt les Articles qe les Countes de Lancestre e de Warrewyke maunderent au Roi, de mettre gent de office e remuer autres, en son hostel, e de garder les Ordinaunces avaunt escrites en touz lour poyntz[5]."

This means that the additional ordinances were drawn up by a committee of the ordainers, the primary duty of which was the detailed reform of the household[6]. These details were not important enough to find a place in the Ordinances. They were applications of the original Ordinances and exemplifications of them and were certainly drawn up after the original Ordinances had been accepted and published[7]. They were in effect applications of the general principles contained in the Ordinances to specific instances, though they may have been a list of Ordinances not observed by the king. The Ordinance concerning gifts by the king[8] was to be maintained, but the gifts given by agreement to Robert de Clifford, Guy Ferre, Edmund[9] de Mauley and William D'Audley were to be excepted from its application[10]. Receipts were to come wholly to the exchequer as was ordained[11]. Two ordainers, the bishop of Norwich

[1] *Ann. Lond.* pp. 198–202.

[2] *Mun. Gildh. Lond.* vol. II, Pt ii, pp. 682–690.

[3] Cant. Cath. MS. K. 11, dorse. [4] Ibid.

[5] *Mun. Gildh. Lond.* vol. II, Pt ii, p. 682.

[6] Cf. *Ann. Lond.* p. 198: "ordinatores tractaverunt de familia et servis regis, et supplicaverunt domino regi forma quae sequitur ut eos ab officio removeret."

[7] Ibid. [8] Ordinance 3. Vide above, p. 372.

[9] *Mun. Gildh. Lond.* vol. II, Pt ii, p. 683, has Robert, but *Ann. Lond.* p. 199, gives the correct Edmund.

[10] *Mun. Gildh. Lond.* vol. II, Pt ii, pp. 682–3.

[11] Cf. Ordinance 4. Vide above, p. 373. *Mun. Gildh. Lond.* vol. II, Pt ii, p. 683.

and Hugh de Courtney, were appointed auditors of the accounts of the alien merchants[1], as provided in the Ordinances[2]. The Ordinance against Gavaston[3] was extended to include all his kindred. They were all to be removed from the king and his service[4]. Other foreigners, some in administrative offices, such as the marshal of the exchequer, others in Cornwall, were to be removed from their offices and ordered to return to their own country[5].

Other articles dealt with the reform of the household. The primary object of some of these was to reduce the expenditure of the household. The porters of the household were to be discharged and there were to be no porters except as in the time of Edward I. All the mariners were to be discharged, and all carters and carts except such as were wanted for the household as in Edward I's time[6].

In others the action was prompted by grievances and wrongs which had been committed. Robert Lewer, the archers and all manner of low persons were to be discharged from the king's wages whether in castles or elsewhere. They were in future only to be employed in his service during time of war. Any wages due to them were not to be paid until they had made satisfaction to those they had wronged[7]. There were persons holding office both in the king's and queen's household who had been introduced by Gavaston. Those who were not fit and proper were to be discharged at the discretion of the steward of the household and the keeper of the wardrobe[8].

A considerable number of the articles were directed against officers of the household or persons about the court[9]. John de Knokyn, Roger his brother, Ralph de Waltham and Richard de la Garderobe were to be discharged[10]. John de Cherleton, who if not actually already chamberlain became that shortly afterwards[11], John de la Beche, John de Sapy, William de Vaux, John de Hothum, who had been Gavaston's deputy as keeper of the forest north of Trent[12] and was also escheator north of Trent[13], and Gerard de Salveyn were all

[1] *Mun. Gildh. Lond.* vol. II, Pt ii, p. 583.
[2] Cf Ordinance 5. Vide above, p. 379.
[3] Cf. Ordinance 20. Vide above, pp. 369–370.
[4] *Mun. Gildh. Lond.* vol. II, Pt ii, p. 683. Cf. *Auct. Malm.* p. 174.
[5] *Mun. Gildh. Lond.* vol. II, Pt ii, pp. 683–4.
[6] Ibid. [7] Ibid. pp. 684–5. [8] Ibid. p. 685.
[9] A summary of a number of the personal articles is given in *Auct. Bridl.* p. 40.
[10] Ibid. p. 685. [11] Vide above, pp. 215–216.
[12] Cf. *Cal. Fine Rolls*, 1307–19, p. 117.
[13] He was appointed 10 December, 1309, and surrendered it on 3 February, 1313 (Tout, *The Place of Ed. II*, p. 362).

to be removed from their offices and from the service of the king in such a way that they should not approach the king[1]. The keeper of the wardrobe, Ingelard de Warle[2] and the escheator south of Trent, Roger de Wellesworth[3], were to be removed from the king and from his service and they were not henceforth to go near the king[4]. Robert Darcy and Edmund Bacon and the others, who had issued forth from the king's palace armed to pursue Despenser the son, were to be removed from the king's household and from his following and were to hold no office under him[5].

Another article in the form of a petition had no connection whatsoever with the Ordinances. The prelates, earls and barons prayed that the king would do right to Walter de Langton about his lands and especially in the matter of his goods, according to the Great Charter and the Ordinances[6].

Other articles dealt with the application of the Ordinances to the administrative system. The sheriffs were to be removed and others appointed, as was provided in an Ordinance[7]. The king was requested to appoint a fit and proper warden for the exchanges, as the then warden was not suitable[8]. Certain officials who had made prises contrary to the Ordinances, to the injury of the king and his people, were to be removed from the king's service[9]. Emery de Friscobaldi was to be removed and his lands seized[10], according to the Ordinance[11]. Richard Damory against whom many complaints were made was to be removed from the king and his office until he had been cleared of the charges[12]. The deputy constable of Bordeaux was to come to render his account[13]. The justices and other officers of the forest, who had not come to render account, were to be distrained to come to account the morrow of St Hilary before the barons of the exchequer[14]. The offices of the forests on both sides of Trent which were not seized into the king's hands according to the Ordinance[15], were to be seized immediately and persons appointed to inquire, hear and

[1] *Mun. Gildh. Lond.* vol. II, Pt ii, p. 685.

[2] Tout, *The Place of Ed. II*, p. 355.

[3] He was appointed 26 April, 1311, and held the office until 30 December, 1312 (Tout, *The Place of Ed. II*, p. 362).

[4] *Mun. Gildh. Lond.* vol. II, Pt ii, p. 686. [5] Ibid.

[6] Ibid. Cf. *Auct. Bridl.* p. 40.

[7] *Mun. Gildh. Lond.* vol. II, Pt ii, p. 687. Ordinance 17. Vide above, p. 376.

[8] *Mun. Gildh. Lond.* vol. II, Pt ii, p. 687. [9] Ibid. [10] Ibid.

[11] Ordinance 21. Vide above, pp. 370–1.

[12] *Mun. Gildh. Lond.* vol. II, Pt ii, p. 687. [13] Ibid. pp. 687–8.

[14] Ibid. p. 688.

[15] Cf. Ordinance 18. Vide above, p. 378.

determine as provided[1]. The officials who had not taken the oath required by the first of the executive clauses of the Ordinances[2] were to do so[3]. The pleas held before the steward and marshals since the making of the restrictive Ordinance[4] were to be held as null[5]. The lands of the Templars had been redelivered to those who held them before the Ordinances. This matter was to be redressed[6]. The king was also asked to appoint that long list of officials of the administration and household which it was ordained should be appointed by the counsel and assent of the barons in parliament[7] according to the form of the Ordinance[8].

These additional ordinances emphasise the weakness of the executive machinery. Many of them are merely repetitions of previous Ordinances. The Ordinance against Beaumont[9] was repeated. His lands in England and elsewhere were to be seized and the kingdom of Man delivered to a good man of English birth[10]. The castle of Bamburgh was to be seized into the king's hands according to the Ordinances[11]. Gavaston had letters of protection and of general attorney which apparently, despite the Ordinance against him, still held good. They were to be recalled and held as of no effect since they were contrary to the Ordinance[12]. The king was not without hope that the time would not be far distant when Gavaston would be in England once more. In accordance with the Ordinance he took into his hands the lands of Gavaston and delivered them to those who were previously officers of Gavaston. The barons detected the plan and required the king to dismiss those officials and appoint others[13]. This was but one way in which the king might succeed in getting round the Ordinances. The very need for these additional ordinances shows the weakness of the baronial position. They were as ineffective as the previous ones.

More than the defects of the Ordinances was shown by the additional articles. These show more clearly baronial policy especially

[1] *Mun. Gildh. Lond.* vol. II, Pt ii, p. 690.
[2] Cf. Ordinance 39. Vide above, p. 380.
[3] *Mun. Gildh. Lond.* vol. II, Pt ii, p. 689.
[4] Cf. Ordinance 26. Vide above, pp. 376–7.
[5] *Mun. Gildh. Lond.* vol. II, Pt ii, p. 689.
[6] Ibid. pp. 689–690.
[7] Cf. Ordinance 14. Vide above, pp. 371–2.
[8] This article which is the last one on the list in *Ann. Lond.* pp. 201–2, and Cant. Cath. MS. K. 11, dorse, is omitted in *Mun. Gildh. Lond.* vol. II, Pt ii, p. 690.
[9] Ordinance 22. Vide above, p. 370.
[10] *Mun. Gildh. Lond.* vol. II, Pt ii, pp. 688–9.
[11] Ibid. p. 689. Vide above, p. 370. Ordinance 23.
[12] *Mun. Gildh. Lond.* vol. II, Pt ii, p. 688.
[13] Ibid. p. 690.

towards the household organisation. The claim to appoint such important officers of the household as the steward, the keeper and controller of the wardrobe, and a keeper of the privy seal was extended to the right to dismiss the pettiest menial and to limit the number of officials employed in the household. Subsequent events showed that the household was in need of drastic internal reform. The household ordinances made in 1318 and 1323[1], prove the necessity for reform. Such reform should not have been the work of a baronial committee working with the definite object of exercising restraint. The wholesale clearance desired of the household officials and servants proves that reform was but a secondary consideration. Royal nominees were to be removed and replaced by baronial partizans. The household was to be made a source of weakness not strength to the king. It was to be a hotbed of partizans of the baronial opposition. Little of the scheme was to become permanent. Even the immediate effects of the Ordinances were not considerable. The personal clauses, which should have been the easiest to make effective, did not succeed. In less than three months after the publication of the Ordinances Gavaston had returned from exile and joined the king once more[2]. Though his triumph was short lived it was not the Ordinances but the Lancaster faction that destroyed him. The events which led up to his destruction too were to rend the unity of the barons and to hurl Pembroke into the king's hands. The result of Gavaston's murder was to make that rather than the Ordinances the main question at issue between king and barons.

An attempt was made to put some of the Ordinances into effect immediately. Writs[3] were issued on 9 October, 1311, "by the king and the whole council," revoking, in accordance with the Ordinances, all grants made in Scotland and Ireland. On the same day Beaumont was ordered to deliver the land of Man to Robert de Leyburn, constable of the castle of Cockermouth[4]. This writ also was issued in accordance with the Ordinance "by the king and the whole council." On 9 October, in fact, the ordainers were able to do as they desired. They had so overcome the king that whatever writs the council wished were issued. Writs were issued ordering that the collection of the new customs should cease in accordance with the Ordinances[5]. On 11 October, schedules were sent to the escheators north and south of Trent ordering them to resume into the king's hands the

[1] Vide below, pp. 535–7. [2] *Ann. Lond.* p. 202.
[3] *Cal. Fine Rolls*, 1307–19, pp. 107–8. [4] Ibid. p. 108.
[5] Ibid. pp. 108–9. *Cal. Close Rolls*, 1307–13, p. 380. *Parl. Writs*, vol. II, Pt i, p. 72 (9 Oct. 1311).

lands contained therein which had been granted since 16 March, 1310[1], when the commission was given to the ordainers. The list of grants contained in these schedules and revoked was lengthy. The grants were in the main to such favourites as Gavaston[2], Beaumont[3], and Oliver de Bordeaux[4]. Resumptions were also ordered by writ of privy seal: the castle and manor of Skipton in Craven granted to Robert de Clifford were recovered in this way[5]. On 23 October, 1311, the king's council was ordered, by privy seal, not to sell the wardship and marriage of Sir John ap Adam to Despenser or any other until the next parliament. If the grant had been made it was to be repealed[6]. On 27 October, the wardship which had been granted to Despenser was resumed into the king's hands[7]. Some of the grants resumed were subsequently regranted with the consent of the ordainers[8], or with the assent of the magnates assembled in parliament[9]. On 9 October and subsequent days several grants of custodies were also made by the council[10].

A grant of the wardship of the lands which had belonged to John ap Adam, which had been resumed, was made in December to Ralph de Monthemer for 6000 marks, "by king with the assent of the ordainers on the information of William de Melton[11]." The king however did not surrender his rights. In a list of appointments to castles made on 29 September, 1311, two days after the Ordinances had been published by the ordainers, appeared the appointments of Richard Damory to the castle of Oxford, and Robert Lewer to the castle of Odiham[12]. Appointments were still made by warrant of privy seal. A citizen of London obtained the exchanges of London and Canterbury in this way on 20 October[13], and Roger de Waterville was given the manor of Tottenham to hold at farm on 27 October[14]. On 22 October the king ordered the treasurer and barons of the exchequer by writ of privy seal to allow Robert de Kendale who held certain Templars' manors at farm to have his goods and chattels therein *saunz nondu empeschement*[15]. In December John de Crombwell went to the exchequer and announced there, on the king's behalf, that the king had ordered him to release a certain prisoner[16].

[1] *Cal. of Chan. Rolls*, 1272–1326, pp. 98–104.
[2] Ibid. p. 102. [3] Ibid. pp. 98, 100, 102. [4] Ibid. pp. 98, 99, 100.
[5] *Cal. Pat. Rolls*, 1307–13, p. 395 (20 Oct. 1311).
[6] Anc. Corresp. vol. XLV, no. 165. Vide App. of Doc. no. 117.
[7] *Cal. Fine Rolls*, 1307–19, p. 109.
[8] *Cal. Pat. Rolls*, 1307–13, p. 407 (16 Dec. 1311). [9] Ibid. p. 408.
[10] *Cal. Fine Rolls*, 1307–19, pp. 104, 106, 109. [11] Ibid. p. 121.
[12] Ibid. p. 103. [13] Ibid. p. 103. [14] Ibid. p. 109.
[15] K. R. Mem. Roll, no. 85, m. 8. [16] Ibid. m. 44.

The household system was not entirely or even considerably superseded.

It was not until 4 December, 1311, that the keepers of the forest north and south of Trent were ordered to take into the king's hands the offices of all keepers, bailiffs and other ministers of the forest pursuant to the Ordinance[1]. Despenser, who had surrendered the keepership of the forest south of Trent on 2 December, the office having been resumed by the king in compliance with the Ordinances[2], appeared at the exchequer on 18 December, before the lieutenant of the treasurer and the barons, seeking a day to account there as he wished to fulfil the Ordinance. A day was accordingly given him, when he duly presented himself[3]. In accordance with the Ordinances, on 29 October, 1311, the escheator south of Trent was ordered to take into the king's hands the lands of Emery de Friscobaldi and its issues[4]. The king however soon afterwards repented of this and a number of conflicting orders appeared[5]. On 20 December, the bishop of Worcester announced on the king's behalf to Norwich, lieutenant of the treasurer, and to the barons of the exchequer in the presence of Robert de Clifford, Henry de Percy and others of the king's council that Peter de Friscobaldi should have the horses, two robes and his armour which were amongst the goods and chattels of the society of the Friscobaldi taken by the sheriff of London by command of the king by Ordinance of the ordainers[6].

The Ordinances were acknowledged in the law courts. Reference was made to the Ordinance dealing with mainprise[7] in the proceedings in the court of exchequer upon a bill presented at the exchequer[8]. Justice Bereford sent a case into parliament "because the new ordinances[9] direct that when the Justices are in doubt about their judgment the cause shall be sent into parliament[10]." Before the justices holding the eyre in Kent it was argued that it was laid down in the new Ordinances that no law should be changed by the king to the delaying of justice[11].

[1] *Cal. Fine Rolls*, 1307–19, p. 117.
[2] Ibid. p. 116.
[3] K. R. Mem. Roll, no. 85, mm. 47, 71 d. L. T. R. Mem. Roll, no. 82, m. 31.
[4] *Cal. Fine Rolls*, 1307–19, p. 107.
[5] *Hist. Essays*, ed. Tout and Tait, 'The Italian Bankers in England and their loans to Edward I and Edward II,' W. E. Rhodes, pp. 148, 151.
[6] K. R. Mem. Roll, no. 85, m. 45 d.
[7] Cf. Ordinance 34. Vide above, pp. 377–8.
[8] Exch. K. R. Bills, 1/5.
[9] A reference to Ordinance 29. Vide above, p. 374.
[10] Seld. Soc., *Year Bk 2–3 Ed. II*, p. 52.
[11] Seld Soc., *Eyre of Kent*, vol. 1, p. 276.

In their claim to assist in the appointment of officials the barons were not very successful immediately after the Ordinances. Their consent was obtained to the appointment of Henry de Percy to the office of the keeper of the forest north of Trent, but the consent was not obtained until after the appointment had been made, and was announced by the note "and afterwards the ordainers consented to the aforesaid[1]."

The king and the barons had a great struggle over the appointment of the treasurer. John de Sandale had been appointed treasurer on 6 July, 1310[2]. On 23 October, 1311, the bishop of Worcester, chancellor, appeared at the exchequer, and having summoned the barons and chamberlains, announced to them on the king's behalf that for certain causes it was not the king's will at present that Sandale should remain any longer in that office[3]. On the same day Walter de Norwich, baron of the exchequer, was appointed to act as treasurer[4]. Norwich was not the king's first choice as lieutenant of the treasurer. Richard de Abingdon's appointment was first ordered, but because he was not in London, Norwich was appointed[5]. No hint was given that this removal was due to baronial pressure. It was certain however that the king, on his part, had no reason to dispense with Sandale's services; and his subsequent reinstatement in that office[6] and later promotion as chancellor prove that his removal was not due to loss of royal favour. Moreover it was not usual for the lieutenants of the treasurer to be appointed by writ of great seal. In view of subsequent proceedings in the exchequer it would seem that the removal was due to the instigation of the barons.

On 23 January, 1312, Walter de Langton, Edward I's treasurer, was appointed treasurer "until the next parliament[7]," the king finding the loophole from the Ordinances in this formula. This appointment of Langton was probably a deliberate move on Edward II's part to strengthen the personnel and organisation of the exchequer against the barons. Langton was an experienced official, well versed in exchequer business and tradition and after his long service under Edward I likely to be a strong royal supporter against the

[1] *Cal. Fine Rolls*, 1307–19, p. 116 (2 Dec. 1311).

[2] *Cal. Pat. Rolls*, 1307–13, p. 234.

[3] K. R. Mem. Roll, no. 85, m. 41. L. T. R. Mem. Roll, no. 82, m. 18.

[4] *Cal. Pat. Rolls*, 1307–13, p. 396. Cf. Brev. Baron. 5 Ed. II; K. R. Mem. Roll, no. 85, m. 8.

[5] Chan. Warr., File 82/2413.

[6] He was reappointed lieutenant of the treasurer on 4 October, 1312. Vide above, p. 120.

[7] *Cal. Pat. Rolls*, 1307–13, p. 413.

barons. At the king's wish, he had been admitted a member of the council on 23 October, 1311[1], and was present at the exchequer with the chancellor and others of the council when Norwich was admitted to act as treasurer on 23 October[2]. On 11 January, 1312, the keeper of the great seal was ordered to inform the bishop in whose hands were his lands and goods, which the king had returned to him[3], and also to make letters under the great seal to Norwich, lieutenant of the treasurer, and the barons of the exchequer ordering them to aid him in recovering his debts[4]. The lieutenant of the treasurer and the barons were similarly ordered by writ of privy seal on 16 January[5]. Nevertheless his appointment as treasurer was unexpected. It could not have been more than a few weeks previously that the prelates, earls and barons had petitioned the king on his behalf[6]. The first writ of appointment apparently produced no effect though a liberate writ for 500 marks dated on 28 January was made on his announcement[7], and another writ to the same effect was issued on 14 March[8]. Meanwhile on 3 March, Norwich had been appointed chief baron, and the barons had been ordered to admit him[9].

The magnates were determined not to allow Langton to act as treasurer, and for the time being they had the advantage. They were at Westminster; the king was in the north. On the morning of 3 April, the bishop came to Westminster to the exchequer of receipt, assembled the barons and chamberlains and others of the exchequer and exhibited the commission under the great seal of his appointment as treasurer. He was prepared to take the proffers of the sheriffs, bailiffs and others in full exchequer when the earls of Pembroke and Hereford, John Botetourte and others in their company, on behalf of the archbishop, bishops and other prelates, earls and barons and the whole commonalty of the realm, appeared and stated how the king had given a commission to ordainers and how the Ordinances had been confirmed and sworn to be observed. Langton was charged with taking the office of treasurer against the Ordinances which required that the treasurer should be made with the assent of the baronage in parliament. Pembroke and Hereford then charged the chamberlains of the exchequer that they should not pay

[1] K. R. Mem. Roll, no. 85, m. 41. L. T. R. Mem. Roll, no. 82, m. 18.
[2] Ibid.
[3] Chan. Warr., File 82/2470. Vide App. of Doc. no. 57.
[4] Chan. Warr., File 82/2471.
[5] Exch. of Pleas, Plea Roll, no. 31, m. 52 d.
[6] Vide above, p. 384.
[7] Liberate Roll, no. 88, m. 2.
[8] *Cal. Pat. Rolls*, 1307–13, p. 440.
[9] Ibid. p. 435. K. R. Mem. Roll, no. 85, m. 18.

out any money or treasure to anyone by whom it could come to the hands of an enemy of the realm. The following day, when the barons entered the little exchequer to counsel on the royal business, the two earls and Botetourte appeared and repeated in part what they had said the previous day and added that no money should be paid to Sir Ingelard de Warle and the others whom the ordainers had requested should be displaced from their offices and from the king's presence[1]. On 4 April the barons wrote to the king giving him an account of the matter[2]. On 12 April the king ordered them to obey Langton as treasurer, and as they wished to escape the king's anger they were in no way to omit to do this[3]. As a result of the threats which had been made against him[4] Langton was afraid to act. On 13 April the king ordered him to fulfil his duty[5]. The result was that while writs were addressed to Langton, the barons and chamberlains of the exchequer, by the assent of the whole council at Westminster, Norwich was recognised as lieutenant of the treasurer by virtue of the commission he had received in October[6]. On 17 May however Norwich was ordered to continue to act as treasurer, Langton having been prevented from entering on the execution of his office by the ordainers[7]. If the ordainers did not assert their right to appoint the treasurer they certainly made it impossible for one to whom they objected to act in that office. The king did not give up the idea of making Langton his treasurer. On 14 April he was ordered to join the king with all speed to give his counsel concerning the king's affairs[8]. A letter which the "administrative" council sent the king by Oliver de Bordeaux advised him to continue calling Langton treasurer "car sire vous nauez uncore fait nul autre[9]." When Langton was excommunicated by the archbishop for the part he was supposed to be taking against the Ordinances[10] the king wrote

[1] K. R. Mem. Roll, no. 85, m. 52. L. T. R. Mem. Roll, no. 82, m. 45. Vide App. of Doc. no. 16.

[2] Ibid.

[3] Madox, *Hist. Exch.* vol. II, p. 38. K. R. Mem. Roll, no. 85, m. 21.

[4] K. R. Mem. Roll, no. 85, m. 52. L. T. R. Mem. Roll, no. 82, m. 45. Vide App. of Doc. no. 16.

[5] *Cal. Close Rolls*, 1307–13, p. 417. *Foedera*, vol. II, p. 164.

[6] Issue Roll, no. 162, m. 2 (1 May, 1312): "Et quia idem Walterus de Norwyco per assensum tocius consilii domini Regis, apud Westmonasterium existentis, locum Thesaurarii tenens virtute commissionis mense Octobris...."

[7] *Cal. Pat. Rolls*, 1307–13, p. 459. K. R. Mem. Roll, no. 85, m. 23.

[8] *Cal. Close Rolls*, 1307–13, p. 458.

[9] Anc. Corresp. vol. XLIX, no. 66.

[10] *Chron. Murimuth*, p. 18. *Flores Hist.* vol. III, pp. 148–9. Wilkins, *Concilia*, vol. II, p. 407.

to the pope on his behalf[1]. The bishop of Worcester, keeper of the great seal, was ordered that in the letters under the great seal to the pope on behalf of Langton "facez nomer meisme Leuesque nostre Tresorer si com nous lui auoms nomez en noz autres lettres qe nous auoms enueiz pur lui a nostre dit seint pere le pape auant ces houres[2]." The king's efforts were in vain. Too much importance can, however, be attached to the baronial success in this instance, though the barons' power and influence were considerable. In November, 1311, the king had ordered that no keeperships were to be sold in the exchequer without the presence of the bishop of Worcester, chancellor[3], and in February, 1312, measures had been taken to ensure the safe-keeping of the palace of Westminster and the exchequer[4].

The means by which the magnates obtained their advantage was not one which was likely to answer on every occasion. All the circumstances were entirely in the ordainers' favour. They were still united. The king was at a safe distance. In the circumstances it is surprising that they were not able to achieve still more.

As early as 12 January, 1312, the king found himself strong enough to order a restricted proclamation of the Ordinances to be made. The sheriffs throughout England were to proclaim that the laws and customs of the kingdom and the Ordinances recently made, so far as they were not prejudicial to the king, should be observed[5]. There is no necessity to enter into the tedious quarrels and the futile attempts at reconciliation which followed the murder of Gavaston. The death of the favourite told in the king's advantage. It removed from the king's immediate circle a source of endless irritation. It distracted attention from the constitutional problem, though even in royal writs the pursuers of Gavaston were still called "the ordainers[6]." The death made Pembroke throw in his lot with the king, and make possible his administration of 1312–16[7], which did not a little to withstand the extremists and support the king against them. The disappearance of Gavaston from the scene also opened the way for the return of others to the king's party. The result was that when concord was made in December, 1312, the only concession the king made was to pardon[8] those who had participated in the

[1] Chan. Warr., File 83/2537 (23 Nov. 1312). *Foedera*, vol. II, p. 167.

[2] Chan. Warr., File 83/2542 (30 Nov. 1312).

[3] K. R. Mem. Roll, no. 85, m. 11 d.

[4] Ibid. m. 49.

[5] *Cal. Close Rolls*, 1307–13, p. 449. *Foedera*, vol. II, p. 154.

[6] *Cal. Pat. Rolls*, 1307–13, p. 553 (22 Feb. 1313).

[7] Vide above, pp. 322–330.

[8] *Stat. of Realm*, vol. I, pp. 169–170. *Foedera*, vol. II, pp. 191–2, 230. *Cal. Pat. Rolls*, 1313–17, pp. 35–36.

pursuit and death of Gavaston. The barons had on the other hand to make humble obeisance, and full restitution of what they had taken at Newcastle, when they had pursued the king and Gavaston, and to endeavour to obtain a subsidy for the Scottish war from parliament[1]. The real victory for the king lay in the omission of all reference to the Ordinances. In this treaty therefore the barons had to surrender temporarily all intention of forcing the king to maintain and abide by the Ordinances, and the king was released from binding himself to observe them in a mutual compact.

In the period immediately following the Ordinances, when the need for them was most imperative, for the ordainers were enthusiastic over their work and the king was in isolation, merely surrounded by his household officials and a few courtiers, with the occasional assistance of a detached magnate like Gloucester[2], the Ordinances did not exercise more than a passing effect upon the administration. If the effect were to be judged by what had been achieved two or three years after the publication of the Ordinances very little importance could be attached to them. In their main object the barons had failed entirely. They had been able to revoke a part of what the king had done between 16 March, 1310, and 5 October, 1311, but they had no assurance that even that small part of their negative work would be permanent. The important principles laid down they were unable to translate into practice. Some of the principles they did succeed in applying fitfully, others they never succeeded in applying. Despite the uncomfortable position in which the king found himself at the beginning of 1314, he could afford to congratulate himself upon his successful resistance to the baronial plans. His position was uncomfortable from external considerations coming partly from Scotland, not because of the baronial opposition. The episode of the Ordinances did not begin with the king's commission of appointment and end with the publication. The whole of the subsequent baronial action and hence of the king's defensive measures may be regarded as a commentary upon the Ordinances. The great program of baronial reform recurred whenever the barons were in the ascendant. They were obeyed and disobeyed in alternation as the barons or king obtained the advantage.

[1] *Foedera*, vol. II, pp. 191–2. [2] Cf. *Ann. Lond.* p. 210.

CHAPTER III

THE EXPERIMENTS (*cont.*)

(ii) *The Lancaster Administration*

The defeat of the king at Bannockburn in 1314 gave Lancaster and his supporters the opportunity they desired. A beaten and discredited king returned from Scotland. His prestige had gone, and his power was seriously diminished. Lancaster had not joined in person the force that fought at Bannockburn. A section of the barons had protested that the campaign was against the Ordinances, which provided that the king should not go out of his kingdom to fight without the consent of all his magnates in parliament[1]. A number of the moderates, the earls of Gloucester, Hereford and Pembroke and others had gone; but other of the magnates had refused to set out in person, though they sent their due service in aid of the king[2]. One chronicler attributes the defeat to the fact that the campaign was contrary to the Ordinances and points out in support that not one of the ordainers who took part in the fight escaped capture or death, except Pembroke, who fled bare without arms[3]. As soon as practicable after the battle a parliament was held at York[4], meeting on 9 September[5]. Before the parliament had met the king was making a rapprochement with Lancaster. On 4 September he wrote asking him to allow the archbishop of Canterbury for his greater security to travel in his company[6]. This prepared the way for the reconciliation which took place at the parliament[7].

The barons urged upon the king that nothing would be well done unless the Ordinances were fully observed[8]. The king accordingly promised in good faith that he would keep the Ordinances[9]. This

[1] *Chron. Mon. de Melsa*, vol. II, p. 330.
[2] Ibid. pp. 330–1.
[3] Ibid. pp. 331–2.
[4] *Ann. Paul.* p. 376. *Auct. Malm.* p. 208. *Chron. Murimuth*, p. 21. *Flores Hist.* vol. III, p. 339.
[5] *Parl. Writs*, vol. II, Pt ii, pp. 128–131.
[6] *Lit. Cantuar.* vol. III, App. p. 395.
[7] *Ann. Paul.* p. 276. *Chron. Lanerc.* p. 211.
[8] *Auct. Malm.* p. 208.
[9] Ibid. *Chron. Lanerc.* p. 211.

did not satisfy the barons. They demanded not the mere observance but the execution of the Ordinances. The king granted the execution; he would deny the earls nothing[1]. Accordingly the chancellor, the treasurer and the sheriffs were removed from their offices and others appointed according to the tenor of the Ordinances[2]. The somewhat fitful tenure of the chancery by the archbishop of Canterbury had come to an end on 31 March, 1314, and from that time the great seal had been in the custody of Osgodby, Bardelby and Ayremynne as keepers[3]. On 26 September, Sandale, now bishop of Winchester, was appointed[4] chancellor. This appointment left open the office of treasurer, and on the same day Walter de Norwich was appointed treasurer "by king and council[5]." In the months of October and November most of the sheriffs were changed[6]. The earls also desired that Despenser, Beaumont and others should leave the king's court. This the king withstood[7], but Despenser, who was an enemy of Lancaster and among the chief and greatest counsellors of the king[8], was compelled to go into hiding[9].

The battle of Bannockburn then had two important results; it gave Lancaster a predominant position in the administration; and it led to a revival of the Ordinances. For nearly two years, within limits, it can be said that the Ordinances were both observed and partly executed. For the execution which took place in the parliament of York in 1314 was but the beginning. Lancaster's share in administration was due to necessity and not to choice on the king's part. He did not trust Lancaster, and Lancaster did not trust him[10]. It would have been inopportune and indeed impossible for the king to dispense with the earl's assistance.

With Lancaster's accession to power, the earl of Warwick also obtained a share in administration. Lancaster and Warwick had always been the extremists amongst the barons. They had been the chiefs of the faction which had put Gavaston to death[11]. So prominent did Warwick become in 1314 that one chronicler records that he was made the chief in the king's council[12]. Though this was probably an exaggeration of his position he certainly was deputed

[1] *Auct. Malm.* p. 208. [2] Ibid. [3] Vide above, pp. 332–3.

[4] *Cal. Close Rolls*, 1313–18, pp. 197–8.

[5] *Cal. Pat. Rolls*, 1313–17, p. 178.

[6] *Cal. Fine Rolls*, 1307–19, pp. 220–1. P. R. O. Lists and Indexes, *List of Sheriffs*, passim.

[7] *Auct. Malm.* p. 208. [8] *Flores Hist.* vol. III, p. 339.

[9] *Auct. Malm.* p. 208. [10] *Chron. Lanerc.* p. 217.

[11] *Chron. Knighton*, vol. I, p. 409.

[12] *Ann. Lond.* p. 232: "factus est princeps consilii regis."

by king and council to assist in administration. On 28 May, 1315, power was given to Warwick, Sandale, chancellor, and Badlesmere to treat with Lancaster and others about the custody of the Scottish marches[1]. On 8 June, 1315, the assent between Badlesmere, constable of Bristol, and the men of that town was made before Lancaster and Warwick and the chancellor[2]. Two days later, an agreement was made at Warwick in the presence of Warwick and the chancellor[3].

During the years 1314–15 Lancaster had a great part in the administration. Messengers frequently passed between him and the king, carrying matters concerning administration. During this period William de Montague went as the king's envoy from Clipston to Wigan to the earl with three squires and one clerk[4]. In June, 1315, the business was pressing enough for Sandale to leave the seal in the custody of keepers to go as envoy from the king at Westminster to Lancaster at Kenilworth[5]. In October, 1315, the king sent William de Melton, keeper of his wardrobe, and Hugh D'Audley, who was beginning to find a place in the royal favour, to the earl at Donnington[6]. The purpose of the journey was to discover his advice upon certain administrative matters. This the earl sent to the king in a schedule on 20 October[7]. The matters which were treated included the service of the magnates in Scottish expeditions, assemblies which the magnates made, and the providing of expenses and provisions for northern expeditions. On these matters the earl gave his advice under the form "il semble au dit conte qe...[8]." The king received the earl's letter and schedule the same day and forwarded a transcript under the privy seal to the archbishop of Canterbury, Hereford, Sandale, and Norwich, treasurer, without whose advice and counsel the king did not wish to proceed. They were ordered to call those of the council they wished, to examine diligently and consider the transcript, to make good advice on them and to certify the king of their decisions plainly without delay[9]. This case of the king consulting Lancaster and then sending his opinion and advice on to the "administrative" council is conclusive proof of the place Lancaster held. He would not attend with diligence the meetings of the council, preferring such consultation.

[1] *Cal. Pat. Rolls*, 1313–17, p. 291.
[2] Anc. Corresp. vol. XXXV, nos. 135 and 135 A.
[3] *Cal. Pat. Rolls*, 1313–17, pp. 296–7.
[4] *Cal. Close Rolls*, 1323–27, p. 441.
[5] Ibid. 1313–18. p. 233.
[6] Anc. Corresp. vol. XXXIV, no. 106. Vide App. of Doc. no. 101.
[7] Ibid.
[8] Ibid.
[9] Chan. Warr., File 93/3513. Vide App. of Doc. no. 62.

On occasion, however, he did attend the "administrative" council. The king on 17 March, 1315, in a writ of privy seal to the archbishop of Canterbury, Lancaster and other good men of the council, commended them for the great diligence with which they had attended the arrangement and execution of the king's weighty business, and requested that the same diligence should be shown, until those matters were ended to the honour and profit of the king and his kingdom[1]. On 19 March, 1315, another writ under the privy seal was sent to the archbishop and the earl and others of the council at Westminster upon complaints of the Cinque Ports about Flemings[2]. It would seem as if at this time the archbishop and Lancaster were at the head of the council. In these writs there was no reference to either the chancellor or treasurer.

The earl's influence was seen in many administrative acts. Orders were issued at his request[3]; appointments made at his instance[4], as well as pardons and safe conducts[5]. The outlawed men of Bristol, at his instance, were given safe conduct in going to Warwick[6] to treat before the earls and the chancellor there[7]. He also obtained favours for himself, such as licences to crenellate[8], and was authorised to send his servants and mariners to purvey corn and other necessaries in Ireland[9]. He besought the king to assign four persons whom he nominated, to inquire into the death of his beloved valet, John de Swynnerton, and at the same time he wrote to the chancellor, asking him to issue no writ to any justices for the hearing of this matter except to those he had named[10]. Another valet of the earl, Ralph de Tydmarsh, found employment in the lands of a deceased tenant in chief[11]. Extensive commissions of lands in several counties were made under the exchequer seal by Norwich at Lancaster's instance[12]. When certain men of the countess of Warwick's household were attached he wrote to the king on the countess' behalf requiring that

1 Anc. Corresp. vol. XLV, no. 190.

2 Ibid. no. 191.

3 *Cal. Close Rolls*, 1313–18, p. 61 (20 June, 1314).

4 *Cal. Fine Rolls*, 1307–19, p. 248 (20 May, 1315).

5 *Cal. Pat. Rolls*, 1313–17, pp. 263, 289, 294 (17 March, 20 May, 4 June, 1315).

6 Ibid. pp. 289, 294 (20 May, 4 June, 1315).

7 Vide above, p. 396.

8 *Cal. Pat. Rolls*, 1313–17, p. 344 (28 Aug. 1315).

9 *Hist. and Municipal Doc. Ireland*, 1192–1320, pp. 388–391 (10 Feb. 1315).

10 Anc. Corresp. vol. XXXV, no. 155. Vide App. of Doc. no. III.

11 Issue Roll, no. 176, m. 6.

12 K. R. Mem. Roll, no. 88, m. 4. L. T. R. Mem. Roll, no. 85, Commiss. m. 3 (12 May, 1315).

the attachments should be released, and the determination of the matter made according to the laws and usages of the realm[1].

Letters which the earl sent to the king received immediate and careful consideration. On 25 October, 1315, such a letter was sent under the privy seal to the archbishop of Canterbury, Sandale, chancellor, and Norwich, treasurer, who were ordered to summon such of the council as they desired, to examine the transcript and to give such counsel as the law and usage of the kingdom demanded, as the earl had required in his letters[2]. Again on 4 December, another letter of the earl's was enclosed under the privy seal to the chancellor, who was to consider it and to execute the required matters, which the king had much at heart, with all possible grace and favour without offending law[3].

Besides occasionally acting in an unofficial capacity of importance in the council Lancaster accepted at least one official position. The question of Scotland was still pressing and required the best energies of the kingdom. On 8 August, 1315, Lancaster was appointed king's lieutenant and chief captain of all the forces in the north[4], probably the result of the deputation the king had sent him a few months before[5], though it was only in June that Pembroke had been appointed to be captain of the forces there[6].

Pembroke's displacement by Lancaster shows the decline in the former's influence. For the time being he was eclipsed by Lancaster. His control of the administration[7] was weakening and he was soon to make an effort to regain it by building up the middle party[8]. Pembroke's eclipse was gradual. He still retained his position in the council[9], but side by side with Pembroke came either Lancaster, or since he seldom felt inclined to take an active part himself, a nominee of his. During this period the magnates made a complaint about the exaction of scutage, and a reply was to be made in the exchequer by the king's council. There came there for this purpose on behalf of the prelates and earls, Pembroke and Hereford and Michael de Meldon, Lancaster's steward[10]. Pembroke on occasion still acted with the magnates and already he was beginning to act in concert with Hereford.

[1] Anc. Corresp. vol. XXXIV, no. 107. Vide App. of Doc. no. 102.
[2] Chan. Warr., File 93/3523. [3] Ibid. File 93/3570.
[4] *Rot. Scot.* vol. I, p. 148. *Parl. Writs*, vol. II, Pt i, p. 161.
[5] Vide above, p. 396.
[6] *Rot. Scot.* vol. I, p. 144. *Parl. Writs*, vol. II, Pt i, p. 158.
[7] Vide above, p. 330. [8] Vide below, pp. 425–434.
[9] Vide below, pp. 405–6, 422. [10] K. R. Mem. Roll, no. 88, m. 145.

The plan of acting from a distance and by deputy was characteristic of the part Lancaster played throughout the reign. It was only under great provocation that he could be stimulated to action; and his periods of activity were always short. During the years 1314–15, however, he took a part in the administration, but his attitude then was rather that of an independent power, conscious of his own strength, than of an official or administrator. At his instance and request, and at the request of other magnates, a convocation of the clergy for the defence of the realm against the Scots was held at Doncaster in 1315[1]. When the king desired the residue of the papal tenth from the bishop of Exeter, he wrote from York on 26 September, asking for payment[2]. On 3 October, Lancaster wrote to the bishop from Berwick. He stated that the king, by the assent of the council, had charged the company of the Bardi with certain purveyance for the business of the Scottish march and asked the bishop to pay them the residue of the papal tenth in payment thereof[3]. This was not the only instance in which a royal writ was supplemented by a letter from the earl. The king wrote similarly to Drokensford, bishop of Bath and Wells, on 26 September, 1314, and the earl's letter followed on 3 October[4].

The independence of Lancaster's position was further emphasised by the petitions addressed to him. The merchants of the city of Chester, whose servants travelling to Gascony, Normandy and Ireland for wine, corn and other merchandise, were continually molested in the parts of North Wales by the command of Adam de Wetenhale, the king's chamberlain there, petitioned Lancaster for such a remedy as would ensure them to go, come, and expose their merchandise when they came to those parts[5]. Another petition addressed to him is still more suggestive of his position. He was informed by his merchant Hugh de Worcester that the king had frequently sought by his letters to the aldermen and bailiffs of Lubeck that right should be done to Hugh or his attorneys for a debt which certain merchants of that town owed him. Nothing had come of these royal requests. Accordingly the earl was asked to ordain a remedy, or to speak to the chancellor, that Hugh might have such a remedy as had been used in similar cases previously[6].

[1] Surtees Soc., *Memorials of Ripon*, vol. II, p. 79. *Letters from North. Regist.* p. 245.

[2] *Regist. de Stapleton*, 1307–1326, pp. 429–430.

[3] Ibid. p. 30.

[4] *Royal Hist. Commiss.* 10th *Rep. App. III, Rep. MSS. Wells Cathedral* [1885], p. 300.

[5] Ancient Petition, no. 4920.

[6] Exch. Misc. 3/2. Vide App. of Doc. no. 40.

Derived partly from Lancaster's position in the administration and partly from the causes which gave Lancaster that position, was the execution of the Ordinances which was a feature of the years 1314–15. The whole credit of such success as the Ordinances obtained then must not be given to Lancaster. His associate Warwick worked towards the same end until his death in August, 1315. Hereford, who was slowly veering round to a moderate if not a royalist position, had been an ordainer and was still prepared to see them put into execution and to assist towards that end. Pembroke too both accepted and approved of the Ordinances and his administrative knowledge and position with the king rendered his aid invaluable. The result was that the Ordinances received a general acceptance not received before or after. Though all the circumstances were in the ordainers' favour and their ascendancy appeared to be complete the king was not powerless. The Ordinances never received the wholehearted acceptance and were never so completely executed as the ordainers intended or hoped, but they exercised most influence in the two years immediately following the king's defeat at Bannockburn.

It had been one of the indispensable concessions granted by the king in the parliament at York in September, 1314, that he would observe and execute the Ordinances[1]. The next parliament, called for 20 January, 1315, at Westminster, which sat until 9 March[2], likewise demanded a confirmation of the Ordinances and of Magna Carta and a perambulation of the forests[3]. The Ordinances were accordingly confirmed[4] and the counties granted a twentieth and the boroughs a fifteenth[5]. That the confirmation and the other concessions were dependent upon the grants of money is certain. On 20 April, 1315, the king ordered the sheriffs throughout England to make proclamation to the effect "that it was the king's intention from the time of the grant of the twentieth granted to him to resist the Scotch invasion, that the requests of the commons concerning the ordinances lately made and approved by the king and for the keeping of Magna Carta and the Charter of the Forests and for making perambulations of the forest shall be observed in all things, and the king has caused persons to be appointed to make the perambulations[6]." Confirmation in parliament without intention to abide thereby was

[1] Vide above, pp. 394–5. [2] *Parl. Writs*, vol. II, Pt i, p. 137.
[3] Ibid. Pt ii, App. pp. 89–92.
[4] *Auct. Bridl.* p. 47. Cf. *Eulog. Hist.* vol. III, p. 195.
[5] *Parl. Writs*, vol. II, Pt ii, App. pp. 89–92. [6] *Cal. Close Rolls*, 1313–18, p. 224.

useless and this writ is therefore interesting and instructive. It was issued after parliament had dispersed: it was issued to that section of the community which was least able to coerce the king, and it was issued without, as far as can be ascertained, any pressure being brought to bear upon the king by council or outside bodies, for it was issued "by king[1]." A *liberate* "until the next parliament" was made to one who had lost his lands in Scotland for his adherence to the king[2]. The king therefore seems to have accepted the position and to have been determined to redeem his promises.

Most of the orders giving effect to the Ordinances were issued in March and April, 1315. Indeed the course of the parliament itself was marked by steps in this direction. On 14 February, Brabazon and his fellow justices of king's bench were ordered to cause the Ordinances to be observed in their court[3]. Several petitions presented to that parliament were endorsed in accordance with the Ordinances. A petition of the chancellor and scholars of Oxford touching prises received this endorsement "Responsum est per ordinationes[4]." One of the abbot of Bardney about a matter pending in the exchequer was answered by the council. It was decided that the treasurer and barons of the exchequer should be ordered to do full justice, both to the king and to the parties, according to right and according to the form of the Ordinances[5]. Another claimed redress for an act committed against Magna Carta and against the Ordinances. Isabel, the widow of Hugh Bardolf, alleged that she had been ousted of her free tenement by Robert Lewer without law. Lewer had purchased a chancery writ by false suggestion, and had seized the lands into the king's hands by writ under the great seal issued by warrant of privy seal. This Isabel claimed was against the form of the Great Charter which stated that neither the king nor his officials should oust anyone of his free tenement without reasonable judgment, and it was also against the form of the Ordinances which the king had accepted, which stated that common right should not be delayed by writ of privy seal[6]. The great council considered that if Isabel could show her charters, she should obtain restitution[7]. In another petition of that parliament, a matter was said to be "encontre la lei et les ordenaunces[8]." Petitioners no less than parliament were looking to the Ordinances for remedies for grievances.

[1] *Cal. Close Rolls*, 1313–18, p. 224. [2] *Cal. Doc. Scotl.* vol. III, p. 77
[3] *Cal. Close Rolls*, 1313–18, p. 148. [4] *Rot. Parl.* vol. I, p. 327.
[5] Ibid. p. 323. [6] Cf. Ordinance 32. Vide above, p. 373.
[7] *Rot. Parl.* vol. I, p. 298. [8] Ibid. p. 290.

The Ordinances were most fully obeyed in the resumption of lands granted by the king since 16 March, 1310, the date of the commission to the ordainers. Almost immediately after the publication of the Ordinances, efforts in this direction had been made[1], though they had not been altogether successful. On 5 March, 1315, schedules containing lists of lands which, in accordance with the Ordinance[2], should be taken into the king's hands, were sent to the escheators north and south of Trent[3]. Some of the resumptions ordered—such as those of Robert de Waterville, Edmund Bacon, Otto Ferre, and the earl of Gloucester[4]—were repetitions of orders made in 1311[5] and not carried into effect. Others, such as those ordering resumptions from Despenser the younger, Pessaign and Alexander de Bikenor[6], were new. The list of resumptions now ordered or repeated if not formidable was heavy, though some were apparently still ineffective. Among those now ordered to be made by the escheator north of Trent was that of the castle and honour of High Peak with its appurtenances, which was held by the earl of Surrey[7]. On 20 April, 1315, the king found it necessary again to order the escheator to resume the castle and honour and to certify the king of what he had done by the bearer of the writ[8].

On 15 March schedules were sent to the treasurer and barons of the exchequer, who were ordered to examine the rolls and memoranda of their office concerning all gifts made by the king to the prejudice of the crown and all pardons and remissions of debts made by him after 16 March, 1310, and to inspect the schedules. All such debts contained in the rolls, memoranda and schedules were to be levied, notwithstanding any remission or pardon. They were also to cause answer to be made to the exchequer for the issues of lands, wardships and marriages pertaining to the king because they had been revoked by the Ordinance[9]. The exchequer almost immediately gave effect to this writ. On 11 April an exchequer writ was issued, by warrant of this writ of great seal and of the schedule from the chancery which the chancellor delivered to the exchequer, to the sheriffs of London ordering them to resume certain rents[10].

[1] Vide above, pp. 386–387.
[2] Cf. Ordinance 7. Vide above, p. 372.
[3] *Cal. Fine Rolls*, 1307–19, pp. 240–4. [4] Ibid. pp. 240, 241.
[5] *Cal. Chan. Rolls*, 1277–1326, pp. 98, 99 (11 Oct. 1311).
[6] *Cal. Fine Rolls*, 1307–19, pp. 241, 242. [7] Ibid. p. 244.
[8] Ibid. p. 240. [9] *Cal. Close Rolls*, 1313–18, p. 167.
[10] K. R. Mem. Roll, no. 88, m. 3 d. L. T. R. Mem. Roll, no. 85, Commiss. m. 2 d. Cf. also *Red Bk. of Exch.* vol. III, p. 841.

The resumptions however did not give universal satisfaction, nor did the king wholly abide by them. One ordered on 5 March, 1315[1], was recommitted during pleasure on 22 June[2]. The earl of Athol petitioned the king for the restoration of his inheritance given on 15 July, 1311, during the Ordinances, contrary to them. The grant had been repealed and he had been deprived of all his lands in Scotland for adhering to the king. By royal command the petition was read in full parliament before the prelates, earls, barons and others, and answer was made that "the earl's ancestor through whom he demanded the inheritance, forfeited all his right against the king and suffered loss, so that the earl could not demand the land as his inheritance, but the king has nevertheless given him other lands of like value because he could not restore the land that he claimed as his inheritance, whereby he ought not to have again what he claims in such manner[3]." The ground taken by Roger de Mortimer of Chirk, who had suffered through the resumptions of 1311[4], was different and more skilful. The king had granted Mortimer the castles and lands of Blaenllyfni and Dinas which the king had purchased from John the son of Reginald. Mortimer claimed that the lands had been given him for his good service to the king and his father. They had nevertheless been seized into the king's hands by virtue of the Ordinances. Mortimer sought restoration "desicome eux ne luy furent pas doner pur damage du Roi, mes pur son service fait et a fair, ne les terres ne sont mie en la Corone, mes sont du purchaz de Roi[5]." The petition was skilfully drawn up and touched important points. The policy in the circumstances was to delay the answer. It was said that, since the lands were taken into the king's hands by virtue of the Ordinances in which it was contained that land of this sort should not be returned to those who had it before without the common assent of the magnates in parliament, because there were not a sufficient number present then, Mortimer should await the next parliament[6]. This was an easy though not a very satisfactory way of overcoming the difficulty.

The necessity for the personal Ordinances against Gavaston and the Friscobaldi had ended. The elder Despenser and Langton now aroused the wrath of the barons, and were removed[7]. Lady de Vescy had apparently ceased to be a source of annoyance or danger, though

[1] *Cal. Fine Rolls*, 1307–19, p. 240.
[2] Ibid. p. 251.
[3] *Rot. Parl.* vol. I, p. 294. The petition was enrolled on the Close Roll, vide *Cal. Close Rolls*, 1313–18, p. 217.
[4] *Cal. Chan. Rolls*, 1277–1326, pp. 99–100.
[5] *Rot. Parl.* vol. I, p. 305.
[6] Ibid.
[7] *Auct. Malm.* p. 209.

an excess of an extent held by her was to be resumed[1]. Beaumont had succeeded in maintaining his position with the king, and the barons still insisted that the personal Ordinance against him should be executed. On 5 March, 1315, the escheator south of Trent was ordered to take into the king's hands the reversion of lands of the value of over £40 which the king had granted to Beaumont[2]. The escheator north of Trent was on the same day ordered to resume the island of Man with all its liberties and appurtenances[3], the previous resumption having apparently been ineffective[4]. These specific orders were followed on the 2nd of April by general orders to the escheators to take into the king's hands all the lands which Beaumont had held on 5 October, 1311[5], as was contained in the Ordinance[6]. Beaumont however continued to be about the court, and the baronial efforts against him were never crowned with success.

The Ordinance which forbade the collection of customs by aliens[7] was also enforced. A French merchant to whom the king had assigned the revenue of the custom of wool in the port of London, in satisfaction of certain debts, appeared by attorney and handed in full exchequer one part of the cocket seal used for the customs of the port of London[8].

In May, 1315, as had been promised in the parliament of Westminster and subsequently by royal proclamation[9], the king issued commissions, in accordance with the Ordinances[10], for perambulations of the forests. Five sets of commissions were issued[11] and it appeared as if full effect was to be given to the Ordinance.

Efforts were also made to ensure the observance of the Ordinance dealing with the pleas of the marshalsea court[12]. In the parliament of Westminster a petition was presented complaining of an attachment made by the steward and marshal for a trespass committed in London. The petitioners told the steward and marshal that they ought not to answer before them for this matter, as the Ordinances ordered otherwise. They were nevertheless taken and imprisoned. The council ordered the steward and marshal to send the record and process *coram Rege* a fortnight after Easter. Meanwhile the

[1] *Cal. Fine Rolls*, 1307–19, p. 242. [2] Ibid. p. 243. [3] Ibid.
[4] Vide above, p. 386. [5] *Cal. Fine Rolls*, 1307–19, p. 238.
[6] Ordinance 22. Vide above, p. 370.
[7] Ordinances 4, 8. Vide above, p. 373.
[8] K. R. Mem. Roll, no. 88, m. 146 d. [9] Vide above, p. 400.
[10] Ordinance 18. Vide above, p. 378.
[11] *Cal. Pat. Rolls*, 1313–17, p. 296 (10 May, 1315).
[12] Ordinance 26. Vide above, pp. 376–377.

petitioners were to be released on sufficient mainprise and the names of the manucaptors were to be sent *coram Rege* at the same time[1] Moreover, on 8 March, 1315, a writ was sent to the steward and marshal of the household stating that amongst the liberties granted to the citizens of London was one that no one should be impleaded outside the city for any plea except one of land held outside. All the liberties of London had been confirmed by Magna Carta and the Ordinances had ordered that Magna Carta should be held in each and every article[2]. The king was unwilling that the citizens should be proceeded against contrary to the tenor of the charters and Ordinances and the steward and marshal were not to draw any citizen in any plea outside the city against the form of the charters and Ordinances[3]

In addition to the retrospective observance of the Ordinance concerning gifts of land, efforts were made to enforce its positive observance. A number of grants were made by the assent of the baronage. A grant of 1000 marks out of the issues of the office of escheator south of Trent from wardship and marriages was made to Norwich, treasurer, on 6 July, 1315, by the assent and counsel of the archbishop of Canterbury, the bishops of St David's, Chichester and Exeter, the earls of Richmond, Pembroke, Hereford and Warwick, and Hugh de Courtney, many others of the council also assisting[4]. The writ was issued by the king and council[5]. The escheator had already been ordered on 12 June, 1315, to cause wardships and marriages to the value of 1000 marks to be sold by the advice of Sandale, chancellor, for this purpose[6]. The pardon which the king had made to the heirs and executors of Anthony, bishop of Durham, of all debts due to the king from the bishop and of the goods taken from them for those debts had been revoked by the Ordinances. On 23 May, 1315, a writ stating that the debts were again pardoned was issued, the pardon being made with the assent of the prelates, earls and barons in parliament assembled at Westminster[7]. The barons were successful too, in securing their own rights and protecting their own interests. When Robert de Clifford died, the wardship of his lands and castles and such parts of the sheriffdom of Westmorland as belonged to him were granted to Warwick, Percy and Badlesmere[8]. It would seem that the part taken by the

[1] *Rot. Parl.* vol. I, p. 315. [2] Ordinances 6, 38. Vide above, p. 369.
[3] *Mun. Gildh. Lond.* vol. I, pp. 301–2.
[4] *Cal. Pat. Rolls*, 1313–17, p. 280. [5] Ibid.
[6] *Cal. Close Rolls*, 1313–18, p. 189.
[7] *Cal. Pat. Rolls*, 1313–17, p. 290.
[8] *Cal. Fine Rolls*, 1307–19, p. 212 (2 Oct. 1314).

council in administration was greater than usual and that the "administrative" council which now had a leavening of barons, such as Lancaster, Warwick, Hereford and Pembroke, was assuming a greater independence of action. The petitions presented to the Westminster parliament of 1315 were answered by the council or the great council without any reference whatsoever to the king[1].

Though the Ordinances were enforced to this extent, and though the barons were taking this part in administration, the king's power in vital matters was not seriously diminished. The household system remained, as far as all practical purposes went, unreformed. All those opportunities which the system gave the king to foil external control he still possessed. While the barons could exercise checks they had not captured the executive. The king, moreover, possessed such resources that at a crisis he could easily override all such checks. All this time the king was gathering strength. The barons had no organization and therefore there could be no hope of permanence. Once the king felt strong enough he might desire and endeavour to shake himself free from a control which if not firm was irksome. As matters stood the tutelage was not oppressive. The administration still depended overwhelmingly upon writs under the privy seal. A writ of 4 December, 1314, under the privy seal to the chancellor is interesting. Its exact purport it is difficult to determine. It furnishes no evidence whether it was the result of baronial pressure or of royal desire. The date of its issue would suggest baronial instigation. Its contents would suggest purely royal origin. The king, for certain reasons, desired to be certified of all manner of matters for which fines were made in his court, and of all manner of things which he had given, granted or assigned for debts, both in lands, rents, wardships, marriages, escheats and reversions, as well as vacancies of bishoprics, abbeys and priories, and what he had released in debts and services and what he had pardoned of franchises in mortmain, forfeitures and other matters for which he could have had fines, from the time in which he first received the government of the kingdom. For this purpose the chancellor was to search the rolls and memoranda of the chancery and to send the results under his seal before Christmas to Melton, keeper of the wardrobe[2]. The

[1] *Rot. Parl.* vol. I, pp. 315, 323, 327.

[2] Chan. Warr., File 90/3203. Vide App. of Doc. no. 60. On the same day the chancellor and treasurer were ordered to search the rolls and memoranda of chancery and exchequer for gifts granted by the king since he gave commission to the ordainers and to certify the king before the next parliament, as the barons had asked him at the parliament of York to repeal these gifts (Chan. Warr.,

purposes for which the barons would desire such a return are plain; but a return desired by the barons would not have been sent to the keeper of the wardrobe. What purposes the king can have had in desiring such a return are obscure. What is important is that, even at the end of 1314, the king could order such a return under his privy seal and that the results should have been returnable to such a purely household officer as the keeper of the wardrobe. It can fairly be said then that the king's initiative in administration was still free and unimpeded, that the household organisation was unencumbered by baronial restrictions and that the personal system but required an opportunity, which it could easily make, to reassume the old position. The household system had not been destroyed. Before one system could be destroyed a substitute had to be provided. The Ordinances had laid down principles and advocated reforms. They had provided no system or machinery. More than four years had now elapsed since the publication of the Ordinances, and the baronial weakness—lack of machinery—was being discovered. The only effective way to exercise control over organised administration, was to superimpose upon it another organisation, baronial rather than royal in origin. There were precedents upon which to build. The next task before the baronial opposition was to provide that organisation. In the parliament of Lincoln in 1316 they set themselves to do this.

File 90/3202; vide App. of Doc. no. 59). A partial return to this writ made by the escheator north of Trent illustrates the difficulty of obtaining permanent redress from the king against his will. The lands were granted, resumed and regranted (P. R. O. Escheators' Acct. 3/18).

CHAPTER IV

THE EXPERIMENTS (*cont.*)

(iii) *The Parliament of Lincoln*, 1316

The parliament which had been summoned for Lincoln on 27 January, 1316[1], was one of the most important of the reign. There were many urgent matters awaiting discussion and decision. The legislative and administrative work which was performed there was considerable; but its greatest significance lay in the official position which the parliament gave the earl of Lancaster. It was one step, though in the circumstances, not one of the utmost practical importance, towards giving the baronial opposition a place of permanence and predominance in the administration. The leader of that opposition was made head of the king's council. The whole work of the parliament is worth review, and the roll of the parliament[2], drawn up by William de Ayremynne, clerk of chancery[3], who was specially appointed and deputed by the king[4], is happily full. As the baronial element was powerful in this parliament, their policy is reflected in much of the work, though the king's influence must not be ignored or belittled.

On 28 January the prelates, earls, and others were assembled in a chamber in the house of the dean of Lincoln, when the king entered and informed them of his intentions by William Inge[5], justice of the common bench. The parliament had been summoned, according to the writs of summons, on account of various weighty matters touching the king and kingdom, especially concerning Scotland. The king desired greatly that the parliament should be held with all possible haste. The prelates, earls, and others had come from distant parts. If their stay was lengthened, it would become very

[1] *Parl. Writs*, vol. II, Pt ii, pp. 152–4.

[2] A full transcript of the roll is given in *Rot. Parl.* vol. I, pp. 350–2, and *Parl. Writs*, vol. II, Pt ii, pp. 156–7. A translation is given in *Parl. Writs*, vol. II, Pt i, pp. 168–170.

[3] The question of the relation of chancery and exchequer to the rolls of parliament will be discussed below, pp. 519–520.

[4] *Rot. Parl.* vol. I, p. 350.

[5] Vide above, p. 68, note 5.

distasteful and burdensome to them because of the scarcity of food—then much more oppressive than usual[1]. The king considering these matters was anxious to shorten the parliament. Because Lancaster, and certain other magnates of the council by whom the king desired to act in these weighty matters, had not yet come, the king desired to defer proceeding until they arrived[2]. It could only have been through pressure from the barons present, or fear of the consequences of proceeding without Lancaster, that the king would have been induced to make this delay. Meanwhile the king desired that the best use should be made of the time. He enjoined the prelates, earls and others to meet from day to day to continue the parliament and to treat other business until the absent magnates should arrive. Sandale, the chancellor, was ordered to receive the proxies and excuses of the prelates and others. With Norwich, treasurer, and William Inge, whom the king associated to him, he was to examine the excuses, allow such as were sufficient and report to the king those who were absent and had not excused themselves or sent proxies[3].

There were other preliminary arrangements which could be made before the coming of the absent magnates. On the same day it was agreed that petitions should be received and hastened as had been the custom in previous parliaments, the last day for receiving them being fixed for 3 February. Receivers of petitions were then appointed; Robert de Askeby, clerk of chancery, and Adam de Lymbergh, remembrancer of the exchequer, for the petitions from England, and Master Edmund de London, clerk of chancery, and Master William de Maldon, chamberlain of the exchequer, for the petitions of Gascony, Wales, Ireland and Scotland. Proclamation of this was made. The chancellor, treasurer, and justices of both benches were ordered to reduce briefly to writing the matters pending before them that could not be determined out of parliament, which were to be reported to parliament to be answered there[4].

The delay proved of no avail. Lancaster was still absent. Accordingly on 6 February, it was decided to proceed upon the petitions until the arrival of the earl and the other magnates[5]. The business was still in part formal and preparatory; the choice of the auditors of the petitions was a matter of importance, but they were appointed. The bishops of Norwich, Chichester and Salisbury,

[1] The year 1315 had seen a serious famine and murrain. Vide *Ann. Lond.* pp. 236–8; *Ann. Paul.* p. 279; *Auct. Bridl.* p. 48; *Auct. Malm.* p. 214; *Chron. Murimuth*, p. 24; *Ann. Monast.* vol. III, *Ann. de Bermund.* p. 470. Vide also *Foedera*, vol. II, p. 268; *Rot. Parl.* vol. I, pp. 295, 340. Vide below, p. 411.

[2] *Rot. Parl.* vol. I, p. 350. [3] Ibid. [4] Ibid. [5] Ibid.

Edmund Deyncourt, Philip de Kyme, John de Insula, baron of the exchequer, Henry le Scrope, justice of the common bench, and Robert de Bardelby, clerk of chancery, were appointed auditors of the petitions from England. The auditors of the Gascon petitions were to be the bishops of Winchester, Exeter and Bath and Wells, William Inge, Master Roger de Rothwell, Richard de Plumstok, Thomas de Cherleton, and Henry de Canterbury. For the petitions from Wales, Ireland and Scotland, Ralph Fitzwilliam, Master William de Bristol, archdeacon of Gloucester, Master John Walwayn, escheator south of Trent, John Bush, Philip de Turvill and John de Insula, clerks, and John de Mutford, justice of assize, were to be auditors[1]. It would be usual and natural for officials and clerks to form the bulk of the auditors, but it was unusual for so few barons to be employed and for those few to be of so little importance. The probable explanation is that a considerable number of the barons as well as Lancaster were absent.

On 7 February answers were made to certain complaints of the clergy by the earl of Hereford in the king's presence and on his behalf. The prelates had previously presented certain petitions touching the state of the church. The earl announced that those answers which had previously been given to petitions and which were sufficient were to be observed. The answers which were considered unsatisfactory should be corrected. To those petitions to which answers had not yet been given, reply should be made as should seem to the prelates, and magnates together with the king's council, best for the well-being of the king, his kingdom and the church[2]. This formed the basis of the *Articuli Cleri* which were published by the king on 24 November, 1316[3].

By 8 February the king was tired of waiting for the absent magnates. On that day, after the bishops of Norwich, Chichester, Exeter and Salisbury had been sworn of the king's council, he made preparations for his departure from Lincoln. The bishops of Norwich and Exeter and the earls of Richmond and Pembroke were named as the king's lieutenants during his absence until the arrival of the earl of Lancaster and the other magnates[4]. Whether the king left Lincoln or not is uncertain, but when parliament next met both king and the hitherto absent magnates were present.

[1] *Rot. Parl.* vol. I, p. 350.

[2] Ibid. Vide also *Letters from North. Regist.* pp. 253–260.

[3] *Stat. of Realm*, vol. I, pp. 171–4. *Cal. Pat. Rolls*, 1313–17, p. 607.

[4] *Rot. Parl.* vol. I, p. 350.

A "full[1]" parliament was held on 12 February in the hall of the dean of Lincoln. Lancaster and the other magnates were now present and the king in full parliament made the cause of the summons of the parliament to be recited. Amongst other reasons it was stated that it had been summoned on account of the condition of the country which had been invaded by the Scottish enemies. The king therefore besought and ordered the prelates, magnates and others of his faithful subjects there present to advise him on these matters and to make him suitable aid. It was thereupon agreed that the prelates and magnates should meet on the morrow in the chapter of Lincoln Cathedral to treat on these matters. The meeting was held and various matters discussed. Finally it was agreed and commanded by the king that they should meet the following day at the convent of the Carmelites to treat of the same affairs[2].

This meeting was duly held, but the matters resolved upon there were not Scottish affairs. It was then agreed that the proclamation fixing a maximum price for provisions[3] should be revoked, and that they should be sold at a reasonable price, as had been the custom before, writs to this effect being made under the great seal[4]. In view of the severe famine which afflicted the land[5], this matter was as urgent as the question of the Scottish war, and the action taken by parliament was wise and justified by the result. On the same day too a statute concerning sheriffs and hundreds was enacted[6]. The statute which dealt with the method of appointing sheriffs[7] and the qualifications for the offices of sheriff and bailiff was made by the king "by the information of his prelates, earls, barons and other great men of the realm...and also by the grievous complaint of the people" and by the assent of the prelates, earls, barons and other great estates[8].

On 17 February the really important business of the parliament commenced. Three days had elapsed since the last meeting, and it

[1] Professor Pollard in *Eng. Hist. Rev.* vol. XXX [1915], pp. 660–2, suggests "open" as the correct translation of *plenum* as applied to parliaments of this time.

[2] *Rot. Parl.* vol. I, pp. 350–1.

[3] This had been made at the Westminster parliament of 1315 (*Rot. Parl.* vol. I, p. 295; *Foedera*, vol. II, p. 206).

[4] *Rot. Parl.* vol. I, p. 351. The writs were not issued until 20 Feb. (*Cal. Close Rolls*, 1313–18, p. 325; *Foedera*, vol. II, p. 286).

[5] Cf. *Chron. Trokelowe*, pp. 93–98; J. Thorold Rogers, *Hist. of Agric. and Prices* [1866], vol. I, pp. 198–9, 230–1, 264.

[6] *Rot. Parl.* vol. I, p. 351.

[7] The statute will be discussed in detail below, pp. 524–6.

[8] *Stat. of Realm*, vol. I, pp. 174–5.

is likely that the interval had been a stormy time. The first business of parliament when it met again was the Ordinances, and it seems as if the interval had been spent in bringing the king to terms. Even after the delay, the barons' triumph was not complete, as the king was able to introduce at least one modifying clause. On 17 February, in the presence of the king, the prelates and magnates, the bishop of Norwich, by the king's command, recited the matters which had been decided, and added that the king wished to observe in all things the Ordinances previously made by the prelates and magnates and accepted by him, and the perambulations of the forest made in the time of Edward I, saving to the king his reasons against those perambulations[1]. Writs were then made about these matters[2].

The same day the bishop also declared on the king's behalf a certain matter touching the earl of Lancaster. The bishop spoke to the earl to remove a certain doubt which he was said to have entertained concerning the king. He assured him that the king bore sincere and entire goodwill towards him and the other magnates and that he held them as his faithful and liege men especially in the royal favour. The king wished Lancaster to be the chief of his council[3] and the bishop asked the earl on behalf of the king, the prelates and the magnates of the realm then present to assume that office effectually, and as he was bound to do, give the necessary advice and aid in the matters of the king and kingdom[4].

This was a great triumph for the baronial opposition; but Lancaster did not accept immediately. The earl thanked the king and humbly besought that he should consider the matter before he gave his reply. The earl was afterwards sworn of the king's council[5]. The acceptance of the office by Lancaster was not unconditional.

For the great love which he bore the king, and for the common profit of the realm and for the Ordinances which he had consented to hold, and to maintain the rightful laws in all points, and in the hope of effecting amendment in several matters touching the household and the estate of the kingdom he consented to be of the king's council with the other prelates, earls and barons. If however the king would not follow his advice and that of the others of the council in the affairs

[1] *Rot. Parl.* vol. I, p. 351.

[2] Ibid. The writs concerning prices were issued on 20 Feb. (*Cal. Close Rolls*, 1313–18, p. 325). Writs touching the Ordinances were issued on 3 and 6 March (ibid. p. 328).

[3] "Quod idem Comes esset de Consilio Domini Regis Capitalis."

[4] *Rot. Parl.* vol. I, p. 351.

[5] Ibid.

touching the household and kingdom after these had been shown to him, the earl could without bad faith, challenge or impropriety discharge himself of his council[1]. In the circumstances this was a perfectly reasonable condition. However much the earl and the barons might gain by becoming of the king's council they thereby lost a certain independence of action. Being of the council involved duties and responsibilities as well as power. Lancaster was prepared to surrender his independence of action and accept the duties and responsibilities which the oath and position of counsellor necessitated only as long as his will prevailed. As soon as the king showed any independence of action or even refused to obey his task master, Lancaster claimed the right to end his responsibilities and duties and, by putting himself outside the council, free himself to undertake what course he should think best against the king. No matter touching the king or the kingdom was to be undertaken without the assent of the earl and the other prelates, earls and barons[2]. The king was to have no independence of action. The council with Lancaster at its head was to assent to every administrative act before it was undertaken.

If any prelate, earl or baron gave any counsel to the king, or did any act which was not to the profit of the king or his kingdom, at the next parliament, according to the advice of the king and his men, he was to be removed, and so from parliament to parliament according to the faults found in them[3]. The object of this third condition was probably to maintain Lancaster's permanent ascendancy in the council. In parliament he might expect a permanent majority but in the council he could not hope for this. Those who proved objectionable or refractory in the council could, under this scheme, be removed at the next parliament.

Lancaster's reply to the king was contained in the form of a bill which was to be entered on the rolls of parliament. The bill was handed to William de Ayremynne, the clerk, by the hand of Norwich, treasurer, and Badlesmere who on the king's behalf ordered him to enrol it word for word[4].

After these important events the parliament continued its normal course, and at last concerned itself with the primary object of its summons—aid for the Scottish war. On 20 February the magnates and community of the realm granted the king for the Scottish war,

[1] *Rot. Parl.* vol. I, p. 351. [2] Ibid. [3] Ibid.

[4] Ibid. pp. 351–2, under the heading "La forme de la Demoere le Counte de Lancastre du Conseil le Roi."

one strong and fencible footman suitably armed from each vill in the kingdom excepting cities, boroughs and royal demesnes. The men of the vills were to provide these foot-soldiers with arms and to pay them their expenses until they should come to the muster, and their wages for 60 days more, each man receiving *4d.* a day. If there was a market in the vill it was to be charged with a greater number of men. The king promised to issue letters to the magnates and community for himself and his heirs, that this grant of foot-soldiers should not prejudice them or their heirs or be drawn into a precedent[1]. By the advice of his magnates the king also ordained that all the service due to him should be summoned to be at Newcastle on 8 July, 1316[2]. The citizens, burgesses and knights of the shire, who were not included in the above grant, granted to the king in aid of the war a fifteenth of the moveable goods of the citizens, burgesses and men of the cities, boroughs and demesnes of the king, both of those which were in the hands of others for term of life and of those which were in the king's own hands[3].

Thus with the grant of subsidies for the war, the parliament of Lincoln ended. Full as were its rolls, one or two items of importance were omitted. A series of ordinances of the utmost importance relating to North and South Wales were issued during the parliament in reply to petitions presented there. The ordinances were entered on the patent rolls and sent under the great seal to the justice of Wales[4]. It was also decided in parliament that all persons having £50 a year in lands or rents or a whole knight's fee of that value, who had held the same for a year, and who were not knights, should receive knighthood. The sheriffs throughout England were ordered to proclaim this in the county courts[5].

Notwithstanding this long catalogue of the work of the parliament of Lincoln, one chronicler finds that nothing was done there[6], and another who knew the chief acts done there, thought that but little had been achieved[7]. Although the king had granted the perambulation of the forest, though Lancaster had been made the principal

[1] *Rot. Parl.* vol. I, p. 351. By a writ of 5 March, 1316, the sheriffs were to acquaint the exchequer at their next proffer what hundreds, cities, boroughs, towns there were in their counties (*Cal. Close Rolls*, 1313–18, p. 327) and from these returns were compiled the Nomina Villarum (vide *Feudal Aids*, vols. I–V passim). On 26 March the muster was announced (*Cal. Pat. Rolls*, 1313–17, pp. 460–2). In a meeting at Lincoln on 29 July, 1316, this grant of fencible men was commuted for a 16th (ibid. pp. 529, 532).

[2] *Rot. Parl.* vol. I, p. 351.

[3] Ibid.

[4] Cf. *Foedera*, vol. II, pp. 283–4.

[5] *Cal. Close Rolls*, 1313–18, p. 327.

[6] *Le Livere de Reis de Brit.* p. 332.

[7] *Auct. Malm.* p. 218.

counsellor of the king and the ordinances of prices had been revoked, so many barons had been employed in suppressing the revolt of Llewelyn Bren in Glamorgan that few had attended the parliament[1].

Inasmuch however as the parliament of Lincoln expressed the policy of the barons in a new phase, it is of the utmost importance. That phase can however be better discussed after the results of the parliament of Lincoln upon the observance of the Ordinances during 1316 and upon the action of Lancaster in the same period have been seen.

The observance of the Ordinances and the ascendancy of Lancaster always seemed to run concurrently. After 1312 the quarrels between the king and Lancaster were mainly due to the king's failure to abide by the Ordinances. The disagreements before the parliament of Lincoln, which were settled there, were due in part to the Ordinances[2]. The earl desired them kept: the king and his ministers were always breaking them as far as possible, especially those concerning prises and the marshalsea[3]. It was inevitable that any rapprochement between king and earl should be consequent upon or followed by a confirmation of the Ordinances[4]. Writs made on 3 March to all the sheriffs ordering them to cause the Ordinances to be proclaimed and observed in their counties were vacated because subsequently issued in another form[5]. In the subsequent issue of 6 March the sheriffs were ordered "to publish as often as need be the ordinances made by the prelates and proceres and approved by the king which the king lately ordered should be observed in all counties and to observe the same and cause them to be observed by others in his bailiwick causing it to be known that the king will punish all transgressors of the same as the king learns that the ordinances are not well observed[6]." This second issue, with its extended terms and its strict injunctions, suggests that the king was at this time desirous of seeing the Ordinances in force and that their non-observance was due not to the king's objection alone but also to lack of respect paid to them by the people generally.

Separate orders were issued relating to various provisions of the Ordinances commanding their enforcement. The sheriffs were ordered to cause proclamation to be made prohibiting anyone taking unjust

[1] *Auct. Malm.* p. 218. For the revolt of Llewelyn Bren vide *Flores Hist.* vol. III, pp. 339–340, 343.

[2] *Ann. Lond.* p. 237.

[3] Ibid.

[4] Vide above, pp. 411–412. Vide also *Ann. Lond.* p. 237.

[5] *Cal. Close Rolls*, 1313–18, p. 328.

[6] Ibid. *Foedera*, vol. II, p. 287.

prises from prelates, men of religion, ecclesiastics, clerks, or laymen, under the penalties contained in a statute of Edward I[1] and in the Ordinances[2]. The collectors of the customs in various parts throughout the realm were ordered to bring to the exchequer "all money collected hereafter from the said custom according to an ordinance made by the prelates, earls and barons of the realm, notwithstanding any orders of the king touching payment therefrom elsewhere or other assignments whatsoever, and to be themselves at the Exchequer a month from Easter next to certify the treasurer and barons thereof of all payments made therefrom by them, and to whom and in what manner[3]." How far this writ would have the effect of countermanding or nullifying writs made by the king to the contrary effect under privy seal or great seal is doubtful, but the king either under pressure or under the influence of an impulse for reform, probably the former, endeavoured to put this particular Ordinance[4] into practice.

In the month of April the council seems to have been in the ascendant. Various writs of that month resuming grants by the king were issued "by the council[5]." When the parliament was sitting various grants had been made with the assent of the council[6]. A grant of a manor for a term of years not yet passed was resumed in this form[7]. The sheriff of York was ordered not to pay henceforth a daily fee and yearly robes from the issue of his county to a servant of queen Isabel, and the treasurer and barons of the exchequer were ordered no longer to allow him that sum in his account[8]. By similar orders the keeper of the castle and honour of Knaresburgh was ordered to resume the close there and the chamberlain of Scotland the castle and county of Roxburgh[9]. Despenser the elder, to whom the king had granted the manor of Salam, was to appear before the council at Westminster with the charter of that grant and to do and receive what should be decided there[10].

Another order which was issued without any formal notice of the council's influence was much more sweeping. The treasurer and barons of the exchequer were ordered to retake into the king's

[1] Cf. *Stat. of Realm*, vol. I, pp. 26–27, 137–8.

[2] *Cal. Close Rolls*, 1313–18, p. 334 (10 April, 1316). The reference is to Ordinance 10. Vide above, p. 379.

[3] *Cal. Fine Rolls*, 1307–19, p. 277 (12 April, 1316).

[4] Ordinances 4, 8. Vide above, p. 373.

[5] *Cal. Fine Rolls*, 1307–19, p. 275 (1 and 6 April, 1316).

[6] *Cal. Pat. Rolls*, 1313–17, pp. 389, 394.

[7] *Cal. Fine Rolls*, 1307–19, p. 275 (1 April, 1316).

[8] Ibid.

[9] Ibid.

[10] Ibid. (6 April, 1316).

hands all grants made to the king's loss and contrary to the Ordinance, for a term of years or at the king's will and to devise them to the king's greater profit[1]. There was at this time probably less need than in the previous year for such general resumptions and enforcement of the Ordinances, as the resumptions and enforcement made after the parliament of Westminster, 1315[2], seem to have had effect. The observance of the Ordinances after the parliament of Lincoln is important, for the terms of issue of the orders dealing with the observance in the counties, with the facts of the resumptions and the enforcement of particular Ordinances show that there was both the need and the desire for their maintenance.

The reconciliation made between the king and Lancaster appeared to many to be the event of greatest importance which occurred at the parliament[3]. Though Lancaster had there been made the chief of the king's council there appears to have been little sincerity about the reconciliation and before a year had passed he was once more in almost armed opposition[4]. Meanwhile he exercised some, though not considerable, influence upon administration. Immediately after the parliament of Lincoln the king seemed anxious and felt it necessary to abide by the terms of the agreement. Transcripts of letters from Scotland and Ireland and a letter from William Inge relating to the serious plight of the men of Berwick were simultaneously sent by the king to Sandale, chancellor, and Norwich, treasurer, and to Lancaster. The king begged Lancaster to send back his counsel and advice[5]. Again on 15 March, 1316, letters from the constable of France were sent to the archbishop, Lancaster and other good men of the council at London under the privy seal. They were to consider the letters and make suitable remedy[6]. Later in March, Lancaster was with the king. Two petitions presented to the king in Lancaster's presence were sent under privy seal on 30 March to the chancellor, treasurer and others of the council[7]. On 31 March he was the first witness to a charter of the earl of Chester[8]. On 28 April power was given to Lancaster, Pembroke, Badlesmere and Robert de Holand to grant safe conducts in the king's name to Robert de Bruce or other men of Scotland to come to England to treat for a truce[9]. This association

[1] *Cal. Fine Rolls*, 1307–19, p. 275 (26 April, 1316).
[2] Vide above, pp. 400–406. [3] Cf. *Auct. Bridl.* p. 49.
[4] *Auct. Malm.* pp. 228–230. Vide below, p. 424.
[5] Chan. Warr., File 93/3594 (26 Feb. 1316).
[6] Anc. Corresp. vol. XXXV, no. 126. Vide App. of Doc. no. 108.
[7] Chan. Warr., File 94/3640. [8] *Cal. Pat. Rolls*, 1313–17, p. 476.
[9] Ibid. p. 450.

in a commission of Pembroke and Badlesmere, who were to become two of the most prominent members of the middle party[1], with Lancaster and his servant Holand is interesting. It is a proof of Lancaster's position at this time that in a commission of four he was able to obtain a place for Holand, who then, certainly, was entirely devoted to his interests. The commission however was vacated because surrendered and cancelled[2]. In the months of June and July the king was again in communication with Lancaster—Alexander le Convers, clerk, receiving expenses for acting as the royal messenger[3].

In effect this period did little more than provide Lancaster with an occasion of exposing his incapacity. He made good use of his opportunity to obtain grants and favours for himself and his partizans. He obtained various licences for alienation in mortmain[4]. When about to go north on the king's service with certain other magnates of the realm he and his company were given permission to enter royal castles, stay there, and go forth as often and whenever they desired[5]. This writ was subsequently surrendered and cancelled[6], probably because the journey was not made[7]. Even writs under the exchequer seal were issued on his behalf, ordering the mayor, seneschals and bailiffs of Drogheda to allow his men to make purveyance there[8]. Lancaster obtained a grant of murage and pavage for a term of seven years for the towns of Leicester and Lancaster[9]. At his instance, Griffith de la Pole, one of his partizans, who had attacked John de Cherleton, the royal chamberlain, received a pardon for all trespasses committed by him in this matter[10]. On the same day as Griffith de la Pole received his pardon, the escheator south of Trent was ordered to restore to him all his lands in Wales and the marches of Wales with their issues, the order being made at Lancaster's request[11]. Robert de Holand who had acquired without licence, 300 acres of wood in fee from the earl which the latter held in chief received a pardon and a licence to retain the grant[12]. Though the writ was issued "by king[13]," there can be little doubt that the pardon was due to Lancaster's influence.

In the light of the events immediately following the parliament of Lincoln, the success or failure of the scheme laid down there can be

[1] Vide below, pp. 425–9. [2] *Cal. Pat. Rolls*, 1313–17, p. 450.
[3] Issue Roll, no. 180, m. 6. [4] *Cal. Pat. Rolls*, 1313–17, pp. 441, 512.
[5] Ibid. p. 453 (1 May, 1316). [6] Ibid [7] Vide above.
[8] *Hist. and Municip. Doc. Ireland*, 1172–1320, p. 390 (11 May, 1316).
[9] *Cal. Pat. Rolls*, 1313–17, p. 512 (13 July, 1316).
[10] Ibid. p. 548 (10 Oct. 1316).
[11] *Cal. Close Rolls*, 1313–18, pp. 369–370 (10 Oct. 1316)
[12] *Cal. Pat. Rolls*, 1313–17, p. 476 (18 June, 1316). [13] Ibid.

judged more accurately. It seems as if the king was induced to accept this scheme as much by external circumstances as by baronial coercion. The pressure from Scotland was becoming increasingly burdensome, and the insistence upon the urgency of Scottish affairs, which the king made in the writs of summons and in the meetings of parliament, is a sufficient indication of the importance attached to that matter. Simultaneously there was the revolt of Llewelyn Bren in South Wales and a grievous famine afflicting the whole land. The bad harvests lessened the royal revenue[1]. Under the pressure of these external circumstances and the discontent they caused, the king felt that an extreme remedy was necessary. In consequence the scheme of making Lancaster the chief of the council[2] was adopted. That scheme probably did not mean the same to the king as to the baronial opposition. To a chronicler it seemed that Lancaster: "juratus fuit de consilio regis, ad addendum et subtrahendum de ordinationibus prius factis, prout regi et regno melius viderit expedire[3]," and the same idea appears to have been present to the mind of Lancaster when he said in the bill detailing the conditions of his acceptance of the position of chief of the council that:

> pur le grant amour qil ad devers son dit seigneur le roi, e pur le commun profit du Roialme e des Ordinances qil ad, sue merci, enterement grante a tenir, e les Leis dreitureles en touz pointz meintenir, et en espeir de mettre amendement de plusours choses nient convenables tochauntes son Hostiel e l'Estat de son Roialme, ad grante destre du Conseil nostre Seigneur le Roi, ovesqes les Prelatz, Countes, e Barons[4].

The acceptance was to be but another opportunity to enforce the Ordinances and reform of the household upon the king. The futility of a temporary committee like that of the ordainers, whose power ended with the acceptance of the Ordinances by the king, was recognised. It was a comparatively easy matter to prepare a scheme of reform and even to get the king to accept it. The problem which confronted the baronial opposition was how to ensure that the accepted reforms would be executed. Coercion could secure the appointment of a committee of reform, coercion could force the king to accept the scheme of reform. But the efficacy of coercion had its limits. Coercion as the continual machinery and motive power of government was impossible. The working of the whole organising

[1] *Reg. J. de Drokensford*, pp. 4–5.

[2] In the bill in which Lancaster laid down his conditions of acceptance, he stated that the king wished him to be "Chief de son Conseil" (*Rot. Parl.* vol. I, p. 351).

[3] *Auct. Bridl.* p. 49.

[4] *Rot. Parl.* vol. I, p. 351.

administration in its minutest details by coercion was worse than useless. A new machinery of restraint had to be devised. The working of the administrative machinery depended upon the household system. There were two courses open. The barons could endeavour to destroy the household system, but if they did that they would have to erect another system of government to take its place. The household system was too strong to be overthrown; and the barons had not an effective alternative to replace it. The other course was to divert the household system into baronial channels, or rather to give the barons a share in and a control over the household system. The barons had seen that action from outside, as in the committee of ordainers, was almost useless. In the parliament of Lincoln they made their first great endeavour to obtain action from the inside. The committee of the ordainers had been something erected outside the existing system; Lancaster was now to take his place at the head of the executive, and as chief of the council rule both king and kingdom.

There were, however, weaknesses in this scheme. The council had hitherto been the servant of the king. It had known no official head. The most considerable and important element in it had been administrative officials. The chancellor and treasurer had hitherto generally been predominant. There were however precedents for lay rather than official heads, for example Pembroke[1] and the archbishop of Canterbury[2]; but both had worked with and on behalf of the king. It was almost certain that Lancaster would work in direct opposition to the royal will. He desired that position to enforce the Ordinances and reform of the household and see that such reforms were executed. It was impossible that the royal and baronial views upon these questions should agree. The earl desired some guarantee that his position as chief of the council should be supreme and lasting and that his will should prevail even against the king's. The conditions he imposed are of the utmost importance. They supply an insight into the policy of the baronial opposition. They show the weaknesses which were inherent in the scheme and were a list of the conditions which Lancaster considered necessary to counteract those weaknesses.

The first condition was in the nature of an ultimatum. If the king would not obey the earl and his council in the advice given him about his household and his kingdom after that had been explained to him, the earl considered himself free to resign his position[3]. The

[1] Vide above, pp. 322–330. [2] Vide above, pp. 331–5.
[3] *Rot. Parl.* vol. I, p. 351. Vide below, p. 422.

motives[1] prompting the earl to resign and so free himself from his duties and obligations as a counsellor were forcible. A brief notice of the effect of the condition upon the king, if accepted and adhered to, is necessary. To prevent Lancaster's resignation, the king had to obey implicitly the commands of the earl and the council. The will of the council rather than that of the king was to prevail. The condition seems to imply that under its terms would come a new or a revised or an additional set of ordinances relating to the household and the kingdom. Such a reform of the household was included in the next experiment of the baronial opposition which was accepted at the parliament of York in 1318[2]. It was unlikely that this foisting of another set of ordinances upon the king in this way would prove effective. Lest the king should supersede the action of the council, it was laid down:

> Et les busoignes tochauntes li e son Roiaume ne seient faites ne perfumes sanz assent de li e des autres Prelatz, Countes, e Barons qi de li conseiller serront ordenetz[3].

Under existing custom, the king could act upon his own initiative. The council was now to be made supreme in all matters and the king was not to act without it. This condition was necessary to give effect to the first, especially in consideration of the ingenuity and ease with which the king created one organisation to take the place of another over which his direct influence was waning. The baronial conception of the council is illustrated. Lancaster stated that the king wished him to act as chief of the council, "en totes les busoignes grosses ou chargauntes touchauntes li e son Roiaume ensemblement ovesqes autres Prelatz, Countes, e Barons[4]." On the acceptance of conditions he promised "destre du Conseil nostre seigneur le Roi, ovesqes les Prelatz, Countes, e Barons[5]."

The third condition laid it down that:

> Si nul des Prelatz, Countes, e Barons en conseillant le dit nostre Seigneur le Roi, ou autre choses fessant qe ne seit al profit de li ou de son Roiaume, qe au prochein Parlement, solonc lavisement nostre Seigneur le Roi e le seon, seient remuetz. Et issint de Parlement en Parlement de eus e de chescun de eus, solom les defautes trouees en eus[6].

Throughout the bill the council is composed of the prelates, earls and barons. Yet from the functions which it has to perform it appears to be the "administrative" and not the great council. No reference whatsoever was made to the official element. It does not follow necessarily that the baronial plan meant its total exclusion. It

[1] Vide above, pp. 412–413. [2] Vide below, pp. 453–5.
[3] *Rot. Parl.* vol. I, p. 351. [4] Ibid. [5] Ibid. [6] Ibid.

certainly meant that the baronial element was to be predominant if not more. The council was to be oligarchical. The king was to submit in all administrative matters to a committee of the oligarchy. For the form of the third condition speaks of the prelates, earls and barons who were ordained to counsel the king, and this in view of precedent[1] and future policy[2] can be read to refer to a committee of the barons appointed by the whole body. The whole matter is immature. The council is not adequately defined. The whole scheme, in fact, appears to be an immature discussion of what was presented in a more perfect form in the parliament of York in 1318[3].

Though the parliament roll gives no indication of the composition of this council, a letter written by Lancaster to the king in July, 1317, upbraiding him for his ill-conduct, recounts how in the parliament of Lincoln a committee had been appointed to guide the king. Because the governance of the realm was guided by people no wise sufficient the king consented that the archbishop of Canterbury, the bishops of Llandaff, Chichester, Norwich and Salisbury, the earls of Pembroke, Hereford, Arundel and Richmond together with the earl of Lancaster and Bartholomew de Badlesmere should make and ordain by the advice of the wise men sworn of the king's council how the estate of his realm might be redressed and the governance of the kingdom and household better ordered. The king had also consented that the unsuitable persons should be removed from him[4]. This was the council of which Lancaster was to be head. The scheme was to take the form of an addition of prelates, earls and barons to the "administrative" council; and it will be remembered that the bishops of Norwich, Chichester and Salisbury had been sworn of the king's council at the parliament[5]. In a council so composed the king had trusty friends in the archbishop, Pembroke and Richmond, and Lancaster's influence even as chief of the council would not have been great. This committee had proceeded to London, where the wisest men of the king's council were, and by their advice there were ordained certain points best suited for the household and the governance of the realm which were sent to the king by Badlesmere and William Inge[6]. The committee of the barons appears to have sat with the "administrative" council of officials and justices at London and made the arrangements and one member of the executive committee and

[1] Vide above, pp. 344–9. [2] Vide below, pp. 448–451, 463–6. [3] Ibid.

[4] A French version of this letter is found in the App. to *Chron. Murimuth*, pp. 271–6; a Latin summary in *Auct. Bridl.* pp. 50–52.

[5] Vide above, p. 410.

[6] *Chron. Murimuth*, pp. 271–6. *Auct. Bridl.* pp. 50–51.

a representative of the "administrative" council carried results of the conference to the king. The scheme as gathered from Lancaster's letter shows progress. As early as 23 March, the earl was presiding over the council. On that day the mayor and aldermen of London appeared before Lancaster, Sandale, chancellor, Norwich, treasurer, and other magnates of the king's council sitting at St Paul's and offered the king the sum of 500 marks for a confirmation of their liberties and £500 for a renewal of certain articles in the form of a charter[1].

The third condition providing for the removal of any member of the council who gave advice or did anything which was not to the profit of the king and his kingdom adds further weight to the suggestion that the king was to be ruled by an oligarchy. Removal in parliament probably meant nothing more than a removal by the general body of barons. It might easily happen that Lancaster's influence would be greater in parliament than in the council, especially in view of the composition of that council. His influence in the council would depend considerably upon the number of officials included in that body. In the "administrative" council, officials would have equal importance with barons. The officials were summoned to parliament in a subordinate capacity. In parliament therefore Lancaster and the barons could obtain the removal of any member, official or baron. What was against their will they would regard as prejudicial to the king and kingdom.

Such a scheme, had it been practicable, would have gone further than previous attempts towards securing the baronial aims. Such restriction as the scheme imposed upon the king's power and action it was unlikely he would submit to for long. Pressure of external circumstances rather than the baronial opposition had induced him to adopt the plan, and it was unlikely that those circumstances would remain constant. The king would not long brook control by a baronial oligarchy. Moreover in the household system there were yet resources to withstand, delay and impede such a scheme. What had happened proved, and what was to happen was to substantiate, that internal control no less than external control could be effective only when and as long as it was imposed with the king's acquiescence and goodwill. This was the line upon which the middle party proceeded. This the Lancastrian faction never realised fully. Mere temporary advantage and transitory success could not prevail against the strength of the organisation which supported the king.

[1] *Cal. Letter Books, E*, pp. 59–60.

On this occasion, of almost greater value to the king than the strength of the household system was Lancaster himself. He was no administrator and could not shake himself free from the inaction of sullen opposition. Even as head of the council he retained the attitude and policy of an opposition leader. As a result the whole scheme came to naught. The Scots, who had proved Edward's undoing in 1314, in 1316 proved the undoing of Lancaster.

The country was no more protected against Scottish invasion with Lancaster at the head of affairs than it had been before. The north had been invaded in June, when the Scots had penetrated as far as Richmond[1]. The king and Lancaster would not co-operate[2]; neither would trust the other. Worse than all it was noticed that the Scots in their ravages spared Lancaster's lands[3]. The suggestion immediately was that Lancaster had connived at the incursions[4]. A suggestion of this nature would strengthen the king's case tremendously. The reciprocal charges of treason which Lancaster and the courtiers levelled at each other[5] increased the tension. The result was that before the end of 1316, Lancaster and the king were again at strife. Each wished to capture the other, and as a result the whole land was greatly disturbed[6]. Additional causes of irritation were soon provided. Lancaster's wife was carried off by the earl of Warenne[7], it was suggested, with the connivance of the king[8]. In September, 1317, a pacification was patched up[9] though a final peace was far from being achieved. Throughout these disputes between the king and Lancaster, Pembroke had been playing his usual part of mediator[10]. Moreover the failure of the scheme of 1316 and Lancaster's subsequent disgrace afforded Pembroke and his associates an opportunity to put their views into practice. Beginning with the year 1316, therefore, a party which endeavoured to mediate between the king and Lancaster grew up. This party was moderate in tone and objected to the virulence and extremity of the Lancastrian faction while it saw clearly that reform was needed. Its methods of setting to work and of achieving its ends were entirely different from those of the Lancaster faction. It profited by the past failures of the baronial opposition and its moderation gave it more possibility of success.

[1] *Chron. Lanerc.* pp. 216–217. [2] *Flores Hist.* vol. III, p. 341.
[3] *Auct. Malm.* pp. 224–5. [4] Ibid. [5] Ibid. p. 224.
[6] *Chartul. St Mary's Abbey, Dublin*, vol. II, *Ann. of Irel.* p. 298.
[7] *Auct. Malm.* p. 228. [8] Stubbs, *Constit. Hist.* vol. II, p. 358, note 4.
[9] *Ann. Paul.* p. 281. *Auct. Malm.* p. 230. *Flores Hist.* vol. III, pp. 180–1.
[10] *Auct. Malm.* pp. 230–1.

CHAPTER V

THE EXPERIMENTS (*cont.*)

(iv) *The Middle Party and its Activities*

Lancaster had failed to secure the baronial objects. The failure of the extremists gave the barons who favoured a moderate policy the opportunity to develop and materialise their views. Accordingly a middle party grew up slowly but naturally. The raw material for the creation of such a party was plentiful. There was a basis of barons who were dissatisfied with the leadership of Lancaster and were not prepared to go his length in factious opposition. To this basis of barons additions could be made from three groups—the administrative officials, the household officials and the king's friends and favourites. It appeared that the craftsman alone was required to model this raw material, and that craftsman was found in the earl of Pembroke. As a result of his skill the middle party reached its height of power and influence at the parliament of York in 1318. After that there was wear and tear. In the parliament of Westminster in 1320 its influence had declined. By 1321 the party as such existed no longer. Pembroke had to fall back once more on a policy of personal mediation.

The middle party was the creation more of Pembroke than of any other person. In his years of predominance 1312–14, his control had proved neither irritating nor irksome. The efficiency of the administration had profited by his skill and ability and the whole country had benefited. One result was that, owing to the aid he had given the king, the Ordinances during this period had not obtained their promised success. This occurred not because Pembroke was out of sympathy with the Ordinances. He had been an ordainer and, despite his rupture with the Lancastrian faction, he retained his respect for them. On the other hand he was not prepared to force the king to extremity. His influence exerted upon the king's behalf strengthened the administration and thus indirectly lessened the need for, and the opportunity to enforce, the Ordinances. The added power and opportunities which Lancaster obtained after the battle of Bannockburn and especially in and immediately after the parliament of Westminster in 1315, threw a shadow over Pembroke. He did not disappear nor did his influence vanish entirely. He still took part in administration, but his influence was declining. Lancaster was in the ascendant. The events which followed the parliament of Lincoln in 1316 gave Pembroke opportunity to reassert his influence. As early as 3 March, 1316, he was associated with the archbishop of Canterbury, the chancellor and treasurer in a writ of privy seal to call the council[1]. Again Lancaster was playing an extreme part and again there was room for a mediator like Pembroke. This time he was not to act alone. There were others dissatisfied with the domination of Lancaster; others saw that their true interests lay in supporting the king. The co-operation of such was welcomed by Pembroke and in a short time he had gathered round him a party which if small in numbers was strong in influence.

Humphrey de Bohun, earl of Hereford, though one of the fiercest of the pursuers of Gavaston had not allowed his factiousness to run riot as Lancaster had. Though often acting with the Lancastrian faction, he had throughout preserved a certain independence of action. He had loyally supported the king at Bannockburn, and in 1315 took a share in the administration quite apart from his Lancastrian connection. The influence he was beginning to have with the king from March, 1315, onwards was reflected in the licences granted at his instance[2] and in grants obtained for himself[3]. By October he had a prominent place in the administrative council. On 20 October, with the archbishop of Canterbury, the chancellor, and treasurer he was ordered to call the council at London to consider certain matters[4]. One matter had reference to letters from Lancaster which Hugh D'Audley and William de Melton, the king's messengers to the earl, had brought. The archbishop and Hereford had previous knowledge of the matter and in company with the council were to give their advice thereon to the king[5]. About the second matter the king sent Master John Walwayn, escheator south of Trent who was a clerk of Hereford's[6], to tell them of the great

[1] Chan. Warr., File 94/3604.
[2] *Cal. Pat. Rolls*, 1313–17, pp. 278, 292–3, 376.
[3] Ibid. pp. 267, 278, 332.
[4] Chan. Warr., File 93/3513, 3515. Vide App. of Doc. nos. 62, 63.
[5] Chan. Warr., File 93/3513. Vide App. of Doc. no. 62.
[6] For the relation between Walwayn and Hereford vide above, pp. 355–6.

outrages and damage which had been done to the king in the castle of Warwick which was in royal hands[1]. In the parliament of Lincoln, Hereford acted as the king's spokesman, answering the petitions of the clergy[2]. About the same time he sat amongst other counsellors, including the bishop of Exeter, Walwayn, John de Mutford, and Baldock with the treasurer and barons of the exchequer, when the mayor of London appeared at the exchequer to answer concerning the disturbance about the Lombards[3]. An early occasion on which he acted with other members of the middle party was on 3 July, 1315, when a confirmation charter of Edward II to Reading Abbey was witnessed by the archbishop of Canterbury, the earls of Richmond, Pembroke, Hereford and Arundel, Badlesmere, and Crombwell, steward of the household[4]. From the year 1316 onwards, until the Despenser war of 1321 caused a re-arrangement of the parties, Hereford acted with the middle party rather than with Lancaster.

One of the most energetic members of the middle party was Bartholomew de Badlesmere, a knight from Kent[5], who held certain lands of the archbishop of Canterbury by serjeanty of being his chamberlain[6]. Badlesmere first obtained a place of importance through the influence of the earl of Gloucester whose knight he was. He frequently received money from the exchequer on his master's behalf[7]. When Gloucester was engaged in the Scottish war, Badlesmere led bands of knights and others in his company[8]. After the death of the earl of Lincoln, when Gloucester became keeper of the realm, Badlesmere took a part in the administration[9]. He also wrote to William de Ayremynne on behalf of John de Chelmsford[10], clerk of the earl of Gloucester[11]. Besides the training in administrative work which he received he also obtained grants of manors from the king at Gloucester's request[12]. A song-writer of the time attributes the death of Gloucester to the treachery of Badlesmere, who seeing

[1] Chan. Warr., File 93/3515. Vide App. of Doc. no. 63.

[2] *Rot. Parl.* vol. I, p. 350. *Parl. Writs*, vol. II, Pt i, p. 169.

[3] L. T. R. Mem. Roll, no. 89, m. 31 d. [4] Camb. Univ. MS. Dd. ix. 38, f. 77 a.

[5] He was one of the knights of the shire from Kent in the parliament of Carlisle (*Cal. Close Rolls*, 1302–7, p. 324).

[6] Round, *King's Serjeants*, pp. 113–114, note 3.

[7] Issue Rolls, no. 144, m. 3; no. 150, m. 5; no. 153, m. 6: "per manus Bartholomew de Badlesmere militis sui."

[8] Chan. Warr., File 1703.

[9] Badlesmere was ordered by Gloucester to go to the treasurer and inform him of a tournament arranged for Lincoln and to make arrangements that it should not be held (Anc. Corresp. vol. XXXVI, no. 200).

[10] Anc. Corresp. vol. XXXVI, no. 60. [11] Chan. Warr., File 1703 passim.

[12] *Cal. Pat. Rolls*, 1307–13, p. 214 (5 March, 1310).

his master beset failed to attempt a rescue[1]. How Badlesmere first obtained his position in the earl of Gloucester's company is uncertain. Badlesmere had already married or was soon to marry a relation of Gloucester's[2], so it is possible he obtained his position through this fact. It is certain that up to the death of Gloucester in 1314, Badlesmere was his servant. He was also somewhat associated with the earl of Hereford and had acted as his deputy constable of England in 1310[3]. In his will made in 1319 the earl left Badlesmere a black steed which he had brought from abroad[4]. Badlesmere had on occasion acted with Lancaster—as in April, 1316, when associated with him in a commission to treat with Bruce[5]—and he had served on the council over which Lancaster had been appointed chief in the parliament of Lincoln[6]. In addition to his association with these earls, Badlesmere had obtained a certain amount of influence at court, probably through Gloucester. He had in fact been associated with the court rather than the baronial opposition since the beginning of the reign. At his request a writ of privy seal was issued on 14 December, 1310, pardoning a fine[7], and another privy seal to the exchequer was issued at his request on 23 January, 1311[8]. Grants under the great seal were made at his instance[9], and he obtained grants of weekly markets and yearly fairs[10] and free warren[11] in his own lands. As early as 28 May, 1308, a manor of Langton's had been granted to him[12] and subsequently various other grants[13]. In June, 1311, he obtained a payment from the exchequer for his expenses in going to the king in Scotland on royal business[14]. At the parliament of Lincoln in 1316 he appeared as a royal messenger[15], and it is probable that Badlesmere was already decidedly on the king's side. Later in the same year he was in close association with Pembroke and others of the middle party.

[1] Camd. Soc., *Polit. Songs*, p. 263.

[2] *Cal. Inq. P. M.* vol. VI, p. 159

[3] *Parl. Writs*, vol. II, Pt ii, p. 40. Madox, *Bar. Angl.* p. 214.

[4] *Arch. Jour.* vol. II [1846], p. 346.

[5] *Cal. Pat. Rolls*, 1313–17, p. 450.

[6] Vide above, p. 422. In view of Badlesmere's antecedents Prof. Tout, *The Place of Ed. II*, pp. 111–114, appears to lay too great stress upon Badlesmere's connection with Lancaster.

[7] Chan. Warr., File 73/1567.

[8] K. R. Mem. Roll, no. 84, m. 22.

[9] *Cal. Charter Rolls*, 1300–26, pp. 183, 272.

[10] Ibid. pp. 282–3

[11] Ibid. p. 283.

[12] K. R. Mem. Roll, no. 81, m. 10 d.

[13] Chan. Warr., File 74/1679. *Abbrev. Orig.* p. 162.

[14] Issue Roll, no. 157, m. 4.

[15] *Rot. Parl.* vol. I, pp. 351–2. *Parl. Writs*, vol. II, Pt i, p. 169.

Pembroke, Hereford and Badlesmere formed the baronial basis upon which the middle party was constructed. Though the end of 1316 saw them still acting as individual supporters of the king, in a few months they were to become united in purpose. In December, 1316[1], Pembroke[2], Badlesmere, and the bishops of Ely and Norwich were commissioned to go on an embassy to John XXII who had recently been elevated to the papal throne. The mission had two objects. It desired papal help against the Scots and a bull to relieve the king of his oath to the Ordinances[3]. The king would naturally choose for such a mission men who felt well disposed to his cause. John de Hothum, bishop of Ely, had been a king's clerk, had acted as Gavaston's deputy as keeper of the forest north of Trent and had been escheator north of Trent[4]. John Salmon, bishop of Norwich, though he had not yet taken any part in the administration, was to obtain office under the middle party. In this mission to Avignon may be found the origins of that party[5]. By the activity of the middle party within two years three of this mission had attained high office. Pembroke sought no great office for himself. He was prepared to stand in the background and direct the activities. Unfortunately, on the return from this mission, Pembroke was captured and imprisoned in France[6]. This delayed the progress of the party for some months. It was not until July, 1317[7], that he was able to return to England. By that time the bishop of Ely was already treasurer[8] and the first step in the plan of the middle party had been secured. Pembroke and Badlesmere had acted in association before this mission[9]; but it drew them closer and on their return they continued to act together. On 13 July, 1317, for instance, the king wrote to them jointly, acknowledging the receipt of their letters and approving of their action in remaining until a certain date for the business concerning John Botetourte[10].

[1] Protections were issued 7 Dec. 1316 (*Cal. Pat. Rolls*, 1313–17, p. 593). Vide Chan. Warr., File 97/3907, power was to be given them under the great seal "issint qe nul de eux eit poair de rien graunter a nully saunz assent de eux touz" (4 Jan. 1317).

[2] His influence was growing. By a privy seal of 4 December, 1316, with the archbishop of Canterbury and the chancellor he was ordered to call the council (Chan. Warr., File 96/3819).

[3] *Auct. Malm* pp. 227–8.

[4] Vide above, pp. 383–4.

[5] Prof. Tout suggests that it was in this mission that the formation of the party occurred (*Place of Edward II*, p. 112).

[6] *Chron. Murimuth*, p. 26. *Foedera*, vol. II, p. 329.

[7] *Cal. Doc. Scotl.* vol. III, p. 108.

[8] *Cal. Pat. Rolls*, 1313–17, p. 657. He was appointed 27 May, 1317.

[9] Ibid. p. 450.

[10] *Cal. Doc. Scotl.* vol. III, p. 108.

The policy of the middle party stands in very marked contrast to that of the Lancastrian faction. The members of that party in common with the baronial opposition in general desired to control the king. They did not seek to do this by harsh means. What they desired was the substance rather than the form of power. It was not to their purpose to provoke unnecessary irritation and ánger in the king. They appeared to be, and acted as, the king's friends. The result was that they gained the king's confidence, and he willingly surrendered the administrative offices into their hands. One of their objects was obtained if they could secure the administrative offices for their partizans or win over the holders of the offices to their views. The king acquiesced in this because the middle party saved him from Lancaster. The middle party saw that it was quite useless to obtain possession of the administrative offices alone. The household controlled the administration. An endeavour was therefore made to secure positions within the household for partizans or supporters of the middle party, or to win over the household officers. The household officers and the courtiers had contributed not a little towards the defeat of previous efforts to control the administration. As long as the administration was ruled by one party and the household by another, conflict between them was inevitable; and the conflict generally resulted in victory for the party which controlled the household. The probability of such conflicts was to be eliminated. The middle party was to have the same influence in the household as in the administration. There was still a third element to be taken into account, the king's friends and favourites. Ultimately most things depended upon those people who, on account of the king's affection or their nearness to him, were able to influence his will and action. Those persons could through the king rule the household and the administration. It was important that the middle party should conciliate or incorporate them.

Of the chief administrative officials at this time, the chancellor, Sandale, since 1316 bishop of Winchester, had been appointed to his office during the baronial reaction following Bannockburn. Though he could not fairly be called a Lancastrian—for he had held high office since the beginning of the reign—he had been too closely associated with Lancaster to prove acceptable to the middle party. Similarly Norwich, treasurer, who was to be superseded by the bishop of Ely[1], had been the candidate supported by the ordainers against

[1] Vide above, p. 429.

Langton[1], and had been appointed treasurer in September, 1314, "by king and council[2]."

The household officials must also be considered. In November, 1316, William de Montague had succeeded John de Crombwell as steward of the household[3]. The office of chamberlain was still held, at least up to 19 April, 1318, by John de Cherleton[4]. The treasurer of the wardrobe was Roger de Northburgh[5], and the keeper of the privy seal Master Thomas de Cherleton[6], the chamberlain's brother.

The three greatest personal influences round the king were Hugh le Despenser the younger, Hugh D'Audley and Roger Damory. The three were married to the Gloucester co-heiresses[7]. Damory had obtained the hand of the youngest sister, Elizabeth, by royal favour[8]. Despenser the younger was slowly working himself into the royal grace[9]. It would have turned out ill if two of the competitors for portions of the Gloucester inheritance had sought the royal favour and the third had held aloof. D'Audley, too, was a courtier. Delivery of the portions of the Gloucester inheritance was not ordered until 25 November, 1317[10], and after that date the three co-partners still maintained their positions at court. The young Despenser, relying partly on his father's influence, and partly upon that of his wife[11], obtained and kept his position at court. When the activities of the middle party are examined it will be found that Despenser frequently acted in association with them[12]. It was in part under their influence that he obtained his great household office[13].

Damory was in royal favour as early as December, 1314, when he obtained a grant of the castle and honour of Knaresburgh[14]. From that time onwards he was the frequent recipient of signs of royal affection. In February, 1315, he obtained the wardship of certain lands of Henry de Percy during the minority of his heir[15]. By March, 1315, his position as one of the king's knights was established. A payment was made from the exchequer to the keeper of the wardrobe for the expenses of the king's household through Roger Damory, knight[16]. In May he was still about the court[17]. In

[1] Vide above, pp. 387–392.
[2] *Cal. Pat. Rolls*, 1313–17, p. 178.
[3] Tout, *The Place of Ed. II*, p. 354.
[4] *Cal. Pat. Rolls*, 1317–21, p. 133.
[5] Tout, *The Place of Ed. II*, p. 355.
[6] Ibid. p. 357.
[7] Cf. *Cal. Pat. Rolls*, 1313–17, p. 660; *Rot. Parl.* vol. I, p. 363; Cotton MS. Nero A. iv (Chron. Landavense), f. 536.
[8] *Flores Hist.* vol. III, p. 194.
[9] Vide above, pp. 90–94.
[10] *Cal. Fine Rolls*, 1307–19, p. 350.
[11] Vide above, pp. 70–91.
[12] Vide below, pp. 437–440.
[13] Vide below, pp. 454–5.
[14] *Cal. Fine Rolls*, 1307–19, p. 225.
[15] Ibid, pp. 234, 237.
[16] Issue Roll, no. 172, m. 6.
[17] Ibid. no. 174, m. 3.

May, 1316, he obtained a grant of £100 for his services in Glamorgan in putting down the revolt of Llewelyn Bren[1]. By January, 1317, he had so improved his position that he obtained a grant of 200 marks to be received annually at the exchequer until the king would provide him with lands or rents to that value[2]. The grant was made to enable him to maintain himself the more fittingly in the king's service[3]. The year 1317 saw a still greater number of grants to Damory. In August, 1316, he had obtained the wardship of the Verdoun lands[4], and in January, 1317, this grant was extended[5]. In March for his good service at Stirling and elsewhere he obtained another wardship[6]. In June, the castle of Knaresburgh, which he held at will on rendering 500 marks yearly at the exchequer, was granted to him for life free of rent[7], though the grant was afterwards surrendered and cancelled. His wife obtained grants of manors[8] and he obtained grants of houses in London[9], manors[10] and hundreds[11]. In October, 1317, he was appointed custodian of Gloucester[12]. He was then first in the royal favour, and during the course of the year 1318 the favour increased rather than diminished. The castles of Corfe[13], Knaresburgh[14], and St Briavel's and the forest of Dean[15] and manors[16] fell to him. As a person near the king he acted as a frequent messenger to the chancellor ordering the issue of writs[17]. His influence with the king was also apparent in writs of privy seal which were issued at his request[18]. If the middle party was to achieve anything it was indispensable that it should obtain his support. In the years 1316–18, Damory was the supreme influence at court, easily out-pacing all his competitors, including the younger Despenser.

There was not room for two persons exercising such an influence as Damory did. D'Audley, his rival, could not hope to out-distance him in the royal favour. As early as November, 1313, he had obtained a grant of land for life[19]. In the parliament of Westminster

[1] K. R. Mem. Roll, no. 89, m. 45. L. T. R. Mem. Roll. no. 86, m. 85.
[2] *Cal. Pat. Rolls*, 1313–17, p. 609. Cf. *Issue Roll*, no. 180, m. 3.
[3] *Cal. Pat. Rolls*, 1313–17, p. 609.
[4] *Cal. Fine Rolls*, 1307–19, p. 294.
[5] Ibid. pp. 316–317.
[6] *Cal. Pat. Rolls*, 1313–17, p. 622.
[7] Ibid. pp. 662–3.
[8] Ibid. pp. 606, 677.
[9] Ibid. p. 640.
[10] Ibid. p. 677.
[11] *Cal. Fine Rolls*, 1307–19, p. 345.
[12] *Cal. Pat. Rolls*, 1317–21, p. 38.
[13] *Cal. Fine Rolls*, 1307–19, p. 353.
[14] Ibid. p. 355.
[15] Ibid. p. 363.
[16] Ibid. p. 355.
[17] Ibid. pp. 332, 339, 340, 361. *Cal. Charter Rolls*, 1300–26, p. 409.
[18] Chan. Warr., File 104/4620. K. R. Mem. Roll, no. 91, Brev. dir. m. 30. L. T. R. Mem. Roll, no. 88, Brev. dir. Hill. m. 4 d.
[19] *Cal. Fine Rolls*, 1307–19, p. 184.

in 1315 he was given custody of lands and tenements[1], a fact which suggests Lancastrian leanings. In April of that year, however, he was sufficiently in the king's favour to act in company with Oliver de Ingham as a messenger ordering payment out of the exchequer[2]. In June the chancellor was ordered by privy seal so well and graciously to hasten the business before him touching Hugh D'Audley, "quil se doyne tenir appaiez par reson et quil puisse returner a nous hastiuement si come nous lui auoms chargez[3]." He also obtained a fee from the king[4], as well as grants of land[5]. Writs of privy seal were issued at his request[6]. In 1318 he obtained a grant of murage for three years for the town of Tonbridge[7], and a pardon was issued at his request[8]. Though his influence was smaller than Damory's, he was still a sufficiently important person for the middle party to desire to incorporate.

This was the raw material from which Pembroke had to build his middle party. He was the master craftsman who had to produce a useful and serviceable article. In addition to welding the various groups—the moderate barons, the administrative officials, the household officials and the king's friends—he had to be careful that no powerful influence like that of the archbishop of Canterbury was alienated[9]. He had to adjust the whole matter with the utmost care. In so diverse a party there were bound to be conflicting interests. These had to be quieted. The task of leader and guide was a difficult one, but Pembroke proved equal to it.

The ways he employed to build up his party and keep it together were various. One of the most interesting was that of a bond. On 24 November, 1317, Damory entered into an indenture[10] with Pembroke and Badlesmere. He undertook to use his utmost diligence and power to induce the king to allow himself to be led and governed by the counsel of Pembroke and Badlesmere and to place faith in

[1] *Rot. Parl.* vol. I, p. 324.
[2] Issue Roll, no. 174, m. 2.
[3] Chan. Warr., File 91/3365.
[4] Issue Roll, no. 183, m. 8.
[5] *Cal. Close Rolls*, 1313–18, p. 541.
[6] K. R. Mem. Roll, no. 91, Brev. dir. m. 15. L. T. R. Mem. Roll, no. 88, Brev. dir. Mich. m. 14.
[7] *Cal. Pat. Rolls*, 1317–21, p. 133.
[8] Ibid. p. 135.
[9] He had to reconcile the courtiers and the officials with the milder elements in the baronial opposition.
[10] One part of this indenture is preserved in Exch. Misc. 4/6. Vide App. of Doc. no. 42. A copy is printed in *Parl. Writs*, vol. II, Pt ii, App. p. 120, and an abridged translation is found *Parl. Writs*, vol. II, Pt i, pp. 202–3. Vide also Introduction, pp. 35–36.

them before all other people, so far as they should counsel him loyally to his honour and profit and that of his crown and kingdom. Moreover Damory promised to govern himself by the same counsels without transgressing them in any particular. He would neither procure for himself or for another, nor assent that the king should give to any man without the assent of Pembroke and Badlesmere, land or to the value of £20 in land, or that the king should do anything of great import which might be prejudicial to him or his crown in any event. If in the absence of Pembroke and Badlesmere the king should endeavour to grant to anyone beyond that value, or do any matter of great import of his own accord which might be prejudicial to him, his crown or his kingdom, Damory was to do all in his power to hinder him. If he could not prevent it in any manner, he was to acquaint Pembroke and Badlesmere before it could take effect so that the three together with one accord should force the king to alter his will. If Damory thought that anyone said or did anything before the king in prejudice, dishonour or damage of Pembroke or Badlesmere so that they should have no influence with the king, he would warn them without delay and work against that person with his best power. To hold and fulfil this agreement well and loyally so that he should never do anything against it, Damory took oath on the Eucharist and bound himself to pay a sum of £10,000 to Pembroke and Badlesmere at their request whenever he proceeded against this agreement. Pembroke and Badlesmere on their part promised in good faith as loyal knights that they would defend, warrant and maintain Damory against all persons whatsoever, saving only the allegiance which they owed the king, and that they like Damory would hold and observe the agreement fully. They bound their heirs and executors and all their goods both movable and immovable, present and to come, to the will of Damory[1]. One part of the indenture was sealed with the seals of Pembroke and Badlesmere and the other part with the seal of Damory[2]. The agreement was to be kept secret, Badlesmere binding himself not to reveal it[3].

Whether this was the first of a series of indentures or one in a series is uncertain. It is possible that it stands alone. In any case it would appear to be the most noteworthy on account of the importance of the persons bound by it. Damory was at this time the supreme

[1] Exch. Misc. 4/6 Vide App. of Doc. no. 42.

[2] Ibid.

[3] *Cal. Pat. Rolls*, 1321–24, p. 21. *Parl. Writs*, Vol. II, Pt i, p. 264. *Foedera*, vol. II, p. 454.

person at court: Pembroke and Badlesmere were also persons of influence there. The pope was writing to Badlesmere as one of the king's counsellors, and exhorting Pembroke to urge the king to pursue a certain action[1]. Already on 3 August, 1317, "the king who thought fit to retain Bartholomew de Badlesmere by him for the benefit of his counsel," for his services, made him a special assignment of 4000 marks[2]. Had the middle party but included these three its influence upon administration must have been considerable. It is certain however that there were many other members of the middle party, and it is possible that there were a number of them bound together by deed.

There is upon the close roll under the date 1 June, 1317, a series of recognisances made in the king's presence at Westminster and enrolled thereon by his order. There were five parties concerned, Despenser the father and his son, Damory, D'Audley and Montague[3]. The five were persons constantly near the king and one held the highest office in the household[4]. Moreover the fact that the recognisances were made in the king's presence is significant. It is possible that they were made with an object similar to that of the indenture between Pembroke, Badlesmere and Damory. The recognisances were entered into by all, who bound themselves to all the others with the exception of the Despensers, who did not bind each other[5]. An agreement for some purpose underlay the recognisances and the natural suggestion is that the purpose was the formation of a court party, a party which became absorbed into the middle party.

While the growth of the middle party had been progressing in various directions, Hereford[6] had been making his position at court firmer. Protections[7] and grants[8] were made at his instance. He obtained licence to demise a manor[9] and obtained grants of wardships[10]. With the archbishop of Canterbury and the bishop of Exeter, on 13 April, 1317, he was ordered to open the approaching parliament, as the king could not attend in person[11]. In February of the same

[1] *Cal. Pap. Letters*, 1304–42, p. 427. [2] *Cal. Pat. Rolls*, 1317–21, p. 14.

[3] *Cal. Close Rolls*, 1313–18, p. 477. Vide also K. R. Misc. 3/6.

[4] Damory, D'Audley and Montague are mentioned as the royal favourites in 1317 (*Flores Hist.* vol. III, p. 178).

[5] *Cal. Close Rolls*, 1313–18, p. 477. Among the acknowledgments of debts due to the earl of Lancaster on 23 Nov. 1318, were considerable sums from Damory, D'Audley and Montague (*Cal. Close Rolls*, 1318–23, pp. 109–110)—a curious commentary upon the above.

[6] Vide above, pp. 426–7. [7] *Cal. Pat. Rolls*, 1313–17, p. 549. [8] Ibid. p. 604.

[9] Ibid. p. 513. [10] *Cal. Fine Rolls*, 1307–19, pp. 281, 284.

[11] *Cal. Pat. Rolls*, 1313–17, p. 634.

year, the king, in Hereford's presence, ordered the treasurer to make a payment to a certain merchant[1]. A further grant of a considerable wardship was made to him in April[2]. His position at court was now strong; but it is not until September, 1317, that he is found acting in intimate association with Pembroke.

At this time the disturbances between the king and Lancaster were again pronounced. The earl was at Pontefract with his forces, the king was at York[3]. It was only by the mediation of Pembroke and the cardinals that a conflict was prevented. The king agreed to have a parliament at Lincoln in the following January[4]. On 24 September, at the instance of Pembroke and Hereford[5] and others, a safe conduct was granted for Lancaster, his followers and adherents. Neither they nor their goods were to be seized. Any who had been arrested were to be released[6]. The writ was issued by the king and council[7]. On the same day power was given to the two earls to liberate any of Lancaster's followers or adherents who had been arrested[8]. Two days later, protection, to continue as long as the coming parliament which the king had conceded, was granted to Lancaster and his followers and adherents, at their request. They were to enjoy freedom from arrest and seizure. Such things as could be redressed in parliament were to be there redressed. Other matters were to be decided by the law of the realm[9]. At the same time an extended power to discharge followers and adherents and to restore their goods was granted to Pembroke and Hereford[10]. Further, on 4 January, in anticipation of the imminent parliament the two earls were again empowered to discharge all persons who might be arrested as followers of Lancaster[11].

This close association of the two earls, begun through common dislike of Lancaster's policy, continued, and it can be fairly said that by the beginning of the year 1318 the essential elements of the middle party had been gathered together. Pembroke, Badlesmere

[1] Issue Roll, no. 180, m. 8. [2] *Cal. Fine Rolls*, 1307–19, p. 329.
[3] *Auct. Malm.* p. 230. [4] Ibid.
[5] In this month Hereford and Pembroke were at Boroughbridge with a force of men and there received the despoiled cardinals from Lancaster (*Chron. Mon. de Melsa*, vol. II, p. 334).
[6] *Cal. Pat. Rolls*, 1317–21, p. 27. [7] Ibid. [8] Ibid.
[9] Ibid. p. 29. "By king," *Parl. Writs*, vol. II, Pt i, p. 201. The original commission is preserved (Exch. Misc. 4/7, m. 1) with the following endorsement: "La commissioun le Roy fait a mounsire Aymar de Valence counte de Pembroke et a mounsire Humphrey de Bohun de redrescer et ordener les gens le Counte de Lancastre qe ils ne soient arestuz de nule parte en le Royalme."
[10] Ibid. [11] *Cal. Pat. Rolls*, 1317–21, p. 69.

and Damory were united by bond. Pembroke and Hereford were united by close political association. Other men and interests were being attracted to the growing party. The first-fruits of the endeavours of that party were obtained in the Treaty of Leake and the parliament of York in 1318. This phase possesses such interesting and important features that it will be discussed separately[1]. Meanwhile the subsequent fortunes of the middle party and, as a result partly of its power and partly of his own ability, Pembroke's further share in the administration, will be treated.

The triumph of the middle party in the parliament of York in 1318 did not end its activities. It continued until 1321 to be the dominant force—its power being emphasised in the parliament of Westminster in 1320[2]. The struggles which arose from the Gloucester inheritance and the policy of the younger Despenser finally broke up the middle party and rallied the wronged barons around Lancaster again. The present endeavour is not to give a chronicle of the activities of the middle party. Its two most important phases--that of the parliament of York of 1318 and of the parliament of Westminster of 1320—are treated separately. The aim is to give a number of instances of the various directions in which individual members of the middle party are seen co-operating. In this way the various members of the party will be discovered.

To a charter of the earl of Surrey granting certain castles and lands to the king on 3 July, 1315, Pembroke and Hereford, Despenser senior, Ralph Basset of Drayton, Crombwell, steward of the household, Despenser junior, Norwich, the treasurer, and a number of justices acted as witnesses[3]. At this time the middle party cannot be said to have existed; but already Pembroke and Hereford were both at court, and the younger Despenser had begun to appear. A subsequent deed of the earl of Surrey to the king made on 25 October, 1317, had as its witnesses the bishops of Winchester, Ely and London, Pembroke and Hereford, Despenser senior, Badlesmere and Crombwell[4]. The bishop of Winchester was still chancellor, the bishop of Ely, a member of the middle party, had already become treasurer[5]; Pembroke and Hereford were still the only earls; the inevitable elder Despenser was still at court; Badlesmere was an important addition; Crombwell, though superseded by the new favourite Montague, still retained his place at court. On 20 February, 1318,

[1] Vide next chapter.
[2] Vide below, pp. 469–472.
[3] *Abbrev. Placit.* p. 324.
[4] *Cal. Close Rolls*, 1313–18, p. 569.
[5] Vide above, pp. 429–430.

the king granted an office in certain forests at the joint request of Damory, Badlesmere and D'Audley[1], a very interesting combination. To a deed of Badlesmere to the king dated 20 March, 1318, there appear as witnesses the archbishop of Canterbury, the bishop of Winchester, chancellor, Pembroke and Hereford, both Despensers, and Montague[2]. The middle party had not yet obtained the office of chancellor for any of its number. Sandale, chancellor, going to treat on the king's behalf with Lancaster, handed over the seal in the presence of the archbishops of Canterbury and Dublin, Hereford, both Despensers, and Badlesmere[3]. Hereford and Badlesmere were becoming as familiar figures at the court as the archbishop of Canterbury and the elder Despenser. The younger Despenser, too, was consolidating his position by constant attendance. The association of Pembroke and Hereford continued, and in January, 1319, they united their prayers to the archbishop of Canterbury to induce him to consecrate Stephen de Gravesend, the newly elected bishop of London[4].

Later in 1319, the bishop of Ely, chancellor, Pembroke and Badlesmere, steward of the household, made a truce with Robert Bruce[5]. The influence of the middle party was by this time supreme. The chief offices of both administration and household were held by chiefs of that party and its greatest asset of all, Pembroke, co-operated with those two heads to secure the truce. The original commission to treat had included one who was already an almost equally potent force, the younger Despenser[6]. Though he held no such definite connection with the middle party as did the steward of the household he acted with them and owed his office to them. It is interesting to note that the commission to treat with the Scots was made by "king and council[7]." In January, 1320, Pembroke, Despenser junior, and Badlesmere jointly acted at the exchequer as the mainpernors of the executors of the late bishop of Winchester[8]. In June of that year in the king's palace at Westminster in the presence of the archbishop of Canterbury, the bishop of Exeter, treasurer, the bishop of London, Pembroke, Hereford, Despenser junior, certain barons of the exchequer and justices of the bench, the king ordered the seals used in England when he had been in France to be carried before

[1] *Cal. Pat. Rolls*, 1317–21, p. 109. [2] *Cal. Close Rolls*, 1313–18, p. 607.
[3] Ibid. p. 619.
[4] Camd. Soc., *Doc. illustr. Hist. of St Paul's*, p. 49.
[5] *Cal. Doc. Scotl.* vol. III, pp. 129–130.
[6] *Cal. Pat. Rolls*, 1317–21, p. 414. [7] Ibid.
[8] K. R. Mem. Roll, no. 93, m. 109. L. T. R. Mem. Roll, no. 90, Manu. Hill. m. 1.

them and they were there broken[1]. There had been by this time a slight re-arrangement of offices; but the presence of Pembroke and Hereford shows that the middle party was still dominant. These brief notices of some of the formal gatherings of the period 1315–20 show that members of the middle party were constantly about the court; often they were in the majority, sometimes every person present was attached to that party.

It was not in formal matters only that the middle party was predominant during this period. It had captured the administrative offices, and in 1318 obtained the two important household offices for its nominees. In the more detailed work of administration the middle party was supreme. Pembroke again took a share in the administration though it was no longer necessary for him to take such a part as in the years 1312–13. He could now work through his friends in office. The king still relied upon his advice, and frequently sought it; while Pembroke took part in various spheres of administration such as the council and the exchequer. Sometimes he acted alone, sometimes in conjunction with one or more of his associates of the middle party. In March, 1319, the king sent, under his privy seal, certain letters to Pembroke, relating to the payment of debts to the Bardi, so that the latter might the more easily obey the royal commands, orders to like effect being sent to the exchequer, which was to aid the merchants[2]. In July of the same year, the newly appointed master moneyer and the new officer for the mint at Canterbury took their oath at the exchequer before the treasurer and barons in Pembroke's presence[3]. The officer for the mint at Canterbury had been appointed by the assent of the treasurer, barons and Pembroke[4]. With Badlesmere and the earl marshal, he went as a solemn deputation to a convocation of the clergy at London seeking aid for the Scottish war[5], and during the Michaelmas term of 1319, the influence of Pembroke and Badlesmere is very visible on the issue roll[6]. On 22 February, 1320, Pembroke was again at the exchequer. He was present when the Bardi handed over two crowns to the chamberlains of the exchequer[7].

When the king on 24 February, 1320, intended going abroad Pembroke was appointed the keeper of the realm during his absence[8].

[1] K. R. Mem. Roll, no. 93, m. 92. L. T. R. Mem. Roll, no. 90, Trin. Rec. m. 9 d.
[2] Anc. Corresp. vol. XLIX, no. 47.
[3] K. R. Mem. Roll, no. 92, Trin. Rec. m. 10. L. T. R. Mem. Roll no. 89, m. 35 d.
[4] Ibid. [5] *Reg. R. de Baldock* (Cantab. and York Soc.), p. 207.
[6] Issue Roll, no. 189 passim. [7] K. R. Mem. Roll, no. 93, m. 77.
[8] *Cal. Pat. Rolls*, 1317–21, p. 425.

Though the writ of appointment was surrendered and cancelled, because the king did not on that occasion go abroad[1], he acted on it. On 1 March, he sent under the privy seal to Norwich, chief baron of the exchequer, a letter from Mortimer, justice of Ireland, in which he was ordered to make full advisement concerning the matter contained therein with the earl of Pembroke, keeper of England, the chancellor and other good men of the council[2]. As keeper of the realm, Pembroke naturally had an all-important part in administration, and the bishop of Norwich, chancellor, was on 7 March ordered to carry out what he bade him on the king's behalf[3]. On 4 June he was again appointed keeper of the realm[4] and took an increasing part in administration. He was ordered to summon the council and settle business there[5]. At the king's command three serjeants-at-arms stayed in his company, their fees being paid at the exchequer[6]. Pembroke asked the chancellor to appoint his nominee to the office of receiver of works at Windsor[7]. In August, 1320, Pembroke was asked his advice on the marriage of the king's brother[8]. At this time, Despenser was so well acquainted with Pembroke's intentions that he was able to tell them to the king before the earl's letters were received[9].

When the barons rose against the Despensers in 1321, Pembroke endeavoured to act the part of a mediator, though the unexpected force of the barons compelled him to acquiesce in their plans[10]. Throughout this trying time the king, who had greater need than ever of the earl's help, sent urgent appeals to come to him. On 1 August the king informed the earl that he had a great desire to see him and have his advice, and begged and charged him specially to be at Westminster the following day, promising to send a boat to Lambeth to meet him[11]. On 31 August, after the barons had carried their point and secured the exile of the Despensers, the king sent one of his clerks to Pembroke to tell him certain things[12]. Though Pembroke probably took a greater part in administration than any other single member of the middle party, except, of course, those who obtained offices in the administration, the share that he took may

[1] *Cal. Pat. Rolls*, 1317–21, p. 425.

[2] K. R. Mem. Roll, no. 93, m. 31. L. T. R. Mem. Roll, no. 90, Brev. dir. Pasch. m. 13.

[3] Chan. Warr., File 110/5321.

[4] *Cal. Pat. Rolls*, 1317–21, p. 454.

[5] Anc. Corresp. vol. XLV, no. 193.

[6] Issue Roll, no. 191, m. 5.

[7] Anc. Corresp. vol. XXXVI, no. 18.

[8] Ibid. vol. XLIX, no. 49.

[9] Ibid.

[10] Vide below, p. 479.

[11] Anc. Corresp. vol. XLIX, no. 50.

[12] Ibid. no. 51. Vide App. of Doc. no. 127.

be fairly said to be a characteristic instance of the policy of that party.

Further proofs of the king's regard for Pembroke are found in the grants which he obtained during the years in which the middle party flourished. For remaining with the king he obtained a grant of 500 marks a year. In consideration of this, he obtained the castle and towns of Hertford and Haverford with all appurtenances to him and his heirs[1]. He also obtained grants of the custody of other castles[2], the lands in England of one who had rebelled against the king in Ireland[3] and various hundreds[4]. In May, 1320, he obtained the important office of keeper of the forest south of Trent[5]. He also received many grants of favours. The debts due to him from the wardrobe were paid in the exchequer[6]. His lands were freed from purveyance[7]. His executors were granted free administration of all his movable goods[8]. Free warren in his demesne lands, weekly markets and yearly fairs were granted[9]. His influence at court was further shown by pardons[10] and licences[11] issued at his request, grants[12] and payments[13] made at his instance, and by writs issued on his information[14]. The middle party obtained for Pembroke the important position he had held before the Lancaster revival after Bannockburn. Though his actual part in administration was not as great, his influence was more widely spread and more productive. The middle party gathered round him as a centre and usually acted under his general direction. He owed his position not to his rank as earl nor his influence as a territorial magnate. He was the ablest of the barons of his time and his position was won by his ability. He had the ability of the moderate, though his leanings inclined him more to the royal side than towards the Lancaster faction.

As the two most important events of the history of the middle party have not been dealt with, it may seem a little premature to enter into a discussion of its policy. Inasmuch, however, as the

[1] *Cal. Pat. Rolls*, 1317–21, p. 47 (4 Nov. 1317).

[2] Berkhamstead (*Cal. Pat. Rolls*, 1317–21, p. 46, 1 Nov. 1317). Mitford (ibid. p. 73, 30 Jan. 1318). Cf. also ibid. 1321–24, p. 37.

[3] *Cal. Pat. Rolls*, 1317–21, p. 397 (9 Sept. 1319).

[4] *Cal. Fine Rolls*, 1319–27, p. 3 (4 Aug. 1319).

[5] Ibid. p. 23 (18 May, 1320). The office was subsequently re-granted in full parliament. Vide below, p. 471.

[6] Issue Roll, no. 195, m. 4.

[7] *Rot. Scot.* vol. 1, p. 187.

[8] *Cal. Pat. Rolls*, 1317–21, p. 388.

[9] *Cal. Charter Rolls*, 1300–26, pp. 391, 408, 415, 435.

[10] *Cal. Pat. Rolls*, 1317–21, p. 594. *Cal. Fine Rolls*, 1319–27, p. 183.

[11] *Cal. Pat. Rolls*, 1317–21, p. 594.

[12] *Cal. Charter Rolls*, 1300–26, p. 415.

[13] Issue Roll, no. 183, m. 12.

[14] *Cal. Charter Rolls*, 1300–26, p. 376.

general aims of the party were well marked, and as in the scheme accepted in the parliament of York and in the subsequent history of the party there were foreign elements introduced, the general outlines of policy can be well considered now. Most of the characteristic features of their policy were revealed before the parliament of York, and the common motives which drew together men so different in aim and position had been established. The party had its birth in the failure of the Lancastrian party after Bannockburn, and especially after the parliament of Lincoln. The extremists had defeated their own ends. If it was to be a choice between an oligarchy controlled by Lancaster or by Edward II there were a number of men among the barons who preferred the king. This was not due to conservative instincts, for Lancaster claimed to be resisting innovations. His desire was to re-establish the old order. It was due to the fact that the king had a definitely organised system of government. The administration might, possibly did, require reform. Lancaster had proved that he did not possess the qualities of a reformer.

Between these extremes the "constitutional" party sprang up. Pembroke, the embodiment of caution and moderation, was its spiritual head. The king trusted Pembroke almost implicitly. He had saved him previously from Lancaster. That the royal confidence was reposed in its leader was a great asset to the new party. Badlesmere, reared in the royalist feelings of Gloucester, co-operated with Pembroke. The husbands of the three Gloucester heiresses had nothing to expect from Lancaster and his following, and they formed an additional source of strength. Hereford, weary of the factiousness of Lancaster and not forgetful that he was bound to the royal house by ties of marriage, was a convert of weight. The household officers, Cherleton, chamberlain, his brother Thomas, keeper of the privy seal, Montague, steward, Northburgh, keeper of the wardrobe, were not opposed to the aims of the new party. Finally a number of prelates, the bishops of Ely and Norwich, and in a less degree the bishops of Exeter and Carlisle[1] and others added stability and dignity. The party desired to lead rather than drive the king. They were mindful of the king's executive power. They knew that with the institutional and prohibitive resources he possessed it would be extremely difficult, if not impossible, for any party to force its will upon the king for any length of time against his wish. Since their aims were moderate, this policy of becoming a part of the household system rather

[1] *Reg. J. de Halton* (Canterbury and York Soc.), vol. I. Intro. T. F. Tout, pp. xxvi, xxvii.

than destroying it was all the more easy to achieve. From within his own court they ruled the king. From the administrative offices they were able to direct the course of the administrative departments. From the council they were able to exercise a general supervision over administration. Since they were in the household there was no room for a party to challenge their influence and to work against them. With all these advantages the possibility of success was considerable. There was no need for them to fear any disturbing factor from king, court, household or administration. The only disturbing factor was Lancaster. It was well nigh useless to hope to conciliate him. It might be possible to remove grounds upon which he could base objection. The endeavours in these directions found expression in the Treaty of Leake and the parliament of York.

The effect of the aim and activity of the middle party upon the king was not serious. He had no deep objection to genuine and sincere reform of the household and administration. Interference with his personal affairs, the murder of his greatest friend, the removal of his companions—to these he objected with all his strength. The middle party attempted to do none of these things. The king's friends and companions were in fact the most substantial part of that party. Under their easy guidance the king was induced to hear reason. Efficient administration was as much the king's desire as that of the baronial opposition. Efficient administration forced upon him at the cost of his personal dignity and loss of independence of action he considered too dearly bought and so resolutely opposed it. When the king's feelings were always respected and when reformers appeared as friends the whole position was altered entirely. The middle party never imposed a burdensome control or restriction upon the king. Its members were his friends and throughout acted as his friends. Thus while the king lost no rights, the middle party was able to exercise a preponderant control over the administration. It is true that this system was not without its weaknesses. Ultimately it was entirely dependent upon the king's will, to resist which the middle party could have resorted only to force. Still as long as they had the king's goodwill they were able to achieve something. The greatest danger of all lay in the possibility of a new favourite arising who would place his own interests before those of the king and administration. Already Hugh le Despenser the son was displacing Roger Damory.

CHAPTER VI

THE EXPERIMENTS (*cont.*)

(v) *The Parliament of York*, 1318

The general plan of operation of the middle party has been illustrated by the object with which the leaders gathered their supporters, and by the normal activity of the party during and after its formation. In the parliament of York the work of the middle party is seen in progress with certain outside influences acting upon it. For in that parliament and especially in the arrangements antecedent to it Lancaster took an effective part. Still the scheme adopted in 1318 was the result of the activities of the middle party, and the success the baronial opposition attained then was at basis their victory. For Lancaster, who during the interval between the parliaments of Lincoln in 1316 and York in 1318 had been a source of endless trouble, was quieted. He was skilfully superseded by Pembroke and his allies.

The pacification which had been made between the king and Lancaster in September, 1317[1], in the execution of which Pembroke and Hereford are first found in intimate political association[2], had included the promise of a parliament which was to meet on 27 January, 1318[3]. The long and intricate negotiations which followed this pacification gave the middle party an opportunity of formulating their schemes more definitely and of putting their aims to the test of practice. On 4 January the meeting of the parliament was postponed until 12 March[4]. The king's supporters feared the result of a parliament in which both king and Lancaster would appear in arms[5]. They thought it better that persons should mediate for a final settlement and then after settlement a parliament could be held more fittingly[6]. In the adoption of this course the middle party probably had a decisive

[1] *Auct. Malm.* p. 230.
[2] Vide above, p. 436.
[3] *Auct. Malm.* p. 230. *Parl. Writs*, vol. II, Pt ii, p. 171.
[4] *Parl. Writs*, vol. II, Pt ii, p. 177.
[5] *Auct. Malm.* p. 233.
[6] Ibid.

voice. They wished to eliminate risk of conflict, and thought that by mediation their ends could be better secured.

Arrangements were accordingly made for a meeting at Leicester[1]. In April the archbishop of Canterbury, the bishops of Norwich, Chichester, Winchester, Llandaff and Hereford, the earls of Pembroke and Hereford, various barons, William de Bereford and Walter de Norwich met at Leicester[2]. The subsequent course of events is confusing. One chronicler states that these met Lancaster's counsellors to treat on various matters[3], another mentions Lancaster amongst those present[4]. Another states that certain articles were discussed and agreed upon at Leicester between Lancaster and the clergy, and were afterwards ordained and confirmed at London by the cardinals, the archbishops of Canterbury and Dublin, and other prelates of the province of Canterbury, and were subsequently returned to the earl at his castle of Tutbury by the bishops of Norwich and Ely[5]. It is certain that the bishop of Winchester was going to Leicester on 29 March[6], and the bishop of Ely also acted as messenger to the earl and on 4 August reached Leicester, being prevented by illness from going further[7]. The articles of agreement incorporated in *Knighton*, which appear to be quite genuine, are of great importance. These articles seem to be those reached by the meeting of prelates and barons at Leicester, which were returned to Lancaster as amended or approved by more formal assembly at London, or probably after their acceptance by the king. The bishops of Ely and Norwich, who submitted them to the earl anew, were royal commissioners.

The negotiations of which these articles were a result supply a valuable commentary to the Ordinances and Lancaster's policy. The first article concerned the gifts given against the Ordinances[8]. All such lands, rents and tenements were to be returned to the king's hands without any regrant. They were to remain there for his profit, and in parliament it was to be decided what could be conveniently given and what could not. To ensure that the lands were not regranted, the earl replied that they should be placed in such suitable custody

[1] *Auct. Malm.* p. 233, mentions this meeting. *Auct. Bridl.* p. 54, called a meeting at Leicester held in April a parliament. *Chron. Knighton*, vol. I, pp. 413–421, gives the proceedings at a meeting at Leicester. These three all appear to refer to one and the same meeting. Ramsay, *Genesis of Lancaster*, vol. I, pp. 90–91, appears to see several meetings at Leicester, one in March and a series in April.

[2] *Auct. Bridl.* p. 54.

[3] *Auct. Malm.* p. 233.

[4] *Auct. Bridl.* p. 54.

[5] *Chron. Knighton*, vol. I, p. 413.

[6] *Parl. Writs*, vol. II, Pt ii, App. p. 122.

[7] *Cal. Close Rolls*, 1313–18, pp. 619–620.

[8] Ordinance 7.

that the full issues should go to the exchequer for the common profit of the king and kingdom, to be spent in defence of the land and not to be wasted or spent to evil purpose as heretofore. The commissioners agreed to this article since it was for the good of the king, the relief of the people and to maintain the peace of the land, but those who had received such gifts were not to suffer harm or punishment for taking them[1]. This did not satisfy the earl. He charged the bishops with bad faith and urged that those who had taken gifts against the Ordinances should be punished in parliament[2]. The commissioners then promised, on the king's behalf, that suitable surety should be made by letters patent for the earl and his followers on coming to the king[3]. The question of surety appeared to touch the earl to the quick. He had done nothing against the king which necessitated such surety. Moreover charters, commissions and letters, which had been made concerning the Ordinances, despite even the excommunication of Winchelsey and all the other prelates, had not been kept. The evil counsellors who surrounded the king were also a source of peril. The earl could not accept such a surety or come to the king while such were near him. Still, he greatly desired to approach the king, and asked the commissioners to ordain such a surety as he could accept[4]. To this the commissioners replied that the prelates and barons who were at Leicester assured the earl and his by their letters[5]. The earl then stated that he was well aware that the prelates and cardinals wished him no harm. It was the deception of the evil counsellors he feared. As for the other magnates who were at Leicester it seemed to him that he could not place much trust in them. Some of them had since taken a new oath, among other things, the earl was informed, to maintain those who gave evil counsel to the king in disinheritance of the crown[6]. The bishops had their answer to this objection: they had made surety to the earl by their letters and by their oaths made privately to him. The surety was full and was protected by the sentence of excommunication of the cardinals. From those whom he suspected, the earl wished to have no surety. The bishops pointed out to the earl that those he suspected would be in parliament the same time as the bishops. Moreover it seemed to them that those suspected should come as men to be punished by award of the peers in parliament, according to the trespass they had made against the

[1] *Chron. Knighton*, vol. I. pp. 413–414.
[2] Ibid. pp. 414–415. Cf. *Auct. Bridl.* p. 54.
[3] *Chron. Knighton*, vol. I, p. 415. [4] Ibid. p. 416. [5] Ibid. [6] Ibid. p. 417.

Ordinances[1]. The bishops then suggested that it was necessary that the king and the earl should meet at a place and time suitable to the king and that the earl on his arrival should do to the king, as to his liege lord, due reverence and obedience as was agreed by the prelates, earls and barons. The earl claimed some share in the determination of the place. It should be good and suitable and above suspicion, as had been agreed at Leicester. As regards due reverence and obeisance, the earl had not heard of anything for which he should make obeisance, but he was prepared to do the reverence and honour to the king which he owed him as his liege man[2]. The question of the earl's safe conduct and surety was further discussed at length, Lancaster referring again to the question of evil counsellors, the relative Ordinance being quoted[3].

The basis of the earl's demand throughout all the negotiations was that the Ordinances should obtain the fullest observance[4]. The removal of evil counsellors, an old complaint, was also revived as was the cry for suitable counsellors[5]. Despenser and his son were likely to prove an obstacle to settlement; Lancaster offered to retain both with a retinue of 200 lances for the term of their lives[6]. Lancaster was obdurate on one point. His quarrel with the earl of Warenne for the abduction of his wife was excepted from the terms of settlement[7].

The parliament which had been postponed to March[8] was further adjourned to 19 June[9], so that the negotiations pending could resolve themselves into a settlement. In June an advance of the Scots into Yorkshire caused the countermanding of the parliament[10]. Early in the month of June, as if to reassure the people, the king accompanied by the archbishop, bishops, earls and barons went to St Paul's and there the bishop of Norwich announced that the king wished to cling to and direct himself in everything by the council and by aid of his earls and barons[11]. By 31 July, 1318, the negotiations appear to have taken a turn for the better, for a pardon was issued to all adherents of Lancaster, excepting those who had participated in the attack upon the cardinal[12]. The pacification was sealed by the Treaty of Leake.

The king with the assent of many magnates and others of his

[1] *Chron. Knighton*, vol. I, pp. 417–418.
[2] Ibid. pp. 418–419. [3] Ibid. pp. 419–421. [4] *Auct. Malm.* p. 233.
[5] *Auct. Bridl.* p. 54. [6] Ibid. p. 55. [7] *Auct. Malm.* p. 233.
[8] Vide above, p. 444. [9] *Parl. Writs*, vol. II, Pt. ii, p. 178. [10] Ibid. 181.
[11] *Ann. Paul.* p. 282. *Flores Hist.* vol. III, p. 184.
[12] *Cal. Pat. Rolls*, 1317–21, p. 199.

council had sent certain prelates, earls and barons from Northampton to the earl of Lancaster to treat with him. The embassy had consisted of the archbishop of Dublin, the bishops of Norwich, Ely and Chichester, the earls of Pembroke and Arundel, Roger de Mortimer, John de Somery, Batholomew de Badlesmere, Ralph Basset and John Botetourte[1], an embassy containing a representative gathering of members of the middle party. It was agreed between them that the bishops of Norwich, Chichester, Ely, Salisbury, St David's, Carlisle, Hereford, and Worcester, the earls of Pembroke, Richmond, Hereford and Arundel, Hugh de Courtney, Roger de Mortimer, John de Segrave, John de Grey, and one of Lancaster's bannerets, to be nominated by him, should remain with the king for a quarter of a year, until his next parliament. Two bishops, one earl, one baron and Lancaster's banneret were to remain constantly with the king. All important matters which could and ought to be done without parliament were to be done by the assent of the committee. If they were done in any other manner they were to be held as evil and redressed in parliament by the award of the peers. All suitable matters were to be redressed by them. From amongst them and others those who ought to stay with the king by quarters were to be chosen in the parliament. The prelates, earls and barons, who had entered into this agreement, undertook, with the will and assent of the king, that he would make release and acquittance to Lancaster, and his men and retinues, of all manner of felonies and trespasses made against the king's peace before 25 July, 1318. The charters of release and acquittance which were to be made were to be simple and without condition, and if better security could be found for them it was to be made at the next parliament, and affirmed there before king and baronage. Lancaster, on his part, granted that he would make release and acquittance to all those who adhered to the king who demanded it for trespass done against his person. This was to be done as soon as the promises were confirmed. He promised that he would not make suit of felony against any of them from the time when they should receive his letters. He saved to himself all the quarrels, actions, and suits which he had against the earl of Warenne, and all those who had assented to and sided with the felonies and trespasses which Warenne had done him against the king's peace.

[1] The indenture made is printed in Cole, *Doc. illustr. Eng. Hist. in 13th and 14th Cent.* pp. 1–2 Cf. also *Cal. Close Rolls*, 1318–23, pp. 112–113; *Foedera*, vol. II, p. 370; *Rot. Parl.* vol. I, pp. 453–4; *Parl. Writs*, vol. II, Pt i, pp. 214–215. The indenture is preserved in Exch. Misc. 4/7 and is sealed with the king's privy seal.

The Ordinances were to be observed and kept as contained under the great seal. This agreement too was to be kept in all points[1]. The agreement was drawn up in the form of an indenture, the prelates, earls and barons sealing one part and Lancaster the other, the date being 9 August[2].

This sealing was the first great triumph of the middle party. Already in the midst of the negotiations with Lancaster, Sandale had been made to surrender the seal which had been obtained for Hothum, bishop of Ely[3], who was already treasurer and, as the grants made to him show, firmly establishing himself in the royal favour. The office of treasurer was given to Master John Walwayn, escheator south of Trent, who was intimately associated with Hereford[4]. Now a number of the middle party, acting as the king's representatives, had treated with Lancaster and obtained his acquiescence to a scheme which sought to ensure permanence to a committee to control the king, the committee containing a majority of members of the middle party It is true that Lancaster stood out in a position of pre-eminence in the negotiations. The treaty was made by the prelates, earls and barons acting with the king's assent on one side, and by Lancaster acting entirely alone on the other. He made the agreement as an almost independent power. The effect of the agreement was to diminish seriously his position and importance. The control of baronial policy was passing from him to the middle party. This indenture set the seal to that transfer of power. Lancaster could hardly have blinded himself to the true state of affairs. By this time the middle party was too important to be ignored. Their victory must have been all the more bitter to Lancaster as it was secured by the very weapons he had wielded so clumsily. For the council appointed to be with the king until the approaching parliament could have found little favour in his eyes. It consisted of the bishops of Ely and Worcester, Pembroke and John de Segrave[5].

The agreement had still to be confirmed in parliament. Before parliament met the personal reconciliation of Edward and Lancaster had taken place. On 14 August the king and earl met at Loughborough and were reconciled to all outward appearances[6]. As a

[1] Cole, *Doc. illustr. Eng. Hist. in 13th and 14th Cent.* pp. 1–2. *Cal. Close Rolls*, 1318–23, pp. 112–113.

[2] Ibid [3] Ibid. 1313–18, p. 619 (11 June, 1318).

[4] Vide above, pp. 355–6.

[5] Cole, *Doc. illustr. Eng. Hist. in 13th and 14th Cent.* p. 13.

[6] *Ann. Paul.* p. 283. *Auct. Bridl.* p. 55. *Chron. Murimuth*, p. 29. *Le Livere de Reis de Brit.* p. 334.

sign of his goodwill the earl entertained the king's friends, even Damory, though Despenser the elder and Warenne he still refused to admit to his grace[1]. Parliament was eventually held at York commencing on 20 October, 1318, and there the whole matter came up again.

This parliament[2] was without exception the most important gathering held during the reign. After a recital of some important matters, the roll of parliament proceeded to give a list of those "qui devoient ordiner les primers poyntz qe sont a treter et parler en parlement sil pleise a nostre seignur le Roi[3]." The list is useful inasmuch as it gives the names of the prelates, earls and barons who were present. The two archbishops were there with the bishop of Ely, chancellor, and the bishops of Norwich, Coventry, Winchester, Worcester, Salisbury, Exeter, Bath, Durham, Carlisle and one other[4]. These with the other bishops when they should come were to ordain on these matters. Lancaster headed the list of earls, which included the earl Marshal, Richmond, Pembroke, Hereford, Arundel, Athol and Angus, with the name of Ralph de Monthemer[5] ending the list, on account of his previous association with the earldom of Gloucester. The list of barons[6] was headed by Despenser the son, and Badlesmere, and included the two Mortimers, Segrave, Courtney, Holand, Somery, Basset and Botetourte[7]. Walter de Norwich found a place among the list of barons[8] and not, as might be expected, among the officials. Significant absentees from the parliament were Warenne and Despenser senior. Of even greater interest than the list of prelates, earls and barons was that of the officials and clerks present. The list of officials was headed by Walwayn, treasurer, and after his name came those of the dean of York, Henry le Scrope, chief justice of king's bench, Northburgh, keeper of the wardrobe, Ayremynne, keeper of the rolls of chancery, Spigurnel, justice of king's bench, Master Thomas de Cherleton, keeper of the privy seal, Gilbert de Toudeby, a king's serjeant, Richard de Ayremynne, a clerk of chancery, Michael de Meldon[9], Lancaster's steward;

[1] *Auct. Malm.* p. 236.

[2] The roll of this parliament was omitted from *Rot. Parl.* and subsequently printed by Cole in *Doc. illustr. Eng. Hist. in 13th and 14th Cent.* pp. 1–46.

[3] Cole, *Doc. illustr. Eng. Hist. in 13th and 14th Cent.* p. 11.

[4] The roll is mutilated here.

[5] Cole, *Doc. illustr. Eng. Hist. in 13th and 14th Cent.* p. 11.

[6] Twenty-three barons composed the list.

[7] Cole, *Doc. illustr. Eng. Hist. in 13th and 14th Cent.* p. 11

[8] Ibid.

[9] Michael de Meldon has been seen before acting as the representative of the earl of Lancaster. In the disturbances resulting from the murder of Gavaston

Roger Beler, already at court, and Geoffrey le Scrope and John de Stonore, king's serjeants, completed the number of the officials who were present[1].

It was first agreed that the points of Magna Carta and the Ordinances should be treated and that they should be read before those assembled. Accordingly Magna Carta was read before them[2]. It was then agreed that Norwich, William de Ayremynne and Michael de Meldon (probably acting as Lancaster's representative) should be charged with the enrolment of the reply which the king made to the petition presented by the prelates, earls and barons concerning the council of the prelates, earls and barons which was to be by the king for quarters according to the form demanded[3]. The archbishop of York and Hereford were sent to the king with the petition[4]. Additions were made to the names of the committee as found in the Treaty of Leake[5]. To the bishops were added by new nomination the bishops of Winchester and Coventry; to the barons there were added Despenser junior, Badlesmere, Mortimer of Chirk, Martin, Somery, Gifford and Botetourte[6].

The assembled prelates, earls and barons next set about the appointment of a committee to make arrangements for the amendment of the household. Hereford, Badlesmere, Mortimer of Wigmore, Somery and Norwich were nominated. To them the king added the archbishop of York and the bishops of Ely and Norwich. These with Hereford and the other four nominated with him the king assigned to perform the matters relating to his household[7].

There still remained the appointment of the committees to act as auditors of petitions. To hear and reply to the petitions of England, Ireland and Wales the bishops of Winchester, Worcester and Carlisle together with Courtney, Martin, Botetourte, Bardelby, Henry de Clif, Toudeby, Geoffrey le Scrope, and Beler were assigned[8]. These summoned to their assistance as in good manner they could summon for this purpose Walter de Norwich and Henry le Scrope[9].

he was continually associated with the barons. The London authorities were ordered not to admit him into the city (*Cal. Close Rolls*, 1307–13, p. 481), and safe conducts were issued to him to treat with the king's council about a pacification (*Cal. Pat. Rolls*, 1307–13, pp. 498, 502). In the parliament of York he appears to act as the effective representative of Lancaster.

1 Cole, *Doc. illustr. Eng. Hist. in 13th and 14th Cent.* p. 12.

2 Ibid.

3 Ibid.

4 Ibid.

5 Vide above, p. 448.

6 Cole, *Doc. illustr. Eng. Hist. in 13th and 14th Cent.* p. 12.

7 Ibid.

8 Ibid.

9 Ibid.: "ad istos vocentur domini Walterus de Norwico, Henricus le Scrop cum bono modo ad hoc vocare poterunt."

For the petitions of Gascony there were assigned the bishops of Coventry and Lichfield, Exeter and Bath and Wells, who called to them because it pleased them to do so, Master Richard de Burton[1].

The parliament opened by the assembled prelates, earls and barons, at the king's request, affirming the articles contained in the indenture made at Leake on 9 August, 1318, an enrolment of that indenture being made[2]. The indenture was accordingly read in the presence of all those assembled and the matters contained in it were carefully considered. The prelates, earls and barons agreed, for the honour of the king and the profit of him and his realm, to beg and request him to assent that two bishops, an earl, a baron, with a baron or banneret of Lancaster's company on his behalf and in his name should be constantly near the king by quarters, to execute and counsel in due manner on all the important matters which could and ought to be executed without parliament until subsequently it could be ordained otherwise in parliament so that no such matter should be executed without the counsel and assent of the prelates, earls and others who should thus remain near the king according to the form of the indenture. Such matters as were done otherwise should be held as naught according to the indenture.

The request was made to the king, who replied that he desired to be counselled in all manners resulting in the honour and profit of him and of his kingdom. Considering that at the time when he received the government of his kingdom, he found his land of Scotland in war against him, which war still continued, that since his accession there had been a war made against him in his land of Ireland, and that many other impeachments had happened and were still happening there and elsewhere in his lordship, it seemed to him that he had the more need for greater and more sufficient counsel near him. He therefore agreed, and wished to have near him prelates, earls and barons to counsel him in the form suggested, provided always that his officials should perform their offices as they ought to according to the law and usages of his kingdom. In the matter of the charters of release and acquittance to Lancaster his men and retinues—as was contained in the indenture—the king with the assent of the prelates, earls and barons and commonalty of his realm in parliament granted pardon to the earl and his retinues, the suit of his peace and what pertained to him by reason of his suit of all manner of felonies and trespasses made against his peace until 7 August last and the pardon

[1] Cole, *Doc. illustr. Eng. Hist. in 13th and 14th Cent.* p. 13: "qui ad eos cum eis placuit vocent Magistrum Ricardum de Burton."

[2] Ibid.

of outlawry to those who asked for it if any outlawry had been pronounced against them, before the making of their charters. In this behalf the king commanded the bishop of Ely, chancellor, to make charters simple and without condition under his great seal for Lancaster and for those named in Lancaster's letters to the chancellor. The king wished and granted that the reference in the indenture to the Ordinances should be held and kept in the suggested form. The king, moreover, ordered that all these matters should be enrolled in the rolls of parliament, and that they should be sent to the chancery and enrolled there[1] and thence by writ of great seal to the places of the exchequer and the two benches to be enrolled there[2], and to be held and kept in due form. The transcript of this enrolment was accordingly handed to the chancellor to be entered in the chancery rolls[3].

After the formal acceptance of this indenture, parliament set to work to effect reforms. It was agreed in full parliament by the king and prelates, earls and barons, and expressly ordered by the king that the prelates, earls and barons should meet together to treat and counsel on the other business touching him or his kingdom and to report their counsel, their advice and their action to the king. They accordingly proceeded to do this[4].

The first matter to which they applied themselves was the amendment and the better array of the household. It seemed to them that it would be well to request and counsel the king to be pleased to order amendment. The committee appointed even contained one who had been a most intimate household officer, Melton, archbishop of York[5]. The king agreed to this advice and arrangement. The administrative officials were considered to discover if they were sufficient. If deemed sufficient, with the agreement of the king, they were to be retained in their offices[6]. The treasurer was first considered, though what decision was reached cannot be gathered from the roll of parliament[7]. As Walwayn was succeeded by Sandale, bishop of Winchester, on 16 November, the appointment being *per consilium*[8], it would seem as if the decision was not altogether in

[1] It was enrolled on Close Roll, 12 Ed. II, m. 22 d.

[2] Cf. *Abbrev. Placit.* p. 332.

[3] Cole, *Doc. illustr. Eng. Hist. in 13th and 14th Cent.* pp. 1–3. *Cal. Close Rolls*, 1318–23, pp. 112–114.

[4] Cole, *Doc. illustr. Eng. Hist. in 13th and 14th Cent.* p. 3.

[5] Vide above, pp. 228–9.

[6] Cole, *Doc. illustr. Eng. Hist. in 13th and 14th Cent.* p. 3.

[7] The roll is quite unreadable here with the exception of a few words.

[8] *Cal. Pat. Rolls*, 1317–21, p. 227. K. R. Mem. Roll. no. 92, Rec. Hill. m. 6. L. T. R. Mem. Roll, no. 89, m. 15.

his favour. Moreover, in a commission of the office of escheator made to Walwayn in 1321 the king stated that he was discharged from the office of treasurer "not on account of his demerit but by the importunity of sundry persons[1]." It may therefore be surmised that he was deemed insufficient[2]. The other officers were next reviewed. Among those found to be sufficient were Henry le Scrope, chief justice of king's bench, Bereford, chief justice of common bench, Norwich, chief baron of the exchequer, who were to retain their offices[3]. Next a number of the household offices came up for consideration. The office of steward of the household, the appointment to which was challenged by Lancaster, was bestowed upon Badlesmere[4]. Lancaster challenged in support of claims he imagined his office of steward of England gave him[5]. Montague, whom Badlesmere had succeeded, was replaced by a more important member of the middle party, but no grievance was found against him. In fact the very next item on the roll was his appointment as seneschal of Gascony[6]. Northburgh, keeper of the wardrobe, Ralph de Monthemer and John de Crombwell, keepers of the forests north and south of Trent respectively, Adam de Herwynton, chief clerk of the common bench, were all maintained in their offices, the king agreeing to this and all the members of the committee assenting to it[7]. To the office of escheator north of Trent, Ralph de Crophill was appointed by the king's agreement and the assent of all the committee[8]. It was pleasing to the king, with the assent of all the committee, that Master Thomas de Cherleton should remain clerk of the privy seal[9]. Similarly Gilbert de Wigton was appointed controller of the wardrobe, and Robert de Kendale was considered sufficient to remain in his office as constable of Dover, and Badlesmere as constable of Bristol[10].

Then followed the consideration of one of the most important appointments of all. "Item le Roi sest acorde par consail et a la requeste de grantz qe Monsire Hugh le Despenser le fuiz demoerge son Chamberleyn et ad jurer etcetra[11]." This appointment which

[1] *Cal. Fine Rolls*, 1319–27, p. 78.

[2] He did not lose the royal favour. On 5 Dec. 1318, the king granted him £100 yearly until a competent benefice should be provided for him (Issue Roll, no. 189, m. 6).

[3] Cole, *Doc. illustr. Eng. Hist. in 13th and 14th Cent.* p. 3.

[4] Ibid. This seems like the drift of the mutilated roll.

[5] Vide above, Introduction, pp. 20–22.

[6] Cole, *Doc. illustr. Eng. Hist. in 13th and 14th Cent.* p. 3. Cf. *Foedera*, vol. II, p. 377.

[7] Cole, *Doc. illustr. Eng. Hist. in 13th and 14th Cent.* pp. 3–4.

[8] Ibid. *Cal. Fine Rolls*, 1319–27, p. 380 (25 Nov. 1318).

[9] Cole, *Doc. illustr. Eng. Hist. in 13th and 14th Cent.* p. 4. [10] Ibid. [11] Ibid.

if granted previously could not have been made many months before[1] and which was almost certainly given under the influence of the middle party, was stated in a much stronger form than the other appointments. It was made by the counsel and at the request of the magnates. John de Sapy, justice of Chester, was considered insufficient by the prelates, earls and barons and they requested the king to appoint another in his place. To this the king replied that the appointment rested with his son the earl of Chester and that Sapy had done nothing for which he should be removed and another appointed[2]. He still acted as justice of Chester in July, 1319[3]. But since Sapy was also constable of Beaumaris and sheriff of Anglesey and Carnarvon the king agreed at the request of the magnates that he should be removed from these offices and another sufficient official appointed, and that an inquest should be held concerning him and his bearing in office as of other sheriffs in England, and that such process should be kept and made to him as to others[4]. It was also decided that the underconstable of Beaumaris should be removed on account of the grievous complaints made of him in that parliament and another good and sufficient officer appointed, and that an inquest should be held of him and his conduct, as of sheriffs. By the counsel and inquest of the same magnates, the king agreed that Richard de Cornwall, clerk of markets, should be removed from his office, another good and sufficient officer appointed in his place and that an inquest should be heard concerning him as concerning the sheriffs and the same process held and kept[5]. After going through various local officials, the central administration was returned to and a statement made concerning the barons of the exchequer.

> Item il plest au Roi solonc le conseil a li done en ceste partie qe Barons suffisantz qe puissent ordiner et governer le place de lexchekier a sa droit y soient et noun plus qe ne covenent par la dite place governer[6].

This general statement suggests an inability or an unwillingness on the part of those who were considering the question of officials to decide on this matter off-hand. The decision was accordingly postponed and left to others[7].

After the officials had been passed in review parliament turned its attention to more general matters. Scottish affairs still demanded

[1] Vide above, p. 93.
[2] Cole, *Doc. illustr. Eng. Hist. in 13th and 14th Cent.* p. 4.
[3] *Thirty-first Report Deputy Keeper*, App. p. 237.
[4] Cole, *Doc. illustr. Eng. Hist. in 13th and 14th Cent.* p. 4.
[5] Ibid. [6] Ibid.
[7] Vide below, p. 461.

attention. It was agreed and assented by the prelates, earls and barons that the king should summon his host at Newcastle-on-Tyne for 10 June, 1319[1]. It was similarly agreed and assented that the next parliament should be held within a month of Easter at York or Lincoln, which could be decided between that time and when it was necessary to issue the writs for the summoning of that parliament, and according to the necessities of the time[2]. The fixing of the next parliament was a judicious move which gave the magnates an opportunity of seeing how far the execution of their decisions and of the agreement of Leake had been carried out.

There were various grievances which oppressed the land to which parliament desired to direct the attention of the king. The prelates, earls and barons and the whole commonalty of the realm made various requests. Various statutes had been made by the king's ancestors, which had been confirmed in his time by the Ordinances for making remedy to the people of England, for the serious wrongs and oppressions committed by sheriffs and bailiffs within franchises and without. The sheriffs and bailiffs did not cease for such from doing wrong but grieved the people more boldly. The baronage and the commonalty of the people accordingly begged the king that all the sheriffs north and south of Trent, except the sheriffs of Northumberland, Westmorland and Cumberland[3], should be removed and other suitable men put in their places, who had not previously been sheriffs, and that they should have sufficient land in the counties in which they were to act[4]. Inquirers were to be assigned to hear and determine the complaints which the people made of the sheriffs, the under-sheriffs and all their officials who had held office during the king's reign. The under-escheators, the officials of the green wax and the king's other bailiffs north and south of Trent, excepting the same three counties, were also to be removed and inquiry by loyal men made into their conduct, as into that of the sheriffs. In this manner the people would be greatly comforted and the king would obtain great profit and honour. Those officials found by inquest to have conducted themselves well and loyally in all matters and in their offices were to be reinstated if they had the requisite landed position[5]. To this request the king gave his assent[6].

[1] Cole, *Doc. illustr. Eng. Hist. in 13th and 14th Cent.* p. 4. [2] Ibid.

[3] An exception probably due to the pressure from Scotland.

[4] According to the Stat. of Lincoln, 9 Ed. II, § 2 (*Stat. of Realm*, vol. I, p. 174). Vide below, pp. 524–6.

[5] Cole, *Doc. illustr. Eng. Hist. in 13th and 14th Cent.* pp. 6–7.

[6] Ibid. p. 7: "Le Roi est assentu."

The prelates, earls and barons too had a complaint and request to make on their own behalf about scutage. The prelates, earls and barons and other tenants, who held their counties, baronies, and other tenements in chief from the king, on finding a certain number of men-at-arms in his war as the service due to him, showed the king that the service had been for them and all their tenants and that for such service they and their ancestors had been accustomed to have a chancery writ to the sheriffs to levy scutage from their tenants. Now a new practice had arisen. The king's ministers by order of the treasurer and barons of the exchequer distrained these tenants to pay 40*s*. to the king for each fee which they held of them. But they would not allow to the tenants-in-chief release of their services which they were still forced to do. They therefore begged the king to order the treasurer and barons of the exchequer to cease to distrain the tenants for that reason, and that such a demand should not be made and that they should have their scutage as accustomed[1]. To this the king did not return an immediate answer. The matter was delayed for deliberation[2]. There was also another sectional request which the barons had to make on the subject of scutage. They could only levy scutage from the tenants by virtue of a royal writ empowering them to do so[3]. The prelates, earls and barons accordingly begged the king for such permission. They asked in the first place that a scutage due in the time of Edward I should be pardoned them; they undertaking to pardon what was due to them. They asked the king to grant them scutage of two marks to be levied that year for the services done at Roxburgh and the following year to have a scutage of two marks for their services when summoned to Berwick for the Scottish war[4]. To these requests the king assented[5].

There was another serious complaint made concerning the local administration. Various oppressions and extortions were made daily from the people by the men who held counties, wapentakes, tithings and other bailiwicks at farm, rendering to the sheriffs a greater sum yearly for those offices beyond the fixed farm which the sheriffs were charged at the exchequer in their accounts. In order to obtain the high farms which they had to pay for their offices and the profits which they made above their farms, they extorted from the people

[1] Cole, *Doc. illustr. Eng. Hist. in 13th and 14th Cent.* p. 7.

[2] Ibid.: "Ceste requeste demoertz sur deliberacion."

[3] Pollock and Maitland, *Hist. of Engl. Law*, pp. 271–4.

[4] Cole, *Doc. illustr. Eng. Hist. in 13th and 14th Cent.* p. 7.

[5] Ibid.: "Le Roi sest assentu."

and impoverished them to make themselves rich, the king not sharing in the profit. On this account the baronage together with the common people begged the king to agree that no sheriff should let to anyone to farm hundreds, wapentakes, tithings, or other offices at a higher farm than came to the king's profit by answer to the exchequer nor otherwise than they were let out at the time of the coronation of Henry III. No holder of a hundred, wapentake, tithing or other office, should have under him in his office more men, on horse or foot, riding or going at the expense of the people otherwise than had been at the coronation of Henry III. If a sheriff or his officers did otherwise they asked that it should be ordained by the king that they should be punished on this account in due manner. If anyone in hundreds, wapentakes, tithings or other offices for term of life or in other manner had done these things, since the time of the Ordinances, the offices should be taken into the king's hand and the sheriffs made to answer for those hundreds, wapentakes, tithings or other offices at the exchequer year by year in their accounts as had been done[1]. The king gave his assent to this request[2].

An important part of the activities of this parliament was concerned with the consideration of gifts which had been made to various people. These were not treated in the narrow spirit of obeying implicitly the relative Ordinance, but by judging each case on its merits. Certain lands which had been granted to Oliver de Bordeaux were to remain to him and his heirs for good service in the form granted by the king. The grant which had been made to him of 100 marks to be received yearly from the exchequer until the king should grant him land to the yearly value of 100 marks, and the gifts and grants made to him since the parliament of Lincoln were cancelled[3]. John de Knokyn was to retain, in the form granted by the king, the land of Ellesmere but other gifts and grants since the parliament of Lincoln were disallowed[4]. About Montague, for his services to Edward I and for those rendered and to be rendered to Edward II, it was agreed that the king's grants to provide him with lands to the value of 200 marks "est bien a suffrir qil estoise a terme de sa vie et estre ceo eit lx li de terre en fee[5]." Of the lands granted to Beaumont in England and Gascony, it seemed to the council, he should hold some, and that the other gifts made should be repealed

[1] Cole, *Doc. illustr. Eng. Hist. in 13th and 14th Cent.* p. 7.
[2] Ibid.: "Le Roi sest assentu."
[3] Ibid. p. 9. This section of the roll was entitled "Des douns etcetera."
[4] Ibid. [5] Ibid.

and vacated[1]. The castle and land of Builth granted to Hereford in September, 1317[2], came up for review. The earl, apparently, claimed to have other right to that land beside the royal grant. Moreover it seemed that the land was of greater value than £112, the sum at which it was assigned. It therefore seemed to the council that the king should inform himself of the earl's right and of his reason, if any, and also that the true value of the land should be found between that time and the next parliament and the matter should be decided by the good advisement of all[3]. Grants to Despenser the son, Damory and D'Audley were considered amongst others[4]. Though a considerable number of the grants made were allowed, full countenance to disobedience of the Ordinances was not to be permitted. It was accordingly laid down in the following form:

> Et fait a remembrer qe acorde est et assentu par le Roi et les autres grantz du counseil qe toutes persones avant nomez qe avant eurent les douns desusdit du grant le Roi ove fee et avoesons par cest assent et acorde les eient expressez a ore par novel fait[5].

Closely connected with this revision of grants was a grant agreed upon in parliament. It was agreed that the bishop of Ely, chancellor, should have the issues of the great seal until the end of the next parliament to meet the expenses to which he was put and by reason of his office. It was also agreed by the king and the other magnates that the king should make a grant to him of the issues during the holding of that parliament[6].

A large number of petitions were presented to this parliament, many of them being of the first importance. Some, such as Langton's lament[7], were of interest. Others dealt with important matters such as the Ordinances[8]. Certain petitions were handed to William de Ayremynne, who had been assigned with others to treat of the matters touching the Flemish and English[9]. Various petitions from clerics were also to be handed over to him[10]. The parliament too in the Statute of York passed useful legislation[11]. This statute was indeed of sufficient importance to be noticed by the chronicler[12], but the real importance to the chronicler of the parliament of York was the scheme confirmed then, and its execution. The appointment of a council to control the king's action, a part of which was to

[1] Cole, *Doc. illustr. Eng. Hist. in 13th and 14th Cent.* p. 10.
[2] *Cal. Charter Rolls*, 1300–26, p. 367 (20 Sept. 1317).
[3] Cole, *Doc. illustr. Eng. Hist. in 13th and 14th Cent.* p. 10.
[4] Ibid. pp. 9–10.
[5] Ibid. p. 10.
[6] Ibid.
[7] Ibid. pp. 4–5.
[8] Ibid. pp. 30–31, 33.
[9] Ibid. p. 27
[10] Ibid. p. 28.
[11] *Stat. of Realm* vol. I, pp. 177–9.
[12] *Auct. Bridl.* p. 56.

be always with him, was noticed, the reason for such a council being found in the necessity of fulfilling the Ordinances which forbade grants by the king or the undertaking of any great or weighty matter without the assent of the barons in parliament[1]. Importance too was attached to the change of ministry which the parliament effected, the steward, treasurer, chamberlain and all sheriffs being removed[2]. The commission for hearing complaints against the king's ministers was commended[3]. The charters of pardon made to Lancaster and his followers for all trespasses and outlawries were also given an importance[4]. The whole result of the parliament had been so salutary that the chronicler saw an omen in the fact that such a visible improvement had taken place in every sphere in the twelfth year of the king's reign. The pope had taken measures against the Scots; there had been a good omen in Ireland in the fall of Edward Bruce; there had been a cessation of the dearth; there was peace between king and earl; and the bad counsellors had been dismissed. Perhaps the prosperity of Edward's reign was at last to begin[5].

Before the general discussion of the scheme and work of the parliament of York is started, the execution of the orders of that parliament and the parliament to be held at York at Easter, 1319, have to be noticed briefly. When the parliament was still sitting many writs under the great seal giving effect to its orders and recommendations had been issued. On 22 October, Lancaster, with the assent of parliament, had been pardoned all felonies and trespasses committed before 7 August[6]. In accordance with the agreement, he sent the chancellor his letters containing the names of his followers and adherents in the form: "Nous vous enuoioms le noun dun vallet de nostre retenaunz Johan de Denum lequel sire nous vous prioms qe vous lui voillez faire auoir chartre nostre seigneur le Roi tiel come est acorde a ceste parlement Deuerwyk[7]." Between 1 and 16 November, 188 of his adherents received their charters made "by the king and council[8]."

Letters patent were made for the grants of land which had been confirmed in parliament[9]. The escheator was ordered to allow

[1] *Auct. Malm.* pp. 236–7.
[2] *Auct. Bridl.* p. 56.
[3] *Auct. Malm.* pp. 238–9.
[4] *Ann. Paul.* p. 284. *Auct. Bridl.* p. 56.
[5] *Auct. Malm.* pp. 237–8.
[6] *Cal. Pat. Rolls*, 1317–21, p. 227: "By King."
[7] Chan. Warr., File 1705, contains 34 such letters.
[8] *Cal. Pat. Rolls*, 1317–21, pp. 233–5. Cf. *Abbrev. Placit.* p. 333.
[9] Cf. *Cal. Pat. Rolls*, 1317–21, pp. 248. *Cal. Charter Rolls*, 1300–26, pp. 297–8 399, 403.

Damory to hold as before the parliament, the wardship of the lands late of Robert de Willoughby, until the next parliament when it was to be ordained what should be done concerning them[1]. Grants by the king were made under the great seal "by the king and petition of council" or "by king and council[2]." The king made a grant of a royal manor immediately outside the city of Oxford with its appurtenances to the Carmelite friars, the grant being made "in fulfilment of a vow made by the king when in danger and with the assent of the parliament at York[3]." The king seems to have observed faithfully the letter of the recommendation and promises made in parliament. The case of the appointments was similar. The new escheator north of Trent was appointed[4]. The sheriffs were removed[5]. The recommendation about the barons of the exchequer was carried out. By writ of privy seal or 2 January, 1319, the treasurer was reminded how it was agreed at the parliament that the barons of the exchequer should be sufficient and not more than was necessary to govern that place. He was ordered, if the place was over-staffed, to advise which of the barons might be best suffered to remain, always allowing Robert de Wodehouse and John de Okham, whom the king considered sufficient and necessary for that place, to remain in peace in their stations[6]. These few instances are typical of the way in which the king faithfully put into execution what had been assented to and agreed.

The parliament which had been provided for in 1318 met at York on 6 May, 1319, and lasted until the 25th of that month[7]. The observance which the king had shown to all the injunctions of the previous parliament had in part removed the necessity of such a meeting, though its purpose came out in a petition which the commonalty of Southampton made complaining that the sheriff of that county had not been removed. The treasurer and barons of the exchequer were ordered to remove him and appoint a suitable man in his place[8]. There were, however, a few items left uncompleted from the previous parliament. The land of the value of £100 given to Damory

[1] *Cal. Fine Rolls*, 1307–19, p. 285: "By King and Council."

[2] *Cal. Charter Rolls*, 1300–26, pp. 395, 396, 399, 403.

[3] *Cal. Pat. Rolls*, 1317–21, p. 237 (21 Nov. 1318): "By King and Council on the information of William de Montague."

[4] *Cal. Fine Rolls*, 1307–19, p. 380 (25 Nov. 1318).

[5] P. R. O. Lists and Indexes, *List of Sheriffs*, passim.

[6] K. R. Mem. Roll, no. 92, Brev. dir. m. 18 d. L. T. R. Mem. Roll, no. 89, m. 81. Vide App. of Doc. no. 27. Cf. Madox, *Hist. Exch.* vol. II, p. 61.

[7] *Parl. Writs*, vol. II, Pt ii, pp. 197. 210.

[8] Cole, *Doc. illustr. Eng. Hist. in 13th and 14th Cent.* p. 53.

for his good service at Stirling, and the wardship and marriage of the heir of Robert de Willoughby, parliament in 1318 had decided should remain in his hands until the next parliament. He was to find surety to answer to the king for the issues in the meantime if it was agreed that the wardship should be recovered into the king's hands[1]. In 1319 it was decided in parliament that the wardships and marriages should be sold to Damory for 2000 marks, but he was to retain the issues which had accrued in the meantime[2]. At the parliament of 1318, D'Audley and Margaret his wife, Gavaston's widow, petitioned the king and his council for the earldom of Cornwall and the lands pertaining to it. They claimed that the king had granted Gavaston the earldom before the Ordinances and that the grant had been made with the assent of his council. They pleaded the Great Charter and the Statute of Westminster II in support of their case[3]. The decision upon the petition was given in the parliament of 1319. After it had been fully treated in parliament, it was then recorded by the prelates, earls, barons and whole community of the realm that it was agreed and ordained at another time by them, that all the grants which had been made to Gavaston and his wife should be revoked and annulled, it was therefore agreed that the earldom and all its appurtenances should remain to the king, quit of D'Audley and his wife and of the issue of Gavaston, and that the charters touching the same should be restored to chancery and annulled and that the enrolments in chancery should also be quashed and annulled. This judgment was to be entered on the rolls of parliament and chancery, and from chancery it was to be sent to the exchequer and both benches to be enrolled[4]. This was accordingly done and the necessary writs and warrants were sent[5]. Subsequently, however, with the assent of the parliament, the king granted Margaret certain lands in dower[6].

In the parliament of York in 1319, Lancaster and his supporters would seem to have appeared in force. A charter of Richard Lovel releasing to the prior of Montague all his right in certain lands was witnessed by, amongst others, Lancaster, Holand, William Trussell and Michael de Meldon[7], and a grant of free warren was made at the

[1] Cole, *Doc. illustr. Eng. Hist. in 13th and 14th Cent.* p. 10. Vide above, pp. 460–1.

[2] *Cal. Fine Rolls*, 1307–19, p. 401.

[3] Ibid. p. 49. *Cal. Close Rolls*, 1318–23, p. 143.

[4] Cole, *Doc. illustr. Eng. Hist. in 13th and 14th Cent.* p. 49. *Cal. Close Rolls*, 1318–23, p. 143. Cf. *Cal. Pat. Rolls*, 1317–21, p. 251.

[5] *Cal. Close Rolls*, 1318–23, pp. 143–4. *Abbrev. Placit.* p. 335.

[6] *Cal. Pat. Rolls*, 1317–21, p. 386 (20 July, 1319).

[7] *Abbrev. Placit.* p. 334.

instance of the earl[1]. Still the middle party seem to have maintained its position in administration. Grants of land and honours were again made with the assent of parliament. With the assent of the prelates, earls and barons and the chief men there present, the king gave to John de Birmingham 200 marks yearly from the county of Louth and the title of earl of Louth, the grants being made because he had been captain of the troop that had defeated Edward Bruce[2]. With the assent of the parliament of York, the king granted to Beaumont his reversion of manors and all things in the county and city of Lincoln[3]. Other grants, including some to Damory and Edmund de Woodstock, the king's brother, were made "by the king and council[4]." The king was still acting up to the undertaking he had given parliament in 1318.

The acceptance of the scheme of government, which had been first arranged at Leake on 9 August, 1318, by the king in the parliament of York marked the triumph of the middle party, the whole course of the parliament being a continued series of victories. Those who negotiated with Lancaster at Leake on the king's behalf were almost without exception members or adherents of that party. The standing council which was created to control the king was overwhelmingly inclined to that side. Though it may have pleased Lancaster's vanity to treat with the king and the remainder of the barons as an independent power, his isolation was keeping him away from any share in the control of government. In 1312 the letters patent granted by Pembroke and his associates to Gavaston were to be shown to the king in Lancaster's presence or those he desired. Then the earl had been a real power, and his independence was only duly and necessarily recognised by Pembroke. Since 1312 Lancaster's influence had risen and then declined appreciably. His banneret, who was to serve on the standing council, though he was to be in constant attendance upon the king, could exercise little influence. His position was insignificant when compared with the four who were first elected to serve. Hothum, bishop of Ely, held the highest administrative office; Cobham, bishop of Worcester, was a man of great eminence and learning; John de Segrave was an important baron and had been keeper of the forest north of Trent[5] and keeper of Scotland[6]. The dominating personality was Pembroke, and his influence would

1 *Cal. Charter Rolls*, 1300–26, p. 412.
2 Ibid. p. 408 (12 May, 1319).
3 *Cal. Pat. Rolls*, 1317–21, p. 351 (25 June, 1319).
4 Ibid. pp. 388, 397. *Cal. Charter Rolls*, 1300–26, p. 416.
5 *Cal. Fine Rolls*, 1307–19, p. 17 (appointed 12 March, 1308).
6 *Foedera*, vol. II, p. 106 (appointed 10 April, 1310).

probably have been supreme. In this council of five, Lancaster's banneret would have been impotent.

The scheme was the most workable which had yet been devised to control the king. In the first place it ensured permanence. The standing council was to consist of eight bishops, four earls and four barons with Lancaster's banneret, who for really practical purposes may be almost ignored. Of these, two bishops, one earl and one baron with the banneret were to act as a committee to stay constantly by the king. Four such committees would thus be secured and each was to remain with the king for a period of three months. The subsequent enlargement of the standing council did away with the symmetry of the scheme. The additional members consisting of two bishops and seven barons added an amount of weight and experience. The bishop of Winchester had been treasurer and chancellor and was soon to be chancellor again. The bishop of Coventry was Edward I's experienced treasurer. Amongst the new barons, Martin had been an ordainer, Mortimer of Chirk had been justice of Wales almost throughout the reign. Badlesmere and Despenser were household officials; Botetourte had been connected in a minor capacity with administration. Gifford and Somery were not of outstanding importance. At whose instigation these additional members were appointed is uncertain. Much can be said in favour of the view that they were appointed by the king and much also in support of the contention that the middle party were responsible.

The idea of a standing council removed the weakness which had been so apparent in the scheme of the ordainers, and efficiency was assured by the system of the committee of five. Unfortunately the relations of the committee to the standing council are not explained. It is unlikely that the standing council was to act merely as a reservoir whence succeeding committees could be obtained. Whether when the king acted against the will of the committee or defied them, the matter was to be referred by the committee to the standing council is uncertain. It is equally uncertain what powers, if any, parliament delegated to the standing council or the committees. Their actions were certainly to be subject to the supervision of parliament, but it is not known whether they were to have full interim authority between sessions of parliament. They were to concern themselves mainly with matters of importance, which could and ought to be done without parliament. It is possible that the committee of five merely represented the minimum of the standing council which should always be with the king. The personnel of that minimum would be changed quarterly but it may have been that any other members of the standing council who desired to act might do so at any time.

Efficient as was the scheme, its effectiveness depended entirely upon one thing—the goodwill of the king. With an unwilling king who actively resisted the interference of such a committee or council, the scheme could result in nothing better than chaos and anarchy. The state of the administration would have been worse than ever. The aim of the middle party was to act with the king's goodwill and co-operation. Throughout the parliament of York this aim underlies all their actions. The value of their policy measured by its results was considerable. To obtain these results, their labours towards providing a suitable council to control and restrain the king's actions was as important as the general motive of their policy, to rule with the king's goodwill. The success of the first condition was dependent upon the success of the general aim. The third condition which occasioned their success was contained in the ability they possessed and the opportunity they had to obtain a fair start for their scheme. The history of the parliament of York is the history of the way in which the scheme contained in the Treaty of Leake was put into operation. The theory of the policy of the standing council was put into execution in the parliament of York.

The parliament of York must not be considered as a legislative assembly. Legislation was the most inconsiderable part of its activities. It must not be considered primarily as concerned with the presenting of petitions or with judicial business, though that formed an important part of its work. The parliament of York stands out in importance as being concerned with administrative work. The most important of its activities was its reform of the administration and the machinery it established for maintaining those reforms. Throughout the reign the baronial opposition had been concerned with the reform of the administration. This had been a leading motive in the appointment of the ordainers; it had been one of the supreme objects of the Ordinances. At the parliament of Lincoln, Lancaster had been made the chief of the council so that he might control the administrative power and action of the king. The primary object of the standing council of 1318 was that it should have a salutary effect upon the administration. In the parliament of York it began to exercise its functions in this direction. The reform of the administration seems to have been generally included in the reform of the household which was so constantly urged. That the barons drew no clear distinction between administrative and household officers is apparent in the parliament of York. The officials were being considered to discover whether they should be retained in office as sufficient or removed. Certain judicial and exchequer officers were first considered, then the steward of the household. The next appointment made was the seneschal of Gascony, followed by a consideration of the keeper of the wardrobe. Administrative officials were returned to and the reappointment of a clerk to be keeper of the privy seal considered. It was in fact quite natural that the barons should have failed to recognise any distinction. They were all the king's officials and at one time not very far distant had all been definitely household officials. Moreover the barons claimed to interfere as much with household officials as with administrative.

The administrative activity of the parliament of York is worthy of further consideration. The most important direction in which it displayed itself was in the consideration of the conduct of ministers. The local administration appeared to be in an almost hopeless state of disorder and abuse. With the king's assent a strong line was taken. All the sheriffs were dismissed. Reform was not sufficient. Past grievances must be redressed and inquiry made into the conduct of the dismissed officials. Other abuses in the local administration were considered and redressed. Other officials, such as the clerk of the market, were subjected to a similar inquiry into their conduct. The review made of the officials of the central administration was still more important. Appointments were renewed, insufficient officers removed and even fresh appointments made. The desire throughout was not capricious interference with royal appointments or power to increase the influence of baronage or parliament. It was genuinely a desire to improve the efficiency of administration. When the question of the number of barons necessary for the efficient administration of the exchequer arose, no endeavour was made to lay down any rule as to how many or who should be retained. It was felt that there was insufficient knowledge of the needs of the exchequer and of the capacity of the barons. The execution of the recommendation was left to the king.

Under the normal conditions of baronial opposition it would have been of the utmost danger to have left any reform to depend upon royal execution. It was felt on this occasion that it could be done safely. The king was not now being forced to reform his administration; he was being led to that point gently and skilfully. Thus in the matter of the barons of the exchequer he ordered the treasurer to make suitable arrangements, though he ordered that two barons in whom he was specially interested should be retained. In the circumstances this was the wisest course. Sandale, then treasurer, had held that office on previous occasions and was the most competent person in the kingdom to decide such a matter. Everything the execution of which was left to depend upon the king was effected. The arrangement made for the subsequent parliament which was to meet about Easter the following year, however judiciously planned, was in the circumstances almost useless because unnecessary. The king was willing to put into execution the decisions of the parliament of York because those decisions had been conceived in a moderate way and because the underlying motives were fair and considerate.

The same note of moderation is struck in the references to, and the treatment of, the Ordinances. It had been a condition in the Treaty of Leake that the Ordinances should be observed as issued under the great seal. The king in the parliament of York granted that they should be observed in that form. Immediately parliament had met it had been agreed that the Ordinances should be treated, and that, together with Magna Carta, they should be read to the assembly. It was the reading of the Great Charter alone that was recorded in the parliament roll. In the administrative work of the parliament, though there was a general observance of the Ordinances, there was no strict adhesion to every letter. This comes out especially in the manner and spirit in which the king's grants of lands to various persons were considered. Most of the persons were allowed to retain a certain amount of what had been granted, though a considerable number of grants were revoked and cancelled. This was travelling very far from Lancaster's demand made but a few months before that those who had accepted grants from the king should be punished. This broad interpretation of the Ordinances was due partly to consideration for the king and partly to expediency. On the one hand, there was no desire to push the king to extremity or to irritate him by strict enforcement of the Ordinances. On the other hand, enforcement of the Ordinances concerning grants would have been most inexpedient, as amongst those whose grants came up for consideration were Hereford, Despenser the son, Damory, D'Audley, Montague and other pillars of the middle party.

The position of the king throughout this time was one of security and ease. The middle party saved him from Lancaster. His interests and feelings were considered, his personal dignity protected, and his prerogative unimpaired. Those who surrounded him were there of his own choice. The officials he had were agreeable to him.

He was relieved of much of the burden of administration without being in danger of being insulted or having his powers curbed. If the composition of the various bodies, the standing council, for instance, is considered it will be seen that the members were nearly all personally acceptable to the king. The committee to amend his household as appointed by parliament consisted of Hereford, Badlesmere, Mortimer of Wigmore, Somery and Norwich. To no single one could the king have had strong objections; the majority stood well in his favour. So great was the consideration shown the king that he was allowed to associate with these five, on his own nomination, the archbishop of York and the bishops of Ely and Norwich. Though surrounded and guided by his friends the king was not helpless. He still retained a certain independence of action even against his friends. To the important demands of the barons in the request on scutage the king gave an answer which delayed the matter, and the further deliberation which he suggested should take place was not to be made in parliament but in the exchequer. The king was however reasonable. To all the requests made in the parliament of York which desired or called for real and adequate reform he gave a willing answer. It seemed at last as if the king, by the aid of the middle party, was to rule at peace and in prosperity. Soon the horizon was darkened by a cloud rising in the household of the king himself. The cloud was the first sign of the storm which was to overwhelm the middle party.

CHAPTER VII

THE EXPERIMENTS (*cont.*)

(vi) *The Parliament of Westminster*, 1320, *and the Exile of the Despensers*

In the parliament of York in 1318 the activity of the middle party was seen with the influence of Lancaster added. In the parliament held at Westminster in 1320, another manifestation of the middle party was given, uninfluenced by Lancaster, and therefore presenting more characteristic features of its aims and ideals. The revolutionary element was entirely absent. The parliament of Westminster of 1320 illustrates an experiment of orderly administration, in which the king was still content to be led gently by the more friendly of the barons acting in harmony with his officials and personal friends. To contrast with the value and peaceful order of the work of the middle party, the parliament of Westminster was followed by the baronial movement which culminated in the exile of the Despensers in 1321. The action of the Despensers made the barons desert the quiet yet valuable results achieved by moderate policy for the coercion and force of the Lancaster faction, with their sundering and deplorable consequences. Yet in this particular instance the violence of the Lancastrians seems to be excused partially by the provocation afforded by the Despensers.

After the parliament of York the middle party still continued to be predominant. Its members still possessed great influence at court. Pembroke had considerable part in administration and in the king's favour[1]. Hereford, too, maintained his position. He obtained grants for himself and his family[2]. He went to Hainault as the king's messenger[3]. For his good service to Edward I the king granted that his executors should have the custody of half his lands and of the marriage of his heir after his death[4]. D'Audley likewise

[1] Vide above, pp. 438–440. [2] *Cal. Charter Rolls*, 1300–26, pp. 376, 390.

[3] *Cal. Close Rolls*, 1318–23, pp. 36. 132.

[4] *Cal. Doc. Scotl.* vol. III, p. 124. *Cal. Pat. Rolls*, 1317–21, p. 391 (4 Sept. 1319).

received a number of marks of royal regard[1], though, as before, Damory was far higher in the king's esteem. Even though Despenser was slowly ousting Damory, he retained his position well. Various grants were made in satisfaction of the land to the value of 100 marks a year which the king had made him[2]. He obtained various grants of free warren[3]. Wardships were granted to him on rendering the yearly extent[4]. For his good services and for the expenses he had incurred in the king's service in Scotland and Wales, 1000 marks of a sum which he owed the king were remitted[5]. On 20 September, 1320, he was granted respite of all his debts at the exchequer and orders were issued that no distress was to be taken from him[6], and similar orders were issued on 20 December[7]. The exchequer of Dublin was ordered to entertain pleas of debt brought by him[8]. The favours conferred were proof of the king's regard and affection.

When parliament opened at Westminster on October 6, 1320[9], the king was still under the guidance of the middle party. The king with the assistance of the archbishop of Canterbury, the bishop of Norwich, now chancellor, the bishop of Exeter, treasurer, the bishops of London, Ely and Coventry and Lichfield, the earl of Pembroke, Edmund de Woodstock and other magnates made arrangements for receiving and hearing petitions[10]. The middle party and its influence were as much reflected in the committees to hear and answer petitions as in the assembly of prelates and others who accompanied the king. Adam de Lymbergh, king's remembrancer, and William de Herlaston, clerk of chancery, were appointed receivers of the petitions of England and Wales. The bishops of London, Chichester and Coventry and Lichfield, the abbot of St Alban's, John de Somery, Richard de Grey, William Herle and John de Stonore, king's serjeant[11], Robert de Bardelby and Henry de Clif, clerks of chancery,

[1] *Cal. Charter Rolls*, 1300–26, p. 395. *Cal. Close Rolls*, 1318–23, p. 81. *Parl. Writs*, vol. II, Pt i, p. 242.

[2] *Cal. Pat. Rolls*, 1317–21, pp. 248, 388. *Cal. Fine Rolls*, 1307–19, p. 391.

[3] *Cal. Charter Rolls*, 1300–26, pp. 400, 428.

[4] *Cal. Fine Rolls*, 1307–19, p. 399.

[5] *Cal. Pat. Rolls*, 1317–21, p. 519 (14 Nov. 1320).

[6] K. R. Mem. Roll, no. 94, m. 7. L. T. R. Mem. Roll, no. 91, Brev. Mich. m. 3 d.

[7] K. R. Mem. Roll, no. 94, m. 39 d. L. T. R. Mem. Roll, no. 91, Brev. Pasch. m. 3 d.

[8] *Cal. Close Rolls*, 1318–23, p. 154 (7 Aug. 1319).

[9] *Parl. Writs*, vol. II, Pt ii, p. 219.

[10] Ibid. Pt i, p. 251. *Rot. Parl.* vol. I, p. 365.

[11] A few days later he became a justice of the Common Bench (*Cal. Pat. Rolls*, 1317–21, p. 508).

and Geoffrey le Scrope, king's serjeant, were appointed to give answers to those petitions. The receivers of the petitions of Ireland, Gascony and the Isles were to be Edmund de London and Henry de Canterbury. The bishops of Bath and Wells, Worcester and Hereford, the abbot of Ramsay, Hugh de Courtney, William Martin, Guy Ferre, Walter de Friskeney, recently appointed baron of the exchequer[1], Jordan Moraunt and Richard de Burton, both of whom were experienced in Gascon affairs, and Gilbert de Toudeby, king's serjeant, were to give answers to them[2]. Lancaster felt himself so completely thrust into the background that he did not attend parliament, though he sent procurators to make excuses for him, amongst whom was Nicholas de Segrave[3].

In this parliament various administrative actions were performed or confirmed. Pembroke's appointment as keeper of the forest south of Trent which had been made on 18 May, 1320[4], until the next parliament, was regranted to him on 13 October by the king in full parliament, by assent of the magnates there[5]. The castle of Dover and the Cinque Ports were on 13 October committed to Badlesmere "by the assent of the prelates, earls, barons and the chiefs of the realm in the present parliament of Westminster[6]." Grants made to Norwich, the bishop of Exeter, and others were made by the king on the petition of the council or by the assent of the parliament[7]. "By assent of the prelates, earls, barons and other chiefs of the realm in the present parliament, summoned at Westminster," Oliver de Bordeaux, king's yeoman, was pardoned for life the whole of the yearly rent of certain lands in the forest of Windsor and the arrears due from him for that rent[8]. The bishop of Exeter, treasurer, was pardoned, with the assent of the parliament, all that pertained to the king for the escape from his prison of clerks who had been indicted before the justices and delivered to him at his request according to the privilege of the clergy[9], and with similar assent the bishop obtained grants for his see[10]. Petitions which the knights, citizens and burgesses presented at the parliament of Westminster were responsible for the issue of commissions of oyer and terminer by the king and council. In pursuance to one petition an ordinance was made by the king and council, and a commission was issued for the trial of persons who had

[1] *Cal. Pat. Rolls*, 1317–21, p. 504 (6 Aug. 1320).
[2] *Parl. Writs*, vol. II, Pt i, p. 251.
[3] *Ann. Paul.* p. 290.
[4] *Cal. Fine Rolls*, 1319–27, p. 23.
[5] Ibid. pp. 34–35.
[6] Ibid. p. 38.
[7] *Cal. Charter Rolls*, 1300–26, pp. 428, 431.
[8] *Cal. Fine Rolls*, 1319–27, pp. 41–42.
[9] *Cal. Pat. Rolls*, 1317–21, p. 517.
[10] *Cal. Charter Rolls*, 1300–26, p. 431.

impeded the administration of justice by threatening jurors, way-laying suitors and entering into illegal confederacies[1]. Commissions of oyer and terminer were granted similarly for the trial of sheriffs and minor local officials who had harassed the people by false appeals and indictments and extorted large sums of money[2]. All these writs which were issued by the assent of parliament were executed quite voluntarily by the king. Many of them indeed were issued by warrants under the privy seal[3]. There is an instance of a writ of 31 July, 1320, enforcing one of the Ordinances, issued by warrant of the privy seal[4]. The king stated that he had recently confirmed the Ordinances and he wished to put them into execution. Accordingly, though he had granted to Stephen de Abingdon, his butler, the king's right prise of all wines, he ordered that he should render account before the treasurer and barons of the exchequer. They were to audit his accounts with all speed and to charge him rigidly with what pertained to his office, notwithstanding the grant. When the accounts had been audited, the king was to be certified so that he might cause to be done what should seem good of his grace[5].

Under the guidance of the middle party the king was still acting in a spirit of good faith and reason. In a writ of 14 November to the exchequer, the king stated that he wished the Ordinances to be inviolably observed[6]. The spirit of the agreement was still being kept, and the administration was going on in an orderly fashion. Strenuous efforts were being made to root out the abuses, especially those of serious disorder in the local administration. There was indeed every possibility that the period of orderly administration and good government inaugurated by the advent into power of the middle party would be continued and would produce lasting effect.

The parliament of Westminster in 1320 was however the last occasion upon which the middle party was in a position to exert any influence. Its total disruption followed fast upon the meeting of parliament. The clouds had been long gathering Indeed the origin of the trouble[7] which broke up the middle party and hurled into the camp of Lancaster those who had for years acted with

[1] *Cal. Pat. Rolls*, 1317–21, p. 548 (27 Nov. 1320).

[2] Ibid. pp. 548–9 (18 Dec. 1320).

[3] *Cal. Fine Rolls*, 1319–27, pp. 41–42. *Cal. Pat. Rolls*, 1317–21, p. 517.

[4] *Cal. Close Rolls*, 1318–23, p. 249.

[5] Ibid. Cf. also *Cal. Fine Rolls*, 1319–27, pp. 23–24.

[6] K. R. Mem. Roll, no. 94, m. 22.

[7] The whole subject of the conduct of the Despenser towards Damory and D'Audley and the other marcher lords is treated at length in the paper on 'The Despenser War in Glamorgan' in the *Trans. R. H. Soc.* vol. IX [1915], pp. 24–44.

Pembroke may be found as far back as November, 1317, when the delivery of the portions of the Gloucester inheritance had been made to Despenser, Damory and D'Audley[1]. Despenser had obtained as his portion the lordship of Glamorgan[2]. He was consumed by an overwhelming ambition and seems to have conceived the idea of consolidating his resources in South Wales and obtaining for himself there a position as powerful as the earls of Gloucester had held. This at least would seem a natural inference from his actions. He pursued on all sides a policy of the most unscrupulous opportunism. The partitioners had been in doubt about the relation of the county of Gwenllwyg, which had been awarded to D'Audley, to Despenser's lordship of Glamorgan. The relations between the county and the lordship were however settled in the partition, and it was decided that in future Gwenllwyg should be held directly from the crown[3]. The doubt, however, was a sufficient ground for Despenser to intervene. Before D'Audley could take homage from the men of Gwenllwyg and Machen, Despenser had made an indenture with them to receive their fealties[4]. Despite the intervention of the royal power, so strong was Despenser's position that D'Audley deemed it advisable to enfeoff him with a portion of those lands[5], the matter being finally settled by an exchange, Despenser giving lands in England in return[6]. Despenser next turned his eyes westwards and obtained a grant for life of the castle and town of Drysllwyn and the land of Cantrev Mawr[7].

The barony of Gower was the next object of Despenser's attentions. William de Brewosa, the lord of Gower, was in straitened circumstances and desired to sell his land, Hereford and the two Mortimers proving willing buyers[8]. Despenser also appeared as a purchaser, and by his influence with the king seemed likely to be successful[9]. John Inge, his sheriff of Glamorgan, had been well instructed in the matter[10]. Brewosa had a daughter whom he had married to John de Mowbray[11], and he had made a grant of the honour of Gower to him

[1] *Cal. Fine Rolls*, 1307–19, p. 350 (15 Nov. 1317).

[2] Exch. Misc. 9/23, formerly Misc. Chan. Roll 3/8

[3] Ibid.

[4] Parl. and Council Proc. (Chan.), File 4/22. *Cal. Pat. Rolls*, 1317–21, p. 103.

[5] *Cal. Pat. Rolls*, 1317–21, p. 257.

[6] Ibid. p. 456 (12 May, 1320).

[7] Regranted with the assent of the parliament of York, 28 Nov. 1318 (*Cal. Pat Rolls*, 1317–21, pp. 225–6, 248).

[8] Trokelowe, *Annal.* p. 107.

[9] Ibid.

[10] Cotton MS. Vesp. F. vii, f. 6. The original letter from Despenser to Inge dated 21 Sept. 1319.

[11] Trokelowe, *Annal.* p. 107. Clark, *Cartae de Glam.* vol. III [1891 edit.],p. 589.

and his heirs with remainder to Hereford and his heirs[1]. By virtue of this grant, Mowbray entered into possession of the castle of Swansea and the barony of Gower. Despenser was aroused and sought to prevent this[2]. The land of Gower had been obtained without licence[3]. On Despenser's suggestion[4], the king ordered the seizure of Gower into his hands[5]. A question of the most serious import was at once raised—the liberties of the march. Despenser's object was to prevent the necessary licence for alienation being given. The marcher lords protested against what they considered a violation of march custom. Despenser maintained that the king had always enjoyed the prerogative that no one should enter into land in the marches without the royal licence[6]. The king's orders to seize Gower were resisted[7].

Despenser's behaviour about Gower was characteristic of his whole policy. Encroachments on the lands of Damory and D'Audley, interference with Hereford and the Mortimers, the disinheritance of Mowbray by a legal quibble and one that affected the whole body of marcher barons, produced the expected effect. Hereford did not consider himself in a position to deal with such a weighty matter alone so he referred it to Lancaster[8]. Thus one of the stalwarts of the middle party once again made his peace with Lancaster and appealed to him against the king and his master the younger Despenser. By the end of 1320 the middle party was already split up. The king was making his preparations to support Despenser. The Welsh castles were being rendered defensible[9]. Despenser had given special instructions as early as September, 1319, about the repair and provisioning of the castles[10]. By 18 January, 1321, the Glamorgan castles were in a state of preparedness and Despenser was looking out for confederations against him[11]. A letter written to the king on 27 February had warned him of the state of affairs among the barons. Lancaster and the barons of the Welsh march had met, and the plot to create disturbances and evils in Wales was already formed[12]. Indeed, as early as 30 January, the king had forbidden Hereford and other barons from making assemblies to treat of affairs of the realm[13].

[1] Dugdale, *Baronage* [1675], p. 420 b, states that the original of this grant was then in existence. Cf. *Ann. Paul.* p. 292.

[2] *Ann. Paul.* p. 293.

[3] *Cal. Pat. Rolls*, 1321–24, p. 21.

[4] *Auct. Malm.* p. 254.

[5] *Cal. Fine Rolls*, 1319–27, p. 40.

[6] *Auct. Malm.* pp. 254–5.

[7] *Cal. Fine Rolls*, 1319–27, pp. 41–42.

[8] *Cal. Pat. Rolls*, 1317–21, p. 567. *Cal. Close Rolls*, 1318–23, p. 292.

[9] *Cal. Close Rolls*, 1318–23, p. 292.

[10] Cotton MS. Vesp. F. vii, f. 6.

[11] Anc. Corresp. vol. XLIX, no. 143.

[12] Ibid. vol. XXXV, no. 8.

[13] *Cal. Close Rolls*, 1318–23, p. 355. *Foedera*, vol. II, p. 442.

Soon the king began to act. On 31 March the land of Builth which the king had granted to Hereford was resumed into the king's hands[1]. On 8 April, sentence of forfeiture was pronounced upon D'Audley at Gloucester[2] and his lands were seized and his chattels forfeited[3]. On 18 April, the castle of Montgomery, which D'Audley held, was seized into the king's hands[4]. The king was himself hovering about the Welsh border, and at the end of March and the beginning of April had been at Gloucester[5]. He had ordered various magnates including Hereford, Damory, Mortimer and Cherleton to appear at Gloucester on 5 April to treat with him[6]. Hereford had not entirely lost the constitutional bias of the middle party. He sent a lengthy reply to the king's command. In the heat of the moment he had told the royal official that he would not come to the king as long as Despenser remained with him. He therefore sent the abbot of Dean to explain his words. He was quite willing to come to the king at his orders, but as long as Despenser the son remained with him he dared not do so. Hereford begged the king to summon a parliament at a time and place where he and Hugh could come with safety and where they could bring forward their complaints and receive judgment. Meanwhile he suggested that Despenser should be committed to the custody of Lancaster. He would mainprise himself, under penalty of all he could forfeit, to lead Despenser to Lancaster and bring him to parliament safely[7].

The king had not been under the guidance and tuition of the middle party for naught. He sent a skilful reply to Hereford taking a high constitutional stand upon the Ordinances, Magna Carta, and his coronation oath. Despenser, the king stated, had been appointed chamberlain by the counsel of the prelates, earls and barons in full parliament at York. To that appointment Hereford had himself consented. No complaint had been made against him in any parliament. The earl need fear no danger in coming to the king for the royal orders were a protection and defence to everyone. It would be unbecoming and dishonest to remove Despenser from the king's company as suddenly as the earl desired. Moreover if he was removed without cause it would be an unjust and evil precedent to the king's other officials. The king had already arranged to discuss with Hereford and other of his subjects a place for holding a parliament

[1] *Cal. Fine Rolls*, 1319–27, p. 50.
[2] *Parl. Writs*, vol. II, Pt ii, App. p. 156.
[3] Sheriffs' Accts. 10/5, 29/13.
[4] *Cal. Pat. Rolls*, 1317–21, p. 575.
[5] Cf. Chan. Warr., Files 113/5599; 114/5602, 5603.
[6] *Cal. Close Rolls*, 1318–23, p. 314.
[7] Ibid. p. 367.

and other business of the kingdom. It would be contrary to Magna Carta, the common law of the land, the Ordinances which he had sworn to observe, and his coronation oath, for the king to commit Despenser to any person without cause, especially as he had presented himself before the king as ready to answer the complaints of everyone in parliament and elsewhere. Hereford and Mortimer of Wigmore were accordingly ordered to meet the king at Oxford three weeks from Easter to treat with him and other magnates and give their counsel[1].

The king's reply, however cleverly conceived, was not calculated to satisfy the earl and his supporters. The baronial demands had been that Despenser should be dismissed or committed to the charge of a chosen person to stand judgment on a certain day to answer what was objected against him. If these demands were not accepted the barons would no longer have the king as ruler, but would refuse homage and fealty and the swearing of anything due to the king and as men without a king, without a ruler and without justice, for lack of justice they would proceed on their authority to the punishment of Despenser and perform such vengeance as they were able on the doers of such evil deeds[2]. Early in May[3] they started to do so. The Glamorgan lands of the Despensers were ravaged and destroyed and then the confederate barons proceeded to his lands in England.

Though the barons of the march could destroy the Despenser property it was doubtful whether they could coerce the king without Lancaster's aid. Lancaster was acquainted with the state of affairs throughout and they had his moral support[4]. He took no active part in the revolt, perhaps because he was just recovering from an illness[5]. Still he took an interest in the outcome and avowed his consent[6]. All things were done by his advice and counsel[7]. He could not have been expected to co-operate enthusiastically with Hereford, Damory, D'Audley and the other barons. As members of the middle party, they had done much to lessen his influence and though in their new position they may have had his open sympathy, it was yet a little early to expect active support. When their endeavours were being crowned with success Lancaster moved.

[1] *Cal. Close Rolls*, 1318–23, pp. 367–8.
[2] *Auct. Malm.* p. 256.
[3] *Flores Hist.* vol. III, p. 344, gives the date as 4 May, 1321, which is approximately right.
[4] *Auct. Malm.* p. 255.
[5] Chan. Warr., File 113/5551.
[6] *Chron. G. le Baker*, p. 11. *Chron. Murimuth*, p. 33. *Le Livere de Reis de Brit.* p. 336.
[7] *Chron. Lanec.* pp. 229–230.

On 24 May, Lancaster held a meeting in the chapter house of the priory of Pontefract when Thomas de Multon, Thomas de Furnivall, Edmund Deyncourt, Henry Fitz-Hugh, Henry de Percy and ten other northern barons and bannerets attended. There, they all agreed to enter into a league for mutual defence, which was confirmed by seal[1]. Lancaster next appealed to a wider constituency. It seemed that the business required the counsel of greater people and especially of the prelates. Accordingly, the archbishop and the other prelates of the province of York were summoned to Sherburn to treat with the others on matters concerning the public good and peace. On 28 June, the appointed day, the archbishop of York, the bishops of Durham and Carlisle, Lancaster, Hereford fresh from the ravage of the Welsh lands of the younger Despenser, abbots and priors, many barons, bannerets and knights from north and south met together in the parish church of Sherburn. By Lancaster's command, John de Bek, knight, read certain articles in their presence[2]. These articles varied very considerably in value. Foremost was put Lancaster's old bugbear of evil counsellors. It was put forward that if those assembled knew of any considerations or grievances to the loss or shame of the people or the crown brought about by the king's evil or unsuitable friends they should be declared before the earl, so that by unanimous consent and common counsel suitable remedy should be provided for such grievances. For it seemed that those who received the offices by which the kingdom ought to be guided, the chancellor, treasurer, chamberlains, justices, keeper of the privy seal[3], escheators, and others who ought to be appointed by election, and had received the offices against the Ordinances were the cause of the new evils and oppressions which bore down the people[4]. It also seemed that a remedy should be provided for a new grievance caused by such officials against the magnates of the land: "videlicet quod illi qui terras et tenementa perquirunt, quae de rege tenentur in capite per servitia consueta, repelluntur, eis forisfacturum suorum omnium imponendo et de aliis qui contra leges terrae per potestatem regis exheredati et exjudicati sunt assensu parium terrae minime requisito[5]," an article which was patently occasioned by the Mowbray incident and which is of interest as foreshadowing a charge against Despenser in his process of exile[6] and a petition presented

[1] *Auct. Bridl.* pp. 61–62. [2] Ibid. p. 62.

[3] "custos sigilli secreti." The summary given of the articles is a translation into Latin of the French original and the official referred to there would probably have been the keeper of the privy not the secret seal.

[4] *Auct. Bridl.* pp. 62–63. [5] Ibid. p. 63. [6] Vide below, pp. 480–1.

in the parliament held to depose Edward II[1]. Another article was concerned with the justices, who by royal commissions and at the instigation of the evil counsellors, inquired into various trespasses, and indicted the magnates of the realm that by their conspiracies they might disinherit them against the common law[2], in oppression of the people, on account of various charges[3]. The appointment of the itinerant justices in London and the issue of *quo waranto* writs—both of which were attributed to the evil counsellors—were considered another grievance. The staple of foreign merchants and treaties which the king had made provided more articles with grievances. The king moreover at the instigation of the same evil counsellors retained all the skilled lawyers in his service, so that if a magnate or another was impleaded by the king, he could not have counsel[4]. After the articles had been read the clergy withdrew to the house of the rector and there drew up their answer[5]. That answer could have given the earl little pleasure. The clergy were quite prepared to aid in resisting the Scots. The other matters it seemed to them should be treated in the next parliament with the king and his liege men. When this reply had been read the assembly broke up[6].

There was however still one matter to be done by the barons. On 28 June an indenture[7] was made at Sherburn in the presence of the archbishop of York, the bishops of Durham and Carlisle and the earls of Lancaster and Angus. Because it was considered that the two Despensers had given the king evil counsel and because the reason which Hereford, the two Mortimers, D'Audley, Damory, Mowbray and others had given had been heard and understood and the earls of Lancaster and Angus, Robert de Holand and various other lords having been informed that Hereford, the Mortimers and other great men of the marches had commenced quarrels against the Despensers and because it seemed that the oppressions of the people would not cease until the Despensers had been captured or banished, the indenture was made. The earls of Angus and other lords undertook to maintain the quarrel with all their power and in strength of this sealed the indenture[8].

With the formal union of Lancaster and the barons of the Welsh march, the break-up of the middle party was complete. Lancaster

[1] Vide below, p. 481. [2] "contra leges usitatas." [3] *Auct. Bridl.* p. 63.
[4] Ibid. pp. 63–64. [5] Ibid. p. 64. [6] Ibid. pp. 64–65.
[7] This indenture is given in Brady, *Cont. of Compl. Hist. of Eng.* [1700], p. 128. Cf. also *State Trials*, vol. 1, p. 25. Brady took it from the Register of Christ Church, Canterbury.
[8] Brady, *Cont. of Compl. Hist. of Eng.* [1700], p. 128.

was again at the head of an almost united baronage. The king was again in almost complete isolation. Even Pembroke had supported the marcher barons secretly[1].

The only person upon whom the blame for the situation can be placed is the younger Despenser. By his overweening ambition, by his disregard of personal friendship and public policy, he had wrecked all Pembroke's plans. In his overthrow Pembroke was quite willing to acquiesce. He was not prepared to see the king utterly humiliated. Accordingly, he adopted once more a mediating policy, but he mediated on condition that the barons obtained their central demand, the exile of Despenser. For the person who thus ruined his carefully thought-out and skilfully laid plans he would have little consideration.

After the devastation of the Despenser property the confederate barons drew near London. The bishops of London, Salisbury, Hereford, Ely and Chichester who attempted to mediate were sent to the king with the demand that the Despensers should be banished and the barons pardoned[2]. After weeks of attempts to compromise the king was finally, on 14 August, forced to submit to these conditions. The submission was brought about largely by Pembroke's mediation[3], though he remained with the king the whole time. The exile was effected in due form[4] and the list of charges brought against the two Despensers gives an insight into the policy and into the position of the barons.

Hugh the son had acted contrary to the scheme accepted at the parliament of York in 1318. By virtue of the position of chamberlain received in that parliament[5], he had drawn to his aid the elder Hugh who was not agreed upon in the parliament as one of the persons who was to stay near the king. Together the father and son had exercised royal power over the king, his officials and the control of the kingdom[6]. The charge made against the younger Despenser of making an indenture to restrain the will of the king[7] was strange coming from the barons who had used the very argument in their own behalf when pursuing Gavaston[8], and strange also coming from Damory in view of his indenture with Pembroke and Badlesmere[9]. The complaint that they had not allowed his magnates to approach the king[10] was

[1] *Chron. G. le Baker*, p. 11. *Chron. Murimuth*, p. 33.

[2] Trokelowe, *Annal.* pp. 108–9.

[3] *Auct. Malm.* pp. 257–9.

[4] *State of Realm*, vol. I, pp. 181–4. *Cal. Close Rolls*, 1318–23, pp. 492–3.

[5] *Stat. of Realm*, vol. I, pp. 181–2.

[6] Ibid.

[7] Ibid. p. 182.

[8] *Auct. Bridl.* pp. 33–34.

[9] Vide above, pp. 433–4.

[10] *Stat. of Realm*, vol. I, p. 182.

sounder. They refused to allow a magnate or a good counsellor to speak to the king or to give good counsel except in their presence and in their hearing[1]. The decisions given were those of Despenser and not of the king. The good and suitable ministers who had been appointed by assent, the Despensers had removed, placing bad officials, who would support them, in their place. The sheriffs, escheators, constables of castles and others who had been appointed by them were unsuitable. Justices who were ignorant of the law of the land had been appointed by them; among the appointments to which the barons objected were those of the elder Despenser, Ralph Basset and John Inge. These were their friends and partizans. They had arranged that the magnates of the realm, including Hereford, Gifford and others should be falsely indicted, because they coveted their lands[2]. By advising the king to march towards Gloucester in their support, an action which was against Magna Carta and the award of the peers, they had promoted civil war[3]. By procuring the death of the Welsh rebel Llewelyn Bren, Hugh the son had accroached royal power and acted in disinheritance of the crown, and inasmuch as Llewelyn had surrendered to Hereford and Mortimer of Wigmore on condition of grace, he had acted in dishonour of the king and of those barons[4]. The disinheritance of barons which they had counselled and secured, especially that of Damory and D'Audley, was made a charge against them[5]. Throughout, the utter selfishness which had characterised their policy, especially that of the son, was made a leading motive of the exile. In the pursuit of their selfish ends it would appear that they had considered neither law nor scruple. The king had granted to the earl of Warwick by letters patent that if he died during the minority of his heirs his executors should have the custody of the lands[6]. At the request and by the assent of the peers of the land the grant had been confirmed in the parliament of Lincoln, after the earl's death. The elder Despenser, with the assistance of his son, obtained the repeal of this deed and secured the wardship of the lands. By their evil counsel they had defeated what the king had granted in his parliament by good counsel with the assent of the peers of the land[7]. This instance of the policy of the Despensers shows how useless grant in parliament was in view of

[1] *Stat. of Realm*, vol. I, p. 182.
[2] Ibid. pp. 182–3. Cf. *Rot. Parl.* vol. II, pp. 11, 12.
[3] *Stat. of Realm*, vol. I, p. 183.
[4] Ibid. Vide above, Introduction, pp. 31–32.
[5] *Stat. of Realm*, vol. I, p. 183.
[6] *Cal. Fine Rolls*, 1307–19, p. 255.
[7] *Stat. of Realm*, vol. I, p. 183.

the king's executive power. The Gower incident provided another charge. They had not allowed the king to take reasonable fines from the peers of the land as had been the custom, but, because they desired to obtain the lands, had put undue hindrances in the way in the hope that they would be forfeited[1]. All these were not merely temporary grievances. This particular question occupied a prominent position in the petitions of the commons on the accession of Edward III. The commons sought that no purchase of lands or tenements held in chief of the king, made without licence, should result in the seizing of those lands into the king's hands as forfeited, but that by ordinance of the common council a certain fine should be levied according to the value of the purchase[2]. To this petition the king assented[3]. By their conduct about the Templar lands and the representations that the magnates had made thereon, it seemed that they had planned that right should not be done except at their will[4]. The younger Despenser had moreover used his office of chamberlain as a means of extorting fines. The elect of bishoprics, abbeys and priories had been unable to approach the king for his grace until they had made fine with him, although they ought of right to have been received by the king. In fact no one who sought anything from the king could obtain it until he had made the necessary fine with Despenser[5]. He interfered with the course of royal justice and released prisoners to his own advantage before the plaintiffs had received their rights[6]. In consideration of all these evil deeds, the peers of the land, earls and barons, awarded in the presence of the king, that both Despensers should be disinherited for ever as disinheritors of the crown and enemies of the king and his people and that they should be exiled from the realm of England without returning at any time except by the assent of the king, and of the prelates, earls and barons given in parliament duly summoned. If they stayed in England after the day fixed for their departure or if they returned they were to be treated as enemies of the king and kingdom[7].

The sentence if severe was hardly unjust. The charges made against the Despensers in the process of exile were substantially true. That they were able to exert such an influence over the king was due to the personal system. They made use of the opportunities they

[1] *Stat. of Realm*, vol. I. pp. 183–4.

[2] *Rot. Parl.* vol. II, p. 9.

[3] Ibid. p. 12.

[4] *Stat. of Realm*, vol. I, p. 184.

[5] Ibid.

[6] Ibid. Cf. Ancient Petition, no. 2759. Vide above, p. 97.

[7] *Stat. of Realm*, vol. I, p. 184. The writs issued on 20 August were "by king and council."

had; that many of these opportunities presented themselves was in no way due to their efforts. Others, including Damory, had had the same opportunities and, according to their ability, had used them. The younger Despenser differed from his predecessors in several points. He showed greater ability in using his opportunities and as a result exaggerated the evils of the system. In his policy he exhibited a greater selfishness and a greater lack of scruple. Consequently the amount of support he alienated and the number of interests he attacked was greater. In 1321 there was not a single baron to support him. More important than all he possessed considerable administrative ability, though his constitutional theories and his administrative schemes were secondary to his ambitions. The most considerable and active part of the baronage was in 1321 ranged in bitter hostility to him; the remainder of the baronage was inactive. He was removed, but he retained the confidence of the king.

In the baronial demands, coupled with the exile of the Despensers, had been pardon for the baronial actions. This also the king had been forced to concede. The barons had been forced by necessity to act without the law in securing the exile. They could not secure their ends by process of law since as they said, "Hugh le Despenser the father and Hugh le Despenser the son had accroached to themselves royal power, and had at their will the king and his ministers and the direction of the law[1]." Since done by necessity, these things, they argued, ought not to be redressed or punished by rigour of law. Indeed, without occasioning great trouble and perhaps worse war in the realm, redress or punishment could not be secured. The barons therefore demanded pardon for their past actions to be made by letters patent without any fee being paid to the chancery[2]. On 20 August, 1321, these letters were issued by the king and council[3]. Pardon was made to Hereford and Warenne, the two Mortimers, Damory, D'Audley, Badlesmere, Mowbray, Gifford, Richard de Grey and several hundred of their adherents[4]. All these principals had been active members of the middle party, and how that party had been broken up by Despenser's aggression receives illumination from this list. With the issue of these pardons the success of the barons was complete.

As a result of this revolt against the Despensers the king's power

[1] *Cal. Close Rolls*, 1318–23, p. 495.

[2] Ibid.

[3] *Cal. Pat. Rolls*, 1321–24, p. 15. On the same day an appointment of a sheriff was made by council (*Cal. Fine Rolls* 1319–27, p. 67).

[4] Ibid. pp. 15–20.

had been seriously threatened. When he had proved unwilling to accede to the baronial demands, they had threatened that if he did not hear their complaints and render satisfaction to their petitions according to justice: "ab homagio suo penitus discederent et alium rectorem sibi praeficerent qui justitiam omnibus faceret et collum nocentium et superborum humiliaret[1]."

Coerced by these threats and by the strong force which the barons had gathered round London[2] the king had given way. Even after parliament had suspended its sittings the king was still ruled by the barons, and writs making appointments were made by king and council[3]. But there was no longer that unanimity between king and barons which had existed under the regime of the middle party. The king was now at deep enmity with the barons. His dignity had been offended, his friends exiled and his action coerced.

The king's view of the whole proceedings is found in the revocation of the pardon to the confederate barons effected at the parliament of York in 1322. In that parliament the prelates, earls, barons, knights of the shire and the commonalty of the realm showed that the pardon was "sinfully and wrongly made and granted, against reason and common right, and against the oath which the king had made at his coronation, and that the assent which they gave to it was given for dread of the great force which the earl of Hereford and the other great confederates brought to the parliament of Westminster, with horse and arms, in affray and abasement of all the people, and that they would not in anywise have assented to it but by reason of the said outrageous and unjust force[4]." They therefore besought the king that he would cause it to be repealed and made void[5]. These reasons, and because it was against Magna Carta wherein it was contained that the king should not deny or delay right or justice to any man, and because it tended to increase crime rather than promote remedy and redress wrong, were considered by the king. But the real motive seems to lie in the fact that it "was made to his displeasure, and great dishonour, and to the blemishing of his royal dignity, and in injury of the rights of other men and that he could not at that time withstand the said force upon the sudden to do right as it behoved him[6]." For these and other reasons, and by the counsel and request of the prelates, earls, barons, knights of shires, and commonalty of the realm, the pardons were revoked[7].

[1] *Auct. Malm.* pp. 258–9.
[2] *Ann. Paul.* pp. 293–6.
[3] *Cal. Fine Rolls*, 1319–27, p. 69.
[4] *Stat. of Realm*, vol. I, p. 185.
[5] Ibid.
[6] Ibid. p. 187.
[7] Ibid. pp. 187–8.

The barons in the exercise of this coercion had acted in direct opposition to that first canon upon which the middle party acted. That party had proceeded upon the view that it was impossible to coerce the king or to control him effectively against his will. Success bought by that means would be but transitory. It was in the revolt against the Despensers that the doctrine of coercion found its strictest and most violent application during the reign of Edward II. He had been coerced by force on previous occasions, and the coercion had, in a short time, proved its utter futility. In the events which followed the exile of the Despensers more than another proof of the futility of coercion was supplied. Within a few months the king had granted his friends safe conducts[1]; a little later, the pardons obtained by coercion were broken and annulled[2]. The reaction went further than mere revocation. For the occasion the king's new energy proved more disastrous to the baronial opposition than the strength of the household system. Almost immediately after the culmination of baronial success, in his personal quarrel with Badlesmere, the king found opportunity to wreak his vengeance upon those who had reduced him to such humiliation. This final struggle of the barons with the king possessed no new feature, and supplies nothing useful towards a consideration of the policy or character of the baronial opposition. It gave but another proof to the already well established fact that the king's power and resources were too great for coercion or control to have any lasting effects. There was immediately a reaction in the king's favour, and this reaction coincided with an unwonted burst of energy on his part. A number of barons with Pembroke at the head again rallied in his support. For the king's cause prospered owing to the efforts of some of his adherents[3]. London sent aid. There was a rapid campaign in the Welsh marches followed by the hurrying northwards of the baronial forces. The north proved loyal. Boroughbridge was the price paid for coercion.

[1] *Cal. Pat. Rolls*, 1321–24, p. 45. [2] *Cal. Close Rolls*, 1323–27, p. 44.
[3] *Chron. Lanerc.* (ed. Maxwell), p. 231.

CHAPTER VIII

THE RESULTS OF THE EXPERIMENTS

The phases of the baronial opposition which provide best instances of their policy have been considered, and before the explanation for the failure of that policy is attempted, the results of their experiments must be mentioned briefly. The Ordinances formed the basic program of the baronial opposition. They contained the ideals which the barons sought to see in administrative operation and legislative force. The results of the experiments of the baronial opposition, starting with the Ordinances of 1311 and concluding with the exile of the Despensers in 1321, will have to be considered from two points, the immediate and the final. Besides the great program of reform of the Ordinances, useful legislation was passed under baronial auspices in the Statutes of Lincoln of 1316 and York of 1318. When the raw material of the baronial plans and their ultimate results have been considered, the final results of the machinery by which the barons sought to attain the execution of their schemes will have to be estimated. Besides the direct influence of the baronial opposition, there were various indirect results which are found in the administrative reforms of the later portion of the reign. Inasmuch as those reforms were composed of various elements and occasioned by various reasons, among which the indirect influence of the baronial opposition was not paramount, they will be considered separately[1].

The achievements of the barons in the parliament of Westminster in August, 1321, mark the last occasion upon which the baronial opposition had any success in their attempts to control the king's action. The years following Boroughbridge were concerned with administrative reforms of the utmost importance and significance, but they were reforms undertaken spontaneously by the king and the administration. The revolution which came in Michaelmas, 1326, and hurled the king from his throne and cost the Despensers their lives, was important rather in its personal phase than as an expression of baronial opposition to the king and his policy and powers. The year 1322 can therefore be taken as a fair time at which to ascertain

[1] Vide below, pp. 511–537.

the results of the various experiments which the baronial opposition had made.

How far the Ordinances were executed has been discussed. The real action of the baronial opposition commenced with the Ordinances; much of their opposition to Gavaston had only a personal significance. The whole of the baronial policy subsequent to the Ordinances, as expressed in Lancaster and his party, was a series of endeavours to obtain their execution. In all negotiations to which he was a party, Lancaster put first and foremost the observance of the Ordinances. The middle party, who had a wider conception of baronial policy, did not bind themselves down as rigidly to a cut and dried scheme.

There were some of the Ordinances to which the king throughout refused obedience. He had been particularly unwilling to obey that which forbade him making grants of land and ordering the restoration of grants made since the appointment of the ordainers[1]. As early as 17 November, 1311, the keeper of a manor was ordered to deliver it to the person from whom it had been resumed into the king's hands by reason of the Ordinances[2]. This regrant was not made purely on the king's initiative, for it had been agreed by the king's council that it should be returned[3]. The council here referred to was hardly that of the ordainers but probably the king's "administrative" council over which the ordainers had not obtained control. On 30 March, 1312, the king ordered further restorations to be made[4]. A similar policy was pursued under the Pembroke administration in the same year when the forest of High Peak and the manors of Torpel and Upton, taken into the king's hands by virtue of the Ordinances, were restored to the earl of Surrey, the writs being issued on Pembroke's information[5]. The ascendancy of the barons was always marked by resumptions, but until the parliament of York in 1318, whenever free from baronial pressure, the king always disobeyed this particular Ordinance. Against the king's will there was no means of enforcing it. After the Treaty of Leake had been made on 10 September, the lands forfeited by the ordainers were granted to D'Audley, "by the assent of the king's kinsman, Aymer de Valence, Earl of Pembroke and other magnates[6]." The triumph of the middle party was heralded by a disobedience to the Ordinances.

[1] Ordinance 7.

[2] *Cal. Close Rolls*, 1307–13, p. 387.

[3] Ibid.

[4] Ibid. pp. 415–416.

[5] *Cal. Fine Rolls*, 1307–19, p. 140 (25 and 26 July, 1312).

[6] Ibid. p. 374 (10 Sept. 1318).

The king was equally opposed to the Ordinance relating to appointments[1]. Had it been given full effect it would have put the control of the administration into the hands of the magnates in parliament, as it was intended to do. Fortunately for the king, it was extremely difficult to enforce its execution. The changes in the office of keeper of the forest south of Trent prove this. At the time of the Ordinances, Despenser the elder was keeper. In compliance with the Ordinances[2] he had to resign, and Robert fitz Payn was appointed in his stead[3]. This appointment was made contrary to the form provided. Fitz Payn was a member of the court party and was still steward of the household in December, 1310[4]. His was intended to be merely an interim appointment until the king could return the office to Despenser. On 14 June, 1312, Despenser was reappointed, the writ being issued on the information of Edmund de Mauley, steward of the household[5]. The king had again contemned the Ordinance. The keeper of the forest north of Trent had previously been reappointed. That office had been held before the Ordinances by Gavaston, to whom it had been granted for life[6]. On 2 December, 1311, Henry de Percy, who had acted with the ordainers in 1310[7], was appointed to that office, the consent of the ordainers being obtained subsequent to the appointment[8]. On 3 April, 1312, it was restored to Gavaston[9], the restoration ignoring the personal Ordinance against[10] him and that dealing with appointments. The appointments to these two offices were made but a few months after the Ordinances, but the king was almost invariably equally successful in this direction. With the notable exception of the way in which they prevented Langton from obtaining the office of treasurer[11], the barons did not succeed in enforcing this Ordinance to any degree until the parliament of York.

The most serious of the personal Ordinances was entirely disregarded in December, 1311, when Gavaston returned to England and the king joined him. The other personal Ordinances were insignificant in comparison with the one directed against Gavaston. They, too, were broken. On 6 October ,1313, the king also abrogated such parts of the Ordinances touching Beaumont and Lady de Vescy as were to their detriment and prejudice[12]. In consideration of this,

[1] Ordinance 14.
[2] Cf. Ordinance 18.
[3] *Cal. Fine Rolls*, 1307–19, p. 116 (2 Dec. 1311).
[4] Tout, *The Place of Ed. II*, p. 353.
[5] *Cal. Pat. Rolls*, 1307–13, p. 464 (1307).
[6] *Cal. Fine Rolls*, 1307–19, p. 73 (1319).
[7] Vide below, pp. 505–6.
[8] *Cal. Fine Rolls*, 1307–19, p. 116.
[9] *Cal. Pat. Rolls*, 1307–13, p. 450.
[10] Ordinance 20.
[11] Vide above, pp. 389–392.
[12] *Cal. Pat. Rolls*, 1313–17, p. 29.

acquittance was made, for greater security, to Lady de Vescy of the farm of the castle of Bamburgh during the whole of her tenure of the castle[1].

The Ordinance which forbade the king to leave the realm[2] was also disregarded. In 1313 the king received an invitation from the king of France to attend the knighting of his son[3]. Edward decided to go. The earls sent to him, advising him not to expose his kingdom to danger by crossing the sea without permission[4]. The king went, but ordered all conservators of the peace and sheriffs throughout England, lest any evil suspicion be propagated in England in consequence of the king's voyage, to proclaim that the journey was undertaken at the request of the pope and the king of France for the reformation of the state of Gascony and not for any other cause, and it was the king's intention to return with all possible speed[5]. What importance the barons attached to this Ordinance is uncertain, but the king had no intention of abiding by it. The campaigns against Scotland undertaken without baronial assent gave proof to this.

Though one of the preliminary ordinances of 1310[6] had ordered that the customs should be paid into the exchequer, on 29 August, 1311, the collectors of the customs of Hull were ordered to pay their receipts to the Bellardi in satisfaction of the king's debts to them[7], and though the preliminary ordinance was confirmed and repeated in October, 1311[8], the collecters were again ordered to pay their receipts to them on 27 August, 1312[9]. The Bellardi were also granted wardship of lands in return for a sum of money paid into the exchequer[10]. It was by ordering payments to be made to the wardrobe that the king disobeyed this Ordinance most frequently. It was important, if the barons were to control the king, that he should be dependent solely upon the exchequer for his revenue. He was able, by various plans, to ensure that money should be paid directly into his wardrobe. Thus for a loan of £500, which the keeper of his wardrobe received from London, the king granted that no tallage should be levied from that town before a certain date[11]. The mayor and

[1] *Cal. Pat. Rolls*, 1313–17, p. 83 (28 Jan. 1314).
[2] Ordinance 9.
[3] *Auct. Malm.* p. 190.
[4] Ibid.
[5] *Cal. Pat. Rolls*, 1307–13, p. 588 (20 May, 1313).
[6] Ordinance 4. Vide above, p. 373.
[7] Cf. *Cal. Pat. Rolls*, 1307–13, p. 386. Cf. *Hist. Essays*, ed. Tout and Tait, p 144.
[8] Ordinances 4, 8.
[9] *Cal. Close Rolls*, 1307–13, p. 476.
[10] *Cal. Fine Rolls*, 13c7–19, p. 106.
[11] Ibid. p. 160 (13 Jan. 1313).

sheriffs of London were ordered to pay 600 marks, for fine levied for pulling down walls near the Tower, to certain Gascon merchants, in payment of wine which the king's butler had purchased from them[1]. In November and December, 1312, the king was finding difficulty in obtaining money for the payment of his household. He therefore made an indenture with the mayor, sheriffs and aldermen of London by which a sum of 1000 marks was to be provided by the city for this purpose. For that money the officials of the city were to have the king's bond under the great seal[2]. In this way immediately after the Ordinances the intention of the ordainers was defeated. Again in February, 1313, they agreed to advance a loan of £1000 to the king's wardrobe[3].

The Ordinance which abolished the new customs and evil tolls[4] was almost consistently obeyed until the year 1322. The king's triumph then was marked by a reimposition of new customs and evil tolls. On 16 June, the collectors in various parts were informed that on account of the need of resisting the attacks of the Scots, which required the king "to pour forth as it were infinite money the merchants of the realm and those staying there" had granted to the king a subsidy on wool, wool fells and hides for one year. They were accordingly to collect them and answer for the issues thereof at the exchequer, the writ being made "by king and council[5]." The new customs on wine were also reimposed, and orders for collection issued on 20 July[6]. The king claimed that as the Ordinances had now been annulled, the new customs ought to be levied[7].

These few instances of the way in which the king disobeyed the Ordinances express his general policy towards that part of the activity of the baronial opposition. His disobedience was immediate, and, if not continuous, was renewed whenever opportunity offered itself. For he considered that the Ordinances were to his loss and prejudice[8]. An examination of the periods when the Ordinances were disobeyed by the king shows that until the parliament of York, except when the king was under the direct influence of the baronial opposition, as after the parliament of Westminster in 1315, the Ordinances were not obeyed. After the parliament of York, the king was ready to listen to reason and rule in accordance with the general spirit and desire of the middle party. The Ordinances were then generally observed.

1 *Cal. Letter Books, E*, pp. 52–53.
2 Ibid. *D*, pp. 301–2.
3 Ibid. pp. 303–4.
4 Ordinance 11.
5 *Cal. Fine Rolls*, 1319–27, p. 135.
6 Ibid. pp. 145–7.
7 Cf *Cal. Fine Rolls*, 1319–27, p. 180.
8 K. R. Acct. 375/8, f. 7.

In a word, coercion by the barons did not produce the desired result; moderation went far towards attaining it. Lancaster was able to effect little; Pembroke did much towards procuring reform of the administration and even of the household.

The final results of the Ordinances cannot be judged until the year 1322, after they had been revoked. For the king did not rejoice at the expense of his enemies. In a memorandum of matters which the king referred to his council[1] before the parliament of York, though the question of the repeal of the Ordinances came first: "Ade primes de Lestatut sur le repeal des Ordenances," that was followed immediately by a concession one would have hardly expected from the king, so soon after his victory over the very power that had sought to enforce the Ordinances to their last letter: "Item de mettre les bons pointz en Estatut." The other matters which were referred by the king to the council were all connected with reforms of administration and legislation. They were to ordain how chattels of felons, waste, deodands, wreck of the sea and other similar profits, which could be levied only in eyre, might be levied year by year to the king's need, as other lords who had such profits by grant of ancient charter levied them to their need. They were to consider how all the balances could be adjusted both for buying and selling, as it was said that all the balances in the realm were false. Other matters to be considered related to the redress of all kinds of beer, of appeals of felonies, of matters connected with the staple and various matters. On all the king desired all his councils to consider how to amend the law for his profit and that of his people. What was agreed was to be put into the form of a statute ready for the approaching parliament[2].

The revocation of the Ordinances was therefore the first matter which came before the parliament which met at York on 2 May[3]. Among the prelates, earls and barons at that parliament were the greater number of the ordainers who were still alive[4], and the king was thus able to strengthen the moral value of the repeal by obtaining their co-operation. Upon examination of the Ordinances by the prelates, earls and barons and by the commonalty of the realm, it was found that by the Ordinances "the royal power of the king was restrained in divers things contrary to what ought to be, to the blemishing of his royal sovereignty and against the estate of the

[1] Parl. and Council Proc. (Chan.), File 5/10. Vide App. of Doc. no. 93.

[2] Ibid.

[3] *Parl. Writs*, vol. II, Pt ii, p. 245.

[4] *Stat. of Realm*, vol. I, p. 189.

crown[1]." By the Ordinances, which had been made by subjects against the royal power, troubles and wars had occurred by which the land had been in peril. It was therefore accorded and established in parliament by the king and by the prelates, earls and barons, and by the whole community of the realm:

> that all the things by the said ordainers ordained and contained in the said ordinances, shall from henceforth for the time to come cease and shall lose their name, force, virtue and effect for ever; the statutes and establishments, duly made by our lord the king and his ancestors, before the said ordinances, abiding in their force[2].

The revocation of the Ordinances did not satisfy the king. He safe-guarded himself for the future. Anything henceforth made by subjects, against the royal power, was to be void and of no avail or force[3]. The sheriffs throughout England were, on 19 May, informed, by letters patent, of the revocation, which was to be read and published in full county court, and observed by them in their offices[4]. Similar writs were sent to the benches ordering publication and observance[5]. Thus the king at one stroke, in proper constitutional form, had revoked the whole program of the Ordinances and all that it involved. Such complete revocation was to be expected. The king before 1318 had only acquiesced in them for short periods under compulsion. After 1318 the acquiescence had been more willing, because strict enforcement of the Ordinances was not insisted upon. The whole idea underlying the Ordinances was repugnant to the king. By them his royal power had been restrained in various ways contrary to what ought to be. The king had been forced to appoint the ordainers. He had been forced to accept the Ordinances. The ordainers had restricted his power in various ways. It was only spasmodically that the king could be forced to execute the Ordinances. Restraint by force the king could not countenance. Accordingly all that had been achieved by force had to be swept away. In this matter the king had the support of the pope. In June, 1322, the pope ordered the archbishop of Canterbury to ascertain the facts touching the Ordinances, which, though made under pretext of reform, were to the diminution and depression of the king's power. Such

[1] *Stat. of Realm*, vol. 1, p. 189. A draft of the revocation made in the council and amended is found in Parl. and Council Proc. (Chan.), File 5/9.

[2] *Stat. of Realm*, vol. 1, p. 189.

[3] The discussion of this important clause is postponed to pp. 513–517.

[4] *Stat. of Realm*, vol. 1, p. 190.

[5] *Abbrev. Placit.* p. 348. The writ and revocation sent to Henry le Scrope and his fellow justices *coram rege* are preserved in K. B. Misc., Class 138, no. 108, mm. 9 and 10.

steps were to be taken as should seem fit for the good of the church and the realm[1].

After revocation, however, such beneficial reforms as the Ordinances had included could be treated on a new basis. The good points were to be put into a statute. But in future they were to owe their force, not to baronial restraint, but to royal statute duly enacted. The Ordinances which had been ordained by the earl of Lancaster and the other magnates of his conspiracy were repealed; but if there was any profitable Ordinance it was to be written and had in the name of a statute[2]. A petition relating to the Ordinances made to the first parliament of Edward III[3] received as its reply:

> Quant a les Ordenaunces, soient veues et examinez, et les bones soient mis en Estatut, et les autres soient oustez[4].

It is interesting to find that the king in the triumph of 1322 took no more violent action than a new and young king, owing his throne to a revolutionary movement engineered largely by the barons, took in 1327. The chroniclers attached more importance to the erection to an earldom of the elder Despenser than to the Ordinances or any other act of this parliament of York[5]. One[6] mentions this revocation of the Ordinances without referring to the new statute which contained the Ordinances of which the king approved. Few seemed to realise the magnanimity of the king in adopting the good reforms of his bitterest enemies. It was a good augury for the new era.

The statute[7], which contained such of the Ordinances as the king approved, is worthy of detailed consideration. Besides being a proof of the king's desire for reform it gave that part of the Ordinances which became final and irrevocable. The preamble stated that it was the king's desire to ordain and establish a matter that should be to the honour of God and of Holy Church, to the profit of himself and his realm, the good keeping of his peace and the tranquillity of his people. He therefore made this establishment by the assent of the prelates, earls, barons and commonalty of the realm assembled in his

[1] *Cal. Pap. Letters*, 1304–42, p. 231.

[2] *Le Livere de Reis de Brit.* p. 344: "e a cel parlement furent repellez les ordinaunces le dit counte de Lancastre qil e autres grauntz de la covine eurent ordinee: e sil y fust trove nul ordinaunce profitable serroit escrit e averoit noun de statut."

[3] *Rot. Parl.* vol. II, p. 7.

[4] Ibid. p. 11.

[5] *Ann. Paul.* p. 303. *Auct. Bridl.* pp. 78–79. *Flores Hist.* vol. III, p. 209. *Chron. Murimuth*, p. 37. *Chron. Mon. de Melsa*, vol. II, p. 345.

[6] *Ann. Paul.* p. 303.

[7] Printed *Rot. Parl.* vol. I, pp. 456–7, App. no. 35. *Cal. Close Rolls*, 1318–23, pp. 537–8, where it is transcribed in full and not calendared. It is omitted from *Stat. of Realm*, vol. I.

parliament at York[1]. After the manner of all important medieval legislation of a general nature, it opened with a reference to the church. Holy Church was to have all its rights and liberties as was contained in Magna Carta and the other statutes that had been made before this time. The king's peace was to be firmly kept throughout his realm so that all could safely go, come and stay according to the law and custom of the realm. What Edward I in his parliament of Westminster in his 28th year had established[2] touching prises and of the manner of the punishment of those who acted against it, was to be held and kept in all its points; each one who wished to complain of something done to him against this establishment should have a writ in chancery suitable to his case. Sheriffs and hundreders were to be appointed according to the form of the statute made in the present king's time at his parliament of Lincoln in his 9th year[3]. The grant which Edward I had made at Westminster, on 27 May in his 34th year[4], touching his forests and indictments made in trespasses of vert and venison was to be held in all its points for ever. Those who felt themselves grieved against the form of the grant were to have the writ in chancery on the matter. What Edward I in his parliament at Westminster in the 28th year of his reign[5] made and established of the estate of the steward and the marshals and of pleas which ought to be held there and concerning cognizance of debts and the office which belonged to the coroner of felony made within the verge should be held and kept in all points for ever. The steward and marshals in future in pleas of trespass, contracts, covenants and debts of which they ought to have cognizance according to the form of the establishment, should receive attorneys as well for defendants as for plaintiffs[6]. If the steward or marshal acted contrary to that establishment or this statute, his action was to be held for naught and he should be punished towards the king by punishment and by ransom. Those who sued the plea should be punished towards the party in double damages. All who wished to complain of things done to him against that establishment or this statute were to have a writ of chancery pleadable before the king, as well against the steward and marshals as against the party[7]. Then followed[8] the Ordinances,

[1] *Cal. Close Rolls*, 1318–23, p. 557.

[2] The transcript in *Cal. Close Rolls*, 1318–23, p. 552, gives the year as the 8th; the transcript in *Rot. Parl.* vol. I, p. 456, gives it as the 28th. The reference must be § ii, Articuli super cartas, 28 Ed. I, *Stat. of Realm*, vol. I, pp. 137–8.

[3] Vide below, pp 524–5. [4] *Stat. of Realm*, vol. I, pp. 147–9.

[5] *Stat. of Realm*, vol. I, p 138, Articuli super cartas, § iii.

[6] Cf. Ordinances 26, 27. [7] *Cal. Close Rolls*, 1318–23, pp. 557–8. [8] Ibid. p. 558.

which had been made concerning the statute of merchants[1], outlawries[2] and appeals[3], which are given verbatim as in the Ordinances.

A number of the clauses in this statute were repetitions of enactments of Edward I; others were Ordinances given a legal form. There was little that was new. The need of the time was administrative reform, not additional legislation. The first essential was that existing legislation should be executed and maintained. This Edward II was now preparing to do. The most important phase of the remainder of his reign was the administrative reforms attempted, and partly achieved. It was upon the exchequer that the best energies of the reformers were spent. The exchequer reforms, with which the name of Walter de Stapleton, bishop of Exeter, treasurer, was so closely connected, were serious attempts to promote order and efficiency in that department. Efforts were also made to reform the household, and the local administration which was in a hopeless state of confusion; and abuse was also attacked. This reforming energy which constituted one of the dominant features of the period 1322–26 owed a good deal to the Ordinances and the baronial attempts to put them into execution. These reforms provide to some extent a justification for the baronial opposition. Such of the Ordinances as had not been actuated by a factious spirit and such as had not been due to selfish baronial aims had attacked real administrative abuses. Even in Lancaster, however petty, narrow and selfish his motives, there had been an underlying desire for reform, apart from baronial aims. A number of these reforms the king willingly incorporated in the statute which he made in the parliament of York in 1322. He had indeed never denied the need of reforms. What he had been resolutely opposed to had been those restrictions of his power, which had accompanied and absorbed the genuine reforms. More important than such part of the Ordinances as was retained was the impulse which they had given to the reforming movement. The Ordinances and the consequent action of the baronial opposition had, at least, shown the imperative need of administrative reform. When the king and his party were free to act unhindered by baronial interference, he and his officials took up these reforms with some amount of energy. The undertaking of these reforms was in part a result of the baronial opposition.

Various legislative measures apart from the Ordinances also

[1] Ordinance 33. [2] Ordinance 35. [3] Ordinance 36.

obtained after 1322. The important Statute of Lincoln, made in 1316, when baronial influence had been strong, was contained in the statute made in 1322. The Statute of York of 1318 also retained its position. To actual reforms the king did not object. Restriction upon his power masquerading as reform he opposed with resolution.

It has been seen that the baronial scheme, in as far as it was contained in a program of reform, left some traces of its influence upon subsequent legislation and administration. The varied machinery by which the barons endeavoured to control the king must be considered separately. There are four definite instances of that machinery which have to be considered. In the first place, there was the machinery which effected the appointment of the ordainers and the work of the ordainers themselves as a committee of reform. Then there was the committee of five which was to secure the execution of the Ordinances. At the parliament of Lincoln new machinery was set up with Lancaster as the head of the council. Lastly in the parliament of York in 1318 there was the standing council with the committee of five. Besides these specific instances there were general and unorganised attempts to control the king, such as the Lancaster administration after Bannockburn and the action of the confederate barons in the parliament at Westminster in 1321. The ultimate basis of all these attempts to control the king, with perhaps the exception of the scheme accepted by the parliament of York, was coercion. In the circumstances it was inevitable that all these schemes should collapse. Apart from the standing council of 1318, which must be treated as an exception from most general statements, there was no element of permanence about them. The direction of the powers of the ordainers had been definitely fixed by the king in the authority giving the barons the right to appoint. The lay section of the ordainers clung together as a body after the duration of these powers but were able to effect little. The executive clauses of the Ordinances, which instructed the appointment of a committee of five to hear complaints against the royal officers, was almost useless as an executive body, and little trace, if any, is left of its action. The scheme of appointing Lancaster as chief of the king's council depended almost entirely upon the action and will of one man. Lancaster was notoriously subject to frequent periods of inaction and was himself no administrator. Little could be expected from a scheme, the efficiency of which depended upon his action. All these schemes possessed such inherent weaknesses, apart from their dependence upon coercion, that successful results could not be expected. It is true that the lords appellant of Richard II's reign and their action had a considerable resemblance to the ordainers of 1310–11. That is not sufficient to relieve the executive clauses of the Ordinances of the charge of sterility. These instances of the machinery of restraint employed in the reign of Edward II had precedents in similar inventions designed for a like purpose under Henry III. This mere fact does not crown with success the efforts made under Henry III. The machinery designed to restrain and control Edward II obtained little effect in the very time of its creation and it grew less immediately. The effect was never complete and always transitory. Of ultimate effect it was completely void. The machinery was temporary and created for specific purposes. It failed to fulfil even those specific purposes. The king's power had not suffered in the slightest as a result of the efforts by the year 1322. Control of the king relying upon coercion and inefficient machinery was impossible.

The machinery set up in the parliament of York in 1318, with its standing council of prelates, earls and barons, and its committee of five, composed of two bishops, one earl, one baron and a banneret of Lancaster's, could not be condemned for the same defects. The committee which was to remain with the king quarterly ensured that there would be permanence of control. The useful work done in the parliament of York gave it a fair start on its way. More important than all, it was started with the co-operation or at least without the avowed or active disapproval of the king. He acquiesced in this scheme because it saved him from something worse. It stood between him and Lancaster. He had no love or respect for a committee of control, as a part of the machinery of government. When the influence of the younger Despenser grew the king followed him and his father rather than the committee. When in 1322 the king's action was free and unimpeded by any danger or threats, no attempt was made to return to any council of control. The "administrative" council composed of the chancellor, treasurer, a number of justices and other officials, with a prelate or magnate associated with them on occasion when the king desired, supplied the royal need as far as advice and administrative detail went. The element of control was unnecessary and improper. Thus machinery of control which was efficient and which did not depend upon coercion, though it had greater temporary success had no greater ultimate result than the less efficient which depended upon coercion.

In addition to the practical objects of the barons and the methods by which they sought to attain their ends, the results of the baronial opposition upon the spirit in which the king approached the problems of administration and legislation must be considered. The barons had shown where reform was necessary and as a measure of mere self-defence, it was the royal policy to achieve some measure of that reform. Thus, while the baronial opposition failed to effect any of the schemes, it cannot be said that all its endeavours ended in total failure. Their opposition resulted in disaster, dishonour, and death to themselves. The battle of Boroughbridge was a debacle. That their schemes had any result was not because of, but despite, the method they employed. They failed to diminish the king's power. They failed to impose constitutional checks upon his action. The attempt of the oligarchy to capture administration failed. But they had pointed to definite and serious grievances in the administration and although unable to effect reform themselves, they had shown the need and suggested the way. The effect of the baronial opposition upon the reforms of the concluding period of the reign can be easily exaggerated. Much was due to the energy and ability of men like Stapleton. The bishop of Exeter was a man of independent views and was probably willing to learn from the experience of the baronial opposition. The baronial opposition in its own downfall left a small heritage of good to the royal administration.

CHAPTER IX

EXPLANATION OF THE BARONIAL FAILURE

The baronial efforts proved unable to achieve their immediate objects. Various suggestions can be put forward in explanation of this failure. First in importance stands the great inherent strength of the royal position. When that weighty consideration is united to inherent defects in baronial policy and especially to weaknesses in its expression and operation, the failure of the barons is appreciated. The human side of the baronial opposition told heavily against success.

The reasons for the ultimate failure of the baronial designs were mainly the same as the reasons which had prevented the execution of the baronial schemes when the barons were in the plenitude of their power. The first of these was the strength of the king's positions. Theoretically the king's power and authority was unassailable. The extent to which the theoretical authority obtained, was dependent upon the king's practical power. Henry III, though his theoretical position was about as complete as that of Edward II, had been driven to greater extremities. Writs had been issued then, not by the king's authority, but on that of the barons, and such witnessings as:

> Per comitem Leycestrie comitem Gloucestrie comitem Marescallum Hugonem le Bigod justiciarium Johannem filium Galfridi Johannem Mansell et alios de consilio regis[1].
>
> Ista litera processit de precepto Hugonis justiciarii Anglie et Egidii de Argentem senescalli regis[2].

were found on the patent roll of Henry III. That Edward II was not driven to such extremity was not due to baronial weakness but to the king's practical strength. Even if the king's prerogative had not increased since the time of Henry III the household system and its intricacies had developed. The reign of Edward I, too, had increased the practical position of the king. The household system was a whole armoury of weapons which enabled the king to foil

[1] Harcourt, *His Grace the Steward*, pp. 132–7, from Pat. Roll, 42 Hen. III. m. 45 (6 July, 1258). Cf. *Cal. Pat. Rolls*, 1247–58, p. 640.

[2] Ibid. Pat. Roll, 42 Henry III. m. 2 (1 Oct. 1258). Cf. *Cal. Pat. Rolls*, 1247–58, p. 652.

the barons at every thrust. Lancaster's constant complaints, that the king was contemning the Ordinances[1], were due to the fact that the king, by virtue of his position, could afford to do so, and by virtue of his resources in the household system had the means of doing so. On January 30, 1321, when the trouble over the Despensers' oppression was approaching its climax and Hereford and others were making treaties and holding gatherings, the king could order that such "ought not to be held without the king's presence or the presence of those of his council appointed by him[2]." Although Hereford and those acting with him included a majority of the middle party, the king could still claim to issue such a writ "by king and council[3]." Even if the king could not enforce the observance of such a writ, it showed his power that on such an occasion, though deserted by those upon whose assistance he had acted for a number of years, he was still able to issue such a writ in such a form.

The chief strength of the king's position lay, however, in its negative power. The king could make writs even if he could not enforce them. The barons had, at times, the force but they could not secure control over the great seal; and behind the great seal the king had the privy seal and the secret seal. In a word, the king's strength depended upon his executive power. It was in execution that the baronial opposition was weak. The vital point in their attempts to exercise restraint was the capture of the executive. It was here that their failure was greatest and most serious in its results. If the king could not secure the enforcement of his own commands, he could yet frustrate baronial action. He could prevent baronial commands having force by refusing to allow them to be given in the normal way. The king could ensure that his commands alone passed the great seal. As long as the king controlled the executive he controlled the administration. If the administrative officers did not obey the commands of the executive, they could be removed by the executive. The control of the central administration by the executive was extremely important and comparatively easy. To mention but one way in which the central administration was maintained in its loyalty, the king secured offices there for his household officials. In the strength of the household system and in the executive power which it assured the king, the barons found a position which they could not overcome.

In these circumstances the barons could not ultimately have been

[1] Cf. *Auct. Bridl.* p. 51.
[2] *Cal. Close Rolls*, 1318–23, pp. 355–6.
[3] Ibid.

successful against the king, but had there not been immediate causes of baronial weakness a greater measure of success might have been attained. There were several weaknesses in the ranks of the barons which told in the king's favour. In a body of such a size and of so diverse interests entire unity was almost impossible. The first consideration of the prelates, who formed so considerable and influential a portion, would be the church and their dioceses. Moreover, many of the prelates had been royal officers and had strong royalist leanings. Amongst the lay baronage there was still greater lack of cohesion. Lancaster's position as leader was not unchallenged. From 1316 onwards there were definitely two parties among the barons, parties that differed in aims and ideals as well as in method. There was disagreement even among the earls who formed the most important part of the committee of ordainers. The earl of Gloucester was definitely royalist by tradition and training. Lincoln was not whole hearted and though an ordainer was sufficiently trusted by the king to be chosen as his regent during his absence in the north when the ordainers were sitting. On his death he was followed as king's lieutenant by Gloucester. About Easter, 1311, an observer of affairs feared a serious riot in London, chiefly from the lower classes, between the partizans of the earls of Gloucester and Lancaster, for Gloucester, who had returned to England, would be in London at that time when the prelates, earls and other ordainers would also be there[1]. Such disagreement even before their scheme was accepted by the king inevitably militated considerably against ultimate success. There was a difference in the degree in which the various barons were prepared to push the king. The strength of the king's position made it important that the barons should show a united front and work with a united purpose. Internal disagreement would encourage the king and improve his position. From the purely baronial point of view it was a cause of weakness that a number of them joined in the king's expeditions, including the Bannockburn campaign, which was undertaken contrary to the Ordinances.

Apart from general lack of cohesion there were a number of occasions on which serious, if not irreparable, harm was done the baronial cause by the defection of a powerful personality. The most serious was the action of Pembroke in 1312, consequent upon the murder of Gavaston. Pembroke then identified himself strongly with the king's policy, undertook almost complete charge of his administration and supported the king against the Lancaster faction.

[1] *Cal. Doc. Scotl.* vol. III, p. 41.

Although Pembroke had been a firm supporter of the Ordinances and had led the opposition to the appointment of Langton as treasurer[1], he never again co-operated heartily with Lancaster, and his influence did more than any other factor to lessen Lancaster's importance and diminish his authority. The creation of the middle party was a direct challenge to Lancaster.

Moreover, in addition to his disputes with Lancaster on matters of public policy, Pembroke had in 1314 a personal dispute with him on the matter of the castle of Thorpwaterville. Pembroke in fact went so far as to gather great numbers of men-at-arms against Lancaster on account of the dispute. On 7 February, 1314, the king ordered him, by privy seal, to cease making such assemblies. He was to settle the business in the king's court according to the law and custom of the realm[2]. Pembroke accordingly purchased a commission of oyer and terminer against certain of Lancaster's men. When the time of meeting came Pembroke's armed men prevented Lancaster's men from coming before the justices[3]. By writ of privy seal Pembroke was on 20 February ordered to prevent this immediately and to allow the king's court to have its course undisturbed[4]. With this writ of privy seal someone about the court wrote, on the king's behalf, a covering letter to Pembroke. He explained how two messengers from Lancaster had come to the king with letters of credence about the dispute. The king answered them that he was shortly to have his council assembled for certain weighty matters and this matter would be treated there. The earl's messengers had complained of Pembroke's men who appeared on the day of the oyer and terminer in force and arms and therefore the writ of privy seal was sent[5]. Subsequently, at the king's request, Pembroke quit-claimed to Lancaster the castle and manor of Thorpwaterville and other manors in Northampton and the New Temple in London[6]. This quit-claim was confirmed on 1 October, 1314[7]. On 3 October in consideration of it the king granted as gift to Pembroke all the lands in Monmouth which Robert de Clifford had held for life[8]. Pembroke was still slow in restoring the muniments connected with this land, and on 6 October the king had to order him to deliver them to Lancaster[9]. Such personal disputes as this within the ranks of the baronage did much to weaken their cause.

[1] Vide above, pp. 389–392.
[2] Anc. Corresp. vol. XLIX, no. 24.
[3] Ibid. no. 25.
[4] Ibid.
[5] Ibid. vol. L, no. 86.
[6] *Cal. Pat. Rolls*, 1313–17, pp. 184–5.
[7] Ibid.
[8] *Cal. Charter Rolls*, 1300–26, p. 242.
[9] Anc. Corresp. vol. XLIX, no. 28.

The dispute which Lancaster had with the earl of Surrey was still more serious and it touched Lancaster's honour. Warenne was not a man of first rate importance and had not taken a considerable part in the baronial schemes. He had been ignored in the appointment of the ordainers but had joined them in their pursuit of Gavaston in 1312. With the murder of Gavaston, he, too, went over to the king's side[1], though his loss did not weaken the barons. It was by the abduction[2], or participation[3] in the abduction, of Lancaster's wife in 1317 that Warenne got into bitter enmity with him. The abduction was not the result of lust but was merely done in despite of the earl[4]. Warenne's action naturally led to war with Lancaster. As early as 28 May gatherings in arms were forbidden[5]. By November, Lancaster had besieged and captured various castles belonging to Warenne in Yorkshire, and, on that behalf, had done many things to the disturbance of the king's peace. The king ordered him to desist from such proceedings and to cause amendment to be made. Whatever complaints Lancaster had against Warenne and others he ought to prosecute in the king's court where the king was prepared to do him justice[6]. Lancaster still harboured his ill-feelings. On 18 June he was ordered not to do anything in breach of the king's peace, as the king understood he was about to occupy the lands of Bromfeld and Yale which belonged to Warenne[7]. In July, 1318, in the midst of the general pacification with the king and his followers, he refused to be reconciled with Warenne[8]. This personal insult was further complicated by a dispute between Lancaster and Warenne over certain lands, which was happily settled by an exchange[9]. On 1 January, 1319, Warenne obtained the royal licence to enfeoff Lancaster of certain lands held in chief and have them redelivered to himself for life, Lancaster obtaining licence to hold for life certain lands in Surrey[10]. On 3 January, Lancaster obtained licence to grant lands to the value of 1000 marks to Warenne for life[11]. Though the whole quarrel seemed terminated, there can have been little really good feeling established. Warenne acted as one of the

[1] *Ann. Lond.* p. 208.
[2] *Ann. Paul.* p. 280. *Auct. Malm.* p. 233. *Flores Hist.* vol. III, pp. 178–9.
[3] *Auct. Bridl.* p. 54.
[4] *Chron. Mon. de Melsa*, vol. I, p. 335.
[5] *Cal. Close Rolls*, 1313–18, p. 469. *Foedera*, vol. II, p. 332.
[6] *Cal. Close Rolls*, 1313–18, p. 575 (3 Nov. 1317).
[7] Ibid. p. 554.
[8] *Auct. Malm.* p. 236.
[9] Ibid. p. 240.
[10] *Cal. Pat. Rolls*, 1317–21, p. 264.
[11] Ibid. Cf. also *Descr. Cat. Ancient Deeds*, vol. III, p. 196. *Cal. Pat. Rolls*, 317–21, p. 319. *Cal. Close Rolls*, 1318–23, p. 68.

earls who sat to try and to condemn Lancaster in 1322[1], and after his death obtained possession of the castle of Holt and all the lands of Bromfeld and Yale which Lancaster held for life of his demise[2]. Though the quarrel between Lancaster and Warenne did not cause such important political results as the alienation of Pembroke, it helped to lessen the power of the baronial opposition. As long as some members of the baronial opposition acted apart from the others, and as long as there were personal disputes within the baronial ranks, its chances of success, however small they may have been, were being further prejudiced.

Lancaster was, of course, pre-eminent among the barons in wealth and position. He was a mighty territorial magnate, the steward of England, and of the royal blood. He gathered round himself a number of barons, bannerets and knights, who because of the favours they received from him, should have been devoted to his interests. Great as was Lancaster's power he had troubles of his own. He found when his hour of need arrived that one, in whom he had placed entire confidence, failed him. Had Lancaster been better served by his supporters and had no troubles of his own distracted his attention and energies from his main object, the baronial opposition, which depended so much upon him, might have achieved a greater success. The earl had bestowed gifts of land and other favours upon one of his knights, Robert de Holand[3]. In the crisis of 1322, Lancaster sent him out to gather forces for him and was relying greatly upon the certain aid he would bring[4]. Holand proved a traitor to the earl, and failed to appear at the appointed time[5]. At the critical moment he deserted to the king[6]: and Holand's was not the only desertion that Lancaster suffered. Harclay himself had been knighted by the earl[7]. Most of the company of his knights also deserted[8], though Holand's was the most serious and disastrous. It was subsequently presented by a local jury that when Lancaster had been defeated at Burton, Holand had on the same day sent several letters to the earl. The jurors were ignorant of the tenor of the letters but they believed that they were for the purpose of drawing his lord away[9]. When the earl

1 *Auct. Bridl.* p. 77.

2 *Cal. Pat. Rolls*, 1321–24, p. 122 (27 May, 1322).

3 *Vict. Co. Hist. Lancaster*, vol. II, p. 198. Cf. *Cal. Inq. P. M.* vol. VII, p. 60.

4 *Chron. Knighton*, vol. I, p. 424. *Auct. Malm.* p. 267.

5 *Chron. Knighton*, vol. I, p. 424. Cf. *Cal. Close Rolls*, 1318–23, p. 525.

6 *Auct. Malm.* p. 267.

7 *Eulog. Hist.* vol. III, p. 196.

8 Camd. Soc., *Polit. Songs*, pp. 270–1.

9 "quod causa fuit detrahendi dominum suum predictum."

was fleeing, Holand pillaged various baronial supporters including D'Audley and the countess of Lincoln and other baronial adherents of their goods to the value of £1000[1]. That Holand's desertion had a serious effect is suggested by a decision concerning him made in the first parliament of Edward III: "Il plest a nostre Seigneur le Roi, et a touz les Grantz du Conseil, qe Sire Robert de Holand ne soit pas eide entre ceaux de la querele[2]." In 1328 he was beheaded at Harrow and his head sent as a present to Henry, earl of Lancaster[3], and this fate was considered a fit punishment for treachery[4].

Even in his own county of Lancaster, the earl had a rising against his authority, when in 1315, Adam de Banaster a knight revolted. Whether the cause of the revolt is to be found in a dispute between Banaster and Robert de Holand[5], or in Banaster's fear of punishment for a murder he had committed[6], or whether he thought he would please the king[7] is uncertain. On 8 October, 1315, Adam de Banaster met various knights and entered into a sworn confederacy with them to live and die together[8]. As they moved about the county they gathered forces and on 23 October made an unsuccessful attempt upon Liverpool. Then separating into parties they plundered and ravaged. They exhibited letters patent under the king's seal stating that they had the king's commission to act as they did. At Manchester, they showed a standard with the king's arms, which they had taken from a church, stating that the king had sent it to them. A small force sent against the rebels was defeated, but when the larger body arrived they were completely routed, after less than an hour's fighting[9]. Banaster was beheaded immediately[10]. The king granted the earl a commission of oyer and terminer to try the rebels[11]. Though the revolt had dealt no serious blow to the earl it must have hampered his power considerably. Lands which had been taken from Banaster's brothers by Lancaster on account of the revolt, they were unable to regain as long as the earl lived. After his death the king and council were petitioned for remedy[12], with some success[13], though a previous

[1] Wm Salt Soc., *Coll.* vol. IX, p. 99. [2] *Rot. Parl.* vol. II, p. 12.
[3] *Ann. Paul.* p. 342. [4] *Chron. Knighton*, vol. I, p. 424.
[5] *Ann. Paul.* p. 279. [6] *Auct. Malm.* p. 214. [7] Ibid.
[8] *Vict. Co. Hist. Lancaster*, vol. II, p. 198, quoting Coram Rege Roll, no. 254.
[9] Ibid. pp. 198–9.
[10] *Ann. Lond.* pp. 236–7. *Ann. Paul.* p. 279. *Auct. Bridl.* p. 48. *Auct. Malm.* p. 215. *Flores Hist.* vol. III, pp. 172–3. *Chron. Hemingburgh*, vol. II, p. 296.
[11] *Cal. Pat. Rolls*, 1313–17, p. 421 (12 Mar. 1315).
[12] *Rot. Parl.* vol. I, p. 414.
[13] Cole, *Doc. illustr. Eng. Hist. in 13th and 14th Cent.* p. 26.

petition in the parliament of York in 1318 had produced no result[1]. Such troubles, as this which Lancaster had, were neither trifling nor disastrous. Added to other causes they acted as a source of weakness to the barons as a whole and thus accounted to some extent for the baronial failure.

More serious than such external sources of weakness, or trouble various barons had on their own account, was one which was internal. The barons allowed personal motives and ends to interfere with their public policy. This fact robbed the baronial opposition of so much that might otherwise have justified it. It degraded the baronial cause and it proved a considerable factor towards the undoing of the baronial plans. The charge of allowing personal motives to rule is a general one which might be almost equally well applied to all the barons. It is against Pembroke that it could be made with least justification. This condition of affairs weakened the stand they took against the favourites, Gavaston and Despenser. Their case was that the favourites were exploiting the king and procuring money from the exchequer, grants of land and other favours. The barons displayed as much selfishness and consideration for their own interests as even the favourites did. The baronial policy was often as much directed by narrow baronial and personal interests as was the royal policy, as directed by the Despensers before the exile in 1321. Often the complaint of the barons against the favourites was produced by mere envy.

The extent to which the barons allowed their own interests to interfere with the aims of the baronial opposition can be illustrated by the career of Henry de Percy, in the period immediately before and after the Ordinances. He had acted with the barons in obtaining the appointment of the ordainers[2]. Before that he had been in attendance at court[3] and soon after he again received the royal favour[4]. On 3 February a writ of privy seal was issued at his request allowing certain persons to plead debts at the exchequer[5]. On 20 March, 1311, he had received the custody of the bishopric of Durham, which was then vacant, the writ being issued by warrant of privy seal[6]. Other lands were also granted to him in March and May[7]. On 4 August,

[1] *Parl. Writs*, vol. II, Pt i, p. 370.

[2] Vide above, p. 360.

[3] *Cal. Pat. Rolls*, 1307–13, p. 83. *Cal. Close Rolls*, 1307–13, p. 225.

[4] Chan. Warr., File 69/1192 (29 Aug. 1310). A writ of p. s. was issued at his instance.

[5] K. R. Mem. Roll, no. 84, m. 20 d.

[6] *Cal. Fine Rolls*, 1307–19, p. 86.

[7] Chan. Warr., Files 75/1748, 1750; 78/2051.

at the instance of Beaumont, he was granted "the chief bailiwick of Holand[1]." He was about the court and acted as the royal messenger to the chancellor, when on 28 August the king restored to Hereford, as his right, the constableship of England, which the king had taken into his hands[2]. On 2 December the office of keeper of the forest north of Trent, which had been surrendered in conformity with the Ordinances, was accepted by him despite the fact that the appointment was not made as provided in the Ordinances, though the ordainers afterwards consented to it[3]. In the same month the castle of Bamburgh was granted to him, the writ being issued on the information of the bishop of Worcester[4]. Percy was acting simply on his own interests without paying any regard to the policy of the ordainers. The crowning act of self-interest committed by him in despite of the Ordinances was when he sold the office of justice of the forest north of Trent to Gavaston, to whom the king restored it on 3 April, 1312[5]. Yet a few weeks later he joined in the pursuit of Gavaston[6]. Percy probably acted in the manner any other baron placed in similar circumstances would have done, for they were all equally selfish. That fact, however, increased rather than diminished the prejudicial effects upon the success of the baronial policy.

As a result the whole baronial policy was vitiated by the worst features. Selfishness bred insincerity and lack of sincerity characterised a considerable portion of the baronial actions. Low as was the general character of the period, its depths were reached by some of the barons. This poverty of character failed to impress the country with the virtues of baronial policy. If the barons were the only considerable section of the community apart from the church, and the people were barely articulate, in a conflict ultimately dependent upon force and numbers the opinion of the people was of considerable moment. The importance of appealing to the people was realised by the king, and he took care that the people should know his side of the case by issuing frequent proclamations, and by prohibiting narrators of false news. When the king set out for his march campaign late in 1321 he ordered the sheriffs to make proclamation for the preservation of the peace and the observance of the statutes of the realm. Immediately after the battle of Boroughbridge, when the malice of the rebels was no longer to be feared, the sheriffs throughout

[1] *Cal. Fine Rolls*, 1307–19, p. 100.
[2] *Cal. Pat. Rolls*, 1307–13, p. 387.
[3] Vide above, p. 389
[4] *Cal. Fine Rolls*, 1307–19, p. 121.
[5] *Cal. Pat. Rolls*, 1307–13, p. 450.
[6] Cf. ibid. p. 486; *Cal. Close Rolls*, 1307–13, p. 469.

England were ordered to make proclamation that the king's peace and the statutes, laws and customs of the realm should be maintained and observed uninjured[1]. The opinion of communities like London was very important. The barons seldom succeeded in impressing the citizens of London with their honesty and for most of the reign of Edward II London supported the king.

The action of the section of the baronage which refused to go in person to fight against the Scots would not appeal generally. Thus the failure of Lancaster, Hereford, Pembroke and Arundel to join the king in 1310[2], because they did not see eye to eye with him on some particular point of policy[3], lacked conviction. The statement of the earls in 1314, that the king should summon a parliament so that general agreement should be obtained concerning what was to be done according to the Ordinances rather than that the matter should be proceeded upon secretly[4], in view of the urgency of the relief of Stirling, was inopportune. The king's refusal to wait was met by a counter refusal of the earls to fight without a parliament, because they did not wish to go contrary to the Ordinances[5]. This, too, probably did not improve the position in the eyes of the people.

The inconsistency of the barons was noted by a chronicler. Writing after the exile of the Despensers and the full pardon his plunderers had exacted from the king, this chronicler said that the makers of the laws had become their perverters. At the parliament of York, Lancaster had made the king pardon his suit of peace, against himself and all his abettors, and yet that same earl had previously sworn to hold certain Ordinances[6] that the king should not remit suit of peace to anyone in cases in which death had happened[7]. The pardons and acquittances which had been made in the parliament of Westminster were similarly questioned[8]. Another chronicler commented upon the prevalence of pride and insolence. Envy, moreover, ruled. The squire strove to get better than the knight, the knight than the baron, the baron than the earl and the earl than the king. Luxury provided desire for more; because what one had was insufficient, therefore men devoted themselves to plunder, spoiling their neighbours. The magnates of the land fell in battle, died without sons and divided their inheritance among daughters, and the name of the father was lost for ever[9]. Whatever may have been the real

[1] *Cal. Close Rolls*, 1318–23, pp. 534–5 (21 Mar. 1322).
[2] *Ann. Paul.* p. 269.
[3] *Chron. Lanerc.* p. 190.
[4] *Auct. Malm.* pp. 200–1.
[5] Ibid.
[6] A reference to Ordinance 28.
[7] *Auct. Bridl.* p. 73.
[8] Ibid.
[9] *Auct. Malm.* p. 207.

cause of the decline in the character of the baronage is immaterial. The decline was there and the lack of character in the barons affected their policy and hence the results of their endeavours.

Another cause that promoted the failure of the baronial schemes lay in the impolicy of the barons' general plan and in the action of individuals. Coercion was useless in the circumstances produced by the king's executive power. As far as individual barons were concerned the ineptitude of Lancaster is the foremost consideration. Lancaster was more than the nominal leader of the barons. In a number of matters he may be said on occasion to have stood for the baronage. The prominent position which he occupied afforded him countless opportunities of showing his incapacity. As an opposition leader he might have attained spasmodic successes. He was liable to frequent periods of inaction, when he remained brooding or angry in one of his estates and failed or refused to take his share either in administration or in opposition. The most fatal instances of his inaction were in the crises of 1321-2 when on two occasions he failed to make any move when action was essential. He did not attempt to march to raise the siege of Leeds Castle[1], and he did not proceed to the marches in time to save the Mortimers[2]. He allowed the king to win the first success and still remained inactive while the king pursued his victorious course towards the Welsh march. His slowness in joining the barons on this occasion was fatal, but was quite in accordance with his character.

The same feature came out in his conduct of administration. Even for the brief occasions when he secured a hold upon the government, he failed to achieve what he should, because of frequent inattention to his duties. He was quite incapable of realising the duties and responsibilities of his position as head of the administration. In this he stands in marked contrast to Simon de Montfort. Lancaster failed to pay serious and continual attention to the needs of administration. He sulked away from court for a great part of the time. Montfort never absented himself from the side of the king[3]. In view of the power in the hands of the king's immediate circle of friends and servants such as the steward, keeper of the wardrobe and keeper of the privy seal, this was an important consideration. One who gave but half-hearted attention to his duty and failed to take the most patent opportunities to secure real, as opposed to nominal, control

[1] *Auct. Malm.* p. 262. [2] *Chron. Mon. de Melsa*, vol. II, p. 340.

[3] Camd. Soc. vol. XV [1840], *Chron. W. de Rishanger*, p. 41: "Comes a rege nunquam se absentavit, nec aliquod magnum sine illo in regno agebatur."

was certain to fail. By remaining always with him Montfort had been able to hold the king in tutelage[1]. The younger Despenser recognised the advisability, almost the necessity, of keeping the whole time in close personal contact with the king, and this he was able to do by his position as chamberlain. It was a matter of complaint against him that no one was allowed to approach the king unless he was also in attendance. This was from Despenser's point of view a precautionary measure and would help to account for his long continued ascendancy over the king. Lancaster would have been more successful had he devoted more attention to this method.

The oligarchy which sought to obtain control over the king was very widely divorced from the commonalty of the realm. They had little in common in aims or interests. There are however several suggestions which seem to contradict this. One chronicler, while admitting that the city of London sent men to aid the king in his siege of Leeds Castle in 1322, said this was done because they dared not refuse the king[2]. The conduct of London throughout the reign hardly supports this. The suggestion that the commons co-operated with the barons to secure the appointment of the ordainers[3] seems to be quite opposed to the facts. On the other hand the commonalty in the first parliament of Edward III prayed the king, the prelates and all the magnates to ask the pope for the canonisation of Lancaster and Winchelsey[4], but such a request at that time can be quite easily understood. Taking the reign as a whole it would be quite fair to say that Edward II did not find the commonalty joining the barons against him. He was not a tyrant, but merely inefficient, hence he did not rouse any deep hostility in the people. Edward's lax rule provided boroughs with opportunities to increase their privileges and extend their boundaries[5].

The commonalty, in fact, frequently complained of the magnates and their conduct. In 1322 the knights of the shire and all the commonalty of the land prayed the king of his grace to assign justices to take fines from those who had adhered to the rebels and enemies, and wished to have grace. The fines were to be proportionate to the amount of their land, and by that means the king would immediately have great profit and the commonalty of his realm would obtain relief[6]. Nor was it only after the triumph of the king in 1322 that

[1] Camd. Soc. vol. XV [1840], *Chron. W. de Rishanger*, p. 41: "regem tenuit in custodia."

[2] *Chron. Mon. de Melsa*, vol. II, p. 341.

[3] Gneist, *Constit. Hist.* vol. II, p. 16.

[4] *Rot. Parl.* vol. II, p. 7.

[5] Cf. M. de W. Hemmeon, *Burgage Tenure in Medieval England* [1914], p. 105, note 7.

[6] Ancient Petition, no. 3955. Vide App. of Doc. no. 135.

the commonalty made complaint. A petition, presented by the commonalty in the parliament at Westminster in 1315, when the barons were powerful, made various complaints against "les grantz seigneurs de la terre." They complained that in pleas of land and other pleas the great lords maintained parties so that those who had the greater force prevailed. Purveyance made by barons passing through the land was also a source of complaint. They entered into the manors and places of Holy Church and others and took without permission and against the will without paying anything, which was against the law and the Ordinances. They prayed that remedy should be made for such outrages as these barons committed[1]. It is not likely that the people had much sympathy with the political action of such barons. For they coerced the people as they attempted to coerce the king. The conduct of the oligarchy made the commonalty support the king. It was better that one should exercise purveyance than the whole baronage. The commonalty therefore chose the lesser evil.

It is doubtful whether these sources of weakness were not in themselves sufficient to condemn the baronial opposition to failure had other conditions been fair. The conditions in the struggle between king and baronage in the reign of Edward II were not equal. The barons had no fair chance because from the very commencement the strength of the king's position was unassailable. Against that position, even under the most favourable circumstances, the barons could not have prevailed. The unfavourable circumstances which the barons created only emphasised their failure. The real cause of that failure is to be found in the strength of the household system. It was a tribute to the strength of that system that it was able to emerge after the reign of Edward II unimpaired. That reign put the strength of the system to its test and it came out triumphant. At the beginning of the reign the barons themselves did not seem to recognise the strength of the system which they were attacking. Conflict with the system taught them that. Accordingly there was a change in the baronial policy. Instead of an effort to destroy that system, an endeavour was made to use it. As a result of the change of policy great success attended, but that success was due to the king rather than to the baronial opposition. The king acquiesced; when he ceased to acquiesce success ended. Whenever the king desired, in execution, he was supreme.

[1] *Rot. Parl.* vol. I, p. 290.

CHAPTER X

THE INFLUENCE OF THE EXPERIMENTS UPON THE ADMINISTRATION

Though the baronial opposition to Edward II was occasioned by, and centred round, the household, it was inevitable that the baronial policy should have a wider application. Attempts to reform the household reacted upon its relations to the administration. It is therefore useful to consider the various changes which took place in the organisation of the administration during the reign and to estimate if these changes were due directly or indirectly to the baronial opposition and its action. The various administrative bodies must now be considered from the point of view of their reform, especially in so far as they were the outcome of, or influenced by, the baronial opposition. That influence must be estimated on parliament, council, chancery and exchequer and the benches, and finally the changes which took place in the household offices must be sketched.

What has been regarded as a landmark in the history of parliament was enacted at the parliament of York in 1322. Before that matter is considered the baronial treatment of parliament must be noted briefly. So little importance did the barons attach to the commonalty that their co-operation was not sought in any shape or form in the appointment of the ordainers or in the making of the Ordinances. That was conceived to be a matter which entirely concerned the prelates, earls and barons or such of them as were prepared to act with the dominant faction. No wider conception was introduced into the Ordinances. It was ordained "that the king shall hold a parliament once in the year or twice if need be, and that at a convenient place[1]." Yet no indication was given whether the commonalty were to be included in these annual or half-yearly parliaments. The reason for their occurrence at such frequent intervals was given. The business laid down as that with which parliament was to concern itself was entirely of a judicial nature. The parliament which the

[1] Ordinance 29.

barons desired was a meeting of magnates to concern itself with hearing pleas which had been delayed in the king's court, with deciding pleas upon which the justices were divided, with hearing complaints against the royal ministers and with providing remedies to petitions[1]. In none of these functions of parliament had the commonalty a share. The commonalty's functions hitherto had been to assent to legislation, to make grants of money, and to present petitions. Not a word was said about any of these functions in the Ordinance concerning parliament.

Other references in the Ordinances to parliament confirm this view. Various officials of the king were to be appointed "by the counsel and assent of his baronage and that in parliament[2]." If it was necessary to appoint an official before parliament met, "then the king shall appoint thereto by the good counsels which he shall have near him until the parliament[3]." The object of the ordainers in this was to obtain control of the administration for the baronage. All the grants which had been given by the king since the appointment of the ordainers were to be repealed, and were not to be given again to the same persons without common consent in parliament. Grants made without the assent of his baronage and that in parliament, were to be void, and the recipient was to be punished in parliament by the award of the baronage[4]. The reference to parliament in the executive clause was to the same effect. In every parliament one bishop, two earls and two barons were to be assigned to hear and determine all complaints made against the king's ministers who should contravene the Ordinances[5]. Parliament was to be essentially a baronial assembly, meeting for the fulfilment of baronial aims. The baronial conception of parliament was almost that of the author of the *Mirror of Justices*, as a body of earls to meet twice a year or oftener if needed, "to hold parliament touching the guidance of the people of God, how the folk should keep themselves from sin, and live in quiet and receive right according to the fixed usages of holy judgment[6]." It is not intended to suggest that the barons did not mean the commonalty to meet. From the premises it is doubtful, and even if it was to meet, the assembly was to be of little importance. Though in the writs for the summons of the parliament of August–October, 1311, the lower clergy, knights of the shire, and citizens and burgesses were included[7] and elsewhere that assembly was described as "the parliament in which the ordi-

[1] Ordinance 29. [2] Ordinance 14. [3] Ibid. [4] Ordinance 7.
[5] Ordinance 40. [6] Seld. Soc., *Mirror of Justices*, p. 8.
[7] *Parl. Writs*, vol. II, Pt ii, App. pp. 37–39.

nances made for the commonweal are to be completed and confirmed[1]," it is extremely doubtful whether the commons had any share in that confirmation. The confirmation probably meant was that of the king who was then to accept the completed work of the ordainers[2]. The barons claimed to be or to represent the whole community of the realm. To them the "commonalty" meant merely the body of barons[3]. A letter, sent to the pope in 1309 from the barons at the parliament of Stamford protesting against the excessive number of papal provisions and other exactions by which the church in England was burdened, was tested: "In cujus rei testimonium sigilla nostra, tam pro nobis quam tota communitate regni et terrarum predictarum, presentibus sunt appensa[4]."

When therefore Lancaster objected to give his counsel, advice and assent to a certain matter, because that ought to be treated in full parliament and in the presence of the peers of the land, and declined to treat outside parliament the things that ought to be treated in parliament[5], he was not claiming any participation for the commons. It was but another way of protesting against the king having a parliament *in cameris*[6]. The objection was to things being done in a small council summoned by the king rather than in parliament before all the peers of the realm. On the other hand the very confusion in functions and power of the great council and parliament suggests that the commonalty had little real and effective share in parliament. The same matter could be equally fittingly discussed and decided upon in great council and parliament and it therefore seems that the part of the commons in parliament was little more than formal.

In contradistinction to the narrowness of the baronial conception, a statement included in the revocation of the Ordinances has been seized upon as a great concession to the commons by the king: the words ran: "But the matters which are to be established for the estate of our lord the king and of his heirs, and for the estate of the realm and of the people, shall be treated, accorded, and established in parliaments by our lord the king, and by the assent of the prelates, earls and barons, and the commonalty of the realm; according as it

[1] *Parl. Writs*, vol. II, Pt i, p. 69.

[2] The question whether the Ordinances were confirmed by the commons is discussed at length by Prof. Tout, *The Place of Ed. II*, pp. 87–91.

[3] Cf. K. R. Mem. Roll, no. 85, m. 52; L. T. R. Mem. Roll, no. 82, m. 45 when Botetourte appeared in the exchequer and spoke on behalf of the "commonalty," vide above, pp. 390–1.

[4] *Reg. R. de Swinfield*, pp. 472–5. Cf. *Ann. Lond.* pp. 161–5.

[5] *Chron. Murimuth*, pp. 275–6. *Auct. Bridl.* pp. 51–52.

[6] *Auct. Malm.* p. 250.

hath been heretofore accustomed[1]." This has been interpreted to mean that what Edward I had devised and called together on occasion without any determinate policy was established permanently as a part of the machinery of government by Edward II[2]. Parliament had previously gained the right to petition for new laws; that right was now made exclusive[3]. It was a rejection of the oligarchical pretensions of the baronage and a grant of a share in legislation to the commons[4]. A later interpretation[5] suggests that the principle which was intended to be conveyed by these words was not intended to cover all legislation but such fundamental constitutional changes of the same nature as had been included in the Ordinances. It drew, in a word, the distinction between ordinary legislation and fundamental law.

It must be remembered that the king instructed his council to draw up this statute which was to repeal the Ordinances[6] and that the council carried out his instructions[7]. The part which the commons took in the passing of this statute was purely formal. Neither the magnates nor the commons had any voice in drawing up the statute. It was the work of the king's council. Moreover the clause which has been taken must be read in the light of the preceding clause:

"And that for ever hereafter all manner of ordinances or provisions, made by the subjects of our lord the king or of his heirs, by any power or authority whatsoever, concerning the royal power of our lord the king or of his heirs, or against the estate of our said lord the king or of his heirs, or against the estate of the crown, shall be void and of no avail or force whatever[8]." This clause was a vindication of the royal power, and after such vindication it is improbable that the king should immediately after bind himself for the future to consult or act by the assent of the prelates, earls and barons and the commonalty of the realm on that very question of fundamental law on which he had vindicated his right. This clause concerns the power of the king and his heirs and his crown. The succeeding clause concerned matters which touched, not the estate of the king and his heirs alone, but the estate of the realm and of the people. The conclusion therefore is that these two clauses stood for something very different.

[1] *Stat. of Realm*, vol. I, p. 189. [2] Stubbs, *Constit. Hist.* vol. II, p. 369.

[3] Figgis, *Divine Right of Kings*, p. 28.

[4] Gneist, *Constit. Hist.* vol. II, p. 21, note 3 a.

[5] *Eng. Hist. Rev.* vol. XXVIII [1913], G. T. Lapsley, 'The Parliament of York,' pp. 118–124.

[6] Parl. and Council Proc. (Chan.), File 5/10. Vide App. of Doc. no. 93.

[7] Parl. and Council Proc. (Chan.), File 5/9. A draft of the Statute of Revocation.

[8] *Stat. of Realm*, vol. I, p. 189.

One has application to the king, his rights and privileges which must not under any circumstances be altered or lessened. The other has a far wider application and significance. It refers to matters which have a direct bearing upon the whole kingdom, legislation, administration, taxation. The Ordinances, besides enforcing the restraint which the king had just condemned, had also been concerned with abuses of legislation, administration and taxation.

The one was therefore not a modification of the previous clause but supplemented it. It added to it and acted as a contrast to it. The narrow personal rights of the king and his crown had been safeguarded. Next came the general and wider rights of the people. The privileges and powers of the king were a personal matter about which he would brook no interference. "The matters which were to be established for the state of the lord king and of the realm and of the people" were matters which concerned the king and people; and they were to have a definite voice in their establishment. They were to be treated, accorded and established by their assent. It is therefore suggested that they refer to general legislation and administration. The suggestion is supported by the fact that the king claimed he was urging nothing new. He was merely setting down definitely in parliament what had been recognised in practice by Edward I. The clause was, in other words, declaratory of existing usage. The matters were to be established "as it hath been heretofore accustomed."

The fact that it was merely declaratory does not minimise its importance. It was of supreme importance that the people should have something more definite than a royal concession, unrecorded and merely at the good will of the king. This the clause gave them. It normalised the exceptional, and perpetuated what might otherwise have proved a mere temporary expedient. Further support of this suggestion is found in the fact that a number of the clauses of the Ordinances which were purely reformatory and dealt with legislative abuses were in this very parliament established by the assent of the prelates, earls and barons and the commonalty of the realm[1]. In the parliament of Westminster in 1324 "the king by the mutual assent of the earls, barons and noblemen, of his regal authority" gave and assigned the Templar lands to the Hospitallers[2]. There was no mention made of the assent of the commonalty here, and it would seem as if the concession was little more than a form. Neither at the present time nor in future was there any prospect of submitting to, or even allowing to, the prelates, earls and barons and commonalty

[1] *Cal. Close Rolls*, 1318-23, p 557. [2] *Stat. of Realm*, vol. I, p. 196.

of the realm interference with or definition of the king's powers and privileges. In this parliament any such interferences by the subjects of the king had been specifically and finally denied force or avail. On the other hand the right granted, or rather the right declared, was put into operation immediately in the assent to the statute which enacted a number of the good points of the Ordinances and re-enacted various provisions of statutes which Edward I had made.

Many objections can therefore be raised to the view that, in the parliament of York, the king granted that fundamental changes of the constitution[1] should only be secured by the assent of the prelates, earls and barons and the commonalty of the realm. The king would hardly have thrust upon the people, in a legislative form, the principle that the power of the crown should be subject to the approval of parliament and that limitation of that power should be approved or disapproved in parliament. The king's position throughout the struggle rather was that no person or body of men had the right to challenge the king's power or impose restraint upon the crown.

Conditions can be conceived in which the king might have found it to his advantage to introduce such a principle. Had he been in extreme fear of serious restriction from the barons he might have deemed it advisable to appeal temporarily to a wider constituency in order to strengthen his position. This involves the question whether the position of the commonalty in parliament in 1322 was such that the king could have expected to derive any benefit from their support. In 1322 the king was in no danger from the barons. There was no need for him to appeal to a wider constituency, and, had he desired to make such an appeal, the position of the commonalty was not of sufficient importance to justify his making it in that direction. The power of the king in 1322, after his decisive victory over the barons, must not be ignored. While it is true that he made only the most moderate use of his great and newly acquired power the vastness of his power must not, on that account, be overlooked. For the moment he required no aid against threatened danger and it is difficult to see what useful purpose could be served by imposing such a considerable limitation, theoretical rather than practical though it was, upon the king's power. If the king's motive in making this concession of a right to assent to changes in fundamental law to prelates, earls and barons and to the commonalty was utility, it was utility wrongly conceived. If the king granted this he was surrendering more in the

[1] This view is set forth by Mr Lapsley, *Eng. Hist. Rev.* vol. XXVIII [1913], pp. 118–124.

hour of victory than the barons had been able to extract from him in long years of struggle. They had sought to impose restraint. According to the new interpretation of this clause the power to impose such restraint was given, if the assent of the prelates, earls and barons and the commonalty of the realm could be obtained. The prelates, earls and barons had been the very people who had endeavoured to exercise that restraint before 1322. The king was therefore thrusting into the hands of the commonalty an instrument which they were not strong enough to use, so that he was in effect surrendering to the barons what they had fought for. On the other hand, it is interesting to note that there is something to be said in favour of the view that it was the king's policy to appeal to a wider constituency. Representatives from Wales were summoned for the first time to this parliament. Edward II was popular in Wales. The Welsh, especially the North Welsh, consistently and loyally supported him. They certainly had no love for the marcher lords who had been so bitterly opposed to the king for nearly two years, and whom the king had now crushed. They would willingly support the royal authority. There was a strong feeling against the Mortimers in Wales[1], and the parliament of York followed immediately upon their defeat and imprisonment.

To sum up, the king at the parliament of York does not appear to have given the prelates, earls and barons and the commonalty of the realm the right to deal with fundamental law. The statute which revoked the Ordinances was made with the purpose of putting an end to the possibility of subjects restraining the royal power contrary to what ought to be and blemishing the royal sovereignty and the estate of the crown. This the king did for the past by repealing the Ordinances. He was determined to provide for the future. This he did by enacting that thereafter anything done by subjects concerning the royal power or the estate of the king or crown should be void and of no force or avail. Having protected his own interests, which were personal to him, he turned to the wider problem of what was established for the estate of himself, his realm and the people. Such matters were to be treated, accorded and established in parliament by the king, and by the assent of the prelates, earls and barons and commonalty as was customary.

Though the action of the baronial opposition had effected little change in parliament, the king's victory was followed by the enunciation, or the declaration, of an important principle. In the position,

[1] Cf. the petition presented in the parliament. *Rot. Parl.* vol. I, p. 400.

composition and functions of the council the results of the baronial opposition and the succeeding royal victory were less apparent than in parliament. This was all the stranger since the council had been a constant cause of irritation to the barons since the reign of Edward I. "The promotion of clerks, the prominence of household officers, the filling of the great ministries with men of the *curia*, and above all the patronage that was enjoyed by the king's personal confidants were sources of a chronic political irritation[1]." The attempts made by the barons to capture or form the council which assisted the king had no permanent results. Such experiments in council-making as were made at the parliaments of Lincoln and York had transitory influence. But the king's "administrative" council[2] went on its course unimpeded even during the triumphs of the baronial opposition, and that phase of the council was in all essentials the same in 1326 as it had been in 1307. If any alteration was visible it was that the personal as opposed to the administrative element was more prominent.

The influence of the baronial opposition and the king's subsequent action upon the two great administrative departments of the chancery and the exchequer resolves itself chiefly into a discussion of the relative positions of the two. If the baronial action is any criterion there was little need of reform in the chancery, and when the king was free to act he did not direct the energy of the reformers to the chancery but to the exchequer. In the circumstances it can be assumed that the chancery was not in need of drastic reform, that it presented no apparent and outstanding abuse in its administrative working and that it therefore remained running on its normal course throughout the reign.

The relative positions of chancery and exchequer will be discussed in some detail[3] because it has been alleged that as a result of the baronial opposition the exchequer sank to a subordinate position and gave way before the supremacy of the chancery. The originator of this view[4] finds that the decisive battle was fought at the parliament of Lincoln in 1316, when the method of the appointment of sheriffs

[1] Baldwin, *King's Council*, p. 93.

[2] The "administrative" council, for instance, carried on its functions when the ordainers were in power. E.g. *Cal. Close Rolls*, 1307–13, p. 315. Cf. Chan. Warr., Files 69/1164; 70/1213; 73/1579, 1600; 77/1929, 1981, etc.

[3] The appointment of sheriffs during the reign of Edward II has been treated in the *Law Quarterly Review*, vol. XXXIII [1917], 'The Statute of Lincoln, 1316, and the Appointment of Sheriffs,' J. C. Davies, pp. 78–86. The argument will be summarised here.

[4] Mr A. Hughes in his paper on 'The Parliament of Lincoln 1316' in the *Trans. R. Hist. Soc.* N. S. vol. x [1896], pp. 41–58.

was decided[1]. This heresy has been accepted by Professor Baldwin[2], who finds that henceforth sheriffs were appointed through the chancery, which gained a signal victory. The triumph of the chancery included the supersession of the exchequer as the custodian of the enrolled records of parliament[3].

This view has been challenged by Professor Tout[4], who fails to find in Edward II's reign "the decisive turning point in a long conflict between the chancery and the exchequer." Indeed he goes further. He sees no trace of such a struggle, but attributes the transference to the chancery of the nomination of sheriffs as a part of the policy of definition and differentiation of function. "There was, in fact, absolutely no reason why the chancery should carry on an imaginary feud with the exchequer. Its enemy was rather in the administrative offices of the household, against which it had a common ally in the exchequer[5]."

While it is certain that William de Ayremynne, a chancery clerk, drew up the rolls of the parliament of Lincoln[6] that is not sufficient ground for suggesting that it marked the complete transference of power from the exchequer to the chancery in all but financial matters. The surviving rolls of the parliaments of 1318 and 1319[7] are exchequer rolls; and other rolls of parliament after 1316 were also derived from that source[8]. While chancery and parliament were closely connected, the rolls being written by chancery clerks and the writs being issued from the chancery, and the chancery has been called "an office of the parliament[9]," the exchequer was also associated with the work of parliament though in different ways. The close connection between the origin and early history of parliament and the financial needs of the crown suggests that the relation to the exchequer, in which account for the parliamentary grants had to be made, must have been close. For long an important business of parliament was to make money grants to the crown—money grants collected and administered by the exchequer. Even in the parliament of Lincoln exchequer officials took a prominent part. In that parliament as receivers of petitions

[1] Mr A. Hughes in his paper on 'The Parliament of Lincoln 1316' in the *Trans. R. Hist. Soc.* N. S. vol. x [1896], p. 43.

[2] Baldwin, *King's Council*, p. 229.

[3] *Trans. R. Hist. Soc.* vol. x [1896], p. 44.

[4] Tout, *The Place of Ed. II*, p. 183.

[5] Ibid. pp. 183–4.

[6] *Rot. Parl.* vol. I, p. 350.

[7] Printed by Cole, *Doc. illustr. Eng. Hist. in 13th and 14th Cent.* pp. 1–54.

[8] P. R. O. Exchequer Rolls of Parliament, nos. 22 and 24 (for 14 and 15 Edward II).

[9] Pike, *Constit. Hist. House of Lords*, p. 295.

for England were appointed Robert de Askeby, clerk of chancery, and Adam de Lymbergh, remembrancer of the exchequer, and for Gascony. Wales, Ireland and Scotland Master Edmund de London, clerk of chancery, and Master William de Maldon, chamberlain of the exchequer[1]. The two offices divided the work. In the parliament of Westminster in 1320[2] an exchequer and chancery official acted jointly as receivers of petitions. Adam de Lymbergh, king's remembrancer of the exchequer, acted in that capacity in the two parliaments, and by his continuous service was as much associated with the work of parliament as any clerk of chancery. Exchequer officials also acted upon the committees which were to hear and answer the petitions presented to parliament. Thus at the parliament of Lincoln amongst the auditors of the petitions for England was John de Insula, baron of the exchequer[3]. In the parliament of York, Norwich, then chief baron of the exchequer, William de Ayremynne, keeper of the rolls of chancery, and Michael de Meldon, steward of the earl of Lancaster, were appointed to arrange the enrolment of the king's reply to the important petition incorporating the Treaty of Leake[4]. As far as parliament was concerned neither in the parliament of Lincoln nor subsequently did the chancery succeed, even if it endeavoured, to oust the exchequer from its position.

In general administration, and especially in the control of the work of the "administrative" council, there is no evidence to prove that the chancery superseded the exchequer. It seems to have depended very much upon the personal character and importance of the men holding the respective positions of chancellor and treasurer which of the two administrative departments was, for the time being, predominant. When for the last years of Edward I, the chancellor was thrown into insignificance by the weight of the great and powerful treasurer, Langton, the exchequer was the more important office. In 1300 it was "testified by the treasurer and by John de Langton the chancellor before the king" that a certain matter was agreed before his council at York, and this was an entry on the chancery roll[5]. On 7 August, 1306, a still more curious entry showing the importance of the treasurer even in the chancery was entered on the close roll: "Memorandum that the aforesaid writs were made at Nottingham by Sir Walter bishop of Coventry and Lichfield the treasurer and were

1 *Rot. Parl.* vol. I, p. 350.
2 *Parl. Writs*, vol. II, Pt i, p. 251. *Rot. Parl.* vol. I, p. 365.
3 *Rot. Parl.* vol. I, p. 350.
4 Cole, *Doc. illustr. Eng. Hist. in 13th and 14th Cent.* p. 12.
5 *Cal. Close Rolls*, 1296–1302, p. 359.

sent under his seal to the chancellor at the abbey of St James without Northampton to be sealed with the great seal in the form aforesaid[1]." Petitions seeking favours were addressed to him as treasurer[2]. Under Edward II writs to summon the "administrative" council were frequently sent to both chancellor and treasurer[3], often to the chancellor alone[4], sometimes to the treasurer[5]. When Stapleton was treasurer and Baldock chancellor, the writs under privy seal issued to them jointly were addressed to the treasurer and chancellor[6]—and the same statement is true of the archbishop of York when he was treasurer[7]. In 1321 a petition was sent by the king to "noz chers et foialx Wautier de Norwiz chief Baron de nostre Excheker et William de Ayremynne[8]," the exchequer official obtaining the first place. The case therefore cannot hold good as far as general administration was concerned.

The crux of the whole matter lies however in the question of the appointment of sheriffs. It may be readily conceded from the very outset that during the latter portion of the reign of Edward I and throughout the reign of Edward II the exchequer was unpopular[9]. A department that conducts the financial administration of the land must almost invariably draw upon itself some amount of unpopularity. The unpopularity of the exchequer at this time had more substantial and reasonable grounds than mere prejudice. The exchequer was in need of urgent reform. Good and efficient administration was stultified there by lack of revenue. The abuses in the local administration reacted upon the exchequer, and the abuses in the exchequer upon the local administration. There was need of drastic reform in the local administration, and the continuous complaints of petitioners against the tyranny of sheriffs[10] and their officers and the endeavours which the baronial opposition made to secure more efficient and less

[1] *Cal. Close Rolls*, 1302–7, p. 411. *Foedera*, vol. I, p. 996.

[2] Exch. Misc. 3/2.

[3] Vide Chan. Warr., Files 58–134 passim.

[4] Ibid.

[5] Vide K. R. and L. T. R. Mem. Rolls for the reign passim.

[6] E.g. Chan. Warr., Files 125/6756, 6792; 129/7173, etc.

[7] E.g. ibid. File 130/7247.

[8] Ibid. File 116/5833.

[9] *Trans. R. Hist. Soc.* vol. x [1896], p. 57.

[10] P. R. O. K. R. Estreats, 140/1 gives some impression of the state of local administration during the reign of Edward II, containing estreats of Hervy de Staunton and the other justices appointed by Edward II to hear and determine the oppressions of sheriffs and their officials, constables, sub-escheators, taxors and sub-taxors. Five different men who had been sheriffs of Worcester were fined in various amounts for trespasses committed by them. The sub-taxors and sub-collectors of taxes in the county of Worcester (the city of Worcester excepted) were fined £500, and so in other counties, those of Gloucester being fined 1450 marks.

grievously abused local administration, and their summary dismissal of all the sheriffs in 1318 show how urgent was the whole problem. In the appointment of sheriffs the exchequer met the local administration. In its unreformed state, with all the patent abuses, the exchequer was not likely to fulfil its functions in the appointment of sheriffs in a good and suitable manner. Moreover that department was not likely to exercise a good influence over the local administration. This, combined with other causes, prompted a change in the appointment of the sheriffs.

Edward I's attempt at reform, by ordering the election of the sheriffs by the counties[1], was soon dropped, and under him the normal method of appointment had been in the exchequer, the commission being under the exchequer seal[2]; and this practice was continued under Edward II[3]. The treasurer and barons of the exchequer of Dublin were in 1303 ordered to appoint a sheriff for the county of Cork by letters patent under the seal of the exchequer, the order to that effect from England being issued under the great seal[4].

It was easy for the king to influence the selection by sending writs of privy seal to the treasurer and barons nominating sheriffs[5], such writs being issued on the request or instance of some baron or other person near him[6]. Walter Reynolds the treasurer[7], the elder Despenser[8] and Egidius de Argentine[9] and others acted as royal messengers ordering the appointment of sheriffs. In January, 1311, Sandale, treasurer, was ordered to perform what Robert fitz Payn should inform him on the royal behalf. Following the writ of privy seal, Robert appeared in the exchequer and on the king's behalf required that the sheriff of Gloucester should be removed and that Nicholas de Kingston should be appointed instead[10]. For the king ordered the

[1] *Stat. of Realm*, vol. I, p. 139, Articuli super cartas, § viii. Cf. *Cal. Close Rolls*, 1302–7, p. 84. Cf. Wm Salt Soc., *Coll.* [1913], pp. 272, 277.

[2] *Trans. R. Hist. Soc.* vol. x [1896], p. 48. This left considerable discretionary power in the hands of the treasurer and was liable to abuse. One of the charges preferred against Langton was that he had taken gifts for bestowing the office of sheriff (Exch. of Pleas, Plea Roll, no. 31, m. 21).

[3] K. R. Mem. Rolls, nos. 81–84 passim. L. T. R. Mem. Rolls, nos. 78–81 passim.

[4] *Cal. Close Rolls*, 1302–7, pp. 115–116 (4 Dec. 1303).

[5] E.g. K. R. Mem. Rolls, no. 81 m. 9; no. 82 mm. 5, 10; no. 83, m. 6; no. 84, mm. 2, 3 d, 4 d. Cf. Madox, *Hist. Exch.* vol. II, pp. 68–70.

[6] K. R. Mem. Roll, no. 84, m. 4 d, m. 31 d (Ralph de Monthemer), m. 27 d (Earl of Warenne), m. 12 (William de Latimer).

[7] Ibid. no. 81, m. 4. L. T. R. Mem. Roll, no. 78, m. 6 d.

[8] K. R. Mem. Roll, no. 82, m. 11.

[9] Ibid. no. 82, m. 4. L. T. R. Mem. Roll, no. 79, m. 4.

[10] K. R. Mem. Roll, no. 84, m. 19.

removal as well as the appointment of the sheriffs[1]. The removal of Henry de Segrave, sheriff of Norfolk and Suffolk, was ordered on account of the grievous complaints made against him, for the people were surprised that the king had suffered him so long[2]. The king later approved of the official who had been appointed to fill his place[3]. The sheriff was sometimes removed "quia tamen Rex certis ex causis non vult quod dictus Johannes de custodia comitatum illorum ulterius se intromittat in aliquo[4]." Sometimes the writ of privy seal ordering removal also included nomination to that office[5]. Walter Hakelut who was sheriff of Hereford and who remained by the royal order in the king's household received a privy seal authorising him to appoint a deputy[6]. Sometimes the writ of privy seal ordering appointment allowed the exchequer officials discretion[7].

One of the Ordinances of 1311 sought to alter the method of appointment. In future sheriffs were to be appointed by the chancellor, treasurer and such others of the council as were present. If the chancellor were not present the sheriffs were to be appointed by the treasurer and barons of the exchequer, and by the justices of the bench. Those who were appointed were to be fit and sufficient and have lands and tenements whereof they could answer to the king and to the people for their actions. Their commissions were to be under the great seal[8]. The chancellor was to be called with the council to assist the treasurer in this particular work, as the chancellor and council sat with and assisted the exchequer officials in other matters[9].

The most important alteration was that in future the commissions were to be made not under the exchequer but under the great seal. The aim of the barons may have been to free the appointments from the king's active interference as well as to improve local administration. The Ordinance was put into execution almost immediately and twenty-one sheriffs were appointed in the presence of Pembroke, the chancellor, the treasurer and barons of the exchequer, the justices of the benches, Despenser and others of the council[10]. Henceforth commissions of appointment appear on the fine roll of the chancery, not the memoranda rolls of the exchequer. Yet it was still the treasurer and barons who made the appointments, though they were issued

[1] Cf. Madox, *Hist. Exch.* vol. II, pp. 68–69.
[2] K. R. Mem. Roll, no. 84, m. 23 d (3 April, 1311).
[3] Ibid. m. 31 d.
[4] Ibid. no. 84, m. 3 d.
[5] L. T. R. Mem. Roll, no 79, m. 65.
[6] Ibid. no. 78, m. 17 d.
[7] K. R. Mem. Roll, no. 83, mm. 8, 26.
[8] Ordinance 17.
[9] Vide above, pp. 266–276.
[10] L. T. R. Mem. Roll, no. 82, schedule attached to m. 20.

under the chancery seal and the king's interference was not stopped[1]. The others only gave the exchequer officials advice in the appointment.

Writs of privy seal about the appointment still went to the treasurer and barons of the exchequer[2]. On 3 April, 1312, they were ordered to discharge the sheriff of Essex and Hertford, who was occupied with other business and could not attend to his office, "et y facez mettre un autre qui soit suffisant et profitable por nous et por nostre poeple. Et ce ne leissez...[3]." On 20 June a similar order was sent concerning the sheriff of Northampton[4]. The sheriff of Devon could not perform the duties of his office owing to illness; another, sufficient and suitable for the king and the people, was to be appointed until the sheriff was sufficiently recovered to attend to his office[5]. These writs under the privy seal were of purely administrative significance, but during the same period the king also sent writs to the treasurer and barons ordering them to allow a sheriff to remain in office until a stated time[6], or ordering the discharge of one who was engaged on the Scottish war at the request of Despenser the younger, in whose company he was serving, the appointment of another suitable in his place, and the receiving of his men to render his account at the exchequer[7].

After the Ordinances, the exchequer appointed in consultation with the justices. The chancery issued the commission under the great seal when required by the exchequer[8].

At the parliament of Lincoln in 1316 the method of appointment ordained in 1311 was enacted in statute form. Sheriffs were to be appointed by the chancellor[9], treasurer, barons of the exchequer and justices and in the absence of the chancellor by the others acting without him. No one was to be appointed to the office unless he had sufficient land in the county where he was sheriff to answer the king and his people. No steward or bailiff of a magnate was to be made

[1] *Law Quart. Rev.* vol. XXXIII, pp. 80–81.

[2] K. R. Mem. Roll, no. 85, m. 16.

[3] Ibid. m. 20.

[4] Ibid. m. 24 d.

[5] Ibid. no. 86, m. 9 d.

[6] Ibid. no. 87, m. 24. L. T. R. Mem. Roll, no. 84, Brev. dir. Pasch. m. 1.

[7] K. R. Mem. Roll, no. 87, m. 31 d. L. T. R. Mem. Roll, no. 84, Brev. dir. Pasch. m. 9 d.

[8] Chan. Files (under arrangement), C, File 11.

[9] The ingenious suggestion, that the chancellor referred to in the law was the chancellor of the exchequer and not the chancellor of England, made by Daines Barrington in his *Observations upon the Statutes* [1766], p. 155, is quite understandable in view of the connection of the sheriff with the exchequer.

sheriff unless he was out of office so that he could give attention to his duties as sheriff. The same rules were to apply to the appointment of hundreders. Insufficient sheriffs or hundreders who held office at that time were to be removed and more suitable officers appointed in their place[1].

After this statute also, the treasurer and barons were still the persons most largely concerned in the appointment of sheriffs. Communication was made with the chancellor when commissions were required to be issued. By privy seal the exchequer was still ordered to appoint and remove. In actual appointment or selection the exchequer was responsible. The chancellor and justices assisted, advised or assented, though since a commission was required, the chancellor had more opportunity to interfere and some sense of supervision over the choice. The chancellor was required by king or exchequer officials to issue the necessary letters under the great seal. The sheriff took his oath of office at the exchequer[2].

At the parliament of York in 1318, at the request of the prelates, earls and barons and the commonalty, the sheriffs throughout England were dismissed and a commission of inquiry promised to consider their conduct[3]. Before the end of that year commissions of inquiry had been issued touching the malpractices and oppressions with which the sheriffs, bailiffs and other ministers of the king were charged[4]. At that parliament, too, in reply to a petition, the chancellor, treasurer and barons of the exchequer and the justices were ordered to assign sheriffs in each county according to the form of the Statute of Lincoln, and the sheriffs were to be enjoined to appoint bailiffs according to the form of that statute only[5].

A writ addressed to Stapleton, treasurer, and Norwich, chief baron, ordered them to make Ingelram Berenger, whom the king wished to be sheriff of Bedford and Buckingham, have his commission under the great seal in due form[6]. The treasurer and barons were ordered to make Roger de Aylesbury have the office of sheriff of Warwick and Leicester to hold in the form required in the king's writ[7]. The

[1] *Stat. of Realm*, vol. I, pp. 174–5.

[2] These suggestions are all supported by detailed evidence in *Law Quart. Rev.* vol. XXXIII, pp. 82–84.

[3] Cole, *Doc. illustr. Eng. Hist. in 13th and 14th Cent.* pp. 6–7.

[4] *Cal. Pat. Rolls*, 1317–21, p. 298 (29 Dec. 1318).

[5] Cole, *Doc. illustr. Eng. Hist. in 13th and 14th Cent.* p. 16.

[6] K. R. Mem. Roll, no. 93, m. 31. L. T. R. Mem. Roll, no. 90, Brev. dir. Pasch. m. 13.

[7] K. R. Mem. Roll, no. 94, m. 47. L. T. R. Mem. Roll, no. 91, Brev. dir. Pasch. m. 2.

sheriffs continued to take their oaths and receive their offices at the exchequer[1]. The king continued too to order the chancellor by writ of privy seal to make the necessary commissions and letters to sheriffs whom he nominated[2].

The Statute of Lincoln was incorporated in the statute made in the parliament of York in 1322 re-enacting various reforms, and this is fairly conclusive proof that the altered method of appointment and commission did not deprive the king of his influence. If the baronial object had been to lessen the king's interference it had not been achieved. The change was probably an attempt to secure fitting officials and improve the terrible condition of local administration. The king employed precisely the same means to interfere with the appointments after 1322. The treasurer and barons were ordered to remove immediately a cousin of Andrew de Harclay, who had been made sheriff of Westmorland, and to put another suitable officer in his place[3]. They were ordered to allow the sheriff of Devon to have his office without removal[4], and to remove the sheriff of Lincoln and appoint another suitable[5]. The confirmation of the Statute of Lincoln in the Statute of Northampton, supports the view that the statute of Edward III did not lessen the king's control, and the suggestion that the motive of the change was a desire and endeavour to improve local administration.

"To sum up: it cannot be said, in light of the practice after the statute, that the Statute of Lincoln gave into the hands of the chancery the appointment of the local official, the sheriff. The whole of the case of those who see a long-continued struggle between chancery and exchequer for supremacy, a struggle culminating in complete victory for the chancery at the parliament of Lincoln, turns upon the power which this statute is supposed to have conferred upon the chancellor....The intention of the framers of the ordinance and the Statute of Lincoln is not important. Whatever their intention may have been, the subsequent practice was for the treasurer and barons of the exchequer, sometimes with the co-operation of the chancellor and the justices, sometimes with the co-operation of the justices only, sometimes acting entirely alone, to make the appointment. The treasurer and barons then took the oath, and required commission from the chancery. The practice was the same when

[1] E.g. K. R. Mem. Roll, no. 92, Rec. Mich. m. 8; Rec. Hill. mm. 1 d, 2; Rec. Pasch. m. 2.

[2] Chan. Warr., File 109/5114.

[3] K. R. Mem. Roll, no. 96, m. 46.

[4] Ibid. no. 101, m. 26 d.

[5] Ibid. no. 102, m. 60 d.

the appointment was made as a regular part of the exchequer business as when it was made on the king's intervention. In the latter case the king might instruct the chancellor to make the commission or he might leave it to the treasurer to do so in the normal way. There was then no great transference of power from the exchequer to the chancery[1]."

In the policy and action of the baronial opposition there is to be noticed a slight depressing tendency. In official records the effect of the Ordinances was nowhere more noticeable than upon the memoranda rolls of the exchequer. Instead of several membranes containing the enrolments of exchequer commissions, less than three appear in the sixth year[2]. The issue under the exchequer seal for other than purely administrative purposes of exchequer business was greatly restricted. The few commissions made were dull and colourless. There were extremely few commissions of land, none of the appointment of sheriffs. Most of the items were concerned with the appointment of inquiries into various matters such as the trespasses of taxors and collectors. A certain depression is also noticed on the issue rolls for the year following the Ordinances[3]. The judicial functions of the exchequer had been restricted by the Ordinance concerning exchequer pleas[4]. On the other hand against this depression, the Ordinances had asserted the supremacy of the exchequer in financial administration. The customs of the realm and all other issues and profits derived were to be paid there[5]. Though payment to the wardrobe was not explicitly mentioned, there can be little doubt that the object was to make all wardrobe revenue pass through the exchequer into the wardrobe. The baronial opposition, however, had comparatively little effect upon the wardrobe when the influence of the Stapleton reforms is taken into account.

Throughout the reign of Edward II the finances had been in a bad state, and even before Stapleton became treasurer the king had made some efforts in administrative reform. Throughout the reign, as the memoranda rolls of the exchequer testify, attention had been paid to the improvement of the financial efficiency of the exchequer. Writs of privy seal were constantly sent to the treasurer and barons touching defects in the administration of exchequer revenue and suggesting ways and means of reform. On 26 March, 1311, while the ordainers were sitting, the king had issued his writ of privy seal to the chancellor

[1] *Law Quart. Rev.* vol. XXXIII, pp. 85–86.

[2] K. R. Mem. Roll, no. 86.

[3] Issue Rolls, nos. 159, 162, 164.

[4] Ordinance 25.

[5] Ordinances 4, 8.

and treasurer ordering a commission for a new official. Those of the king's council who were with him had advised that he should appoint an escheator of cities and boroughs. The king thought much of the loyalty and ability of his clerk, Master John de Percy, and wished that he should become the escheator of cities and boroughs. Accordingly the chancellor and treasurer were to arrange between them a commission for Master John for that office. The commission was to be as good, full, and suitable for the time of his ancestors as for his time that the royal right should not be delayed, and that the king should endure no loss by default of this commission. Because the office was new and there was no fee appointed for it, the chancellor and treasurer were to assign such a fee as they considered suitable, having regard to the losses and expenses of that office[1]. Though no execution seems to have been made to the writ by the chancellor and treasurer, it is interesting as showing the king's effort towards administrative reform.

About this time the problem of enrolment of exchequer accounts and debts also received the king's attention. On 21 March, 1312, from York the king ordered the treasurer, barons and chamberlains of the exchequer "to inspect and cause to be observed in the exchequer a writ of the late king's issued in the twelfth year of his reign, to the treasurer, barons and chamberlains ordering that the bodies of counties, farms and profits of the same counties, the farms of serjeanties, of assarts, cities, boroughs, towns and other farms whatsoever should be enrolled in the exchequer, and that debts should be attermined under certain forms, and other leviable debts enrolled, and that other things should be observed in the exchequer for the better government of the same[2]." This writ was not the result of the action of baronial opposition, for it was issued on the information of Edmund de Mauley, steward of the household[3]. At the same time the treasurer and barons were ordered to cause all accounts to be rendered with all speed, to rouse the officials of the exchequer to their duty and to order them to make daily reports[4]. Again in 1318 a number of groups of clerks were appointed to arrange the debts owing to the king, and to classify them into those which were recoverable and those which were irrecoverable[5]. In June, 1319, the exchequer officials were ordered to inform the king what lands and profits had

[1] Chan. Warr., File 76/1839. K. R. Mem. Roll, no. 84, m. 24 d. Vide App. of Doc. no. 54.

[2] *Cal. Close Rolls*, 1307–13, p. 417. *Foedera*, vol. II, p. 160.

[3] Ibid. [4] Ibid. [5] Issue Roll, no. 186, m. 6.

come to the king from his father, what were then in his hands and in the possession of others, the nature and true value of the tenure[1]. The king appeared to be preparing to undertake a thorough reorganisation. A long writ under the privy seal was issued on 31 October, 1319, which foreshadowed coming exchequer ordinances and touched such important topics as the presentation of the wardrobe accounts at the exchequer, the behaviour of the exchequer clerks and officials, prohibition of the discharge of debts, the care of rolls, prohibition of payment or assignment without special order, the procedure when bailiffs had paid money direct to the wardrobe, and a visit of the king's council twice a year to the exchequer[2]. These instances suffice to show that attention had been paid to administrative reform before Stapleton's day.

It was after the appointment of Stapleton[3] to the office of treasurer on 18 February, 1320, that the real reform began. His first period of office was unfortunately short, as it closed on 25 August, 1321. He became treasurer again under happier auspices on 10 May, 1322, and held that office until 3 July, 1325[4], when he was followed by the archbishop of York. His interest in reform did not end with the surrender of his office, and as late as July, 1326[5], he was still associated with the exchequer when the king asked him to attend there to treat with the officials how the articles provided and agreed upon by him and them should be kept at the exchequer for the business of accounts and other matters[6]. The bishop was in fact one of the most trusty of the king's officials though he had never followed the king blindly. He had maintained an independence of view and action which stood out notably in that time. The queen's taunt in December, 1325, that he was acting to win the favour of the young Despenser, and that he was of his accord and humbly obedient to him[7], was, in the circumstances, quite unjustified. The zeal which Stapleton applied to his work of administrative reform was unfortunately not allowed to attain all its rewards. The revolution of 1326 which ended the king's reign also ended those reforms and brought in its train the murder of the reformer. A final conclusion upon his merits is therefore unlikely to do him full justice.

[1] *Cal. Close Rolls*, 1318–23, p. 196.

[2] K. R. Mem. Roll, no. 93, m. 9 d. L. T. R. Mem. Roll, no. 90, Brev. dir. Mich. m. 5 d. Vide App. of Doc. no. 29.

[3] For an appreciation of Stapleton vide *Reg. W. de Stapleton*, 1307–26, Preface, pp. xviii–xxviii.

[4] Tout, *The Place of Ed. II*, pp. 332–3.

[5] K. R. Mem. Roll, no. 102, m. 65 d.

[6] Ibid.

[7] Anc. Corresp. vol. XLIX, no. 188.

Stapleton's first short period of office was marked by the preparation for reform. Preparations were made for the proper arrangement of the exchequer records. The treasurer and barons and chamberlains of the exchequer were ordered "to appoint such of the king's clerks as shall be necessary to survey, dispose of and put under a proper state before Michaelmas the king's things in his treasury in the Tower of London and the rolls, books and other memoranda touching the exchequer of the times of his progenitors which the king understands are not so well disposed as is needed for him and the common weal[1]." This order was made on 7 August, 1320, and at the same time the treasurer and chamberlains were ordered to pay the clerks assigned for this purpose their reasonable expenses[2]. These orders were issued by warrant of the privy seal, thus showing the king's interest in the work[3]. The previous day orders had been issued for the making of a "calendar divided into title of all processes, letters and instruments and rolls touching the duchy of Acquitaine in order to have fuller memory thereof in future[4]."

The time for performing the task was short, and officials were set to work upon it immediately. The two chamberlains were assigned with two clerks each to arrange the rolls, memoranda and all other things in the king's treasury in the Tower of London, and to put them into a suitable state[5]. At the same time eleven clerks were busily engaged making estreats of debts due to the king[6]. Right on into April with various other clerks they were engaged in the array of the rolls and other things in the king's chapel in the Tower of London[7]. At the same time clerks were making extracts in the chancery, exchequer, and wardrobe of all grants which the king had made since his first year[8]. Before the work was completed the bishop had ceased to be treasurer; a start however had been made which was to be resumed on his reappointment.

Soon after the commencement of Stapleton's second period of office, the complete calendar of Gascon documents which had been ordered to be made in August, 1320, and handed into the treasury by him on 16 November[9] was on 4 December, 1322, delivered by the

[1] *Cal. Close Rolls*, 1318–23, p. 258. [2] Ibid. [3] Chan. Warr., File 111/5363.

[4] *Cal. Close Rolls*, 1318–23, p. 319. The matter is discussed by Prof. Tout, *The Place of Ed. II*, pp. 189–193.

[5] Issue Roll, no. 191, m. 8.

[6] Ibid. m. 7. [7] Ibid. no. 193, m. 4. [8] Ibid. m. 2.

[9] Ibid. no. 200, m. 1. At the same time the book of gifts which the king had made during his whole reign, a book of transcripts, a book of arrentions of the forest and a book "de parliamentis" were handed in.

exchequer to Baldock, keeper of the privy seal[1]. On 3 December the treasurer and chamberlains were ordered from York to cause all bulls and other charters, deeds and memoranda touching the king and his estate in England, Ireland, Wales and Scotland and Ponthieu in the treasury and elsewhere to be arranged and calendared[2]. The treasurer and chamberlains were to appoint sufficient persons to do this work[3]. Already clerks were at work searching and arranging and collecting in due order "cartas scripta et cetera munimenta in certis castris et aliis locis infra regnum Anglie" and had been so employed since the previous Easter term[4]. Stapleton set about the immediate appointment of clerks for the purpose. John Deuery together with Elias de Johnston and Roger de Sheffield was assigned to search, arrange and place the records in a certain calendar by divers titles according to the information of Master Henry de Canterbury assisting them[5]. It was Master Henry de Canterbury with the assistance of Elias de Johnston and others who had drawn up the calendar of Gascon records[6] and his experience was to be used again. A year later these clerks were still engaged in their work[7]. The final result of the work was "Bishop Stapleton's Calendar[8]." It was a monument of labour and besides the present historical value, it must have been of the utmost use at the time and for the purpose for which it was made.

The arranging and calendaring of exchequer records was however but preparatory work. Stapleton also issued a number of reforming ordinances[9]. The first of these ordinances under the title "the articles ordained and provided for the arrangement of matters in the exchequer" was issued on 14 June, 1323, as an ordinance of the king and council[10]. Professor Tout finds that "the idea at its root was that the incredible confusion of the exchequer accounts and the deplorable arrears of the accounting were due, not only to the

[1] The calendar is now to be found in P. R. O. Misc. Bks of Excheq. T. R. vol. CLXXXVII, ff. 1 et seq. It is discussed by Prof. E. Déprez in *Mélanges offerts à M. Charles Bémont* [1913], pp. 225–242, 'Le Trésor des Chartres de Guyenne sous Edouard II.'

[2] *Cal. Close Rolls*, 1318–23, p. 688.

[3] Ibid.

[4] Issue Roll, no. 220, m. 1.

[5] Ibid. m. 6.

[6] *Cal. Pat. Rolls*, 1321–24, p. 5.

[7] Issue Roll, no. 206, m. 6.

[8] The calendar is printed in Palgrave's *Ancient Kalendars and Inventories of the Exchequer*, vol. I, pp. 1–155.

[9] Their importance is stated at length, *Red Book of Exch.* vol. III, pp. cccxxxix–cccxlix (ed. H. Hall).

[10] *Cal. Close Rolls*, 1318–23, p. 662. The ordinance is printed with a translation in *Red Book of Exch.* vol. III, pp. 848–907, Vide Madox, *Hist. Exch.* vol. II, pp. 270–1.

embarrassed finances of the crown, but also to the old-fashioned and unbusinesslike way in which the accounts were kept[1]." Business was continually increasing, and with business the bulk of the records. The documents of the treasurer's remembrancer's department, the great rolls of the exchequer[2], the various documents delivered into the exchequer had all increased to from five to ten times their usual bulk[3]. All these writs of privy and great seal had to be enrolled on the memoranda rolls of the exchequer and hence increased its bulk, and they were filed. The need for array and calendaring the records becomes apparent.

As reforms it was ordained that "foreign accounts" should henceforth be enrolled separately. The irrecoverable debts of the king were to be written only in the "exannual roll" and then only once and not carried to succeeding rolls. The exchequer staff was to be increased. Definite functions were assigned to the two remembrancers. Restrictions were put upon the hearing of pleas in the exchequer. No official was to account by attorney and no exchequer officer was to act as attorney[4]. These reforms were supplemented in 1324 by other ordinances of the king and council issued on 6 May[5]. Various offices of the household were separated from the wardrobe and made to account directly to the exchequer. A definite time for the accounting of the wardrobe was fixed.

A third exchequer ordinance was issued on 30 June, 1326[6]. The archbishop of York was then treasurer and must take some of the credit for the reforming measures, but the ordinances had been made with the advice of Stapleton whose opinion the king held in the greatest respect[7]. Much of these ordinances was concerned with re-enactments of those of 1323. Among the new ordinances were those which provided that sheriffs' accounts should be held in full exchequer, that the treasurer and barons should exercise half yearly control over the remembrancers, that the chancellor and keeper of the privy seal should enrol annually all writs for payment in the exchequer, that the sheriffs should not be changed as often as they had been[8].

All the reforms in administration in the exchequer during this

[1] Tout, *The Place of Ed. II*, p. 193.

[2] The name applied to the "pipe roll." On the origin of the name pipe roll see *Eng. Hist. Rev.* vol. XXVI [1911], pp. 329–330, J. H. Ramsay.

[3] *Red Book of Exch.* vol. III, pp. 884, 860, 862–4.

[4] Ibid. pp. 848–907. [5] Ibid. pp. 908–929. [6] Ibid. pp. 930–969.

[7] K. R. Mem. Roll, no. 102, m. 56, where a long writ of privy seal to the treasurer and barons under date 17 April, 1326, gives some idea of the part Stapleton took in the arrangement of these ordinances.

[8] *Red Book of Exch.* vol. III, pp. 930–969.

period were not contained in these ordinances. On 9 June, 1323, ordinances made by the king and council were sent to the keepers of the great seal which ordered the manner in which estreats were to be made by the chancery to the exchequer and also how the justices and other officials were to make estreats[1]. Instructions sent by the bishop of Exeter to William de Ayremynne, a keeper of the great seal, concerning extents and administration of the forfeited lands also displayed that treasurer's administrative care and ability[2]. Early in 1326 transcripts of the rolls containing the exchequer ordinances of 1323 and 1324 were being made[3], and other matters which had been accorded and provided for the administration of the exchequer were on 23 July, 1326, ordered to be sent to the exchequer and such as referred to the chancery were to be kept in all their points in that department[4]. With all these reforms Stapleton was definitely connected.

Other alterations were also made with which his connection is not so certain. In 1323 and 1324 the arrangement of two escheators north and south of Trent was superseded by the arrangement of eight local escheators and the plan held until 1327[5]. A still more important change was made in 1324 which was attributed in a chronicler to Roger Beler, baron of the exchequer[6]. On 16 June, 1324, the king sent an important writ of privy seal to the treasurer and barons of the exchequer[7]. The exchequer was to be separated into two divisions and the officials divided between them, the change to take effect on 18 June "pur plus prestement deliuerer nostre poeple a lour esement et a nostre profit." The change had been previously ordered to take place on 11 June and apparently a number of the exchequer officers did not like the scheme and had hindered it. Norwich was to be chief baron of one part with Robert de Aylleston and Edmund de Passelewe as barons, and Beler chief baron in the new place with Humphrey de Walden, William de Euerdon and William de Fulbourn as barons. By counsel between them another suitable person was to be appointed to keep the great roll in place of William de Euerdon[8]. All the business relating to the north was to be done in the place in which

[1] Chan. Warr., File 123/6550 A, 6550 B, 6550 C. Cf. *Stat. of Realm*, vol. I, pp. 190–2.
[2] Chan. Warr., File 1705.
[3] Issue Roll, no. 216, m. 1.
[4] Chan. Warr., File 132/7450.
[5] Tout, *The Place of Ed. II*, p. 200.
[6] *Flores Hist.* vol. III, pp. 231–2.
[7] K. R. Mem. Roll, no. 97, Brev. dir. Trin. m. 4.
[8] He was appointed baron on the day the separation was to take effect, 18 June, 1324 (*Cal. Pat. Rolls*, 1321–24, p. 429). The appointment of Humphrey de Walden was also dated 18 June, 1324 (ibid.).

Norwich and his barons were, and the business of the south in the place under Beler and his barons. This condition was to last until the king should order otherwise. The treasurer and chancellor were to assign clerks under them who could act in their offices in the one place and the other, as was ordained, engrossers and remembrancers. Strict injunctions ordering the change to be made at the appointed day were issued[1]. The chronicler's statement that Beler was the originator of the scheme seems fairly well established. He was to become chief baron instead of baron, and with the larger staff was to conduct the business of the south. Moreover while the business of the north for Trinity term in that year, the seventeenth of the reign, was entered on the old memoranda roll, the business of the south was immediately separated and a new memoranda roll for the south for the Trinity term of the seventeenth year was made[2]. The new arrangement was continued for two years and seems to have come to an end with the death of Beler in 1326[3]. For the eighteenth and nineteenth years of Edward II there were two annual memoranda rolls of the king's and treasurer's remembrancers, one for the south and one for the north[4]. In the twentieth year the normal course was resumed and there was again one king's remembrancer's roll and one treasurer's remembrancer's roll[5]. These instances represent in a fair measure the various alterations which the reforming impulse, occasioned in part by the baronial opposition though chiefly by the need of reform, produced in the exchequer.

Little effect was produced upon the judicial benches either by the baronial opposition or the subsequent royal action. Some of the Ordinances had concerned grievances connected with the hearing of pleas. Such reforms as had been advocated were remedial, and some were maintained after the king's triumph in 1322. The restriction imposed upon the judicial functions of the exchequer and marshalsea court acted in favour of the common law courts and checked their rivals. The Statute of York in 1318 had been concerned with a number of judicial grievances and provided relief[6]. Orders concerning

[1] K. R. Mem. Roll, no. 97, Brev. dir. Trin. m. 4.

[2] K. R. Mem. Roll, no. 98. In the L. T. R. Series this roll was incorporated in the old one, L. T. R. Mem. Roll, no. 94, which therefore contains the business in K. R. Mem. Rolls, nos. 97 and 98.

[3] He was killed near Leicester on 19 Jan. 1326 (*Ann. Paul.* p. 310; *Chron. Knighton*, vol. I, p. 432; *Flores Hist.* vol. III, p. 232; cf. also *Cal. Close Rolls*, 1323–27, p. 550; *Cal. Fine Rolls*, 1319–27, pp. 381–2).

[4] K. R. Mem. Rolls, nos. 99–102. L. T. R. Mem. Rolls, nos. 95–98.

[5] K. R. Mem. Roll, no. 103. L. T. R. Mem. Roll, no. 99.

[6] *Stat. of Realm*, vol. I, pp. 177–9.

new rules or the maintenance of old laws were sent to the justices as the result of petitions. Thus a petition of the commonalty of England in 1315 that protection should not be allowed in a plea of felony, and especially touching the death of a man, received the reply: "Mandetur Justiciariis de utroque banco et Justiciariis ad diversas felonias in Regno audiendas et terminandas et Justiciariis ad Gaolas deliberandas assignatis quod non allocent protectiones Regis in casu felonie[1]." In the same parliament in answer to a writ an extended application of the statute of fines was ordered: and a writ to that effect sent to the justices: "Ordinatum est et preceptum per Dominum Regem et ejus Concilium, quod Statutum de Finibus extendat se tam ad antiquos Fines ante editionem Statuti, quam post editionem ejusdem levatos. Et super hoc dirigitur breve Justiciariis ad placita Regis tenenda assignatis, sub tenore qui sequitur...[2]."

In the parliament of Westminster in 1320 the commonalty petitioned because persons indicted of homicide and committed to the prison of the marshal of the bench were mainprised though this was against the law. Those who had complaints were to obtain writs from chancery, and the Statute of York was to be sent to the justices to be kept[3]. Except by remedy provided by statute, ordinances, writ and endorsement, no important alteration appears within the judicial offices.

The effect of the action of the baronial opposition and the royal policy after 1322 upon the household offices remains to be considered. There was undoubtedly need for very considerable reform in the household; and its disordered state was one of the cries of the baronial opposition. Lancaster's policy may in fact be embodied in the phrase "reform of the household." At the time of the Ordinances there seemed no clear conception of how that reform could be secured and maintained. A number of the household offices were to be appointed by the barons. An implication that the privy seal should be separated from the office of the controller of the wardrobe, restriction in the jurisdiction of the household court, and reform in the manner of taking prises form a complete catalogue of the attempts made in the Ordinances themselves to reform the household. To a great extent the policy of the ordainers seemed to be directed rather against the personal, than towards the permanent, reform of the household. In the additional ordinances, they endeavoured to remove from the household those men who were objectionable to themselves, though no organised scheme of reform was presented. In the parliament of

[1] *Rot. Parl.* vol. I, pp. 291, 324. [2] Ibid. pp. 295–6. [3] Ibid. p. 372.

York in 1318, under the influence of the middle party, a committee was appointed to reform the household. In 1318 ordinances dealing with reform of the household were issued[1]. These ordinances were not made by the committee appointed in parliament but by Badlesmere, steward of the household, Despenser, chamberlain, Northburgh, treasurer, and Gilbert de Wigton, controller of the wardrobe, who made them by the king's command. The ordinances were made:

> Pour ceo qe les officers del lostiell nostre seignour le roi ount estez toutz iours en arere, et noun certein de ceo qils deueront faire et prendre du roi, par reason de leur officez, par quoy due examinement dez ditez officers ne poiat estre fait, ne les officers chargez si come estre deuoient, a grand damage et dishonour du roi et en desarament de soun hostiell; et nostre dit seignour le roi, eiant regard al estat de son dit hostiell meyns bien garde, et a ses chosez en autre manere despenduez qi estre ne duissent[2].

There was no suggestion that the ordinances were in any way the result of baronial pressure; they were drawn up by the chief household officials. They were read and assented to before the king and in the presence of the archbishop of York, the bishop of Ely, chancellor, the bishops of Norwich and Salisbury, Henry le Scrope and Henry Spigurnel, justices[3]. There was uncertainty as to the various offices and the ordinances were concerned with their definition. Definition rather than reform was in fact the keynote of these ordinances. The uncertainty which was expressed in the preamble was to be superseded by precise rules as to the functions and rewards of the household officers. They were concerned with the domestic and not the political phase of the household. In June, 1323, another ordinance of the household[4] was made and assented to, in the presence of the king, by Melton, archbishop of York, Stapleton, bishop of Exeter, treasurer, Norwich, Beler and other barons of the exchequer, and others of the king's council[5]. As these names might lead one to expect, this ordinance was mainly concerned with the way in which accounts of the household were to be drawn up and presented, a subject which was also dealt with in the exchequer ordinances of 1324[6]. It was therefore seen that the king was not opposed to reforms of the household. Indeed in November, 1312, he had instructed Pembroke, Despenser the elder and Sandale to consider and ordain "coment nostre meignee puisse mieltez estre sustenue"

[1] The household ordinances of 1318 are printed as an Appendix to Prof. Tout's *The Place of Ed. II*, App. 1, pp. 270–314.

[2] Tout, *The Place of Ed. II*, App. 1, p. 270.

[3] Ibid.

[4] The household ordinances of 1323 printed op. cit. App. 1, pp. 314–318.

[5] Tout, *The Place of Ed. II*, App. 1, p. 314.

[6] Vide above, p. 532.

on account of the great complaints which were made of it[1]. What he was resolutely opposed to was reform in such a personal matter forced upon him by the barons with a partly political object. Disinterested reform, or reform with the object of increasing efficiency or removing abuses, he accepted. The reforms, or definitions amounting to reforms, which were accomplished by the ordinances of 1318 and 1323 had no political significance, but increased the efficiency of the domestic administration of the household. The baronial Ordinances of 1311 dealing with the household were not altogether unsuccessful. The Ordinance about the marshalsea court was re-enacted in the statute or establishment of 1322. The keeper of the king's privy seal[2] became, though not immediately, distinct from the controller of the household.

The effects of the baronial opposition upon the different administrative departments, were they considered in 1322, would not have been considerable. The baronial schemes proved failures. The great reforms and changes were made after 1322 and were the work of the king acting on the direction and under the guidance of a number of administrators of the highest ability. It was then that the reorganisation and reform of the exchequer took place. It was after the defeat of the baronial opposition, too, that the declaration was made in the parliament of York concerning the place of the commonalty. The baronial opposition may, however, be said to have had this share in those reforms—the opposition had shown where the grievances lay. Their policy had been too completely negative for them to suggest remedies. Even had they been able to provide suitable remedies, while the king and the household system behind him were opposed to those remedies, little could have been achieved. Reform of the administration to be effective must come from within and be accepted voluntarily. It was the royal administration, and reforms ought not to come from the barons but from the king. The baronial endeavours showed the king the need. When he was freed from that opposition he endeavoured to profit by the experience he had undergone and reforms were introduced.

[1] Anc. Corresp. vol. XLIX, no. 15. Vide App. of Doc. no. 123.

[2] Prof Tout throws out the interesting suggestion that Baldock when chancellor endeavoured to subordinate this office to the chancery preliminary to an amalgamation. (*The Place of Ed. II*, pp. 166–7.)

CONCLUSION

The reign of Edward II ended in a revolution as violent, illogical and cruel as any such movement in English history. Its violence and cruelty were the direct result of the heartless and selfish policy the Despensers had pursued since their triumph in 1322. It was illogical, because the heir to the throne overthrew his father's government by the aid and support of the remnant of the baronial opposition. The aggression of the younger Despenser, especially his endeavour to create a great and centralised power in Wales[1], was a leading cause of the revolution. The unpopularity of the administration and its officials was equally potent. It was a baronial movement, for though London seized the opportunity the crisis presented for savage riot and murder, the people appear merely to have acquiesced. The leaders of the movement were Mortimer of Wigmore and Henry de Lancaster, lord of Kidwelly, the very men whose interests and possessions were threatened by Despenser's Welsh policy. Yet the revolution was not a defeat for the household system of government and its details do not contradict any of the claims which have been put forward in support of the strength of that system.

The conflict of the reign was administrative. The foremost cause of the baronial opposition was administrative, and though a certain amount of "popular" discontent was caused by financial troubles, that discontent rarely found expression, and in the great struggle of the reign can be ignored. The barons pursuing an oligarchical policy came into conflict with the royal theory and position. It was a struggle between baronial ideas and royal authority and reality. The baronial theory was but little less powerful than the royal theory of government. But the household system of administration had all the strength of a well-established organism behind it. Against the strength of that system the barons strove in vain. At every turn and twist of baronial policy there was some instrument of the household

[1] This is emphasised by Professor Tout, *The Place of Edward II*, pp. 153–5. A few of the enormous grants to Despenser in pursuit of this policy are found in *Cal. Pat. Rolls*, 1321–24, p. 214; 1324–27, pp. 95, 116; *Cal. Charter Rolls*, 1300–26, pp. 448, 449, 450, 451, 461, 467, 469, 478.

system to meet it. If there was not an existing instrument available a new one could be devised or a new use found for an old one. The ability of the household system to provide new checks was one of its greatest assets. It was the breath which gave life to the organism of the administrative system. When the inherent strength of the household system was added to this ability to provide new instruments and counter strokes, the completeness of the royal power is seen and the real reasons for the failure of the baronial opposition made apparent.

In the reign of Edward II conditions demanded that the confusion of business, which had been a marked feature of the administrative system, should cease. Definition and differentiation were to supersede confusion. There were confusion and uncertainty in the purely household offices, there were confusion and uncertainty in the administrative offices and confusion was worse confounded in the inter-relations between the household and the administrative offices. Confusion meant an insistent need and demand for reform. The exchequer had acted as a secretariat, as an executive, as a court of common law. A demand arose, partly from the ineffective way in which the financial business was transacted because of the employment of the exchequer officials on other than financial business, partly from other sources, that the exchequer should confine itself to finance. In that sphere, however, it was to become supreme. There was to be no parallelism between wardrobe and exchequer. The wardrobe was to account to the exchequer.

The natural tendency of the time was in accord with this need and demand for definition. Feudal custom was being transformed. The old feudal contract had broken down. It was necessary that the obligations of lord and vassal should be defined. The paper constitutions which were so prevalent from the reign of Henry III onwards are another manifestation of the same tendency. About the same time it was found necessary to give definite form to the financial attributes of the king's prerogative and the statute *De Prerogativa Regis*[1] was made. It was one thing to make an enactment and quite a different matter to secure observance to it. Yet it was important that custom was being superseded by enactment.

The reign of Edward II came between the reigns in which important and well marked characteristics strike the eye. Edward I sought to make England whole within her own borders. His policy towards his Celtic neighbours, towards law and order, towards the barons, all

[1] *Stat. of Realm*, vol. I, pp. 226–7.

had this object in view. Edward III inaugurated a period of foreign expansion and found on the fields of France an outlet for his own energies and those of his barons and people. Edward II's father is known to history as the creator of parliament; Edward II's son is hardly less renowned for his victories abroad and the splendour of his reign at home. Attention has concentrated upon outwardly visible effects and ostentation. Edward II's reign has been considered of little importance because it contained no thrilling personalities and events. His reign has an importance of his own, an unique importance to be discovered only by a study of the intricacies of the administrative methods and processes of his time. Without that study the action of the baronial opposition becomes almost unintelligible. By the application of administrative study to the interpretation of political history, the baronial opposition to Edward II becomes a vital phase in the development of the administration and constitution of England and the reign has an importance as considerable as it is unexpected. The study of the reign presented here as based upon an examination of the administrative documents of the reign, has taken the form of a statement of the policy which they reveal, with perhaps less than necessary attention to the previous and future history of that policy. This was, partly, inevitable, but a brief word must be said about the past and future.

However capable the successor of Edward I had been, his task would have been a difficult one. It was not so much the usual unfortunate position of the successor of a great king. It was partly that in the institutional and constitutional as well as in the political aspects the successor would have to meet the reaction after centralisation and rapid constitutional development. Edward I's policy had not been national but royal or rather anti-baronial. The barons had been restive during his later years. Edward I's reign stood between the revolutionary doctrines of Montfort and the Provisions of Oxford and the equally revolutionary doctrines of Lancaster and the Ordinances. His reign was the breathing space between the two periods. In that breathing space he had achieved much, yet not all he had sought. The revival of the revolutionary doctrine was not a mere repetition of the same arguments in similar circumstances. A vast difference was apparent. More attention was paid to administrative matters.

Edward II's reign was still concerned largely with the old problems of the thirteenth century. It was not a struggle of parliament or people against the king. People and parliament were almost entirely ignored by the baronage, though they obtained a little more recognition from the king. The struggle was between royal position and baronial rights. These rights the king refused to admit. The administrative significance of the struggle is greater than its constitutional importance. The position of parliament is not fundamental in the consideration of the question and the struggle could be well understood with little reference to that body. The council was of far greater importance than parliament.

When the barons sought to restrain the king they found that the great source of opposition against which they had to contend lay in the household system. The barons might have attacked the strength of that system in two ways. In the first place they might have aimed at an entire separation and differentiation between the household and the administration. They might have lessened the control which the household exercised over the government. Any part which they night have obtained in, or any control they might have obtained over, the government would have resulted in the diminution of household control over the government. In the second place, the barons might have endeavoured to weaken the sources of strength of the household system by decreasing its independence in various directions. Its action as the executive with its instruments of the privy and secret seals and its verbal orders might be restricted. Its financial independence in the wardrobe and the chamber might be curtailed. Its independence in justice might be defined and limited. Its officials might be rendered responsible to another authority than the king. The barons endeavoured to achieve success along these different lines. A clear distinction between what was household and what was administrative they did not draw. At the time any such distinction would have been almost impossible. The barons did not seek to control the administration alone. The household was the key to the position, and over the household they claimed to exercise as complete an influence as over the administration. Household and administration were to contemporary eyes the same.

That in the household there were outstanding grievances is fairly apparent on every side. There was lack of definition, confusion of duties, uncertainty and extravagance. If the king did not reform it himself, upon whom was the duty to fall? The barons' interpretation was that it was their duty. The king did not deny the need of reform. He denied that it was the right of the barons to interfere in his personal affairs. He had the resources to maintain that position, for he could frustrate if not prevent baronial action.

In the series of experiments in which the barons sought to put their plan into action, there is discernible a change in tactics and a development in policy. The Ordinances as a scheme of government were not surrendered, for as a program of reform they were of great value. Modifications and omissions had to be made: the outline of the scheme remained intact. It was in the methods by which the barons sought to secure the execution of their schemes and in their general attitude towards the household system that the change occurred. The baronial division into the two camps of Lancaster and Pembroke marked the change, though Lancaster's policy did not remain static. Lancaster consistently urged the observance of the Ordinances and with equal consistency urged the removal of the "evil counsellors" by whom the king was surrounded. The best features of baronial policy appear in the work of Pembroke and the middle party and it was that section that achieved a fair measure of success. The motive which underlay their plan was good and their execution of the plan for long well-conceived.

The best that can be said of the baronial opposition in general is that it sought to subject the king, no less than his people, to the rule of law. The great principle contained in Magna Carta that the king was under the law, was very open to misinterpretation, and the policy of the barons partly lay them open to this charge. Viewed from the best light the aims of the opposition were to secure the omnipotence of law and to lessen the powers the king might exercise to the detriment, or in negation, of law. To royal partizans the baronial aims were something very much worse. They were to make the king and crown dependent upon and subject to the will of the baronage. There were undoubtedly strong oligarchical tendencies in the barons, and the attempt made by them to obtain control over the great offices of government and their experiments to control the king by a committee can be easily so interpreted. On the other hand, they can be regarded equally well as efforts to secure the operation of the principle which they urged of the obedience of the king to law. In other words the struggle resolved itself once more into the eternal question of the control of the executive. The barons desired to control the executive to secure a wider end, the control of the whole government. The work which Henry II had done had been too well done for feudalism to remain unaffected or for it ever to revive in its previous form. It was no longer an effort by a feudal caste to render itself locally independent or to rule the suzerain. The fight now took the form of an effort by a narrow and powerful oligarchy to obtain the share they claimed their ancestors had exercised in the government. There appear to be two considerations which contributed to the oligarchical principle as expressed in the thirteenth century, and subsequently: the hereditary officers of the court and the title, rank and position of the earls. Both these considerations played their part during the reign of Edward II.

The downfall and death of the king in 1326–7 meant no weakening of the household system. The administration of the queen and her son was no less personal than Edward II's had been. The system remained; the figures changed. Mortimer took the place in the court and administration which had been occupied by the younger Despenser. When the reaction against Edward II was most violent—in the first parliament of his son—the commonalty presented various petitions which echoed the cries of the baronial opposition. They sought that certain ancient debts should be pardoned[1], an alteration made in the administration of debts[2] and that suitable men and wise, appointed by the barons, should be with the king to give him good counsel, and to be removable by parliament for misdeeds[3]. Such policy was however but temporary in its operation and effect. It was also enacted in that parliament that those who had been disinherited by the Despensers, Baldock and Stapleton were to have actions before the king, the justices of king's bench, with two bishops, two earls and two barons or one of each rank associated with them[4]. This association of magnates was not to be a restrictive measure but purely judicial and the king himself often gave magnates a place in judicial and administrative courts. In fact in the eighteenth year of Edward II when the king was supreme the council of prelates and magnates chosen to treat concerning the journey of the king to Gascony had advised:

> Et sire quant a larray de vostre realme Dengleterre y semble sire a mesmes ceux qi a mon seigneur vostre filz come a vostre lieu tenant soient assignez deux Erceuesqes quatre Euesqes deux countes et quatre Barons qi soient entendantz a son conseil ouesqes voz ministres des places et ouesqes autres qi purront estre appellez solenc ce qe homme verra qe les busoignes demanderont les queux prelatz countes et Barons soient sire sil vous plest nomez par vous Et de ceux sire pur ce qils ne purront mie touz contennement demorer endressement entour lui par conseil des queux les autres soient appellez quant mestre serra[5].

This was put forward as a serious and practical proposal when the king's position was very strong and it was in reality a sign of strength not weakness. Though the new government was weak in 1327 the

[1] *Rot. Parl.* vol. II, pp. 8, 11. [2] Ibid. [3] Ibid. pp. 10, 12.

[4] *Stat. of Realm*, vol. I, p. 253. *Stat. Westm.* I, 1 Ed. III, § 3.

[5] Anc. Corresp. vol. XLIX, no. 89.

household system was unimpaired and administration ran its normal course in almost all directions. The exchequer maintained its position and was ordered to appoint under exchequer seal "some of the king's subjects sworn of his council" to extend certain manors[1].

Such minor encroachments as were then made did little to impair the efficiency, and they were more than recovered very shortly. Edward III's government was as personal and the household influence as general as in the previous reign. This was inevitable, for all the household's sources of strength remained intact. The king and the household retained the ability of substituting vigorous for formalised instruments. Under Edward III the service of the privy seal was better organised[2]. As Edward II had used the secret seal, so under Edward III in the griffin seal and signet[3] new instruments of the royal will were found.

Though a number of the particular features which characterised the baronial opposition during the reign of Edward II reappeared in the work of the Lords Appellant of Richard II's day, and although in that time as in the time of James II the precedents of Edward's reign were searched and discussed, the varying circumstances make any profound similarity almost impossible. The particular phase baronial opposition took in the reign of Edward II was dictated largely by the administrative circumstances of the time. The personal character of the king, of the "curialists," of the administrative officers and of the barons also had due influence. It was a conflict of principle.

Even in the debacle at the end of the reign the royal principle was triumphant. The baronial theory lacked effective machinery. During the reign of Edward II it had lacked leaders of constructive ability. The series of experiments which endeavoured to rule the king, by lessening the control and independence of the household, by endeavouring to capture now the household, now the executive, now both, had lacked the spark of genius. As constructive statesmanship they were weak and inconclusive means of attacking the household system and its sway. Yet it seems difficult to discover what means could have overcome or threatened that system of government with its independence in executive, finance, justice and official staffs, and with its comprehensive control of the administration. Out of the wreck of baronial schemes the king was able to borrow somewhat. Out of a period of stress if not strain the household system emerged triumphant, secure and virile.

[1] *Cal. Close Rolls*, 1323–27, p. 622.
[2] E. Déprez, *Études de Dipl. Ang., Le Sceau Privé, etc.* p. 23. [3] Ibid. pp. 86–94.

APPENDIX OF DOCUMENTS

NOTE

The arrangement of a number of documents, such as this Appendix, offers a very difficult problem. An organised arrangement according to their subject or administrative significance would have been the best method to adopt, but it was almost impossible on account of the dual nature of the thesis. When everything had been considered, the best decision seemed to be to place the documents as in the Public Record Office classes. The documents have therefore been divided into three divisions, those of the great administrative departments of the Exchequer and of the Chancery and those included under the omnibus heading of Special Collections. This plan has its defects, but in the circumstances seemed the best adapted for the present purpose.

The documents therefore appear in the Appendix in the following order:

I. *Exchequer Records.*

- (i) K. R. and L. T. R. Memoranda Rolls.
- (ii) Exchequer Miscellanea.
- (iii) K. R. Exchequer Bills.
- (iv) K. R. Exchequer Accounts.
- (v) Issue Rolls.
- (vi) Exchequer of Pleas, Plea Roll.

II. *Chancery Records.*

- (i) Chancery Miscellanea.
- (ii) Chancery Warrants.

III. *Special Collections.*

- (i) Parliamentary and Council Proceedings (Chancery).
- (ii) Ancient Correspondence.
- (iii) Ancient Petitions.
- (iv) Duchy of Lancaster, Ancient Correspondence.
- (v) K. B. Miscellanea.

The documents have been transcribed verbatim and extended. Following the plan of Mr Hilary Jenkinson no effort has been made to correct the scribe's mistakes and a purely literal rendering of the documents as written has been aimed at. Where a word occurs in full in a document it is extended according to that spelling throughout the document. Where the same word occurs in full in different spellings in the same document it is extended according to the more normal or frequent of those spellings. Thus where aũ occurs several times and auoir once aũ is always extended in that document as auoir; where q̃ is found once as que and once or more as qe it is always extended in that document as qe. Though the documents reveal considerable variation that must most frequently be attributed to the scribe rather than to the transcriber. Spaces denote either irrelevant material or a mutilated document.

To increase the utility of the Appendix a short description of each document has been added. This compensates to some extent for the lack of arrangement under subjects.

I. EXCHEQUER RECORDS

1. **Letter from treasurer to barons of exchequer enclosing king's writ and ordering execution.** [K. R. Mem. Roll, no. 81, m. 14 d. L. T. R. Mem. Roll, no. 78, m. 16 d.]

A son cher ami sire William de Carleton Baron de Lescheker nostre seigneur le Rey Gauter Renaud Tresorer nostre seigneur le Rey saluz et cheres amistez Je vous envoy enclos denz cestes un bref qe me vint de par nostre seigneur le Rey y ce Lundy a Totenham et vous pri qe hastiuement unes cestes lettres facez execution de meismes le bref en touz poyntz solonc le mandement nostre seigneur le Rey et selonc ce quil est contenu en meismes le bref Nostre seigneur vous gard Escrit a Totenham icest Lundy au vespre.

2. **Writ of privy seal to exchequer officials to inquire into misdeeds of Langton, Edward I's treasurer.** [K. R. Mem. Roll, no. 81, m. 18. L. T. R. Mem. Roll, no. 78, m. 21.]

Thesaurario Baronibus et Camerariis per Regem.

Edward par la grace de dieu Roi Dengleterre Seignour Dirlande et Ducs Daquitaine as Tresorier et as Barons et as Chaumberleins de nostre Escheqer saluz Pur ceo qe nous voloms qe Wauter de Langeton Euesqe de Cestre nad gaires Tresorier nostre cher pere qui dieux assoille soit procheinement aresone et acoupe deuant nos Justicz de trespas et mesprisiouns et damages qil fist a nostre dit pere en son temps et a nous et as autres qe voudront suire vers lui tant comme il feust Tresorier nostre dit pere vous maundoms et chargoms en la foi qe vous nous deuez et sur quant qe vous nous deuez et sur quant qe vous nous porrez forfaire qe vous toutz et chescoun de vous auisez si estreitement comme vous porrez par tottes les maneres des remenbraunces qe vous sauerez et facez mettre en escrit toutz les mesfaitz et damages qe le dit Euesqe fist a nostre dit pere tant comme il feust son Tresorier al Escheker et aillours comme en torceneuses allouaunces faus enroulementz et procuraunt faus iugementz pernant champert des dettes nostre dit pere pur les faire paier a la foitz la tierce partie a la foitz la quarte partie en graunt esclaundre et damage de nostre dit pere et damage du poeple et en appropriant auxi a lui grant foison de Tresor nostre dit pere le quel il fist les ministres du Roialme paer a son hostel et en autres lieus a sa volente aillours qe a la rescette del dit Escheqer ou les issues du Roiaume deussent auer este paez et en acquitant trop legerment les ministres du Roiaume de leur accountes et asseant les fermes du Roiaume a meindre pris qe eles ne valount pur douns et pur presenz qe lui furent donez et de totes les autres mesprisions qe vous porrez sauoir et enquer de lui et de totes cestes choses et de quantqe vous porrez sauoir certifiez distinctement et apertement nostre cher et foial monsire William de Bereford qi nous auoms assigne de resceuire oier et trier totes les pleintes qe hom vodra faire del dit Euesqe ausi bien pur nostre profit comme pur ceaux du poeple qi se vodront pleindre de li E ne lessez en nule manere afaire ceo qe est de susdit sicom nous vous chargeoms sur les sermentz qe vous nous auez fait et sur la foi et la ligeaunce qe vous nous deuez issint qe nous puissons sauoir par ceo coment nous porroms et deueroms fier de vous Donne sutz nostre priue seal a Langele le xxvii iour de Nouembre Lan de nostre Regne primer.

3. **Writ of privy seal to council at London enclosing petition and ordering remedy.** [K. R. Mem. Roll, no. 81, m. 35 d. L. T. R. Mem. Roll, no. 78, m. 68 d.]

Pro Rogero de Mortuo Mari.

Edward par la grace de dieu etcetera a noz chers et foialz les honurables pieres en dieu par la meisme grace Johan Euesqe de Cicestre nostre Chancellier Wauter Eslit de Wyrcestre confermez nostre Tresorier monsire Johan de Brytaigne Counte de Richemont nostre cher cousin monsire Hugh le Despenser et autres bones gentz de nostre consail a Loundres saluz Nous vous enueoms cy de denz enclos une peticion qe nous est baillie par monsire Roger de Mortimer seingneur de Chirk et vous maundoms qe sour les choses contenuez en meisme La peticion lui facez tut Le remedie qe vous purrez solonc la ley et lusage de nostre Roiaume et sil y eit chose qe depende en nostre grace si nous enauisez par vos lettres de la grace qe nous enpussoms faire en bone manere Donne souz nostre priue seal a Wyndesore le xiiij de Juyl Lan de nostre regne secund.

4. **Ordinance made in parliament about king's mines in Devon.** [K. R. Mem. Roll, no. 82, m. 55. L. T. R. Mem. Roll, no. 79, m. 41.]

Deuonscire Ordinacio pro minera Regis.

Deuonscire ffait a remembrer qe ordine est par lonurable pere en dieu sire Wauter par la grace de dieu Euesqe de Wyrcestre Trosorier nostre seigneur le Roi en la presence sire Johan de Sandale Chaunceller sire William de Carleton sire Thomas de Cantebrigge Sire Rogere de Hengham mestre Richard de Abyndon Mestre Johan de Euerdon Barouns del Escheqier et plusours autres del consail du dist nostre seigneur Le Roi en son parlement le terme de seint Michel lan de son regne secund qe Roberd de Thorp seit gardein de la minere le Roi en Byrelond et en Deuenesire et des autres mineres qil purra faire cerhcier es parties de Deuenesire ou il entendra faire le profist le Roi et qe Johan de Repple clerk seit countreroullour des dites mineres...... Cest endenture fust faite a Westmoustre Le xij iour de Decembre lan auauntnomee.

5. **Execution by council of writ of privy seal to treasurer and barons.** [K. R. Mem. Roll, no. 82, m. 56 d. L. T. R. Mem. Roll, no. 79, m. 41.]

Lincolnscire.

Dominus Rex mandauit hic breue suum quod est inter comunia de hoc anno in hec verba: Edward par la grace de dieu Roi Dengleterre Seigneur Dirlaund et Ducs Dacquitaigne au Tresorier et as Barouns de nostre Escheqier salutz Nous vous maundoms qe a Robert de Wayneflet qui se dit Abbe de Bardenaye et as moignes qe demoerent en sa compaignie facez assigner ascune Eglise ou autre rente de la dite Abbaye dount il puissent estre sustenuz en alant vers la court nostre seint pere le pape pur purchacer lestat du dist Robert sicome il verra qe face a faire Donne souz nostre priue seal a Wyndesore le xxix iour de Decembre Lan de nostre regne secund Et pretextu huius breuis tractato isto negocio coram Johanne Episcopo cicestrense Cancellario Anglie Thesaurario et Baronibus Johanne de Britannie comite Richemund Hugone le Despenser et aliis de consilio Regis modo xxj die Januario concordatum est per idem consilium quod manerium de Barton...assignetur eidem Abbati....

6. **Memorandum of exhibition of letters close to exchequer officials and council.** [K. R. Mem. Roll, no. 82, m. 65 d. L. T. R. Mem. Roll, no. 79, m. 89.]

De Rogero de Ryuers liberando Turri Londonii.

Memorandum quod cum Rogerus de Ryuers venit hic ad scaccarium coram Johanne de Sandale tenente locum Thesaurarii et Baronibus assidentibus eis Rogero le Brabaunzoun Willelmo de Bereford Henrico Spygournel Justiciariis domini Regis et aliis de consilio domini Regis modo die Jouis xxvj die Junij et exhibuit predicto tenenti locum Thesaurarii quasdam litteras clausas.

7. **Writ of privy seal to earl of Lincoln to summon council to discuss arrangements for a parliament and certify king.** [K. R. Mem. Roll, no. 83, m. 10 d.]

Henrico de Lacy comiti Lincolnie per Regem.

Edward par la grace de dieu etcetera a nostre trescher cousyn et foial monsire Henri de Lacy counte de Nicole salutz Sachez qe par nostre conseil qe nous auioms a Euerwyk nous auoms ordene de faire somoundre nostre grant parlement destre a Euerwyk le demayn procheyn apres la Chaundeleur por treter de la busoigne Descoce et dautres diuerses busoignes solonc lauisement qe nous aueroms de vous et dautre bone gentz de nostre consail Par quei nous vous maundoms qe si tost come vous porretz bonement entendre appelletz a vous nostre Tresorier et autres de nostre conseill qi vous veez qi facent appeller et auisez en quele maniere et de quel endreit il nous couendra ceo parlement deliuerer et soit tut ordeine deuaunt vous et mys en escrit le arrai de nostre parlement issint qil nous couiegne mye demorrier illosqes por parlementer outre x iours ou xij au plus et nous facetz a sauoir par vos lettres au plus tost qe vous porrez bonement come vous auerez la busoigne ordene Donne souz nostre priue seal a Ribbestan le iiij iour de Novembre lan de nostre regne tierz.

8. **Writ of privy seal to exchequer officials enjoining secrecy.** [K. R. Mem. Roll, no. 83, m. 11.]

Baronibus per Regem.

Edward par la grace de dieu au Tresorier Chaunceler et as Barons de nostre Escheqier salutz Come nous eoms entenduz qe le conseil et les busoigne qe nous touchent qe sont tretez deuant vous a nostre dit Escheqier soient trop souent descouerez et pupplietz par la ou il afferreit point a grant damage de nous et en arrerissement de noz dites busoignes vous mandoms fermement enioignauntz qe entre vous ordenetz issint qe a nostre dit Escheqier ne en les places ou vous auetz noz busoignes a ordener et tretir ne suffriez entre vous nul autre venir forsqe ceaux qi sont a ceo iurriez Et si par auenture il vous couiegne auoir plus deyde de clerks ou dautres qui ne sont auant iurriez les facetz iurrier et chargier par leurs sermentz si auaunt come vous verrez qe face a faire qe bien et lealment feront et celeront Les choses qe nous touchent quiqil soient de vos clers ou de autres qui illoeqes vendront ou demurront pur acountes oir ou autres busoignes faire que nous touchent Donne souz nostre priue seal a Euerwik le xxvj iour Doctobre Lan de nostre regne tierz.

9. **Writ of privy seal to allow debts to be recovered at exchequer.** [K. R. Mem. Roll, no 83, m. 14 d.]

Thesaurario et Baronibus pro Willelmo Seruat.

Edward par la grace de dieu et cetera au Tresorer et as Barons de nostre Escheker saluz Nous voillantz faire grace especiale a nostre cher marchand William Seruat vous mandoms qe vous receuez le dit William ou son attorne a pleder deuant vous a nostre Escheker por recouerer les dettes qe lui sount dues selonc la ley et Lusage de meisme lescheker totes les foiz qe vous verrez qe face a faire Donne souz nostre priue seal a la Groue le xx iour Janeuoir Lan de nostre regne tierz.

10. **Letter from treasurer to barons to hasten accounts and make allowances.** [K. R. Mem. Roll, no. 83, m. 22.]

Baronibus per Thesaurarium.

Saluz et treschieres amistez Pur ceo qe nostre seigneur le Roi vous ad maunde par ses lettres qe vous hastez les acountes de marchaundz de ffriscombaud et qe vous leur facez allowaunce des gages de ceux quil ount mis a receuire les custumes des Leynes quires et peaux Launtz vous maundoms de par le dit nostre seigneur le Roi qe vous hastez les ditz acountes et leur facez allowaunce des ditz gages solome le maundement nostre seigneur le Roi auauntdit E ceo ne lessez en nule manere Nostre seigneur vous eit en sa garde Escrit a Oxenford le ix iour de Maij.

11. **Writs of privy seal to barons to entertain king's pleas only.** [K. R. Mem. Roll, no. 83, m. 22 d.]

Baronibus per Regem.

Edward par la grace de dieu et cetera as Barons de nostre Eschekier saluz Nous vous mandoms qe vous ne tiegnez desoremes a nostre dit Eschekier nul play fors qe tantsolement ceux qe touch nous meismes et la dite place mais entendez a oir et a deliurerer les acontes qe y sont a deliuerer et les autres busoignes touchantes nostre profit demesne totes autres busoignes leissez donne souz nostre priue seal a Wodestok le xij iour de Maij Lan de nostre regne tierz.

12. **Writ of privy seal to treasurer not to act in a matter until further orders.** [K. R. Mem. Roll, no. 83, m. 26.]

Thesaurario per Regem.

Edward par la grace de dieu et cetera al honurable pere en dieu Wauter par la meisme grace Euesqe de Wircestre saluz Nous vous mandoms qe vous ne ordenez ne ne facez rien endroit du chastel de Cokermue tant qe vous eneez autre mandement de nous Donne souz nostre priue seal a Wyndesores le xxxj iour de may lan de nostre regne tierz.

13. **Writ of privy seal to treasurer and barons to entertain a plea of assault upon servant of a king's clerk.** [K. R. Mem. Roll, no. 83, m. 27.]

Baronibus pro Willelmo de Melton.

Edward par la grace de dieu et cetera au Tresorier et as Barons de nostre Eschekier saluz Nous auoms entenduz par la moustrance William de Melton nostre clerc qui demoert pres de nous en nostre seruise par nostre especial comandement que Johan Caperoun et Robert Mel un cheual du dit William pris de xl mark nad gaires trouez en la cite de Londres en la moyn dun corretter a qui il laueit fait bailler a vendre a force et armes et contre la volunte du dit William et du garzon qui lauoit en garde pristrent et amenerent et meisme le garzon batirent defolerent et malement treterent et autre outrage se soint au dit nostre clerc en despit de nous et grant damage du dit nostre clerc et countre nostre pees Par quoi nous vous mandoms que par breef de meisme nostre Eschekier ou par bille facez faire attacher les ditz Johan et Robert ou quil soient trouez issint qil soient deuant vous a nostre dit Eschekier lendemain de la Trinite procheine auenir pur respundre a nous du dit despit et a nostre dit clerc du trespas et damage auantditz Et receuoz nostre dit clerc ou sun attorne a pledeer deuant vous pur le trespas auantditz a ceste foiz de nostre grace especiale et enfacez faire acomplissement de droit as ditz partyes selonc la ley et lusage du dit Escheker nouncontrestant le mandement qe nous vous feismes nad gaires que vous ny tenissez nul play sil ne touchat nous en la dite place Donne souz nostre priue seal a Wyndesore le v iour de Juyn lan de nostre Regne tierz.

14. Writ of privy seal to treasurer and barons to hear pleas at exchequer. [K. R. Mem. Roll, no. 83, m. 27.]

Baronibus pro Priore et fratribus Predicatoribus de Londinio.

Edward par la grace de dieu et cetera au Tresorer et as Barouns de nostre Escheker saluz Por ce qe noz chers en dieu le Prior et les freres precheours de Londres nous ont fait entendantz quil se sentent mout greuez empeschez et damagez par diuers gentz aussibien endreit des purueances quil sount faire par eux et par leur amys pur leur sustenance come dautres choses qe leur sont donees des aumoisnes des bones gentz et du plus par reson de ce qe les trespassours ne poent estre legerement chastiez par la commune ley de nostre Reaume Nous voillanz faire grace especiale as ditz freres en cele partie vous mandoms qe quele houre qe le Priour du dit lieu ou son lieu tenant se vodre pleyndre a vous a nostre dit Eschekier des tieles maners de greuaunces empeschementz et damages et des autres greuances qe hom leur eit feit auant ces houres ou feront de cy enauant les facez sanz delay a la suite du dit Priour ou de son attorne redrescer et amender deuant vous au dit Escheker solonc la key et Lusage de meisme Lescheker Donne souz nostre priue seal a Westmouster le xiij iour Juyn lan de nostre regne tierz.

15. Writ of privy seal to exchequer concerning sale of wardships. [K. R. Mem. Roll, no. 85, no. 11 d.]

Edward par la grace de dieu et cetera au lieu tenant nostre Tresorier et as Barons de nostre Eschekier salutz Nous vous mandoms et chargeoms fermement enioygnantz qe les gardes qe soit escheues et escherront en nostre meyn ne vendetz a nulli santz la presence Leuesqe de Wircestre nostre Chaunceller et les gardes qe vous frez liuerer en paement des dettes qe nous deuoms facez liuerer a la vereie value en la foi qe vous nous deuetz Donne souz nostre priue seal a Westmouster le xxv iour de Nouembre lan de nostre regne quint.

16. Certification by exchequer to king of baronial interference with exchequer business. [K. R. Mem. Roll, no. 85, m. 52. L. T. R. Mem. Roll, no. 82, m. 45.]

Certificacio facta Domino Regi de adventu quorundam comitum ad scaccarium.

Die lune modo in crastino clausi pasche superuenerunt super proffrum vicecomitum Balliuorum et aliorum in pleno scaccario Adomarus de Valencia comes Penbrok Humfridus de Bohum comes Hereford Johannes Boteturte miles et alii in comitiua eorum minantes Waltero de Langton couuentriensi et lichfeldiensi Episcopo Thesaurario si amplius se intromitteret de officio Thesaurarie super quo Barones de scaccario certificarunt Regem in forma que subsequitur:

Sire y cest lundy lendemeyn des Oytaues de Pasqes Leuesqe de Cestre vynt par matyn a Westmonstier a vostre Escheqier de la resceite et assembla od li nous et les chamberleyns et les autres de Lescheqier et moustra commission de vostre grant seal par la quele vous lui auiez commys loffice de Tresorier et sassist oue nous et oue les autres de Lescheqier aresceuire le profre des viscontes Baillifs et autres gentz qi furent venues pur le dit proffre dit qe les auantditz deux contes et li y vyndrent depar Lerceuesqe Euesqes et autres Prelatz Contes et Barons et par toute la communalte du Roiaume et rehercea comment vous meismes nadgaires grantastes as certaines gentz poair dordener sur lestat de vostre Roiaume et les ordenances qe celes gentz auoient faites auiez acortez et fait publier et a y celes fermement garder et tenir aussibien Prelatz comme Contes et Barons comme autres feurent sermentez et demanda del dit Euesqe de Cestre sil eust fait le serment en meisme la manere et Leuesqe dit qe oyl et adonqes dit meisme celi monsire Johan depar la dite communalte qe Leuesqe feust parmis desicomme il sist la fesant loffice de Tresorier contre les dites ordenances qe volent qe Tresorier soit fait par assent du Barnage et ce en parlement et mes ne se entremeist de cel office par quoi pys ne li auenist Et meisme cel li rehercerent les ditz Contes de Pembrok et de Hereford et disient plus outre et chargerent et chargerent (*sic*) le Chaumberleyns de vostre Escheqier qe eux si come il se vousisent garder santz damage ne liurassent nuls deniers ne autre tresor del vostre a nul homme par qui ils deuenissent a les meyns lenemy du Roiaume Et meisme les contes apres ceo desoient qe leur entencion ne feust mye ne leur volunte qe voz busoignes de la place se delaiassent en nul poynt einz se preissent a vostre profist et a deliuerance du poeple par tut en due manere Et cestes choses dites ils disoient a deux hommes qi esteint illoesqes ouesqes eux deuant nous vous Tabelions tesmoignez les choses qe vous auez cy oi et les mettetz en Instrument publik et ensi sire sen departirent Et lendemeyn venismes a Lescheqier et comme nous feussoms entrez en vostre petit Escheqier por conseiller sour voz busoignes les deux Contes et ledit monsire Johan y vyndrent et rehercerent en partie ce quil auoient le iour deuaunt et quant a ceo quil auient auant dit qe vostre Tresor ne soit liuerez a tiel par il peusse deuenir en meyn del enemy du Roiaume il disoient qe ce est a entendre qe nulle liuree ne se face a sire Ingelard ne a autre qi vous meismes a la requeste des ditz ordenours faistes oustier des office quil tyndront et dentour vous Estre ce sire le dit Lundy vynt deuant nous sire Johan de Sandale nadgaires vostre Tresorier et fesoit une demostraunce qe il feust fait entendaunt a vous quil feust mort et qe vous par tant auiez fait prendre en vostre meyn ses terres et ses chateux et se dit estre prest daconter et de gre faite si rien vous deiue et pria deliueraunce de ses terres et ses chateux de quoi nous lui deismes qe rien ne poioms faire por ce qe nous ne sauiens mye la cause del seisir Sur ceste choses auantdites pleise a vostre seignurie comander voz voluntez Sire nostre seigneur vous domt bone vie et Lounge et encresse voz honurs Escrit a Wemoustre le iiij iour Daueril.

17. Letter from exchequer to king about council's advice about certain bulls.
[K. R. Mem. Roll, no. 85, m. 55 d.]

Domino Regi.

Sire nous feismes nad gaires assembler mestre Wautier de Thorp et Mestre Gilbert de Middelton et autres de vostre consail a Loundres

Justices et Clercs pur consailler sur acunes bulles qe nous auoms trouees en vostre tresorie tochauntes vostre profit des queles nous enuoioms a vous les transecritz par vostre clerk mestre William de Maldon qui est charge par vostre dit consail de vous dire plus pleinement de bouche leur auisement en cele partie et ce sire pleise a vostre seignorie entendre ce qe vostre dit clerk vous monsterra depar nous quant a lestat de la Chaumberlaynrie de Northgales qest amayntenant santz garde sour queus choses pleise a vostre seignorie comander voz voluntez sire nostre seigneur vous doynt bone vie et longe et escresse vos honurs Escrites a Westmoustier le secund iour de Juyn.

18. Notification to exchequer officials by earl of Hereford, constable of England, of his appointment of a marshal of the exchequer with request to admit. [K. R. Mem. Roll, no 86, m. 30.]

Baronibus per comitem Hereford.

A ses chiers amys et bien amez Sire Johan de Sandale lieu tenaunt Le Tresorier nostre seigneur Le Roi et as Barons de Leschekier nostre seigneur Le Roi auauntdit Hunfrai de Bohun counte de Hereford et Dessex et Conestable Dengleterre salutz et chieres amistes Porce sires qe nous auoms assigne nostre chier et bien ame clerk sire Roger de Beruers destre en nostre lieu en loffice qe apent a nous a Leschekier nostre seigneur le Roi auandit auxi come vous bien sauez vous prioms si chierement come nous pooms qe nostre dit clerk voillez resceuire et estre amys et eidauntz en les busoignes qil auera a faire pur nous et por nos autres amys en tieu manere qe nous vous soioms le plus chierement tenutz A dieu qui vous eit en sa garde.

19. Case of trespass against king before council at exchequer. [K. R. Mem. Roll, no. 86, m. 76 d. L. T. R. Mem. Roll, no. 83, Recorda S. Hill. m. 1 d.]

Cornubia. De Johanne de Bedewynde occasionato de transgressione facta domino Regi.

Presente coram Adomaro de Valencia comite Pembroch Johanne de Sandale tenente locum Thesaurarii et Baronibus et aliis de consilio modo die veneris proximo post festum sancti Hillarii in scaccario Johanne de Bedewynde clerico nuper vicecomite Cornubie Antonius de Pessaigne mercator Regis presens etcetera dicit pro Rege contra eundem Johannem de Bedewynd quod idem Johannes nuper in pleno comitatu suo tento apud Lostwythyel tempore quo fuit vicecomes Cornubie palam dicebat dominum Regem malos habuisse consiliarios et male consultum fuisse quando ipse dominus Rex concessit eidem Antonio empcionem stagminis in Comitatum Cornubie ad opus Regis inueniendo insufficienciam in ipso domino Rege et consilio suo etcetera in contemptum ipsius domini Regis etcetera.

Item dicit quod postquam dominus Rex assignauerat predictum Antonium ad emendum stagmen in Cornubia predictus Johannes factam domini Regis improbans in hac parte tractatum habuit cum mercatoribus parcium illarum et promisit quod pro suo ei dando faceret dictum Antonium et alios quibus dominus Rex concesserat empcionem stagminis etcetera amoueri ab empcione illa et eandem empcionem committi mercatoribus parcium illarum in contemptum domini Regis etcetera.

Item dicit quod postquam dominus Rex assignauit eidem Antonio empcionem stagminis etcetera dictus Johannes inerit de loco in Locum ubi stagminarii operabantur ad minam stagminis extrahendam etcetera et ipsos operarios inducebat et procurabit quod de operacionibus suis huius modi cessassent etcetera ad dampnum domini Regis et contemptum etcetera Et petit pro domino Rege quod idem Johannes super premissis responderet domino Regi.

20. Exchequer writ of summons before exchequer officials and council. [K. R. Mem. Roll, no. 86, m. 140.]

Mandatum est Johanni de Hothum firmiter iniungendo quod omnibus aliis pretermissis visis presenti in propria persona sua veniat ad scaccarium Regis apud Westmonasterium cum omnia celeritate qua poterit ad audiendum et faciendum quod tenens locum Thesaurarii et Barones de eodem scaccario et alij de consilio Regis ibidem ei iniungent ex parte Regis Et hoc nullatenus omittat Et habeat ibi tunc hoc breue Teste Johanne de Sandale tenente locum Thesaurarii etcetera x die Octobris. per consilium.

Consimili modo mandatum est	Roberto de Wylughby Radulpho de Crophull Nicholas de Kyngeston Alexandri de Caue Jacobo de Norton	Teste ut supra.

21. Letter of archbishop of Canterbury conveying instructions to lieutenant of treasurer. [K. R. Mem. Roll, no. 87, m. 41 d. L. T. R. Mem. Roll, no. 84, Brev. dir. Bar. Trin. m. 10.]

Johanni de Sandale tenenti locum Thesaurarii per Walterum Archiepiscopum Cantuariensem.

Sire il ne affiert mye a nous si comme vous bien sauez de soer illoques pur oir et trier les leys ne pur doner iuggementz de terre ne dautre chose par quoy il ne couient mye qe nul de vous se excuse en tieu manere qe vous ne osez rien faire sanz nous mes nous mandoms et comandoms as toutz enquantqe a nous affiert qe chescun face droit et ley a haste remedie de toutes greuances Et quant a la busoigne qe feust oir mame qe touche le counte de Lancastre il nous semble qil est bon qe home face droit et reson santz dalay si ensi ne soit qe le R'oy meismes ne se melle ou qil eit mande a respiter la chose Et ne nous entendez de nulle busoigne qe soit affaire Car nous ne pooms en nulle manere venir pur ceo qe nous sumes assiez busoignons de ordener nostre estat daler vers le Roy quanqe nous pooms purchacer amour et unite entre li et ces bones gentz.

22. Writ of privy seal to treasurer and barons to summon council to consider grievances of archbishop of Canterbury. [K. R. Mem. Roll, no. 88, m. 17 d.]

Baronibus pro Archiepiscopo Cantuariense.

Edward par la grace de dieu etcetera au lieu tenant du Tresorer et as Barons de nostre Escheqer salutz Por ceo qe Lerceuesqe de Canterbure nous ad fait moustrer par sa peticion qe un torceuous iugement est passe encontre lui et ses gentz a grant greuance de son estat et contre les fraunchises de sa eglise de Canterbure vous mandoms qe veues cestes lettres apelez a vous nos Justices de lun Baunk et del autre et les autres bones gentz de nostre conseil celes parties et oiez les resons et les greuances le dit Erceuesqe de ses gentz lour facez sur ce la couenable remedie solonk droit et reson nient countre esteaunt le iugement auaunt passe Donne souz nostre seal secret a Euerwyk le xxvij iour de Juyl lan de nostre regne Oytisme.

23. Writ of privy seal to council at London to respite a matter to be tried in king's presence. [K. R. Mem. Roll, no. 91, Brev. dir. m. 37. L. T. R. Mem. Roll, no. 88. Brev. dir. Hill. m. 13 d.]

Baronibus pro Stephano de Abyndon.

Edward par la grace de dieu etcetera au Tresorer Barons et autres bones gentz de nostre conseil a Londres saluz Nous vous mandoms qe les choses dont nostre cher seriant Estephne Dabyndon nostre Butiller est empeschez deuant vous a la suite de nous et des marchantz vineters Dengleterre et de Guiene tant come meismes les choses touchent a nous facez mettre en respit sanz rien faire tantqe meismes les choses puissent estre triez en nostre presence issint totes voyes qe le dit Estephne respoigne a suite dautre si nul voille de rien parler vers luy estoise a dreit solonc ley et reson et facez charger noz seriantz qil soyent eidantz au dit Estephne por le dreit de son office meintenir Et de ceste chose le facez deliuerer a plus en haste qe vous unqes porrez issint qil puisse entendre a noz purueances faire si come il en est chargez et qil ne soit delayez ne nous deserm par cele encheson Donne souz nostre priue seal a Shene le xviij iour ffeuerer lan de nostre regne unzime.

24. Writ of privy seal to barons enclosing schedule of names to whom writs under exchequer seal were to be made for the custody of certain lands. [K. R. Mem. Roll, no. 91, Brev. dir. m. 37. L. T. R. Mem. Roll, no. 88, Brev. dir. Hill. m. 13 d.]

Baronibus per Regem.

Edward par la grace de dieu etcetera Nous vous enueoms cy dedeinz enclos un escrouet contenant les nouns daucunes gentz de nostre houstel qe nous auoms assignetz par lettres de nostre priue seal a faire seisyr et prendre en nostre meyn aucuns casteux manoirs terres et tenementz od les appurtenances les queux Margarete iadys Royne Dengleterre nostre treschere mere tint de nostre heritage le iour qele moreust es countez contenuz en le dit escrouet et a meismes les chasteux manoirs terres et tenementz sauement garder issint qil nous respoignent des issues a nostre dit Escheqier pur les despens de nostre houstel tantqe nous en eyoms autrement ordenez et vous mandoms qe regardez meisme lestrouet solonc la tenour dicel facez faire commissions souz le seal de meisme nostre Eschekier as ditz gentz iointement et seueraument a faire seisir a prendre en nostre meyn les ditz chasteux manoirs terres et tenementz od les appurtenances et a les faire sauuement garder en la fourme auantdite Et facez faire aussint semblables commissions as autres au remenant des chasteux terres et tenemenz qe nostre dite mere tint de nostre heritage le iour qele moreust solonc ceo qe vous verrez qe plus soit a nostre profist Donne souz nostre priue seal a Wyndesore le xx iour de ffeuerer lan de nostre regne unzisme Tenor cedule talis est: monsire Johan de Hausted est assigne defaire seisir en la meyn le Roi touz les chasteux terrez tenementz od les appurtenancez en Countez de Wiltesire....

25. Writ of privy seal to treasurer and barons to remove unqualified sheriff and appoint a sufficient person. [K. R. Mem. Roll, no. 91, Brev. dir. m. 60 d. L. T. R. Mem. Roll, no. 88, Brev. dir. Trin. m. 4 d.]

Baronibus pro Rege.

Edward par la grace de dieu Roi Dengleterre Seigneur Dirlaund et Ducs Daquitayne au Tresorer et as Barons de nostre Escheqier salutz Pur ceo qe nous auoms entenduz qe celuy qest viscounte de Kent nad forsqe cink marchees de terre en dit countez par quai il nest suffissaunt destre nostre viscounte illoqes solonc ceo qe ad este ordine auaunt ces houres par nous e par nostre counseil vous mandoms qe si ensi soit adonqe luy facez remuer hors du dit office e y mettre un autre suffissaunt et couenable pur nous et pur nostre people Donez soutz nostre priue seal a Wodestok le xxvj iour de Juyn lan de nostre Roialme unzisme.

26. Writ of privy seal to treasurer containing instructions about payments out of exchequer. [K. R. Mem. Roll, no. 92, Brev. dir. Mich. m. 12. L. T. R. Mem. Roll, no. 89, m. 71 d.]

Thesaurario per Regem.

Edward par la grace de dieu et cetera al honurable piere en dieu Johan par la meisme grace Euesqe de Wyncestre nostre Tresorer salutz Por ce qil nous busoigne auer graunt foeson de deniers aussibien pur les despens de nostre houstel come pur aucunes grosses et chargeauntes busoignes qe nous auoms a faire vous mandoms qe pur maundement qe vous veigne de nous desore ne facetz assignement a nulli de quele condicion qil soit sil ne face expresse mencion de cesty nostre maundement einz touz les deniers qe vous porrez faire leuer soient liuerez pur les despens de nostre dit houstel et pur noz autres busoignes issint qe nous ne soioms escriez par pays pur defaute de paiement ne noz dites busoignes arreries ne destourbees tantqe nostre estat soit mielz releuez Et ce ne lessez Donne souz nostre priue seal a Euerwyk le xxviij iour de Nouembre lan de nostre regne douzisme.

27. Writ of privy seal to the treasurer to retain certain two as barons. [K. R. Mem. Roll, no. 92, Brev. dir. m. 18 d. L. T. R. Mem. Roll, no. 89, m. 81.]

Thesaurario per Regem.

Edward par la grace de dieu et cetera al honurable piere en dieu Johan par la meisme grace Euesqe de Wyncestre nostre Tresorier saluz Il vous doit souenir coment a Euerwik a nostre darrein parlement fust nadgairs assentuz qe les Barouns de nostre Eschekier deuient estre suffissaunz et nient plus qe ne couenent pur la place gouerner par quoi vous mandoms qe si vous veez qe la place soit trop chargee adonqes auisez vous des queux des Barons de nostre dit Eschekier hom se purra mielz soeffrir et facez ce qest acordez issint totez foitz qe noz chers clercs Robert de Wodehous et Johan de Okham queux nous tenoms suffissaunz et necessaires pur cele place y demoergent en pees en lour estatz Donne soutz nostre priue seal a Beuerle le secound iour de Janeuoir lan de nostre regne xij^{me}.

28. Instructions to exchequer officials about disbursements, conveyed by king's chamberlain and steward. [K. R. Mem. Roll, no. 92, Brev. dir. m. 25 d. L. T. R. Mem. Roll, no. 89, m. 88.]

Episcopo Wintoniensi Thesaurario per Regem.

Edward par la grace de dieu etcetera al honeurable piere en dieu Johan par meisme la grace Euesqe de Wincestre nostre Tresorer saluz come piece ad vous mandissiens par lettres de nostre graunt seal qe vous ne feissez paiement ne assignement a nuly si ce ne fust pur les despenses de nostre houstiel ou qe vous en eussez especial mandement de nous fesaunt expresse mencion du dit mandement et eoms chargez nos chers et foiaux monsire Hughe le Despenser le puisnez nostre Chaumberlein et monsire Bertelmeu de Baddlesmere seneschal de nostre houstiel vous dire plus pleinement nostre volente des dites choses et dautres qe nous touchent dount nous leur auoms enioignt vous mandoms qe les ditz monsire Hugh et monsire Bertilmeu ou lun de eux creez fiablement de ce qe il vous endirront ou dirra de par nous Donne souz nostre priue seal a Euerwik le v iour de ffeuerer lan de nostre regne douzisme.

Credencia ipsorum Hugonis et Bartholomei dicta prefato Thesaurario in presencia Walteri de Norwico Baronis de Scaccario Heruici de Staunton Cancellarii de eodem scaccario magistri Jacobi de Ispannia et magistri Willelmi de Maldon Camerariorum etcetera talis est—Le Rey voet qe toutz les assignementz faitz a les creaunceours le Rei des dettes le Rey auant qe les brefs vindrent au Tresorer et as Chaumberleyns a suspendre tieux assignementz e paiementz estoisent et soient les allowaunces de tieux assignementz faites al Escheqier en due manere sicome auaunt ad este fait Item le Rey voet qe la ou le Tresorer qi ore est ad emprompertez deniers ou apromtpera al oeps le Rey pur les busoignes le Rey qe de ceux deniers soit paiement ou couenable assignement fait al Excheqier a les creaunceours le Rey sicome auant ad este usez en tieu cas Item le Rey voet qe toutz les ministres del Excheqier soient entendauntz et responauntz au dit Tresorer en totes choses qe touchent son office sicome auaunt ount este as autres Tresorers en temps passez.

29. Writ of privy seal to exchequer officials containing instructions about exchequer business. [K. R. Mem. Roll, no. 93, m. 9 d. L. T. R. Mem. Roll, no. 90, Brev. dir. Mich. m. 5 d.]

Baronibus pro Rege.

Edward par la grace de dieu Roi Dengleterre Seigneur Dirlaunde et Ducs Dacquitaigne au Tresorier Barouns et chaumberleins de nostre

Eschekier salutz Nous vous mandoms et chargeoms fermement enioignauntz sur la foy qe vous nous deuetz et le serment qe vous nous auetz fait qe vous facetz duement guier et garder lestat de nostre dit Escheqier et totes les choses qe leuiz sount a deliuerer ou pur temps auenir serront pur nous ou autre facetz esploiter solom les leys et les usages de meisme la place et qe totes maneres des acountes qe leuiz sont a rendre aussibien de Garderobe Gascoigne Irlaunde come de aillours soient hastetz sauntz faire desport a nuly de quel estat qil soit sauntz especial maundement de nous Et qe vous Tresorier et Barons facetz clercs et toutz autres qe quel estat qe eux soient qui en la place seruent en seruir deuient bien et peniblement faire ceo qe a chescun de eux appent et si ascun y soit qe ne le face soit de ceo par vous repris et chastiez en due manere ou de tout ostez si le fait le demaunde Et voloms et vous chargeoms qe a entre vous ne facetz desore a terminer nule dette qe soit de ferme ne de fin pur chose achatee de nous ne darrerage dacounte ne autre dette clere qe bonement peusee estre leuee del dettour ou ses meinpernours ou plegges si les eyt sauntz tresgraunt greuance de eux si a ceo faire ne eietz especial maundement de nous mes totes les dettes qe clerement sont dues a nous soient leuetz par totes les maneres qe hom les deuera couenablement leuer sauntz respit de ceo graunter a nuly si bone cause ne soit a le respiter ou qe nous de nostre grace le commandoms affaire Et bien vous auisetz a entre vous qe tieux respitz soient si remembrez a nostre dit Escheqier qe nous les peussoms sauer quant nous voudroms A ceo commandoms et chargeoms en la fourme susdite vous auauntditz Tresorier et Chaumberleins qe par entre vous facetz duement vostre office a la receite et ne soufferetz la ne en nostre Tresorie nul entrer en nul manere qe par reson entrer ne y deuie ne nul a veer ne manier liueres roules ne autres remembrances qe leuiz sont forsqe noz iuretz Et facetz totes les choses en tresourie queles qelles soient qe charge portent veer et mettre en tiel array come appent et ce en manere qe hom peusee sauer ces qelles sont et les auer et prestement trouer quele houre qe nous les voudroms auer pur nous ou pur autre qe par voucher ou en autre manere de ceo deyue estre eide Et qe nul paiement ne assignement desore se face a nostre dit Eschekier en nule manere a nuly sauntz especial mandement de nous de nostre grant seal ou de priue qe mencion face de celui a qi paiement ou assignement faire se deuera et de combien mes totes foitz si visconte Baillif ou autre eit paietz au Gardein de nostre Garderobe a nostre oeps ceo qil deust auer paietz a nostre dit Eschekier et de ceo eit lettres ouertes du Gardein a vous qe le tesmoigne ou qe visconte Baillif ou autre qest tenutz a respondre a nostre Escheqier de ferme ou en autre manere eit fait mises en coustages en purueance de vitailles ou de autre chose a nostre oeps par comandement de nous des issues de sa baillie et de ceo acounte en Garderobe et dilleqes eit bille tesmoignaunce ce qe duz li soit par tiele encheson facetz tieles lettres et billes duement allouer quele houre qeles soient a nostre dit Escheqier moustrez et allouance dicelles demaunde et qe ceo face sauntz nuli delaier de sa allouance auer en tieu cas mes par autre manere ne soit desore assignement ne paiement fait a nostre Escheqier si de ceo ne eietz mandement de nous en la manere susdite Et sachetz certeinement qe nous auoms ia ordinetz deuuoier chescun an certeines gentz de nostre conseil priue queux nous plerra a ce assigner a nostre dit Escheqier deux foitz en lan a meyns ou plus solonc ce qe nous verroms qe face a faire a veer et sauer la receite et lissue de meisme nostre Eschekier en presence de vous Tresorier et Chaumberleins et des Barons queux il leur semble qi a ce facent a apeler et meismes ceux facent remembrer sommairement lestat tiel come troue serra et le nous reportent secrement et aussi qil veent coment cest nostre maundement en toutz pointz auera este tenutz et garde et qils nous reportent ceo qe eux en aueront trouez affaire ent ceo qe nous verroms qe soit a faire par reson Cest nostre maundement facetz enrouller a nostre grant Eschekier et Leschekier de la recette en manere qe souent par entre vous soit veu et entenduz Et ceo pur rien en lessetz Donne soutz nostre priue seal a Euerwik le darrein iour Doctobre Lan de nostre regne treszisme.

30. **Writ of privy seal to chief baron to consider with council transcripts of letters from justice of Ireland.** [K. R. Mem. Roll, no. 93, m. 31. L. T. R. Mem. Roll, no. 90, Brev. dir. Pasch. m. 13.]

Baronibus pro Rege.

Edward par la grace de dieu Roi Dengleterre Seigneur Dirlaunde et Ducs Daquitaine a nostre cher et foial monsire Wautier de Norwyz Chief Baroun de nostre Escheqier salutz Nous vous enuoiems cy dedenz enclos le transescrit dunes lettres qe nous vindrent de nostre cher cousyn et foial monsire Roger de Mortimer nostre Justice Dirlaunde tuchantes une enqueste prise et retourne en nostre Court sur aucunes choses qe les gentz de nostre ville de Dyuelyn suent deuers nous et vous mandoms qe en plener auisement sur ce qest contenuz en le dit transescrit quele houre qe nostre cher cousin et foial monsire Aymer de Valence conte de Pembrok nostre Gardein Dengleterre et nostre Chanceler et vous et nos autres bones gentz de nostre conseil soiez ensemble ordinez sur ce ce qe vous verrez qe mielz enface a faire Donne souz nostre priue seal a Roucestre le primer iour de marz Lan de nostre regne treszime.

31. **Writ of privy seal to barons to make no payments of the tenth without king's verbal order.** [K. R. Mem. Roll, no. 93, m. 53 d. L. T. R. Mem. Roll, no. 90, Brev. dir. Trin. m. 13.]

Baronibus pro Rege.

Edward par la grace de dieu etcetera Nous vous mandoms qe des deniers qe vous vendront ore de la disme ne facez paiement ne assignement a nuly de quele condicion qil soit sanz ceoqe nous meismes vous comandoms de bouche Et ce en nule manere ne lessez Donne souz nostre priue seal a Caterigge le ix iour Daugst lan de nostre regne xiiij^me^.

32. Schedule of payments not to be allowed without king's special order. [L. T. R. Mem. Roll, no. 90, Schedule Rec. Hill. m. 4 d.]

Les parceles southescrites ne poent estre allowez a monsire Antoygne de Pessaigne por nous sauntz especial mandement du Roy

. . . .

Item pur deners paiez a monsire Roger Damori
m[l]m[l]D li. de tournoys

Item a monsire Hugh Daudele m[l]m[l] tournoys

Item pur deners paiez a monsire Luk de fflisk Cardinal du mandement Leuesque Dely de monsire le Counte de Pembrok et de monsire Berthelmeu de Badlesmere
iiij^{c} li. sterling

. . . .

Item pur le damage de quatre mille liures enpromtee du Noel iuqes a la saint Johan lan disme du mandement monsire Wautier de Norwitz Leuesqe Dely le Counte de Pembrok monsire Berthelmeu de Badlesmere
CCCiiij^{xx} li. sterling.

. . . .

33. Writ of privy seal to treasurer and barons about certain ordinances relating to accounts. [K. R. Mem. Roll, no. 94, m. 34. L. T. R. Mem. Roll, no. 91, Brev. dir. Hill. m. 4 d.]

Baronibus pro Rege.

Edward par la grace de dieu etcetera Au Tresorer et as Barons de nostre Eschequier salutz Nous vous reneuoms ci dedeinz enclos la remembrance qe vous nous enuoiastes contenant aucunes ordenances touchantes les acountes auxi bien du temps nostre cher piere qi dieux assoille come de nostre et vous fesoms sauoir qe les dites ordenances ne feurent unqes faites de nostre assent ne de nostre commandement par quoi vous mandoms qe quantqe vous trouetz paiez par vertu des dites ordenances facetz charger de prest sur ceux qe lount resceu issint qil nous en soient tenuz a respoundre come de dette et desore mes ne paiez rien ne alouez pur les ordenances auantdites saunz especial maundement de nous Donne soutz nostre priue seal a ffulham le iij iour de ffeuerer Lan de nostre regne xiiij[me]. Et memorandum quod memorandum de quo fit mencio in breuia consuitur eidem breui et remanet in custodia marescalli.

34. Writ of privy seal to exchequer officials to appoint a cursitor baron. [K. R. Mem. Roll, no. 95, m. 16 d. L. T. R. Mem. Roll, no. 92, m. 47 d.]

Baronibus pro Rege.

Edward par la grace de dieu etcetera A nostre cher et foial Wautier de Norwiz gardein del office de nostre Tresorier et as Barons de nostre Eschekier saluz Por ceo qe nous voloms qe un dentre vous ditz Barons aille ouesqe par pays pur choses touchantes la dite place si come nous deismes nadgueres de bouche a vous auant dit Wautier vous mandoms qe veues cestes lettres saunz delai ordenez un dentre vous bon et conissaunt des dites choses et lui chargez depar nous qil viegne a nous a plus en haste qe unques purra apparaillez et arraiez de nous suire quele part qe nous ailloms pur les choses auantdites Et ceo en nulle manere ne lessez Donne souz nostre priue seal a Marlawe le x iour de Decembre lan de nostre regne xve.

35. **Writ of secret seal to exchequer officials about king's progress in Welsh march.** [K. R. Mem. Roll, no. 95, m. 17 d. L. T. R. Mem. Roll, no. 92, m. 48 d]

Baronibus pro Rege.

Edward par la grace de dieu et cetera Au Gardein del office de nostre Tresorèr et as Barons de nostre Eschekier saluz Nous vous fesoms a sauoir qe cheuauchauntz par pais pur oustier et redrescer les oppressions faites a nostre poeple sumes venuz a Salopbure ou les Mortumers Luncle et le Neueu y ce Vendredi le xxij iour de Janeuer sont venuz a nous humblement conisauntz et regeauntz deuant les Countes et Barouns et noz autres bones gentz lour mal port deuers nous et se sount mis a nostre volunte haut et bas et nous les auoms a ceo resceu et bioms aler outre vers les parties de Lodelawe pur droit faire et a conforter nostre poeple par quoi vous mandoms et chargeoms qe vous soiez tendres de nos droitures et de noz leys garder et meintenir car noz bosoignes vount bien par decea et esperoms qe les irront par amendement de iour en autre a honur de nous et de touz nos amis od leuere de dieu Donne souz nostre secre seal a Salopbure le xxij iour de Janeuer lan de nostre regne xv[me].

36. **Writ of privy seal to exchequer officials to victual castles.** [K. R. Mem. Roll, no. 95, m. 18. L. T. R. Mem. Roll, no. 92, m. 49.]

Baronibus pro Rege.

Edward par la grace de dieu etcetera a nostre cher et foial Wautier de Norwyz Gardeyn de loffice de nostre Tresorer et as Barons et Chaumberleins de nostre Escheqer saluz Pur ceo qe nous sumes en alaunt sur lesploit de noz busoignes et diuerses nous les volent vous maundoms qe saunz delai facez ordener en tiel manere qe noz chasteux deriere nous soient si suffisaument vitaillez et garniz qe mal ne peril ne y peusse auenir Et ce en nulle manere ne lessez Donne souz nostre priue seal a Cirencestre le xxj iour de Decembre Lan de nostre regne xv[me]. Et memorandum quod execucio huius mandati sit sicut plenius continetur alibi in hiis memorandis inter breuia retornabilia de termino sancti Michaelis.

37. **Writ of secret seal to younger Despenser, bishop of Exeter, treasurer, and Robert de Baldock, chancellor, about a charter of Henry de Lancaster.** [K. R. Mem. Roll, no. 97, Brev. dir. Pasch. m. 2.]

Baronibus pro Henrico de lancastre.

Edward par la grace de dieu et cetera A noz chers et foial Hugh le Despenser nostre neueu leuesqe Dexcestre nostre tresorier et Mestre Robert de Baldok nostre Chauncellier saluz Nous auoms biens entenduz voz lettres que vous nous auez enuoiez endroit dune chartre que vous auez trouez taunsoulement fesaunt mencion des terres que nous auoms grantez a nostre cher cosyn Henri de lancastre et de nulles autres et voloms bien que vous facez liuerer a nostre dit cosyn mesme cele chartre si vous veez que nous le puissoms faire saunz prejudice de nous et destourbaunce de noz actions Donne souz nostre secre seal a ffulmere le tierce iour Daueril lan de nostre regne xvij^me^.

38. Writ of privy seal to treasurer and barons ordering the separation of the exchequer. [K. R. Mem. Roll, no. 97, Brev. dir. Trin. m. 4.]

Baronibus per Regem de separacione scaccarii.

Edward par la grace de dieu et cetera As Tresorier et Barons de nostre Escheqier saluz Vous deuez bien entendre par reson coment nous auoms meinte foitz chargez et fait charger qe la place de nostre Escheqer feust seueree en la fourme qe vous estoit auant liuere par escrit et qe les ministres assignez en cele place issint seuerez eussent este en lour places en fesant lour office lendemain de la Trinite prochein passe pur plus prestement deliuerer nostre poeple a lour esement et a nostre profit la quele chose nest pas uncore fait dont nous nous enmerueilloms et sumes mal paiez Par quoi vous mandoms et chargeoms en la foi et la ligeaunce qe vous nous deuez et sicome entre vous touz voillez eschure nostre indignacion qe les places soient seuereez et les ministres en lour places soient solonc la fourme auant ordene y ce lundy prochein apres les utaues de la Trinite sanz plus delai tout soit il qe les places entre cy et la ne puissent estre suffisctument apparailles par la laschesce de vous Tresorier et des onerours qe sont desouz vous Et qe vous sachez pleinement nostre entencion en ceste chose vous fesoms sauer qe nostre volente est qe vous Wautier de Norwyz demoergez chief Baron en la place qe vous ore tenez et qe mestre Robert de Ailleston et Edmon de Passele demoergent Barons pres de vous en mesme la place et qe vous Roger Beler soiez chief Baron en la nouelle place et qe sire Humfrei de Valeden et sire William de Euerdon et sire William de ffoubourne demoergent Barons pres de vous en meisme la place et par comun consail dentre vous par la foi qe vous nous deuez facez metter couenable persone au grant roulle en lieu le dit sire William de Euerdon et si voloms qe solonc ce qe les Contez de nostre roialme sont partiz par remembraunces qest deuers vous les gentz des Contez deuers le North et les ministres et les busoignes qe sont assignez vers celes parties soient esploitez en cele place qe vous Wautier de Norwyz et vous compaignons tendrez et ceux deuers le Suth en la place qe vous Roger et voz compaignons tendrez et ce a nostre volente et iesqes atant qil nous pleise autrement ordener Et vous Tresorier et Chaunceler le Lescheqier purueez et assignez clercs souz vous qe pussent seruir en voz offices en lune place et lautre issint qil y soient ordenez engrossers et remembrancers solonc ce qe vous verrez qe mielx soit a nostre profit Par qoi vous chargeoms derichief qe cestes choses soient faites et mis en execucion au iour auant nomez sanz plus delaier et qentre vous ne le mettez pas en delay Car nous ne le soeffroms point Et voloms qentre vous facez le serment qe nous auoms baille a nostre Tresorier pur fair a nous sicome il vous chargera en nostre noun Et ce en nulle manere ne lessez Et nous auoms fait faire commissions as ditz Humfrey et William de Euerdon qe ne ont mye uncore en commissions doffice de Baron de nostre dit Escheqer Donne souz nostre priue seal a nostre Tour de Londres le xvj iour de Juyn lan de nostre regne xvij[me].

39. Letters patent under the privy seal acknowledging receipt of a sum of money in the chamber. [Exchequer Miscellanea, 3/2.]

Edward par la grace de dieu Roi Dengleterre Seigneur Dirlaunde et Ducs Daquitaine A touz ceux qi cestes lettres verront saluz Sachez nous auoms resceu en nostre chaumbre le iour de la date de cestes par les meyns nostre cher clerc William de langeley de nostre bien amez Johan de Porter gardein de nostre manoir de Neweport en essex Cent liures des issues de sa dite baillie des queux Cent liures nous voloms qil eit due allouance sur son acounte En tesmoignance de queu chose nous auoms fait faire cestes noz lettres patentes Donne souz nostre priue seal a Westmouster le xj iour de ffeuerer lan de nostre regne xviij[me].

40. Petition of a merchant to earl of Lancaster. [Exch. Misc. 3/2.]

A treshonorable seyngeur Counte de Lancestre prie sun marchaunt si luy plest Hugh de Wyrcestre qe come nostre seigneur le Roi plusors foiz eit prie par ses lettres as Aldermans et baillifs de la ville de Lubyk qe eux...ent dreiture au dite Huwe ou ses attornez dune dette de quatreunz liuers en la quele Henri de Hatthorp et Johan Statere marchans de la ville de Lubyk luy sunt tenuz par lour escrit pur morz de luy achatez a Londres et le dit Aldermans et baillifs ren ne unt fait a les priers nostre seigneur le Roy par la ou les dites marchanz furent trouez en lour poer quant les lettres nostre seigneur le Roi furent liueres a eux mes faille de droit outrement qe pleise a vostre seignorie ceo ordener ascun remedie ou dire au Chaunceler qi le dit Hugh peusse auoit tel remedie come ad este use en semblable cas auant ces hures.

41. Letter from earl of Pembroke to his clerk ordering allowance in an account. [Exch. Misc. 4/1.]

Aymar de Valence Counte de Pembrok Seigneur de Weisak e de Montignak a nostre chier clerc sire Henri de Stachesdene salutz Nous vous mandoms qe vous facez alouer a nostre bien ame Creancer Nicholas Amyet Trente et deux Liures Deux soutz e vyt deners de Paris en la fferme del Estank Daberual Les queux deners il ad fait deliurer por nostre hostiel par la mein sire Arantier Alisaundre nostre Chapeleyn E ceo ne lessez Escripte a Pontoyse le Primer Jour de Juyl Lan del Incarnacion mil Trois Centz et Tresze.

(Endorsed)

littera pro Nichol Miete xxxij li. ij s. viij d. lib. domino Waltero Capellano domini.

42. Indenture to restrain the king. [Exch. Misc. 4/6.]

Fait a remembrer qe le Jour de la date de ceste Endenture monsire Roger Damary Cheualer promyst en boune foy come loyau Cheualer aus nobles homes monsire Aymar de Valence Conte de Pembrok et a monsire Berthelmeu de Badlesmere ce qui est contenuz Cest assauoir quil mettra tote sa diligence et son loyau poair deuers nostre segneur le Roy parquoi il se laisse mener et gouuerner par les conseaus des ditz Conte et monsire Berthelmeu et qe il croie les conseaus de eus deus sur totes autres gentz terrienes tant come bien et loiaument le consailleront a honor et profyt de lui de sa corone et de son Roiaume et par meismes les conseaus se gouuernera le dit monsire Roger et ne les trespassera en nul poynt Et ne procurera par lui ne par autre ne sauera nassentera qe nostre segneur le Roy doygne a home viuant sanz lassent des ditz Conte et monsire Berthelmeu terre ne auoir outre vynt liuerees de terre on la value auoir ne qe nostre dit segneur le Roy face autre chose de grant chearge qui soit preiudiciele a lui na la corone en nul caas Et se aensuits estoit qe nostre segneur le **Roy** voudra terre ou auoir doner en absence des diz Conte et monsire Berthelmeu a quiquonqe ce fust autre la value dessusdite ou autre besoigne de grant chearge faire de lui meismes qui en preiudice fust de lui de sa corone ou de son Roiaume le dit monsire Roger mettra tout son loyau poair a ce destourber tout sus Et se destourber nel pourra en nulle manere il le fera sauoir aus ditz Conte et monsire Berthelmeu deuant qe effect seu preigne si qe adont eus toutz trois sefforcent dun accord a ostier le segneur de cele volentie Et si le dit monsire Roger sentist qe nul deist ou feist chose deuers nostre segneur le Roy en preiudice deshonor ou damage des ditz Conte et monsire Berthelmeu dont leur estat puist estre de riens empirez deuers nostre segneur le Roy il leur en guarnira sanz nul delay et le destourbera a tout son loyau poair Et a cestes couuenances bien et loiaument tenir et accomplir sicome dessus est dyt et de non faire ne venir iamais alencontre le dit monsire Roger a iure sur le corps dieu et estre ceo se ad oblige en dys mille liures desterlyns a payer aus ditz Conte et monsire Berthelmeu a leur requeste quiele hore a quant il deist feist ou venist en nul poynt contre les couuenances dessus dites Et les ditz Conte et monsire Berthelmeu ont parmys en bonne foy come loyaus Cheualers qe il defendrent guaranteront et meintendront le dit monsire Roger contre totes gentz de quele condicion qui il soient sauue la ligeance quil douient a nostre segneur le Roy tant come le dit monsire Roger tendra et obseruera pleynement les couuenances dessus dites Et a ceo ont oblige eus leur heirs leur Executours et touz lur biens moebles et nonmoebles presentz et auenir a la volentie le dit monsire Roger En tesmoigne des quiex choses lune part de ceste Endenture est sealee des seaus les ditz conte et monsire Berthelmeu et lautre du seal le dit monsire Roger entrechainablement Donne a Londres le vintisme quart Jour de Nouembre Lan de regne nostre segneur le Roy Edward unzisme.

43. **Letter from Edward, prince of Wales, to Walter Reynolds about money for the expenses of his household.** [Exch. Misc. 5/2, m. 4.]

Domino Waltero Reginaldi.

A sire Wauter Reignaud etcetera Pur ceo qe nostre seigneur le

Roy est si corouce deuer nous par reson del Euesqe de Cestre qil ad defendu qe nous ne veignoms en son hostel ne nul de nostre meisnee e ad aussint defendu a ses gentz de sun hostel e del escheker quil ne nous doignent ne prestent riens pur la sustenance de nostre hostel vous mandoms qe vous mettez consail de nous enuoier deners a grant haste pur la sustenaunce de nostre hostel e ne mustrez rien des busoignes qe nous touchent al Euesqe de Cestre ne a nul de ceux del Escheker en nule manere E mandez nous aussint ore e autres choses qe apendent a nostre garderobe Donne souz etcetera.

44. Judgment upon the Mortimers. [Exch. Misc. 24/12.]

Pronunciacio et reddicio Judicij super Rogerum de Mortuo Mari le uncle et Rogerum de Mortuo Mari le Neueu in prisona domini Regis in Turre Londonii detentos facte par Walterum de Norwico Willelmum de Herle Walterum de ffriskeney Johannem de Stonore et Hamonem de Chiggewell Justiciarios domini Regis ad hoc assignatos et ex hac de causa de mandato ipsius domini Regis congregatos apud Westmonasterium die lune in Crastino sancte Petri Aduincula anno regni dicti domini Regis Edwardi fili domini Regis Edwardi sexto decimo.

. . . .

Pur ceo qe vous Rogier le Mortimer Luncle homme lige nostre seigneur le Roi et sa Justice de Guales estoiez et Jurree du counsail nostre seigneur le Roi countre vostre homage foi et ligeaunce et encontre nostre seigneur le Roi vostre seigneur lige leuastes de guerre oduesqes Humfrei de Bohun iadis Counte de Hereford Rogier Damari Bertelmeu de Badlesmere Johan Giffard de Brimmesfeld et Henri Tyes Tretres et enemys le Roi et du Roialme et oduesqes eux treterousement preistes la ville et le chastel nostre seigneur le Roi de Gloucestre et les biens le Roi el dit chastel trouez felonessement desrobbastes et de illuqes come Treitre et enemy oue vostre Banere desplie come de guerre cheuauchastes tantqe a la ville nostre seigneur le Roi de Briggenorth et la dite ville treiterousement come Treitre le Roi assaillistes et enemiablement preistes sur les gentz le Roi et partie de ses gentz illuqes tuastes et partie nasuerastes et la ville treterousement alumastes et graunt partie ardistes a banere desplie come de guerre et apres et deuant en la Roialme nostre seigneur le Roi come de guerre oue vostre banere desplie en destruyant et desrobbant le poeple nostre seigneur le Roi et du Roialme cheuauchastes armez Les queux tresons felonies roberies homicides arsons mauueistez et cheuaucheez as Baneres despliez' sount notoires et conuz el Roialme et nostre seigneur le Roi ceo recorde sur vous par quoi agard ceste Court qe pur les Tresons soiez treynez et pur les arsons roberies homicides et felonies soiez penduz.

45. Bill to the treasurer and barons of exchequer about imprisonment in Newgate and execution thereon. [K. R. Exch. Bills, 1/5, 12 Edward II.]

Au Tresorer et as Barons del Escheqere nostre Seigneur le Roy ceo pleynt Auneys de Cicestre de Rauff Balaunter William Pikeman iadis seriaunt de Londres qe la diste Auneys priste et attacha le Samadi en le veyle de la Trinite Lan du regne le Roy Edward fitz le Roy Edward disime en le Real Chymyn en la Roperye prede la Eglise de Touxs Seynt le graunt et le mena a la prison de Neugate et illeouqes la emprisona del Samady auandit tanqe le Jeoudi procheyn suaunt en mesme lan a gref damages la dite Auneys de quaraunte Liueres de quei ele prie remedie.

(Endorsed)

aduocatur capcionem per preceptum Willelmi de Monte acuto senescalli et per billam marescalli.

presens coronator die martis post purificationem.

Preceptum est vicecomiti quod capiat Agnetus de Cycestre si inuenta fuerit in balliua nostra Et eam saluo custodiret Et quod habet corpus eius coram senescallo et marescallo domini Regis apud Westmonasterium hac instanti die Sabbati proximo post Penticostem ubicunque etcetera ad respondendum Ricardo de Dorkyng in placito transgressionis.

(Endorsed)

Irrotulatur.

Non presens.

46. Indenture of Maurice de Berkeley for defence of Berwick. [K. R. Exch. Acct, 68/2, no. 10.]

ffait a remembrer qe le xviij iour Daueril Lan du regne nostre seigneur le Roi Edward filz le Roi Edward viij^me^ a Westmoustre deuaunt nostre dit seigneur le Roy en presence Lerceuesqe de Canterbire les Countes de Richemond de Pembroke et de Hereford Chauncellier et Tresorier et autres du conseil monsire Moriz de Berkele emprist la garde de la ville de Berewik sur Twede et come gardein de meisme la ville a demorer y de la feste de Pentecost prochein auenir par tout lan prochein des adonqes suaunt pur mille Liures en deniers et quatre cheuaux darmes et deux hauberghs queux il auera du doun le Roy et auera en sa compaignie vint hommes darmes bien montez et apparaillez a sa troueure de meyne en touz pointz dount il serra luy quynt de Cheualier denz meisme le noumbre et le Roi luy soit tenuz en restor de cheuaux si nul auera parduz en son seruise illoeqes duraunt meisme le temps entre les dites milles Liures et de les m^l^ li. auantdites receuera le dit monsire Moriz vendroit a Londres auaunt son aler celes parties CC li. et C marcs en cheuaux ou en autres choses qe le Roi luy fera engottre des marchaundz en Londres estre les quatre cheuaux qe le Roi luy dona et auera mandement as Taxours et Coillours du vintisme en Contez de Gloucestre destre paiez par eux de CCCL marcs des primers deniers qil leueront du dit vintisme et de V^c^li. du remenaunt serra le dit monsire moriz paiez de CCL marcs a la touz seintz prochein auenir et de CCL marcs a la Purification nostre dame prochein suaunt et a la quinzeme de Pasqe prochein swaunt CCL marcs Et pur ce qe le dit monsire Moriz de bone volunte et franchement od emprys cele garde en le meschief et peril qe ore de mostrent en la garde auantdite le Roi eauntz a ce regard de sa curteisie luy ad grantez outre les dites M[l] li. de luy regarder de vj[c]li. des procheignes gardes et mariages qe cherront en sa mein apres la seint Michel prochein auenir Et est a entendre qe nostre seigneur le Roy trouera le remenant des gentz darmes et a pe la garnisture de meisme la ville cest assauer entour CCC homes darmes et des gentz a pee tantqe de nombre come il couyent resnablement pur meisme la garde as gages nostre seigneur le Roy susdit Et nostre seigneur le Roy doit enueer vitailles a la dite ville pur la sustenance des gentz qi il demorrent en garnesture par durerses foiz sicome il verra qe face affaire pur la sauue garde de meisme la ville En tesmoignance de queu chose est faite ceste endenture dount lune partie sealee du priue seal nostre dit seigneur le Roy demoert deuers le dit monsire Moriz et lautre partie du seal le dit monsire Moriz demoert en la garderobe nostre seigneur le Roy auantdit.

47. Indenture of John Darcy the nephew, as sheriff of Lancaster. [K. R Exch. Acct, 68/2, no. 17.]

ffait a remembrer qe le xiij[e] iour de ffeuerer Lan du regne nostre seigneur le Roi Edward xvj[me] monsire Johan Darcy le Neueu receust loffice du visconte du Countez de Lancestre et emprist a demorer sur la sauue garde du dit Countez et a greuer les enemys nostre dit seigneur le Roi tant come il purra od quaraunte hommes darmes dont soi sysme de cheualer et vint hobelours as gages le Roi acoustumez tant come ensi plerra au dit nostre seigneur le Roi sur quels il receust deuant meyn lxxviij li. viij s. En tesmoignance de queu chose le priue seal nostre dit seigneur le Roi et le seal le dit monsire Johan as partiez de ceste endenture soit mys entrechaungeablement Donne a Euerwik le iour et lan dessus escriptz.

48. Writ of privy seal to mayor and bailiffs of Lincoln to pay £20 from their farm to clerk of great wardrobe. [K. R. Exch Acct, 377/10.]

Edward par la grace de dieu Roi Dengleterre Seigneur Dirlaunde et Ducs Daquitaine au Meire et as Baillifs de Nicole saluz Come nostre bien amez Rauf Destokes clerc de nostre grant garderobe soit chargez a faire purueance de diuerses choses qe appendent a son office et de les faire venir hastiuement en nostre garderobe pur les despens de nostre houst vous mandoms qe au dit Rauf ou a son attornez porteur de cestes facez hastiuement liuerer vint liures sur la ferme de la dite ville du terme de la seint Michel prochein auenir por la dite purueance faire Et ce en nulle manere ne lessez issint qe nous ne soioms desseruz par vostre defaute Et receuiez de celi a qi vous les auerez liuerez ses lettres patentes tesmoignantes la receite de la dite somme par tesmoignance de queles et de cestes nous vous enferoms auer due allouance en vostre dite ferme du terme auantdit Donne souz nostre priue seal a Notingham le xxvij iour de Juyl Lan de nostre regne unzisme.

(Endorsed)
particule Maioris et Balliuorum Lincolnie mensibus Augusti Septembris et Octobris anno xi Intrantur.

Et de nouo extracta.

hic sunt tres littere continente xx li. sub sigillo Roberti de Rissheten et Elye de Wherelte solute anno xj° per Maiorem et balliuos Lincolnie super offico Radulphi de Stok clerici magne garderobe.

49. **Admission of bishop of Winchester as lieutenant of treasurer.** [Issue Roll, no. 220, Pt ii, Mich. 20 Ed. II, m. 1.]

Memorandum quod xiiij die mensis Nouembris anno xx° Johannes Wyntoniensis Episcopus venit ad scaccarium et tulit ibidem quoddam mandatum patens sub sigillo Edwardi filij Regis primogeniti cuius tenor talis est

Edwardus dei gratia Rex Anglie et Dominus Hibernie Baronibus et Camerariis suis de scaccario salutem Cum pro eo quod venerabilis pater Willelmus Archiepiscopus Eboraciensis nuper Thesaurarius scaccarij predicti circa diuersa negocia in partibus borialibus est occupatus quo minus indendere possit ad ea que ad officium illud in dicto scaccario pertinent exercenda Constituerimus venerabilem patrem Johannem Wyntoniensem Episcopum Tenentem locum Thesaurarii scaccarij predicti quousque de officio illo aliter duxerimus ordinandum percipiendo in eodem officio dum illud sic tenuerit feodum consuetum prout in litteris nostris patentibus prefato Episcopo inde confectis plenius continetur Vobis mandamus quod ipsum Episcopum ad officium illud admittatis et ei in hiis que ad officium predictum pertinent intendatis in forma predicta Teste Edwardo filio nostro primogenito Custode regni nostri apud Hereford sexto die Nouembris anno regni nostri vicesimo.

Pretextu cuius mandati predictus Episcopus admissus est ad officium supradictum et irrotulatur ad scaccarium termino Michelis anno xx° Rotulo sexto.

50. **Writ of privy seal to exchequer notifying pardon of a debt.** [Exch. of Pleas, Plea Roll, no. 31, m. 9.]

Middlesex.

Postea Rex mandauit hic breue suum de priuato sigillo quod est inter comunia de anno secundo in hec verba

Edward par la grace de dieu etcetera au lieu tenaunt nostre Tresorer et as Barouns de nostre Escheqer saluz Come as nostre grace especiale eioms relessez et pardonez a Henry Longynogh de Kenygnton Lxxv s. qe homme li demande a nostre oeps pur un gorz quil tynt a ferme de Wauter de Langeton Euesqe de Cestre nad guerres Tresorer nostre chier piere qui dieux assoille vous maundoms qe des ditz lxxv s. facez Le dit Henry estre quites a nostre dit Escheqer solonc nostre doun et releisse auantditz Donne souz nostre priuee seal a Langele Le quint iour Daueril Lan de nostre regne secund.

Ideo cesset execucio de predictis denariis Leuandis etcetera.

II. CHANCERY DOCUMENTS

51. Ordinance of the household of lord and lady Willoughby d'Eresby. [Chan. Misc. 3/33.]

Lordenance del hostiel mon seigneur et ma dame le v iour de Janeuoir a Eresby lan xij.

Au primer qil ysoit un hostiel pur moun seigneur et ma dame Monsire Johan de Sturmyn seneschal et en eide de li et en sa absence Henri de Chelreye et en lur absence Alain de Medfeld deuaunt qi et le garderober sil ysoit soient les despens del hostiel abreuez chescune nuyt mes lengrosser de la compte demoerge tantqe le dit monsire Johan et Henri ysoit.

William de Oterhampton garderober od deux chiuaux et serra chief auditour dacompte

Sir Richard Olyuer clerc des offices et lieu tenant le garderober quant il est hors et acountera et serra a la liuere dauenies

. . . .

Sire Hugh de Byford chapelain et aumoner le seigneur et eidera escrire lettres et altres choses quant mestier serra e en absence del garderober countrerollera les despens del hostiel e abreuira les despens del hostiel mon seigneur quant il va hors del hostiel et de ceo acountera a garderober deuant seneschal del hostiel

. . . .

E toutz les despens del hostiel et de garderobe soiont quatre foitz lan surueuz et examinez par le haut seneschal et les seneschal del hostiel ou altres ou altre come yplerra et seigneur dasigner et ordiner.

(Endorsed)

Ordinacio hospicij.

52. Minutes of council about government of Scotland. [Chan. Misc. Bdle 22, no. 12/26.]

(2 Ed. II. orders in council relating to the government of Scotland.)

. . . .

Item assentu est par le conseil qe le ferme de le ville de seint Johan de Perth soit assigne as les Burgeis de mesmes ville pur deux anz pur amenderet redrescer et afforcer lenclosture et les aucuns forces de meisme la ville.

. . . .

De priuato sigillo

Acorde est qe mandement soit fait de par le Roy au Chamberleyn Descoce qil face veer la defaute du Chastel de Dunde qe sur les defautes qe y serrent troue il face mettre le bon consail qil purra et face tout qe meisme le Chastel soit.

De priuato sigillo

Item soit mande a Richard de Brymmesgraue gardein des vitailles de Berewyk qil face garnir le Chaustel...des dites victualles et buller ausint as gentz des...en paiement totes les homes qe le Chamberlyn....

53. Return to writ ordering search of rolls and memoranda of chamber. [Chan. Misc. Bdle 49, no. 2/27.]

Pretextu breuis huic consuti ego Henricus de Greystok scrutatus rotulis et memoranda camere domini Regis in custodia mea existentibus compertum est per quandam extentam manerij de Chilternelangeley factam coram Umfrido de Walden die sabbati in festo Invencionis sancte Crucis anno regni Regis Edwardi patris domini Regis nunc xiij per sacramentum xij iuratorum quod Nicholaus de Passelewe tenet dimidium feodum militis in Swanborne in comitatu Bukenhamsir et debet sectam Curie de tribus septimanis in tres septimanas Et compertum est inter memoranda camere predicte quandam litteram patentem predicte Nicholai sigillo suo consignatam in hec verba Sachent toutes gentz qe ie Nichol de Passelewe ai fait fealte a Richard de Cokham gardein de fees assigne a la chambre nostre seigneur le Roi par les terres et tenementz queuz ie teynk en la ville de Swanbourne queux sont tenuz de nostre seigneur le Roi en...de son manoir de Chilternelangeley pur un dimi fee de morteyn par homage fealte et relief quant il escherra En tesmoignance qe quele chose iai mys mon seal Donne a Swanbourne le quinzisme iour de Nouembre Lan nostre seigneur le Roi Edward tierz puis le conquest dis et oytisme.

54. Writ of privy seal to chancellor and treasurer about appointment of an escheator of cities and boroughs. [Chan. Warr. File 76, no. 1839[1].]

Edward par la grace de dieu Roi Dengleterre Seigneur Dirlaunde et Ducs Daquitaine a nos chers et foiaux Lonurable Pere en dieu Wauter par la meisme grace Euesqe de Wincestre nostre Chancellier et Johan de Sandale nostre Tresorier saluz Por ce que et ceuz qui sont pres de nous de nostre consail nous ont consailiez que nous faceoms ordener un Eschetour des Citez et des Bourgs de nostre Roiaume et nous nous fioms molt de la loiaute et de lauisement nostre cher clerc maistre Johan de Percy si voloms que le dit maistre Johan soit nostre Eschetour des Citez et Bourgs auantditz Et vous mandoms que vous facez ordener entre vous une commission au dit maistre Johan pur le dit office si bone si large et si couenable aussibien pur le temps passe de noz ancestres come de nostre temps que nostre droit ne y soit delaiez ne que nous eyoms damage par defaute de cele commission Et pur ce que cel office est nouel et il ny ad uncore nul certeyn fee assigne pur meisme loffice vous mandoms que vous assignez au dit maistre Johan pur le dit office tiel fee come vous verrez que soit couenable pur nous et pur li eantz regard as mises et despens quil li couendra faire en loffice auantdit Donne souz nostre priue seal a Berewyk sur Twede le xxvj iour de Marz Lan de regne nostre quart.

(Endorsed)

[1] Vide also K. R. Mem. Roll, no. 84, m. 24 d.

55. Writ of privy seal to chancellor that escheator of Wales shall be appointed by justice of Wales. [Chan. Warr. File 76/1857.]

Edward par la grace de dieu Roi Dengleterre Seigneur Dirlaunde et Ducs Daquitaine al honurable pere en dieu Wauter par la meisme grace Euesqe de Wircestre nostre Chancellier saluz Nous auoms entenduz qe nostre cher et foial monsire Wauter de Gloucestre nostre Eschetour dela Trente par li ou par aucuns ses souz Eschetours usent aucunes choses es parties de Gales qe ne appartienent mie a son office par quoi nous voloms et vous mandoms qe as enquestes qe le dit monsire Wauter ou nul de ses souz Eschetours ount pris ou prendrent des choses touchantes loffice descheterie es dites parties de Gales ne doignez nule foi ne nen facez rien Car nous voloms qe nostre cher et foial monsire Roger de Mortimer nostre Justice de Gales ou celi quil ad a ce deputez depar nous use cel office en sa baillie selonc la ley et lusage de celes parties et qe as enquestes quil prendra et retournera a vous en ditz manere vous doignez foi et nemie as autres des choses qe sont en sa baillie Donne souz priue seal a Berewyk sur Twede le primer iour de Aueril Lan de nostre regne quart.

56. Writ of privy seal to chancellor prohibiting commission of inquiry. [Chan. Warr. File 82/2430.]

Edward par la grace de dieu Roi Dengleterre Seigneur Dirlande et Ducs Daquitaine al honurable piere en dieu Wauter par la meisme grace Euesqe de Wycestre nostre Chaunceller Por ce qe nous auoms entenduz qe monsire Griffith de la Pole seut deuers nostre conseil dauer une commission hors de nostre Chauncellerie denquerre si les terres de Powis soient tenues en Galescherie ou de la corone Dengleterre et cele busoigne touche molt la dignete de nostre coroune a la quele garder nous sumes tenuz vous mandoms et chargeoms fermement enioignantz qe vous ne facez faire nulle commission denquerre coment les dites terres sont tenues sanz especial mandement de nostre bouche Et facez sercher les roulles de nostre Chauncellerie et nous certifiez quel an Griffith Gwenonewyn et quel an monsire Oweyn son filz fesoient homage a nostre piere ou a nostre Ael pur la Baronie de Powys susdite. Donne souz nostre priue seal a Wyndesore le xxviij iour Doctobre Lan de nostre regne quint.

57. Writ of privy seal to two chancery clerks to search chancery rolls. [Chan. Warr. File 82, no. 2470.]

Edward par la grace de dieu Roi Dengleterre Seigneur Dirlande et Ducs Daquitaine a nos chiers et feals Adam de Osegoteby et Roberd de Bardelby Clers de nostre Chauncelrie ou a un de eux salutz Purce qe nous auoms rendu a Leuesque de Cestre tutes ses terres et ses tenementz et ses autres biens et les dites terres et tenementz furent nad gerres translatez en diuers meins vous maundoms qe vous facez sercher les Roules de nostre Chauncelerie pur sauoir en qui meins les dites terres furent bailles et en certefiez le dit Euesque issint quil nous puisse auiser as queus nous deuoms escriuere pur faire le dit Euesque auer la deliuerance des dites terres Done de souz nostre priue seal a Cnareborgh le xj iour de Janeuer Lan de nostre Regne quint.

58. **Petition of German merchants in England and writ of privy seal to keeper of great seal enclosing it to be considered by council.** [Chan. Warr. File 86/2849–50.]

A nostre Seigneur le Roy prient les marchanuz de Almayngne reperaunz en soun Realme Dengleterre oue lour marchaundises qe sount et de aunciene temps unt este en fraunchz en la terre Dengleterre par le grant nostre Seigneur le Roy qi ore est e par le grant de ses auncestres qe il lour voyle de grace graunter bref a chaunceler et a soun counsayle qil soynt meyntenuz en son Reaume solum lour fraunchyses et aunciens usages come en la forme de lour chartres pleynement est contenuz et qe decele fraunchise ne soient houstez par nul de ses ministres.

Edward par la grace de dieu Roi Dengleterrc Seigneur Dirlande et Ducs Daquitaine Al honurable pere en dieu Wauter par la meisme grace Eslit de Canterbure confermez gardein de nostre grant seal saluz Nous vous enueoms enclos de deinz cestes lettres une peticion qe nous feut baillee par les marchandz de Alemaigne repairantz en nostre Reaume et vous mandoms qe veue et examinee la dite peticion par vous et les autres de nostre conseil facez faire sur les choses qe y sont contenues selonc ce qe vous verrez qe face afaire par reson Done souz nostre priue seal a Westmoster le xxviij iour de Nouembre Lan de nostre regne septisme.

59. **Writ of privy seal to chancellor and treasurer to search rolls and remembrances of chancery and exchequer for gifts made by king.** [Chan. Warr. File 90/3202.]

Edward par la grace de dieu Roi Dengleterre Seigneur Dirlande et Ducs Daquitaine A noz chers et foiauz Johan de Sandale nostre Chauncellier et Wautier de Norwyz nostre Tresorer Por ce qe les Prelatz Contes et Barons de nostre Realme nous requiserent nadgaires a nostre parlement Deuerwyk qe nous vousissiens repeller touz les douns et reles qe nous auoms fait des terres tenementz baillies gardes mariages dettes et seruices puis le temps qe nous donasmes poair as aucuns des ditz Prelatz Contes et Barons de ordeiner de Lestat de nostre Roialme et de nostre houstel par quoi nous voloms estre certifiez et auisez des ditz douns et reles vous mandoms qe serchez les roulles et remembrances de nostre Chauncellerie et de nostre Eschekier nous certifiez distinctement et apertement a plus en haste qe vous purrez de touz les douns et reles qe nous auoms fait puis le temps du dit poair grante de terres tenementz baillies gardes mariages dettes et seruices et as queuz et de quoi et en quele forme si qe nous puissoms estre auisez auant nostre prochein parlement ce qe en fait afaire Donne souz nostre priue seal a Berkhamstede le iiij iour de Decembre Lan de nostre regne oytisme.

60. Writ of privy seal to chancellor to search rolls and remembrances of chancery for grants made by king, certifying keeper of wardrobe. [Chan. Warr. File 90/3203.]

Edward par la grace de dieu Roi Dengleterre Seigneur Dirlaunde et Ducs Daquitaine a nostre cher et foial Johan de Sandale nostre Chancellier Por ceo qe par aucunes certeines causes nous voloms estre certifiez de toutes maneres de choses dount fyns ount este faites en nostre Court et de totes maneres de choses qe nous auoms done graunte ou assigne por dettes auxibien de terres rentes gardes mariages eschetes et reuersions come de vacacions de Eueschees Abbeies Priortes et qe nous auoms relesse de dettes ou de seruices en guerre et qe nous auoms graunte de pardone de fraunchises en mortissementz forfaitures et dautres choses queles qe elles soient dount nous deueriens ou puissens auoir en fyns en nostre dite Court de tout le temps puis qe nous receumes primerement le gouernement de nostre Roiaume taunt qe en cea vous maundoms qe serchez les roules et les autres remembrances de nostre Chauncellerie de quantqe il y en a remembrance enuoiez a nostre cher clerc William de Melton Gardein de nostre Garderobe la certificacion distinctement et apertement souz vostre seal issint quil layt auant ceste procheine feste de Noel Donne souz nostre priue seal a Berkhamstede le quart iour de Decembre Lan de nostre regne oytisme.

61. Writ of privy seal to chancellor enclosing transcript of roll ordering execution thereof. [Chan. Warr. File 92/3443.]

Edward par la grace de dieu Roi Dengleterre Seigneur Dirlande et Ducs Daquitaine a nostre cher clerc et foial Johan de Sandale nostre Chauncelier Nous vous enueoms souz nostre priue seal le transescrit dun roulle qe nostre cher clerc Roger de Northburgh nous porta depar vous et autres bones gentz de nostre conseil contenaunt aucunes busoignes qe esteient ordenez a Nicole puis nostre darrein departir dilloeqes ensemblement od nostre assent sur les busoignes auantdites et vous mandoms qe meismes les busoignes tant come a vouz ent appartirint facez mettre en esploit saunz nul delay solenc nostre assent auantdit Donne souz nostre priue seal a Lermitoire le viij iour de Septembre Lan de nostre regne neuisme.

62. Writ of privy seal to archbishop of Canterbury, earl of Hereford, chancellor and treasurer, to summon council to consider letters from earl of Lancaster. [Chan. Warr. File 93/3513.]

Edward par la grace de dieu Roi Dengleterre Seigneur Dirlaunde et Ducs Daquitaine a noz chers et foiaux lonurable pere en dieu Wauter par la meisme grace Erceuesqe de Caunterbire Primat de tote Engleterre monsire Humfray de Bohun Counte de Hereford nostre cher frere Johan de Sandale nostre Chaunceller et Wauter de Norwyz nostre Tresorer saluz Nous vous fesoms sauer qe y cest Lundy le vyntisme iour de cesti moys Doctobre a sautre bien de deinz le Nuyt nous vindrent lettres de nostre cher cousin et foial monsire Thomas Counte de Lancastre les queux noz chers et foiaux monsire Hugh Daudele et William de Melton qui alerent nadgaires en nostre message au dit Counte sur certeines bosoignes dount vous auantditz Erceuesqe et Counte de Hereford bien sauez nous enueerent hastiuement deinz les queles estotit enclose une endenture contenant les respounses le dit Counte de Lancestre as articles de la dite messagerie les transcriptz des queles lettres et endenture nous vous enueoms en un Roulle souz nostre priue seal ensemblement od le transcript des lettres qe les dit Hugh et William nous ount enueez de lour conseil et auis sur les bosoignes auantdites Et pur ceo qe nous ne voloms mie ouerir en meismes les bosoignes sanz le conseil et lauisement de vous vous mandoms qe veues cestes lettres facez appeller a vous les autres de nostre conseil qi vous verrez qi appeller y facent et examinez diligeaument et entenduz les ditz transcriptz eez sur les choses qe y sount contenues bon auisement et nous certifiez saunz delay distinctement et apertement par voz lettres et par le porter de cestes de voz conseuix et de voz auys en les dites bosoignes et quoi vous semble qe nous en deueroms mielz faire Issint qe nous ensoioms hastiuement certefiez sicome vous amez nostre honeur Donne souz nostre priue seal a Sautre le xx iour de Octobre Lan de nostre regne Neuisme.

63. **Writ of privy seal to archbishop of Canterbury, earl of Hereford, chancellor and treasurer, to summon council to consider outrages committed.** [Chan. Warr. File 93/3515.]

Edward par la grace de dieu Roi Dengleterre Seigneur Dirlaunde et Ducs Daquitaine a noz chers et foiauz lonurable pere en dieu Wauter par la meisme grace Erceuesqe de Caunterbire Primat de tote Engleterre monsire Humfray de Bohun Counte de Hereford nostre cher frere Johan de Sandale nostre Chaunceller et Wauter de Norwyz nostre Tresorer saluz Nous enueoms a vous nostre cher clerc mestre Johan de Walewayn nostre Eschetour de cea Trente pur vous mostrer aucuns grantz outrages et despitz qe nous ount este faitz ore tart en le Chastel de Warrewyk qe est en nostre main et vous mandoms et chargeoms en la foy qe vous nous deuez qe appellez a vous les autres de nostre conseil qi vous verrez qi appeller y facent et oie et entendre pleinement la mostrance qe le dit mestre Johan vous envoudra faire mettez y si bon et si hastif conseil et remedie qe les dites outrages et despitz soient bien et reddement puniz selom ley et reson et qe nostre honour et nostre estat y soient sauuez et maintenuz en touz pointz Donne souz nostre priue seal a Sautre le xx iour de Octobre Lan de nostre regne Neuisme.

64. **Writ of privy seal to chancellor and treasurer referring certain matters to consideration of council.** [Chan. Warr. File 93/3594.]

Edward par la grace de dieu Roi Dengleterre Seigneur Dirlaunde et Ducs Daquitaine a noz chers et foiaux Johan de Sandale nostre Chaunceller et Wauter de Norwyz nostre Tresorer saluz Nous enueoms a vous par Rauf de Tarente nostre vallet les transescritz des lettres qe nous sont venues Dirlande et Descoce et unes lettres qe furent enuees a monsire William Inge de grant meschef de noz gentz a Berewyk et vous mandoms et chargeoms si auant come nous peoms qe des choses contenues en la copie susdite vostre conseil et auisement nous facez sauer par le dit Rauf a pluis en haste qe vous porrez et especiaument coment il vous semble qe nous deuoms respondere as lettres qe nous sont venues hors dirlande et la dite copie facez monstrer a nostre conseil et sur les choses contenue en y cele bonement voillez conseiller Et nous auoms mandez par monsire Robert de Kendale a nostre cher cousin le comte de Lancastre totes les lettres sicome y vyndrent a nous et lui auoms prie qil enremande a nous son conseil et son loement Donne souz nostre priue seal a Clipston le xxvj iour de ffeuerer lan de nostre regne neuisme.

65. **Writ of privy seal to three chancery clerks ordering their presence with great seal.** [Chan. Warr. File 95/3739.]

Edward par la grace de dieu Roy Dengleterre Seigneur Dirlaunde et Ducs Daquitaine A noz cher clercs William de Ayremynne Robert de Bardelby et Robert de Askeby saluz Nous vous mandoms qe vous soiez a nous a Crayk od nostre graunt seal y ce Mardy le xix iour de cesty moys Doctobre a nostre leuer Et ce en nule manere ne lessez et les clercs demoergent en pees a Euerwyk Donne souz nostre priue seal a Crayk le xviij iour Doctobre Lan de nostre regne disme.

66. **Writ of privy seal to three chancery clerks ordering their presence with great seal and seal for bishopric of Durham, vacant.** [Chan. Warr. File 95/3752.]

Edward par la grace de dieu Roi Dengleterre Seigneur Dirlaunde et Ducs Daquitaine a noz chers clercs William de Ayremynne Robert de Bardelby et Robert de Askeby saluz Nous vous mandoms qe veues cestes lettres veignez a nous au plus en haste qe vous porrez bonement od nostre graunt seal et od le seal ordeinez pur la vacacion de Leuesche de Duresme et facez venir ouesqe vous nostre cher clerc Adam de Brom a receuire en nostre presence loffice de Chauncellier de la dite Euesche duraunte ceste vacacion et a faire le serment sicome appent Donne souz nostre priue seal a Neuburgh le xxiiij iour Doctobre Lan de nostre regne disme.

67. **Writ of privy seal to chancellor and baron of exchequer to summon council to consider schedule enclosed from council of queen.** [Chan. Warr. File 103/4552.]

Edward par la grace de dieu Roi Dengleterre Seigneur Dirlaunde et Ducs Daquitaine a honorable piere en dieu Johan par meisme la grace Euesqe de Wincestre nostre Chaunceler et monsire Wautier de Norwyz Baroun de nostre Escheqer salutz Nous vous enuoioms cy dedeinz enclose une escrowette contienante aucuns articles qe nous fu baillie par le counseil nostre treschere compaigne Isabelle Roine Dengleterre et vous maundoms qe appellez a vous ceux de nostre counseil qi vous verrez qi soient a appelle facez regarder le dite escrowette et ceo qe y est contenuz ordeinez ent hastiuement ceo qe vous verrez qe soit affaire pur le profit de nous et de nostre dite compaigne Donne souz nostre priue seal a Shene le xix iour de ffeurer lan de nostre regne unzisme.

68. Writ of privy seal to chancellor repeating an order for a commission under great seal. [Chan. Warr. File 105/4712.]

Edward par la grace de dieu Roi Dengleterre Seigneur Dirlaunde et Ducs Daquitaine A Lonurable piere en dieu Johan par la meisme grace Euesqe de Wincestre nostre Chaunceller saluz Come nadgaires vous mandissiens par noz autres lettres qe la commission si nulle feust faite de nostre grant seal a autre qe a nostre cher Bacheler monsire Wautier de Graas de loffice de viscounte des Countez de Surreie et de Sussex feissez repeller saunz delay et de meisme loffice faire renoueller la commission le dit monsire Wautier de quoi vous nauez uncore rien voluz faire a ce qe nous auoms entenduz dont nous nous merueilloms molt et nous tenoms durement a mal paiez vous mandoms derechief et chargeoms fermement qe veues cestes lettres saunz nul delay facez auer au dit monsire Wautier la dite commission en due forme Et ce en nulle manere ne lessez Donne souz nostre priue seal a Westmoustre le xxx iour de Maij Lan de nostre regne unzisme.

69. Writ of privy seal to keepers of great seal prohibiting them from receiving a fine. [Chan. Warr. File 116/5832.]

Edward par la grace de dieu Roi Dengleterre Seigneur Dirlaunde et Ducs Daquitaine as Gardeins de nostre grant seal saluz Por ce qe nous auoms entenduz qe Johane qe feust la femme Thomas de Lodelowe cheualier qest a dieu commaundez qi tint de nous en chief sest mariee saunz nostre conge par qai les terres et tenementz meisme cele Johane sount seisiz en nostre mein vous maundoms pur cel trespas ne receuez de lui nulle fin tantqe vous en eiez autre maundement de nous Donne souz nostre priue seal a Biflet le iij iour Doctobre Lan de nostre regne xvme.

70. Writ of privy seal to keepers of great seal to summon council to consider statute. [Chan. Warr. File 116/5857.]

Edward par la grace de dieu Roi Dengleterre Seigneur Dirlaunde et Ducs Daquitaine As Gardeins de nostre grant seal saluz Pur ceo qe nous auoms entenduz qe Johane qe feust la feme Thomas de Loudelawe qi est a dieu comandez et qi tint de nous en chief est rauie et mariee sauntz nostre conge vous mandoms qe appellez a vous noz Justices et autres de nostre consail qi vous verrez qi facent appeller facez regarder lestatut fait sur teux rauisementz si nous en doioms auoir suyte face ordiner outre tieu remedie pur nous en ceo cas come vous verrez qe ley et reson purrount soeffrir et qe cel exces ne soit despuniz Donne souz nostre priue seal a nostre Tour de Londres le xviij iour de Octobre Lan de nostre Regne quinzisme.

71. Writ of privy seal to keepers of great seal not to issue writs touching property of Eleanor la Despenser. [Chan. Warr. File 116/5890.]

Edward par la grace de dieu Dengleterre Seigneur Dirlaunde et Ducs Daquitaine As Gardeins de nostre grant seal saluz Nous vous mandoms qe vous soeffrez nul brief issir hors de nostre Chauncellerie souz nostre dit seal touchant la purpartie nostre chere Niece Alianore la Despenser soer et une des heirs Gilbert de Clare iadis Counte de Gloucestre qi est a dieu commandez la quele purpartie est en nostre mein par certeines enchesons et si nul brief soit issu touchant la dite purpartie facez mander par brief souz nostre dit seal a celi a qi dit brief est issuz qil sursese de execucion faire tant come meisme la purpartie demoert en nostre mein Donne souz nostre priue seal a Westmoustre le xiij iour de Nouembre Lan de nostre regne xv[me].

72. Writ of privy seal to William de Ayremynne to bring chancery to king. [Chan. Warr. File 117/5948 and 5949.]

Edward par la grace de dieu Roi Dengleterre Seigneur Dirlaunde et Ducs Daquitaine A nostre cher clerc William de Ayreminne saluz Por grosses et chargeaunces busoignes qe nous auoms affaire vous maundoms et chargeoms qe toutes autres choses lessees veignoz a nous od nostre grant seal et les clercs de nostre chauncellie si en haste come vous unqes purrez Et ce en nulle manere ne lessez Donne souz nostre priue seal a Hereford le primer iour de ffeuerer Lan de nostre regne xv[me].

73. Writ of privy seal to keepers of great seal to issue writs on nomination of Hugh le Despenser. [Chan. Warr. File 117/5995.]

Edward par la grace de dieu Roi Dengleterre Seigneur Dirlaunde et Ducs Daquitaine As Gardeins de nostre grant seal saluz Nous vous enueoms cy dedeinz enclose une bille contenaunte matire daucunes commissions et lettres qe nous voloms qe soient faites et vous mandoms qe regarde la dite bille sur ce qe y est contenuz facez faire commission et lettres souz nostre dit seal tenuz et tieles et a tieles persones come nostre cher Neueu et foial Hugh le Despenser le filz vous voudra nomer et deuiser depar nous Done souz nostre priue seal a Rothewell le xxv iour de April lan de nostre regne xv[me].

74. Writ of privy seal to keepers of great seal appointing a chancery clerk. [Chan. Warr. File 121/6390.]

Edward par la grace de dieu Roi Dengleterre Seigneur Dirlaunde et Ducs Daquitaine as Gardeins de nostre grant seal saluz Por ce qe nous voloms qe nostre cher clerc mestre Johan de Hildesle demoerge en nostre Chauncellerie as robes et a bouche en Court come un de noz douze clers qe y demoerent vous maundoms qe ostez mestre Johan de Blebury receuiez dentre vous nostre dit clerc en lieu de lui sicome desus est dit Et ce ne lessez Donne souz nostre priue seal a Pountfreint le xij iour de ffeuerer Lan de nostre regne xvj[me].

75. Writ of privy seal to keepers of great seal to attach a Hospitaller and try before council. [Chan. Warr. File 122/6433.]

Edward par la grace de dieu Roi Dengleterre Seigneur Dirlaunde et Ducs Daquitaine As Gardeins de nostre grant seal saluz Por ce qe nous auoms entenduz qe un frere alien del hospital seint Johan de Jerusalem qi se dit visitour deputez est venuz en nostre roiaume od bulles et autres lettres preiudicieles a nous et a nostre roiaume vous maundoms qe le dit frere facez attacher et venir deuant nous et nostre conseil selonc lauisement de nostre cher et foial Roger Beler Baron de nostre Escheqier qi nous auoms chargez de ceste busoigne Donne souz nostre priue seal a Knaresburgh le primer iour de Marz lan de nostre regne xvj^me^.

76. Writ of privy seal to keepers of great seal prohibiting issue of a writ. [Chan. Warr. File 122/6464.]

Edward par la grace de dieu Roi Dengleterre Seigneur Dirlaunde et Ducs Daquitaine As Gardeins de nostre grant seal saluz Nous vous maundoms par certeines resons qe pur nully suyte ne facez garaunt souz nostre dit seal pur deliuerer le Chastel de Brigge Wauter hors de nostre meyn saunz nous ent auiser deuant Donne souz nostre priue seal a Horton le xxiiij iour de Marz Lan de nostre regne xvj^me^.

77. Writ of privy seal to chancellor to summon council to make process against Henry de Beaumont. [Chan. Warr. File 123/6542.]

Edward par la grace de dieu Roi Dengleterre Seigneur Dirlande et Ducs Daquitaine Al honurable pere en dieu Johan par la meisme grace Euesqe de Norwyz nostre Chaunceller saluz Nous vous mandoms qe appellez a vous noz chers et foiaux Henri Lescrope et William de Bereford chiefs Justices de noz Baunks et autres de nostre conseil qe vous verrez facez mettre en couenable forme les proces et agard nadgaires faitz deuant nous et nostre conseil a Bysshopthorp contre Henri de Beaumont et les facez enrouller en vostre place et en nostre Baunk et aillors selonc ce qe nostre cher et bien amez sergeant Geffrey Lescrope qi nous ent auoms chargez vous dirra plus pleinement depar nous Donne souz nostre priue seal a Bysshopthorp le iiij iour de Juyn Lan de nostre regne xvj^me^.

78. Writ of privy seal to chancellor to summon council to consider inquisitions. [Chan. Warr. File 124/6699.]

Edward par la grace de dieu Roi Dengleterre Seigneur Dirlaunde et Ducs Daquitaine A nostre cher clerc Mestre Robert de Baldok Ercedeakne de Middlesex nostre Chauncellier saluz Nous vous enueoms souz nostre priue seal aucunes enquestes prises deuaunt noz chers et bien amez clercs Mestre Robert de Aylleston gardein de nostre priue seal et Robert de Holden touchauntes nostre manoir de Skypton en Crauene et autres diuerses trespas come plus pleinement piert par meisme les enquestes et vous maundoms fermement eniognauntz qe vous meismes lenquestes et appelle deuaunt vous Ceux qi la chose touche oiez et terminez totes les choses contenues en les dites enquestes enfeisant dreit a touz saunz nul esparnier en la foi qe vous nous deit Donne souz nostre priue seal a Colnie le tierz iour de Octobre Lan de nostre regne xvij^me^.

79. Writ of privy seal to chancellor to issue a commission. [Chan. Warr. File 125/6752.]

Edward par la grace de dieu Roi Dengleterre Seigneur Dirlaunde et Ducs Daquitaine A Mestre Robert de Baldok Ercedeakne de

Middlesex nostre Chaunceller saluz Nous vous maundoms qe veues cestes lettres maundez a noz chers et foialx Robert de Ailleston gardein de nostre priue seal et a Johan de Stonore la commission dont nous vous chargeasmes a vostre departir de nous Donne souz nostre priue seal a Rauenesdale le xxv Jour de Nouembre Lan de nostre regne xvij^me^.

80. Petition from king's servants to steward of household. [Chan. Warr. File 129/7114.]

Honurable Seigneur Seneschal nostre Seigneur le Roy Dengleterre vous moustrent William Dautree William Spenay William de la Sale qui ount serui nostre seigneur le Roi qore est et son piere deuant luy qui dieux assoille a terme de xxx aunz et plus Nostre Seigneur le Rey qore est lour...graunte lur garreysons pur lour longe seruices come tesmoigne est en la Chauncellerie en Abbeyes et en Espitelles Sire ils ount suy a les dites mesons oue lettres de la Chancellerie et ils ne les volunte pas receuire oi les lettres ne soient plus chaergantz Pur la quele chose sire ils vous priount pur dieu qe vous voillez mustrer lur estat a nostre seigneur le Roy qils eient plus chargeantes lettres a les dites mesons ou ils ount este oue les lettres le Roy auant ces houres.

81. Writ of privy seal to chancellor not to appoint to vacant church reserved to chamber. [Chan. Warr. File 132/7441.]

Edward par la grace de dieu Roi Dengleterre Seigneur Dirlande et Ducs Daquitaine a nostre cher clerc Mestre Robert de Baldok Ercediakne de Middlesex nostre Chauncellier saluz Por ce qe nous auoms entenduz qe leglise de Beford en Holdrenesse est voide et appurtenante a nostre doneson par reson des terres reseruez a nostre Chambre vous mandoms qe vous ne la donez a nulli Donne souz nostre priue seal a Ledes le xv iour de Juyn Lan de nostre regne xixme.

82. Writ of privy seal to chancellor not to issue writs touching Welsh lands of Hugh le Despenser. [Chan. Warr. File 134/7546.]

Edward par la grace de dieu Roi Dengleterre Seigneur Dirlaunde et Ducs Daquitaine A Lonurable (piere en dieu Johan par meisme la grace) Euesqe Dely nostre Chauncellier saluz Nous vous mandoms qe vous ne soeffrez nul brief passer (hors de nostre Chauncellerie countre) nostre cher Neueu et foial monsire Hugh le Despenser le Puisnez touchant ses terres en Gales por le...sanz seu et especial comandement de nous Donne souz nostre priue seal a Euerwik le iij iour de Aueril Lan de nostre (regne xivme).

83. Bill under privy seal. [Chan. Warr. File 909.]

Dominus Rex concessit Roberto de Snodhull officium Marescalcie coram Justiciariis de Banco eiusdem domini Regis tenendum ad voluntatem ipsius Regis eodem modo quod Robertus Poun illud officium tenuit quam quidem concessionem dominus Rex fecit eidem Roberto ad instanciam domine Regine Anglie consortis sue.

84. Writ of secret seal to keepers of great seal containing instructions about form of certain writs. [Chan. Warr. File 1329/33.]

Edward par la grace de dieu Roi Dengleterre Seigneur Dirlaunde et Ducs Daquitaine As Gardeins de nostre grant seal salutz Nous vous mandoms qeu les commissions qe vous auez fait faire par nostre comandement de seisier en nostre mein les terres qe furent a Hugh le Despenser le piere et le fuitz soit fait mencion qe ceuz qui sont assignez depar nous eient poair de garder et dordiner des dites terres solonc ce qil verront qe melz soit a profist de nous Et soit mandez a eux par nostre bref clos qil nous certefient des biens et chateux esloignez hors des dites terres puis la veille de Lassompcion nostre dame prochein passee Donne souz nostre secre seal a Westmouster le xxvj iour Daust Lan de nostre regne xvme.

85. Warrant from steward of household for letters of protection under great seal. [Chan. Warr. File 1648, no. 30 c.]

fiant si placet protectiones pro Radulfo le Botiller et Johanne de Iustanes milite Hugone de Godington Roberto de Brumsthulf et Hugone de Kemesey vadlet domini Radulfi et Philipo de Iustances valet dicti Johannis qui profecturi sunt in obsequium domini Regis versus partes Vasconie.

per Ricardum Dammory Senescallum hospicij Regis.

86. Warrant from keeper of wardrobe for writ of purveyance. [Chan. Warr. File 1648, no. 59.]

Salutz come a lui meismes Cher ami ieo vous pri qe vous facez faire une commission desutz le grant seal nostre seigneur le Roi pur maistre Andreu le Chaundeler et Rauf de Brantyngham de prendre cire encre et autres choses pertenances al office de Lespicerie et cariage pur meismes celes carier al oeps nostre dit seigneur le Roi pur ses deners prestement paianz en sa garderobe A dieu qe vous eit en sa garde.

per Custodem Garderobe Regis.

87. Informal warrant for a writ ordering payment. [Chan. Warr. File 1703.]

Seit fet bref au Taxours et quillours del xx et xv en le Counte de Kauntebrugge qe de deners qil ount leue de les auauntditz xx et xv facent paier a William Poleter del hostel nostre seygneur le Roy sur son office C liures en resceuiaunt de lui sa lettre patente teigmoinaunce la resseyte Escrit a Loundres le v iour de Aueril.

87 a. Writ of privy seal to the justice of Wales ordering his service in Scotland. [Chan. Warr. File 1703.]

Edward par la grace de dieu Roy Dengleterre Seigneur Dirlande et Ducs Daquitaine a nostre cher et foil monsire Roger de Mortemer nostre Justice de Gales salutz Nous auoms bien entenduz les lettres qe vous nous auez enueez et vous mercioms molt et sauoms bon gre de ceo qe vous estes totes foiz prest de venir en nostre seruise a nostre mandement et vous mandoms et chargeoms fermement enioignantz qe vous viegnez a nous en nostre guerre Descece si en haste et si efforcement come vous porrez Et ceo en nule manere ne lessez Donne souz nostre priue seal a Dukelande le xvij iour de Maii lan etcetera.

87 b. Warrant of steward of household to chancery clerks for letters of protection. [Chan. Warr. File 1703]

ffiat protectiones sub magno sigillo Regis pro Johanne de Enefeld et Audoeno Gough et Johanne de Luk seruientibus Regis predicti ad arma qui profecturi sunt in obsequium ipsius Regis ad partes Scocie.

Domino Ade de Osgoteby per Edmundum de malo lacu senescallum hospicii Regis.

88. Informal warrants for writs under great seal. [Chan. Warr. File 1704.]

Salutem dominus Rex dedit licentiam domino Nicholao de Neuill succidendam ducenti quercus in bosco suo de Aldewerk qui est contiguus foreste domini Regis de Galtres et comodum suum inde faciendum precepit quo michi quod hoc vobis nunciarem ut sibi inde literas sub magno sigillo faciat vale.

faites faire une comissioun au Meir et a Baillif de Hertepool et Roger de Gosewyk qil facent apparailler une Neyf ouesqe seisaunte hommes bien armes et lur vitaille pur quarainte iours issint qils soient prestes yce dimaynge a vespre et le Roi les alleura sur la maletoute et de ce faites fere bref au Custumers de la maletoute.

89. Informal warrants for writs under great seal. [Chan. Warr. File 1705.]

Wygornie ffiat commissio de Cancellario Nicholao Russel de officio vicecomitis qui est in manu Regis ratione minoris etatis heredis Guidonis de bello campo nuper comitis Warrewyk Ita quod de exitu inde etcetera prestitit sacramentum in scaccario.

Sire le Roy vult qe vous maundet breef a Henri de Perci qil certifie le Rey si il eit arestut Johan de Dalton e si il soit arestuz le qele larest e set par cause de son prospre fait ou pur sa aerdaunce as autres e si pur son prospre fet adonkes pur qele fet e si pur aerdaunce pur quele aerdaunce e a qi la aerdaunce se fet.

Sire le Roy veut qe vous facez protectiouns pur monsire Wauter de Beauchaump et pur monsire Wauter de Gloucestre son fuitz.

depar Robert de Haustede.

Le Roi comande au viscont de Kent qil face auoir au Mair de Sandewyk cente homes que...Mair voile choser bien armez dimeyn apres la feste Translacion sancte Thome sanz deley.

III. SPECIAL COLLECTIONS

90. Minutes of council. [Parl. and Council Pr. (Chan.), File 4, no. 9.]

(4 Ed. II. Memoranda of arrangements for the King's expedition to Scotland.)

. . . .

Item soit fait commission au Counte de Nicole destre Gardein et lieu tenant le Roi en Engleterre tantqe...le Roi en Escoce et soit mandez aussint par brefs clos en chescun Contez Dengleterre pur le......qe chescun endende et obeisse a lui come au Gardein et lieutenant le Roy Item les ordenances faites par les ordenours soient mandez au Chaunceller et il enface brefs......contez......les dites ordenances soient gardees et tenues en touz pointz mais le......des mens Euerwyk et reserue a li voudra doner gardes et mariages.......

91. Council's endorsement to royal will. [Parl. and Council Pr. (Chan.), File 4, no. 13.]

Le Roi voet qe sire Edmund de Eyncourt sire Johan de Crumbwell et sire Johan de Hothum seient assigne de oier et de terminer auxibien pur le Roi come pur autres les trespasses qe sire Johan de Segraue et ses ministres de la foreste de la Trente et autres gentz de sa meigne par poair et auowerie de luy ont fait as plusors gentz de denz la dite foreste par reson de sa baillie tancome il fut Justice de meisme la foreste et Gardayn du Chastel de Notingham come as autres du Counte de Leycestre cest asauoir en prises cariages diuerses extorsions et autres plusors greuances et damages fetes a eux.

(Endorsed)

Il semble au conseil nostre Seigneur le Roy qe bon est qe sire Lambert de Trikingham seit assigne ouesqes eux Issi qe toutz treis ou deis de ceo entendent des queux le dit sire Lambert soit totes voies un i.

92. Petition of commonalty of England about conduct of sheriffs. [Parl. and Council Pr. (Chan.), File 4/20.]

A nostre seignour le Roi et a soun Counsail moustre la Comunialte dengleterre qe come les viscountes et suruiscountes en lour countez pernunt ffeetz Robes en pensiouns ceo est asauoir asoms pernunt sessaunte Robes et quartre vynt feez et pensiouns en meyme le Counte et ascuns dieux Centz et les suruiscountes en pernent meyme les feez Robes et pensions a plus pres come eux poient en pursiwauntz lour meistres Dount la poure people ne poient auer nule manere de reisoun ne de dreit en countre nul de ceux oue qi les auaunditz viscountes et suruiscountes sount demorretz Et neynt eiaunt regard al estatut de Nichole qe veet qe nul ne seit seneschal ne baillif ne du fee de graunt seignour qe enprendreit le office mes qil seit tiel qil pusse de tut atendre al office pur lealment le Roi et le poeple Dount la dite communialte prie al dit nostre seignour le Roi qe de ceste duresce lour seit fait remedie.

(Endorsed)

Seit fait bref as Tresorer et Barons sur le statut de Nicole et qe il le facent tenir a la sute de ceus qe se vodrent plaindre.

Irrotulatur.

Coram magno consilio.

93. Agenda of matters referred by king to council before parliament of York, 1322. [Parl. and Council Pr. (Chan.), File 5/10.]

(15 Ed. II, Memoranda of matters referred by king to Council.)

—ffait aremembre des choses souzescrites—

Ade primes de Lestatut sur le repeal des Ordenances

Item de mettre les bons pointz en Estatut

Item de remedi contre faus retours des baillifs des ffranchises

Item de ordener coment les chateus des felons et futifs an et wast deodands wrec de mer et autres tiels profitz qe ne se lieuent forsqe en Eyre peussent estre leuez de an en an al eops le Roi sicome autres seigneurages les lieuent a lour eops qe tiels profitz pernant par chartre en dantiquite

Item de mettre tutes balaunces enfyn auxibien pur vendre come pur achater car hom dist qe tutes les balaunces du Roialme sont fauses fors celes qe sont de feures a grant damage des grantz et a commun poeple

Item de redrescer tutes les mesmes de blec vin et de ceruise par tut le Roialme et de mettre confitna tours sur ceo en chescun Countee en autre garde

Item de ordener coment la mort dun homme cest plegement leuent en un Countee et mort en un autrė Countee serra venge a dreiture fait des felons

Item de remedie qe ceux qi sont appellez de felonie en un Countee de faitz qe sont fait en meisme le Countee et se alloignent hors du Contee apres lappel

Item en meisme la manere de ceux qi sont appelle par pronours de fait fait en foreins Counteez et sont troue en meisme le Contee en lappel est fait

Item de prenours qe appellent gentz demoerrantz en foreins Counteez de felonies faites en foreins Countees

Item daccourter le temps a mettre en certein de bref de dreit assiser de nouele disseine et mort dauncestre......le point de la grant Chartre qe v...qe nul chief Seigneur eyt garde del heir son tenaunt......iesqe atant qil eyt pris ou homage

Item lestaple des lenies et de ordener qe draps soient faitz en Engleterre

Item del user des riches pellures estrescer

Item de ordener remedi contre ceux qui emportent les biens des grant seigneurs et des autres quant eux gisent en lour moriant et tost apres la mort deuant qe les biens viegnant as les mains des executurs et cel cas auient souent.

Et fait asauoir qe le Roi voet qe chescun sage de son conseil soupense de ces pointz......qe peussent amender la ley pur le profist du Roi et du poeple et part eux soit accordez de les......qe serra accorde soit mis en fourme de statut ou mestier est de statut ou de faire autre remedie la ou autre remedie suffira et qe tiele chose issi mise en fourme soit monstre al Roi issint qil sen peusse...... le parlement pur plus tost deliuerer le poeple qe veignent au parlement.

94. List of council at Thorp. [Parl. and Council Pr. (Chan.), File 45/13.]

Les nouns de ceux qi furent au conseil a Thorp y ceo Lundi a Lendemeyn as oytaues de la Trinite.

Lerceuesqe Deuerwik
Leuesqe de Excetre
Labbe de Seleby[1]
Le Counte de Kent
Le Counte de Penebrok
Le Counte de Wyncestre
Le Counte Dascell
Monsire Hugh le Despenser le filz
Le Dean Deuerwik
Le Seigneur de Sully
Sire William de Ros
Sire William Latimer
Sire Henri filtz Hugh
Sire Randolf Datre
Sire ffouk le filtz Waryn
Sire Antoigne de Lucy
Sire Johan de Haryngton
Sire Simon Warde
Sirê Oliuer de Ingham
Sire Richard de Hudleston
Sire Adam de Swynlington
Sire Rauf de Cobham
Sire Hugh de Louther
Sire William Ridel
Nicholas de Langeton Meyre Deuerwik
Richard de Emeldon Meyre de Noef Chastiel sur Tyne[2]

Sire Wautier de Norwiz
Sire William de Bereford
Sire Henri Lescrop
Sire Herui de Staunton
Mestre Robert de Baldok
Sire William de Ayremynne
Sire William de Herle
Sire Roger Beler
Sire Wautier de ffriskeneye
Sire Robert de Malberthorp
Mestre Richard de Cestre
Sire Roger de Waltham
Mestre Henri de Clyff
Sire Adam de Brome
Mestre Johan de Hildresle
Gilbert de Toutheby
Geffrey Lescrop

[1] Inserted in margin. [2] A space of about an inch divides the list here.

Johan de Denom
Le Confessour nostre seigneur le Roi
William de Herlaston
Sire Johan de Weston
Sire Giles de Beauchaump
Sire Robert de Morby
Sire Johan Stormy

95. Writ of privy seal to chamberlain of North Wales about payments to troops for Scotland. [Anc. Corresp. vol. XXXII, no. 76.]

Edward par la grace de dieu Roy Dengleterre Seigneur Dirlaunde et Ducs Daquitaine a nostre Chaumberleyn de Caernaruan saluz il vous deit souener coment nous vous auoms plusures foiz auaunt ces houres maundez qe vous feissez leuer saunz delay totes les dettes qe nous sount dues dedeinz vostre baillie et qe des deners entsourdauntz et auxint des issues de mesmes vostre baillie feissez paier gages as gentz de celes parties qe vendreient deuers nous pur lespleit de nostre guerre descoce Et pur ceo qe nous auoms ia maunder les dites gentz estre a nous a Neef chastel sur tyne la veille de seint Jake prochein auener vous maundoms et chargeoms fermement enioignantz qe vous lour facez prestement paier lour gages tanqe iloeqes issint qil ne seient delaiez ne nous deserniz par vostre defaute Qar sachez qe sils ne y veignent mye prestement au dit iour nous nous tendroms estre deceuz par vous Done souz nostre priue seal a Hathelseie le xvj iour de Juyn lan de nostre Regne quinzisme.

96. Draft of writ of privy seal ordering withdrawal of a suit from ecclesiastical court. [Anc. Corresp. vol. XXXII, no. 91.]

Edward par la grace de dieu Roy Dengleterre Seigneur Dirlande et Ducs Daquitaine a son cher et foyal Johan de ffereres salutz Por ceo qe nous auoms entendu qe vous un plai de lai fee dount la conissance apent purement a nostre Curt suez en la curt crestiene ver Thomas Conte de Lancastre en grand preiudice de nous et de nostre Reaume a blemissement de nostre Corone e de nostre dignete Royale as queux sauuer meintenir e garder vous estes tenuz a liez par le serement qe vous nous auez fait vous mandoms e enioignoms en le homage qe vous nous auez fait e la foi qe vous nous deuez e le cerement auandyt e sur forfeture de quantqe vous nous poez forfere qe vous par vous ne par autre le dyt play ne suez en la Curt crestiene auantdite e si nule suite enauez fait ou mande a faire sanz delay le repelez a faitz repeler E vous meismes soyez deuant nous a trois simoines de la seint Michel ou qe nous seoms pur fere e receuire en les choses auantdites ceo qe droit enserra E nous adunqes serroms prestz de vous fere dreit en cele busoigne si auant come le conissance apent a nous e a nostre Curt E eyez illoeqes cest bref.

97. Writ of privy seal sent to William Inge to attend to a commission of oyer and terminer notwithstanding other orders. [Anc. Corresp. vol. XXXII, no. 110.]

Edward par la grace de dieu Roi Dengleterre Seigneur Dirlande et ducs Daquitaine a nostre cher et foial monsire William de Inge saluz

Come nous eoms assignez vous ensemblement oue aucuns noz autres foiaux noz Justices a oir et terminer aucuns trespas nadgaires par les gentz de la ville de Lenne faitz a nostre cher et foial monsire Robert de Mouhaut a ce qest dit et nous desiroms qe cele busoigne feut haste tant com hom purra bonement vous mandoms qe sanz nul delay entendez a perfaire la dite busoigne selonc la ley et lusage de nostre Roiaume nouncontrestant queuqe autre mandement qe nous vous eoms fait auant ces houres Donne souz nostre priue seal a Westmoster le xxvj iour de Nouembre Lan de nostre regne septisme.

98. Letters of credence to pope for royal messenger. [Anc. Corresp. vol. XXXII, no. 120.]

A Lapostoille de par le Roi Dengleterre salutz etcetera Sire nous enueoms a la presence de vostre sayntete Maistre Raymond de Pyns nostre chier et ame clerc et consaillier et vous prioms qe vous le vueillez oir benignement et piablement crerre de ce quil vous dirra de par nous vaille vostre sayntete etcetera Donne a Canterbire le xx Jour de ffeuerer Lan etcetera.

99. Writ of privy seal ordering deposit of charters in wardrobe. [Anc. Corresp. vol. XXXII, no. 140.]

Edward par la grace de dieu Roy Dengleterre Seigneur Dirlaunde et Ducs Daquitayne a nostre bien ame Meistre Robert de Leycet saluz Nous vous mandoms qe totes les chartres lettres escritz et autres monumentz qe vous auez en garde et qe touchent le chastel de Lumole nous facez hastiuement venir issint qe nous les eioms en nostre Garderobe a la quinzeine de ceste seint Michel procheinement auenir ou qe nous seioms en Engleterre Et ce ne leissez en nule maniere Donne souz nostre priue seal a Clipston le xvj iour de Septembre Lan de nostre regne primier.

100. Letters from town of Bristol to king informing him of action of baronial opposition. [Anc. Corresp. vol. XXXIII, nos. 58 and 59.]

A lur tresnoble et treslige seigneur Sire Edward par la grace de dieu Roi Dengleterre Seigneur Dirlaunde et Ducs Daquitaine les seons liges gentz Mair et la Communalte de sa ville de Bristut humblement soi recommendunt Tresnoble nostre seigneur vous fasoms a sauer qe ycest Lundi le xxvj^{me} jour de Maij drein passe le Counte de Hereford et les autres Barouns de ses allietz nous maunderunt par un frere Menur qe nous donassoms foi et creaunce a lui de ceo qil nous dirroit de bouche saunz lettre de par eux et seigneur la creaunce fust ycele quele nous vous enuoiomz enclose deintz ceste lettre de quele chose il vodroit son respouns auoir de vous qil porreit certe fier au dit Counte et les Barouns entre cy et Jeodi en la feste de la Asseencion et nous ne volums seigneur de ceo respoums doner suaunt qe nous sachoms vostre volunte endroit de ceste chose maiz garderoms bien et sauuement vostre dite ville a vostre eops guei aueigne si deu plest Par quei tresnoble seigneur si vous plest de ceste chose voillez estre et volunte de ceo a nous commaunder Le seigneur tut pussaunt vous sauue lige seigneur et gard a touz iours.

Le Lundi prochein auaunt la feste de seint Austin Lan du regne le Roi Edward quatourzime vynt frere Morice de Penkoyt en countre sa volunte maunde par le Counte de Hereford monsire Rogier de Mortymer le unkle monsire Rogier de Mortimer le neuew monsire Rogier Damory monsire Morice de Berkeleigh et les autres Barouns de lur allietz et fist a sauer au Mair et autres bones gentz de Bristut qe les auauntditz Countes et Barouns lur maund a sauer par lui qe pur lur preu et lur profist qil veoillent garder la ville qe nuls gentz de armes nomenient aliens ne entrunt pur peril qe porreit auenir a nostre seigneur le Roi et a eux mesmes E qil sei veoillent ensurer les Counte et Barouns auauntditz sil veoillent estre de lur assent pur commun profist du Roi et du Realme et euz sei veoillent ensurer deuers la ville en quele manere qeux veoillent mesmes ordenier qe par encheson de eux nul mal nauerunt maiz lur garderunt de mal en contre toutez gentz solomc lur poier Dautrepart veoillent remembrer de quel poier et de quele alliaunce il sunt de quele volunte et grant qil sount il trouerent bien qe ceo serra pur profist du Roi et du Roialme et pur ceo no soient il pas dussuz par nules promesses de nullui de contreestier les auauntnomez E veoillent prendre garde comment celui qe auoit le Chastel en garde sei euala et lessa le dist chastel saunz garde si noun de trois hommes et ceo aliens dount autres poireint legerement entrier cei damage et huntage de nostre seigneur le Roi E de ceste chose veoillent remaunder lur volunte par le dist frere ou ascun de eux mesme par lettre de souz lur seal.

101. Letter from earl of Lancaster to king enclosing indenture. [Anc. Corresp. vol. XXXIV, no. 306.]

A son treshonurable seigneur si lui plest par le soen Conte de Lancestre quantque seet et poet donurs er reuerences Trescher sire nous resceusmes voz lettres de creance a nostre Chastel de Donynton la dymenge prochein apres la feste seint Luke et auoms en tendre sire ce qe sire William de Melton et monsire Hugh Daudele nous ont dit depar vous et enuoioms trescher sire a vostre hautesce cy de denz un escrowet de nostre response endentez a la dite creance qe nous semble a nostre entendement pur le myelz Trescher sire nostre seigneur vous gard touz iours en honur Escrit a nostre Chastel de Donynton le xx iour Doctobre.

Endenture

Endroit de ce qe nostre seigneur le Roine entent poynt qe les grantz seigneurs ne se apparaillent point de venir vers le North a lor custages sicome feust parle a Nichole pur le commun profit du Roialme il semble au Counte qil ne sauera mye bien consoiller sur cel taunt quil eyent en certeyn responduz a nostre seigneur le Roi.

Endroit des assemblees qe les grantz seigneurs fount Il semble au dit Counte qe nostre seigneur le Roi ne deit de ce faire force si ce ne feust a damage de lui ou de son Roialme la queu chose il nentent pas qe soit et sil entend fist il le feroit a sauer a nostre seigneur le Roi et le destourberoit a la meilloure manere quil porrent

Endroit de ce qe le Tresorer ad responduz quil nad mye deners a trouer custages a nostre seigneur le Roi pur sa a...deuers la North cest yuer Il semble au dit Counte qe aussibien p...nostre seigneur le Roi faire myses deuers North come deuers de Suth Et feust ensi entenduz qe la demoere deuers le North ne deust mye estre...qil ne puissent endurer Car lent de la force de la feust qe nostre seigneur le Roi et les Barons...rerent le forte par bref garnissement.

Et le dit Counte fait assauoir a nostre seigneur le Roi qun est prest a demeoer vers le North en le manere qe le granta as Nicole........

102. Letter from earl of Lancaster to king on behalf of countess of Warwick. [Anc. Corresp. vol. XXXIV, no. 107.]

A son treshonurable seigneur depar son Counte de Lancestre quantquil siet et poer donurs et de reuerences Treschier sire pur ceo qe nous auoms entenduz par la Countesse de Warrewyk qe les dames et des damoyseles de sa Chambre et les gentz de son houstel sount attachez par vostre Eschetour de cea Trente pur laloignance la damoisele de Milton de Gillesland la quele se esloigna de son enidegre a ceo qe nous auoms entendu Par quoi trescher sire a vostre hautesce requerroms quil vous plest ceaux attachementez relesser etcetera dommander le triement de cel bosoigne selonc les loys et les usages de nostre Roialme Trescher sire nostre seigneur vous garde en bone vie et longe Escrit a nostre Chastel de Donynton le xxiij iour Doctobre.

103. Certification by exchequer to king in reply to writ of privy seal. [Anc. Corresp. vol. XXXV, no. 27.]

Treshonurable et tresredoute Seigneur vous nous mandastes nadgers par brief de vostre priue seal donne a Notingham le vij iour de Juyl darrein passe qe nous vous certifisoms soutz le seal de vostre dit Escheqier de combien vous solier estre respoundu par an a vostre dit Escheqier pur la baillie du fee de Peuerell en les Countez de Notingham et de Derby Sur quoi pleise a vostre hautesce sauoir qe serchez les roules et remembraunces de meisme vostre Escheqier auoms troueer qe vous auez este respoundre a vostre dit Escheqier de quatorze marcs par an de la ferme et la baillie des honurs de Peuerell es les Countez de Notingham et de Derby par Johan de Dunesley nadgaires baillif illoeqes trescher seigneur dieu vous doun bone vie et longe et encresce voz honurs Escrit a Euerwyk le xxviij iour de Juyl.

104. Letter from council on commissions for taxors. [Anc. Corresp. vol. XXXV, no. 46.]

Sire ie vous enuoi deux peire de lettres encloses denz cestes qe une vindrent du Conte de Warrewyk et pur ce quil semble a nous du consail nostre seignur le Roy par decea qe bon est a faire la priere le Conte pur mult des resunz vous pri si vous plaist facez faire deux noueles commissions en noun des iiij taxours ausi come est dessous escrit

In comitatu Wigornie — Dominus Robertus de Bracy
Osebertus de Apetoft

In comitatu Warrewyk Robertus de Stok
Thomas de Garshale

Et enuoiez me sire ceux briefs si enhaste come vous poez qar le ceus est mult court Nostre seigneur vous ait en sa garde

Escrit a Londres le iour de La Tiphayne matin.

105. Letter from earl of Cornwall to chancellor requesting writs. [Anc. Corresp. vol. xxxv, no. 56.]

Al honorable pierre en dieu Sire Johan par la grace de dieu Euesqe de Cicestre Chancelier nostre seigneur le Roy Pieres de Gauastoun Conte de Cornewaille salutz Honeurs et treschers amistez Sire nous vous prioms especialment qe vous sil vous plest nous voilletz faire auoir deux briefs par le portor de cestes solom ceo qe vous porretz voir par la peticioun qe nous vous enuoioms enclose dedenz cestes si faire le poetz par reson Sire Nostre seigneur vous gard Donne a Knaresbourgh Le vj iour de Nouembre.

106. Warrant for a commission of oyer and terminer. [Anc. Corresp. vol. xxxv, no. 68 A.]

Norhampton Assignentur Petrus Malorre Willelmus Buteneleyn et Johannes Louel de Suttescumbe Justiciarii ad inquirendum audiendum et terminandum qui malefactores et pacis perturbatores insultum fecerunt in Willelmum Poy et in Ricardum de Esseby Pellinarum et ipsos verbauerunt wulnerauerunt et felonice interfecerunt apud Norhampton et de eorum fautoribus receptatoribus vim et auxilium prebentibus et de aliis circumstanciis etcetera Et non dicatur in breui contra pacem nostram set contra pacem tantum quia felonia facta fuit tempore patris Regis nunc Et fiat breue patens modo quo debet fieri in omnibus set quod fiat mencio quod si omnes interesse non possint tunc Petrus Malorre cum uno eorum procedat etcetera Et fiat breue clausum vicecomiti Norhamptonscire quod ad certos dies et loca etcetera Et quod eis sit intendens etcetera pro deo bene expediantur et sient facta breuia.

107. Letter from earl of Gloucester, king's lieutenant, to chancellor ordering prohibition of tournament. [Anc. Corresp. vol. xxxv, no. 93.]

Al honurable piere en deu et son cher ami sire Wauter par la grace de dieu Euesqe de Wyrecestre Chancellier nostre seigneur le Roi Gilbert de Clare Counte de Gloucestre et de Hertford saluz et cheres amistez ffait nous est entendant qe aucune gentz vient ioustier a Thorrok es parties Dessex ycest Lundy prochein auenir Par quoi vous prioms qe vous facez mander au visconte de Essex quil aille en propre persone et face defendre par sa baillie sur forfaiture de qantqe hom purra forfaire deuers nostre seigneur le Roi qe nul homme ne soit si hardi de iouster tornoier bordoier ne autre fait darmes haunter ne faire priueement ne apertement taunt comme nostre seigneur le Roi est en sa guerre descoce sanz especial congie de li Nostre sire vous gard Escrite a Augre le xv jour Daueril.

108. Writ of privy seal to council to reply to letters from constable of France. [Anc. Corresp. vol. xxxv, no. 126.]

Edward par la grace de dieu Roi Dengleterre Seigneur Dirlaunde et Ducs Daquitaine A noz chers et foialx lonurable piere en dieu Wauter par la meisme grace Erceuesqe de Canterbire Primat de tote Engleterre monsire Thomas Counte de Lancastre nostre cher cousin et noz autres bones gentz de nostre conseil a Loundres salutz Nous vous enueoms enclose deinz cestes lettres deuz peire de lettres qe nous sont venues de monsire Gauchelin de Castellion Conestable de ffrance Et vous mandoms qe entendues meismes les lettres ordeinez de faire tieu respounse au dit Conestable et de mettre tieu conseil et remedie sur les choses qe sont contenues es dites lettres come vous verrez qe soit a honur et profit de nous et de nostre Roiaume Donne souz nostre priue seal a Oueston le xv iour de Marz Lan de nostre regne Neuisme.

109. Letter from earl of Lancaster to chancellor requesting that only his nominees should be included in a commission. [Anc. Corresp. vol. xxxv, no. 155.]

A sages homme et soun cher amy sire Johan de Sandal Chaunceler nostre seignur le Roy Thomas Counte de Lancastre et de Leicestre Seneschal Dengleterre salutz et treschers amitez Pur ce sire qe nous auoms prie a nostre seignur le Roy qil voille assigner monsire Johan de Hastang monsire Willeime de Datre monsire Hugh de Louthre et monsire Willeime de Trussel de Notehurst denquere de la mort nostre cher et bien ame souereyn vallet Johan de Swynnerton a ceux qil trouroit coupables doir et terminer de cel mort vous prioms sire cherementes qe nul bref ne ysse pur la deliuerrance de nuli recte de cel mort a altre Justice forsqe a les auantnomez Et ceste chose sire ne voillez lesser pur lamor de nous Done a nostre Chastel de Donynton le dirrein iour de Septembre.

110. Letter from earl of Pembroke to chancellor, ordering, on king's behalf, a writ of liberate. [Anc. Corresp. vol. xxxv, no. 168.]

Al honurable piere en dieu sire Johan par la grace de dieu Euesqe de Wincestre et Chaunceler nostre seigneur le Roy Aymar de Valence Counte de Pembrok seigneur de Wesiak et de Mountignak saluz et bone amour de nostre seignur Nous vous maundoms depar nostre seignur le Roi qe vous facez un liberate au Tresorier de xx mars les queux nostre dit seignur le Roi ad assigne ala dame de ffernyngdraght pur sa sustenaunce tauntqe autre chose soit ordeine de son estat A dieu seigneure qui vous gard.

111. Informal warrant to chancery for issue of writs. [Anc. Corresp. vol. xxxvi, no. 155.]

Sires Pur ceo qe Williame Cokerel de Hadleye en suffouk qi fuist enditez des Parks nostre seygneur le Roy de Hangleye en la Counte de Suffouk auauntdist e de Berdefeld en le Counte Dessex ad fet un fin deuers le dist nostre seygneur le Roy Le Roy voet qe a quel houre qe le dist Williame ou autre depar luy vous porte la fourme de son enditement qe vous luy facez sa chartre tiele cume aplot de lendictement auauntdit E ausint sires qil eyt Bref au viscounte Dessex qil soyt deliures hors de prisoun Sires ceste chose voillet faire si en haste come vous purretz pur lamour de moy Sires nostre seigneur vous doyne bone vie et lunge.

112. Writ of secret seal to William de Ayremynne explaining king's action. [Anc. Corresp. vol. xxxvi, no. 209.]

Edward par la grace de dieu Roi Dengleterre Seigneur Dirlaunde et Ducs Daquitaine a nostre cher clerc William de Ayremynne saluz Nous vous sauoms moit bon gre de la diligence et pemblece qe vous mettez en noz busoignes deuers vous et vous prioms et chargeoms especialment qe ce continuez sicome nous nous fioms de vous Et si par cas diuerse nouelle vous veigne de ce qe nous nous treoms vers les parties de Gloucestre ne le chargez Car nous ne sauoms nouelle de celes parties ne de aillours deuers nous si bone noun dieux mercy mes aloms laundroites pur veer le pays et chiuaucer nostre terre sicome feust acordez auaunt vostre departir de nous Donne souz nostre secre seal a Westmoustre le primer iour de Marz Lan de nostre regne xiiiime.

113. Informal summons to a council. [Anc. Corresp. vol. xxxvii, no. 88.]

Sire sache ie nostre seignur le Roy me mande par monsire Hugh le Despenser yceo Mardi deuers le vespre qe ieo vous mandasse hastiuement depar lui qe vous fussez en toutes maneres y ceo Mescredi a oure de prime as freres Prechours a Londres pur parler de aucunes bosoignes qe sunt hastiues les queles il ad charge le dit monsire Hugh de vous dire E pur ceo sire ne voillez en nule manere lesser qe vous ny seiez adonqes Nostre seignur vous gard.

114. Anonymous letter about ordinances. [Anc. Corresp. vol. xxxvii, no. 110.]

Trescher sire por ce qe ie obliay her de vous enueer lordenance faite par les ordenours quant ie vous enueay la lettre et le roule souz le priue seal pur la grant presse quil y auoit entre nous si vous enuoy ie meisme lordenance en close deinz ceste lettre Trescher sire nostre seigneur vous eit en sa garde Escrit a Suleby le tierz iour de Augst.

115. Writ of privy seal to count of Flanders recommending business of valet. [Anc. Corresp. vol. xlv, no. 144.]

Edward par la grace de dieu Roi Dengleterre Seigneur Dirlaunde et Ducs Daquitaine a noble homme nostre trescher amy monsire Robert Counte de ffiaundres saluz Nous recomendoms a vous especiaument nostre cher vadlet Giles de la Mote et vous prioms affectuousement qe en les busoignes qe nostre dit vadlet ad afaire deuers vous par reson du fied quil tient de vous li voillez faire la grace et la bounte qe vous porrez bonement pur amour de nous en tieu manere qe nostre dit vallet puisse sentir qe ceste nostre requeste li vaille Donne souz nostre priue seal a Certeseye le secund iour de Septembre Lan de nostre regne secund.

116. Writ of privy seal to earl of Lincoln to summon council to consider affairs of Aquitaine. [Anc. Corresp. vol. XLV, no. 149.]

Edward par la grace de dieu Roi Dengleterre Seigneur Dirlaunde et Ducs Daquitaine a nostre cher coson et foial monsire Henri de Lacy Conte de Nicole saluz Nous vous enueoms sealle de nostre priue seal un Roule contenant plusours articles des choses qe nous touchent en la dite duchee et vous mandoms qe a vostre primere venue a Londres apres ceste precheine seint Michiel facez assembler nostre grant consail cest asauoir nostre Chanceller Tresorer Justices Barons de nostre Eschekier et autres de nostre consail et facez examiner bien et diligeaument les ditz articles et a chescun dyceux ordenez entre vous et eux si bon et si couenable remedie comme vous sauerez et porez et comme vous verrez qe face affaire a honeur et a profit de nous Donne souz nostre priue seal a Neumostre le viij iour de Septembre Lan de nostre regne quart.

117. Writ of privy seal to council at London about sale of wardship. [Anc. Corresp. vol. XLV, no. 165.]

Edward par la grace de dieu Roi Dengleterre Seigneur Dirlaunde et Ducs Daquitaine a noz chers et foiaux les bones gentz de nostre conseill a Loundres saluz Nous vous mandoms qe la garde des terres ne le mariage de heir monsire Johan ap Adam ne de sa compaigne ne vendez a monsire Hugh le Despenser ne a autre tantqe a nostre prochein parlement apres ceste touz seintz et si vous les eiez venduz au dit monsire Hugh ou a autre sanz delay facez repeller la dite vente issint qe nule nouellete ne soit fait auant nostre parlement auantdit Donne souz nostre priue seal a Westmouster le xxvij iour Doctobre lan de nostre regne quint.

118. Writ of privy seal to earl of Pembroke and Hugh le Despenser ordering letters of acquittance for money paid into chamber. [Anc. Corresp. vol. XLV, no. 171.]

Edward par la grace de dieu Roi Dengleterre Seigneur Dirlaunde et Ducs Daquitaine a noz chers et foiaux monsire Aymer de Valence Conte de Pembrok nostre Cousin et monsire Hugh le Despenser saluz Por ce qe nous auions mie plente de deniers ore a par meismes deuers nous si auoms receu en nostre Chambre de nostre bien amez Alexandre de Compton nostre Gardein des manoirs des Templers es Contez de Leycestre et de Warrewyk quarante mars des issues des ditz manoirs de vous mandoms qe des ditz deniers li facez auoir noz lettres daquittance en due fourme Donne souz nostre priue seal a Wundesore le xxiij iour de Nouembre Lan de nostre regne sisme.

119. Writ of secret seal to earl of Pembroke to issue writ. [Anc. Corresp. vol. XLV, no. 176.]

Edward par la grace de dieu Roi Dengleterre Seigneur Dirlaunde et Ducs Daquitaine a nostre cher cousin monsire Aymar de Valence Cunte de Penbrok saluz Purceo qe vous nous mandastes de la chose qe nous grauntames a Note de la Dose a tenir a nostre volunte qe vous est auis qe ceo est nostre profit qil la eit a terme de sa vie vous mandoms qe nous voloms qil la eit a terme de sa vie et de ceo qe vous luy facez auoir ses lettres solenc ceo qe apent Donne souz nostre secre seal au Park de Wyndesore le vij iour de may lan de nostre regne sisme.

120. Writ of privy seal to earls of Richmond and Hereford to consider and advise with archbishop of Canterbury on payment of a debt. [Anc. Corresp. vol. XLV, no. 186.]

Edward par la grace de dieu Roi Dengleterre Seigneur Dirlaunde et Ducs Daquitaine a noz chiers et feaux monsire Johan de Bretagne Conte de Richemond nostre cher Cousin et monsire Hunfrey de Bohun Conte de Hereford et de Essex nostre cher frere saluz Comme auant ces heures nous vous eussiens charge que vous regardissiez que on feist a la dame de felinges raison et grace de sa demande de la debte que nous deuiens a son seigneur si que nostre honneur y feust et sur a vous nous aiez rescript par voz lettres que il semble as Contes de Pembrok Warrewyk Aroundel et a vous que nous estiens tenuz par raison de ce que son seigneur se mist du tout hors de souspecon quant il morust en nostre seruice et que nostre Tresorier a respondu que il ne puet sa besoigne esploiter sanz garant et que nostre chancelier neu uuont garaunt faire sanz nostre commandement sicomme en voz dites lettres plus plainement est contenuz Nous vous mandoms que vous veez par bon auisement dentre lonurable pere en dieu Lerceuesque de Canterbire et vous combien nous soumes tenuz a paier a la dite dame de la dite debte a faire raison a li y a deschara nostre conscience en ce cas aianz requart a toutes les choses que y appartiennent a charger en deuue maniere Et de la somme dargente que nous li serons tenuz a paier par lauisement dessus dit facez dire a nostre dit Chancelier depar nous que il face brief de garant a nostre dit Tresorier tiel comme appartient en ce cas Donne souz le seal nostre trescher Compaigne Reine Dengleterre pour ce que nous nauiens pas nostre priue seal empris de nous quant ces lettres furent faites au Park de Wyndesore le xvj jour de Marz Lan de nostre regne huitisme.

(Endorsed)

Mestre Johan de Weston Chaumberleyn Descoce testmoigna ceste chose Westmoustre le septisme iour de May deuant Lerceueske les Contes de Richemond Hereford Pembrok et Warewyk.

121. Writ of privy seal to treasurer enclosing letter on which he is to ordain. [Anc. Corresp. vol. XLV, no. 188.]

Edward par la grace de dieu Roi Dengleterre Seignour Dirlaunde et Ducs Daquitaine a nostre cher et foial monsire Wautier de Norwiz nostre Tresorer salutz Nous vous enuoioms unes lettres qe nous vyndrent de Bonifaz de Salutz tochaunt le droit de nostre chapelle de Tikhull vous maundoms qe de la dite lettre yordenez ce qe vous verrez qe mieltz soit pur nostre droit et honeur sauuer et qe le dit Boniface ysoit mys en possession de sa eglise sicome il deuera estre de droit Donne souz nostre secre seal a Langele Le utisme iour Daust Lan de nostre Regne Neofyme.

122. Writ of secret seal to earl of Pembroke to remedy a matter with council. [Anc. Corresp. vol. XLV, no. 207.]

Edward par la grace de dieu Roi Dengleterre Seigneur Dirlaunde et Ducs Daquitaine A nostre cher cosin et foial Aymer de Valence Counte de Pembrok saluz Trescher cosin nous vous eneuoms ci dedeinz enclose une lettre qe nous vint de noz burgeys de Rauenese-rodde quele nostre bien amez Robert Heleward portour de cestes nous porta et vous maundoms qe regardee la dite lettre et oy pleinement ce qe le dit portour vous voudra dire outre touchaunt la dite busoigne facez ordeiner od nostre conseil deuers vous tiele remede come vous verrez qe fait affaire selonc droit et reson issint qe par colour de damager les flemmeyns hom ne face mie tieles duresces as marchauntz venauntz en nostre roialme Donne souz nostre secre seal a Pount-freint le xij iour de ffeuerer Lan de nostre regne xvj^{me}.

123. Writ of privy seal to earl of Pembroke, Hugh le Despenser, John de Sandale to ordain for better ordering of king's followers. [Anc. Corresp. vol. XLIX, no. 15.]

Edward par la grace de dieu Roi Dengleterre Seigneur Dirlaunde et Ducs Daquitaine A noz chers et foiaux monsire Aymer de Valence Conte de Pembrok nostre cher Cousin monsire Hugh le Despenser et Johan de Sandale saluz Por ce qe nous auoms cy grantz pleintes de ce qe nostre meignee nest mye sustenue ne nostre sale tenue sicome aferoit dont il nous poys durement vous mandoms et chargeoms qe vous regardez et ordenez coment nostre dite meignee puisse mieltz estre sustenue Issint qe ce soit honurs a nous Et en nule manere ne leissez qe ceste chose en soit faite si en haste come vous purrez Donne souz nostre priue seal a Wyndesore le xvij iour de Nouembre Lan de nostre regne sysme.

124. Writ of secret seal to earl of Pembroke on public and private business. [Anc. Corresp. vol. XLIX, no. 21.]

Edward par la grace de dieu Roi Dengleterre Seigneur Dirlaunde et Ducs Daquitaine A nostre cher et bien ame Cosin monsire Aymer de Valence Counte de Pembrok saluz Endroit de ceo qe vous nous suez mandez par voz lettres qe il resemble bien a nostre cher Neueu le Counte de Gloucestre qe nous mandames por le Cardinal et Leuesqe de Peiters quil feuissent a nous iceo Lundy a Shene Vous mandoms qe nous ne puissoms mander par enchesoun qe nous ne sumes mais priuement oue deux bachilliers Par quei vous mandoms qe vous ordenez leuesqe de Wyrcestre ou acun autre depar nous qe puisse la message faire Issint qe les ditz Cardinal et Leuesqe soient a nous as ditz lieu et iour Endroit de la grade et mariage qe vous nous auez priez del heir monsire Johan de Benstede vous mandoms qe nous le vouchoms bien sauue en vous qar ceo qe vous auez nous le tenouns bien tout nostre Et nule rien ne nous grere meis ceo qe la chose est si petyt Donne souz nostre secre seal au Park de Wyndesores le xxvj iour de Janeuoir Lan de nostre regne vj.

125. Writ of privy seal to earl of Pembroke summoning him to a preliminary meeting of council before parliament. [Anc. Corresp. vol. XLIX, no. 23.]

Edward par la grace de dieu Roi Dengleterre Seigneur Dirlande et Ducs Daquitaine a nostre cher Cousin et foial monsire Aymar de Valence Conte de Pembrok saluz Trescher cousin pur ce qe nous voloms auoir conseil et auisement de vous et daucuns autres des priuez de nostre conseil auant nostre prochein parlement sur les bosoignes qe se deuerent treter et faire a meisme nostre parlement vous prioms et chargeoms sicome nous nous fioms de vous qe vous soiez a nous a Certeseye le Lundy prochein apres la feste de Lexaltacion de la seinte croiz procheine auenir pur parler et treiter des les bosoignes auantdites Et ce en nulle manere ne leissez Donne souz nostre priue seal a Wyndesore le xxviij iour Daugst Lan de nostre regne septisme.

126. Writ of privy seal summoning earl of Pembroke to king to give advice. [Anc. Corresp. vol. XLIX, no. 34.]

Edward par la grace de dieu Roi Dengleterre Seigneur Dirlaunde et Ducs Daquitaine A nostre cher cousin et foial monsire Aymer de Valence Counte de Pembrok saluz Trescher cousin por ce qe nous auoms totes foitz trouez vostre conseil bon et profitable es choses qe nous auoms en affaire et nous auoms a exploiter aores aucunes grosses busoignes es queux nous voudtiens auoir vostre conseil et vostre auisement vous prioms trescher cousin et chargeoms especiament qe veues cestes lettres totes autres choses lessees voillez venir a nous a Westmoustre si en haste come vous porrez pur nous conseiller sur noz busoignes auant dites Et ce ne voillez lesser pur amour de nous Donne souz nostre priue seal a Westmoustre le xj iour de May lan de nostre regne neuisme.

127. Writ of secret seal to earl of Pembroke to give credence to royal messenger. [Anc. Corresp. vol. XLIX, no. 51.]

Edward par la grace de dieu Roy Dengleterre Seigneur Dirlaunde et Ducs Daquitaine a nostre cher Cousin et foial Le Counte de Pembrok salutz Trescher Cousin nous enuoions a vous nostre cher Clerk William de Cusance portour de cestes de vous monstrer depart nous ascunes choses dount nous lui auons chergez a qi voillez foi et creaunce doner de ceo qil vous dirra depar nous Donne souz nostre secre seal le darrein iour Daugst Lan de nostre regne xv[me].

128. Letter from treasurer to chamberlains to pay writ of liberate. [Anc. Corresp. vol. L, no. 25.]

Gautier Reynaud Tresorer nostre seignur le Roy as Chamberlayns del Escheker saluz Jeo vous mand qe quele oure qe les ffreres Prechours et Menours de Oxeneford et de Cantebrigge vous portent brief de Liberate del argent qil sunt acoustume de receuoir al Escheker a cest terme de la saint Michiel qe vous les facez paier issint qil ne soient delaie A dieu qe vous gard Escrit a Roucestre le v iour doctobre en lan du Regne nostre seignur le Roy Edward secund.

129. Letter from treasurer to chamberlains to pay money to wardrobe. [Anc. Corresp. vol. L, no. 38.]

Johan de Sandale Tresorer nostre seigneur le Roi as Chaumberleins de Lescheker saluz Nous vous mandoms qe hastiuement veues cestes lettres facez enueer par sire William Druel portour de cestes quatre Centz liures pur les despens del hostel nostre seigneur le Roi auantdit enchargeant sire Ingelard de Warle Tresorer de la Garderobe nostre dit seigneur le Roi en due fourme Escrit a Northampton le xxx iour de Juil Lan du regne nostre dit seigneur le Roi quart.

130. Letter from treasurer to chamberlains ordering payment to be charged to wardrobe. [Anc. Corresp. vol. L, no. 39.]

Johan de Sandale Tresorier nostre seigneur le Roi aş Chamberleins de Leschekier nostre dit seigneur saluz Je vous mank qe veues ces lettres facez liueree au portour de cestes xx mars en partie de deners qe hom deit a William de Tolouse pur cheuaux achatez de li al oeps le Roi Et enchargez sire Ingelard de Warlee Gardein de la Garderobe nostre dit seigneur le Roi Et ce ne soit leissez A dieu qui vous gard Escrit a Northampton le xxxj iour de Juyl.

131. Letter from treasurer to steward of household and treasurer of wardrobe to allow expenses of messenger conveying money. [Anc. Corresp. vol. L, no. 41.]

A noz chers amis monsire Barthelomeu de Badelsmere seneschal nostre seigneur le Roi et sire Rogier de Northburgh Tresorer de sa Garderobe Johan par la suffrance de dieu Euesqe de Wyncestre Tresorer meisme nostre seigneur le Roi salutz come a nous meismes oue la beneiceon de dieu et la nostre Nous vous enueons par Johan de Egmere portour de cestes deux mille et cink centz marts al oeps le Roi et lui auoms fait liuerer douze marcs sur le cariage faire et sur ses despenses et pur ceo qe le chemyn est molt perillouse si lui coment il lower gentz par faire sauf condut selonc ceo qe il est charge depar nous vous prioms qe vous eiez regard a ceo la et lui facez allower totes choses resonablement Nostre seigneur vous gard Escrite a Loundres le xiij iour de Juyl.

132. Informal warrant to exchequer ordering payment to Friscobaldi. [Anc. Corresp. vol. L, no. 114.]

Salutz Jeo vous maunk depar nostre seigneur le Roi qe endreit de $m^{l}m^{l}m^{l}$ mars ou populus qe sount en Tresorie facez liurer vewes cestes lettres a Lapin de la compaignie de ffriscombaud les $m^{l}m^{l}m^{l}$ mars en partie de paemente de ceo qest due a la compaignie de ffriscombaud et x^{m} mars Et le m^{l} mars qe demorent outre facez garder tantqe ieo y veigne pur les despens del hostel nostre seigneur le Roi Et ceste chose ne lessez en nule manere qar nostre seigneur le Roi la me ad comaunde A dieu Escrites a Wymedlon le xxv iour de Mai.

133. Informal warrant to exchequer ordering payment to keeper of wardrobe. [Anc. Corresp. vol. L, no. 115.]

Salutz Jeo vous maunk depar le Roi qe vous facez liurer a sire Ingelard Gardeyn de la Garderobe m^{l} mar issint quil le eit uncore ceste noite Et ce ne lessez en nule manere Nostre seigneur vous garde Escrites a Kenynton le xxvj iour de May.

134. Letter to earl of Kent advising that orders under the great and privy seals only be executed. [Anc. Corresp. vol. LIV, no. 17.]

Salutz et chers amistez.

Nous vous engarnisoms et auisoms qe vous ne tiegnez nuly seal ne mandement qe vous poet venir pur garant a faire noueltez dont damage preiudice si en nul peril poent estre au Roi ou a sa terre ou vous estes si noun le mandement nostre dit seigneur le Roi par son grant seal ou le priue et ensi est il bion qe vous garnisatz touz ceux qe ont gardes en la terre ou vous estes Et tiegnez cestes choses et diez a touz ceux as queux vous les dirrez qeux le tiegnent secrees A dieux etcetera Escritz a Eltham le xxj iour de Juyn.

William Latimer
Johan de Wisham
Lembergh[1]
Monsire Rauf Basset de Drayton } Au Counte de Kent.
Monsire Rauf de Cobham
Sire Adam de Lymbergh

135. Petition from knights of shire and commonalty of land that justices be appointed to take fines from rebels. [Ancient Petition, no. 3955.]

A nostre seigneur le Roy priount les Chiualers des Countez et tote la Commune de sa terre qe luy pleyse de sa grace assigner auskuys Justices de prendre fyn de touz ceux qe furount aerdaunz a ces Rebelles et Enemys qe vodrount venir de gree et conustre laerdaunce et faire fyn au Roi pur lur trespas......lur power et la quantite de lur terres et par tieu manere porra le Roi hastiuement auoir graunt profist et se commune de sa terre estre esee.

(Endorsed)
Auis est au conseil si il plest au Roi qe ceo serreit afaire.
Coram Rege.

136. Letters patent under privy seal acknowledging debt and assigning payment. [Ancient Petition, no. 4426.]

Edward par la grace de dieu Roi Dengleterre Seigneur Dirlaunde et Ducs Daquitaine a touz ceaux qui cestes lettres verrount saluz Sachez nous estre tenuz a nostre cher marchaund Wautier de Gosewyk Burgeys de Berewyk sur Twede en treis Centz liures qe nous receumes de lui de prest et Cent et vint et cynk mars les queux il emprist a paer pur nous a monsire Roger de Moubray des queux soumes nous voloms et grauntoms qe le dit Wauter soit paez des primeres issues de la graunt custume de Hertelpol Entesmoignance de queu chose nous auoms fait faire cestes noz lettres patentes Donne souz nostre priue seal a Berewyk sur Twede le xiij^{me} iour de Juyl lan de nostre regne quint.

(Endorsed)
Irrotulatur.
Coram Rege.

[1] Cancelled.

137. Petition from royal servant for reward referred to steward of household, keeper of wardrobe and king's confessor. [Ancient Petition, no. 4717.]

A nostre seigneur le Roi et a soun Conseil humblement mostre et prie Thome le Bokeler qe come il ad serui le Roi Edward qe dieux assoille et nostre Seigneur le Roi qore est et dieu gard par tout son temps de guerre et grant trauail ad en et parte en lour seruice parount il ne pust mesmes sustenir si noun parmi socour et grace de nostre seigneur le Roi Pleise a lui et a soun consail lui reguerdoner de soun grant trauail et prest est a commandement du dit nostre seigneur le Roi si come auant cest houre ad este solom soun poer.

(Endorsed)

Sewe deuant le Seneschal Garderober et le Confessour le Roi qi sunt assignez etcetera qe eux sainsent de son trauail et du temps qil ad trauaille outre certifient nostre seigneur le Roi.

Irrotulatur.

Coram Rege.

138. Letters patent of earl of Lancaster on behalf of earl of Hereford concerning Gavaston quarrel. [Duchy of Lancaster, Anc. Corresp. no. 13.]

A toutz ceaux qi ceste lettre verront ou orront Thomas Counte de Lancestre et de Leicestre Seneschal Dengleterre salutz en nostre seigneur Sachiez nous estre tenuz a defendre a sauuer monsire Hunfrey de Booun Counte de Hereford et Dessex des damages qe lui porront auenir endroit de la querele touchant Sire Pierres de Gauastone auxi bien devers le Roi come devers toutz autres a tout nostre poair E voloms et assentoms qe du dit sire Pierres soit fait come de Lenemi du Roi et du Roiaume et de son poeple Et nous promettoms fiablement de viure et morir en eide et en defens du dit Counte en la querele susdite E de ceo lui auoms asseoure par nostre serment sur saintes Ewangeilles En tesmoigne de cestes choses nous lui auoms fait faire cestes noz lettres patentes seallez de nostre seal Escrit a Warrewik le xviij iour de Juyn Lan du regne nostre seigneur le Roi Edward fuiz au tresnoble Roi Edward quint.

(Endorsed)

Vacatur.

139. Writ of privy seal to justices of king's bench to try prior of Llantony. [K. B. Misc., Class 138, no. 112, m. 277.]

A Heruy Destaunton et ses compaignons Justices de nostre Baunk par le Roy.

Edward par la grace de dieu Roi Dengleterre Seigneur Dirlande et Ducs Daquitaine A noz chers et foiaux Heruy Destaunton et ses compaignons Justices de nostre Baunk saluz Come pur aucuns articles et diuerses plaintes qe nous furent baillez de William de Pynnebury Priour de la Maison de Lantony de Gloucestre de son port quel deust auoir este nouncouenable deuers nous en temps auant ces houres feismes venir le dit Priour deuant nous en nostre presence a Gloucestre et li feismes examiner sur les poyntz et les articles auantditz lui quel en nostre presence conuseit totes les choses queles nous vous enueoms encloses de deinz cestes et vous mandoms qe veues et examinees les choses susdites facez a nostre suyte tieu proces deuers le dit Priour et les autres qi sont acusez deuant nous par la reconissance du dit Priour selounc la lei et la custume de nostre realme come appent Issint totes foitz qe vous ne pursuiez mie deuers eaux par tiele voie qils portent iugement de vie ne de membre sils soient atteintz Kar les articles et les plaintes nous furent liuerez par aucunes gentz de Religion et le dit Priour examinez deuant nous par aucunes gentz de seinte eglise queux nous ne voloms mie qils offendent lour estatz deuers seinte eglise pur lour reconissaunce ne examinementz auantditz Donne souz nostre priue seal a Gloucestre le xx iour de Janeuoir Lan de nostre regne xvij^me^.

(Endorsed)

De inquirendo apud Gloucestriam.

Ista littera liberata fuit Heruio de Stanton apud Hereford v die ffebruarii hora vesperarum per manus Ade Leonard cursoris ex missione Dunaldi nuncij domini Regis ut idem Adam dicit.

LIST OF SOURCES

A. PRINTED BOOKS

I. State Publications.

(a) *Record Commission.*

Statutes of the Realm. Vol. I. [1810.]
Rotuli Parliamentorum. Vols. I and II.
Foedera. Vols. I and II. [1816–18.]
Parliamentary Writs and Writs of Military Summons. Vol. II, Pts i and ii. [1830.]
Documents illustrative of English History in the thirteenth and fourteenth Centuries. Ed. H. Cole. [1844.]
Abbreviatio Placitorum. [1811.]
Rotulorum Originalium in Curia Scaccarii Abbreviatio. [1805.]
Ancient Kalendars and Inventories of the Treasury of the Exchequer. Ed. Sir F. Palgrave. Vol. I. [1836.]
Testa de Nevill. [1807.]
Rotuli Scotiae. Vol. I. [1814.]
Placita de Quo Warranto. [1810.]

(b) *Calendar Series.*

Calendar of the Patent Rolls:

Henry III.	Vol. I.	1216–1225.	Vol. V.	1258–1266.
	Vol. IV.	1247–1258.		
Edward II.	Vol. I.	1307–1313.	Vol. IV.	1321–1324.
	Vol. II.	1313–1317.	Vol. V.	1324–1327.
	Vol. III.	1317–1321.		

Calendar of the Close Rolls:

Edward I.	Vol. I.	1272–1279.	Vol. IV.	1296–1302.
	Vol. II.	1279–1288.	Vol. V.	1302–1307.
	Vol. III.	1288–1296.		
Edward II.	Vol. I.	1307–1313.	Vol. III.	1318–1323.
	Vol. II.	1313–1318.	Vol. IV.	1323–1327.

Calendar of the Fine Rolls:

Edward II.	Vol. II.	1307–1319.	Vol. III.	1319–1327.

Calendar of the Charter Rolls:
Vol. III. 1300–1326.

Calendar of Inquisitions Post-Mortem:

Vol. IV.	29–35	Edward I.	Vol. VI.	10–20	Edward II.
Vol. V.	1–9	Edward II.	Vol. VII.	1–9	Edward III.

Calendar of Various Chancery Rolls. 1277–1326.
Descriptive Catalogue of Ancient Deeds. Vols. I–V.
Calendar of Papal Registers. Vol. II. 1305–1342.
Inquisitions and Assessments relating to Feudal Aids. 5 Vols.

(*c*) *Public Record Office Lists and Indexes.*

No. 1. Index of Ancient Petitions. [1892.]
No. 9. List of Sheriffs. [1898.]

(*d*) *Rolls Series, Chronicles and Memorials.*

Chronicles of the Reigns of Edward I and Edward II. Ed. W. Stubbs.
Vol. I. Annales Londonienses.
Annales Paulini.
Vol. II. Commendatio Lamentabilis Johannis de Londonia.
Auctore Bridlingtoniensi.
Auctore Malmesberiensi.
Chronicle of Adam Murimuth with the Chronicle of Robert of Avesbury.
Flores Historiarum. Vol. III.
Chronica Monasterii de Melsa. Vol. II.
Le Livere de Reis de Brittanie.
Johannis de Trokelowe et Henrici de Blaneforde Chronica et Annales.
Munimenta Gildhallae Londoniensis.
Vol. I. Liber Albus. Vol. II, Parts i and ii. Liber Custumarum.
Eulogium Historiarum. Vol. III.
Thomae Walsingham Historia Anglicana.
The Chronicle of Pierre de Langtoft. Vol. II.
Chronica Magistri Rogeri de Houedene. Vol. III.
Historic and Municipal Documents of Ireland.
Matthaei Parisiensis Chronica Majora. Vols. III, IV.
Historical Papers and Letters from the Northern Registers.
Registrum Palatinum Dunelmense. Vols. I, II, IV.
Henrici de Bracton de Legibus et Consuetudinibus Angliae. Vols. I, II, VI.
Chartularies St Mary's Abbey, Dublin. Vol. II.
Chronicle of Henry Knighton. Vol. I.
Memoranda de Parliamento. 1305. Ed. F. W. Maitland.
The Red Book of the Exchequer. Ed. H. Hall. Vol. III.
Letter Books of the Monastery of Christchurch, Canterbury. Vols. I, III.
Polychronicon Ranulphi Higden. Vol. VIII.
Annals of Loch Cé Vol. I.
The Historians of the Church of York and its Archbishops.
Memorials of St Edmund's Abbey. Vol. II.
Willelmi Rishanger Chronica et Annales.
Annales Monastici.
Vol. I. Annales de Burton.
Vol. III. Annales Monasterii de Bermundeseia.
Registrum Epistolarum Fratris Johannis Peckham. Vol. III.
Year Books:
20–21 Edward I. 33–35 Edward I.
21–22 Edward I. 14 Edward III.
30–31 Edward I. 14–15 Edward III.
32–33 Edward I. 15 Edward III.

(*e*) *Deputy Keeper Reports.*

9th Report. [1848.]
31st Report. [1870.]

(*f*) *Other Government Reports.*

Report on Dignity of Peer. Vol. I. [1829.]
Royal Historical Commission, 10th Report, Appendix 3. Report on MSS. in Wells Cathedral. [1885.]

(*g*) *Scottish Record Publications.*

Calendar Documents relating to Scotland preserved in the Public Record Office. Ed. J. Bain. Vols. II, III. [1884–7.]

(*h*) *Irish Record Publications.*

Annals of Ulster. Vol. II. [1893.]
Chartae, Privilegia et Immunitates. [1829–30.]

2. Publications of Learned Societies and Periodicals.

(*a*) *Publications of the Selden Society.*

Vol. 2. Select Pleas in Manorial Courts. Ed. F. W. Maitland. [1888.]
Vol. 5. The Leet Jurisdiction in the city of Norwich. Ed. W. Hudson. [1891.]
Vol. 7. The "Mirror of Justices." Ed. F. W. Maitland. [1893.]
Vol. 8. Select passages from Bracton and Azo. Ed. F. W. Maitland. [1894.]
Vol. 9. Select Coroner's Rolls. Ed. C. Gross. [1895.]
Vol. 13. Select Pleas of the Forest. Ed. J. G. Turner. [1899.]
Vol. 17. Year Book, 1–2 Edward II. Ed. F. W. Maitland. [1903.]
Vol. 18. Borough Customs. Vol. I. Ed. Miss M. Bateson. [1904.]
Vol. 19. Year Book, 2–3 Edward II. Ed. F. W. Maitland. [1904.]
Vol. 20. Year Book, 3 Edward II. Ed. F. W. Maitland. [1905.]
Vol. 22. Year Book, 3–4 Edward II. Ed. F. W. Maitland and J. G. Turner. [1907.]
Vol. 23. Select Cases concerning the Law Merchant. Ed. C. Gross. [1908.]
Vol. 24. Eyre of Kent. Vol. I. Ed. F. W. Maitland, L. W. V. Harcourt and W. C. Bolland. [1909.]
Vol. 26. Year Book, 4 Edward II. Ed. J. G. Turner. [1911.]
Vol. 27. Eyre of Kent. Vol. II. Ed. W. C. Bolland, F. W. Maitland, and L. W. V. Harcourt. [1912.]
Vol. 29. Eyre of Kent. Vol. III. Ed. W. C. Bolland. [1913.]

(*b*) *Publications of the Surtees Society.*

Vol. 9. Historiae Dunelmensis Scriptores Tres. Robert de Graystanes. [1839.]
Vol. 67. Memorials of Fountains Abbey. Vol. II, Pt i. [1876.]
Vol. 78. Memorials of Ripon. Vol. II. [1884.]
Vol. 98. Beverley Chapter Act Book. Vol. I. [1897.]
Vol. 113. Records of Northern Convocation. [1906.]
Vol. 117. Percy Cartulary. [1909.]

(*c*) *Publications of the Camden Society.*

O. S. Vol. 6. Political Songs. Ed. T. Wright. [1839.]
O. S. Vol. 15. The Chronicle of William de Rishanger. Ed. J. O. Halliwell. [1840.]
O. S. Vol. 28. The French Chronicle of London. Ed. G. J. Aungier. [1844.]
O. S. Vol. 34. De Antiquis Legibus Liber. Ed. T. Stapleton. [1844.]
N. S. Vol. 26. Documents relating to St Paul's Cathedral. Ed. W. S. Simpson. [1880.]
3rd S. Vol. 9. The State Trials of 1289–1290. Ed. T. F. Tout and H. Johnstone. [1906.]

(*d*) *Publications of the Canterbury and York Society.*

Vol. 5. Registrum Ade de Orleton, 1317–1327. Ed. A. T. Bannister. [1908.]
Vol. 6. Registrum Ricardi de Swinfield, 1283–1317. Ed. W. W. Capes [1909.]
Vol. 7. Registrum Radulphi Baldock, etc. 1304–1338. Ed. R. C. Fowler. [1911.]
Vols. 12–13. Registrum Johannis de Halton, 1292–1334. 2 Vols. Intro. T. F. Tout. [1913.]

(*e*) *Other Bishops' Registers.*

Registrum Johannis de Drokensford. 1309–1329. (Somerset Record Society.) Ed. Bishop Hobhouse. [1887.]
Registrum Johannis de Sandale, etc., 1316–1323. (Hampshire Record Society.) [1897.]
Registrum Walteri de Stapleton, 1307–1326. (Episcopal Registers of the Diocese of Exeter.) Ed. F. C. Hingeston-Randolph. [1892.]

(*f*) *Society of Antiquaries.*

Liber Quotidianus Contrarotulatoris Garderobe. 28 Edward I. [1787.]
Liber Niger Regis Edwardi IV. [1790.]

(*g*) *Oxford Historical Society.*

Vol. 17. Wood's City of Oxford. Vol. II. Ed. A. Clark. [1890.]
Vol. 20. Grey Friars at Oxford. Ed. A. G. Little. [1891.]
Vol. 32. Collectanea. Vol. III. [1896.]
Vol. 33. Cartulary of the Monastery of St Frideswide. Vol. II. [1896.]

(*h*) *Royal Historical Society.*

Transactions, New Series. Vol. 10. [1896.]
Transactions, Third Series. Vol. 9. [1915.]

(*i*) *English Historical Review.*

Vol. 1. [1886.]
Vol. 21. [1906.]
Vol. 22. [1907.]
Vol. 23. [1908.]
Vol. 24. [1909.]
Vol. 25. [1910.]
Vol. 26. [1911.]
Vol. 28. [1913.]
Vol. 30. [1915.]

(*j*) *The British Archaeological Association.*

Archaeological Journal:

Vol. 2. [1846.] Vol. 34. [1877.]
Vol. 15. [1858.] Vol. 36. [1879.]
Vol. 21. [1864.]

(*k*) *William Salt Archaeological Association.*

Collections:

Vol. 6, Pt. i. [1885.] Vol. 10. [1889.]
Vol. 7. [1886.] Vol. 11. [1890.]
Vol. 9. [1888.]

Historical Collections, Staffordshire. Ed. J. G. Wedgewood. [1911.]
,, ,, ,, [1912.]
,, ,, ,, [1913.]

(*l*) *Miscellaneous Society and Serial Publications.*

Chronicon de Lanercost. Ed. J. Stevenson. (Maitland Club.) [1839.]
Chronica de Mailros. Ed. J. Stevenson. (Bannatyne Club.) [1835.]
Chronicon Walteri de Hemingburgh. Vol. II. Ed. H. S. Hamilton. (English Historical Society.) [1849.]
Odericus Vitalis. (Patrologia, Migne. Vol. 188.)
Calendar of Letter Books of the City of London, Letter Books C, D, E. [1901–3.]
Victoria County History:

Lancaster. Vol. II. [1908.]
London. Vol. I. [1909.]

Law Quarterly Review. Vol. 33. [1917.]
Juridical Review:

December, 1901. March, 1902.

Scottish Historical Society:

Vol. 44. Miscellany. Vol. II. [1904.]

Historical Society for West Wales:

Transactions. Vol. I. [1911.]

Middlesex and Hertfordshire Notes and Queries. Vol. II. W. J. Hardy. [1896.]

3. Private Authors.

Adams, G. B. The Origin of the English Constitution. [1912.]
Allen, J. Enquiry into the Rise and Growth of the Royal Prerogative. [1830.]
Ashley, J. W. Economic History. Vol. I. 4th Ed. [1909.]
Baldwin, J. F. The King's Council in England during the Middle Ages. [1913.]
Barrington, Daines. Observations upon the Statutes. [1766.]
Bémont, C. Simon de Montfort. [1884.]
Brady, Robert. A Continuation of the Complete History of England. [1700.]
Brequigny's Lettres du Roi. Vol. I. [1839.]
Campbell, Lord. Lives of the Lord Chancellors. Vol. I. [1845.]
Caxton's Chronicle. [1480.]
Chadwick, H. M. Origin of the English Nation. [1907.]

Chadwick, H. M. Studies in Anglo-Saxon Institutions. [1905.]
Chronicon Galfridi le Baker. Ed. E. M. Thompson. [1889.]
Clark, G. T. Cartae et alia Munimenta de Glamorgan. Vol. III. [1891 Ed.]
Cobbett's Complete Collection of State Trials. Vol. I. 1163–1600. [1809.]
Coke, Sir Ed. Reports, 7th part. [1608.]
Davis, H. W. C. England under the Normans and Angevins. [1909.]
Déprez, Eugène. Études de Diplomatique Anglaise, Le Sceau Privé, etc. [1908.]
—— 'Le Trésor des Chartres de Guyenne sous Edouard II,' in Mélanges offerts à M. Charles Bémont. [1913.]
Dimitresco, M. Pierre de Gavaston. [1898.]
Dowell, S. History of Taxation. Vol. I. 2nd Ed. [1888.]
Dugdale, W. Baronage. [1675.]
Eyton, R. W. Antiquities of Shropshire. Vol. IX. [1859.]
Figgis, J. N. The Divine Right of Kings. 2nd Ed. [1914.]
Foss, Ed. Judges of England. Vol. III. [1851.]
Gardiner, S. R. Short History of England. 2nd Ed. [1891.]
Gneist, R. History of the English Constitution. Vol. II. [1891.]
Hall, Hubert. Customs Revenue of England. Vol. II. [1885.]
Harcourt, L. W. V. His Grace the Steward and Trial by Peers. [1907.]
Hemmeon, M. de W. Burgage Tenure in Medieval England. [1914.]
Holdsworth, W. S. History of English Law. 3 Vols. [1903–1909.]
Jenks, Ed. Edward Plantagenet. [1902.]
Kerly, D. M. History of Equity. [1890.]
Lang, A. History of Scotland. Vol. I. [1900.]
Langlois, C. V. Textes Relatifs à l'Histoire du Parlement. [1888.]
Lapsley, G. T. The County Palatine of Durham. [1900.]
Liber Assisarum, 8 Edward III. [1678.]
McIlwain, C. H. The High Court of Parliament and its Supremacy. [1910.]
McKechnie, W. S. Magna Charta. 2nd Ed. [1914.]
Madox, T. History of the Exchequer. 2 Vols. [1769.]
—— Baronia Anglica. [1741.]
—— Formulare Anglicanum. [1702.]
—— Firma Burgi. [1726.]
Maitland, F. W. Bracton's Note-book. 3 Vols. [1887.]
Makower, F. Constitutional History of the Church of England. [1895.]
Maxwell, H., Sir. The Chronicle of Lanercost. [1913.]
Michel, F. Histoire des Ducs de Normandie et des Rois Dangleterre. [1840.]
Migne, J. P. Lexicon Manuale ad Scriptores Mediae et Infimae Latinitatis.
Morris, J. E. Welsh Wars of Edward I. [1901.]
Nichols, F. M. Britton. 2 Vols. [1865.]
Oman, C. W. C. Art of War in the Middle Ages. [1905.]
Pike, L. O. Constitutional History of the House of Lords. [1894.]
Plummer, C. Fortescue, Governance of England. [1885.]
Pollock and Maitland. History of English Law. 2nd Ed. 2 Vols. [1911.]
Prothero, G. W. Life of Simon de Montfort. [1877.]

Ramsay, J. H. The Genesis of Lancaster. Vol. I. [1913.]
—— The Dawn of the Constitution. [1908.]
Riley, T. H. Memorials of London. [1868.]
Rogers, J. E. T. History of Agriculture and Prices. Vol. I. [1866.]
Round, J. H. The Commune of London. [1899.]
—— The King's Serjeants and Officers of State. [1911.]
Selden, J. Titles of Honour. 3rd Ed. [1672.]
—— Fleta, Commentarius. [1647.]
Select Essays in Anglo-American Legal History. Vol. II. [1908.]
Staunford, W. An Exposition of the King's Prerogative. [1567.]
Stubbs, W. Constitutional History. Vol. I. 6th Ed. [1897.] Vol. II. Library Ed. [1880]; 4th Ed. [1896.]
—— Select Charters. 9th Ed. Ed. H. W. C. Davis. [1913.]
Thoms, W. J. Book of the Court. [1838.]
Tout, T. F. The Place of Edward II in English History. [1914.]
—— Edward I. [1893.]
—— Political History. 1216–1377. [1905.]
Tout and Tait. Historical Essays. [1907.]
Twysden, R. Historiae Anglicanae Scriptores Decem. [1652.]
Viollet, P. Institutions Politiques. Vol. III. [1903.]
Wharton, H. Anglia Sacra. Vol. I. [1691.]
Wilkins, D. Concilia. Vol. II. [1737.]

B. MANUSCRIPT AUTHORITIES

I Public Record Office.

(*a*) *Exchequer Records.*

King's Remembrancer Memoranda Rolls. 1–20 Edward II. Nos. 81–103.
Lord Treasurer's Remembrancer Memoranda Rolls. 1–20 Edward II. Nos. 78–99.
Issue Rolls. 1–20 Edward II. Nos. 141, 143, 144, 146, 150, 152, 153, 155, 157, 159, 162, 164, 166, 167, 170, 172, 174, 176, 180, 181, 183, 184, 186, 187, 189, 191, 193, 195, 196, 198, 200, 202, 206, 207, 210, 213, 216, 217, 218, 219, 220, 1323, 1325.
Receipt Rolls, nos. 173, 1772.
Liberate Rolls. 1–20 Edward II. Nos. 84–103.
Enrolment of Wardrobe Accounts, L. T. R. Roll, no. 2.
King's Remembrancer's Accounts 15/1, 16/4, 68/1, 68/2, 114/2, 211/6, 256/1, 309/18, 373/30, 374/7, 374/12, 375/1, 375/4, 375/5, 375/6, 375/8, 376/11, 377/10, 377/17, 378/6, 379/7, 379/11, 379/17, 380/4, 506/16, 506/25.
Escheator's Account 3/18.
Sheriff's Accounts 10/5, 29/13, 49/8.
Miscellanea of Exchequer 2/40, 3/2, 3/6, 4/1, 4/6, 4/7, 5/2, 9/23, 24/12.
K. R. Exchequer Bills 1/5, 1/6, 1/7.
K. R. Exchequer Brevia Baronibus. 5 Edward II.
Exchequer of Pleas, Plea Roll, no. 31.
K. R. Estreats 140/1.
Pipe Roll, no. 171.
Miscellaneous Books of Exchequer, Treasury of Receipt. Vol. 187.

(*b*) *Chancery Records.*

Chancery Warrants, Files 58–134, 909, 1328–29, 1648–51, 1703–6.
Chancery Miscellanea 3/33, 22/6 (6), 22/10 (8), 22/10 (8 *a*), 22/12 (26), 24/3 (16), 25/2 (11), 25/2 (12), 51/1 (14), 59/3 (71), 59/3 (99), 64/1 (28), 64/3 (77), 64/3 (78), 64/6 (143), 64/7 (196), 68/8 (187), 86/14 (328), 88/1 (8), 138.
Placita in Cancellaria, File 1/2 (3).
Chancery Files (under arrangement) C, Files 9–12.

(*c*) *Special Collections and Miscellaneous.*

Ancient Correspondence, Volumes 32, 33, 34, 35, 36, 37, 45, 49, 50, 54, 58.
Ancient Petitions, nos. 119, 160, 361, 414, 559, 1320, 1725, 1944, 2053, 2062, 2064, 2273, 2282, 2481, 2749, 2759, 2760, 2761, 2762, 2766, 3813, 3819, 3841, 3955, 3982, 4051, 4052, 4106, 4259, 4426, 4605, 4660, 4717, 4719, 4720, 4730, 4913, 4920, 5459, 5656, 5694, 5911, 7778, 10895, 11856, 13027.
Parliamentary and Council Proceedings (Chancery), Files 4/3, 4/9, 4/13, 4/19, 4/20, 4/22, 5/2, 5/6, 5/9, 5/10, 33/14, 45/13, 45/15.
Parliamentary and Council Proceedings (Exchequer), File 2/4, roll no. 17.
Duchy of Lancaster, Ancient Correspondence, no. 13.
King's Bench, Class 138, no. 68/108.
Marshalsea Court, Plea Roll, no. 3.
Minister's Account 1287/1.
Statute Roll, no. 2.
Exchequer Rolls of Parliament, nos. 22, 24.

2. British Museum.

Cotton MSS.:

Vespasian F. vii.
Nero A. iv.
Nero C. iii.
Nero C. viii.
Cleopatra C. iii.

Stowe MS. 553.
Additional MS. 22,923.

3. Cambridge University Library.

Dd. vii. 6. Dd. ix. 38. Ee. iv. 4. Ee. v. 31. Gg. i. 15. Ii. vi. 8. Mm. i. 33.
Additional MS. no. 3129.

4. Library of Canterbury Cathedral.

MS. K 11.

5. Corpus Christi College Library.

MS. no. 258.

INDEX

For Product Safety Concerns and Information please contact our EU representative GPSR@taylorandfrancis.com Taylor & Francis Verlag GmbH, Kaufingerstraße 24, 80331 München, Germany

Batch number: 08153782

Printed by Printforce, the Netherlands